Also by William J. Bennett

COUNTING BY RACE: *Equality from the Founding Fathers to Bakke* (with Terry Eastland)

OUR CHILDREN AND OUR COUNTRY: *Improving America's Schools and Affirming the Common Culture*

THE DE-VALUING OF AMERICA: *The Fight for Our Culture and Our Children*

THE BOOK OF VIRTUES: *A Treasury of Great Moral Stories*

Edited, with Commentary, by

William J. Bennett

SIMON & SCHUSTER

New York London Toronto Sydney Tokyo Singapore

The
MORAL
COMPASS

•

*Stories for a
Life's Journey*

SIMON & SCHUSTER
Rockefeller Center
1230 Avenue of the Americas
New York, NY 10020

Copyright © 1995 by William J. Bennett
All rights reserved,
including the right of reproduction
in whole or in part in any form.

SIMON & SCHUSTER and colophon are registered trademarks
of Simon & Schuster Inc.

A leatherbound signed first edition of this
book has been published by Easton Press.

Designed by Karolina Harris
Picture Research by Natalie Goldstein

Manufactured in the United States of America

1   3   5   7   9   10   8   6   4   2

Library of Congress Cataloging-in-Publication Data
The moral compass : stories for a life's journey /
edited with commentary by William J. Bennett.
p.   cm.
Sequel to: Book of virtues.
1. Literature—Collections.   2. Conduct of life—
Literary collections.   I. Bennett, William John, 1943–
PN6014.M36   1995
808.8'038—dc20   95-4783
CIP
ISBN 0-684-80313-5

To America's teachers:

in homes, schools, and churches

Contents

	INTRODUCTION	11
ONE	HOME AND HEARTH	17
TWO	INTO THE WORLD	131
THREE	STANDING FAST	243
FOUR	EASING THE PATH	361
FIVE	MOTHERS AND FATHERS,	
	HUSBANDS AND WIVES	481
SIX	CITIZENSHIP AND LEADERSHIP	591
SEVEN	WHAT WE LIVE BY	697
	ACKNOWLEDGMENTS	813
	INDEX	815

Introduction

LIKE *The Book of Virtues,* this book aims to aid in the task of the moral education of the young. *The Book of Virtues* identified and examined ten traits of character—self-discipline, compassion, responsibility, friendship, work, courage, perseverance, honesty, loyalty, and faith. In this volume we find those same virtues, but this time we meet them in a different place: the stages of a life's journey.

Children learn most of their first character lessons in the home, which is where this book begins. Those early lessons stay with children as they make their way into the world, shaping the way they see life, and to a large degree determining whether they live it well. Later, as young people and then as adults, through various stages of life, they must make countless choices that call the virtues into play. As the chapters of this book unfold, we witness many of those choices and their implications. The stories and poems in these pages can serve as reference points on a moral compass, giving our children a clearer sense of direction in matters of right and wrong, helping to guide their actions in day-to-day living, as well as in those occasional, momentous decisions required of every individual.

The basic assumption underlying this volume is that much of life is a moral and spiritual journey, and that we undertake it, at least in large part, to find our way morally and spiritually. Thus it makes no sense to send young people forth on such an endeavor having offered them only some timid, vacillating opinions or options about conduct in the hope that in the course of their wanderings, they will stumble onto some more definite personal preferences which will become their "values." We must give our children better equipment than that. We must raise them *as moral and spiritual beings* by offering them unequivocal, reliable standards of right and wrong, noble and base, just and unjust. " 'Tis virtue . . . which is the hard and valuable part to be aimed at in education," the philosopher John Locke reminded us, "and not a forward pertness of any little arts of shifting. All other considerations and accomplishments should give way and be postponed to this." The stories in this book aim at clear concepts of good and bad without hesitation or apology. They treat life as a moral endeavor.

Of course, sound character education cannot come solely through hearing and reading stories, no matter how great they are. The training of the heart and the mind toward the good involves much more. (We would do well to remember that the Greek word *charakter* means "enduring marks," traits that can be formed in a person by an almost infinite number of influences.) Moral education must involve following rules of good behavior. It must involve developing good habits, which come only through repeated practice. And character training must provide example by placing children in the company of responsible adults who show an allegiance to good character, who demonstrate the clear difference between right and wrong in their own everyday habits.

Nevertheless, the books and stories we share with our children can be important moral influences. They can be invaluable allies for parents and teachers; as President Charles W. Eliot of Harvard observed, "In the campaign for character, no auxiliaries are to be refused." Literature can be a crucial part of a home, school, community, or culture's *ethos*—another ancient Greek term meaning the distinguishing character or guiding beliefs, the habits of the denizens. As every parent and teacher knows, children love stories. Even in an age of computer games and electronic toys, there is still resonant power in the phrase "Once upon a time . . ." And so *what* we choose to read to our children matters a great deal. Legends, folktales, sacred stories, biographies, and poems can introduce the youngest children to the virtues; they can clarify notions of right and wrong for young people; and they can serve as powerful reminders of mankind's best ideals all the way through adulthood. More than one great man or woman at a critical instant has recalled a simple fable, a familiar verse, a childhood hero.

Philosophers, theologians, and poets have long regarded wisdom as the sibling virtue of morality. If an individual is to do good, the tenets of the heart must be informed and directed by a well-ordered mind. In fact, the classical Greek thinkers regarded prudence as one of the fundamental virtues; to them, the word meant not circumspection, as it does to us today, but rather the ability to govern and discipline oneself by the use of reason. It meant being able to recognize the right choice in specific circumstances, and it was the intellectual virtue that made it possible to put the moral virtues into action. The reader will find stories involving such practical wisdom scattered throughout this book; knowing them may help us handle some of the tough situations that crop up in everyday life. Furthermore, there are many stories in this book that deal with a grander notion of wisdom, stories that help us try to gain even some ultimate knowledge of self, of our fellow human beings, and of God's will. These stories may aid in arriving at a guiding philosophy of life. They have been selected with this standard in mind.

Originally I had not intended to put together a second collection of moral stories, and agreed to do so only at the urging of readers who loved the material they found in *The Book of Virtues* and wrote to ask for more. I confess, however, that I began this project with a certain degree of doubt in my mind. Even though the quarry of wonderful literature is deep, and *The Book of Virtues* had barely scratched the surface, I still wondered how difficult it would be to assemble a second volume that would equal the first in terms of offering timeless stories that both instruct and entertain. As it turned out, my doubts proved to be groundless.

In order to dig a bit deeper into that mine of wonderful literature, I decided to take a close look at some of the books American children were reading in their homes and schools around the turn of the twentieth century. The wealth of material was astonishing, and it comprises a large part of this volume. Much of it, after a little updating for the modern ear (and abridging to meet restrictions of an anthology), is every bit as instructive *and* entertaining today as it was one hundred years ago.

I think that in some ways this is a more interesting collection than *The Book of Virtues.* Many of these stories seem to me more intriguing and more imaginative than those in the first volume. There are more stories of the spirit, more stories from the deeper recesses of the human heart. I think readers will find a greater number of unfamiliar stories in this volume; I hope this book will help today's public discover some old tales that were favorites in another era but have slipped out of the modern, popular canon. There are also many stories and characters here (the Gordian knot, the race from Marathon, the triumph of Florence Nightingale) that we adults already know—or should know—and want to pass on to our children. As Wordsworth put it, "What we have loved, others will love, and we will teach them how." In this respect, I hope this book is a contribution to our cultural as well as to our moral literacy.

Although this book is grounded solidly in the heritage of Western Civilization, there are many countries, many cultures, many traditions represented here. Like the American people, these stories come from all over the globe, and they serve a valuable purpose in our collective consciousness. Many of these stories have been handed down from generation to generation for hundreds of years. They have stood the test of time. They contain the wisdom of the ages.

Although the chapters in this book are arranged according to different stages of life, the reader should not conclude that the stories in any one section are meaningful only to certain ages or groups (that is, that Chapter One is only for youngsters still at home, or that Chapter Five is only for married people). On the contrary, I think there is something for every age in every chapter. For example, even young children need to hear stories about what it is like to be a spouse or a parent so they can begin to be aware of the joys and responsibilities that will come when they, too, begin their own families. And adults can profit by re-reading and reminding themselves of the first, basic lessons life offers, not only because it will help them teach their own young children but also because those first lessons are often the most important ones, the ones even we adults need to attend to again and again.

Some chapters address certain virtues more than others. Chapter Three, for example, which is meant to help in facing the tough times of life, concentrates largely on perseverance and courage. Chapter Four, which inspires us to help each other along life's journey, deals mostly with compassion. Clearly, these virtues are valuable at any age, and so are most of the stories in those sections. The book's seven chapters are not strictly chronological phases of life; on the contrary, much of life is a process of repeating our ventures, our plans, our aspirations, learning and growing with each new effort.

As in *The Book of Virtues,* I have tried to arrange each chapter so that the easier material comes first; when selections share certain themes and lessons, however, I have grouped those readings together. In short, this book, like its predecessor, is mainly for browsing, for finding favorite stories and passages, for reading out loud to each other, for memorizing snatches of verses. And I hope that most of these stories are ones both young and old can enjoy, especially together.

Although most of the ideas and themes in this book are as old and universal as human nature, it would be difficult to put together such a collection without keeping in mind some of the specific currents in today's culture. As Flannery O'Connor observed, "You have to push as hard as the age that pushes against you." I have therefore included, for example, many stories about families—and how to keep them strong—because of the current plight of that institution. The decline of the American family constitutes perhaps the greatest long-term threat to our children's well-being; we should not hesitate to place before young people examples that help instill a reverence for the blessings and duties of home and hearth. The reader will also find some stories dealing with gratitude and ingratitude. In today's public discourse, there seems to be little expression of the former, and much time given to the latter in the form of griping and complaining and pointing fingers. Sometimes we need to remind ourselves that thankfulness is indeed a virtue. Gratitude is something we very much need to show.

The most encouraging feedback I received about *The Book of Virtues* was that children—not just their parents—love those old stories and ask to hear them again and again. I hope this book delights and entertains just as much and that these stories help young people understand that virtues are not bothersome things that take all the fun out of life. Rather, I hope these wonderful stories and verses will help them understand that virtues can make life worthwhile, can help in the tasks of both meaning and content-ment. Children should know that loving life and living well go hand in hand. "Through our great good fortune, in our youth our hearts were touched with fire," Justice Oliver Wendell Holmes wrote of his own childhood. "It was given to us to learn at the outset that life is a profound and passionate thing." I hope this book inspires readers to remember that life is a profound and passionate journey, and I hope it can be a compass of sorts to help guide the way.

I would like to thank Bob Asahina for his now customary scru-tiny, wisdom, and fine editing; Sarah Pinckney, Bob's colleague at Simon and Schuster, for her patience, cooperation, and helpfulness; and Bob Barnett for sagacious counsel and clinical judgment on the vagaries of contracts and the ways of negotiation. I am once again indebted to John Cribb for his energy, imagination, good taste, and prodigious efforts at home, in libraries, and on countless plane rides. He is the keeper of the story vault. At that he has no equal.

Finally, to my family again I offer my thanks. John and Joseph were the audience in mind and sometimes actually in place as this book was put together. I hope they like it. Elayne's love and counsel were the most important mainstay for this as for so many of my other work projects. "Her candle goeth not out by night," and the readers of this book are the beneficiaries.

One

·

HOME
AND
HEARTH

ALL children need bread and shelter. But a true home, of course, is much more than that. Children also need love and order and, because they are not born knowing the difference between right and wrong, a place where they can begin to develop a moral sense. The transmission of virtues is one important reason for a home, and attention to the virtues is one of the important ties that bind a family together. "It is the peculiarity of man, in comparison with the rest of the animal world," Aristotle wrote, "that he alone possesses a perception of good and evil, of the just and the unjust, and of other similar qualities; and it is association in these things which makes a family."

And so home is the place where we receive our first instruction in the virtues. It is our first moral training ground, the place where we can come to know right from wrong through the nurturing and protective care of those who love us more than anyone else. Our character takes shape under the guidance of the *do*s and *don't*s, the instructions, the exhortations we encounter around the house. Equally important, our moral sense emerges under the influence of examples set by mother, father, sisters, and brothers. In the familiar world of home and hearth, we learn the habits of virtue that will fortify us when we venture into the world.

In this chapter we find some of these lessons of home and hearth. We find family members helping each other along, and looking toward each other for help. We find siblings showing what "brotherhood" and "sisterhood" really mean. We see children learning about chores and responsibilities and self-sacrifice, and learning to help parents out of love. We encounter young hearts giving loving obedience. We witness the growth of conscience, of a desire to live up to the expectations of those who love us. We witness how our loyalty and courage and perseverance see families through hard times with a love that can overcome any number of obstacles.

Of course, no home is perfect. Home can be the place where we get our first look at vices as well as virtues. And, unfortunately, some homes are simply not good places—not all homes are havens; not all hearths have a warm glow. But *all* homes teach lessons, even if they are the wrong kind of lessons. And so even though many homes do not resemble the best ones we find in these pages, the stories here are no less valuable because they give us all something at which to aim. They remind us of the kind of conditions families need and the attention children deserve. We set these examples before our eyes in order to keep raising our sights and our efforts.

These first lessons stay with us long after we leave home. In our affections and our memories, they remain forever a part of us, often the most cherished part of us. "Where shall a man find sweetness to surpass his own home and parents?" Odysseus asks in Homer's *Odyssey*. "In far lands he shall not, though he find a house of gold." The early experiences of home become a moral compass point, guiding and instructing us for the rest of life's journey.

And in one sense, the moral journey that begins with leaving home is the search for opportunities to offer others the same nurture and love we received in our own childhood. The memory of home becomes a past, an experience, an ideal we seek to re-create in our later lives, and in the new lives we shepherd into the world. We build our own homes, offer our own lessons, nurture our own children in the strength and knowledge once gained beside the first warm hearth of home.

HUSH, LITTLE BABY

The first notes we hear are those cradle songs that spring from a parent's heart. Lullabies abound in every age and every culture. By such promises of nurture and protection babies find trust to rest and grow.

> Hush, little baby, don't say a word,
> Papa's going to buy you a mockingbird.
> And if that mockingbird won't sing,
> Papa's going to buy you a diamond ring.
> If that diamond ring turns brass,
> Papa's going to buy you a looking glass.
> If that looking glass gets broke,
> Papa's going to buy you a billy goat.
> If that billy goat won't pull,
> Papa's going to buy you a cart and bull.
> If that cart and bull turns over,
> Papa's going to buy you a dog named Rover.
> If that dog named Rover won't bark,
> Papa's going to buy you a horse and cart.
> If that horse and cart fall down,
> You'll still be the sweetest baby in town!

•

CRADLE SONG

Johannes Brahms

> Lullaby and good night, with roses bedight,
> With lilies bedecked, is baby's wee bed.
> Lay thee down now and rest, may thy slumber be blest,
> Lay thee down now and rest, may thy slumber be blest.

•

SWEET AND LOW

Alfred Tennyson

Sweet and low, sweet and low,
　Wind of the western sea,
Low, low, breathe and blow,
　Wind of the western sea!
Over the rolling waters go,
Come from the dying moon, and blow,
　Blow him again to me;
While my little one, while my pretty one, sleeps.

Sleep and rest, sleep and rest,
　Father will come to thee soon;
Rest, rest, on mother's breast,
　Father will come to thee soon;
Father will come to his babe in the nest,
Silver sails all out of the west
　Under the silver moon:
Sleep, my little one, sleep, my pretty one, sleep.

•

WHAT BRADLEY OWED

Adapted from Hugh T. Kerr

**Home is the place where first lessons are learned. And it is the
place where much of what you do, you do for love.**

There was once a boy named Bradley. When he was about
eight years old, he fell into the habit of thinking of everything in
terms of money. He wanted to know the price of everything he saw,
and if it didn't cost a great deal, it did not seem to him to be worth
anything at all.

But there are a great many things money cannot buy. And some
of them are the best things in the world.

One morning when Bradley came down to breakfast, he put a little piece of paper, neatly folded, on his mother's plate. His mother opened it, and she could hardly believe it, but this is what her son had written:

Mother owes Bradley:	
For running errands	3 dollars
For taking out the trash	2 dollars
For sweeping the floor	2 dollars
Extras	1 dollar
Total that Mother owes Bradley	8 dollars

His mother smiled when she read that, but she did not say anything.

When lunchtime came she put the bill on Bradley's plate along with eight dollars. Bradley's eyes lit up when he saw the money. He stuffed it into his pocket as fast as he could and started dreaming about what he would buy with his reward.

All at once he saw there was another piece of paper besides his plate, neatly folded, just like the first one. When he opened it up, he found it was a bill from his mother. It read:

Bradley owes Mother:	
For being good to him	nothing
For nursing him through his chicken pox	nothing
For shirts and shoes and toys	nothing
For his meals and beautiful room	nothing
Total that Bradley owes Mother	nothing

Bradley sat looking at this new bill, without saying a word. After a few minutes he got up, pulled the eight dollars out of his pocket, and placed them in his mother's hand.

And after that, he helped his mother for love.

•

NAILS IN THE POST

M. F. Cowdery

**In this tough story from a Civil War-era school reader, we find
another kind of lesson that some homes offer. Here is a father
giving his son stern but loving moral instruction.**

There was once a farmer who had a son named John, a boy
very apt to be thoughtless, and careless about doing what he was
told to do.

One day his father said to him, "John, you are so careless and
forgetful, that every time you do wrong, I shall drive a nail into this
post, to remind you how often you are naughty. And every time you
do right I will draw one out." His father did as he said he would,
and every day he had one and sometimes a great many nails to
drive in, but very seldom one to draw out.

At last John saw that the post was quite covered with nails, and
he began to be ashamed of having so many faults. He resolved to
be a better boy, and the next day he was so good and industrious
that several nails came out. The day after it was the same thing, and
so on for a long time, till at length only one nail remained. His
father then called him, and said: "Look, John, here is the very last
nail, and now I'm going to draw it out. Are you not glad?"

John looked at the post, and then, instead of expressing his joy,
as his father expected, he burst into tears. "Why," said the father,
"what's the matter? I should think you would be delighted; the nails
are all gone."

"Yes," sobbed John, "the *nails* are gone, but the *scars* are there
yet."

So it is, dear children, with your faults and bad habits; you may
overcome them, you may by degrees cure them, but the scars remain. Now, take my advice, and whenever you find yourselves
doing a wrong thing, or getting into a bad habit, stop at once. For
every time you give in to it, you drive another nail, and that will
leave a *scar* on your soul, even if the nail should be afterwards
drawn out.

•

NORTHWEST PASSAGE

Robert Louis Stevenson

There is no better place to begin learning about bravery than in the safe confines of home. For many children, the first great adventure is that long, perilous journey up the stairs to bed. Making it can be a first exercise in courage.

1. GOOD NIGHT

When the bright lamp is carried in,
The sunless hours again begin;
O'er all without, in field and lane,
The haunted night returns again.

Now we behold the embers flee
About the firelit hearth; and see
Our faces painted as we pass,
Like pictures, on the window glass.

Must we to bed indeed? Well then,
Let us arise and go like men,
And face with an undaunted tread
The long black passage up to bed.

Farewell, O brother, sister, sire!
O pleasant party round the fire!
The songs you sing, the tales you tell,
Till far tomorrow, fare ye well!

2. SHADOW MARCH

All round the house is the jet-black night;
    It stares through the windowpane;
It crawls in the corners, hiding from the light,
    And it moves with the moving flame.

Now my little heart goes a-beating like a drum,
    With the breath of the bogy in my hair;
And all round the candle the crooked shadows come,
    And go marching along up the stair.

The shadow of the balusters, the shadow of the lamp,
    The shadow of the child that goes to bed—
All the wicked shadows coming, tramp, tramp, tramp,
    With the black night overhead.

3. IN PORT

Last, to the chamber where I lie
My fearful footsteps patter nigh,
And come from out the cold and gloom
Into my warm and cheerful room.

There, safe arrived, we turn about
To keep the coming shadows out,
And close the happy door at last
On all the perils that we past.

Then, when Mama goes by to bed,
She shall come in with tiptoe tread,
And see me lying warm and fast
And in the Land of Nod at last.

•

THE HILL

Laura E. Richards

**Brothers and sisters help each other along, first up backyard hills,
and later up life-long climbs.**

I cannot walk up this hill," said the little boy. "I cannot possibly
do it. What will become of me? I must stay here all my life, at the
foot of the hill. It is too terrible!"
    "That is a pity!" said his sister. "But look, little boy! I have

found such a pleasant game to play. Take a step, and see how clear a footprint you can make in the dust. Look at mine! Every single line in my foot is printed clear. Now, you try, and see if you can do as well!"

The little boy took a step.

"Mine is just as clear!" he said.

"Do you think so?" said his sister. "See mine, again here! I tread harder than you, because I am heavier, and so the print is deeper. Try again."

"*Now* mine is just as deep!" cried the little boy. "See! Here, and here, and here, they are just as deep as they can be."

"Yes, that is very well," said the sister, "but now it is my turn; let me try again, and we shall see."

They kept on, step by step, matching their footprints, and laughing to see the gray dust puff up between their bare toes.

By and by the little boy looked up.

"Why," he said, "we are at the top of the hill!"

"Dear me!" said his sister. "So we are!"

•

THE THREE BILLY GOATS GRUFF

This familiar Norse tale is about an age-old job for big brothers—
looking out for little brothers.

Once upon a time there were three billy goats who lived in a meadow at the foot of a mountain. They were all three brothers, and their last name was Gruff.

One fine day they said to each other, "Let's go up on the hillside, and eat grass, and make ourselves fat."

The youngest of the three started out first. After a while, he came to a bridge. Now the little billy goat did not know it, but under this bridge lived a terrible Troll, with eyes as big as a saucer, and a nose as long as a poker. As the Smallest Billy Goat Gruff went trip-trap, trip-trap over the bridge, the Troll roared out, "WHO'S THAT tripping over my bridge?"

"It's I, the Smallest Billy Goat Gruff. I'm going up on the hillside to eat grass, and make myself fat."

"Well, I'm coming to gobble you up!" roared the Troll.

"Oh, don't do that! I'm so little, I'll make scarcely a mouthful. My brother the Middle-Sized Billy Goat Gruff will be along soon. He'll make a much better meal. You'd better wait for him."

"Very well, be off with you!" said the Troll.

So the little goat ran on, trip-trap, trip-trap, across the bridge and up on the mountain, where he was safe.

Pretty soon, along came the second Billy Goat Gruff.

He went *trip-trap, trip-trap,* over the bridge.

"WHO'S THAT tripping over my bridge?" roared the Troll.

"It's I, the Middle-Sized Billy Goat Gruff. I'm going up on the hillside to eat grass, and make myself fat."

"Well, I'm coming to gobble you up!" roared the Troll.

"Oh, don't do that! I'm not very big, and I won't make much of a meal. My brother the Big Billy Goat Gruff will be along soon. He'll make a much better dinner. You'd better wait for him."

"Very well, be off with you!" said the Troll.

So the Middle-Sized Billy Goat Gruff ran on, *trip-trap, trip-trap,* across the bridge and up on the mountain, where he was safe.

After a while, along came the Big Billy Goat Gruff. *TRIP-TRAP, TRIP-TRAP* he went over the bridge, and it creaked and groaned under his weight.

"WHO'S THAT tripping over my bridge?" roared the Troll.

"IT'S I, THE BIG BILLY GOAT GRUFF!" said the billy goat in a big voice of his own.

"Well, I'm coming to gobble you up!" roared the Troll.

"HO! HO!" laughed the Big Billy Goat Gruff. "You don't say so! Well, come along! I'll crush you to bits, body and bones!" That's what Big Billy Goat Gruff said in his big, rough voice.

Up came the Troll. He jumped on the bridge and put down his big, bushy head and ran at the billy goat. The Big Billy Goat Gruff put down his head and ran at the Troll, and they met in the middle of the bridge.

But the Big Billy Goat Gruff's head was harder than the Troll's, so he knocked him down, and thumped him about, and took him up on his horns, and threw him over the edge of the bridge, into the river below! The Troll sank out of sight, and no one ever saw him again.

Then the Big Billy Goat Gruff went up on the hillside with the other Billy Goat Gruffs, who knew all along their big brother would punish the terrible Troll. And they all ate grass, and ate grass, and ate grass, until they were so fat they could hardly walk home.

•

BEAUTIFUL HANDS

Adapted from Lawton B. Evans

Happy homes need helpful hands.

Some young girls were talking by the brook, boasting of their beautiful hands. One of them dipped her hands in the sparkling water and the drops looked like diamonds falling from her palms.

"See what beautiful hands I have! The water runs from them like precious jewels," said she, and held up her hands for the others to admire. They were very soft and white, for she had never done anything but wash them in clear, cold water.

Another one of them ran to get some strawberries and crushed them in her palms. The juice ran through her fingers like wine from a wine press until her fingers were as pink as the sunrise in the early morning.

"See what beautiful hands I have! The strawberry juice runs over them like wine," said she, and she held up her hands for the others to admire. They were very pink and soft, for she had never done anything but wash them in strawberry juice every morning.

Another one gathered some violets and crushed the flowers in her hands until they smelled like perfume.

"See what beautiful hands I have! They smell like violets in the deep woods in the spring time," said she, and she held up her hands for the others to admire. They were very soft and white, for she had never done anything but wash them in violets every morning.

The fourth girl did not show her hands but held them in her lap. An old woman came down the road and stopped before the girls. They all showed her their hands and asked her which were the most beautiful. She shook her head at each one and then asked to see the hands of the last girl, who held hers in her lap. The last girl raised her hands timidly for the old woman to see.

"Oh, these hands are clean, indeed," said the old woman, "but they are hard from toil. These hands have been helping Mother and Father dry the dishes, and sweep the floor, and wash the windows, and weed the garden. These hands have been taking care of the baby, and carrying hot tea to Grandma, and showing little brother how to build his blocks and fly his kite. Yes, these hands have been busy making the house a happy home, full of love and care."

Then the old woman fumbled in her pocket and brought out a ring set with diamonds, with rubies redder than strawberries, and turquoise bluer than violets.

"Here, wear this ring, my child. You deserve the prize for the most beautiful hands, for they have been the most helpful."

And the old woman vanished, leaving the four girls still sitting by the brook.

•

THE BROWNIES

Adapted from Juliana Horatia Ewing

In English folklore, brownies are good-natured fairies or elves who perform services at night, such as washing, mending, and sweeping. Juliana Horatia Ewing wrote this widely loved tale about the little people, in the mid-nineteenth century. The story helped inspire Robert and Agnes Baden-Powell to found the junior branch of the Girl Guides movement in England (now called the Brownie Girl Scouts in the United States).

"Children are a burden," said the tailor to himself as he sat at his bench, stitching away.

"Children are a blessing," said the kind old lady who sat knitting at the window. "It is the family motto. The Trouts have had large families and good luck for generations."

It was the tailor's mother who spoke. She knew the history of the whole family going back years and years, and which of the Trouts were buried under which old stones in the graveyard. And she had an endless supply of tales about ghosts and fairies and hobgoblins and such, much to her grandchildren's delight.

"Children are a blessing!" she declared again.

"But look at Tommy," the tailor argued. "That boy does nothing but whittle sticks from morning till night. I almost have to lug him out of bed in the mornings. If I send him on an errand, he loiters. If I give him a little chore to do, he does it unwillingly and with such poor grace that it would be far better for me to do it myself. He's not a bad one, mind you, I'm not saying that. But he's not much help, and I did hope he would be a blessing rather than a burden."

"Well, there's still Johnny," the old lady murmured.

"Johnny's too young to be much of a help right now," Mr. Trout replied. "And he won't turn out any different from Tommy if his older brother doesn't stop leading him by the nose."

Now, the thing the boys loved more than anything else in the world was to hear their grandmother tell them the old stories of times gone by. One evening as they sat beside the fire, she told them about a brownie who used to live in the Trout house and help them with the work.

"What was he like, Granny?" Tommy asked.

"Like a little man, they say, my dear."

"What did he do?"

"He came in before the family was up, and swept up the hearth, and lit the fire, and set out the breakfast, and tidied the room, and did all sorts of housework. Sometimes he weeded the garden or threshed the corn. He saved endless trouble. But he never would be seen, and was off before anyone could catch him. The family could hear him laughing and playing about the house sometimes, though."

"Did they give him any wages, Granny?"

"No, my dear. He did it for love. They left a glass of water for him overnight, and now and then a bowl of bread and milk or cream. He liked that, for he was very dainty."

"Oh, Granny! Where did he go?"

"I don't know, dear."

"I wish he'd come back!" both boys cried at once.

"He'd tidy the room," said Johnny.

"And sweep the floor," said Tommy.

"And wash the dishes," said Johnny.

"And pick up our toys," said Tommy.

"And do everything!" they both decided. "We wish he hadn't gone away."

"Well, there are plenty of brownies," the old lady said. "Perhaps the Trouts will have another someday."

"But how do we get one?" Tommy asked.

"Only the Old Owl knows that, my dear. You'd have to ask her."

That night, when they crawled into bed, little Johnny was soon in the land of dreams, but Tommy could not get the thought of the brownie out of his mind.

"There's an owl living in the old shed by the pond," he thought. "It may be the Old Owl herself, and she knows, Granny says. When Father's gone to bed and the moon rises, I'll go."

Soon the moon rose like gold, and went up into the heavens like silver, flooding the moors with a pale ghostly light and painting black shadows under the stone walls. Tommy crept softly out of bed, through the kitchen, and out onto the moor.

It was a glorious night, although everything but the wind and Tommy seemed asleep. The stones, the walls, and the gleaming lanes were intensely still. The church tower in the valley seemed awake and watching, but silent. The houses in the village all had their eyes shut, that is, their window blinds down, and it seemed to Tommy as if the very moors had drawn white sheets over themselves and lay sleeping too.

"Hoot! Hoot!" said a voice from the woods behind him. Somebody else was awake, then.

"It's the Old Owl," said Tommy—and there she came, swinging heavily across the moor with a flapping, stately flight, and sailed into the shed by the pond. Though Tommy ran hard, she was in the shed some time before him. When he got inside, there sat the Old Owl, blinking down at him with yellow eyes.

"Come up! Come up!" she said hoarsely.

She could speak then! Beyond all doubt it was *the* Old Owl, and none other. Tommy shuddered.

"Come up here! Come up here!" said the Old Owl.

The Old Owl sat on a beam that ran across the shed. Tommy had often climbed up for fun; he climbed up now, and sat face to face with her, and thought her eyes looked as if they were made of flame.

"Now, what do you want?" said the owl.

"Please," said Tommy, who felt rather reassured, "can you tell me where to find the brownies, and how to get one to come and live with us?"

"Oohoo!" said the owl, "that's it, is it? I know of two brownies."

"Hurrah!" said Tommy. "Where do they live?"

"In your house," said the owl.

Tommy was aghast.

"In our house!" he exclaimed. "Whereabouts? Let me rummage them out. Why do they do nothing?"

"One of them is too young," said the owl.

"But why doesn't the other work?" asked Tommy.

"He is idle, he is idle," said the Old Owl, and she gave herself such a shake as she said it, that her fluff went flying through the shed, and Tommy nearly tumbled off the beam in his fright.

"Then we don't want them," he said. "What is the use of having brownies if they do nothing to help us?"

"Perhaps they don't know, as no one has told them," said the owl.

"I wish you would tell me where to find them," said Tommy. "I could tell them."

"Could you?" said the owl. "Oohoo! Oohoo!" Tommy couldn't tell whether she was hooting or laughing.

"Of course I could," he said. "They might be up and light the fire, and spread the table, and that sort of thing, before Father comes down. Besides, they could *see* what was wanted. The brownies did all that in Granny's mother's young days. And then they could tidy the room, and sweep the floor, and wash the dishes, and pick up my toys. Oh! there's lots to do."

"So there is," said the owl. "Oohoo! Well, I can tell you where to find one of the brownies, and if you find him he will tell you where his brother is. But this depends upon whether you feel equal to undertaking it, and whether you will follow my directions."

"I am quite ready to go," said Tommy, "and I will do as you tell me. I feel sure I could persuade them. If they only knew how everyone would love them if they made themselves useful!"

"Oohoo! Oohoo!" said the owl. "Now pay attention. You must go to the north side of the pond when the moon is shining and turn yourself around three times, saying this charm:

> Twist me, and turn me, and show me the Elf!
> I looked in the water and saw . . .

Then you look in the pond, and if you see the brownie, you must think of a word that will finish the rhyme. If you do not see the brownie, or if you fail to think of the word, it will be of no use."

"Is the brownie a merman, that he lives underwater?" asked Tommy, wriggling himself along the beam.

"That depends on whether he has a fish's tail," said the owl, "and this you can discover for yourself."

"Well, the moon is shining, so I shall go," said Tommy. "Good-bye, and thank you, ma'am." And he jumped down and went, saying to himself as he ran, "I believe he is a merman all the same or else how could he live in the pond? I know more about brownies than Granny does, and I shall tell her so." For Tommy was somewhat opinionated, like other young people.

The moon shone very brightly on the center of the pond. Tommy knew the place well, for there was a fine echo there. Around the edge grew rushes and water plants, which cast a border of shadow. Tommy went to the north side and turning himself three times, as the Old Owl had told him, he repeated the charm:

> Twist me, and turn me, and show me the Elf!
> I looked in the water and saw . . .

Now for it! He looked in and saw . . . the reflection of his own face.

"Why, there's no one but myself!" said Tommy. "And what can the word be? I must have done it wrong."

"Wrong!" said the echo.

Tommy was most surprised to find the echo awake at this time of night.

"Hold your tongue!" he said. "Matters are provoking enough by themselves. Belf! Celf! Delf! Felf! Gelf! Helf! Jelf! What rubbish! There can't be a word to fit. And then to look for a brownie and see nothing but myself!"

"Myself!" said the echo.

"Will you be quiet?" said Tommy. "If you told me the word, there would be some sense to your interference. But to roar 'Myself!' at me, which neither rhymes nor fits—it does rhyme, though, as it happens. How very odd! And it fits, too:

> Twist me, and turn me, and show me the Elf!
> I looked in the water and saw myself!

What can it mean? The Old Owl knows, as Granny would say. I shall go back and ask her."

"Ask her!" said the echo.

And so he did. He went back to the shed, and there sat the Old Owl as before.

"Oohoo!" said she, as Tommy climbed up. "What did you see in the pond?"

"I saw nothing but myself," Tommy said indignantly.

"And what did you expect to see?" asked the owl.

"I expected to see a brownie," said Tommy. "You told me so."

"And what are brownies like, pray?" inquired the owl.

"The one Granny knew was a useful little fellow, something like a little man," said Tommy.

"Ah," said the owl, "but at present this one is an idle little fellow, something like a little man. Oohoo! Oohoo! Are you quite sure you didn't see him?"

"Quite," answered Tommy sharply. "I saw no one but myself."

"Hoot! Hoot! How touchy we are! And who are you, pray?"

"I'm not a brownie," said Tommy.

"Don't be too sure," said the owl. "Did you find the rhyme?"

"No," said Tommy. "I could find no word with any meaning that would rhyme but 'myself.' "

"Well, that rhymes," said the owl. "What else do you want?"

"I don't understand," said Tommy humbly. "You know I'm not a brownie, am I?"

"Yes, you are," said the owl, "and a very idle one too. All children are brownies."

"But I couldn't do work like a brownie," said Tommy.

"Why not?" inquired the owl. "Couldn't you sweep the floor, light the fire, spread the table, tidy the room, wash the dishes, and pick up your own toys? As you said, there's lots to do."

"Please," said Tommy, "I should like to go home now, and tell Johnny. It's getting cold, and I am so tired!"

"Very well," said the Old Owl. "I think I had better take you."

"I know the way, thank you," said Tommy.

"Just lean against me," insisted the owl. "Lean with your full weight, and shut your eyes."

Tommy lay his head against the Old Owl's feathers. He had a vague idea that she smelled of heather and thought it must be from living on the moor. He shut his eyes and leaned with his full weight, expecting that he and the owl would certainly fall off the beam together. Down . . . feathers . . . fluff . . . he sank and sank. He could feel nothing solid. He jumped up with a start to save himself, opened his eyes, and found that he was sitting in bed, with Johnny sleeping at his side! But ·even odder was that it was no longer moonlight but early dawn.

"Get up, Johnny," he cried. "I've got a story to tell you!" And while Johnny sat up and rubbed his eyes open, Tommy told him everything.

And from that day forward, the Trout household had two of the most useful brownies in the whole land.

•

MR. NOBODY

Does this man live at your house? This is a great poem to help teach responsibility. It's fun to read out loud too.

> I know a funny little man,
>   As quiet as a mouse,
> Who does the mischief that is done
>   In everybody's house!
> There's no one ever sees his face,
>   And yet we all agree
> That every plate we break was cracked
>   By Mr. Nobody.
>
> 'Tis he who always tears our books,
>   Who leaves the door ajar,
> He pulls the buttons from our shirts,
>   And scatters pins afar;
> That squeaking door will always squeak
>   For, prithee, don't you see,
> We leave the oiling to be done
>   By Mr. Nobody.
>
> He puts damp wood upon the fire,
>   That kettles cannot boil;
> His are the feet that bring in mud,
>   And all the carpets soil.
> The papers always are mislaid,
>   Who had them last but he?
> There's no one tosses them about
>   But Mr. Nobody.

The finger-marks upon the door
By none of us are made;
We never leave the blinds unclosed,
To let the curtains fade.
The ink we never spill, the boots
That lying round you see
Are not our boots; they all belong
To Mr. Nobody.

•

THE TREE THAT WAS LONESOME

Home is shelter from storms—all sorts of storms.

There was once an old oak tree that had stood for a long time in the forest.

Many years before, a great storm had swept through the forest. This storm had left the oak only a crooked, ugly tree. It was no longer straight and beautiful like the others. Each spring it covered its ugliness with new green leaves. In the fall the leaves turned to a pretty crimson cloak. But the winds of the forest always swept by. They carried the leaf cloak of the old oak tree away with them. Then it was left with nothing to cover its ugliness.

After years and years, the old oak tree began to feel hollow. It felt as if its heart as well as its body were hurt. The wind sighed through its bare branches one fall when it was very, very old indeed. It made the old oak speak. "No one wants me. I am of no more use in the world," the oak said.

Tap, tap, rap-a-tap-tap! That was Mr. Red-headed Woodpecker. He was hammering at the trunk of the old oak tree. Tap, tap! He hammered and drilled. He worked until he had made a little round front door. It led into his winter house in the trunk of the tree. He had found a ready-made pantry there. It was full of grubs for himself and his family to eat when the cold days came. The walls of his house were warm. It was snug and cozy.

"How grateful I am for this hollow tree," sang Mr. Red-headed Woodpecker.

Whisk, whirr! That was Bobby Squirrel. He ran up the trunk of the old oak tree until he came to the round hole that was his little front window. Bobby Squirrel peeped inside. Oh, how comfortable and snug was the little house that he saw! He lined it with moss. Where the bark stuck out and made shelves, Bobby Squirrel laid piles and piles of nuts. They were ready to feast upon when the cold days came. He would be able to live there, warm in his fur overcoat and well fed. He would be safely sheltered until spring came.

"How grateful I am for this hollow tree," chattered Bobby Squirrel.

Then a strange thing happened to the tree. The beating of the wings of the bird and the happy heart of the little squirrel inside it warmed it. They made the heart of the old oak tree full of joy.

Instead of sighing in the wind, the old oak tree's boughs sang with happiness. The fall rains had left tears on the ends of its twig fingers. Now they turned to diamonds until its twig hands sparkled with them. The snow covered its ugly body with a cloak of white. The starlight at night and the sun in the day time set a crown upon its head.

In all the forest there was no tree more glad, or more beautiful, than the old oak tree.

•

THE PRINCE'S HAPPY HEART

A close-knit and loving home is worth more than a kingdom, as the little prince discovers in this story.

I

Once upon a time there was a little Prince in a country far away from here. He was one of the happiest little Princes who ever lived. All day long he laughed and sang and played. His voice was as sweet as music. His footsteps brought joy wherever he went. Every one thought that this was due to magic. Hung about the Prince's neck on a gold chain was a wonderful heart. It was made of gold and set with precious stones.

The godmother of the little Prince had given the heart to him when he was very small. She had said as she slipped it over his curly head: "To wear this happy heart will keep the Prince happy always. Be careful that he does not lose it."

All the people who took care of the little Prince were very careful to see that the chain of the happy heart was clasped. But one day they found the little Prince in his garden, very sad and sorrowful. His face was wrinkled into an ugly frown.

"Look!" he said, and he pointed to his neck. Then they saw what had happened.

The happy heart was gone. No one could find it, and each day the little Prince grew more sorrowful. At last they missed him. He had gone, himself, to look for the lost happy heart that he needed so much.

II

The little Prince searched all day. He looked in the city streets and along the country roads. He looked in the shops and in the doors of the houses where rich people lived. Nowhere could he find the heart that he had lost. At last it was almost night. He was very tired and hungry. He had never before walked so far, or felt so unhappy.

Just as the sun was setting the little Prince came to a tiny house. It was very poor and weather stained. It stood on the edge of the forest. But a bright light streamed from the window. So he lifted the latch, as a Prince may, and went inside.

There was a mother rocking a baby to sleep. The father was reading a story out loud. The little daughter was setting the table for supper. A boy of the Prince's own age was tending the fire. The mother's dress was old. There were to be only porridge and potatoes for supper. The fire was very small. But all the family were as happy as the little Prince wanted to be. Such smiling faces and light feet the children had. How sweet the mother's voice was!

"Won't you have supper with us?" they begged. They did not seem to notice the Prince's ugly frown.

"Where are your happy hearts?" he asked them.

"We don't know what you mean," the boy and the girl said.

"Why," the Prince said, "to laugh and be as happy as you are, one has to wear a gold chain about one's neck. Where are yours?"

Oh, how the children laughed! "We don't need to wear gold hearts," they said. "We all love each other so much, and we play that this house is a castle and that we have turkey and ice cream for supper. After supper mother will tell us stories. That is all we need to make us happy."

"I will stay with you for supper," said the little Prince.

So he had supper in the tiny house that was a castle. And he played that the porridge and potato were turkey and ice cream. He helped to wash the dishes, and then they all sat about the fire. They played that the small fire was a great one, and listened to fairy stories that the mother told. All at once the little Prince began to smile. His laugh was just as merry as it used to be. His voice was again as sweet as music.

He had a very pleasant time, and then the boy walked part of the way home with him. When they were almost to the palace gates, the Prince said:

"It's very strange, but I feel just exactly as if I had found my happy heart."

The boy laughed. "Why, you have," he said. "Only now you are wearing it inside."

•

WE THANK THEE

Blessings of the home often last longer when we remember to be grateful for them. Gratefulness is too often a forgotten virtue in our day.

> For mother-love and father-care,
> For brothers strong and sisters fair,
> For love at home and here each day,
> For guidance lest we go astray,
>   Father in Heaven, we thank Thee.
>
> For this new morning with its light,
> For rest and shelter of the night,
> For health and food, for love and friends,
> For ev'rything His goodness sends,
>   Father in Heaven, we thank Thee.

•

THE GOLDEN WINDOWS

Retold by Laura E. Richards

We often dream of the splendors of faraway places, but on inspection those attractions are seldom as precious as home.

All day long the little boy worked hard, in field and barn and shed, for his people were poor farmers, and could not pay a workman; but at sunset there came an hour that was all his own, for his father had given it to him. Then the boy would go up to the top of a hill and look across at another hill that rose some miles away. On this far hill stood a house with windows of clear gold and diamonds. They shone and blazed so that it made the boy wink to look at them. But after a while the people in the house put up shutters, as it seemed, and then it looked like any common farmhouse. The boy supposed they did this because it was supper-time; and then he would go into the house and have his supper of bread and milk, and so to bed.

One day the boy's father called him and said: "You have been a good boy, and have earned a holiday. Take this day for your own; but remember that God gave it, and try to learn some good thing."

The boy thanked his father and kissed his mother. Then he put a piece of bread in his pocket, and started off to find the house with the golden windows.

It was pleasant walking. His bare feet made marks in the white dust, and when he looked back, the footprints seemed to be following him, and making company for him. His shadow, too, kept beside him, and would dance or run with him as he pleased; so it was very cheerful.

By and by he felt hungry, and he sat down by a brown brook that ran through the alder hedge by the roadside, and ate his bread, and drank the clear water. Then he scattered the crumbs for the birds, as his mother had taught him to do, and went on his way.

After a long time he came to a high green hill; and when he had climbed the hill, there was the house on the top. But it seemed that the shutters were up, for he could not see the golden windows. He came up to the house, and then he could well have wept, for the windows were of clear glass, like any others, and there was no gold anywhere about them.

A woman came to the door, and looked kindly at the boy, and asked him what he wanted.

"I saw the golden windows from our hilltop," he said, "and I came to see them, but now they are only glass."

The woman shook her head and laughed.

"We are poor farming people," she said, "and are not likely to have gold about our windows. But glass is better to see through."

She bade the boy sit down on the broad stone step at the door, and brought him a cup of milk and a cake, and bade him rest. Then she called her daughter, a child of his own age, and nodded kindly at the two, and went back to her work.

The little girl was barefooted like himself, and wore a brown cotton gown, but her hair was golden like the windows he had seen, and her eyes were blue like the sky at noon. She led the boy about the farm, and showed him her black calf with the white star on its forehead, and he told her about his own at home, which was red like a chestnut, with four white feet. Then when they had eaten an apple together, and so had become friends, the boy asked her about the golden windows. The little girl nodded, and said she knew all about them, only he had mistaken the house.

"You have come quite the wrong way!" she said. "Come with me, and I will show you the house with the golden windows, and then you will see for yourself."

They went to a knoll that rose behind the farmhouse, and as they went the little girl told him that the golden windows could only be seen at a certain hour, about sunset.

"Yes, I know that!" said the boy.

When they reached the top of the knoll, the girl turned and pointed; and there on a hill far away stood a house with windows of clear gold and diamonds, just as he had seen them. And when they looked again, the boy saw that it was his own home.

Then he told the little girl that he must go. He gave her his best pebble, the white one with the red band, that he had carried for a year in his pocket; and she gave him three horse-chestnuts, one red like satin, one spotted, and one white like milk. He kissed her, and promised to come again, but he did not tell her what he had learned. He went back down the hill, and the little girl stood in the sunset light and watched him.

The way home was long, and it was dark before the boy reached his father's house; but the lamplight and firelight shone through the windows, making them almost as bright as he had seen them from the hilltop. When he opened the door, his mother came to kiss him, and his little sister ran to throw her arms about his neck, and his father looked up and smiled from his seat by the fire.

"Have you had a good day?" asked his mother.

Yes, the boy had had a very good day.

"And have you learned anything?" asked his father.

"Yes!" said the boy. "I have learned that our house has windows of gold and diamonds."

•

THE LEGEND OF THE CHRIST CHILD

Adapted from a retelling by Elizabeth Harrison

This beautiful old story reminds us that in homes where love is, God is.

Once upon a time, long, long ago, on the night before Christmas, a little child was wandering all alone through the streets of a great city. There were many people in the street, fathers and mothers, sisters and brothers, uncles and aunts, and even gray-haired grandfathers and grandmothers, all of whom were hurrying home with bundles of presents for each other and for their little ones. Fine carriages rolled by, express wagons rattled past, even old carts were pressed into service. All things seemed in a hurry and glad with expectation of the coming Christmas morning.

From some of the windows bright lights were already beginning to stream, until it was almost as bright as day. But the little child seemed to have no home, and wandered about listlessly from street to street. No one took any notice of him, except perhaps Jack Frost, who bit his bare toes and made the ends of his fingers tingle. The north wind, too, seemed to notice the child, for it blew against him and pierced his ragged garments through and through, causing him to shiver with cold. Home after home he passed, looking with longing eyes through the windows in upon the glad, happy children, most of whom were helping to trim the Christmas trees for the coming morrow.

"Surely," said the child to himself, "where there is so much gladness and happiness, some of it may be for me." So with timid steps he approached a large and handsome house. Through the windows he could see a beautiful Christmas tree already lighted. Many presents hung upon it. Its green boughs were trimmed with gold and silver ornaments. Slowly he climbed up the broad steps and gently rapped at the door.

It was opened by a tall and stately footman. He had a kindly face, although his voice was deep and gruff. He looked at the little child for a moment, then sadly shook his head and said, "Go down off the steps. There is no room here for such as you." He looked sorry as he spoke. Through the open door a bright light shone, and the warm air, filled with the fragrance of the Christmas pine, rushed out from the inner room and greeted the little wanderer like a kiss. As the child turned back into the cold and darkness, he wondered why the footman had spoken thus, for surely, thought he, those little children would love to have another companion join them in their joyous Christmas festival. But the little children inside did not even know that he had knocked at the door.

The street grew colder and darker as the child passed on. He went sadly forward, saying to himself, "Is there no one in all this great city who will share the Christmas with me?" Farther and farther down the street he wandered, to where the homes were not so large and beautiful. There seemed to be little children inside of nearly all the houses. They were dancing and frolicking about. Christmas trees could be seen in every window, with beautiful dolls and trumpets and picture-books and balls and tops and other wonderful toys hung upon them.

In one window the child noticed a little lamb made of soft, white wool. Around its neck was tied a red ribbon. It had evidently been hung on the tree for one of the younger children. The little wanderer stopped before this window and looked long and earnestly at the beautiful things inside, but most of all was he drawn toward the white lamb.

At last, creeping up to the windowpane, he gently tapped upon it. A little girl came to the window and looked out into the dark street where the snow had now begun to fall. She saw the child, but she only frowned and shook her head, and said, "Go away and come some other time. We are too busy to take care of you now." Back into the dark, cold street he turned again. The wind was whirling past him and seemed to say, "Hurry on, hurry on, we have no time to stop. 'Tis Christmas Eve and everybody is in a hurry tonight."

Again and again the child rapped softly at door or window-pane. At each place he was refused admission. One mother feared he might have some ugly disease which her darlings would catch; another father said he had only enough for his own children, and none to spare for beggar brats. Still another told him to go home where he belonged, and not to trouble other folks.

The hours passed; the night grew later, and the wind colder, and the street darker. Farther and farther the little one wandered. There was scarcely anyone left on the streets by this time, and the few who remained did not notice the child. Suddenly ahead of him there appeared a bright, single ray of light. It shone through the darkness into the child's eyes. He looked up, smiling, and said, "I will go where the little light beckons. Perhaps they will share their Christmas with me."

Hurrying past all the other houses he soon reached the end of the street and went straight up to the window from which the light was streaming. The house was old and small, but the child cared not for that. The light seemed still to call him in. From what do you suppose the light came? Nothing but a candle which had been placed in an old cup with a broken handle, in the window, as a glad token of Christmas Eve. There was neither curtain nor shade at the small, square window, and as the little child looked in he saw standing upon a neat, wooden table a small Christmas tree. The room was plainly furnished, but it was very clean. Near the fireplace sat a sweet-faced mother with a little two-year-old on her knee and an older child beside her. The two children were looking into their mother's face and listening to a story. She must have been telling them a Christmas story, I think. A few bright coals were burning in the fireplace, and all seemed light and warm within.

The little wanderer crept closer to the windowpane. So sweet was the mother's face, so loving seemed the little children, that he took courage and tapped gently, very gently, on the door. The mother stopped talking, the little children looked up. "What was that, Mother?" asked the little girl at her side.

"I think it was some one tapping on the door," replied the mother. "Run quickly and open it, dear, for it is a bitter cold night to keep anyone waiting in this storm."

"Oh, Mother, I think it was the bough of the tree tapping against the windowpane," said the little girl. "Do please go on with our story."

Again the little wanderer tapped upon the door.

"My child! My child!" exclaimed the mother, rising. "That cer-

tainly was a rap on the door. Run quickly and open it. No one must be left out in the cold on Christmas Eve."

The child ran to the door and threw it wide open. The mother saw the ragged stranger standing without, cold and shivering, with bare head and almost bare feet. She held out both hands and drew him into the warm, bright room. "You poor dear child," was all she said, and, putting her arms around him, she drew him close to her breast. "He is very cold, my children," she exclaimed. "We must warm him."

"And," added the little girl, "we must love him and give him some of our Christmas, too."

"Yes," said the mother, "but first let us warm him."

The mother sat down beside the fire with the child on her lap, and her own two little ones warmed his half-frozen hands in theirs. The mother smoothed his tangled curls, and, bending low over his head, kissed the child's forehead. She gathered the three little ones close to her and the candle and the firelight shone over them. For a moment the room was very still. I think she must have been praying. Then she whispered to the little girl, who ran into the other room and returned with a bowl of bread and milk for the little stranger.

By and by the little girl said, softly, to her mother, "May we not light the Christmas tree, and let him see how beautiful it looks?"

"Yes," replied the mother. With that she seated the child on a low stool beside the fire, and went herself to fetch the few simple ornaments which from year to year she had saved for her children's Christmas tree.

And as they busied themselves about the tree, they began to notice that the room had filled with a strange and wonderful light.

Brighter and brighter it grew, until it shone like the sun; from floor to ceiling all was light as day. And when they turned and looked at the spot where the little wanderer had sat, it was empty. There was nothing to be seen. The child was gone, but the light was still in the room.

"Children," the mother said quietly, "I believe we have had the Christ Child with us tonight."

And she drew her dear ones to her and kissed them, and there was great joy in the little house.

•

MY TWO HOMES

Henry Hallam Tweedy

Many children feel at home in their house because they know it is part of God's house.

Of all the houses in the world
    The one that I love best
Is that in which I wake and play
    And lay me down to rest.

My father built it by his toil;
    My mother makes it home;
You cannot find a lovelier place
    No matter where you roam.

The rooms are clean and bright and fair
    With pictures, books, and toys,
And food, and clothes, and beds, and chairs
    For all the girls and boys.

We children work and care for it,
    And help to keep it clean,
Our palace of true happiness,
    Where mother reigns as queen,

And father guards us with his strength,
   A wise and gracious king,
To whom we pay the honor due,
   And glad obedience bring.

So full of love and joy it is,
   So safe and bright and warm,
I would not go too far from it
   Lest I should come to harm.

And yet when I go out of doors
   And look up at the sky,
I know I'm in my Father's house,
   And that His love is nigh.

For God is Father—Mother, too!
   The world is my big home;
The green grass is the carpet,
   And the blue sky is the dome.

On every side are pictures;
   The fields are full of food;
And all the things that God has made
   Are beautiful and good.

He keeps me by His mighty power,
   He loves me as His child;
His paths are bright with happiness,
   His laws are just and mild.

And all His children in this house,
   So wonderful and fair,
Should love each other, learn His truth,
   And trust His love and care.

I thank thee, Father, for these homes,
   Where we may dwell with Thee,
And cast out fear, and share the joys
   Thou givest full and free.

•

THE MATSUYAMA MIRROR

This charming Japanese tale was popular with American children
around the turn of the twentieth century. It was handed down
from parent to child in Japan over many generations, and dates
to a time when people living outside of cities knew nothing of
mirrors or their uses. It reminds us that in many ways, we grow
up in our parents' image. We hope their virtues become our
virtues.

I

Long ago there lived, in a quiet spot in far away Japan, a young
man and his wife. They had one child, a little daughter, whom they
loved dearly. I cannot tell you their names, for they have been long
since forgotten; but the name of the place where they lived was
Matsuyama.

It happened once, while the little girl was still a baby, that the
father had to go to the great city, the capital of Japan, upon some
business. It was too far for the mother and her little baby to go, so
he set out alone, after bidding them good-by and promising to
bring them home some pretty present.

The mother had never been farther from home than the next
village, and she could not help being a little frightened at the
thought of her husband taking such a long journey; and yet she was
a little proud, too, for he was the first man in all that countryside
who had been to the big town where the King and his great lords
lived, and where there were so many beautiful and curious things
to be seen.

At last the time came when she might expect her husband
back, so she dressed the baby in her best clothes, and herself put
on a pretty blue dress which she knew her husband liked.

You may fancy how glad this good wife was to see him come
home safe and sound, and how the little girl clapped her hands,
and laughed with delight, when she saw the pretty toys her father
had brought for her. He had much to tell of all the wonderful things
he had seen upon the journey, and in the town itself.

"I have brought you a very pretty thing," said he to his wife. "It
is called a mirror. Look and tell me what you see inside." He gave

to her a plain, white, wooden box, in which, when she opened it, she found a round piece of metal. One side was white like frosted silver, and ornamented with raised figures of birds and flowers; the other was bright as the clearest crystal. Into it the young mother looked with delight and astonishment, for from its depths was looking at her a smiling, happy face.

"What do you see?" again asked the husband, pleased at her astonishment, and glad to show that he had learned something while he had been away.

"I see a pretty woman looking at me, and she moves her lips as if she were speaking, and—dear me, how odd, she has on a blue dress just like mine!"

"Why, it is your own face that you see," said the husband, proud of knowing something that his wife didn't know. "That round piece of metal is called a mirror. In the town everybody has one, although we have not seen them in this country place before."

The wife was charmed with her present, and for a few days could not look into the mirror often enough, for you must remember that this was the first time she had seen a mirror, so of course it was the first time she had ever seen the reflection of her own pretty face. But she considered such a wonderful thing far too precious for everyday use, and soon shut it up in its box again, and put it away carefully among her most valued treasures.

II

Years passed, and the husband and wife still lived happily. The joy of their life was their little daughter, who grew up the very image of her mother, and who was so dutiful and affectionate that everybody loved her. Mindful of her own little passing vanity on finding herself so lovely, the mother kept the mirror carefully hidden away, fearing that the use of it might breed a spirit of pride in her little girl.

She never spoke of it; and as for the father, he had forgotten all about it. So the daughter grew up as simple as the mother had been, and knew nothing of her own good looks, or of the mirror which would have reflected them.

But by and by a sad misfortune came to this happy little family. The kind mother fell sick; and, although her daughter waited upon her day and night, with loving care, she got worse and worse, until at last there was no hope but that she must die.

When she found that she must so soon leave her husband and

child, the poor woman felt very sorrowful, grieving for those she was going to leave behind, and most of all for her little daughter.

She called the girl to her and said, "My darling child, you know that I am very sick; soon I must die, and leave your dear father and you alone. When I am gone, promise me that you will look into this mirror every night and every morning. There you will see me, and know that I am still watching over you." With these words she took the mirror from its hiding place and gave it to her daughter. The child promised, with many tears, and so the mother, seeming now calm and resigned, died a short time after.

Now this obedient and dutiful daughter never forgot her mother's last request, but each morning and evening took the mirror from its hiding place, and looked in it long and earnestly. There she saw the bright and smiling vision of her lost mother; not pale and sickly as in her last days, but the beautiful young mother of long ago. To her, at night, she told the story of the trials and difficulties of the day; to her, in the morning, she looked for sympathy and encouragement in whatever might be in store for her.

So day by day she lived as in her mother's sight, striving still to please her as she had done in her lifetime, and careful always to avoid whatever might pain or grieve her.

Her greatest joy was to be able to look in the mirror and say, "Mother, I have been today what you would have me be."

Seeing her every night and morning, without fail, look into the mirror, and seem to hold converse with it, her father at length asked her the reason for her strange behavior.

"Father," she said, "I look in the mirror every day to see my dear mother and to talk with her." Then she told him of her mother's dying wish, and how she had never failed to fulfill it. Touched by so much simplicity, and such faithful, loving obedience, the father shed tears of pity and affection. Nor could he find it in his heart to tell the child that the image she saw in the mirror was but the reflection of her own sweet face, becoming more and more like her dear mother's, day by day.

•

THE APRON STRING

Laura E. Richards

The much-derided apron string can come in handy, especially when its fibers are the virtues we've learned at home. Those bonds stay with us.

Once upon a time a boy played about the house, running by his mother's side; and as he was very little, his mother tied him to the string of her apron.

"Now," she said, "when you stumble, you can pull yourself up by the apron-string, and so you will not fall."

The boy did that, and all went well, and the mother sang at her work.

By and by the boy grew so tall that his head came above the window-sill; and looking through the window, he saw far away green trees waving, and a flowing river that flashed in the sun, and rising above all, blue peaks of mountains.

"Oh, Mother," he said, "untie the apron-string and let me go!"

But the mother said, "Not yet, my child! Only yesterday you stumbled, and would have fallen but for the apron-string. Wait yet a little, till you are stronger."

So the boy waited, and all went as before; and the mother sang at her work.

But one day the boy found the door of the house standing open, for it was spring weather. He stood on the threshold and looked across the valley, and saw the green trees waving, and the swift-flowing river with the sun flashing on it, and the blue mountains rising beyond. And this time he heard the voice of the river calling, and it said "Come!"

Then the boy started forward, and as he started, the string of the apron broke.

"Oh! how weak my mother's apron-string is!" cried the boy; and he ran out into the world, with the broken string hanging beside him.

The mother gathered up the other end of the string and put it in her bosom, and went about her work again; but she sang no more.

The boy ran on and on, rejoicing in his freedom, and in the fresh air and the morning sun. He crossed the valley, and began to climb the foothills among which the river flowed swiftly, among rocks and cliffs. Now it was easy climbing, and again it was steep and craggy, but always he looked upward at the blue peaks beyond, and always the voice of the river was in his ears, saying "Come!"

By and by he came to the brink of a precipice, over which the river dashed in a cataract, foaming and flashing, and sending up clouds of silver spray. The spray filled his eyes, so that he did not see his footing clearly; he grew dizzy, stumbled, and fell. But as he fell, something about him caught on a point of rock at the precipice-edge, and held him, so that he hung dangling over the abyss; and when he put up his hand to see what held him, he found that it was the broken string of the apron, which still hung by his side.

"Oh! how strong my mother's apron-string is!" said the boy. And he drew himself up by it, and stood firm on his feet, and went on climbing toward the blue peaks of the mountains.

•

FOUR DAUGHTERS

This story from South America reminds us that the habits we learn in the home are the habits we carry with us into the world.

There once lived a mother who had four daughters, named Margarita, Emilia, Carmen, and Maria. The three eldest children were lazy and rude and rarely obeyed their mother. Only the youngest, Maria, did what she could to be a loving daughter.

The time came when the mother called her children together.

"You are growing older now, and so am I," she told them. "I will not be able to take care of you forever. You must learn to work so you can make your own ways in the world someday. So I have chores for each of you to do. Margarita, you must dust away the cobwebs. Emilia, you must sweep the floor. Carmen, you must rake the yard. And Maria, you must weed in the garden."

But Margarita, the eldest daughter, scowled.

"Dust? I can't be expected to dust!" she hooted. "I need my

beauty sleep." She packed her bag and left the house to find some quiet place to lay down her head.

Emilia, the next daughter, threw up her arms and paced the room in circles.

"I don't know how to sweep," she grunted. "I'm sure I can't learn how. I'm going for a stroll in the countryside. It's much more pleasant there."

She packed her bags and left the house.

Carmen, the next daughter, banged her fist on the table.

"I don't know how to work either!" she shrieked. "I've got better things to do, you know. I'm moving to town. People there know how to have fun."

She too packed her bags and left the house with a frown.

Only Maria, the youngest daughter, put on a smile.

"Don't worry, Mother," she said. "I'll work in the garden and plant as many flowers as it will hold, and sell them in town at market. That way I can stay with you and take care of you as you grow old."

Time passed, and Maria kept her word. Her garden flourished, as did her trade at the marketplace, and she made enough money to give some comfort to her mother.

But at last the day came when the old woman sensed her time had come. She sent Maria to find her sisters so she might tell them good-bye.

Marie found Margarita asleep in the shady forest.

"Mother is ill and asks you to come home," she told her.

"I'm sleeping right now," Margarita yawned. "It's much too early. Tell her I'll come later."

Maria found Emilia wandering the countryside, searching the fields for scraps of food left from the harvest.

"I don't have time to come home," she said. "I'm hoping to pick up some dinner."

Maria found Carmen walking the town lanes and alleys, knocking on door after door, looking for handouts.

"I can't come home just now," she muttered. "No one feels generous today. I must keep knocking if I am to eat." She turned her back to rap on another door.

Maria returned to her mother, who grieved at her daughters' fates.

"My Margarita will live in the darkness of the forest for the rest of her life, sleeping the days away," she cried. "My Emilia will spend her life wandering aimlessly, content to live on what lies on the ground. My Carmen will knock and knock for the rest of her days, grubbing for morsels. Only you, Maria, will be welcomed and beloved by all."

The old woman closed her eyes and drew her last breath.

And her prophecy came true.

After her death, Margarita became an owl, and to this day she dwells in the darkest parts of the forest, sleeping the days away.

Emilia turned into a ugly vulture, and now circles the country skies, hoping to dine on whatever she finds lying on the ground.

Carmen changed into a woodpecker, and you can still hear her knocking and knocking all day long, grubbing for morsels.

As for little Maria, she is still hard at work in her garden, tending her flowers, sipping the nectar from their silky cups. And everywhere she goes, she is welcomed and beloved, for Maria turned into a hummingbird.

•

THE NEW LEAVES

Adapted from Laura E. Richards

Here's a great story for the New Year that will help children understand what "turning over a new leaf" means. Better to learn good habits in the home than out in the world, where turning the leaves may be much tougher.

"Wake up!" said a clear little voice. Tommy woke, and sat up. At the foot of the bed stood a boy about his own age, all dressed in white, like fresh snow. He had very bright eyes, and he looked straight at Tommy.

"Who are you?" asked Tommy.

"I am the New Year!" said the boy. "This is my day, and I have brought you your leaves."

"What leaves?" asked Tommy.

"The new ones, to be sure!" said the New Year. "I hear bad accounts of you from my Daddy—"

"Who is your Daddy?" asked Tommy.

"The Old Year, of course!" said the boy. "He said you asked too many questions, and I see he was right. He says you are greedy, too, and that you sometimes pinch your little sister, and that one day you threw your reader into the fire. Now, all this must stop."

"Oh, must it?" said Tommy. He felt frightened, and did not know just what to say.

The boy nodded. "If it does not stop," he said, "you will grow worse and worse every year, till you grow up into a Horrid Man. Do you want to be a Horrid Man?"

"N-no!" said Tommy.

"Then you must stop being a horrid boy!" said the New Year. "Take your leaves!" And he held out a packet of what looked like notebook paper, all sparkling white, like his own clothes.

"Turn over one of these every day," he said, "and soon you will be a good boy instead of a horrid one."

Tommy took the leaves of paper and looked at them. On each leaf a few words were written. On one it said, "Help your mother and father!" On another, "Pick up your toys!" On another, "Stop tracking mud across the floor!" On another, "Be nice to your little sister!" And on still another, "Don't fight Billy Jenkins!"

"Oh!" cried Tommy. "I *have* to fight Billy Jenkins!" He said—"

"Good-by!" said the New Year. "I shall come again when I am old to see whether you have been a good boy or a horrid one. Remember,

> "Horrid boy makes horrid man.
> You alone can change the plan."

He turned away and opened the window. A cold wind blew in and swept the leaves out of Tommy's hand. "Stop! stop!" he cried. "Tell me—" But the New Year was gone, and Tommy, staring after him, saw only his mother coming into the room. "Dear child!" she said. "Why, the wind is blowing everything about."

"My leaves! My leaves!" cried Tommy. Jumping out of bed, he looked all over the room, but he could not find one.

"Never mind," said Tommy. "I can turn them just the same, and I mean to. I will not grow into a Horrid Man." And he didn't.

THE NIGHT WIND

Eugene Field

At home that guardian of virtue we call conscience takes root. It talks to us often, even when we don't ask it to.

Have you ever heard the wind go "Yooooo'"?
  'Tis a pitiful sound to hear.
It seems to chill you through and through
  With a strange and speechless fear.
It's the voice of the night that broods outside
  When folks should be asleep;
And many and many's the time I've cried
To the darkness that brooded far and wide
  Over the land and the deep:
"Whom do you want, O lonely night,
That you wail the long hours through?"
And the night would say in its ghostly way:
      "Yoo—oo—oo—oo! Yoo—oo—oo—oo!
        Yoo—oo—oo—oo!"

My mother told me long ago
  (When I was a little lad),
That when the night went wailing so,
  Somebody had been bad.
And then, when I was snug in bed,
  Whither I had been sent,
With the blankets drawn up around my head,
I'd think of what my mother'd said,
  And wonder what boy she meant.
"And who's been bad today?" I'd ask
Of the wind that hoarsely blew.
And that voice would say in its awful way:
      "Yoo—oo—oo—oo! Yoo—oo—oo—oo!
        Yoo—oo—oo—oo!"

That this was true I must allow—
    You'll not believe it though!—
Yes, though I'm quite a model now,
    I was not always so.
And if you doubt what things I say,
    Suppose you make the test;
Suppose when you've been bad some day,
And up to bed you're sent away
    From mother and the rest—
Suppose you ask, "Who has been bad?"
And then you'll hear what's true.
For the wind will moan in its ruefullest tone:
    "Yoo—oo—oo—oo! Yoo—oo—oo—oo!
    Yoo—oo—oo—oo!"

•

THE GARDEN OF THE FROST FLOWERS
Retold by Frances Jenkins Olcott

Home is a place of protection from very real dangers beyond the doorstep—dangers from nature and dangers from man. This sad story in which a child dies, retold from a poem by William Cullen Bryant, reminds children that when they are young, they must not stray too far alone, and they must take seriously their parents' warnings.

THE PROMISE MADE

In the olden time, long, long ago, there dwelt on a mountain side a cottager, his wife, and his little girl named Eva. A lovely spot was their home, for near it was a glen through which dashed a brook fringed with many sweet-smelling Spring flowers.

But then Winter came, the little brook was fringed with other blossoms. Strange white ones with crystal leaves and stems grew there in the clear November nights. For when the Winter Winds blew hard, down from the mountain top came a troop of Little People of the Snow. A beautiful Fairy race they were, with bright locks, and voices like the sounds of steps on crisp Snow. With

trailing robes they came, some flying through the air, others tripping lightly across the icy fields.

They threw spangles of silvery Frost upon the grass and edged
the brook with glistening parapets. They built crystal bridges over
the stream, and, touching the water, turned its face to glass. Then
they shook, from their full laps, so many Snowflakes that they covered the whole world with a soft blanket.

Now Eva had often heard about these Little People, but she
had never seen them. One Mid-Winter day, when she was twelve
years old, she dressed herself warmly to play in the Snow.

"Do not stay too long," said her mother, as she wrapped her
furry coat around the child and put on her fur boots. "Do not stay
too long, for sharp is the Winter Wind. And go no farther than the
great Linden Tree on the edge of our field."

All this Eva promised, and went skipping from the house. Now
she climbed the rounded snow swells that felt firm with Frost beneath her feet, and now she slid down them into the deep hollows.
So she played alone and was happy.

But as she was clambering up a very high drift, she saw a tiny
maiden sitting on the Snow. Lily-cheeked she was, with flowing
flaxen hair and blue eyes that gleamed like Ice, while her robe
seemed of a more shadowy whiteness than her cheeks.

When she saw Eva, this tiny creature bounded to her feet, and
cried: "Oh, come with me, pretty Friend. I have watched you often,
and know how well you love the Snow, and how you carve huge-
limbed Snowmen, Lions, and Griffins. Come, let us ramble over
these bright fields. You shall see what you have never seen before."

So Eva followed her new friend. Together they slid down drifts
and climbed white mounds, until they reached the spot where the
great Linden Tree stood.

"Here I must stop," said Eva, "for I promised my mother I
would go no farther."

But the little Snow Maiden laughed.

"What!" cried she. "Are you afraid of the Snow? of the pure
Snow? of the innocent Snow? It has never hurt any living thing.
Surely your mother made you promise that because she thought
you had no one to guide you. I will show you the way and bring
you safely home."

By such smooth words Eva was won to break her promise, and
she followed her new playmate. Over glistening fields they ran, and
down a steep bank to the foot of a huge Snowdrift or Hill of Snow.

There the Winds had carved a shelf of driven snow, that curtained a wide opening in the hill.

"Look! Look! Let us enter here!" cried the little creature merrily. "Come, Eva, follow me."

IN THE GARDEN OF FROST FLOWERS

Straight under the shelflike curtain Eva and the little Snow Maiden crept, and walked along a passage with white walls. Above them in the vaulted roof were set Snow Stars that cast a wintry twilight over all.

Eva moved with awe and could not speak for wonder; but the little Snow Maiden, laughing gayly, tripped lightly on before. Deeper and deeper they went into the heart of the Hill of Snow. And now the walls began to widen; and the vaulted roof rose higher and higher, until it expanded into a great white dome above their heads.

Eva looked about her. She stood in a large white garden, where everything seemed to be spun out of delicate silent Frost.

At her feet grew snow-white plants with lacelike leaves and spangled flowers. At her side Palm Trees reared their stately white columns tufted with frosted plumes. Huge Oaks, with icelike trunks, waved their transparent branches in the silent air, while their gnarled roots seemed anchored deep in glistening banks. Light sprays of Myrtle, and snowy Roses in bud and bloom, drooped by the winding walks.

All these things—flowers, leaves, and trees—seemed delicately wrought from stainless alabaster. Up the trees ran Jasmine vines with stalks and leaves as colorless as their blossoms. All this Eva saw with wonder and delight.

"Walk, softly, dear Friend," said the little Snow Maiden. "Do not touch the frail creation round you, nor sweep it with your skirt.

"Now, look up, and behold how beautifully this Garden of Frost Flowers is lighted. See those shifting gleams that seem to come and go so gently. They are the Northern Lights that make beautiful our Winter Palace.

"Here on long cold nights I and my comrades, the Little People of the Snow, make this garden lovely. We guide to this place the wandering Snowflakes and, piling them up into many quaint shapes, bid them grow into stately columns, glittering arches, white trees, and lovely flowers of Frost.

"But come now, dear Eva, and I will show you a far more wonderful sight."

THE DANCE OF THE LITTLE PEOPLE OF THE SNOW

As she spoke, the little Snow Maiden led her to a windowpane of transparent ice set in the Snow wall.

"Look," said she, "but you may not enter in."

Eva looked.

Lo! she saw a glorious, glistening palace hall from whose lofty roof fell stripes of shimmering light, rose-colored, and delicate green, and tender blue.

This light flowed downward to the floor, enveloping in its rainbow hues a joyous multitude of tiny folk, whirling in a merry dance. Silvery music sounded from cymbals of transparent Ice skillfully touched by tiny hands.

Round and round they flew beneath the dome of colored lights, now wheeling and now turning. Their bright eyes shone under their lily brows. Their gauzy scarfs, sparkling like snow wreaths in the Sun, floated in the dizzy whirl.

Eva stood entranced in wonder, as all these Little People of the Snow, dancing and whirling in the colored lights, swept past the icy windowpane.

Long she gazed, and long she listened to the sweet sounds that thrilled the frosty air. Then the intense cold around her numbed her limbs, and she remembered the promise to her mother.

THE PROMISE BROKEN

"Alas!" she cried, "too long, too long am I lingering here! Oh, how wickedly I have done to break my promise! What must they think, the dear ones at home?"

With hurried step she found the snowy passage again, and followed it upward to the light, while the little Snow Maiden ran by her side, guiding her feet.

When she reached the open air once more, a bitter blast came rushing from the clear North, chilling her blood, and she shrank in terror before it. But the little Snow Maiden, when she felt the cutting blast, bounded along, uttering shouts of joy, and skipping from drift to drift. And she danced around Eva, as the poor child wearily climbed the slippery mounds of frozen snow.

"Ah me!" sighed Eva at last, "Ah me! My eyes grow heavy. They swim with sleep."

As she spoke, her lids closed, and she sank upon the ground and slept.

Then near her side sat the little Snow Maiden, watching her slumber. She saw the rosy color fade from Eva's rounded cheeks, and the child's brow grow white as marble, while her breath slowly ceased to come and go. All motionless lay her form; and the little Snow Maiden strove to waken her, plucking her dress, and shouting in her ears, but all in vain.

Then suddenly was heard the sound of steps grating on the Snow. It was Eva's parents searching for their lost child. When they found her, lying like a fair marble image in her deathlike sleep, and when they heard from the little Snow Maiden how she had led Eva into the Garden of Frost Flowers, their hearts were wrung with anguish.

They lifted the dear child up and bore her home. And though they chafed her limbs and bathed her brow, she never woke again. The little maid was dead.

Now came the funeral day. In a grave dug in the glen's white side they buried Eva, while from the rocks and hills around a thousand slender voices rose, and sighed, and mourned, until the echoes, taking up the strains, flung them far and wide across the icy fields.

From that day the Little People of the Snow were never seen again. But all during the long, cold Winter nights, invisible tiny hands wove around Eva's grave frost wreaths, and tufts of silvery rime shaped like flowers one scatters on a bier.

•

JOSEPH AND HIS BROTHERS

*Retold by J. Berg Essenwein
and Marietta Stockard*

Joseph embodies the true spirit of brotherhood: his love was so
great, he not only forgave but saved those who betrayed him, and
made for them a new home. The story is from the book of Genesis
in the Bible.

Long ago, in the land of Canaan, there lived a rich shepherd
and farmer called Jacob. He had great flocks and many servants. He
had also twelve sons, and the best loved of his sons was Joseph.
Perhaps it was because Joseph himself was always gentle and obedient; perhaps it was because of his beautiful mother, Rachel, who
had died when the little brother, Benjamin, was born; but at any
rate, Jacob loved Joseph deeply and tenderly.

His brothers grew angry and jealous because of this great love.
"Our father will give him all of his riches, and make him ruler over
us," they said.

When Joseph was seventeen years old, his father gave him a
beautiful coat of many colors. He walked among his brothers
dressed in the coat, and they grew more jealous and angry still.
Sometimes he talked to them of strange dreams he had, which
seemed to mean that some day he would be more rich and powerful than they. This made them hate him bitterly.

At last, one day when they had driven their flocks· to pastures
which were far away from home, Jacob called Joseph to him and
said: "Go see whether it be well with thy brethren and with the
flocks; and bring me word again."

Joseph was always glad to serve his father, so he set out toward
Shechem to find his brothers. But they had driven their flocks still
farther away, and Joseph wandered in the fields for a long time
before he came to them.

When they saw him far off, the jealousy which had been making their hearts more wicked each day grew into hatred so black
that they began to plan to murder their own brother. But Reuben,
the oldest of the brothers, determined to save Joseph if he could.

He seemed to agree with them, and said: "Let us cast him into this pit here in the wilderness and leave him." He meant to return, however, and send Joseph away home to their old father.

As Joseph drew near to them, his brothers began to mock him. "Behold the dreamer!" they scoffed. "Let us now see what will become of his dreams!" They caught him and with rough hands stripped off his beautiful coat, and threw him into the deep pit. Then they sat near and ate their food, laughing at Joseph's cries and pleadings.

While they sat there, a caravan of merchants came along the highway. Their camels were loaded with spices and myrrh which they were carrying down into Egypt.

"Come," said Judah, "let us sell Joseph to these Ishmaelites. They will carry him down into Egypt, and we shall never see him again. We shall be rid of him, and still we shall not have his blood upon our hands."

The brothers agreed, and lifted Joseph from the pit. He begged most piteously to be allowed to go back home, but they hardened their hearts, and sold him for twenty pieces of silver. Then the Ishmaelites set him upon a camel, and carried him away into the strange land of Egypt.

Reuben came back to the pit and found Joseph gone. He rent his clothes in his great grief, but the other brothers said: "We are well rid of him. Now he will never rule over us."

They took Joseph's coat and tore it, then dipped it in the blood of a kid so that their father would think some wild beast had slain his son. When Jacob saw the coat, he mourned most piteously.

Meantime, the Ishmaelites continued their journey down into Egypt, carrying the lonely lad. But God comforted him in his dreams. He remembered too the teaching of his father, and faith and courage stayed in his heart.

When they arrived in Egypt, Joseph was sold to Potiphar, who was an officer of the king, called Pharaoh. Soon Joseph's gentle ways and comely looks caused him to be loved and trusted by all. Whatever he did prospered, so the Egyptian captain saw that God was with him, and he made him the overseer of his house. There Joseph learned the customs of the land, he learned to command men, and learned the needs of the country.

But the happy, prosperous days soon came to an end. The wife of Potiphar filled her husband's mind with wicked lies concerning Joseph, and caused him to be thrown into prison. Some servants of

Pharaoh who had angered him were in the prison at this time, and Joseph talked with them so wisely that they knew that his knowledge came from God.

Two long years went by, and at last Pharaoh was troubled by strange dreams and needed counsel. The chief butler, who had been in the prison with Joseph, remembered his great wisdom. "Send for that young Hebrew prisoner," he said to King Pharaoh; "he will interpret your dream."

Then Pharaoh sent and called Joseph. He was brought from his dungeon and placed before the king. He listened to the king's strange dream of seven lean cows coming from the river and devouring seven fat cows; of seven blasted ears of corn springing up and devouring seven ears that were full and good. And God gave Joseph the wisdom to know the meaning of the dream.

"O King," he said, "there are seven years of great plenty at hand, but these seven years will be followed by seven years of famine in the land. Let the king command that food be gathered and stored during the seven years of plenty."

Pharaoh believed Joseph's words and made him chief ruler in the land. Only the king himself was greater than he. He gave him riches and power, and the high-born maiden Asenath for his wife.

In the seven years that followed, Joseph caused great storehouses to be built and filled with grain, so when the years of famine came there was bread in Egypt, but in no other land. People came from all the neighboring countries into Egypt to buy bread.

Now the aged Jacob heard that there was bread in Egypt, so he sent his ten sons there. Benjamin, the youngest son, he sent not. He feared that evil might befall this other son of his beloved Rachel, the mother of Joseph.

The ten brothers journeyed down to Egypt, and stood before the governor of the land. They bowed down before him, not knowing that the rich and powerful governor was their own brother whom they had sold to the Ishmaelites long years before. But Joseph knew them, and he remembered the dreams of his boyhood. He felt glad for the strange, hard things which had come to him, because through them this day had become possible.

His heart yearned for his own people, but he wished to test his brothers, so he spoke to them roughly and accused them of being spies. "You say you have a younger brother at home. Go fetch him so that I may know you are true men."

When they would not promise to fetch Benjamin, he threw them into prison for three days. Then they stood before him again, and at first talked among themselves in deep distress. At last they told Joseph about their brother whose anguish they had not heeded when they sold him into slavery long years before. "It is because of our guilt that this sorrow has come upon us," they said.

Joseph went out from them and wept at their words, but he felt that the time had not yet come for him to make himself known to them. So he caused Simeon to be bound and kept as a hostage, then he filled their sacks with corn and sent them back to Canaan. But every man's money was secretly placed in the mouth of his sack.

The brethren were filled with wonder and fear when they found it there. They returned to Jacob, their father, and told him all that had befallen them; and his heart was troubled for his children.

At last the food was all gone, and unless they would starve they must return to Egypt, so Jacob at last consented to send Benjamin with them as the strange man had demanded. He sent rich presents, too, and double the money for the grain he wanted to buy, hoping thus to please the powerful governor.

When at last the brothers stood before Joseph, and he saw Benjamin with them, he ordered the ruler of his house to make ready a great feast for them. They bowed themselves to the ground before him, and told him of the money in their sacks.

"Fear not," he said, "the God of your father hath given you treasure."

He brought out to them Simeon, whom he had kept as a hostage, and treated them with great kindness. At last he sent them on their way again, and as before, every man's money was placed in his sack. But in the sack of Benjamin, Joseph's own drinking cup was placed.

When they had gone out of the city, Joseph sent his steward after them, and he said: "Why have you rewarded evil for good? You have taken away the cup from which my lord drinks."

He compelled them to open their sacks, and when the cup was found in the sack of Benjamin, they cried out in great distress, and hastened back to the city. They threw themselves at Joseph's feet and begged for the liberty of their young brother.

Judah said: "His brother is dead, and he alone is left of his mother, and his father loves him." Judah begged that he be made a servant in the lad's place.

Then Joseph knew that their hearts were no more filled with jealousy and selfishness, and he cried out to them: "I am Joseph, your brother. Grieve no more that you sold me, for God did send me before you to preserve life."

Then he kissed his brothers and showed great love for them. "Go," he said, "fetch our father and all your households down from Canaan. The best part of the land of Egypt shall be yours."

Joseph's brothers did as he commanded. They journeyed down into Egypt, and made their homes there. Then at last Jacob held Joseph's children in his arms and blessed them, and there was great happiness between them throughout all their days.

●

The Place of Brotherhood

This beautiful Jewish story reminds us that home should be the place where we learn about selflessness and how to practice it with those closest to us. King Solomon built the Temple of Israel to house the Ark of the Covenant in the tenth century B.C.

In the days of King Solomon there lived two brothers who reaped wheat in the fields of Zion. One night, in the dark of the moon, the elder brother gathered several sheaves of his harvest and left it in his brother's field, saying to himself: "My brother has seven children. With so many mouths to feed, he could use some of my bounty." And he went home.

A short time later, the younger brother slipped out of his house, gathered several sheaves of *his* wheat, and carried it into his brother's field, saying to himself: "My brother is all alone, with no one to help him harvest. So I'll share some of my wheat with him."

When the sun rose, each brother was amazed to find he had just as much wheat as before!

The next night they paid each other the same kindness, and still woke to find their stores undiminished.

But on the third night, they met each other as they carried their gifts into each other's fields. Each threw his arms around the other and shed tears of joy for his goodness.

And when Solomon heard of their love, he built the Temple of Israel there on the place of brotherhood.

THREE THINGS

Here are three important levers, the ones that raise children, raise efforts, and raise hearts and minds.

> I know three things must always be
> To keep a nation strong and free.
> One is a hearthstone bright and dear,
> With busy, happy loved ones near.
> One is a ready heart and hand
> To love and serve and keep the land.
> One is a worn and beaten way
> To where the people go to pray.
> So long as these are kept alive,
> Nation and people will survive.
> God keep them always everywhere—
> The home, the heart, the place of prayer.

•

CORNELIA'S JEWELS

*Adapted from retellings by James Baldwin
and William J. Sly*

Cornelia was the daughter of Scipio Africanus, a famous Roman
general who defeated Hannibal and the Carthaginians. She married Tiberious Sempronius Gracchus, a powerful consul, and lived
amid the lavish trappings of the Roman nobility. After her husband
died, however, she had to sell most of her property and learn to
live simply. This Roman legend about Cornelia's real wealth takes
place in the second century B.C.

It was a bright morning in the old city of Rome many hundred
years ago. Two brothers were playing in a garden when their
mother, Cornelia, called them into the house.

"A friend is coming to dine today," she told them. "She is very
rich, and she will show us her jewels."

Soon the woman arrived. Her fingers sparkled with rings. Her
arms glittered with bracelets. Chains of gold hung about her neck,
and strands of pearls gleamed in her hair.

"Did you ever see anyone so pretty?" the younger boy whispered to his brother. "She looks like a queen!"

They gazed at their own mother, who was dressed only in a
white robe. Her hands and arms were bare, and for a crown she
had only long braids of soft brown hair coiled about her head. But
her kind smile seemed to light her face more than any bright stone
could.

"Would you like to see some more of my treasures?" the rich
woman asked. A servant brought a box and set it on a table. When
the lady opened it, there were heaps of blood red rubies, sapphires
as blue as the sky, emeralds as green as the sea, diamonds that
flashed like sunlight.

The brothers looked long at the gems.

"Ah!" whispered the younger. "If only our mother could have
such beautiful things!"

At last, however, the box was closed and carried away.

"Tell me, Cornelia," the rich woman said with a pitying smile,
"is it true you have no jewels? Is it true you are too poor?"

Cornelia smiled. "Not at all," she said. "I have jewels far more valuable than yours."

"Then let me see them," the lady laughed. "Where are they?"

Cornelia drew her boys to her side.

"These are my jewels," she smiled. "Are they not far more precious than your gems?"

The two boys, Tiberius and Caius Gracchus, never forgot their mother's pride and love and care. Years later, when they had become great statesmen of Rome, they liked to think of this scene in the garden. And when the Roman people erected statues to honor the brothers, they did not forget to pay tribute to the woman who showed them how to be wise and good. The Romans inscribed her tomb this way: "Cornelia, Mother of the Gracchi."

●

THE STORY OF THE FIRST DIAMONDS

Retold by Florence Holbrook

In all times and places, the dearest thing is the tear of mother love.

The chief of an Indian tribe had two sons, whom he loved very dearly. This chief was at war with another tribe, and one dark night two of his enemies crept softly through the trees till they came to where the two boys lay sound asleep. The warriors caught the younger boy up gently, and carried him far away from his home and his friends.

When the chief woke, he cried, "Where is my son? My enemies have been here and have stolen him."

All the Indians in the tribe started out in search of the boy. They roamed the forest through and through, but the stolen child could not be found.

The chief mourned for his son, and when the time of his death drew near, he said to his wife, "Moneta, my tribe shall have no chief until my boy is found and taken from our enemies. Let our oldest son go forth in search of his brother, and until he has brought back the little one, do you rule my people."

Moneta ruled the people wisely and kindly. When the older son was a man, she said to him, "My son, go forth and search for your brother, whom I have mourned these many years. Every day I shall watch for you, and every night I shall build a fire on the mountain top."

"Do not mourn, Mother," said the young man. "You will not build the fire many nights on the mountain top, for I shall soon find my brother and bring him back to you."

He went forth bravely, but he did not come back. His mother went every night to the mountain top, and when she was so old that she could no longer walk, the young men of the tribe bore her up the mountain side in their strong arms, so that with her own trembling hand she could light the fire.

One night there was a great storm. Even the brave warriors were afraid, but Moneta had no fear, for out of the storm a gentle voice had come to her that said, "Moneta, your sons are coming home to you."

"Once more I must build the fire on the mountain top," she cried. The young men trembled with fear, but they bore her to the top of the mountain.

"Leave me here alone," she said, "I hear a voice. It is the voice of my son, and he is calling, 'Mother, Mother.' Come to me, come, my boys."

Coming slowly up the mountain in the storm was the older son. The younger had died on the road home, and he lay dead in the arms of his brother.

In the morning the men of the tribe went to the mountain top in search of Moneta and her sons. They were nowhere to be seen, but where the tears of the lonely mother had fallen, there was a brightness that had never been seen before. The tears were shining in the sunlight as if each one of them was itself a little sun. Indeed, they were no longer tears, but diamonds.

The dearest thing in all the world is the tear of mother-love, and that is why the tears were made into diamonds, the stones that are brightest and clearest of all the stones on the earth.

•

THE BOY WHO KISSED HIS MOTHER

Eben E. Rexford

As many a philosopher, biographer, and poet has considered, there seems to be an age-old, life-long link between the virtues of men and their love for their mothers.

> She sat on the porch in the sunshine,
>   As I went down the street—
> A woman whose hair was silver,
>   But whose face was blossom sweet,
> Making me think of a garden,
>   Where, in spite of the frost and snow
> Of bleak November weather,
>   Late, fragrant lilies grow.
>
> I heard a footstep behind me,
>   And the sound of a merry laugh,
> And I knew the heart it came from
>   Would be like a comforting staff
> In the time and the hour of trouble,
>   Hopeful and brave and strong;
> One of the hearts to lean on
>   When we think that things go wrong.
>
> I turned at the click of the gate-latch
>   And met his manly look;
> A face like his gives me pleasure,
>   Like the page of a pleasant book;
> It told of a steadfast purpose,
>   Of a brave and daring will—
> A face with a promise in it
>   That God grant the years fulfill.
>
> He went up the pathway singing.
>   I saw the woman's eyes
> Grow bright with a wordless welcome,
>   As sunshine warms the skies.

"Back again, sweetheart mother,"
　　He cried, and bent to kiss
The loving face that was lifted
　　For what some mothers miss.

That boy will do to depend on,
　　I hold that this is true—
From lads in love with their mothers
　　Our bravest heroes grew.
Earth's grandest hearts have been loving hearts,
　　Since time and earth began,
And the boy who kissed his mother
　　Is every inch a man.

●

ABOUT ANGELS

Laura E. Richards

Here is a story about a true guardian angel, the kind who watches over us from the moment we come into the world.

"Mother," said the child, "are there really angels?"

"The Good Book says so," said the mother.

"Yes," said the child. "I have seen the picture. But did you ever see one, Mother?"

"I think I have," said the mother, "but she was not dressed like the picture."

"I am going to find one!" said the child. "I am going to run along the road, miles, and miles, and miles, until I find an angel."

"That will be a good plan!" said the mother. "And I will go with you, for you are too little to run far alone."

"I am not little any more!" said the child. "I have trousers; I am big."

"So you are!" said the mother. "I forgot. But it is a fine day, and I should like the walk."

"But you walk so slowly, with your lame foot."

"I can walk faster than you think!" said the mother.

So they started, the child leaping and running, and the mother stepping out so bravely with her lame foot that the child soon forgot about it.

The child danced on ahead, and presently he saw a chariot coming towards him, drawn by prancing white horses. In the chariot sat a splendid lady in velvet and furs, with white plumes waving above her dark hair. As she moved in her seat, she flashed with jewels and gold, but her eyes were brighter than her diamonds.

"Are you an angel?" asked the child, running up beside the chariot.

The lady made no reply, but stared coldly at the child. Then she spoke a word to her coachman, and he flicked his whip, and the chariot rolled away swiftly in a cloud of dust, and disappeared.

The dust filled the child's eyes and mouth, and made him choke and sneeze. He gasped for breath, and rubbed his eyes; but presently his mother came up, and wiped away the dust with her blue gingham apron.

"That was not an angel!" said the child.

"No, indeed!" said the mother. "Nothing like one!"

The child danced on again, leaping and running from side to side of the road, and the mother followed as best she might.

By and by the child met a most beautiful maiden, clad in a white dress. Her eyes were like blue stars, and the blushes came and went in her face like roses looking through snow.

"I am sure you must be an angel!" cried the child.

The maiden blushed more sweetly than before. "You dear little child!" she cried. "Some one else said that, only last evening. Do I really look like an angel?"

"You *are* an angel!" said the child.

The maiden took him up in her arms and kissed him, and held him tenderly.

"You are the dearest little thing I ever saw!" she said. "Tell me what makes you think so!" But suddenly her face changed.

"Oh!" she cried. "There he is, coming to meet me! And you have soiled my white dress with your dusty shoes, and pulled my hair all awry. Run away, child, and go home to your mother!"

She set the child down, not unkindly, but so hastily that he stumbled and fell; but she did not see that, for she was hastening forward to meet her lover, who was coming along the road. (Now if the maiden had only known, he thought her twice as lovely with the child in her arms; but she did not know.)

The child lay in the dusty road and sobbed, till his mother

came along and picked him up, and wiped away the tears with her blue gingham apron.

"I don't believe that was an angel, after all," he said.

"No!" said the mother. "But she may be one some day. She is young yet."

"I am tired!" said the child. "Will you carry me home, Mother?"

"Why, yes!" said the mother. "That is what I came for."

The child put his arms round his mother's neck, and she held him tight and trudged along the road, singing the song he liked best.

Suddenly he looked up in her face.

"Mother," he said, "I don't suppose *you* could be an angel, could you?"

"Oh, what a foolish child!" said the mother. "Who ever heard of an angel in a blue gingham apron?" And she went on singing, and stepped out so bravely on her lame foot that no one would ever have known she was lame.

•

APPIUS

Retold by H. Twitchell

This Roman legend reminds us that life provides opportunities for children to return the love and nurture given to them by their parents. The story echoes an even earlier incident that has become one of the immortal images of classical literature—that of Aeneas, the founder of Rome, bearing his aged father, Anchises, out of the burning ruins of Troy at the close of the Trojan War.

At the time when the Roman Republic was nearing its ruin and the Empire was about to be born, many innocent persons fell victims to the general misrule. They were proscribed and banished for the slightest offense, and their property was confiscated by the state.

Among the proscribed ones was an old man who had always been held in great respect by all. He had twice served as consul, and had grown old and infirm in the service of the state. When the

Triumvirs who ruled Rome decreed that he should leave the city forever, he could scarcely believe that men could be so ungrateful.

He had not the strength to undertake a long journey, so he decided to remain in his house, although he knew that his disobedience would be punished by death.

His son, young Appius, who was absent from the city, heard of the danger threatening his venerable parent. He hastened home at once to try to save his father, who at first refused to listen to his plea.

"Why should I seek death in a foreign land, when I can find it here?" he said. "With my infirmities, I could not get beyond the walls, even if I wished to do so. I should be killed in the streets, and I would rather die in my bed."

The evening of the last day that he was to be permitted to remain came. The son again urged his father to save himself.

"I know you cannot walk," said the boy, "but I can carry you. Trust yourself to me, and strength will be given me to bear you out of the city."

The father at last yielded to his son's entreaties. Taking his precious burden on his back, Appius walked through the streets of Rome, applauded by the multitude. Moved by the sight of this filial devotion, those in power did not interfere with the passage of the pair.

The hour was fast approaching when the old man was to meet death if found within the city walls, and the two were yet a long way from the gates. The boy bent under his load, and his strength was nearly exhausted. Still he pressed on, cheered by the cries of the populace, and a few seconds before the expiration of the allotted time, he passed out of the city.

Still the old consul was not safe, as he was not to remain in Roman territory. Under cover of night, Appius carried him to the seashore, where they embarked for Sicily.

This devoted act was inscribed in the annals of the Republic, so that it might not be forgotten. When Appius became a man, he was recalled to Rome, where he held many important positions.

•

THE LITTLE GIRL WHO DARED

Henry W. Lanier

This story reminds us that home is where your loved ones are, even in a prairie schooner crossing the desert. And it reminds us that love of family is the engine of much courage in the world. The scene is one in a chain of incidents that led to the most famous disaster of the overland pioneer crossings. Virginia Reed's act of love and bravery had enormous consequences for the Donner Party. Later, in the winter of 1846–1847, when snows trapped the group in the Sierra Mountains, Virginia's father led relief efforts to save his family and former comrades. Forty of the eighty-seven emigrants survived the cold and hunger, little Virginia among them.

Three years before the gold discovery at Sutter's Mill drew thousands across the continent, a prairie caravan was laboring over the desolate Nevada sandhills, west of the Humboldt River.

It was composed of a party of more than eighty men, women, and children, who had split off from a large caravan at Fort Bridger, lured by reports of a much shorter route. Among them was James T. Reed, with his wife and daughter, and two families named Donner.

Reed's oxen, crazed with thirst, had dashed off into the wastes of Salt Lake Desert, and disappeared forever. Indians had just stolen more oxen at the Humboldt sink. The travelling was exhausting. Men's nerves had become frazzled.

Another of the endless succession of sand dunes appeared ahead.

The cattle were so weary that it had become customary to put a double team to each wagon in pulling up these sandy hills; and since this made twice the number of trips, it was very exasperating to the teamsters.

Wearily the drivers halted, and prepared to unhitch and double up. But one man, named Snyder, swore he wouldn't bother with it; he started his oxen up the incline with shouts and loud crackings of his whip. The straining beasts labored up the slope, the heavy wagon wheels sinking deep in the soft, binding sand. It was too much, even for their patient strength. They stopped, exhausted and blown. The driver's utmost urgings and savage lashings could not force them a foot farther.

Wild with sullen rage, Snyder began to belabor the poor beasts unmercifully. Reed, who had gone on over the brow of the hill to pick out a road ahead, came back to witness the man's brutal abuse of the meek creatures, who, with gasping breath and rolling eyes, tried to shrink away from the blows which he rained on their heads and shoulders with the butt end of his heavy whip handle.

The useless cruelty was too much for Reed. He tried to quiet the driver, who was working himself into a frenzy where it seemed probable he would kill one or more of the oxen outright.

This interference snapped Snyder's already quivering nerves. Leaping to the wagon tongue, he turned his fury on Reed. Three times he brought his hickory handle savagely down on the other man's head, till the blood streamed from the scalp wounds.

Instinctively, Reed's wife rushed forward. Snyder was blind with rage by this time; the next blow fell upon her head.

Seeing the maniac raise his bludgeon for still another blow, Reed drew his hunting knife, and tackled him as if he were the wild beast he was imitating. The quick thrust entered Snyder's side, killing him almost instantly.

The men of the party held an informal court. The dead body spoke more loudly to them than the provocation which had brought on the tragedy. With a cowardice that declared for the uttermost penalty, yet strove to dodge the direct responsibility, the majority came to a singular and frightful decision.

A committee announced to Reed that he was to go forth alone into the surrounding desert, with nothing but the clothes he wore.

This meant death by slow torture. Without food, water, gun, ammunition, or bedding, a solitary man in that encompassing infinity of sand had nothing to expect but to perish through starvation and the unspeakable, lingering agonies of thirst. But it enabled his judges to preserve a faint pretense of his having wandered off of his own volition.

Reed refused. Any man who had come across those hundreds of miles of desert would unhesitatingly have chosen to stand up before a firing squad in preference to this protracted suicide.

But his overwhelmed wife, catching desperately at any straw, begged him so piteously to take this forlorn chance, that he finally accepted the verdict.

Mrs. Reed's pleadings made his executioners relent to the extent of permitting him to take a horse, instead of going on foot.

So he fared forth under the blazing sun to meet what seemed like an inexorable sentence.

Wife and twelve-year-old daughter watched him disappear into the pitiless desert. Then they went back to their own wagon, where the sight of every article seemed to bring a fresh pang. The leaders of the party were human enough, and they tried to show a rough sympathy for the suffering pair, but it was only too evident that any open professions were a painful mockery. They presently withdrew and the mother and daughter were left as alone and isolated as if there were some contagious disease in their canvas-roofed home on wheels.

Automatically, habit drove them to preparations for supper. Trying to support each other by encouraging hopes that deceived neither, they choked down the rough food.

Presently, Virginia, who had disappeared for a short while before sundown, looked up at her mother's tearstained face.

"Mamma," said she resolutely, "I'm going out to find Father and take him something to eat as well as his gun and pistols."

"What do you mean, child?" exclaimed Mrs. Reed. "You can't find your father."

"Yes, I can," insisted the girl. "I'm not going alone; I've asked Milt, and he's going with me."

Mrs. Reed protested. It seemed like merely adding a last horror to this nightmare day.

But twelve-year-old Virginia had made up her mind. She knew the Vigilance Committee had stationed guards to see that no attempt was made to interfere with the punishment; she was full of childish tremors at the thought of the night-enfolded desert and the wild beasts that howled through the darkness; but her daddy was out there with nothing to eat—and she was going to do something to help him no matter what happened.

When the camp was quiet and all the children who might run in were asleep, she got together what their scanty stock offered—a piece of bacon, some crackers, coffee, and sugar. A tin cup, the gun and pistols, and some ammunition were collected. Next a lantern and a supply of matches.

Her mother lay helpless, watching these preparations in increasing doubt.

"How will you find him this dark night?" she whispered.

"I'll look for the horse's tracks and follow them."

The woman shook her head hopelessly.

But just then soft footsteps sounded outside. They listened, breathless. A gentle rap came against the wagon.

"That's Milt now," whispered Virginia.

Carefully she gathered up the weapons and handed them to a silent figure outside. In silence she hugged her mother, who murmured a few words of prayer. Descending cautiously, she and the friendly Milton set out on their difficult mission.

The flare of many fires lit up little circles in the encompassing blackness, amid which the canvas wagoncovers loomed with ghostly dimness. Taking advantage of the shadows, they crept toward the outer edge of the circle.

Ahead the flickering light of the fires showed the guard, tramping back and forth, the only moving sign of life in the whole encampment. To one side of him the shadow of the wagons stretched out into the solid black wall of the solitudes that surrounded all.

Lying flat, they wormed their way noiselessly forward to pass this danger point. A horse stamped restlessly behind. The sentry stopped short. Virginia and Milton froze to the ground like frightened partridge chicks. The man scanned the motionless camp; he turned for a long gaze outward into the void night; then he resumed his monotonous beat.

Hardly daring to draw a breath, the two again wriggled ahead, serpent-wise. The guard was left behind. They ventured to crawl on hands and knees. They were out into the open: rising to their feet, they hastened on across the sand, and were swallowed up in the sea of darkness.

When they had reached a safe distance Virginia touched her companion's arm.

"Let's light the lantern," she whispered.

Standing between it and the camp, Milton lit the candle in the lantern. The girl took it and, covering it with her skirt so that it shone only downward, began to walk to and fro, searching this tiny moving circle of illumination for the horse's footprints.

It was hard to find. Back and forth and farther out she looked in vain. The care necessary to prevent a flash of the lantern's light from reaching the guard and at the same time scrutinize every foot of the ground was confusing amid the obscurity. They had slowly worked their way completely around the camp when a low exclamation of delight came from Virginia.

There was a hoofprint in the loose sand. Kneeling down, she

made sure. A little farther on the marks were plain. Relieved and eager, they hastened in that direction.

It was a long journey, with no landmarks to show the progress, and the inevitable loss of time when they occasionally lost the trail. Mile after mile they followed these mute guides, which seemed to lead on into an endless nowhere. The mournful howls of marauding coyotes made the child shudder every time they moaned across the plain. The shrill, savage screech of a mountain lion seemed even more threatening, as it split the silence close beside them. She knew well that there were prowling wolves about, dangerous on their night roamings. Even Milton, who scorned these night prowlers like any stout frontier boy, stopped paralyzed with fear when, a little later, another sound came which was made by no wild beast, but a far more dangerous animal; they judged it to mean the presence, not far off, of one of the Indian bands who had been lurking about their advance to pick off straggling humans or cattle.

But even this most excruciating terror of childhood was not as compelling as the thought of her father, alone and hungry and unarmed among these dangers.

They stopped for a few moments, dreading to hear the warwhoop. All was silent. Virginia started on again.

For what seemed like hours they labored on.

At last the girl gave a cry, pointing ahead.

"There's Papa!" she exclaimed.

Milton scanned the blackness. "It's a fire, sure enough."

Neither gave vent to the thought which presently flashed upon them that the tiny point of light off there might be kindled by the Indians who loomed so large in their minds. Reassuring themselves by again studying the footprints that had led them so far, they hurried toward this beacon.

A disconsolate figure sat hunched over in front of the blaze, head between hands.

As the two drew near it suddenly sprang up, and Reed gazed wonderingly out from his circle of light, expecting some attack.

And then a slender little figure, dropping the lantern to the ground, sped out of the encircling blackness into her daddy's arms.

Sorely against her will, Virginia started back for the camp with her companion at the first break of dawn.

But she had the proud satisfaction of seeing her father, with the fresh courage and confidence she had brought him, ride off westward with better than a fighting chance of escape.

The Donner party which had cast him out was destined, after a ghastly struggle, to leave half its members dead among the cruel snows of the winter Sierras; but plucky little Virginia was one of the half which finally reached the pleasant valleys of California.

•

DR. JOHNSON AND HIS FATHER

James Baldwin

English poet, critic, essayist, and lexicographer Samuel Johnson (1709–1784) was regarded by many contemporaries as the leading man of letters of his time. His reputation for brilliant and witty conversation remains unsurpassed to this day. The man of great learning added this realization to his store of wisdom: An opportunity for love and duty brushed aside in childhood can live as a deep regret long into adulthood. As recounted in this moving story, Johnson's father was a respected but rather unsuccessful bookseller.

I

It is in a little bookshop in the city of Lichfield, England. The floor has just been swept and the shutter taken down from the one small window. The hour is early, and customers have not yet begun to drop in. Out of doors the rain is falling.

At a small table near the door, a feeble, white-haired old man is making up some packages of books. As he arranges them in a large basket, he stops now and then as though disturbed by pain. He puts his hand to his side, coughs in a most distressing way, then sits down and rests himself, leaning his elbows upon the table.

"Samuel!" he calls.

In the farther corner of the room there is a young man busily reading from a large book that is spread open before him. He is a very odd-looking fellow, perhaps eighteen years of age, but you would take him to be older. He is large and awkward, with a great round face, scarred and marked by a strange disease. His eyesight must be poor, for, as he reads, he bends down until his face is quite near the printed page.

"Samuel!" again the old man calls.

But Samuel makes no reply. He is so deeply interested in his book that he does not hear. The old man rests himself a little longer and then finishes tying his packages. He lifts the heavy basket and sets it on the table. The exertion brings on another fit of coughing; and when it is over he calls for the third time, "Samuel!"

"What is it, Father?" This time the call is heard.

"You know, Samuel," he says, "that tomorrow is market day at Uttoxeter, and our stall must be attended to. Some of our friends will be there to look at the new books which they expect me to bring. One of us must go down on the stage this morning and get everything in readiness. But I hardly feel able for the journey. My cough troubles me quite a little, and you see that it is raining very hard."

"Yes, Father; I am sorry," answers Samuel; and his face is again bent over the book.

"I thought perhaps you would go down to the market, and that I might stay here at the shop," says his father. But Samuel does not hear. He is deep in the study of some Latin classic.

The old man goes to the door and looks out. The rain is still falling. He shivers, and buttons his coat.

It is a twenty-mile ride to Uttoxeter. In five minutes the stage will pass the door.

"Samuel, will you not go down to the market for me this time?"

The old man is putting on his great coat.

He is reaching for his hat.

The basket is on his arm.

He casts a beseeching glance at his son, hoping that he will relent at the last moment.

"Here comes the coach, Samuel." And the old man is choked by another fit of coughing.

Whether Samuel hears or not, I do not know. He is still reading, and he makes no sign nor motion.

The stage comes rattling down the street.

The old man with his basket of books staggers out of the door. The stage halts for a moment while he climbs inside. Then the driver swings his whip, and all are away.

Samuel, in the shop, still bends over his book.

Out of doors the rain is falling.

II

Just fifty years have passed, and again it is market day at Uttox-eter.

The rain is falling in the streets. The people who have wares to sell huddle under the eaves and in the stalls and booths that have roofs above them.

A chaise from Lichfield pulls up at the entrance to the market square.

An old man alights. One would guess him to be seventy years of age. He is large and not well-shaped. His face is seamed and scarred, and he makes strange grimaces as he clambers out of the chaise. He wheezes and puffs as though afflicted with asthma. He walks with the aid of a heavy stick.

With slow but ponderous strides he enters the market place and looks around. He seems not to know that the rain is falling.

He looks at the little stalls ranged along the walls of the market place. Some have roofs over them and are the centers of noisy trade. Others have fallen into disuse and are empty.

The stranger halts before one of the latter. "Yes, this is it," he says. He has a strange habit of talking aloud to himself. "I remember it well. It was here that my father, on certain market days, sold books to the clergy of the county. The good men came from every parish to see his wares and to hear him describe their contents."

He turns abruptly around. "Yes, this is the place," he repeats.

He stands quite still and upright, directly in front of the little old stall. He takes off his hat and holds it beneath his arm. His great walking stick has fallen into the gutter. He bows his head and clasps his hands. He does not seem to know that the rain is falling.

The clock in the tower above the market strikes eleven. The passersby stop and gaze at the stranger. The market people peer at him from their booths and stalls. Some laugh as the rain runs in streams down his scarred old cheeks. Rain is it? Or can it be tears?

Boys hoot at him. Some of the ruder ones even hint at throwing mud; but a sense of shame withholds them from the act.

"He is a poor lunatic. Let him alone," say the more compassionate.

The rain falls upon his bare head and his broad shoulders. He is drenched and chilled. But he stands motionless and silent, looking neither to the right nor to the left.

"Who is that old fool?" asks a thoughtless young man who chances to be passing.

"Do you ask who he is?" answers a gentleman from London. "Why, he is Dr. Samuel Johnson, the most famous man in England. It was he who wrote *Rasselas* and the *Lives of the Poets* and *Irene* and many another work which all men are praising. It was he who made the great *English Dictionary,* the most wonderful book of our times. In London, the noblest lords and ladies take pleasure in doing him honor. He is the literary lion of England."

"Then why does he come to Uttoxeter and stand thus in the pouring rain?"

"I cannot tell you. But doubtless he has reasons for doing so." And the gentleman passes on.

At length there is a lull in the storm. The birds are chirping among the housetops. The people wonder if the rain is over, and venture out into the slippery street.

The clock in the tower above the market strikes twelve. The renowned stranger has stood a whole hour motionless in the market place. And again the rain is falling.

Slowly now he returns his hat to his head. He finds his walking stick where it had fallen. He lifts his eyes reverently for a moment, and then, with a lordly, lumbering motion, walks down the street to meet the chaise which is ready to return to Lichfield.

We follow him through the pattering rain to his native town.

"Why, Dr. Johnson!" exclaims his hostess, "we have missed you all day. And you are so wet and chilled! Where have you been?"

"Madam," says the great man, "fifty years ago, this very day, I tacitly refused to oblige or obey my father. The thought of the pain which I must have caused him has haunted me ever since. To do away the sin of that hour, I this morning went in a chaise to Uttoxeter and did do penance publicly before the stall which my father had formerly used."

The great man bows his head upon his hands and sobs.

Out of doors the rain is falling.

•

THE WOUNDED PINE TREE

Babrius

This fable is told by Babrius, a Greek poet who penned several
Aesop-like fables around the second century.

Deep in the forest, a woodcutter was cutting down a stout old
pine. With each blow of his ax, the giant tree shuddered and cursed
the cold, hard steel that splintered its side.

It was a tough old tree. After a while the woodsman inserted a
large, wooden wedge into the cut in order to pry the trunk apart.
He pounded away at the wedge; amid a great ripping and splinter-
ing, the noble pine toppled and hurtled toward the ground. As it
fell, it groaned:

"How can I blame the ax, which is no kin of mine, as much as
this wicked wedge, which is my own brother?"

*Pain inflicted by outsiders is never so terrible as suffering
caused by one's own kin.*

•

A FATHER'S RETURN

This wonderful story is told in many different versions in African
folklore. This one reminds us that the essence of home and hearth
is one soul reaching for another. And it reminds us that the need
of a son for his father ought to be one of the strongest ties that
bind a family.

There once was a man who considered himself the happiest
man alive because he had a loving wife and four healthy sons. The
oldest son was named Keen-Eyes because he could follow tracks
through field and jungle better than anyone else in the village. The
second son was known as Sharp-Ears because he knew best the call
of every creature in the wilderness. The third son was named
Strong-Arms because he never failed to win any contest of strength.

The fourth son was only a baby, but his father was sure the boy would grow up to be as skilled and devoted as his brothers.

One morning the family woke to discover the father had disappeared. By nightfall he had not returned, and the next morning brought no sign of his whereabouts.

They talked it over and wondered where he might have gone.

"Perhaps he decided to go visit our uncle," said Keen-Eyes, shrugging his shoulders.

"Or maybe he went to the festival in the next village," suggested Sharp-Ears.

"Or he may have gone into the hills, to enjoy the cool mountain breezes," said Strong-Arms.

Their mother remained quiet and shook her head uncertainly.

Another day passed, then a week, and still their father did not return. Sometimes his sons wondered out loud where he might have gone, but after a while they did not talk about it any longer. They feared he was dead.

But the youngest son had no such thoughts, and one morning, as he sat on his mother's lap, he opened his mouth and spoke his first words:

"Where is Father? I want to see my father."

His older brothers gazed at him.

"That's right," said Keen-Eyes. "Where is Father?"

"Some harm may have come to him," said Sharp-Ears.

"We really should go look for him," suggested Strong-Arms.

The three older brothers started out at once, following a path deep into the jungle.

"Look, he came this way," pointed Keen-Eyes. "I can see his tracks on the trail." He led his brothers over hills and into valleys, through fields and woods, farther and farther from home. But at last the tracks disappeared, and even Keen-Eyes lost the trail.

"We must give up," he declared.

"Wait!" urged Sharp-Ears. "I hear someone crying out."

He led his brothers even deeper into the wilderness, farther than they had ever ventured before, pausing every now and then to strain for the sound only he could hear.

At last they came upon a river, and beside it lay their father, holding a growling leopard at bay with his spear!

"We must save him!" yelled Strong-Arms, and without waiting for his brothers he threw himself onto the pouncing beast and crushed it in his mighty grasp.

"You came just in time," gasped their father. "I came into the jungle to hunt but fell and hurt my leg. I could not make it home. I've lived on what food I could find, but my strength was failing, and the leopard had moved in for the kill."

His sons dressed his wounded leg, brought food to build his strength, and carried him home to their village. Everyone listened to the story of how Keen-Eyes, Sharp-Ears, and Strong-Arms had saved their father, and everyone praised their skill and devotion.

But the fame went to the brothers' heads, and they began to argue among themselves about who was the most responsible for their father's rescue.

"If it were not for me, we would never have known which way to look," boasted Keen-Eyes. "I followed his trail deep into the jungle."

"Yes, but you lost it," reminded Sharp-Ears. "I heard him crying out and led us to the river."

"But what good would that have done if I had not been there?" asked Strong-Arms. "I was the one who killed the leopard and saved our father from certain death."

They debated among themselves, and at last asked their father himself to decide who was the most responsible for his return.

He listened to their arguing and then raised his hand for quiet.

"To all three of you I owe my life," he told them, "for you each played a part in my rescue. But if you ask which of my sons did the most to bring me home, I must tell you it is not you, Sharp-Eyes, nor you, Keen-Ears, not even you, Strong-Arms. The one who truly brought me home is here."

He took his youngest son into his arms.

Then everyone recalled that this was the son whose first words had been, "Where is Father?" It was the little boy's loving heart that had brought his father home.

•

SIMON'S FATHER

Guy de Maupassant

This nineteenth-century story of a boy without a father has truths
for all times, perhaps most poignantly for the late twentieth century, when fatherlessness is epidemic. Little boys want to be men,
but they need good men to show them how. The lucky boys have
such men as fathers.

Noon had just struck. The school door opened and the youngsters tumbled out, rolling over each other in their haste to get out
quickly. But instead of promptly dispersing and going home to
dinner as was their daily wont, they stopped a few paces off, broke
up into knots and set to whispering.

The fact was that that morning Simon, the son of La Blanchotte,
had, for the first time, attended school.

They had all of them in their families heard talk of La Blanchotte; and, although in public she was welcome enough, the mothers among themselves treated her with compassion of a somewhat
disdainful kind, which the children had caught without in the least
knowing why.

As for Simon himself, they did not know him, for he never
went abroad, and did not go galloping about with them through
the streets of the village or along the banks of the river. Therefore,
they loved him but little; and it was with a certain delight, mingled
with considerable astonishment, that they met and that they recited
to each other this phrase, set afoot by a lad of fourteen or fifteen
who appeared to know all, all about it, so sagaciously did he wink.
"You know . . . Simon . . . well, he has no father."

La Blanchotte's son appeared in his turn upon the threshold of
the school.

He was seven or eight years old. He was rather pale, very neat,
with a timid and almost awkward manner.

He was on the point of making his way back to his mother's
house when the groups of his schoolfellows perpetually whispering
and watching him with the mischievous and heartless eyes of children bent upon playing a nasty trick, gradually surrounded him and
ended by enclosing him altogether. There he stood fixed amidst

them, surprised and embarrassed, not understanding what they were going to do with him. But the lad who had brought the news, puffed up with the success he had met with already, demanded, "How do you name yourself, you?"

He answered, "Simon."

"Simon what?" retorted the other.

The child, altogether bewildered, repeated, "Simon."

The lad shouted at him, "One is named Simon something . . . that is not a name . . . Simon indeed."

And he, on the brink of tears, replied for the third time, "I am named Simon."

The urchins fell a-laughing. The lad triumphantly lifted up his voice. "You can see plainly that he has no father."

A deep silence ensued. The children were dumbfounded by this extraordinary, impossible monstrous thing—a boy who had not a father; they looked upon him as a phenomenon, an unnatural being, and they felt that contempt, until then inexplicable, of their mothers for La Blanchotte grow upon them. As for Simon, he had propped himself against a tree to avoid falling and he remained as though struck to the earth by an irreparable disaster. He sought to explain, but he could think of no answer for them, to deny this horrible charge that he had no father. At last he shouted at them quite recklessly, "Yes, I have one."

"Where is he?" demanded the boy.

Simon was silent. He did not know. The children roared, tremendously excited; and these sons of toil, most nearly related to animals, experienced that cruel craving which animates the fowls of a farmyard to destroy one among themselves as soon as it is wounded. Simon suddenly espied a little neighbor, the son of a widow, whom he had always seen, as he himself was to be seen, quite alone with his mother.

"And no more have you," he said, "no more have you a father."

"Yes," replied the other, "I have one."

"Where is he?" rejoined Simon.

"He is dead," declared the brat with superb dignity, "he is in the cemetery, is my father."

A murmur of approval rose amidst the scapegraces, as if this fact of possessing a father dead in a cemetery had caused their comrade to grow big enough to crush the other one who had no father at all. And these rogues, whose fathers were for the most part evil-doers, drunkards, thieves and ill-treaters of their wives, hustled each other as they pressed closer and closer, as though they, the legitimate ones, would stifle in their pressure one who was beyond the law.

He who chanced to be next to Simon suddenly put his tongue out at him with a waggish air and shouted at him, "No father! No father!"

Simon seized him by the hair with both hands and set to work to demolish his legs with kicks, while he bit his cheek ferociously. A tremendous struggle ensued between the two combatants, and Simon found himself beaten, torn, bruised, rolled on the ground in the middle of the ring of applauding vagabonds. As he arose, mechanically brushing his little shirt all covered with dust with his hand, someone shouted at him, "Go and tell your father."

He then felt a great sinking in his heart. They were stronger than he was, they had beaten him and he had no answer to give them, for he knew well that it was true that he had no father. Full of pride he attempted for some moments to struggle against the tears which were suffocating him. He had a choking fit, and then without cries he commenced to weep with great sobs which shook him incessantly. Then a ferocious joy broke out among his enemies, and, naturally, just as with savages in their fearful festivals, they took each other by the hand and set about dancing in a circle about him as they repeated as a refrain, "No father! No father!"

But Simon quite suddenly ceased sobbing. Frenzy overtook him. There were stones under his feet. He picked them up and with all his strength hurled them at his tormentors. Two or three were struck and rushed off yelling, and so formidable did he appear that the rest became panic stricken. Cowards, as a crowd always is in the presence of an exasperated man, they broke up and fled. Left alone, the little thing without a father set off running toward the fields, for a recollection had been awakened which brought his soul to a great determination. He made up his mind to drown himself in the river.

He remembered, in fact, that eight days before a poor devil who begged for his livelihood, had thrown himself into the water because he had no more money. Simon had been there when they had fished him out again; and the sight of the fellow, who usually seemed to him so miserable, and ugly, had then struck him—his pale cheeks, his long drenched beard and his open eyes being full of calm. The bystanders had said, "He is dead."

And someone had said, "He is quite happy now."

And Simon wished to drown himself also because he had no father, just like the wretched being who had no money.

He reached the neighborhood of the water and watched it flowing. Some fishes were sporting briskly in the clear stream and occasionally made a little bound and caught the flies flying on the surface. He stopped crying in order to watch them, for their housewifery interested him vastly. But, at intervals, as in the changes of a tempest, altering suddenly from tremendous gusts of wind, which snap off the trees and then lose themselves in the horizon, this thought would return to him with intense pain, "I am about to drown myself because I have no father."

It was very warm and fine weather. The pleasant sunshine warmed the grass. The water shone like a mirror. And Simon enjoyed some minutes the happiness of that languor which follows weeping, in which he felt very desirous of falling asleep there upon the grass in the warmth.

A little green frog leapt from under his feet. He endeavored to catch it. It escaped him. He followed it and lost it three times following. At last he caught it by one of its hind legs and began to laugh as he saw the efforts the creature made to escape. It gathered itself up on its large legs and then with a violent spring suddenly stretched them out as stiff as two bars; while, its eye wide open in its round, golden circle, it beat the air with its front limbs which worked as though they were hands. It reminded him of a toy made with straight slips of wood nailed zigzag one on the other, which by a similar movement regulated the exercise of the little soldiers stuck thereon. Then he thought of his home and next of his mother, and overcome by a great sorrow he again began to weep. His limbs trembled; and he placed himself on his knees and said his prayers as before going to bed. But he was unable to finish them, for such hurried and violent sobs overtook him that he was completely overwhelmed. He thought no more, he no longer saw anything around him and was wholly taken up in crying.

Suddenly a heavy hand was placed upon his shoulder, and a rough voice asked him, "What is it that causes you so much grief, my fine fellow?"

Simon turned round. A tall workman with a black beard and hair all curled, was staring at him good naturedly. He answered with his eyes and throat full of tears, "They have beaten me . . . because . . . I . . . have no . . . father . . . no father."

"What!" said the man smiling, "why, everybody has one."

The child answered painfully amidst his spasms of grief, "But I ... I ... I have none."

Then the workman became serious. He had recognized La Blanchotte's son, and although but recently come to the neighborhood he had a vague idea of her history.

"Well," said he, "console yourself, my boy, and come with me home to your mother. They will give you ... a father."

And so they started on the way, the big one holding the little one by the hand, and the man smiled afresh, for he was not sorry to see this Blanchotte, who was, it was said, one of the prettiest girls of the countryside, and, perhaps, he said to himself, at the bottom of his heart, that a lass who had erred might very well err again.

They arrived in front of a little and very neat white house.

"There it is," exclaimed the child, and he cried "Mamma."

A woman appeared and the workman instantly left off smiling, for he at once perceived that there was no more fooling to be done with the tall pale girl who stood austerely at her door as though to defend from one man the threshold of that house where she had already been betrayed by another. Intimidated, his cap in his hand, he stammered out, "See, madam, I have brought back your little boy, who had lost himself near the river."

But Simon flung his arms about his mother's neck and told her, as he again began to cry, "No, Mamma, I wished to drown myself, because the others had beaten me ... had beaten me ... because I have no father."

A burning redness covered the young woman's cheeks, and, hurt to the quick, she embraced her child passionately, while the tears coursed down her face. The man, much moved, stood there, not knowing how to get away. But Simon suddenly ran to him and said, "Will you be my father?"

A deep silence ensued. La Blanchotte, dumb and tortured with shame, leaned herself against the wall, both her hands upon her heart. The child, seeing that no answer was made him, replied, "If you do not wish it, I shall return to drown myself."

The workman took the matter as a jest and answered laughing, "Why, yes, I wish it certainly."

"What is your name, then?" went on the child, "so that I may tell the others when they wish to know your name?"

"Phillip," answered the man.

Simon was silent a moment so that he might get the name well into his head; then he stretched out his arms quite consoled as he said; "Well, then, Phillip, you are my father."

The workman, lifting him from the ground, kissed him hastily on both cheeks, and then made off very quickly with great strides.

When the child returned to school next day he was received with a spiteful laugh, and at the end of school when the lads were on the point of recommencing, Simon threw these words at their heads as he would have done a stone, "He is named Phillip, my father."

Yells of delight burst out from all sides.

"Phillip who? . . . Phillip what? What on earth is Phillip? Where did you pick up your Phillip?"

Simon answered nothing; and immovable in faith he defied them with his eye, ready to be martyred rather than fly before them. The schoolmaster came to his rescue and he returned home to his mother.

During three months, the tall workman, Phillip, frequently passed by the Blanchotte's house, and sometimes he made bold to speak to her when he saw her sewing near the window. She answered him civilly, always sedately, never joking with him, nor permitting him to enter her house. Notwithstanding which, being, like all men, a bit of a coxcomb, he imagined that she was often rosier than usual when she chatted with him.

But a fallen reputation is so difficult to recover and always remains so fragile that, in spite of the shy reserve La Blanchotte maintained, they already gossiped in the neighborhood.

As for Simon, he loved his new father much, and walked with him nearly every evening when the day's work was done. He went regularly to school and mixed with great dignity with his schoolfellows without ever answering them back.

One day, however, the lad who had first attacked him said to him, "You have lied. You have not a father named Phillip."

"Why do you say that? demanded Simon, much disturbed.

The youth rubbed his hands. He replied, "Because if you had one he would be your mamma's husband."

Simon was confused by the truth of this reasoning, nevertheless he retorted, "He is my father all the same."

"That can very well be," exclaimed the urchin with a sneer, "but that is not being your father altogether."

La Blanchotte's little one bowed his head and went off dreaming in the direction of the forge belonging to old Loizon, where Phillip worked.

This forge was as though entombed in trees. It was very dark there, the red glare of a formidable furnace alone lit up with great flashes five blacksmiths, who hammered upon their anvils with a terrible din. They were standing enveloped in flame, like demons, their eyes fixed on the red-hot iron they were pounding; and their dull ideas rose and fell with their hammers.

Simon entered without being noticed and went quietly to pluck his friend by the sleeve. He turned himself round. All at once the work came to a standstill and all the men looked on very attentive. Then, in the midst of this unaccustomed silence, rose the little slender pipe of Simon; "Phillip, explain to me what the lad at La Michande has just told me, that you are not altogether my father."

"And why that?" asked the smith.

The child replied with all its innocence, "Because you are not my mamma's husband."

No one laughed. Philip remained standing, leaning his forehead upon the back of his great hands, which supported the handle of his hammer standing upright upon the anvil. He mused. His four companions watched him, and, quite a tiny mite among these giants, Simon anxiously waited. Suddenly, one of the smiths, answering to the sentiment of all, said to Phillip, "La Blanchotte is all the same a good and honest girl, and stalwart and steady in spite of her misfortune, and one who would make a worthy wife for an honest man."

"That is true," remarked the three others.

The smith continued, "Is it this girl's fault if she has fallen? She had been promised marriage and I know more than one who is much respected today, and who sinned every bit as much."

"That is true," responded the three men in chorus. He resumed, "How hard she has toiled, poor thing, to educate her lad all alone, and how much she has wept since she no longer goes out, save to go to church, God only knows."

"This also is true," said the others.

Then no more was heard than the bellows which fanned the fire of the furnace. Phillip hastily bent himself down to Simon. "Go and tell your mamma that I shall come to speak to her."

Then he pushed the child out by the shoulders. He returned to his work and with a single blow the five hammers again fell upon their anvils. Thus they wrought the iron until nightfall, strong, powerful, happy, like hammers satisfied. But just as the great bell of a cathedral resounds upon feast days above the jingling of the other bells, so Phillip's hammer, dominating the noise of the others, clanged second after second with a deafening uproar. And he, his eye on fire, plied his trade vigorously, erect amid the sparks.

The sky was full of stars as he knocked at La Blanchotte's door. He had his Sunday blouse on, a fresh shirt, and his beard was trimmed. The young woman showed herself upon the threshold and said in a grieved tone, "It is ill to come thus when night has fallen, Mr. Phillip."

He wished to answer, but stammered and stood confused before her.

She resumed, "And still you understand quite well that it will not do that I should be talked about any more."

Then he said all at once, "What does that matter to me, if you will be my wife!"

No voice replied to him, but he believed that he heard in the shadow of the room the sound of a body that sank down. He entered very quickly; and Simon, who had gone to his bed, distinguished the sound of a kiss and some words that his mother said very softly. Then he suddenly found himself lifted up by the hands of his friend, who, holding him at the length of his herculean arms, exclaimed to him, "You will tell them, your schoolfellows, that your father is Phillip Remy, the blacksmith, and that he will pull the ears of all who do you any harm."

On the morrow, when the school was full and lessons were about to begin, little Simon stood up quite pale with trembling lips. "My father," said he in a clear voice, "is Phillip Remy, the blacksmith, and he has promised to box the ears of all who do me any harm."

This time no one laughed any longer, for he was very well known, was Phillip Remy, the blacksmith, and was a father of whom anyone in the world would have been proud.

•

FATHER

Edgar Guest

Often we do not fully recognize some of the important lessons of
home and hearth until those who have taught us are gone.

> Used to wonder just why father
>   Never had much time for play,
> Used to wonder why he'd rather
>   Work each minute of the day.
> Used to wonder why he never
>   Loafed along the road an' shirked;
> Can't recall a time whenever
>   Father played while others worked.
>
> Father didn't dress in fashion,
>   Sort of hated clothing new;
> Style with him was not a passion;
>   He had other things in view.
> Boys are blind to much that's going
>   On about 'em day by day,
> And I had no way of knowing
>   What became of father's pay.
>
> All I knew was when I needed
>   Shoes I got 'em on the spot;
> Everything for which I pleaded,
>   Somehow, father always got.
> Wondered, season after season,
>   Why he never took a rest,
> And that *I* might be the reason
>   Then I never even guessed.
>
> Father set a store on knowledge;
>   If he'd lived to have his way
> He'd have sent me off to college
>   And the bills been glad to pay.

That, I know, was his ambition:
   Now and then he used to say
He'd have done his earthly mission
   On my graduation day.

Saw his cheeks were getting paler,
   Didn't understand just why;
Saw his body growing frailer,
   Then at last I saw him die.
Rest had come! His tasks were ended
   Calm was written on his brow;
Father's life was big and splendid,
   And I understand it now.

•

THE DROVER'S WIFE

Henry Lawson

In this story by Australian writer Henry Lawson (1867–1922), our hearts are touched by a lone mother's struggle to make a safe place for her children. And we are moved by her young son's final determination that he will be there for his family. This is a tale from another age and another side of the world that remains all too relevant to our time and culture.

The two-roomed house is built of round timber, slabs, and stringy-bark, and floored with split slabs. A big bark kitchen standing at one end is larger than the house itself, verandah included.

Bush all round—bush with no horizon, for the country is flat. No ranges in the distance. The bush consists of stunted, rotten native apple-trees. No undergrowth. Nothing to relieve the eye save the darker green of a few she-oaks which are sighing above the narrow, almost waterless creek. Nineteen miles to the nearest sign of civilization—a shanty on the main road.

The drover, an ex-squatter, is away with sheep. His wife and children are left here alone.

Four ragged, dried-up-looking children are playing about the house. Suddenly one of them yells: "Snake! Mother, here's a snake!"

The gaunt, sun-browned bushwoman dashes from the kitchen, snatches her baby from the ground, holds it on her left hip, and reaches for a stick.

"Where is it?"

"Here! gone into the wood-heap!" yells the eldest boy—a sharp-faced urchin of eleven. "Stop there, Mother! I'll have him. Stand back! I'll have the beggar!"

"Tommy, come here, or you'll be bit. Come here at once when I tell you, you little wretch!"

The youngster comes reluctantly, carrying a stick bigger than himself. Then he yells, triumphantly:

"There it goes—under the house!" and darts away with club uplifted. At the same time the big, black, yellow-eyed dog-of-all-breeds, who has shown the wildest interest in the proceedings, breaks his chain and rushes after that snake. He is a moment late, however, and his nose reaches the crack in the slabs just as the end of its tail disappears. Almost at the same moment the boy's club comes down and skins the aforesaid nose. Alligator takes small notice of this, and proceeds to undermine the building; but he is subdued after a struggle and chained up. They cannot afford to lose him.

The drover's wife makes the children stand together near the doghouse while she watches for the snake. She gets two small dishes of milk and sets them down near the wall to tempt it to come out; but an hour goes by and it does not show itself.

It is near sunset, and a thunderstorm is coming. The children must be brought inside. She will not take them into the house, for she knows the snake is there, and may at any moment come up through a crack in the rough slab floor; so she carries several armfuls of firewood into the kitchen, and then takes the children there. The kitchen has no floor—or, rather, an earthen one—called a "ground floor" in this part of the bush. There is a large, roughly-made table in the centre of the place. She brings the children in, and makes them get on this table. They are two boys and two girls —mere babies. She gives them some supper, and then, before it gets dark, she goes into the house, and snatches up some pillows and bedclothes—expecting to see or lay her hand on the snake any minute. She makes a bed on the kitchen table for the children, and sits down beside it to watch all night.

She has an eye on the corner, and a green sapling club laid in readiness on the dresser by her side; also her sewing basket and a copy of the *Young Ladies' Journal*. She has brought the dog into the room.

Tommy turns in, under protest, but says he'll lie awake all night and smash that blinded snake.

His mother asks him how many times she has told him not to swear.

He has his club with him under the bedclothes, and Jacky protests:

"Mummy! Tommy's skinnin' me alive wif his club. Make him take it out."

Tommy: "Shet up, you little—! D'yer want to be bit with the snake?"

Jacky shuts up.

"If yer bit," says Tommy, after a pause, "you'll swell up, an' smell, an' turn red an' green an' blue all over till yer bust. Won't he, Mother?"

"Now then, don't frighten the child. Go to sleep," she says.

The two younger children go to sleep, and now and then Jacky complains of being "skeezed." More room is made for him. Presently Tommy says: "Mother! listen to them (adjective) little possums. I'd like to screw their blanky necks."

And Jacky protests drowsily.

"But they don't hurt us, the little blanks!"

Mother: "There, I told you you'd teach Jacky to swear." But the remark makes her smile. Jacky goes to sleep.

Presently Tommy asks:

"Mother! Do you think they'll ever extricate the (adjective) kangaroo?"

"Lord! How am I to know, child? Go to sleep."

"Will you wake me if the snake comes out?"

"Yes. Go to sleep."

Near midnight. The children are all asleep and she sits there still, sewing and reading by turns. From time to time she glances round the floor and wallplate, and, whenever she hears a noise, she reaches for the stick. The thunderstorm comes on, and the wind, rushing through the cracks in the slab wall, threatens to blow out her candle. She places it on a sheltered part of the dresser and fixes up a newspaper to protect it. At every flash of lightning, the cracks between the slabs gleam like polished silver. The thunder rolls, and the rain comes down in torrents.

Alligator lies at full length on the floor, with his eyes turned towards the partition. She knows by this that the snake is there. There are large cracks in that wall opening under the floor of the dwelling-house.

She is not a coward, but recent events have shaken her nerves. A little son of her brother-in-law was lately bitten by a snake, and died. Besides, she has not heard from her husband for six months, and is anxious about him.

He was a drover, and started squatting here when they were married. The drought of 18— ruined him. He had to sacrifice the remnant of his flock and go droving again. He intends to move his family into the nearest town when he comes back, and, in the meantime, his brother, who keeps a shanty on the main road, comes over about once a month with provisions. The wife has still a couple of cows, one horse, and a few sheep. The brother-in-law kills one of the latter occasionally, gives her what she needs of it, and takes the rest in return for other provisions.

She is used to being left alone. She once lived like this for eighteen months. As a girl she built the usual castles in the air; but all her girlish hopes and aspirations have long been dead. She finds all the excitement and recreation she needs in the *Young Ladies' Journal,* and Heaven help her! takes a pleasure in the fashion-plates.

Her husband is an Australian, and so is she. He is careless, but a good enough husband. If he had the means he would take her to the city and keep her there like a princess. They are used to being apart, or at least she is. "No use fretting," she says. He may forget sometimes that he is married; but if he has a good cheque when he comes back he will give most of it to her. When he had money he took her to the city several times—hired a railway sleeping compartment, and put up at the best hotels. He also bought her a buggy, but they had to sacrifice that along with the rest.

The last two children were born in the bush—one while her husband was bringing a drunken doctor, by force, to attend to her. She was alone on this occasion, and very weak. She had been ill with a fever. She prayed to God to send her assistance. God sent Black Mary—the "whitest" gin in all the land. Or, at least, God sent King Jimmy first, and he sent Black Mary. He put his black face round the door post, took in the situation at a glance, and said cheerfully: "All right, missus—I bring my old woman, she down alonga creek."

One of the children died while she was here alone. She rode nineteen miles for assistance, carrying the dead child.

It must be near one or two o'clock. The fire is burning low. Alligator lies with his head resting on his paws, and watches the wall. He is not a very beautiful dog, and the light shows numerous old wounds where the hair will not grow. He is afraid of nothing on the face of the earth or under it. He will tackle a bullock as readily as he will tackle a flea. He hates all other dogs—except kangaroo-dogs—and has a marked dislike to friends or relations of the family. They seldom call, however. He sometimes makes friends with strangers. He hates snakes and has killed many, but he will be bitten some day and die; most snake-dogs end that way.

Now and then the bushwoman lays down her work and watches, and listens, and thinks. She thinks of things in her own life, for there is little else to think about.

The rain will make the grass grow, and this reminds her how she fought a bush fire once while her husband was away. The grass was long, and very dry, and the fire threatened to burn her out. She put on an old pair of her husband's trousers and beat out the flames with a green bough, till great drops of sooty perspiration stood out on her forehead and ran in streaks down her blackened arms. The sight of his mother in trousers greatly amused Tommy, who worked like a little hero by her side, but the terrified baby howled lustily for his "mummy." The fire would have mastered her but for four excited bushmen who arrived in the nick of time. It was a mixed-up affair all round; when she went to take up the baby he screamed and struggled convulsively, thinking it was a "blackman"; and Alligator, trusting more to the child's sense than his own instinct, charged furiously, and (being old and slightly deaf) did not in his excitement at first recognize his mistress's voice, but continued to hang on to the moleskins until choked off by Tommy with a saddle strap. The dog's sorrow for his blunder, and his anxiety to let it be known that it was all a mistake, was as evident as his ragged tail and a twelve-inch grin could make it. It was a glorious time for the boys; a day to look back to, and talk about, and laugh over for many years.

She thinks how she fought a flood during her husband's absence. She stood for hours in the drenching downpour, and dug an overflow gutter to save the dam across the creek. But she could not save it. There are things that a bushwoman cannot do. Next morning the dam was broken, and her heart was nearly broken too, for she thought how her husband would feel when he came home and saw the result of years of labour swept away. She cried then.

She also fought the pleuro-pneumonia—dosed and bled the few remaining cattle, and wept again when her two best cows died.

Again, she fought a mad bullock that besieged the house for a day. She made bullets and fired at him through cracks in the slabs with an old shotgun. He was dead in the morning. She skinned him and got seventeen-and-sixpence for the hide.

She also fights the crows and eagles that have designs on her chickens. Her plan of campaign is very original. The children cry "Crows, Mother!" and she rushes out and aims a broomstick at the birds as though it were a gun, and says "Bung!" The crows leave in a hurry; they are cunning, but a woman's cunning is greater.

Occasionally a bushman in the horrors, or a villainous-looking sundowner, comes and nearly scares the life out of her. She generally tells the suspicious-looking stranger that her husband and two sons are at work below the dam, or over at the yard, for he always cunningly inquires for the boss.

Only last week a gallows-faced swagman—having satisfied himself that there were no men on the place—threw his swag down on the verandah, and demanded tucker. She gave him something to eat; then he expressed his intention of staying for the night. It was sundown then. She got a batten from the sofa, loosened the dog, and confronted the stranger, holding the batten in one hand and the dog's collar with the other. "Now you go!" she said. He looked at her and at the dog, said "All right, mum," in a cringing tone, and left. She was a determined-looking woman, and Alligator's yellow eyes glared unpleasantly—besides, the dog's chawing-up apparatus greatly resembled that of the reptile he was named after.

She has few pleasures to think of as she sits here alone by the fire, on guard against a snake. All days are much the same to her; but on Sunday afternoon she dresses herself, tidies the children, smartens up baby, and goes for a lonely walk along the bush track, pushing an old perambulator in front of her. She does this every Sunday. She takes as much care to make herself and the children look smart as she would if she were going to do the block in the city. There is nothing to see, however, and not a soul to meet. You might walk for twenty miles along this track without being able to fix a point in your mind, unless you are a bushman. This is because of the everlasting, maddening sameness of the stunted trees—that monotony which makes a man long to break away and travel as far as trains can go, and sail as far as ship can sail—and further.

But this bushwoman is used to the loneliness of it. As a girl-wife she hated it, but now she would feel strange away from it.

She is glad when her husband returns, but she does not gush or make a fuss about it. She gets him something good to eat, and tidies up the children.

She seems contented with her lot. She loves her children, but has no time to show it. She seems harsh to them. Her surroundings are not favorable to the development of the "womanly" or senti-mental side of nature.

It must be near morning now; but the clock is in the dwelling-house. Her candle is nearly done; she forgot that she was out of candles. Some more wood must be got to keep the fire up, and so she shuts the dog inside and hurries round to the wood-heap. The rain has cleared off. She seizes a stick, pulls it out, and—crash! the whole pile collapses.

Yesterday she bargained with a stray blackfellow to bring her some wood, and while he was at work she went in search of a missing cow. She was absent an hour or so, and the native black made good use of his time. On her return she was so astonished to see a good heap of wood by the chimney, that she gave him an extra fig of tobacco, and praised him for not being lazy. He thanked her, and left with head erect and chest well out. He was the last of his tribe and a King; but he had built that wood-heap hollow.

She is hurt now, and tears spring to her eyes as she sits down again by the table. She takes up a handkerchief to wipe the tears away, but pokes her eyes with her bare fingers instead. The hand-kerchief is full of holes, and she finds that she has put her thumb through one, and her forefinger through another.

This makes her laugh, to the surprise of the dog. She has a keen, very keen, sense of the ridiculous; and some time or other she will amuse bushmen with the story.

She had been amused before like that. One day she sat down "to have a good cry," as she said—and the old cat rubbed against her dress and "cried too." Then she had to laugh.

It must be near daylight now. The room is very close and hot because of the fire. Alligator still watches the wall from time to time. Suddenly he becomes greatly interested; he draws himself a few inches nearer the partition, and a thrill runs through his body. The hair on the back of his neck begins to bristle, and the battle-light is in his yellow eyes. She knows what this means, and lays her hand on the stick. The lower end of one of the partition slabs has a large crack on both sides. An evil pair of small, bright bead-like eyes glisten at one of these holes. The snake—a black one—comes slowly out, about a foot, and moves its head up and down. The dog lies still, and the woman sits as one fascinated. The snake comes out a foot farther. She lifts her stick, and the reptile, as though suddenly aware of danger, sticks his head in through the crack on the other side of the slab, and hurries to get his tail round after him. Alligator springs, and his jaws come together with a snap. He misses, for his nose is large, and the snake's body close down in the angle formed by the slabs and the floor. He snaps again as the tail comes round. He has the snake now, and tugs it out eighteen inches. Thud, thud comes the woman's club on the ground. Alligator pulls again. Thud, thud. Alligator gives another pull and he has the snake out—a black brute, five feet long. The head rises to dart about, but the dog has the enemy close to the neck. He is a big, heavy dog, but quick as a terrier. He shakes the snake as though he felt the original curse in common with mankind. The eldest boy wakes up, seizes his stick, and tries to get out of bed, but his mother forces him back with a grip of iron. Thud, thud—the snake's back is broken in several places. Thud, thud—its head is crushed, and Alligator's nose skinned again.

She lifts the mangled reptile on the point of her stick, carries it to the fire, and throws it in; then piles on the wood and watches the snake burn. The boy and dog watch too. She lays her hand on the dog's head, and all the fierce, angry light dies out of his yellow eyes. The younger children are quieted, and presently go to sleep. The dirty-legged boy stands for a moment in his shirt, watching the fire. Presently, he looks up at her, sees the tears in her eyes, and, throwing his arms round her neck exclaims:

"Mother, I won't never go drovin'; blarst me if I do!"

And she hugs him to her wornout breast and kisses him; and they sit thus together while the sickly daylight breaks over the bush.

●

A WORN PATH

Eudora Welty

Often love of one's own summons the most miraculous human strengths. In this splendid story, an old woman's love for her grandson quietly knocks down all obstacles the world sets before her, including her own frailty and suffering.

It was December—a bright frozen day in the early morning. Far out in the country there was an old Negro woman with her head tied in a red rag, coming along a path through the pinewoods. Her name was Phoenix Jackson. She was very old and small and she walked slowly in the dark pine shadows, moving a little from side to side in her steps, with the balanced heaviness and lightness of a pendulum in a grandfather clock. She carried a thin, small cane made from an umbrella, and with this she kept tapping the frozen earth in front of her. This made a grave and persistent noise in the still air, that seemed meditative like the chirping of a solitary little bird.

She wore a dark striped dress reaching down to her shoe tops, and an equally long apron of bleached sugar sacks, with a full pocket: all neat and tidy, but every time she took a step she might have fallen over her shoelaces, which dragged from her unlaced shoes. She looked straight ahead. Her eyes were blue with age. Her skin had a pattern all its own of numberless branching wrinkles and as though a whole little tree stood in the middle of her forehead, but a golden color ran underneath, and the two knobs of her cheeks were illumined by a yellow burning under the dark. Under the red rag her hair came down on her neck in the frailest of ringlets, still black, and with an odor like copper.

Now and then there was a quivering in the thicket. Old Phoenix said, "Out of my way, all you foxes, owls, beetles, jack rabbits, coons and wild animals! . . . Keep out from under these feet, little bob-whites. . . . Keep the big wild hogs out of my path. Don't let none of those come running my direction. I got a long way." Under her small black-freckled hand her cane, limber as a buggy whip, would switch at the brush as if to rouse up any hiding things.

On she went. The woods were deep and still. The sun made the pine needles almost too bright to look at, up where the wind rocked. The cones dropped as light as feathers. Down in the hollow was the mourning dove—it was not too late for him.

The path ran up a hill. "Seem like there is chains about my feet, time I get this far," she said, in the voice of argument old people keep to use with themselves. "Something always take a hold of me on this hill—pleads I should stay."

After she got to the top she turned and gave a full, severe look behind her where she had come. "Up through pines," she said at length. "Now down through oaks."

Her eyes opened their widest, and she started down gently. But before she got to the bottom of the hill a bush caught her dress.

Her fingers were busy and intent, but her skirts were full and long, so that before she could pull them free in one place they were caught in another. It was not possible to allow the dress to tear. "I in the thorny bush," she said. "Thorns, you doing your appointed work. Never want to let folks pass, no sir. Old eyes thought you was a pretty little *green* bush."

Finally, trembling all over, she stood free, and after a moment dared to stoop for her cane.

"Sun so high!" she cried, leaning back and looking, while the thick tears went over her eyes. "The time getting all gone here."

At the foot of this hill was a place where a log was laid across the creek.

"Now comes the trial," said Phoenix.

Putting her right foot out, she mounted the log and shut her eyes. Lifting her skirt, leveling her cane fiercely before her, like a festival figure in some parade, she began to march across. Then she opened her eyes and she was safe on the other side.

"I wasn't as old as I thought," she said.

But she sat down to rest. She spread her skirts on the bank around her and folded her hands over her knees. Up above her was a tree in a pearly cloud of mistletoe. She did not dare to close her eyes, and when a little boy brought her a plate with a slice of marble-cake on it she spoke to him. "That would be acceptable," she said. But when she went to take it there was just her own hand in the air.

So she left that tree, and had to go through a barbed-wire fence. There she had to creep and crawl, spreading her knees and stretching her fingers like a baby trying to climb the steps. But she talked loudly to herself: she could not let her dress be torn now, so late in the day, and she could not pay for having her arm or her leg sawed off if she got caught fast where she was.

At last she was safe through the fence and risen up out in the clearing. Big dead trees, like black men with one arm, were standing in the purple stalks of the withered cotton field. There sat a buzzard.

"Who you watching?"

In the furrow she made her way along.

"Glad this not the season for the bulls," she said, looking sideways, "and the good Lord made his snakes to curl up and sleep in the winter. A pleasure I don't see no two-headed snake coming around that tree, where it come once. It took a while to get by him, back in the summer."

She passed through the old cotton and went into a field of dead corn. It whispered and shook and was taller than her head. "Through the maze now," she said, for there was no path.

Then were was something tall, black, and skinny there, moving before her.

At first she took it for a man. It could have been a man dancing in the field. But she stood still and listened, and it did not make a sound. It was as silent as a ghost.

"Ghost," she said sharply, "who be you the ghost of? For I have heard of nary death close by."

But there was no answer—only the ragged dancing in the wind.

She shut her eyes, reached out her hand, and touched a sleeve. She found a coat and inside that an emptiness, cold as ice.

"You scarecrow," she said. Her face lighted. "I ought to be shut up for good," she said with laughter. "My senses is gone. I too old. I the oldest people I ever know. Dance, old scarecrow," she said, "while I dancing with you."

She kicked her foot over the furrow, and with mouth drawn down, shook her head once or twice in a little strutting way. Some husks blew down and whirled in streamers about her skirts.

Then she went on, parting her way from side to side with the cane, through the whispering field. At last she came to the end, to a wagon track where the silver grass blew between the red ruts. The quail were walking around like pullets, seeming all dainty and unseen.

"Walk pretty," she said. "This the easy place. This the easy going."

She followed the track, swaying through the quiet bare fields, through the little strings of trees silver in their dead leaves, past cabins silver from weather, with the doors and windows boarded shut, all like old women under a spell sitting there. "I walking in their sleep," she said, nodding her head vigorously.

In a ravine she went where a spring was silently flowing through a hollow log. Old Phoenix bent and drank. "Sweet-gum makes the water sweet," she said, and drank more. "Nobody know who made this well, for it was here when I was born."

The track crossed a swampy part where the moss hung as white as lace from every limb. "Sleep on, alligators, and blow your bubbles." Then the track went into the road.

Deep, deep the road went down between the high green-colored banks. Overhead the live-oaks met, and it was as dark as a cave.

A black dog with a lolling tongue came up out of the weeds by the ditch. She was meditating, and not ready, and when he came at her she only hit him a little with her cane. Over she went in the ditch, like a little puff of milkweed.

Down there, her senses drifted away. A dream visited her, and she reached her hand up, but nothing reached down and gave her a pull. So she lay there and presently went to talking. "Old woman," she said to herself, "that black dog come up out of the weeds to stall you off, and now there he sitting on his fine tail, smiling at you."

A white man finally came along and found her—a hunter, a young man, with his dog on a chain.

"Well, Granny!" he laughed. "What are you doing there?"

"Lying on my back like a June-bug waiting to be turned over, mister," she said, reaching up her hand.

He lifted her up, gave her a swing in the air, and set her down. "Anything broken, Granny?"

"No sir, them old dead weeds is springy enough," said Phoenix, when she had got her breath. "I thank you for your trouble."

"Where do you live, Granny?" he asked, while the two dogs were growling at each other.

"Away back yonder, sir, behind the ridge. You can't even see it from here."

"On your way home?"

"No sir, I going to town."

"Why, that's too far! That's as far as I walk when I come out myself, and I get something for my trouble." He patted the stuffed bag he carried, and there hung down a little closed claw. It was one of the bob-whites, with its beak hooked bitterly to show it was dead. "Now you go on home, Granny!"

"I bound to go to town, mister," said Phoenix. "The time come around."

He gave another laugh, filling the whole landscape. "I know you old colored people! Wouldn't miss going to town to see Santa Claus!"

But something held old Phoenix very still. The deep lines in her face went into a fierce and different radiation. Without warning, she had seen with her own eyes a flashing nickel fall out of the man's pocket onto the ground.

"How old are you, Granny?" he was saying.

"There is no telling, mister," she said, "no telling."

Then she gave a little cry and clapped her hands and said, "Git on away from here, dog! Look! Look at that dog!" She laughed as if in admiration. "He ain't scared of nobody. He a big black dog." She whispered, "Sic him!"

"Watch me get rid of that cur," said the man. "Sic him, Pete! Sic him!"

Phoenix heard the dogs fighting, and heard the man running and throwing sticks. She even heard a gunshot. But she was slowly bending forward by that time, further and further forward, the lids stretched down over her eyes, as if she were doing this in her sleep. Her chin was lowered almost to her knees. The yellow palm of her hand came out from the fold of her apron. Her fingers slid down and along the ground under the piece of money with the grace and care they would have in lifting an egg from under a setting hen. Then she slowly straightened up, she stood erect, and the nickel was in her apron pocket. A bird flew by. Her lips moved. "God watching me the whole time. I come to stealing."

The man came back, and his own dog panted about them. "Well, I scared him off that time," he said, and then he laughed and lifted his gun and pointed it at Phoenix.

She stood straight and faced him.

"Doesn't the gun scare you?" he said, still pointing it.

"No, sir, I seen plenty go off closer by, in my day, and for less than what I done," she said, holding utterly still.

He smiled, and shouldered the gun. "Well, Granny," he said, "you must be a hundred years old, and scared of nothing. I'd give you a dime if I had any money with me. But you take my advice and stay home, and nothing will happen to you."

"I bound to go on my way, mister," said Phoenix. She inclined her head in the red rag. Then they went in different directions, but she could hear the gun shooting again and again over the hill.

She walked on. The shadows hung from the oak trees to the road like curtains. Then she smelled wood-smoke, and smelled the river, and she saw a steeple and the cabins on their steep steps. Dozens of little black children whirled around her. There ahead was Natchez shining. Bells were ringing. She walked on.

In the paved city it was Christmas time. There were red and green electric lights strung and crisscrossed everywhere, and all turned on in the daytime. Old Phoenix would have been lost if she had not distrusted her eyesight and depended on her feet to know where to take her.

She paused quietly on the sidewalk where people were passing by. A lady came along in the crowd, carrying an armful of red-, green- and silver-wrapped presents; she gave off perfume like the red roses in hot summer, and Phoenix stopped her.

"Please, missy, will you lace up my shoe?" She held up her foot.

"What do you want, Grandma?"

"See my shoe," said Phoenix. "Do all right for out in the country, but wouldn't look right to go in a big building."

"Stand still then, Grandma," said the lady. She put her packages down on the sidewalk beside her and laced and tied both shoes tightly.

"Can't lace 'em with a cane," said Phoenix. "Thank you, missy. I doesn't mind asking a nice lady to tie up my shoe, when I gets out on the street."

Moving slowly and from side to side, she went into the big building, and into a tower of steps, where she walked up and around and around until her feet knew to stop.

She entered a door, and there she saw nailed up on the wall the document that had been stamped with the gold seal and framed in the gold frame, which matched the dream that was hung up in her head.

"Here I be," she said. There was a fixed and ceremonial stiffness over her body.

"A charity case, I suppose," said an attendant who sat at the desk before her.

But Phoenix only looked above her head. There was sweat on her face, the wrinkles in her skin shone like a bright net.

"Speak up, Grandma," the woman said. "What's your name? We must have your history, you know. Have you been here before? What seems to be the trouble with you?"

Old Phoenix only gave a twitch to her face as if a fly were bothering her.

"Are you deaf?" cried the attendant.

But then the nurse came in.

"Oh, that's just old Aunt Phoenix," she said. "She doesn't come for herself—she has a little grandson. She makes these trips just as regular as clockwork. She lives away back off the Old Natchez Trace." She bent down. "Well, Aunt Phoenix, why don't you just take a seat? We won't keep you standing after your long trip." She pointed.

The old woman sat down, bolt upright in the chair.

"Now, how is the boy?" asked the nurse.

Old Phoenix did not speak.

"I said, how is the boy?"

But Phoenix only waited and stared straight ahead, her face very solemn and withdrawn into rigidity.

"Is his throat any better?" asked the nurse. "Aunt Phoenix, don't you hear me? Is your grandson's throat any better since the last time you came for the medicine?"

With her hands on her knees, the old woman waited, silent, erect and motionless, just as if she were in armor.

"You mustn't take up our time this way, Aunt Phoenix," the nurse said. "Tell us quickly about your grandson, and get it over. He isn't dead, is he?"

At last there came a flicker and then a flame of comprehension across her face, and she spoke.

"My grandson. It was my memory had left me. There I sat and forgot why I made my long trip."

"Forgot?" the nurse frowned. "After you came so far?"

Then Phoenix was like an old woman begging a dignified for-giveness for waking up frightened in the night. "I never did go to school, I was too old at the Surrender," she said in a soft voice. "I'm an old woman without an education. It was my memory fail me. My little grandson, he is just the same, and I forgot it in the coming."

"Throat never heals, does it?" said the nurse, speaking in a loud, sure voice to old Phoenix. By now she had a card with something written on it, a little list. "Yes. Swallowed lye. When was it?—January—two, three years ago—"

Phoenix spoke unasked now. "No, missy, he not dead, he just the same. Every little while his throat begin to close up again, and he not able to swallow. He not get his breath. He not able to help himself. So the time come around, and I go on another trip for the soothing medicine."

"All right. The doctor said as long as you came to get it, you could have it," said the nurse. "But it's an obstinate case."

"My little grandson, he sit up there in the house all wrapped up, waiting by himself," Phoenix went on. "We is the only two left in the world. He suffer and it don't seem to put him back at all. He got a sweet look. He going to last. He wear a little patch quilt and peep out holding his mouth open like a little bird. I remembers so plain now. I not going to forget him again, no, the whole enduring time. I could tell him from all the others in creation."

"All right." The nurse was trying to hush her now. She brought her a bottle of medicine. "Charity," she said, making a check mark in a book.

Old Phoenix held the bottle close to her eyes, and then carefully put it into her pocket.

"I thank you," she said.

"It's Christmas time, Grandma," said the attendant. "Could I give you a few pennies out of my purse?"

"Five pennies is a nickel," said Phoenix stiffly.

"Here's a nickel," said the attendant.

Phoenix rose carefully and held out her hand. She received the nickel and then fished the other nickel out of her pocket and laid it beside the new one. She stared at her palm closely, with her head on one side.

Then she gave a tap with her cane on the floor.

"This is what come to me to do," she said. "I going to the store and buy my child a little windmill they sells, made out of paper. He going to find it hard to believe there such a thing in the world. I'll march myself back where he waiting, holding it straight up in this hand."

She lifted her free hand, gave a little nod, turned around, and walked out of the doctor's office. Then her slow step began on the stairs, going down.

•

"ONE, TWO, THREE!"

Henry Cuyler Bunner

The play of kindred spirits across generations can be one of the great blessings of family. In our time, it is an irony that even though people live to record numbers of years, many children do not know the joy of playing with their grandparents.

It was an old, old, old, old lady,
    And a boy that was half past three;
And the way that they played together
    Was beautiful to see.

She couldn't go running and jumping,
    And the boy, no more could he;
For he was a thin little fellow,
    With a thin little twisted knee.

They sat in the yellow twilight,
    Out under the maple tree;
And the game that they played I'll tell you,
    Just as it was told to me.

It was Hide and Go Seek they were playing,
    Though you'd never have known it to be—
With an old, old, old, old lady,
    And a boy with a twisted knee.

The boy would bend his face down
    On his one little sound right knee,
And he'd guess where she was hiding,
    In guesses One, Two, Three!

"You are in the china closet!"
    He would cry, and laugh with glee—
It wasn't the china closet;
    But he still had Two and Three.

"You are up in Papa's big bedroom,
    In the chest with the queer old key!"
And she said: "You are *warm* and *warmer;*
    But you're not quite right," said she.

"It can't be the little cupboard
    Where Mamma's things used to be—
So it must be the clothespress, Gran'ma!"
    And he found her with his Three.

Then she covered her face with her fingers,
    That were wrinkled and white and wee,
And she guessed where the boy was hiding,
    With a One and a Two and a Three.

And they never had stirred from their places,
    Right under the maple tree—
This old, old, old, old lady,
    And the boy with the lame little knee—
This dear, dear, dear old lady,
    And the boy who was half past three.

•

THESEUS AND THE STONE

*Adapted from retellings by Charles
Kingsley and Nathaniel Hawthorne*

Home is the place to build strength and resolve before going out
into the world. Plutarch and Appolodorus, among other ancient
writers, have left us accounts of how the Greek hero Theseus
journeyed toward manhood.

In the old city of Troezen, in Greece, there lived long ago a
princess named Aithra. She had one young son named Theseus, the
bravest lad in all the land. Aithra smiled whenever she looked at
him, but it was a sad kind of smile, for the boy had never seen his
father, who lived far across the sea.

One day she took her son into a grove which stood behind the temple. She led him to a tall oak, beneath whose shade grew arbutus and lentisk and purple heather bushes. There she sighed, and said, "Theseus, my son, go into that thicket, and at the base of the tree you will find a great flat stone. Lift it and bring me what lies underneath."

Theseus pushed his way through the thick bushes, seeing they had not been moved for many years. And searching among their roots he found a great flat stone, all overgrown with ivy and moss.

He tried to lift it, but he could not. He tried till the sweat ran down his brow from heat and the tears from his eyes for shame, but all was to no avail. At last he came back to his mother and said, "I have found the stone, but I cannot lift it. Nor do I think any man could in all Troezen."

His mother sighed and said, "The gods wait long, but they are just. Let it be for another year. The day may come when you will be a stronger man than lives in all Troezen."

And when a full year was past she led Theseus again up to the temple and bade him lift the stone, but he could not.

Then she sighed and said the same words again, and again they went home together. The next year they made the same pilgrimage, but Theseus could not lift the stone then, nor the year after. He longed to ask his mother the meaning of the stone and what might lie underneath it, but her face was so sad he had not the heart to ask.

Meanwhile the rock seemed to be sinking farther and farther into the ground. The moss grew over it thicker and thicker, until at last it looked almost like a soft green seat, with only a few gray knobs of granite peeping out. The overhanging trees, also, shed their brown leaves upon it, as often as the autumn came, and at its base grew ferns and wildflowers and vines, which crept over its surface. To all appearance the rock was as firmly fastened as any other portion of the earth's substance.

But as impossible as the task looked, Theseus was growing certain he would someday get the upper hand of the stone.

"Mother, it has moved!" he cried, after one of his attempts. "The earth around it is a little cracked!" And he showed her the place where he thought the stem of a flower had been partly uprooted by the movement of the rock. Aithra only sighed, for she knew the time was coming when she must send her son forth among the perils of the world.

So in order to grow strong Theseus spent all his days in wrestling and boxing and taming horses, and hunting the boar and the bull, and chasing goats and deer among the rocks, till upon all the mountains there was no hunter so swift as Theseus.

And when his eighteenth year was past, Aithra led him again to the temple, and said, "Theseus, lift the stone this day, or never know who you are."

And Theseus went into the thicket and stood over the stone and tugged at it—and it stirred! His spirits swelled within him, and he said, "If I break my heart in my body, it shall come up." He wrestled with the sluggish stone, straining every sinew, as if it were a living enemy. He heaved, he lifted. He resolved now to succeed, or else perish there and let the rock be his gravestone forever! Aithra stood gazing at him, and clasped her hands, partly with a mother's pride and partly with a mother's sorrow. And slowly the great rock rose from the bedded moss and earth, uprooting the shrubs and flowers along with it, and was turned on its side. Theseus had conquered!

And when he looked beneath the stone, on the ground lay a sword of bronze, with a hilt of glittering gold, and by it a pair of golden sandals. He caught them up and burst through the bushes like a wild boar, and leaped to his mother, holding them high above his head.

When she saw them she wept in long silence, hiding her face in her shawl, and Theseus stood by her wondering, and wept also, although he knew not why. And when she was tired of weeping she lifted her head and said, "Bring what you have found, and come with me where we can look down upon the sea."

They went outside the sacred wall and looked down over the bright blue sea. Aithra pointed across the water and said: "There is Attica, where the Athenian people dwell. It is a fair place, a land of olive oil and honey, the joy of gods and men. What would you do, son Theseus, if you were king of such a land?"

Then his heart grew great within him, and he said: "If I were king of such a land, I would rule it wisely and well in wisdom and in might, that when I died all would weep over my tomb and cry, 'Alas for the shepherd of his people.' "

Aithra smiled and said: "Your father is King Aegeus of Athens. When he went to be king, he bade me treat you as a child until you should prove yourself by lifting this heavy stone. That task accomplished, you are to put on his sandals. in order to follow in your father's footsteps, and to gird on his sword, so that you may fight giants and dragons, as King Aegeus did in his youth. And you are to go to him in Athens and say, 'The stone is lifted.' "

But Theseus wept. "Shall I leave you, O my mother?" he cried.

She answered, "Weep not for me. That which is fate must be, and grief is easy to those who do naught but grieve."

Then she kissed Theseus and wept over him, and went into the temple, and Theseus saw her no more.

•

IN THE UTTERMOST PARTS OF THE SEA
Hans Christian Andersen

As we go out into the world, we find that lessons we've learned and loved at home stay with us and sustain us. Virtues travel well. The title of this beautiful Hans Christian Andersen story comes from Psalm 139: "If I take the wings of the morning, and dwell in the uttermost parts of the sea, even there shall Thy hand lead me, and Thy right hand shall hold me."

Some large ships were sent up toward the North Pole, for the purpose of discovering the boundaries of land and sea, and of trying how far men could make their way.

A year and a day had elapsed. Amid mist and ice had they, with great difficulty, steered farther and farther. The winter had now begun; the sun had set, one long night would continue during many, many weeks. One unbroken plain of ice spread around them; the ships were all fast moored to it. The snow lay about in heaps and had even shaped itself into cubiform houses, some as big as our barrows, some only just large enough for two or three men to find shelter within. Darkness they could not complain of, for the Northern Lights—Nature's fireworks—now red, now blue, flashed unceasingly, and the snow glistened so brightly.

At times when it was brightest came troops of the natives, strange-looking figures, clad in hairy skins, and with sledges made out of hard fragments of ice. They brought skins to exchange, which the sailors were only too glad to use as warm carpets inside their snow houses, and as beds whereon they could rest under their snowy tents, while outside prevailed an intensity of cold such as we never experience during our severest winters. But the sailors remembered that at home it was still autumn, and they thought of the warm sunbeams and the leaves still clinging to the trees in varied glories of crimson and gold. Their watches told them it was evening and time for rest, and in one of the snow houses two sailors had already lain down to sleep. The youngest of these two had with him his best home treasure, the Bible that his grandmother had given him at parting. Every night it lay under his pillow. He had known its contents from childhood, and every day he read a portion; and often as he lay on his couch, he recalled to mind those holy words of comfort, "If I should take the wings of the morning, and remain in the uttermost parts of the sea, even there should Thy hand lead me, and Thy right hand should hold me."

These sublime words of faith were on his lips as he closed his eyes, when sleep came to him, and dreams with sleep—busy, swift-winged dreams, proving that though the body may rest, the soul must ever be awake. First he seemed to hear the melodies of songs dear to him in his home. A mild summer breeze seemed to breathe upon him, and a light shone upon his couch, as though the snowy dome above him had become transparent. He lifted his head and behold! The dazzling white light was not the white of a snow wall; it came from the large wings of an angel stooping over him, an angel with eyes beaming with love. The angel's form seemed to spring from the pages of the Bible, as from the pitcher of a lily blossom. He extended his arms and lo! The narrow walls of the snow hut sank back like a mist melting before the daylight. Once again the green meadows and autumnal-tinted woods of the sailor's home lay around him, bathed in quiet sunshine. The stork's nest was empty, but the apples still clung to the wild apple tree. The blackbird whistled in the little green cage that hung in the lowly window of his childhood's home. The blackbird whistled the tune he had taught him, and the old grandmother wound chickweed about the bars of the cage, as her grandson had been wont to do. The smith's pretty young daughter stood drawing water from the well, and as she nodded to the grandmother, the latter beckoned to her, and held up a letter to show her, a letter that had come that morning from the cold northern lands, from the North Pole itself,

where the old woman's grandson now was—safe under God's protecting hand. And the two women, old and young, laughed and
wept by turns—and he the while, the young sailor whose body was
sleeping amid ice and snow, his spirit roaming in the world of
dreams, under the angel's wings, saw and heard it all, and laughed
and wept with them. And from the letter these words were read
aloud, "Even in the uttermost parts of the sea, His right hand shall
hold me fast"; and a sweet, solemn music was wafted round him,
and the angel drooped his wings. Like a soft protecting veil they fell
closer over the sleeper.

The dream was ended; all was darkness in the little snow hut,
but the Bible lay under the sailor's head, faith and hope abode in
his heart. God was with him, and his home was with him, "even in
the uttermost parts of the sea."

•

CHRISTMAS AT SEA

Robert Louis Stevenson

**Often it is hard to leave, but we go knowing that home and hearth
make a point on our compass for the rest of life's journey.**

The sheets were frozen hard, and they cut the naked hand;
The decks were like a slide, where a seaman scarce could stand,
The wind was nor'-wester, blowing squally off the sea;
And cliffs and spouting breakers were the only things a-lee.

They heard the surf a-roaring before the break of day:
But 'twas only with the peep of light we saw how ill we lay.
We tumbled every hand on deck instanter, with a shout,
And we gave her the maintops'l, and stood by to go about.

All day we tacked and tacked between the South Head and the
    North;
All day we hauled the frozen sheets, and got no further forth;
All day as cold as charity, in bitter pain and dread,
For very life and nature we tacked from head to head.

We gave the South a wider berth, for there the tide-race roared;
But every tack we made we brought the North Head close aboard;
So 's we saw the cliffs and houses, and the breakers running high,
And the coastguard in his garden, with his glass against his eye.

The bells upon the church were rung with a mighty jovial cheer;
For it's just that I should tell you how (of all days in the year)
This day of our adversity was blesséd Christmas morn,
And the house above the coastguard's was the house where I was
    born.

O well I saw the pleasant room, the pleasant faces there,
My mother's silver spectacles, my father's silver hair;
And well I saw the firelight, like a flight of homely elves
Go dancing round the china-plates that stand upon the shelves!

And well I knew the talk they had, the talk that was of me,
Of the shadow on the household and the son that went to sea;
And O the wicked fool I seemed, in every kind of way,
To be here and hauling frozen ropes on blesséd Christmas Day.

They lit the high sea-light, and the dark began to fall.
"All hands to loose topgallant sails!" I heard the captain call.
"By the Lord, she'll never stand it," our first mate Jackson cried.
. . . "It's the one way or the other, Mr. Jackson," he replied.

She staggered to her bearings, but the sails were new and good,
And the ship smelt up to windward just as though she understood.
As the winter's day was ending, in the entry of the night,
We cleared the weary headland, and passed below the light.

And they heaved a mighty breath, every soul on board but me,
As they saw her nose again pointing handsome out to sea;
But all that I could think of, in the darkness and the cold,
Was just that I was leaving home and my folks were growing old.

•

THE HAMPSHIRE HILLS

Eugene Field

As this beautiful story reminds us we go into the world wisely, go
through the world bravely, and go out of the world peacefully
when we start with the great fortification that is home.

One afternoon many years ago two little brothers named Seth
and Abner were playing in the orchard. They were not troubled
with the heat of the August day, for a soft, cool wind came up from
the river in the valley over yonder and fanned their red cheeks and
played all kinds of pranks with their tangled curls. All about them
was the hum of bees, the song of birds, the smell of clover, and the
merry music of the crickets. Their little dog Fido chased them
through the high, waving grass, and rolled with them under the
trees, and barked himself hoarse in his attempt to keep pace with
their laughter. Wearied at length, they lay beneath the bellflower
tree and looked off at the Hampshire hills, and wondered if the
time ever would come when they should go out into the world
beyond those hills and be great, noisy men. Fido did not understand it at all. He lolled in the grass, cooling his tongue on the
clover bloom, and puzzling his brain to know why his little masters
were so quiet all at once.

"I wish I were a man," said Abner, ruefully. "I want to be
somebody and do something. It is very hard to be a little boy so
long and to have no companions but little boys and girls, to see
nothing but these same old trees and this same high grass, and to
hear nothing but the same bird songs from one day to another."

That is true," said Seth. "I, too, am very tired of being a little
boy, and I long to go out into the world and be a man like my
gran'pa or my father or my uncles. With nothing to look at but those
distant hills and the river in the valley, my eyes are wearied; and I
shall be very happy when I am big enough to leave this stupid
place."

Had Fido understood their words he would have chided them,
for the little dog loved his home and had no thought of any other
pleasure than romping through the orchard and playing with his
little masters all the day. But Fido did not understand them.

The clover bloom heard them with sadness. Had they but listened in turn they would have heard the clover saying softly: "Stay with me while you may, little boys; trample me with your merry feet; let me feel the imprint of your curly heads and kiss the sunburn on your little cheeks. Love me while you may, for when you go away you never will come back."

The bellflower tree heard them, too, and she waved her great, strong branches as if she would caress the impatient little lads, and she whispered: "Do not think of leaving me: you are children, and you know nothing of the world beyond those distant hills. It is full of trouble and care and sorrow; abide here in this quiet spot till you are prepared to meet the vexations of that outer world. We are for *you*—we trees and grass and birds and bees and flowers. Abide with us, and learn the wisdom we teach."

The cricket in the raspberry hedge heard them, and she chirped, oh! so sadly: "You will go out into the world and leave us and never think of us again till it is too late to return. Open your ears, little boys, and hear my song of contentment."

So spake the clover bloom and the bellflower tree and the cricket; and in like manner the robin that nested in the linden over yonder, and the big bumblebee that lived in the hole under the pasture gate, and the butterfly and the wild rose pleaded with them, each in his own way; but the little boys did not heed them, so eager were their desires to go into and mingle with the great world beyond those distant hills.

Many years went by; and at last Seth and Abner grew to manhood, and the time was come when they were to go into the world and be brave, strong men. Fido had been dead a long time. They had made him a grave under the bellflower tree—yes, just where

he had romped with the two little boys that August afternoon Fido lay sleeping amid the humming of the bees and the perfume of the clover. But Seth and Abner did not think of Fido now, nor did they give even a passing thought to any of their old friends—the bellflower tree, the clover, the cricket, and the robin. Their hearts beat with exultation. They were men, and they were going beyond the hills to know and try the world.

They were equipped for that struggle, not in a vain, frivolous way, but as good and brave young men should be. A gentle mother had counselled them, a prudent father had advised them, and they had gathered from the sweet things of Nature much of that wisdom before which all knowledge is as nothing. So they were fortified. They went beyond the hills and came into the West. How great and busy was the world—how great and busy it was here in the West! What a rush and noise and turmoil and seething and surging, and how keenly did the brothers have to watch and struggle for vantage ground. Withal, they prospered; the counsel of the mother, the advice of the father, the wisdom of the grass and flowers and trees, were much to them, and they prospered. Honor and riches came to them, and they were happy. But amid it all, how seldom they thought of the little home among the circling hills where they had learned the first sweet lessons of life!

And now they were old and gray. They lived in splendid mansions, and all people paid them honor.

One August day a grim messenger stood in Seth's presence and beckoned to him.

Who are you?" cried Seth. "What strange power have you over me that the very sight of you chills my blood and stays the beating of my heart?"

Then the messenger threw aside his mask, and Seth saw that he was Death. Seth made no outcry; he knew what the summons meant, and he was content. But he sent for Abner.

And when Abner came, Seth was stretched upon his bed, and there was a strange look in his eyes and a flush upon his cheeks, as though a fatal fever had laid hold on him.

"You shall not die!" cried Abner, and he threw himself about his brother's neck and wept.

But Seth bade Abner cease his outcry. "Sit here by my bedside and talk with me," said he, "and let us speak of the Hampshire hills."

A great wonder overcame Abner. With reverence he listened, and as he listened a sweet peace seemed to steal into his soul.

"I am prepared for Death," said Seth, "and I will go with Death this day. Let us talk of our childhood now, for, after all the battle with this great world, it is pleasant to think and speak of our boyhood among the Hampshire hills."

"Say on, dear brother," said Abner.

"I am thinking of an August day long ago," said Seth, solemnly and softly. "It was so *very* long ago, and yet it seems only yesterday. We were in the orchard together, under the bellflower tree, and our little dog—"

"Fido," said Abner, remembering it all, as the years came back.

"Fido and you and I, under the bellflower tree," said Seth. "How we had played, and how weary we were, and how cool the grass was, and how sweet was the fragrance of the flowers! Can you remember it, brother?"

"Oh, yes," replied Abner, "and I remember how we lay among the clover and looked off at the distant hills and wondered of the world beyond."

"And amid our wonderings and longings," said Seth, "how the old bellflower tree seemed to stretch her kind arms down to us as if she would hold us away from that world beyond the hills."

"And now I can remember that the clover whispered to us, and the cricket in the raspberry hedge sang to us of contentment," said Abner.

"The robin, too, carolled in the linden."

"It is very sweet to remember it now," said Seth. "How blue and hazy the hills looked; how cool the breeze blew up from the river; how like a silver lake the old pickerel pond sweltered under the summer sun over beyond the pasture and broom-corn, and how merry was the music of the birds and bees!"

So these old men, who had been little boys together, talked of the August afternoon when with Fido they had romped in the orchard and rested beneath the bellflower tree. And Seth's voice grew fainter, and his eyes were, oh! so dim; but to the very last he spoke of the dear old days and the orchard and the clover and the Hampshire hills. And when Seth fell asleep forever, Abner kissed his brother's lips and knelt at the bedside and said the prayer his mother had taught him.

In the street without there was the noise of passing carts, the cries of tradespeople, and all the bustle of a great and busy city; but, looking upon Seth's dear, dead face, Abner could hear only the music voices of birds and crickets and summer winds as he had

heard them with Seth when they were little boys together, back
among the Hampshire hills.

WE ARE SEVEN

William Wordsworth

**This moving poem reminds us that families remain together even
after death.**

A simple child,
That lightly draws its breath,
And feels its life in every limb,
What should it know of death?

I met a little cottage girl:
She was eight years old, she said;
Her hair was thick with many a curl
That clustered round her head.

She had a rustic, woodland air,
And she was wildly clad;
Her eyes were fair, and very fair;
Her beauty made me glad.

"Sisters and brothers, little maid,
How many may you be?"
"How many? Seven in all," she said,
And wondering looked at me.

"And where are they? I pray you tell."
　　She answered, "Seven are we;
And two of us at Conway dwell,
　　And two are gone to sea;

"Two of us in the churchyard lie,
　　My sister and my brother;
And, in the churchyard cottage, I
　　Dwell near them with my mother."

"You say that two at Conway dwell,
　　And two are gone to sea,
Yet ye are seven! I pray you tell,
　　Sweet maid, how this may be."

Then did the little maid reply,
　　"Seven boys and girls are we;
Two of us in the churchyard lie
　　Beneath the churchyard tree."

"You run about, my little maid;
　　Your limbs they are alive;
If two are in the churchyard laid,
　　Then ye are only five."

"Their graves are green, they may be seen,"
　　The little maid replied:
"Twelve steps or more from my mother's door,
　　And they are side by side.

"My stockings there I often knit;
　　My kerchief there I hem;
And there upon the ground I sit,
　　And sing a song to them.

"And often after sunset, sir,
　　When it is light and fair,
I take my little porringer,
　　And eat my supper there.

"The first that died was Sister Jane;
　　In bed she moaning lay,

Till God released her of her pain;
    And then she went away.

"So in the churchyard she was laid;
    And, when the grass was dry,
Together round her grave we played,
    My brother John and I.

"And when the ground was white with snow,
    And I could run and slide,
My brother John was forced to go,
    And he lies by her side."

"How many are you, then," said I,
    "If they two are in heaven?"
Quick was the little maid's reply:
    "O Master! we are seven."

"But they are dead; those two are dead!
    Their spirits are in heaven!"
'Twas throwing words away; for still
The little maid would have her will,
    And said, "Nay, we are seven!"

•

PRAYER FOR HOME AND FAMILY

Robert Louis Stevenson

This beautiful prayer sums up, I think, what family life should be. I read it for the first time recently, and hope to make it familiar in the Bennett home.

Lord, behold our family here assembled. We thank Thee for this place in which we dwell; for the love that unites us; for the peace accorded us this day; for the hope with which we expect the morrow; for the health, the work, the food, and the bright skies, that make our lives delightful; for our friends in all parts of the earth.

Let peace abound in our small company. Purge out of every heart the lurking grudge. Give us grace and strength to forbear and to persevere. Offenders, give us the grace to accept and to forgive offenders. Forgetful ourselves, help us to bear cheerfully the forgetfulness of others.

Give us courage and gaiety and the quiet mind. Spare to us our friends, soften to us our enemies. Bless us, if it may be, in all our innocent endeavors. If it may not, give us the strength to encounter that which is to come, that we may be brave in peril, constant in tribulation, temperate in wrath, and in all changes of fortune, and down to the gates of death, loyal and loving one to another.

As the clay to the potter, as the windmill to the wind, as children of their sire, we beseech of Thee this help and mercy for Christ's sake.

Two

·

INTO
THE
WORLD

BEFORE long, the time comes when we leave the safety and security of home and venture into the world on our own. At first we go forth slowly, step by step, reaching new milestones without quite realizing they are leading us on toward independence—the first trip across the street without anyone to hold our hand, the first day at school, the first slumber party at a friend's house, the first summer job, a first rite of passage at church or temple, and on and on until suddenly we look back and discover we've left home far behind. It dawns on us that the world is wide and often unfamiliar, and our journey has only begun. George Eliot recorded how all young people surely feel when they reach that place of poignant recognition: "They had entered the thorny wilderness, and the golden gates of their childhood had forever closed behind them."

This chapter helps us get ready for that time. It helps us with those first faltering steps across home's threshold and into the world beyond. The lessons offered here can serve as guides to help us choose the right paths; they can be supports to make our footing a bit more sure in a world that does not always deal gently with missteps. Life can be a rough and tough journey; the ground can be hard, the air can get cold. So here we find a few lessons that will help us get into and keep the good habits we'll need for the long haul. We find stories, for example, about watching what we say, and about how good manners will take us further. We discover a few things about facing duty, getting on with a job, and doing good work. We see the value of controlling our appetites, our tempers, and our egos. We'll need these lessons in self-discipline and re-sponsibility if we're to last the whole journey.

Not all the lessons the world teaches are moral truths, and by

no means are all of the stories in this chapter lessons in moral
virtue. As we travel forward, we need to know some other rules of
the road too, ones having to do with how the world works. It can
be a complicated place, and it's not always enough simply to be
good; sometimes you need to act *smart* as well. As the gospel of
Matthew says, "wise as serpents, harmless as doves." And so here
we find a few stories that add to our store of practical, everyday
wisdom, stories illustrating intellectual virtues at work. We discover
the importance of knowing our own—and other people's—
strengths and weaknesses. We learn about using what we've earned
and what we've been given to good advantage, about recognizing
what's good for us and what will only bring trouble, about asking
when fights are worthwhile and when clearly they are not. We see
there are times to take advice and times to rely on our own good
judgment.

At times, the world can be a dangerous place. We encounter
all sorts of strangers. Sometimes they are kind but sometimes they
are not, and it pays to be ready. In this chapter, then, we find stories
reminding us that there are those waiting to lay traps for us. We
meet some people who want everything—including what's ours—
and will do anything to get it. We learn a few things about honesty
and dishonesty, and pick up a few pointers on choosing the right
kind of friends. These lessons in prudence are important, we discover, because the virtues are not always in abundant supply.

Our journey may be a bit smoother and safer if we go armed
with these examples. They may help us see more clearly and wisely,
and so keep out of harm's way. Of course, we *will* make a few
wrong turns and fall into a few traps. In fact, we learn wisdom and
virtue from our failures as much as from our successes. And as
someone once observed, anyone who never made a mistake never
made a discovery either. But since the world can be a stern taskmas-
ter, the examples we find in this chapter may at least help soften
the blows. And if nothing else, they'll help us learn that though we
make mistakes, we don't make them alone. And most of our mistakes aren't fatal. For most wrong paths taken, there is a way back
to the crossroads to try again, another day.

HOW FIVE LITTLE ANGELS LOST THEIR WINGS

Mary Stewart

This is a story about going from one world into another, and the attitudes and dispositions with which we face that new world. It's about choosing smiles over tears, and effort over complaint and regret.

Five little angels perched upon the golden bar of Paradise peering down curiously at the world below.

"See it shine in the sunshine, like a ball of fire!" cried one.

"See it dance around, like this—" exclaimed another, springing off the bar and flying around in a circle.

"Look at the gay colors, like broken bits of rainbow!" cried the third. "They must be the earth flowers. I like them better than the flowers of Paradise, all gold and silver!"

"Do you see those tiny white spots?" asked the fourth. "St. Joan of Arc told me those were flocks of sheep. They are so sweet, she says. She took care of them when she was a shepherdess upon the earth."

"Listen, listen!" cried the fifth. "That is a sound we never hear in Paradise! What is it?"

They all listened, their bright angel faces growing puzzled and troubled.

It was the sound of a child crying.

"Oh, let us fly right down to him and comfort him!" cried one.

"Yes, let us tell him that Heaven is near and angels are guarding him and let us take him a little star for a present!" suggested another.

"We have no feet; we could not walk upon the earth and he might not know how to play with us," objected the third.

"Look!" cried the fourth. "It is growing dark upon the earth; there are clouds around it hiding the stars. There must be many children who are afraid or lonely, for listen, now!"

The sobs and whimpers of many children rose to their ears. Perhaps the happy children were all asleep, for there was no sound of laughter or singing.

"Come, come!" cried the fifth little angel. "Let us fly to Gabriel, the guardian of the angels' nursery. He loves all small things, babies and angels, and he will give us feet so that we can run upon the earth and play with the lonely children."

Gabriel was bending over a great bed of silver lilies when the five little angels came flying toward him. They were all talking at once.

"Please, dear Gabriel, we want to fly down to earth!"

"Oh, give us some little legs and feet that we may play in the meadows with the earth children who are crying!"

"We want to tell the lonely children that Heaven is close to them always!"

"Ah, Gabriel, listen to the weeping children and send us right down to them that we may make them smile."

The little angels fluttered about the big beautiful one, who stood straight and shining as a great lily himself, his wings folded like closed petals.

"Little angels, listen," he said, and his voice was music. "It is a long, dangerous journey which you wish to take. It is hard to live on the earth and remain an angel. Every time you are cross or selfish a feather from your wings will fly back to Paradise. If you lose them all you will never be able to return. The children below need you, but those who need you the most do not live in green fields and tend the sheep; they live in ugly cities, in houses where the sun seldom finds his way. Can you keep your golden smiles and your angel wings there?"

"Yes, yes, dear Gabriel! Listen to these sad sounds, and help us to hurry away!"

Out of the golden box where gifts for newborn babies are kept Gabriel took five pairs of small legs and feet. The toes were all pink and dimpled and the five angels were filled with delight. They put them on and danced about, clapping their hands and fluttering their wings.

"All the children upon the earth will be dancing like this before we come home!" they cried. "Now, dear Gabriel, are we ready?"

Gabriel stooped over and kissed each one upon his forehead.

"Keep the blue of the skies in your eyes, the light of Heaven in your smiles and love in your hearts!" he said.

"Farewell, farewell!" they cried. "Here is a shining cloud to carry us down. Watch us and listen; you will hear no sounds of tears tomorrow night!"

But alas! The little angels were so excited over their journey and the strange sights of the world that they kept putting off the work they had come to do.

Reaching the earth just as the sun rose they fell into a meadow full of daisies and buttercups. Of course they had to try their new feet, dancing over the flowers; they had to answer the calls of the birds, and gaze at their own reflections in the pool. By that time they were tired—a feeling they had never known in Paradise—and they lay down in the long grass to sleep. When they woke the moon was shining and the only sound they heard was "Kerchonk! Kerchonk!" from the gay young frogs. Laughing with merriment they ran to the stream and waded down it, splashing their pink toes in the silver water and imitating the frogs.

So the days went by. Their wings were invisible to the people of the world and passersby thought them merely beautiful children, the most beautiful they had ever seen. For a time the angels were not hungry for our kind of food and when they were they walked boldly up to a palace and asked for part of the feast that was going on.

"What princely children!" exclaimed the guests. "Your family, of course?" they asked the old King.

Now the old King had had very ugly, disagreeable children who had grown up and had equally hideous and cross children of their own. He was delighted with the looks of the little angels in the starry clothes and was glad to receive them as part of the royal family. They were given all the sweets they could eat, crowns were placed upon their heads, and at first they had a splendid time. Then they were put in charge of teachers who tried to make them study out of dull books.

"We know more than any books; have we not come from Paradise?" they asked each other. They tore up the books and stamped upon them and, all unnoticed by them, a few feathers flew back to Heaven.

Then their star robes grew dingy and the old King, who spoiled them and let them have whatever they wished, ordered the finest clothes in the kingdom made for them.

Proudly the angels strutted around in purple and gold, eating the richest food, playing all the time and never contented. Every day feathers drifted back to Gabriel's garden, but the angels did not mind.

"Wings are of no use to us here," they said. "We can have whatever we want and when we wish to return to Paradise we will."

They had forgotten the lonely children they came to play with, the frightened, sick children they had longed to comfort.

One day, discontented with everything, they were playing in the royal garden at sunset.

"These roses have thorns on them!" cried one angel pulling an enormous crimson rose to bits.

"Those lilies don't stand straight!" scolded another, tearing down a splendid white lily.

"This butterfly won't stay still long enough to let me catch him!" complained the third.

"Look at this one; it is far bigger and I will catch it!" cried the fourth. He chased the gorgeous black and orange butterfly over the garden, trampling down whole beds of fragrant flowers as he ran.

"Ah see, I have it!" he cried. "It shall follow me wherever I go!"

He opened his clenched hand in which he had crushed the poor butterfly. Its wings were broken and its color rubbed. It crawled painfully over the angel's hand, and the child began to cry. They were the first tears an angel had ever shed, and the others looked bewildered and frightened. Suddenly they remembered when they had heard a child cry before. It was in Paradise when, leaning over the golden bar, they had heard the lonely earth children and had longed to comfort them.

"We had wings once too," cried an angel. "We have lost them, like this butterfly, and we are not of any use either!"

The littlest angel began to cry also.

"I want to fly back to Paradise!" he sobbed. "We are all too little to be left here alone!"

In a bed of lilies they all gathered, watering the crushed flowers with their tears. They were lonely and ashamed. "What must Gabriel think of us now?" they wailed.

Then the fifth angel sprang up.

"Tears don't help a bit!" he cried. "We are still angels and there are many children who need us. We cannot go back to Paradise, but listen to me. We can make the world so like Heaven that we won't be lonely here anymore!"

"Let us start right off!" cried the other angels, struggling to their feet.

"Brave little angels! What will they do next?" asked Gabriel, looking down upon them and smiling.

Out through the garden gates in the moonlight the five ran, and as they thought again their angel thoughts, tiny wings began to sprout from their shoulders. No one saw the wings, at least no grown-up person did. But perhaps you have seen them. I am sure you have heard them fluttering near you!

For from that moment the angels lived with the children of the earth. They sought them far and near. Whenever a child is ill, wherever a child is lonely or sorrowful, one of the five little angels is by his side in a flash, bringing smiles and laughter to his eyes instead of tears. We hear their angel voices in the songs of the happy children; we see the five little angels in eyes that dream, in smiles of love and of courage everywhere.

Their wings are quite grown out now; they could fly back to Paradise if they wished, but they are so blissful in bringing Heaven to the children of the earth that they never think of leaving.

"Dear little angels," said Gabriel watching and listening. "May the blessing of Heaven be with you day and night!"

•

GRANDFATHER STORK

Katharine Pyle

The next three poems are fanciful, but they carry a very real message. Disregard the advice and directions of those who love you, and the world may instruct you in a much harsher way.

> A very naughty boy was John;
> He quarrelled with his food,
> And would not eat his bread and milk,
> As all good children should.
> It grieved his kind mamma to see
> How thin and thinner grew
> Her little John, in spite of all
> That she could say or do.
> Above the chimney Father Stork
> Heard all that Johnny said,
> And how each day he pushed away
> The bowl of milk and bread.
> And so it was, when kind mamma
> Had left the house one day,

In through the kitchen door he came
   And carried John away.
Upon the roof the little storks
   Live high up in the sky,
And far below them in the street
   They hear the folks go by.
The old stork brings them, in his beak,
   The eels and frogs for food;
But these he will not let them have
   Unless they're very good.
Such things poor Johnny could not eat;
   And as he sat and cried,
He thought of all the bread and milk
   He used to push aside.

"If I were only home again,
  I would be good," he said,
"And never, never turn away
  From wholesome milk and bread."
If little John was thin before,
  Now thinner every day
He grew, until you'd think the wind
  Would carry him away.
So, when at last he was so lean
  His bones seemed poking through,
There came a sudden gust of wind,
  And, puff! away he blew.
And when it blew him to the street,
  How fast he hurried home!
And, oh, how glad his mother was
  To see her Johnny come!
But gladder still she was to find
  That he had grown so good,
And never now would turn away
  From wholesome simple food.

•

OLD MOTHER WEBTOES

Katharine Pyle

"Oh please, mamma," said little Jane,
  "May I go out to play?"
"No, no," her mother answered her,
  "I fear 'twill rain today."
"With my umbrella green," said Jane,
  "I will not mind the wet."
But still mamma replied, "No, no;
  A cold I fear you'd get."
But oh, Jane was a naughty girl!
  On her own way intent;
Soon as mamma had turned away,
  Out in the street she went.

The streets were wet and lonely;
    No children there at play;
Only old Mother Webtoes
    The frog abroad that day.
Now little Jane she seizes,
    In spite of all her cries,
And green umbrella, Jane and all,
    Away with her she flies.
Far, far off in the river,
    Upon a moisty stone,
Old Webtoes and her children
    Live in a hut alone;
And Jane's big green umbrella
    Old Webtoes hides away.
She makes her sweep, she makes her scrub;
    Jane has no time to play.
She spreads a bed of rushes,
    Where Jane may sleep at night,
And wakes her in the morning
    As soon as it is light.
"Get up," cries Mother Webtoes;
    "The breakfast you must get."
"Oh let me stay in bed," says Jane;
    "The floor is cold and wet."
But Mother Webtoes stamps her foot,
    And makes the child arise;
But as Jane sobs, behind the door,
    Ah, what is this she spies?
It is her green umbrella;
    She sets it now afloat,

And down the river in it sails,
   As if it were a boat.
"Oh Mother Webtoes, only look,"
   She hears the young frogs scream;

"The little girl you brought to us
   Is sailing down the stream."
But Jane is quite too far away
   For them to catch her then,
And when at last she drifts ashore
   She sees her home again.

She rushes to her mother's arms
   With sobs and streaming eyes—
"Oh Mother, Mother dear, forgive
   Your naughty Jane," she cries.

•

THE LITTLE FISH THAT WOULD NOT DO AS IT WAS BID

Ann Taylor

"Dear mother," said a little fish,
  "Pray is not that a fly?
I'm very hungry, and I wish
  You'd let me go and try."

"Sweet innocent," the mother cried,
  And started from her nook,
"That horrid fly is put to hide
  The sharpness of the hook."

Now, as I've heard, this little trout
  Was young and foolish, too,
And so he thought he'd venture out,
  To see if it were true.

And round about the hook he played,
  With many a longing look,
And—"Dear me," to himself he said,
  "I'm sure that's not a hook.

"I can but give one little pluck;
  Let's see, and so I will."
So on he went, and lo! it stuck
  Quite through his little gill.

And as he faint and fainter grew,
  With hollow voice he cried,
"Dear mother, had I minded you,
  I need not now have died."

•

TWENTY FROGGIES

George Cooper

A great event in every young life is that long-awaited first day of
going to school. This little poem helps us get ready.

Twenty froggies went to school,
Down beside a rushy pool,
Twenty little coats of green,
Twenty vests all white and clean.

"We must be in time," said they,
"First we study, then we play;
That is how we keep the rule,
When we froggies go to school."

Master Bullfrog, brave and stern,
Called his classes in their turn,
Taught them how to nobly strive,
Also how to leap and dive.

Taught them how to dodge a blow,
From the sticks that bad boys throw.
Twenty froggies grew up fast,
Bullfrogs they became at last.

Polished to a high degree,
As each froggie ought to be.
Now they sit on other logs,
Teaching other little frogs.

•

GOING TO SCHOOL

John Martin

It makes all the difference when a young mind goes to school
with this thought: The opportunity to learn is one of the great
blessings of life.

> Dear God, a schoolday comes again,
>   With many things for me to do.
> Please bless my Heart and guide my Brain
>   And make me thoughtful, strong, and true.
> My lessons may seem dull to me,
>   And study hours long and dry,
> But if You help me, then I'll see
>   How fast those useful hours fly.
>
> O God, go forth with me today,
>   And help my Head and guide my Hand,
> For You are wise and know a way
>   To make me learn and understand.
> Open my Heart and Eyes to see
>   How kind is every study hour;
> For each one offers Gifts to me
>   Like Wisdom, Patience, Love, and Power.
>   Amen.

•

IN *ADAM'S* FALL . . .

From The New England Primer

Here are a few of the famous rhymes that introduced generations
of seventeenth- and eighteenth-century schoolchildren to the alphabet. These verses remind us that in times past, children en-
countered their first lessons within the framework of hard-nosed

realities. First, life is no easy road. Second, each human being ventures down that road possessing a morally responsible soul. These little rhymes may be outdated as a way of learning to read and write, but modern parents and teachers will find the old lessons of mortality and immortality still worth pondering.

> In *Adam*'s fall,
> We sinned all.
>
> Heaven to find,
> The *Bible* mind.
>
> The *Cat* does play,
> And after slay.
>
> The *Dog* doth bite
> A thief at night.
>
> The Idle *Fool*
> Is whipped at school.
>
> As runs the *Glass,*
> Man's life doth pass.
>
> *Job* feels the rod
> Yet blesses God.
>
> Young pious *Ruth*
> Left all for truth.
>
> Young *Samuel* dear
> The Lord did fear.
>
> *Time* cuts down all,
> Both great and small.
>
> While *Youth* do cheer
> Death may be near.

•

THE FOX AND THE CAT

It's not necessarily *how much* you know, but *what* you know, that counts.

It happened once that the cat met Mr. Fox in the wood, and because she thought he was clever and experienced in all the ways of the world, she addressed him in a friendly manner.

"Good morning, dear Mr. Fox! How are you, and how do you get along in these hard times?"

The fox, full of pride, looked at the cat from head to foot for some time, hardly knowing whether he would deign to answer or not. At last he said: "Oh, you poor whisker wiper, you silly piebald, you starveling mouse hunter! What has come into your head? How dare you ask me how I am getting on? What sort of education have you had? How many arts are you master of?"

"Only one," said the cat meekly.

"And what might that one be?" asked the fox.

"When the dogs run after me, I can jump into a tree and save myself."

"Is that all?' said the fox. "I am master of a hundred arts, and I have a sackful of cunning tricks in addition. But I pity you. Come with me, and I will teach you how to escape from the dogs."

Just then a huntsman came along with four hounds. The cat sprang trembling into a tree, and crept stealthily up to the topmost branch, where she was entirely hidden by twigs and leaves.

"Open your sack, Mr. Fox! Open your sack!" cried the cat, but the dogs had gripped him, and held him fast.

"Oh, Mr. Fox!" cried the cat, "you with your hundred arts, and your sackful of tricks, are held fast, while I, with my one, am safe. Had you been able to creep up here, you would not have lost your life."

Cat

•

THE TONGUE AND HOW TO USE IT

Retold by F. J. Gould

Discipline in what we say (especially what we say about others)
is one of the most important kinds of training. There are some
words that can't be recaptured once they've escaped.

Saint Philip Neri, a beloved priest of sixteenth-century Rome,
was sought out by the rich and poor, the noble and common
people alike, for his ability to look into hearts and minds.

A young lady once went to the good man, Saint Philip Neri, to
confess her sins. He knew one of her faults only too well. She was
not a bad-hearted girl, but she often talked of her neighbors, and
spoke idle tales about them. These tales were told again by others,
and much harm was done, and no good.

Saint Philip said: "My daughter, you do wrong to speak ill of
others, and I order you to perform penance. You must buy a fowl
in the market. Then walk out of the town, and as you go along the
road pull the feathers from the bird and scatter them. Do not stop
until you have plucked every feather. When you have done this,
come back and tell me."

She said to herself that this was a very singular punishment to
suffer. But she made no objection. She bought the fowl, walked out,
and plucked the feathers as she had been bidden. Then she went
to Saint Philip and reported what she had done.

"My daughter," said the Saint, "you have carried out the first
part of the penance. Now there is a second part."

"Yes, Father?"

"You must now go back the way you came and pick up all the
feathers."

"But, father, this cannot be done. By this time the wind has
blown them all ways. I might pick up some, but I could not possibly
gather up all."

"Quite true, my daughter. And is it not so with the unwise
words that you let fall? Have you not often dropped idle tales from
your lips, and have they not gone this way and that, carried from
mouth to mouth until they are quite beyond you? Could you possibly follow them, and recall them if you wanted to do so?"

"No, Father."

"Then, my daughter, when you are inclined to say unkind things about your neighbor, close your lips. Do not scatter these light and evil feathers by the wayside."

•

WORDS ARE WONDERFUL THINGS

Mrs. E. R. Miller

Keep a watch on your words, my darling,
    For words are wonderful things;
They are sweet like the bees' fresh honey,
    Like the bees they have terrible stings;
They can bless like the warm, glad sunshine,
    And brighten a lonely life;
They can cut, in the strife of anger,
    Like an open, two-edged knife.

•

THE TALKATIVE TORTOISE

*Adapted from a retelling
by Sara Cone Bryant*

This story comes from a collection of ancient fables from India known as *The Fables of Bidpai.* It underscores the importance of knowing when to keep your mouth shut.

Once upon a time, a Tortoise lived in a pond with two Ducks, who were her very good friends. She enjoyed the company of the Ducks, because she could talk with them to her heart's content. The Tortoise liked to talk. She always had something to say, and she liked to hear herself say it.

After many years of this pleasant living, the pond became very low, in a dry season, and finally it dried up. The two Ducks saw that they could no longer live there, so they decided to fly to another region, where there was more water. They went to the Tortoise to bid her goodbye.

"Oh, don't leave me behind!" begged the Tortoise. "Take me with you. I must die if I am left here."

"But you cannot fly!" said the Ducks. "How can we take you with us?"

"Take me with you! Take me with you!" said the Tortoise.

The Ducks felt so sorry for her that at last they thought of a way to take her. "We have thought of a way which will be possible," they said, "if only you can manage to keep still long enough. We will each take hold of one end of a stout stick, and you take the middle in your mouth. Then we will fly up in the air with you and carry you with us. But remember not to talk! If you open your mouth, you are lost."

The Tortoise said she would not say a word, she would not so much as move her mouth, and she was very grateful. So the Ducks brought a strong little stick and took hold of the ends, while the Tortoise bit firmly on the middle. Then the two Ducks rose slowly in the air and flew away with their burden.

When they were above the treetops, the Tortoise wanted to say, "How high we are!" But she remembered, and kept still.

When they passed the church steeple she wanted to say, "What is that which shines?" But she remembered, and held her peace.

Then they came over the village square, and the people looked up and saw them. "Look at the Ducks carrying a Tortoise!" they shouted. And everyone ran to look.

The Tortoise wanted to say, "What business is it of yours?" But she didn't.

She heard the people shout, "Isn't it funny! Isn't it strange! Look at it! Look!" And she began to grow angry. But she kept her mouth shut.

Then the people began to laugh. "Did you ever see such a funny sight in all your life?" they jeered.

And the Tortoise could stand it no longer.

She opened her mouth and yelled, "Be quiet, you stupid—"

But before she could say any more, she had fallen to the ground.

And that was the end of the Tortoise.

•

THE WISE OLD OWL

Someone once observed that we have two ears and one mouth
and should learn to use them in that proportion.

> A wise old owl sat in an oak,
> The more he heard the less he spoke;
> The less he spoke the more he heard.
> Why aren't we all like that wise old bird?

•

THE TWELVE MONTHS

Retold by James Baldwin

Politeness, etiquette, good manners, civility—the habits these
words represent are underrated and underused in our time. This
old story from eastern Europe illustrates how far those habits can
take you.

A very long time ago there were two little girls who lived in a
little house with a cross old woman.

One of the little girls was named Dobrunka. She was the
daughter of the cross woman, and she was as cross as her mother.

The other little girl was very pretty, and she was as good as she
was pretty. But Dobrunka and her mother were very unkind to her.
Her name was Katinka.

Now Dobrunka was idle and lazy, and she sat in the house and
did nothing all day long.

But Katinka was kept very busy. She did the sweeping and the
cooking and the spinning and the weaving and the milking and the
churning.

Every day the cross woman with whom she lived scolded her,
and sometimes she punished her. Dobrunka scolded her, too, and
set hard tasks for her to do.

One day in January Dobrunka said, "Here, Katinka! Go out into the woods and pick a bunch of violets for me. I want them to wear in my hair."

"A bunch of violets!" answered Katinka. "Why, it is winter, and violets do not grow in the snow."

"Hold your tongue and do as I tell you," said Dobrunka.

"Yes," said the cross woman, "go into the woods; and if you come back without the violets, you shall be punished."

Poor Katinka went into the woods. Her shoes were thin and worn. She had not so much as a shawl to throw over her shoulders.

The wind blew cold. The ground was covered with snow. There was not even a path among the trees.

Do you wonder that the child wept?

She lost her way. She was hungry and very cold. Night was coming on.

As she was climbing a little hill she saw a light among some big rocks in front of her. Could it be a fire? How she wished she could warm herself by it!

Yes, it was a fire—a great blazing fire, built in the mouth of a little cave.

Katinka went nearer.

Around the fire she saw twelve white stones, and on each stone a strange-looking person was sitting. Each person wore a long cloak that covered his shoulders and body and even his feet. Over his head a hood was drawn.

Katinka saw that three of the cloaks were white like snow, three were green like the leaves of the trees in summer, three were yellow like the wheat in harvest time, and three were purple like ripe grapes.

The child was not afraid.

"Please, good men," she said, "may I warm myself at your fire? I am almost dead with cold."

"Certainly, dear child," said one who wore a white cloak. "Come and sit with us. We are the Twelve Months."

"I thank you, Mr. Month," said Katinka; and she went forward and stood by the one who had spoken. Then to this one she said, "I think you must be January."

"You are right," he said. "But who are you, and why do you come here in the deep snow?"

"I am looking for violets," Katinka answered.

"For violets, indeed!" cried January. "This is not the time for them. They do not grow in the snow."

"I know it," said Katinka, "but the woman I live with said I must bring some or she would punish me. Can you tell me where I can find them?"

January did not answer. But he stood up and spoke to one of the green-cloaked fellows.

"Brother March," he said, "it is for you to help this poor child."

March arose, and oh, how the wind blew! Then he stirred the fire with his long staff.

As the flames curled up, warm and bright, the snow melted and the trees began to bud. Then green grass sprang up every- where, and pretty flowers bloomed in sunny places.

"Now, dear child," said March, "gather your violets quickly."

Katinka ran joyfully here and there and picked as many as her hands could hold. She was now quite warm; she had forgotten the cold and the snow.

"Thank you, Mr. March," she said. "Thank you, Mr. January. Thank you all."

Then she ran quickly home through the snow.

Think of the surprise of Dobrunka and her mother!

"Where did you get those things?" asked the woman.

"I found them in the woods," said Katinka. "The ground under the bushes was covered with them."

Dobrunka took the violets, but she did not so much as thank the poor child.

The next morning the cross girl thought of something else. She wanted some strawberries. Nothing would do but she must have some strawberries.

"Katinka," she said, "go into the woods and get some ripe red strawberries for me."

"Why, it is winter," said Katinka, "and strawberries do not grow in the snow."

"Hold your tongue and do as I tell you," said Dobrunka.

"Yes," said the cross woman, "go out and gather some straw- berries; and if you come back without them you shall be punished."

Then she pushed the child out into the snow and shut the door behind her.

Katinka went far into the woods, looking for the light she had seen the day before. She was very tired, when all at once she saw the mouth of the little cave right before her.

The fire was burning bright and warm, and the Twelve Months were sitting in their places, with their long cloaks over their shoul- ders.

"Please, good men," she said, "may I warm myself at your fire? I am almost dead with cold."

"Certainly, dear child," said January. "But why have you come back to us today?"

"I am looking for strawberries," answered Katinka.

"For strawberries, indeed!" cried January. "This is not the time for strawberries."

"I know it," said the child, "but the woman I live with said I must bring some or she would punish me. Can you tell me where I can find them?"

Then January said, "Brother June, it is for you to help the child."

June arose. His cloak was yellow as gold, and his hood was covered with roses.

He stirred the fire with his staff. The cheery blaze flamed up. The snow melted. The trees put on their leaves. The fields were green. The sun was warm. Summer had come.

"Now gather your strawberries quickly, my child," said June.

Katinka filled her apron with the ripe red fruit. She had forgotten that it was ever winter.

"Thank you, Mr. June. Thank you, Mr. January. Thank you all," she said.

Then she ran quickly home through the snow.

Think of the surprise of Dobrunka and her mother!

"Where did you get those things?" asked the woman.

"Out yonder in the woods," said Katinka. "There were so many that the ground was red with them."

Dobrunka and her mother took the strawberries and ate every one of them. But they never so much as thanked the poor child.

On the third morning the cross girl had another fancy. She

wanted some red apples. Nothing would do but she must have
some red apples.

So Katinka was sent out into the snow-covered woods to get
them.

She found the little cave without any trouble. The Twelve
Months were still sitting around their fire.

"Welcome again, dear child," said January. "Come and warm
yourself."

When she was quite warm and happy, he said, "Now tell us
why you have come to us this third time."

Katinka told him about the red apples, and how she would be
punished if she did not carry some home.

"Brother September," said January, "it is your turn to help this
child."

September stood up. His beard was long and gray. His cloak
was purple. On his head was a wreath of autumn leaves.

He stirred the fire with his staff. The flames leaped up. The
snow melted. The ground was warm and dry. Crickets chirped in
the tall grass. The trees were dressed in beautiful colors—red,
brown, and gold. It was autumn.

"Now gather your apples quickly, dear child," said September.

Katinka looked up. An apple tree full of the finest fruit was
before her.

She shook it. A red apple fell at her feet. She shook it again.
Another red apple fell at her feet.

"Hurry home, Katinka," said September.

She picked up the two apples and turned to go.

"Thank you, Mr. September. Thank you, Mr. January. Thank
you all," she said.

Think of the surprise of cross Dobrunka and her mother!

"Apples right off the tree in January!" they cried. "Where did
you get them?"

"Out yonder in the woods. The tree is so full that it looks like
a red cherry tree in summer."

"And you brought only two!" cried Dobrunka. "You ate all the
rest on the way."

"Oh, no, Dobrunka. I was allowed to shake the tree only twice,
and these two apples were all that fell."

"Begone! You do not tell the truth," said the cross girl, and she
struck Katinka with her hand.

Then she and her mother ate the apples, but did not thank the
one who brought them.

"The finest fruit I ever tasted," said the mother.

"Yes, and I wish I had more," said Dobrunka.

"What a pity to leave a tree full of them in the woods," said the mother. "Katinka must milk the cows now, or I would send her right back to gather the rest."

"Mother, give me my fur cloak," said Dobrunka. "I will go out and find the tree myself. I will shake it so hard that all the apples will fall into my lap."

The mother did not want her to go. Night was coming. It was cold. But Dobrunka would not listen.

She wrapped her fur cloak around her. She drew her hood over her head. She hurried out into the woods.

Dobrunka soon lost her way. The ground was all covered with snow. There was not so much as a footpath anywhere.

After a while she saw a light far up on the side of a hill.

She climbed and climbed. She climbed through the snow till she was very tired.

At last she came to the little cave and saw the Twelve Months sitting around their blazing fire.

Without so much as saying "Good evening," she pushed forward, in front of them, and began to warm herself.

"Why have you come here?" asked January. "What is it you are looking for?"

"That is none of your business, old gray-head," answered the unmannerly girl.

January's face grew dark. He lifted his staff. He spoke one word to his brothers.

All at once the fire went out. The cave was nowhere to be seen. The Twelve Months had vanished.

Dark clouds covered the sky. More snow began to fall. The wind roared in the trees.

What could cross Dobrunka do now? Where could she find shelter from the storm and the night?

She stumbled about among the trees and the rocks. She called for help, but no one heard her.

All night long the cross mother waited and watched for Dobrunka.

She stood at the window and looked out at the snow. She listened to the roar of the wind.

In the morning she put on her fur cloak and her hood. "I must go and find Dobrunka," she said.

She hurried out into the great woods. The snow was still falling. The wind was still blowing. There was not even a track to be seen.

"Dobrunka! Dobrunka!" she called. But Dobrunka did not hear. She would never answer her.

At home Katinka was busy with her spinning wheel. Now and then she went to the door and looked out and listened.

"I wish they would come," she said to herself.

At noon she cooked a fine dinner. She set the table. She waited and waited.

But no one came to eat with her.

The snow was still falling. The wind was still blowing.

In the evening she milked the cows and fed the chickens. She made a fresh fire. She brushed the hearth. She set the two chairs before it.

"I fear that something has happened to them," she said.

She went to the door again. The snow was still falling. The wind was still blowing. Another dark night had come.

Day after day Katinka waited, but no word did she ever hear of the cross woman or of cross Dobrunka.

As there was no one else to claim it, the house was now her own. So also were the cows and the chickens and the pretty garden, and the green fields on both sides of the house.

She was busy, busy, busy, all the time. But she was her own mistress, and no cross words were heard in her house.

The Twelve Months did not forget the child.

March brought violets to her door every year.

April watered the fields and made the grain sprout and grow.

May brought sunshine and nesting birds and soft balmy winds.

June remembered to bring plenty of red strawberries.

July ripened the wheat.

August brought loads of sweet hay to Katinka's barn.

September gave her ripe apples, and allowed her to shake the trees as much as she wished.

October brought many a basket of purple grapes into her kitchen.

November found everything housed and safe for the winter.

December filled the child's arms with Christmas presents.

January made the fire glow in the chimney and covered the roof of the house with a soft white blanket.

And even February brought good gifts to the gentle child. Can you guess what they were?

Thus kind Katinka lived a happy and contented life, and everybody loved her. As the old saying has it, she had spring in her heart, summer in her fields, autumn in her orchard, and winter at her door.

•

RULES OF BEHAVIOR

Hearts, like doors, will open with ease
To very, very little keys,
And don't forget that two of these
Are "I thank you" and "If you please."

•

HOW THE BRAZILIAN BEETLES GOT THEIR COATS

Retold by Elsie Eells

Don't estimate other people's strengths and weaknesses too quickly, particularly by judging only appearances. Often you'll be surprised at how wrong you are, as we see in this tale from Brazil.

In Brazil the beetles have such beautifully colored, hard-shelled coats upon their backs that they are sometimes set in pins and necklaces like precious stones. Once upon a time, years and years ago, they had ordinary plain brown coats. This is how it happened that the Brazilian beetle earned a new coat.

One day a little brown beetle was crawling along a wall when a big gray rat ran out of a hole in the wall and looked down scornfully at the little beetle. "O ho!" he said to the beetle, "how slowly you crawl along. You'll never get anywhere in the world. Just look at me and see how fast I can run."

The big gray rat ran to the end of the wall, wheeled around,

and came back to the place where the little beetle was slowly crawling along at only a tiny distance from where the rat had left her.

"Don't you wish that you could run like that?" said the big gray
rat to the little brown beetle.

"You are surely a fast runner," replied the little brown beetle
politely. Her mother had taught her always to be polite and had
often said to her that a really polite beetle never boasts about her
own accomplishments. The little brown beetle never boasted a
single boast about the things she could do. She just went on slowly
crawling along the wall.

A bright green and gold parrot in the mango tree over the wall
had heard the conversation. "How would you like to race with the
beetle?" he asked the big gray rat. "I live next door to the tailor
bird," he added, "and just to make the race exciting I'll offer a
brightly colored coat as a prize to the one who wins the race.
You may chose for it any color you like and I'll have it made to
order."

"I'd like a yellow coat with stripes like the tiger's," said the big
gray rat, looking over his shoulder at his gaunt gray sides as if he
were already admiring his new coat.

"I'd like a beautiful, brightly colored new coat, too," said the
little brown beetle.

The big gray rat laughed long and loud until his gaunt gray
sides were shaking. "Why, you talk just as if you thought you had a
chance to win the race," he said, when he could speak.

The bright green and gold parrot set the royal palm tree at the
top of the cliff as the goal of the race. He gave the signal to start and
then he flew away to the royal palm tree to watch for the end of the
race.

The big gray rat ran as fast as he could. Then he thought how
very tired he was getting. "What's the use of hurrying?" he said to
himself. "The little brown beetle cannot possibly win. If I were
racing with somebody who could really run it would be very different." Then he started to run more slowly, but every time his heart
beat it said, "Hurry up! Hurry up!" The big gray rat decided that it
was best to obey the little voice in his heart so he hurried just as
fast as he could.

When he reached the royal palm tree at the top of the cliff he
could hardly believe his eyes. He thought he must be having a bad
dream. There was the little brown beetle sitting quietly beside the
bright green and gold parrot. The big gray rat had never been so

surprised in all his life. "How did you ever manage to run fast enough to get here so soon?" he asked the little brown beetle as soon as he could catch his breath.

The little brown beetle drew out the tiny wings from her sides. "Nobody said anything about having to run to win the race," she replied, "so I flew instead."

"I did not know that you could fly," said the big gray rat in a subdued little voice.

"After this," said the bright green and gold parrot, "never judge anyone by his looks alone. You never can tell how often or where you may find concealed wings. You have lost the prize."

Then the parrot turned to the little brown beetle who was waiting quietly at his side. "What color do you want your new coat to be?" he asked.

The little brown beetle looked up at the bright green and gold parrot, at the green and gold palm trees above their heads, at the green mangoes with golden flushes on their cheeks lying on the ground under the mango trees, at the golden sunshine upon the distant green hills. "I choose a coat of green and gold," she said.

From that day to this the Brazilian beetle has worn a coat of green with golden lights upon it.

And until this day, even in Brazil, where the flowers and birds and beasts and insects have such gorgeous coloring, the rat wears a dull gray coat.

●

THE PIG BROTHER

Laura E. Richards

Hearing the truth from friends or strangers may sometimes shame us. Like many medicines, shame may not feel good, but its bitter taste can help set us straight. This is a great story for those who can't remember to pick up their toys, clothes, or dirty dishes.

There was once a child who was untidy. He left his books on the floor, and his muddy shoes on the table. He put his fingers in the jam pots, and spilled ink on his best shirt. There was really no end to his untidiness.

One day the Tidy Angel came into his nursery.

"This will never do!" said the Angel. "This is really shocking. You must go out and stay with your brother while I set things right here."

"I have no brother!" said the child.

"Yes, you have!" said the Angel. "You may not know him, but he will know you. Go out in the garden and watch for him, and he will soon come."

"I don't know what you mean!" said the child, but he went out into the garden and waited.

Presently a squirrel came along, whisking his tail.

"Are you my brother?" asked the child.

The squirrel looked him over carefully.

"Well, I should hope not!" he said. "My fur is neat and smooth, my nest is handsomely made and in perfect order, and my young ones are properly brought up. Why do you insult me by asking such a question?"

He whisked off, and the child waited.

Presently a wren came hopping by.

"Are you my brother?" asked the child.

"No indeed!" said the wren. "What impertinence! You will find no tidier person than I in the whole garden. Not a feather is out of place, and my eggs are the wonder of all for smoothness and beauty. Brother, indeed!" He hopped off, ruffling his feathers, and the child waited.

By and by a large Tommy Cat came along.

"Are you my brother?" asked the child.

"Go and look at yourself in the glass," said the Tommy Cat haughtily, "and you will have your answer. I have been washing myself in the sun all the morning, while it is clear that no water has come near you for a long time. There are no such creatures as you in my family, I am humbly thankful to say."

He walked on, waving his tail, and the child waited.

Presently a pig came trotting along.

The child did not wish to ask the pig if he were his brother, but the pig did not wait to be asked.

"Hallo, brother!" he grunted.

"I am not your brother!" said the child.

"Oh, yes, you are!" said the pig. "I confess I am not proud of you, but there is no mistaking the members of our family. Come along, and have a good roll in the barnyard! There is some lovely black mud there."

"I don't like to roll in mud!" said the child.

"Tell that to the hens!" said the pig brother. "Look at your hands, and your shoes, and your shirt! Come along, I say! You may have some of the pig swill for supper, if there is more than I want."

"I don't want pig swill!" said the child, and he began to cry.

Just then the Tidy Angel came out.

"I have set everything right," she said, "and so it must stay. Now, will you go with the Pig Brother, or will you come back with me, and be a tidy child?"

"With you, with you!" cried the child, and he clung to the Angel's dress.

The Pig Brother grunted.

"Small loss!" he said. "There will be all the more swill for me!" And he trotted on.

•

THE CAT AND THE PARROT
Retold by Sara Cone Bryant

Some people want everything—what belongs to them, to you, to me, to everyone. Here is unbridled appetite, the kind that knows no self-discipline.

Once there was a cat and a parrot. And they had agreed to take turns asking each other to dinner. First the cat should ask the parrot, then the parrot should invite the cat, and so on. It was the cat's turn first.

Now the cat was very stingy. He provided nothing at all for dinner except a pint of milk, a little slice of fish, and a biscuit. The parrot was too polite to complain, but he did not have a very good time.

When it was his turn to invite the cat, he cooked a fine dinner. He had a roast of meat, a pot of tea, a basket of fruit, and, best of all, he baked a whole basketful of little cakes—little, brown, crispy, spicy cakes! Oh, I should say as many as five hundred. And he put four hundred and ninety-eight of the cakes before the cat, keeping only two for himself.

Well, the cat ate the roast, and drank the tea, and sucked the fruit, and then he began on the pile of cakes. He ate all the four hundred and ninety-eight cakes, and then he looked round and said: "I'm hungry; haven't you anything to eat?"

"Why," said the parrot, "here are my two cakes, if you want them."

The cat ate up the two cakes, and then he licked his chops and said, "I am beginning to get an appetite. Have you anything to eat?"

"Well, really," said the parrot, who was now rather angry, "I don't see anything more, unless you wish to eat me!" He thought the cat would be ashamed when he heard that, but the cat just looked at him and licked his chops again, and slip! slop! gobble! Down his throat went the parrot!

Then the cat started down the street. An old woman was standing by, and she had seen the whole thing, and she was shocked that the cat should eat his friend. "Why, cat!" she said, "how dreadful of you to eat your friend the parrot!"

"Parrot, indeed!" said the cat. "What's a parrot to me? I've a great mind to eat you, too." And before you could say "Jack Robinson," slip! slop! gobble! Down went the old woman!

Then the cat started down the road again, walking like this, because he felt so fine. Pretty soon he met a man driving a donkey. When he saw the cat he said, "Get out of my way, cat. I'm in a hurry and my donkey might tread on you."

"Donkey, indeed!" said the cat. "Much I care for a donkey! I have eaten five hundred cakes, I have eaten my friend the parrot, I have eaten an old woman—what's to hinder my eating a miserable man and a donkey?"

And slip! slop! gobble! Down went the old man and the donkey.

Then the cat walked on down the road, jauntily, like this. After

a little, he met a procession, coming that way. The king was at the head, walking proudly with his newly married bride, and behind him were his soldiers, marching, and behind them were ever and ever so many elephants, walking two by two. The king felt very kind to everybody, because he had just been married, and he said to the cat, "Get out of my way, pussycat, get out of my way—my elephants might hurt you."

"Hurt me!" said the cat, shaking his fat sides. "Ho, ho! I have eaten five hundred cakes, I have eaten my friend the parrot, I have eaten an old woman, I have eaten a man and a donkey; what's to hinder my eating a beggarly king?"

And slip! slop! gobble! Down went the king; down went the queen; down went the soldiers—and down went all the elephants!

Then the cat went on, more slowly. He had really had enough to eat now. But a little farther on he met two crabs, scuttling along in the sand. "Get out of our way, pussycat," they squeaked.

"Ho, ho ho!" cried the cat in a terrible voice. "I have eaten five hundred cakes, I have eaten my friend the parrot, I have eaten an old woman, a man with a donkey, a king, a queen, his men-at-arms, and all his elephants; and now I'll eat you too."

And slip! slop! gobble! Down went the two crabs.

When the crabs got down inside, they began to look around. It was very dark, but they could see the poor king sitting in a corner with his bride on his arm; she had fainted. Near them were the men-at-arms, treading on one another's toes, and the elephants, still trying to form in twos—but they couldn't, because there was not room. In the opposite corner sat the old woman, and near her stood the man and his donkey. But in the other corner was a great pile of cakes, and by them perched the parrot, his feathers all drooping.

"Let's get to work!" said the crabs. And, snip, snap, they began to make a little hole in the side, with their sharp claws. Snip, snap, snip, snap, till it was big enough to get through. Then out they scuttled.

Then out walked the king, carrying his bride; out marched the men-at-arms; out tramped the elephants, two by two; out came the old man, beating his donkey; out walked the old woman, scolding the cat; and last of all, out hopped the parrot, holding a cake in each claw. (Remember, two cakes were all he wanted.)

But the poor cat had to spend the whole day sewing up the hole in his coat!

•

GREEDY

Sydney Dayre

Often we are guilty of the same sins we see in others.

A greedy fellow? I should say!
They passed the apples round this way
And then he snatched—he couldn't wait—
The biggest one upon the plate.

Such greediness I do despise!
I had been keeping both my eyes
Upon that apple, for, you see,
The plate was coming, next, to me.

'Twas big and mellow, just the kind
A greedy chap would like to find.
He laughed as if he thought it fun—
I meant to take that very one.

•

THE FRIEND OF A FRIEND OF A FRIEND

There are some people who seek any connection or pretext, no matter how tenuous, to get something for themselves. The reward for such behavior should be equally tenuous.

Djuha is a widely loved "wise fool" of Arab folklore.

One day a friend who loved to hunt came to visit Djuha.
"I've brought you a rabbit I just caught," he said proudly as he stepped into the house. "It will make a fine dinner."
Djuha gladly cooked the rabbit into a stew, and they sat down to a fine feast.
The very next day a stranger knocked on Djuha's door.
"Who are you?" inquired Djuha.

"I'm a neighbor of your friend the hunter, who brought you the rabbit yesterday," he said.

Djuha politely invited him inside and set a dinner before him.

"These are the leftovers of our rabbit stew," Djuha said, and the visitor ate heartily.

The very next day another stranger knocked on Djuha's door.

"Who are you?" asked Djuha.

"I'm a cousin of the neighbor of your friend the hunter, who brought you the rabbit," he explained.

"Come in," said Djuha. He sat the man at the table, and set before him a bowl of hot water.

"What's this?" asked the stranger.

"That," said Djuha, "is water boiled in the very same pot as the rabbit of my friend who is the neighbor of your cousin."

•

SPIDER'S TWO FEASTS

Those who can't put their desires in order often get trapped between them. This folk tale comes from Africa.

Long ago, back in the days when animals could talk just as easily as you and I, Spider looked very different than he does now. Today, of course, he has a big, fat head and a big, fat body, with a little, bitty waist in between where his eight long legs stick out. In olden days, though, Spider did not have such a trim waistline. He was big and plump all over. This is the story of how his belly got so thin.

One day Spider was walking through the forest when he met Hare hopping down the path.

"Good morning," called Spider. "Why are you hopping so fast?"

"Don't you know?" asked Hare. "Upstream Town is giving a wedding feast. They'll be eating soon. Everyone is invited."

Spider was so happy, he danced a little dance on his eight long legs.

"How lucky for me," he thought, patting his plump belly. "There'll be yams and fish, and rice and beans. I can eat all I want!"

At once he started toward Upstream Town.

Just then he met Fox trotting the other way.

"Good morning," called Spider. "Why are you trotting so fast?"

"Haven't you heard?" asked Fox. "Downstream Town is giving a harvest feast. They'll be serving soon. Everyone is invited."

Now Spider was so happy, he jumped in the air and flipped a little flip with his eight long legs.

"Two feasts!" he thought, rubbing his fat belly. "I am very happy. I'll go to both! I'll hurry to Downstream Town and fill my stomach. Then I'll run to Upstream Town and fill it again!"

So he turned and started toward Downstream Town.

But before long, a new thought made him stop in his tracks.

"I wonder where the food will be served first?" he thought. "I must go to that town and eat as much as I can. Then I can hurry to the other town in time for my second feast. But how can I know which village will eat first?"

Spider sat down on a rock to ponder his problem. If he went the wrong way, he might miss a whole feast! The terrible thought made his plump belly growl and his eight long legs tremble all over.

Then suddenly he had an idea.

He ran home as fast as he could and found two long ropes. Then he called two of his children and took them to a place on the river halfway between Upstream Town and Downstream Town.

Spider tied one long rope around his waist and gave the other end to his son.

"Take this rope to Upstream Village," he said. "When the feast begins, pull hard, and I will know to come."

Then Spider tied the other long rope around his waist too, and gave the end to his daughter.

"Now, you take your rope to Downstream Village," he told her. "When the feast begins there, pull hard, and I will know to come."

So Spider's son went to Upstream Village with his long rope, and Spider's daughter went to Downstream Village with her long rope, and Spider sat down in between.

"Now I'll know who serves food first," he gloated, smacking his lips. "I can go there and eat my fill, and then go to the second village and have another feast!"

He was very pleased with himself.

An hour passed, but nothing happened. Another hour passed, and still Spider felt no tug on either rope. His plump belly began to growl again, and he started to grow angry.

But then Spider got a rude surprise, because Upstream Village and Downstream Village began their feasts at the same time! Spider's son tugged on his rope in Upstream Village, and Spider's daughter tugged on her rope in Downstream Village, and poor Spider was caught in between.

Now, Spider's children were young and strong, and when their father failed to come, each began pulling harder and harder. Spider just bobbed back and forth in one place, with the ropes around his waist getting tighter and tighter. His children kept pulling, harder and harder, and the ropes kept squeezing Spider, tighter and tighter. Spider waved his eight legs in the air for help, but no one saw him, because they were all at the feasts.

Finally the feasts were over. Spider's children stopped pulling and hurried back to where they had left their father. They found him lying on the ground, gasping for breath, for the ropes had squeezed his big, plump waist thinner than a stick!

And when they took the ropes off, Spider stayed that way. To this day, he has a skinny little waist between his big, fat head and his big, fat body.

And whenever people see him, they think of how he tried to have two feasts at once.

•

FORTUNE AND THE BEGGAR

Ivan Krylov

Philosophers have noted that human desires often increase with the means of their gratification. The next two tales show the principle in action. Many times we want to say, "Just a little more ... more ... more." Wisdom teaches us when to say, "Enough."

The first story comes from Russian fable writer Ivan Krylov (1768–1844).

One day a ragged beggar was creeping along from house to house. He carried an old wallet in his hand, and was asking at every door for a few cents to buy something to eat. As he was grumbling at his lot, he kept wondering why it was that folks who had so much money were never satisfied but were always wanting more.

"Here," said he, "is the master of this house—I know him

well. He was always a good businessman, and he made himself wondrously rich a long time ago. Had he been wise he would have stopped then. He would have turned over his business to someone else, and then he could have spent the rest of his life in ease. But what did he do instead? He took to building ships and sending them to sea to trade with foreign lands. He thought he would get mountains of gold.

"But there were great storms on the water. His ships were wrecked, and his riches were swallowed up by the waves. Now his hopes all lie at the bottom of the sea, and his great wealth has vanished like the dreams of a night.

"There are many such cases. Men seem to be never satisfied unless they can gain the whole world.

"As for me, if I had only enough to eat and to wear I would not want anything more."

Just at that moment Fortune came down the street. She saw the beggar and stopped. She said to him: "Listen! I have long wished to help you. Hold your wallet and I will pour this gold into it. But I will pour only on this condition: All that falls into the wallet shall be pure gold; but every piece that falls upon the ground shall become dust. Do you understand?"

"Oh, yes, I understand," said the beggar.

"Then have a care," said Fortune. "Your wallet is old, so do not load it too heavily."

The beggar was so glad that he could hardly wait. He quickly opened his wallet, and a stream of yellow coins was poured into it. The wallet soon began to grow heavy.

"Is that enough?" asked Fortune.

"Not yet."

"Isn't it cracking?"

"Never fear."

The beggar's hands began to tremble. Ah, if the golden stream would only pour forever!

"You are the richest man in the world now!"

"Just a little more," said the Beggar. "Add just a handful or two."

"There, it's full. The wallet will burst."

"But it will hold a little more, just a little more!"

Another piece was added, and the wallet split. The treasure fell upon the ground and was turned to dust. Fortune had vanished. The beggar had now nothing but his empty wallet, and it was torn from top to bottom. He was as poor as before.

●

THE STONE LION

*Adapted from a retelling
by W. P. O'Connor*

This tale is from Tibet.

Once there were two brothers who lived with their mother in a large house on a farm. Their father was dead. The older brother was clever and selfish, but the younger was kind and gentle. The older brother did not like the younger because he was honest and never would cheat to get the best of a bargain, so one day he said to him: "You must go away. I cannot support you any longer."

So the younger brother packed all his belongings and went to bid his mother goodbye. When she heard what the older brother had done, she said: "I will go with you, my son. I will not live here any longer with so hard-hearted a man as your brother."

The next morning the mother and the younger brother started out together. Toward night they came to a hut at the foot of a hill. It was empty except for an axe, which stood behind the door. But they managed to get their supper, and stayed in the hut all night.

In the morning they saw that on the side of the hill near the hut was a great forest. The son took the axe, and went up on the hillside and chopped enough wood for a load to carry to the town on the other side of the hill. He easily sold it, and with a happy heart brought back food and some clothing to make them both comfortable.

"Now, Mother," he said. "I can earn enough to keep us both, and we shall be happy here together."

Day after day he went out and cut the wood, and at night carried it to the village and sold it. And they always had plenty to eat and what they needed to make them happy and comfortable.

One day the boy went farther up the hill than he had ever gone before in search of better timber. As he climbed up the steep hillside, he suddenly came upon a lion carved from stone.

"Oh!" thought the boy, "this must be the guardian deity of this mountain. I will make him some offering tomorrow."

That night he bought two candles, and carried them to the lion.

He lighted them and put one on each side of the lion, praying that his own good fortune might continue.

As he stood there, suddenly the lion opened his great stone mouth, and said: "What are you doing here?"

The boy told him the story of his hard-hearted brother, and how he and his mother had left home, and were living in the hut at the foot of the hill.

When he had heard the story, the lion said: "If you will bring a bucket here tomorrow, and put it under my mouth, I will fill it with gold for you."

The next day the boy brought the bucket and put it under the lion's mouth.

"You must be very careful to tell me when it is nearly full," said the lion, "for if even one piece of gold should fall to the ground, great trouble would be in store for you."

The boy was very careful to do exactly as the lion told him, and soon he was on his way home to his mother with a bucketful of gold.

They were so rich now that they bought a large, beautiful farm, and went there to live. Everything the boy undertook seemed to prosper. He worked hard and grew strong; and before many years had passed he was old enough to marry and bring a bride to the home. But the mother still lived with them, and they were all very contented and happy.

At last the hard-hearted brother heard of their prosperity. He too had married and had a little son. So he took his wife and the little boy, and went to pay his younger brother a visit. It was not long before he had heard the whole story of their good fortune, and how the lion had given them all the gold.

"I will try that, too," he said.

So he took his wife and child and went to the very same hut his brother had lived in, and there they passed the night.

The very next morning he started out with a bucket to visit the Stone Lion.

When he had told the lion his errand, the lion said: "I will do that for you, but you must be very careful to tell me when the bucket is nearly full; for even if one little piece of gold touches the ground, great misery will surely fall upon you."

Now the older brother was so greedy that he kept shaking the bucket to get the gold pieces closer together. And when the bucket was nearly full he did not tell the lion, as the younger brother had done, for he wanted all he could get.

Suddenly one of the gold pieces fell upon the ground.

"Oh," cried the lion, "a big piece of gold is stuck in my throat. Put your hand in and get it out. It is the largest piece of all."

The greedy man thrust his hand at once into the lion's mouth —and the lion snapped his jaws together.

And there the man stayed, for the lion would not let him go. And the gold in the bucket turned into earth and stones.

When night came, and the husband did not come home, the wife became anxious, and went out to search for him. At last she found him, with his arm held fast in the lion's mouth. He was tired, cold, and hungry. She comforted him as best she could, and brought him some food.

Every day now the wife must go with food for her husband. But there came a day when all the money was gone, and the baby was sick, and the poor woman herself was too ill to work. She went to her husband and said: "There is no more food for you, nor for us. We shall all have to die. Oh! if we had only not tried to get the gold."

The lion was listening to all that was said, and he was so pleased at their misfortune that he began laughing at them. And as he laughed, he opened his mouth, and the greedy man quickly drew out his hand, before the lion had a chance to close his jaws again!

They were glad enough to get away from the place where they had had such ill luck, and so they went to the brother's house once more. The brother was sorry for them, and gave them enough money to buy a small place, and there the hard-hearted brother took his family and lived.

The younger brother and his wife and his mother lived very happily in their beautiful home, but they always remembered the Stone Lion on the hillside, who gave them their good fortune.

THE MAN WHO LOVED MONEY
BETTER THAN LIFE

Retold by Mary H. Davis and Cheow-Leung

Greed is a very powerful emotion. It can sting, it can wound, it can break—it can kill. This tale is from China.

In ancient times there was an old woodcutter who went to the mountain almost every day to cut wood.

It was said that this old man was a miser who hoarded his silver until it changed to gold, and that he cared more for gold than anything else in all the world.

One day a wilderness tiger sprang at him, and though he ran, he could not escape, and the tiger carried him off in its mouth.

The woodcutter's son saw his father's danger, and ran to save him if possible. He carried a long knife, and as he could run faster than the tiger, who had a man to carry, he soon overtook them.

His father was not much hurt, for the tiger held him by his clothes. When the old woodcutter saw his son about to stab the tiger he called out in great alarm: "Do not spoil the tiger's skin! Do not spoil the tiger's skin! If you can kill him without cutting holes in his skin we can get many pieces of silver for it. Kill him, but do not cut his body."

While the son was listening to his father's instructions the tiger suddenly dashed off into the forest, carrying the old man where the son could not reach him, and he was soon killed.

And the wise man who told this story said, "Ah, this old man's courage was foolishness. His love for money was stronger than his love for life itself."

•

THE LITTLE LOAF

Refusing to grab for all you can is a virtue. Sometimes it's a virtue
that even brings a reward. This story comes from a Civil War–era
school reader.

Many years ago, there was a great famine in Germany, and the
poor people suffered from hunger. A rich man who loved children
sent for twenty of them and said: "In this basket there is a loaf of
bread for each of you. Take it and come back again every day till
the famine is over. I will give you a loaf each day."

The children were very hungry. They seized the basket and
struggled to get at the largest loaf. They even forgot to thank the
man who had been kind to them. After a few minutes of quarreling
and snatching for bread, everyone ran away with his loaf except
one little girl named Gretchen. She stood there alone at a little
distance from the gentleman. Then, smiling, she took up the last
loaf, the smallest of all, and thanked him with all her heart.

Next day the children came again, and they behaved as badly
as ever. Gretchen, who would not push with the rest, received only
a tiny loaf scarcely half the size of the others. But when she came
home and her mother began to cut the loaf, out dropped six shining
coins of silver.

"Oh, Gretchen!" exclaimed her mother, "this must be a mistake. The money does not belong to us. Run as quickly as you can
and take it back to the gentleman."

So Gretchen carried it back, but when she gave the gentleman
her mother's message, he said: "No, no, it was not a mistake. I had
the silver baked into the smallest loaf in order to reward you.
Remember that the person who is contented to have a small loaf
rather than quarrel for a larger one will find blessings that are
better than money baked in bread."

•

THE MISER

Aesop

To a large degree, the value of our possessions depends on how we use them.

A miser had a lump of gold, which he buried in the ground, coming to the spot every day to look at it.

One day, finding that it was stolen, he began to tear his hair and lament loudly.

A neighbor, seeing him, said, "Pray do not grieve so. Bury a stone in the hole and fancy it is the gold. It will serve you just as well, for when the gold was there you made no use of it."

THE DOG IN THE MANGER

Aesop

This fable about selfishness is the origin of the phrase "dog in the manger."

A dog was lying in a manger full of hay.

A horse, a cow, a sheep, and a goat came one by one and wanted to eat some of the hay. But the dog sprang up growling and snarling, and would not let them have so much as a mouthful.

"What a selfish beast," said the cow to her companions. "He cannot eat the hay himself, and yet neither will he let those who can."

People often begrudge others what they themselves cannot enjoy.

•

THE TOWN MOUSE AND THE COUNTRY MOUSE
Retold by Sara Cone Bryant

We sometimes tell ourselves that other people's lives are easier than our own. The truth is that every life has its share of hard knocks; as Ishmael notes in *Moby Dick,* "The universal thump is passed around." Giving thanks for your own blessings is usually more productive than longing for someone else's life.

This tale is a widely loved fable from Aesop.

Once a little mouse who lived in the country invited a little mouse from town to visit him. When the little Town Mouse sat down to dinner he was surprised to find that the Country Mouse had nothing to eat except barley and grain.

"Really," he said, "you do not live well at all. You should see how I live! I have all sorts of fine things to eat every day. You must come to visit me and see how nice it is to live in the town."

The little Country Mouse was glad to do this, and after a while he went to town to visit his friend.

The very first place that the Town Mouse took the Country Mouse to see was the kitchen cupboard of the house where he lived. There, on the lowest shelf, behind some stone jars, stood a big paper bag of brown sugar. The little Town Mouse gnawed a hole in the bag and invited his friend to nibble for himself.

The two little mice nibbled and nibbled, and the Country Mouse thought he had never tasted anything so delicious in his life. He was just thinking how lucky the Town Mouse was, when suddenly the door opened with a bang, and in came the cook to get some flour.

"Run!" whispered the Town Mouse. And they ran as fast as they could to the little hole where they had come in. The little Country Mouse was shaking all over when they got safely away, but the little Town Mouse said, "That is nothing; she will soon go away and then we can go back."

After the cook had gone away and shut the door, they stole softly back, and this time the Town Mouse had something new to show. He took the little Country Mouse into a corner on the top shelf, where a big jar of dried prunes stood open. After much tugging and pulling they got a large dried prune out of the jar on to the shelf and began to nibble at it. This was even better than the brown sugar. The little Country Mouse liked the taste so much that he could hardly nibble fast enough. But all at once, in the midst of their eating, there came a scratching at the door and a sharp, loud *meow!*

"What is that?" said the Country Mouse. The Town Mouse just whispered, "Sh!" and ran as fast as he could to the hole. The Country Mouse ran after, you may be sure, as fast as *he* could. As soon as they were out of danger the Town Mouse said, "That was the old cat. She is the best mouser in town—if she once gets you, you are lost."

"This is very terrible," said the little Country Mouse. "Let us not go back to the cupboard again."

"No," said the Town Mouse, "I will take you to the cellar; there is something special there."

So the Town Mouse took his little friend down the cellar stairs and into a big cupboard where there were many shelves. On the shelves were jars of butter, and cheeses in bags and out of bags. Overhead hung bunches of sausages, and there were spicy apples in barrels standing about. It smelled so good that it went to the little Country Mouse's head. He ran along the shelf and nibbled at a cheese here, and a bit of butter there, until he saw an especially rich, very delicious-smelling piece of cheese on a queer little stand in a corner. He was just on the point of putting his teeth into the cheese when the Town Mouse saw him.

"Stop! stop!" cried the Town Mouse. "That is a trap!"

The little Country Mouse stopped and said, "What is a trap?"

"That thing is a trap," said the little Town Mouse. "The minute you touch the cheese with your teeth something comes down on your head hard, and you're dead."

The little Country Mouse looked at the trap, and he looked at the cheese, and he looked at the little Town Mouse. "If you'll excuse me," he said, "I think I will go home. I'd rather have barley and grain to eat in peace and comfort, than have brown sugar and dried prunes and cheese—and be frightened to death all the time!"

So the little Country Mouse went back to his home, and there he stayed all the rest of his life.

•

THE DISCONTENTED STONECUTTER

There is a big difference between healthy ambition and consuming envy. In this old Japanese tale we see the latter, always longing for something in the distance.

Once upon a time in Japan, there was a poor stonecutter, named Hofus, who used to go every day to the mountainside to cut great blocks of stone. He lived near the mountain in a little stone hut, and worked hard and was happy.

One day he took a load of stone to the house of a rich man. There he saw so many beautiful things that when he went back to his mountain he could think of nothing else. He began to wish that he too might sleep in a bed as soft as down, with curtains of silk and tassels of gold. And he sighed:

"Ah me! Ah me!
If Hofus only were rich as he!"

To his surprise, the voice of the Mountain Spirit answered:

"Have thou thy wish!"

When Hofus returned home that evening his little hut was gone, and in its place stood a great palace. It was filled with beautiful things, and the best of all was a bed of down, with curtains of silk and tassels of gold.

Hofus decided to work no more. But he was not used to being idle, and time passed slowly—the days seemed very long.

One day as he sat by the window he saw a carriage dash past. It was drawn by snow-white horses. In it sat a prince, while before and behind were servants in suits of blue and white. One was holding a golden umbrella over the prince.

When the stonecutter saw this, he began to feel unhappy, and he sighed:

"Ah me! Ah me!
If Hofus only a prince might be!"

And again the same voice that he had heard on the mountain answered:

"Be thou a prince!"

Straightway Hofus was a prince. He had servants dressed in crimson and gold, and he rode in a carriage with a golden umbrella over his head.

For a short time he was happy, but one day, as he walked in the garden, he saw that the flowers were drooping, and the grass was dry and brown. And when he rode out he felt the hot sun burn him in spite of his umbrella.

"The sun is mightier than I," thought he, and then he sighed:

"Ah me! Ah me!
If Hofus only the sun might be!"

And the voice answered:

"Be thou the sun!"

Straightway the great sun he became. He burned the grass and rice fields; he dried up the streams. Rich and poor alike suffered from the terrible heat.

One day a cloud came and rested in front of him and hid the earth from his sight. He was angry and cried:

"Ah me! Ah me!
If Hofus only a cloud might be!"

And the voice answered:

"Be thou a cloud!"

Straightway a cloud he became. He floated before the face of the sun and hid the earth from it.

Then day after day the cloud dropped rain. The rivers overflowed, and the rice fields were covered with water. Towns were swept away. Only the great rocks on the mountainside stood unmoved midst the flood.

The cloud looked at them in wonder, then he sighed:

"Ah me! Ah me!
If Hofus only a rock might be!"

And the voice answered:

"Be thou a rock!"

Straightway a rock he became. Proudly he stood. The sun could not burn him and the rain could not move him.
"Now, at last," he said, "no one is mightier than I."
But one day he was awakened from his dreams by a noise— tap! tap! tap!—down at his feet. He looked and there was a stonecutter driving his tool into the rock. Another blow and the great rock shivered; a block of stone broke away.
"That man is mightier than I!" cried Hofus, and he sighed:

"Ah me! Ah me!
If Hofus only the man might be!"

And the voice answered:

"Be thou thyself!"

And straightway Hofus was himself again—a poor stonecutter, working all day upon the mountainside and going home at night to his little hut. But he was content and happy, and never again did he wish to be other than Hofus the stonecutter.

•

HOW HIPPO WAS HUMBLED

Here is an African story about self-absorption. Being stuck on yourself is not a good place to be.

Once upon a time, long ago, Hippopotamus was the most beautiful creature of all the beasts in the bush. She had soft, shiny fur and fine, silky eyelashes. Her ears were long and slender, and her tail, which she loved to wave high in the air, was the thickest and bushiest tail anyone had ever seen.

In those days Hippo did not live in the dark river waters, as she does now. She lived on land so all the other animals could see what a handsome creature she was. She used to sit by the river's edge all day long, waving her thick, bushy tail and staring at her own reflection in the water.

"How beautiful I am!" she would sigh, turning this way and that so she could admire her own features. "What silky fur! What stunning ears! What a magnificent tail! I am by far the most admirable beast in the bush!"

Then one day an awful fire rose deep in the bush. The hot winds spread flames in every direction, and all the animals fled toward the river, where Hippo gazed happily at her own image.

The elephants thundered by, thrashing their trunks in despair.

The giraffes galloped past, craning their long necks to see the flames close behind.

The lions bounded by, roaring the alarm.

"Ah," Hippo said to herself, "they've all come to admire me."

She gazed happily at her reflection and never saw the flames raging closer and closer.

"I hope they all notice my fine, silky lashes," she remarked, leaning over the water.

But just then a spark caught her long, bushy tail, which she happened to be waving so proudly.

"Help!" she cried, hopping around and around, trying to blow out the flames. But it did no good.

"Help!" she yelled. "Help! My soft, shiny fur will catch on fire!"
And it did.

So of course she did the only thing she could to save herself. She hopped right into the river, where she sank to the bottom and held her breath as long as she dared. When she finally came up for air, the bush fire had burned itself out.

Hippo dragged herself out of the water and sat down on the bank.

"That was awful," she moaned. "I'm soaked to my bones, and there's mud all over my shiny fur coat. I must look like a mess."

She leaned over the water to gaze at herself.

But who was this bald, wrinkled creature staring back at her? Hippo gasped.

Her shiny fur coat was burned away! Her fine, silky eyelashes were singed, baring two bulging, beady eyes. Her slender, long ears had shriveled into two ugly stubs. And worst of all, her thick, bushy tail was gone!

Poor Hippo was so ashamed, she jumped right back into the river to hide herself from the other animals. She stays in the water to this day, poking only her eyes and nose above the surface, and coming out only at night when no one can see her.

●

ARACHNE

Retold by Flora Cooke

It's important to do your best. But it's also important to remember that there is almost always someone who can do the same thing just as well, if not better. The ancients considered excessive pride, or hubris, a fatal character flaw.

Arachne was a beautiful maiden who had wonderful skills in weaving and embroidery. The nymphs left their groves and fountains to gather round her loom. The naiads came from the rivers and the dryads from the trees, and never tired of watching her.

She took the wool as it came from the backs of the newly washed sheep and formed it into rolls. She separated it with her deft fingers, and carded it until it looked as light and soft as a cloud. She twirled the spindle in her skillful hands and wove the web. Often she embroidered it with her needle in beautiful, soft colors.

Arachne's father was famed throughout the land for his skill in coloring. He dyed her wool in all the hues of the rainbow.

Her work was so wonderful that people said, "Surely Athena must have taught this maiden." But Arachne proudly denied this. She could not bear to be thought a pupil even of the goddess of the loom.

"If Athena thinks she can weave better than I, let her try her skill with mine," said she boastfully. "If I fail, I will pay the penalty."

In vain her father told her that perhaps Athena, unseen, guided her hands. Arachne would not listen, and would thank no one for her gift, for vanity had turned her head. She said again, "Let Athena try her skill with mine if she dares."

One day as she was boasting to the nymphs of the beauty of

her work, an old woman appeared before her and advised her to accept her rare gift humbly. Arachne looked at the old woman angrily and said, "Keep your advice for others, old dame. I do not need it."

But the old woman said, "Listen to me. I have great age and much experience, and I have come to warn you. Until now, Athena has aided you, asking for no gratitude, but she can help you no more until you grow less selfish and vain. Above all, I advise you to ask forgiveness of Athena. Perhaps she may yet pardon your selfish pride. Challenge your fellow mortals, if you will, but do not, I beg of you, seek to compete with the goddess."

But Arachne said, "Begone. I fear not Athena, no, nor anyone else. Nothing would please me so much as to weave with Athena, but she is afraid to weave with me."

Then suddenly the old woman threw aside her cloak, and there before Arachne's very eyes stood a tall, majestic, gray-eyed goddess, crowned with a golden helmet.

"Athena is here," she said. Then the nymphs bent low in homage, but Arachne stood erect. She grew pale but gave no other sign of fear.

"Come, foolish girl, since you wish to try your skill with me," said Athena, "let the contest begin."

Both went quickly to work, and for hours their shuttles flew swiftly in and out. Athena used the sky for her loom, and in it she wove a picture too beautiful to describe. If you wish to know more about it, look at the western sky when the sun is setting.

She was still merciful, and at length she began a smaller web nearer to Arachne's loom. In this she wove a warning, showing how other boastful mortals had failed when they dared to compete with the gods. She hoped that the girl would even yet repent her rashness. But Arachne refused this last chance to save herself. She would not lift her eyes from her own work.

Her weaving was so fine and beautiful that even Athena was forced to admire it. The figures upon it seemed ready to speak and to live, but into her web she had woven many of the faults and failings of the gods, and her work was full of spite.

When the task was finished, Arachne lifted her eyes to Athena's work. Instantly she knew that she had failed. Ashamed and miserable, she tried to hang herself in her own web, but Athena cried, "Stay, wretched and perverse girl. You shall not die. You shall live to do the work for which you are best fitted. You and your children shall be among the greatest spinners and weavers upon the earth.

You shall be the mother of a great race, which shall be called spiders. Wherever men shall see your web, they shall destroy it even as I destroy yours." And as she spoke, the goddess with her shuttle tore the maiden's wonderful web from top to bottom.

Then Athena touched Arachne's forehead with her spindle thrice, and she became smaller and smaller, until she was scarcely larger than a fly.

And from that day to this Arachne and her family have been faithfully spinning and weaving, but they do their work so quietly and in such dark places that few people know what marvelous webs they weave. Some early morning, you may see their webs gleaming with dew, spread across the grass or hanging between the branches of a tree.

•

THE GOLD BREAD

Adapted from a retelling by Kate Douglas Wiggin and Nora Archibald Smith

Some people think they are better than everyone else, and therefore deserve better. But as this young bride learns to her regret, expecting too much can lead to too little.

In many places, bread symbolizes home and family (an ancient idea preserved in our custom of serving cake at wedding celebrations). In some eastern European countries, the bride is greeted in her new home with bread and salt.

Once upon a time there was a widow who had a beautiful daughter. The mother was modest and humble; the daughter, Marienka, was pride itself. She had suitors from all sides, but none satisfied her. The more they tried to please her, the more she disdained them.

One night, when the poor mother could not sleep, she took her beads and began to pray for her dear child, who gave her more than one care. Marienka was asleep by her side. As the mother gazed lovingly at her beautiful daughter, Marienka laughed in her sleep.

"What a beautiful dream she must have to laugh in this way!"

said the mother. Then she finished her prayer, hung her beads on the wall, laid her head on the same pillow with her daughter, and fell asleep.

"My dear child," said she in the morning, "what did you dream last night that you laughed so?"

"What did I dream, mama? I dreamed that a nobleman came here for me in a copper coach, and that he put a ring on my finger set with a stone that sparkled like the stars. And when I entered the church, the people had eyes for no one but the blessed Virgin and me."

"My daughter, my daughter, that was a proud dream!" said the mother, shaking her head. But Marienka went out singing.

The same day a wagon entered the yard. A handsome young farmer in good circumstances came to ask Marienka to share a peasant's bread with him. The mother was pleased with the suitor, but the proud Marienka refused him, saying, "Though you should come in a copper coach and put a ring on my finger set with a stone that sparkled like the stars, I would not have you for a husband." And the farmer went away storming at Marienka's pride.

The next night the mother awoke, took her beads, and prayed still more earnestly for her daughter, when behold! Marienka laughed again as she was sleeping.

"I wonder what she is dreaming," said the mother, who prayed, unable to sleep.

"My dear child," she said the next morning, "what did you dream last night that you laughed aloud?"

"What did I dream, mama? I dreamed that a nobleman came here for me in a silver coach, and that he offered me a golden diadem. And when I entered the church, the people looked at me more than they did at the blessed Virgin."

"Hush! you are blaspheming. Pray, my daughter, pray that you may not fall into temptation."

But Marienka ran away to escape her mother's sermon.

The same day a carriage entered the yard. A young lord came to entreat Marienka to share a nobleman's bread with him.

"It is a great honor," said the mother. But vanity is blind.

"Though you should come in a silver coach," said Marienka to the new suitor, "and should offer me a golden diadem, I would not have you for a husband."

"Take care, my child," said the poor mother. "Pride is a device of the Evil One."

"Mothers never know what they are saying," thought Marienka, and she went out shrugging her shoulders.

The third night the mother could not sleep for anxiety. As she lay awake, praying for her daughter, behold! Marienka burst into a loud fit of laughter.

"Oh!" said the mother, "what can the unhappy child be dreaming now?" And she continued to pray till daylight.

"My dear child," said she in the morning, "what did you dream last night?"

"You will be angry again if I tell you," answered Marienka.

"No, no," replied the mother. "Tell me."

"I dreamed that a noble lord, with a great train of attendants, came to ask me in marriage. He was in a golden coach, and he brought me a dress of gold lace. And when I entered the church, the people looked at nobody but me."

The mother clasped her hands. Marienka, half dressed, sprang from the bed and ran into the next room, to avoid a lecture that was tiresome to her.

The same day three coaches entered the yard, one of copper, one of silver, and one of gold, the first drawn by two horses, the second by four, and the third by eight, all caparisoned with gold and pearls. From the copper and silver coaches alighted pages dressed in scarlet breeches and green jackets and cloaks, while from the golden coach stepped a handsome nobleman all dressed in gold. He entered the house, and, bending one knee on the ground, asked the mother for her daughter's hand.

"What an honor!" thought the mother.

"My dream has come to pass," said Marienka. "You see, mother, that, as usual, I was right and you were wrong."

She ran to her chamber, tied the betrothal knot, and offered it smilingly as a pledge of her faith to the handsome lord, who, on his side, put a ring on her finger set with a stone that sparkled like the stars, and presented her with a golden diadem and a dress of gold lace.

The proud girl ran to her room to dress for the ceremony, while the mother, still anxious, said to the bridegroom, ' My good sir, what bread do you offer my daughter?"

"Among us," said he, "the bread is of copper, silver, and gold. She can take her choice."

"What does this mean?" thought the mother. But Marienka had no anxiety. She returned as beautiful as the sun, took her lover's arm, and set out for the church without asking her mother's blessing. The poor woman was left to pray alone on the threshold, and when Marienka returned and entered the carriage, she did not even turn around to look at her mother or to bid her a last farewell.

The eight horses set off at a gallop and did not stop till they reached a huge rock, in which was a hole as large as the gate of a city. The horses plunged into the darkness, the earth trembled, and the rock cracked and crumbled. Marienka seized her husband's hand.

"Don't be alarmed, my fair one. In a moment it will be light."

All at once a thousand lights waved in the air. The dwarfs of the mountain, each with a torch in his hand, came to salute their lord, the King of the Mines. Marienka learned for the first time her husband's name. Whether he was a spirit of good or evil, at least he was so rich that she did not regret her choice.

They emerged from the darkness, and advanced through bleached forests and mountains that raised their pale and gloomy summits to the skies. Firs, beeches, birches, oaks, rocks, all were of lead. At the end of the forest stretched a vast meadow, the grass of which was of silver; and at the bottom of the meadow was a castle of gold, inlaid with diamonds and rubies. The carriage stopped before the door, and the King of the Mines offered his hand to his bride, saying, "My fair one, all that you see is yours."

Marienka was delighted. But it was impossible to make so long a journey without being hungry. It was with pleasure, therefore, that she saw the mountain dwarfs bring in a table, everything on which glittered with gold, silver, and precious stones. The dishes were marvelous—side dishes of emeralds, and roasts of gold on silver trays. Everyone ate heartily except the bride, who begged her husband for a little bread.

"Bring the copper bread," said the King of the Mines.

Marienka could not eat it.

"Bring the silver bread," said he.

Marienka could not eat it.

"Bring the gold bread," said he, at length.

Marienka could not eat it.

"My fair one," said the King of the Mines, "I am very sorry. But what can I offer you? We have no other bread."

The bride burst into tears. Her husband laughed aloud. His heart was of metal, like his kingdom.

"Weep, if you like," he cried, "it will do you no good. What you wished for you possess. Eat the bread that you have chosen."

And so the rich Marienka lives in her underground castle, always hungry, and always hunting in vain for a few roots growing down into the earth, ones she might be able to eat.

But once a year, in the springtime, when the ground opens to receive the fruitful rain, Marienka returns to earth. Dressed in rags, pale and wrinkled, she begs from door to door, only too happy when anyone throws her a crust. And thus she receives from a few kind souls what she lacks in her palace of gold—a little bread and a little pity.

•

THE DISCONTENTED PIG

Retold by Katherine D. Cather

Almost every worthwhile job requires at least a little unpleasant or inconvenient work. But running away from it won't make things easier. Contentment is not synonymous with effortlessness.

This story comes from Thuringia, an ancient region of Germany.

Ever so long ago, in the time when there were fairies, and men and animals talked together, there was a curly-tailed pig. He lived by himself in a house at the edge of the village, and every day he worked in his garden. Whether the sun shone or the rain fell he hoed and dug and weeded, turning the earth around his tomato vines and loosening the soil of the carrot plot, until word of his fine vegetables traveled through seven counties, and each year he won the royal prize at the fair.

But after a time the little pig grew tired of the endless toil.

"What matters it if I do have the finest vegetables in the kingdom," he thought, "since I must work myself to death getting them to grow? I mean to go out and see the world and find an easier way of making a living."

So he locked the door of his house and shut the gate of his garden and started down the road.

A good three miles he traveled, till he came to a cottage almost hidden in a grove of trees. Lovely music sounded around him and Little Pig smiled, for he had an ear for sweet sounds.

"I will go look for it," he said, following in the direction from which it seemed to come.

Now it happened that in that house dwelt Thomas, a cat, who made his living playing the violin. Little Pig saw him standing in the door pushing the bow up and down across the strings. It put a thought into his head. Surely this must be easier and far more pleasant than digging in a garden!

"Will you teach me to play the violin, friend cat?" he asked.

Thomas looked up from his bow and nodded his head.

"To be sure," he answered. "Just do as I am doing."

And he gave him the bow and fiddle.

Little Pig took them and began to saw, but squeak! quang! No sweet music fell upon his ear. The sounds he heard were like the squealing of his baby brother pigs when a wolf came near them.

"Oh!" he cried. "This isn't music!"

Thomas, the cat, nodded his head.

"Of course not," he said. "You haven't tried long enough. He who would play the violin must work."

"Then I think I'll look for something else," Piggywig answered, "because this is quite as hard as weeding my garden."

And he gave back the bow and fiddle and started down the road.

He walked on and on, until he came to a hut where lived a dog who made cheese. He was kneading and molding the curd into cakes, and Little Pig thought it looked quite easy.

"I think I'd like to go into the cheese business myself," he said to himself. So he asked the dog if he would teach him.

This the dog was quite willing to do, and a moment later Little Pig was working beside him.

Soon he grew hot and tired and stopped to rest and fan himself.

"No, no!" exclaimed the dog, "you will spoil the cheese. There can be no rest time until the work is done."

Little Pig opened his eyes in amazement.

"Indeed!" he replied. "Then this is just as hard as growing vegetables or learning to play a violin. I mean to look for something easier."

And he started down the road.

On the other side of the river, in a sweet green field, a man was taking honey out of beehives. Little Pig saw him as he crossed the bridge and thought that of all the trades he had seen, this suited him best. It must be lovely there in the meadow among the flowers. Honey was not heavy to lift, and once in a while he could have a mouthful of it. He ran as fast as he could go to ask the man if he would take him into his employ.

This plan pleased the bee man as much as it pleased the pig.

"I've been looking for a helper for a year and a day," he said. "Begin work at once."

He gave Little Pig a veil and a pair of gloves, telling him to fasten them on well. Then he told him to lift a honeycomb out of a hive.

Little Pig ran to do it, twisting his curly tail in the joy of having at last found a business that suited him. But buzz, buzz! The bees crept under his veil and inside his gloves. They stung him on his fingers, his mouth, his ears, and the end of his nose, and he squealed and dropped the honey and ran.

"Come back, come back!" the man called.

"No, no!" Little Pig answered with a big squeal. "No, no, the bees hurt me!"

The man nodded his head.

"Of course they do," he said. "They hurt me too! That is part of the work. You cannot be a beekeeper without getting stung."

Little Pig blinked his beady eyes and began to think hard.

"It seems that every kind of work has something unpleasant about it. To play the violin you must practice until your arm aches. When you make cheese you dare not stop a minute until the work is done, and in taking honey from a hive the bees sting you until your head is on fire. Work in my garden is not so bad after all, and I am going back to it."

So he said goodbye to the bee man and was soon back in his carrot patch. He hoed and raked and weeded, singing as he worked, and there was no more contented pig in all that kingdom. Every autumn he took his vegetables to the fair and brought home the royal prize, and sometimes, on holidays, the cat and the dog and the bee man came to call.

•

THE BLIND MEN AND THE ELEPHANT

**Learning how to work with others is one of the most important
lessons confronting us as we begin to make our way through life.
Cooperation moves us along faster and further.**

There lived in India six friends who were all blind.

Now India, of course, is a land of that greatest of land beasts,
the elephant. But, naturally, since these friends were all blind, they
did not know what an elephant looks like.

One day they were sitting together talking when they heard a
great roar.

"I believe that is an elephant in the street," one said.

"Now is our chance to find out what kind of creature the
elephant is," said another.

So they all went into the street.

The first blind man reached out and touched the elephant's
ear.

"Ah," he said to himself, "the elephant is a rough, wide thing.
It is like a rug."

The second blind man felt the elephant's trunk.

"Now I understand," he thought. "The elephant is a long,
round thing. It is like a giant snake."

The third blind man touched the elephant's leg.

"Well, I wouldn't have guessed it," he said. "The elephant is
tall and firm, just like a tree."

The fourth blind man felt the elephant's side.

"Now I know," he thought. "The elephant is wide and smooth,
like a wall."

The fifth blind man put his hands on the elephant's tusk.

"The elephant is a hard, sharp animal, like a spear," he
decided.

The sixth blind man touched the elephant's tail.

"Well, well," he said. "It gives a mighty roar, but the elephant
is just a thing like a long, thin rope."

Afterward the six blind friends sat down again to talk about the
elephant.

"It is rough and wide, like a rug," said the first.

"No, it is long and round, like a snake," said the second.

"Don't be silly," laughed the third. "It is tall and firm, like a tree."

"No, it is not," growled the fourth. "It is wide and smooth, like a wall."

"Hard and sharp, like a spear!" shouted the fifth.

"Long and thin, like a rope!" yelled the sixth.

And so a fight started. Each one insisted he was right. He had touched it with his own hands, hadn't he?

The owner of the elephant heard all the shouting and came to see what the fuss was about.

"Each of you is right, and each of you is wrong," he told them. "One man may not be able to find the whole truth by himself—just a small part of it. But if we work together, each adding our own piece to the whole, we can find wisdom."

•

ALL GOD'S CREATURES HAVE WORK TO DO

This clever tale from southeast Asia helps us learn the difference between first-rate work and second-rate effort. It is good reading before starting a job.

Two cousins grew up side by side from the day they both entered the world. They learned to crawl and toddle together, and later how to run and swim and play ball and all the other things boys do together. They were constant and devoted friends.

But eventually they began to drift apart, as sometimes happens as even good friends move through life. One cousin took to his books, found a certain delight in learning, studied hard, and passed his exams with flying colors. The other cousin decided books weren't such good companions. He skipped school a good bit so he could continue to swim and play ball, ignored his lessons, and ended up failing his exams.

As is usually the way of the world, fortune rewarded the first cousin, who ended up becoming an adviser to the king himself.

The second cousin soon found himself employed as an oarsman on his majesty's royal yacht.

One day the king and all his royal advisers embarked on a journey up the river. They sat under a wide canopy in the bow of the boat, where the breeze was best, and discussed affairs of state as the yacht moved along.

The sight of his cousin sitting at ease with royalty irked the oarsman no end.

"Look at that lazy fellow, lounging there in the shade, while I must break my back in the sun," he thought as he rowed. "What gives him the right to sit up there, any more than me? After all, aren't we both God's creatures?"

The more he thought about it, the angrier he grew.

"Look at those useless louts," he began grumbling to his fellow oarsmen. "They call themselves advisers, but all they do is sit and gab. Why should we sweat so hard to push their carcasses against the current? There's nothing fair about it. They ought to be back here rowing too. Aren't we all God's creatures?"

That evening, they tied to shore to make camp. Everyone ate and fell asleep quickly.

The oarsman woke in the middle of the night to find a firm hand shaking him by the shoulder. It was the king himself.

"There's a strange noise coming from over there," he said, pointing. "I can't get to sleep from wondering what it is. Please go find out."

The oarsman jumped off the boat and ran up a hill. He came back a few minutes later.

"It's nothing, Your Majesty," he said. "A cat has just given birth to a litter of noisy kittens."

"Ah, I see," said the king. "What kind of kittens?"

The oarsman had not looked to see. He ran up the hill again and came back.

"Siamese," he said.

"And how many kittens are there?" the king inquired.

Again, the oarsman had not noticed. He went back.

"Six kittens," he reported.

"How many males and how many females?" the king asked.

The oarsman ran back once again.

"Three males and three females," he cried, beginning to lose his breath.

"I see," said the king. "Come with me."

They tiptoed to the bow of the boat, where the king woke the oarsman's cousin.

"There's a strange noise up on that hill," he told him. "Go find out what it is."

The adviser disappeared into the darkness and returned in a moment.

"It is a newborn litter of kittens, Your Majesty," he said.

"What kind of kittens?" the king asked.

"Siamese," answered his adviser.

"How many?"

"Six."

"How many males and how many females?"

"Three males and three females. The mother gave birth in an overturned barrel just after we arrived. The cats belong to the mayor of the village. He hopes they have not disturbed you, and invites you to come take your pick if the court is in need of a royal pet."

The king looked at the oarsman.

"I overheard your grumbling earlier today," he said. "Yes, we are all God's creatures. But all God's creatures have work to do. I had to send you to shore four times for answers. My adviser went only once. That is why he is my adviser, and you must row the boat."

•

THE MAN AND HIS PIECE OF CLOTH

Retold by P. V. Ramaswami Raju

Rarely does lasting satisfaction come through escape. Living in the world means living with its responsibilities and cares, as this fable from India reminds us.

A man in the East, where they do not require as much clothing as in colder climates, gave up all worldly concerns and retired to a wood, where he built a hut and lived in it.

His only clothing was a piece of cloth which he wore round his waist. But, as ill-luck would have it, rats were plentiful in the wood, so he had to keep a cat. The cat required milk to keep it, so a cow had to be kept. The cow required tending, so a cow-boy was employed. The boy required a house to live in, so a house was built for him. To look after the house a maid had to be engaged. To provide company for the maid a few more houses had to be built and people invited to live in them. In this manner a little township sprang up.

The man said, "The further we seek to go from the world and its cares, the more they multiply!"

•

THE STORY OF THE TWO FRIENDS
Retold by Rosetta Baskerville

Am I wise, or am I a fool? That is the central question of this wonderful tale from Uganda. The question itself sets us on the road toward wisdom. The story is largely about work, and the instruction this young boy receives from the animals in the forest is not very different from the advice the young James Madison and his College of New Jersey classmates got from their teacher, Dr. Witherspoon: "Do not live useless and die contemptible."

Once upon a time there were a potter and his wife who had one child, a little boy, and as he grew older they were grieved to see that he was different from all other children.

He never played with them, or laughed, or sang. He just sat alone by himself. He hardly ever spoke to his parents, and he never learned the nice polite manners of the other children in the village. He sat and thought all day, and no one knew what he thought about, and his parents were very sad.

The other women tried to comfort the potter's wife. They said, "Perhaps you will have another baby, and it will be like other children." But she said, "I don't want another baby. I want this one to be nice." And the men of the village tried to cheer the potter. "Strange boys often become great men," they said. And one old man said, "Leave the boy alone. We shall see whether he is a wise man or a fool."

The potter went home and told his wife what the men had said, and the boy heard him, and it seemed to wake him up. He thought it over for a few days, and at last one morning at dawn he took his stick in his hand and went into the forest to think there.

All day he wandered about, and at last he came to a little clearing on the side of a hill from which he could look down over the country. The sun was setting over the distant blue hills, and everything was touched with a pink and golden light, and deep shadows lay on the banana gardens and forests in the distance. But the boy saw none of these things. He was footsore and weary and miserable, and he sat down on a fallen log, tired out with his long day. Suddenly a lion came out into the clearing.

"What are you doing here all alone?" he said severely.

"I am very miserable," said the boy, "and I have come into the forest to think, for I do not know whether I am a wise man or a fool."

"Is that all you think about?" said the lion.

"Yes," answered the boy, "I think about it night and day."

"Then you are a fool," said the lion decidedly. "Wise men think about things that benefit the country." And he walked away.

An antelope came bounding out into the clearing and stopped to stare at the boy.

"What are you doing here?" he asked.

"I am very miserable," answered the boy. "I don't know whether I am a wise man or a fool."

"Do you ever eat anything?" said the antelope.

"Yes," said the boy, "my mother cooks twice a day, and I eat."

"Do you ever thank her?" said the antelope.

"No, I have never thought of that," answered the boy.

"Then you are a fool," said the antelope. "Wise men are always grateful." And he bounded off into the forest again.

Then a leopard came up and looked suspiciously at him.

"What are you doing here?" he asked crossly.

"I am very miserable," answered the boy. "I don't know if I am a wise man or a fool."

"Do they love you in your village?" asked the leopard.

"No, I don't think they do," said the boy. "I am not like other boys. I don't know them very well."

"Then you are a fool," said the leopard. "All boys are nice; I often wish *I* were a boy. Wise men mix with their fellows and earn their respect." And he walked off sniffing.

Just then the big gray elephant came shuffling along the forest path, swinging his tail as he walked, and picking a twig here and a leaf there as he passed under the trees.

"What are you doing here all alone in the jungle when the sun is setting?" he asked. "You should be at home in your village."

"I am very miserable," said the boy. "I don't know if I am a wise man or a fool."

"What work do you do?" asked the elephant.

"I don't do any work," said the boy.

"Then you are a fool," said the elephant. "All wise men work." And he swung away down the path which leads to the pool in the forest where the animals go to drink, and the boy put his head down in his hands and cried bitterly, as if his heart would break, for he did not know what to do.

After a little while he heard a gentle voice by his side. "My little brother, do not cry so; tell me your trouble." The boy raised his tear-stained face and saw a little hare standing by his side.

"I am very miserable," he said. "I am not like other people, and nobody loves me. I came into the forest to find out whether I am a wise man or a fool, and all the animals tell me I am a fool." And he put his head in his hands again and cried more bitterly than ever.

The hare let him cry on for a little while, and then he said: "My little brother, do not cry anymore. What the animals have told you is true. They have told you to think great thoughts, to be grateful and kind to others, and, above all, to work. All these things are great and wise. The animals are never idle, and they marvel to see how men, with all their gifts, waste their lives. Think how surprised they are to see a boy like you, well and strong, doing nothing all day, for they know that the world is yours if you will make it so."

The sun had set behind the distant hills and the soft darkness was falling quickly over the forest, and the hare said: "Soon it will be chilly here. You are tired and hungry, and far from your village. Come and spend the night in my home and we will talk of all these things."

So they went into the forest again, and the hare brought the boy water in a gourd and wonderful nuts to eat, and made him a soft bed of dry leaves.

And they talked of many things till the boy said, "My father is a potter, and I think I should like to be a potter too."

"If you are, you must never be content with poor work," said the hare. "Your pottery must be the best in the country. Never rest until you can make really beautiful things; no man has any right to send imperfect work out into the world."

"Nobody will believe in me when I go home; they will think I am mad," said the boy.

And the little hare answered: "Man's life is like a river, which flows always on and on. What is past is gone forever, but there is clear water behind. No man can say it is too late, and you are only a boy with your life before you."

"They will laugh at me," said the boy.

"Wise men don't mind that," said the hare. "Only fools are discouraged by laughter; you must prove to them that you are not a fool. I will teach you a song to sing at your work. It will encourage you:

> "When the shadows have melted in silver dawn,
> Farewell to my dreams of play.
> The forest is full of a waking throng,
> And the treetops ring with the birds' new song,
> And the flowers awake from their slumber long,
>   And the world is mine today.
>
> "My feet are sure and my hands are strong.
> Let me labor and toil while I may.
> When the sun shall set in a sea of light,
> And the shadows lengthen far into the night,
> I shall take the rest which is mine by right,
>   For I'll win the world today."

In the early morning the hare went with the boy to the edge of the forest and they swore an oath of friendship, which is as sacred in the jungle as among men, and the hare said: "Come back sometimes and see me, and we will spend a long day together in the forest. Come to this place and sing my song, and the birds will tell me you are there if I am too far away to hear."

So the boy went back to his village, and found his mother digging in the garden; he knelt down and greeted her as all nice children do, and saw how pleased she was. Then he went to his father, and said: "I want to be a potter. Teach me your work and I will try to learn it." And the potter was very much pleased to think that he would have a son to take on his trade after him, and all the people in the village heard and they rejoiced with the potter and his wife.

The boy worked hard, and after years he became a famous potter, and people came from all parts of the country to buy his pottery, for everyone knew that he never sold anything that was not beautiful and well made.

He made beautiful black pottery, and sometimes he put a design in white on it, and everything he made was good.

But sometimes the old dark moods would return and he would feel sick of his work and all the people round him, and then he would go away at dawn to the edge of the forest and sing the hare's song, and the little hare would come running down the forest path, and the two friends would spend a long day together, while the man would shake out his heart and all its sorrows to the hare, and he never failed to get love and comfort and encouragement in return, and went back to his work full of hope.

This all happened many years ago. Nowadays men think they are much wiser than the animals, but sometimes you may see a strange look in the eyes of an animal, as if it would say, "That man thinks he is wise, but he is only a fool." And the animals in the forests and jungles and in our houses watch everything we do, and they marvel when they see how some men waste their lives.

•

The Unfruitful Tree

Friedrich A. Krummacher

Chronic, selfish suspicion rarely wins happy success. A generous, optimistic spirit makes it easier to take the risks that lead to real reward.

A farmer had a brother in town who was a gardener, and who possessed a magnificent orchard full of the finest fruit trees, so that his skill and his beautiful trees were famous everywhere.

One day the farmer went into town to visit his brother, and was astonished at the rows of trees that grew slender and smooth as wax tapers.

"Look, my brother," said the gardener, "I will give you an apple tree, the best from my garden, and you, and your children, and your children's children shall enjoy it."

Then the gardener called his workmen and ordered them to take up the tree and carry it to his brother's farm. They did so, and the next morning the farmer began to wonder where he should plant it.

"If I plant it on the hill," said he to himself, "the wind might catch it and shake down the delicious fruit before it is ripe; if I plant it close to the road, passersby will see it and rob me of its luscious apples; but if I plant it too near the door of my house, my servants or the children may pick the fruit."

So, after he had thought the matter over, he planted the tree behind his barn, saying to himself, "Prying thieves will not think to look for it here."

But behold, the tree bore neither fruit nor blossoms the first year nor the second. Then the farmer sent for his brother the gardener, and reproached him angrily, saying: "You have deceived me and given me a barren tree instead of a fruitful one. For, behold, this is the third year and still it brings forth nothing but leaves!"

The gardener, when he saw where the tree was planted, laughed and said: "You have planted the tree where it is exposed to cold winds, and has neither sun nor warmth. How, then, could you expect flowers and fruit? You have planted the tree with a greedy and suspicious heart. How, then, could you expect to reap a rich and generous harvest?"

•

YOUR MISSION

Ellen Gates

We can go into the world with this certainty: There is much worthwhile work waiting for every one of us. But we must go to it. And when we take it up, we should remember these words from Ecclesiastes: "Whatsoever thy hand findeth to do, do it with thy might."

If you cannot on the ocean,
   Sail among the swiftest fleet,
Rocking on the highest billows,
   Laughing at the storms you meet,
You can stand among the sailors,
   Anchored yet within the bay;
You can lend a hand to help them,
   As they launch their boats away.

If you are too weak to journey
   Up the mountain, steep and high,
You can stand within the valley,
   While the multitude go by.
You can chant in happy measure,
   As they slowly pass along;
Though they may forget the singer,
   They will not forget the song.

If you have not gold and silver
   Ever ready to command,
If you cannot toward the needy
   Reach an ever-open hand,
You can visit the afflicted,
   O'er the erring you can weep;
You can be a true disciple
   Sitting at the Saviour's feet.

If you cannot in a conflict
   Prove yourself a soldier true,
If where the fire and smoke are thickest
   There's no work for you to do,
When the battlefield is silent,
   You can go with careful tread;
You can bear away the wounded,
   You can cover up the dead.

Do not stand then idly waiting
   For some greater work to do;
Fortune is a lazy goddess,
   She will never come to you.
Go and toil in any vineyard,
   Do not fear to do or dare;
If you want a field of labor,
   You can find it anywhere.

•

FOR YOU AND ME

Laura E. Richards

There is no shortage of people who are filled with all sorts of explanations about why they can't help doing what they do. They act, as Shakespeare put it, as though they were "villains on necessity, fools by heavenly compulsion." The truth is that your best guardian angels (whether they be parents, teachers, ministers, or friends) are the ones who don't buy bad excuses.

"I have come to speak to you about your work," said the Angel-who-attends-to-things. "It appears to be unsatisfactory."

"Indeed!" said the man. "I hardly see how that can be. Perhaps you will explain."

"I will!" said the Angel. "To begin with, the work is slovenly."

"I was born heedless," said the man. "It is a family failing which I have always regretted."

"It is ill put together, too," said the Angel. "The parts do not fit."

"I never had any eye for proportion," said the man. "I admit it is unfortunate."

"The whole thing is a botch," said the Angel. "You have put neither brains nor heart into it, and the result is ridiculous failure. What do you propose to do about it?"

"I credited you with more comprehension," said the man. "My faults, such as they are, were born with me. I am sorry that you do not approve of me, but this is the way I was made. Do you see?"

"I see!" said the Angel. He put out a strong white hand, and taking the man by the collar, tumbled him neck and crop into the ditch.

"What is the meaning of this?" cried the man, as he scrambled out breathless and dripping. "I never saw such behavior. Do you see what you have done? You have ruined my clothes, and nearly drowned me besides."

"Oh yes!" said the Angel. "This is the way *I* was made."

•

INDUSTRY AND SLOTH

Procrastination is not neutral between action and inaction. Procrastination *is* inaction.

A lazy young man, asked why he lay in bed so long, jocosely answered: "Every morning of my life I hear cases in court. Two fine damsels, named Industry and Sloth, are at my bedside, as soon as I awake, presenting their different cases. One entreats me to get up, the other persuades me to lie still; and then they alternately give me various reasons why I should rise and why I should not. As it is the duty of an impartial judge to hear all that can be said on both sides, I am detained so long that before the pleadings are over it is time to go to dinner."

•

RIP VAN WINKLE

Adapted from Washington Irving

Don't sleep your life away.

At the foot of the Catskill Mountains lies a little village of great antiquity, having been founded long ago by the Dutch. And in one of these houses, there lived many years since, while the country was yet a province of Great Britain, a simple, good-natured fellow by the name of Rip Van Winkle.

Now, the great error in Rip's composition was an aversion to all kinds of profitable labor. It could not be from want of perseverance, for he would sit on a wet rock, with a rod as long and heavy as a Tartar's lance, and fish all day without a murmur, even though he would not be encouraged by a single nibble. He would carry a fowling piece on his shoulder for hours together, trudging through woods and swamps, and up hill and down, to shoot a few squirrels or wild pigeons. Or he would assist the children of the village in their sports, make their playthings, fly their kites and shoot their marbles, and tell them long stories of ghosts and witches. Whenever he went dodging about the village, he was surrounded by a troop of them hanging onto his pants and clambering up his back.

He would never refuse to assist a neighbor even in the roughest toil, such as husking Indian corn, or building stone fences. The women of the village, too, used to employ him to run their errands, and to do such little odd jobs as their less obliging husbands would not do for them. In a word, Rip was ready to attend to anybody's business but his own. As to doing family duty, and keeping his farm in order, he found it impossible.

In fact, he declared it was of no use to work on his farm; it was the most pestilent little piece of ground in the whole country. Everything about it went wrong, and would go wrong, in spite of him. His fences were continually falling to pieces. His cow would go astray or get among the cabbages. Weeds were sure to grow quicker in his fields than anywhere else. The rain always made a point of setting in just as he had some outdoor work to do. And so his estate had dwindled away under his management, acre by acre, until there was little more left than a mere patch of potatoes. His children, too, were as ragged and wild as if they belonged to nobody, and promised to inherit the habits, with the old clothes, of their father.

Yes, Rip was one of those happy mortals who take the world easy, and would rather starve on a penny than work for a pound. If left to himself, he would have whistled his life away in perfect contentment. But his wife kept continually dinning in his ears about his idleness, his carelessness, and the ruin he was bringing on his family. Morning, noon, and night, her tongue was incessantly going. Rip had but one way of replying to lectures of that kind. He would shake his head, cast up his eyes, take his gun in hand, and stroll away into the woods with his old dog, Wolf, where he could enjoy some peace and quiet.

One day, on one such ramble with Wolf, he wandered far into the highest parts of the Catskills, shooting at squirrels and admiring the scenery. Before he knew it, the mountains began to throw their long blue shadows over the valleys. He saw it would be dark long before he could reach the village, and he heaved a heavy sigh when he thought of encountering the terrors of Dame Van Winkle.

He was about to descend when he heard a strange, unearthly voice calling his name: *Rip Van Winkle! Rip Van Winkle!*

Wolf bristled his back. Rip looked around but could see nothing but a crow winging its solitary flight across the mountain. He turned to descend again, when he heard the same cry ring through the still evening air: *Rip Van Winkle! Rip Van Winkle!*

And suddenly he saw a strange figure toiling slowly up the rocks, bending under the weight of something he carried on his back. He was a short, square-built old fellow, with thick, bushy hair and a grizzled beard. He was dressed in the antique Dutch fashion with a broad belt and buckles on his shoes and big, baggy britches gathered in at the knees. He bore on his shoulder a stout keg that seemed full of liquor, and made signs for Rip to approach and assist him with the load.

Rip complied with his usual alacrity and followed the old gnome, who spoke not a word but clambered farther up a narrow gully.

Deeper and deeper into the mountains they climbed, through a steep gorge. As they ascended, Rip every now and then heard long rolling peals, like distant thunder, although the sky was perfectly clear.

At last they came to a sort of amphitheater, surrounded by boulders and cliffs. And here new wonders presented themselves, for on a level spot in the center was a company of short, bearded men, all dressed in the same quaint Dutch fashion, with broad belts and high-crowned hats with feathers, red stockings, and wooden shoes. They were playing at ninepins, and whenever the balls rolled along the green turf, they echoed along the mountains like rumbling peals of thunder.

As Rip and his companion approached, they suddenly stopped their play, and stared at him with such statuelike gazes that his heart turned within him, and his knees knocked together. His companion now poured the keg's contents into cups, and made signs to Rip to wait among the company. As he did so the little men drank, wiped their beards, and in silence returned to their game.

By degrees Rip's awe subsided. He even ventured to taste the beverage, which he found to have excellent flavor. He was naturally a thirsty soul, and was soon tempted to try some more. One taste provoked another. He repeated his visits to the keg so often that at length his senses were overpowered, his eyes swam in his head, his head gradually declined, and he sank snoring upon the turf.

It was a bright, sunny morning when he woke. The birds were hopping and twittering among the bushes, and an eagle was wheeling aloft, breasting the pure mountain breeze. There was no sign of the strange little man with the keg of liquor, or the woebegone party at ninepins.

"Surely," thought Rip, "I have not slept here all night." He whistled for Wolf, but the dog had disappeared. He looked around for his gun, but in place of his well-oiled weapon, he found a rusty, worm-eaten old firelock, and he was vexed to think the little men of the mountain must have stolen his gun, and perhaps his dog too, and left him this sorry exchange.

As he rose to walk he found himself stiff in the joints. "These mountains do not agree with me," he thought.

With some difficulty he started down the mountainside, through the gorge he and his companion had ascended the previous evening. He was astonished to find that, whereas it had been dry as a bone before, a mountain stream now foamed through its bottom, leaping from rock to rock.

"I must have come up a different way," thought Rip. "This can't be right."

But at last he reached the village. As he approached he grew bewildered, for the place was greatly altered. There were houses and streets he had never seen before. Strange names were over the doors, and unfamiliar faces at the windows—everything was strange.

He met a number of people he did not know, which surprised him, for he thought himself acquainted with everyone in the country round. Their dress, too, was of a strange fashion. They all stared at him, and invariably stroked their chins when they saw him, which caused Rip to do the same—when, to his astonishment, he found his beard had grown a foot long!

A troop of children gathered at his heels, hooting after him, and pointing at his beard. He made his way to his own house and could not believe his eyes. It had gone to decay—the roof fallen in, the windows shattered, and the doors off the hinges. He called for his wife and children. The lonely chambers rang for a moment with his voice, and then all again was silence.

He hurried to his old resort, the village inn—but it too was changed. The sign of King George was still there, under which he had smoked many a peaceful pipe. But the king's coat had been changed from red to blue, the head was decorated with a cocked hat instead of a crown, and the legend underneath now read GENERAL WASHINGTON.

A crowd of people was there, as usual, but Rip knew none of them. And they were talking about things which meant nothing to his poor, addled brain—rights of citizens, elections, liberty, Bunker Hill.

They gazed with some curiosity at Rip and his long, grizzled beard, and at length crowded round him, and asked whom he was seeking.

"Where's Nicholas Vedder?" inquired Rip.

"Why, Nicholas Vedder, he is dead and gone these sixteen years!"

"Where's brother Brom Dutcher?"

"He went off to the army and never came back."

"Where's Van Brummel, the schoolmaster?"

"He went off to the wars too, was a great militia general, and is now in Congress."

Rip's heart died away at hearing these sad changes, and it dawned on him that he must have been asleep for years and years. But he cried out in despair, "Does nobody here know Rip Van Winkle?"

"Oh, Rip Van Winkle!" exclaimed two or three. "Oh, to be sure, that's Rip Van Winkle yonder, leaning against the tree."

And to his amazement he saw a precise counterpart of himself, just as he had been on the day he went up the mountain—apparently as lazy, and certainly as ragged. It was his own son! His daughter was there too; she had married a stout, cheery farmer, whom Rip recognized as one of the urchins who used to climb on his back. But his wife had long since passed away.

Rip's children gave him a home, and he became the most popular old man in the village. He took his place once more on the bench at the inn door, and people never grew tired of hearing him tell his strange story of how he slept his life away.

And who were the strange company of little gnomes who played at bowling that long-ago evening when Rip fell asleep? It is said they were spirits of the crew of old Henry Hudson, who first explored that region, and gave his name to its great river and valley. And even to this day, when the thunderstorm of a summer afternoon rolls across the Catskill Mountains, people say it is just old Henry and his fellows at their game of ninepins again.

•

THE INGRATITUDE AND INJUSTICE OF MEN TOWARDS FORTUNE

Jean de La Fontaine

It's easy to take credit for successes we meet as we journey into the world. The harder and nobler habit is accepting responsibility for failures as well.

A merchant, trading o'er the seas,
  Became enriched by every trip.
No gulf nor rock destroyed his ease;
  He lost no goods from any ship.

To others came misfortunes sad,
  For Fate and Neptune had their will.
Fortune for him safe harbors had;
  His servants served with zeal and skill.

He sold tobacco, sugar, spices,
  Silks, porcelains, or what you please;
Made boundless wealth (this phrase suffices)
  And "lived to clutch the golden keys."

'Twas luxury that gave him millions:
  In gold men almost talked to him.
Dogs, horses, carriages, postillions,
  To give this man seemed Fortune's whim.

A friend asked how came all this splendor.
  "I know the 'nick of time,' " he said,
"When to be borrower and lender:
  My care and talent all this made."

His profit seemed so very sweet,
  He risked once more his handsome gains.
But, this time, baffled was his fleet:
  Imprudent, he paid all the pains.

One rotten ship sank 'neath a storm,
  And one to watchful pirates fell;
A third, indeed, made port in form,
  But nothing wanted had to sell.

Fortune gives but one chance, we know;
  All was reversed, his servants thieves.
Fate came upon him with one blow,
  And made the mark that seldom leaves.

The friend perceived his painful case.
  "Fortune, alas!" the merchant cries.
"Be happy," says his friend, "and face
  The world, and be a little wise.

To counsel you is to give health:
  I know that all mankind impute
To Industry their peace and wealth,
  To Fortune all that does not suit."

Thus, if each time we errors make,
  That bring us up with sudden halt,
Nothing's more common than to take
  Our own for Fate or Fortune's fault.

Our good we always make by force,
  The evil fetters us so strong;
For we are always right, of course,
  And Destiny is always wrong.

•

THE DANCING HORSES OF SYBARIS
Retold by James Baldwin

From the ancient Greek city Sybaris we get the modern word
"sybarite," meaning someone devoted to luxury or pleasure. Singing and dancing and having fun are fine, but as we see here,
preparation for life must include readiness for sterner stuff as well.
This story takes place around 510 B.C.

In the south of Italy there was once a flourishing Greek colony
called Sybaris. The town was well situated for commerce, the surrounding country was very fertile, the climate was the finest in the
world, and for some centuries the Sybarites were industrious and
enterprising, carrying on a profitable trade with other countries
and heaping up immense wealth. But too much good fortune finally
proved their ruin. Little by little they lost their habits of labor and
thrift and, instead, gave themselves up to pleasure. Finally, leaving
all kinds of necessary work to their slaves, they laid aside the cares
of life, and spent their days in eating and drinking, in dancing and
in listening to fine music, or in attending the circus and watching
the feats of acrobats and performing animals.

It is said, indeed, that prizes were offered to any man who
would invent some new kind of amusement. A certain flute player
hit upon the idea of teaching the horses to dance, and since those
creatures were as fond as their masters of pleasure, he found it a
very easy thing to do. It was not long before the sound of a pipe
would set the heels of every warhorse in the country to beating
time with it. Imagine, if you please, a whole nation of dancing
people and dancing horses—what a free-from-care time of it they
must have had!

But the most pleasant summer must come to an end, even for
grasshoppers. The Sybarites had for neighbors a community of hard
workers, students, and tradesmen, called Crotoniates, who lived
temperately, drank water from the original Croton River, listened
to lectures by Pythagoras, and looked with longing eyes upon the
fair gardens and stately white palaces of Sybaris. The Crotoniates
several times came to blows with the Sybarites; but as their army
was much smaller, and they had no cavalry whatever, they were

beaten in every battle. Their foot soldiers were of no use at all when opposed to the onsets of the Sybarite warhorses.

But true worth is sure to win in the end. When a spy reported to the Crotoniates that he had seen all the horses in Sybaris dancing to the music of a pipe, the Croton general saw his opportunity at once. He sent into the Sybarite territories a large company of shepherds and fifers armed with nothing but flutes and shepherds' pipes, while a little way behind them marched the rank and file of the Crotoniate army. When the Sybarites heard that the enemy's forces were coming, they marshaled their cavalry—the finest in the world at that time—and sallied forth to meet them.

They thought it would be fine sport to send the Crotoniates scampering back across the fields into their own country, and half of Sybaris went out to see the fun. What an odd sight it must have been—a thousand fancifully dressed horsemen, splendidly mounted, riding out to meet an array of unarmed shepherds and a handful of ragged foot soldiers!

The Sybarite ladies wave their handkerchiefs and cheer their champions to the charge. The horsemen sit proudly in their saddles, ready at a word to make the grand dash—when, hark! a thousand pipes begin to play not "Yankee Doodle" or "Rule Britannia" but the national air of Crotona, whatever that may be. The order is given to charge; the Sybarites shout and drive their spurs into their horses' flanks—what fine sport it is going to be! But the war steeds hear nothing, care for nothing, but the music. They lift their slender hoofs in unison with the inspiring strains.

And now the armed Crotoniates appear on the field, but the pipers still pipe, and the horses still dance—they caper, curvet, caracole, pirouette, waltz, trip the light fantastic hoof, forgetful of everything but the delightful harmony. The Sybarite riders have been so sure of the victory that they have taken more trouble to ornament than to arm themselves. Some of them are pulled from their dancing horses by the Crotoniate footmen; others slip to the ground and run as fast as their nerveless legs will carry them back to the shelter of the city walls. The shepherds and fifers retreat slowly toward Crotona, still piping merrily, and the sprightly horses follow them, keeping step with the music.

The dancing horses cross the boundary line between the two countries; they waltz over the Crotoniate fields, they caracole gaily through the Crotoniate gates, and when the fifers cease their playing the streets of Crotona are full of fine warhorses!

Thus it was that the Sybarites lost the fine cavalry of which they had been so proud. The complete overthrow of their power and the conquest of their city by the Crotoniates followed soon afterward —for how, in any contest between so idle and so industrious a community, could it have been otherwise?

•

THE MAN WHO LOVED WAR TOO MUCH

Adapted from a retelling by F. J. Gould

Courage and perseverance are great virtues to bring to a struggle, but only when the struggle has a worthy aim. From the restless fighting of Pyrrhus (319–272 B.C.) we get the expression "Pyrrhic victory," a win gained at too great a cost. This retelling is based on an account by the ancient historian Plutarch.

Once Pyrrhus, king of Epirus in ancient Greece, was listening to two flute players. One played a lively melody, the other a somber tune. When they were done, one of the musicians asked the king which air he liked best.

"Neither," answered Pyrrhus. "The song I like best is the song of sword clashing on sword, and the tune of an arrow leaving the bow."

Pyrrhus loved the joy of battle. He was too restless to stay in his own land and look after the comfort of his own people. His passion was to subdue foreign kingdoms, to add more and more territories to his own. He longed to conquer as Alexander the Great had conquered. As soon as one war was done, he began another, and though he was often beaten, he never shrank from fighting again.

Eventually he made up his mind to pit his strength against Rome. He readied his fleet and prepared to sail. Just before he went aboard, a friend said to him: "The Romans are fierce fighters. But even if the gods favor you, and you beat them, what will you do then?"

"I shall go up and down Italy, and every town will surrender to me."

"And what then?"

"Next, I'll make myself master of the fruitful isle of Sicily."

"Will that be the end?"

"No. Then I'll be ready to cross the sea to Africa and capture the great city of Carthage."

"And after that?"

"I'll march against Macedonia, a country I've long wished to add to my domain."

"And after that?"

"Why, after that, we shall take our ease, make merry, and give thanks for our great fortune."

"Then had we not better take our ease, make merry, and give thanks for our fortune now, instead of looking for so many fights? Why not rest now, instead of seeing so many lands ruined, so many lives lost?"

Pyrrhus turned away from his friend.

He landed on the shores of Italy with a vast army. The Romans marched forward to meet him. The fighting was furious. Battle after battle raged. After one great contest the day belonged to Pyrrhus, but the loss of life was dreadful. As he walked the field, surveying the heaps of dead, one of his officers congratulated him on the triumph.

Pyrrhus smiled grimly. "One more victory like this," he said, "and we are ruined." From that time, a battle won at too great a price has been called a Pyrrhic victory.

At last he was forced to leave Italy, and then to abandon Sicily, and so he took ship and carried his beaten army—what was left of it—back to Epirus. Still he could not rest. He went to war with

Macedonia and conquered the land of Alexandria, but the Macedonian king managed to regain his kingdom. Pyrrhus went to the Peloponnesus and fought against the Spartans, but they drove him from their territory. The fighting went on and on.

The last campaign was against the Greek city of Argos. The end was inglorious. The battle raged through the streets, and Pyrrhus was in the thick of it. An old woman threw a tile from the roof of her house, and it struck the warrior king on the head. He staggered, stunned and defenseless. The enemy closed in. Seconds later he was dead.

And so he was never able to "take his ease, make merry, and give thanks for his great fortune."

•

WOO SING AND THE MIRROR

Retold by Mary H. Davis and Cheow-Leung

This story from China illustrates an ancient proverb from that land: The fire you kindle against another often burns you more than it burns him. For some people, controlling temper is the hardest kind of self-discipline.

One day Woo Sing's father brought home a mirror from the great city.

Woo Sing had never seen a mirror before. It was hung in the room while he was out at play, so when he came in he did not understand what it was, and thought he saw another boy.

This made him very happy, for he thought the boy had come to play with him.

He spoke to the stranger in a very friendly way, but received no reply.

He laughed and waved his hand at the boy in the glass, who did the same thing, in exactly the same way.

Then Woo Sing thought, "I will go closer. It may be that he does not hear me." But when he began to walk, the other boy imitated him.

Woo Sing stopped to think about these strange actions, and he said to himself, "This boy mocks me; he does everything that I do." And the more he thought about it, the angrier he became, and soon he noticed that the boy became angry too.

So Woo Sing grew very much enraged and struck the boy in the glass, but he only hurt his hand and he went crying to his father.

The father said, "The boy you saw was your own image. This should teach you an important lesson, my son. Try not to lose your temper with other people. You struck the boy in the glass and hurt only yourself.

"Now, remember that in real life when you strike without cause you will hurt yourself most of all."

THE AMERICAN BOY

Theodore Roosevelt

Many boys and young men want everyone to think they are tough. Well, here is the right kind of toughness. This old-fashioned essay with its old-fashioned language expresses sentiments much in need today. It was written by one of our toughest presidents.

Of course what we have a right to expect of the American boy is that he shall turn out to be a good American man. Now, the chances are strong that he won't be much of a man unless he is a good deal of a boy. He must not be a coward or a weakling, a bully, a shirk, or a prig. He must work hard and play hard. He must be clean-minded and clean-lived, and able to hold his own under all circumstances and against all comers. It is only on these conditions that he will grow into the kind of American man of whom America can be really proud. . . .

There is no need for a boy to preach about his own good conduct and virtue. If he does he will make himself offensive and ridiculous. But there is urgent need that he should practice decency; that he should be clean and straight, honest and truthful, gentle and tender, as well as brave. If he can once get to a proper understanding of things, he will have a far more hearty contempt for the boy who has begun a course of feeble dissipation, or who is untruthful, or mean, or dishonest, or cruel, than this boy and his fellows can possibly, in return, feel for him. The very fact that the boy should be manly and able to hold his own, that he should be ashamed to submit to bullying without instant retaliation, should, in return, make him abhor any form of bullying, cruelty, or brutality.

The boy can best become a good man by being a good boy—not a goody-goody boy, but just a plain good boy. I do not mean that he must love only the negative virtues; I mean he must love the positive virtues also. "Good," in the largest sense, should include whatever is fine, straightforward, clean, brave, and manly. The best boys I know—the best men I know—are good at their studies or their business, fearless and stalwart, hated and feared by all that is wicked and depraved, incapable of submitting to wrongdoing, and equally incapable of being aught but tender to the weak and helpless. A healthy-minded boy should feel hearty contempt for the coward, and even more hearty indignation for the boy who bullies girls or small boys, or tortures animals. One prime reason for abhorring cowards is because every good boy should have it in him to thrash the objectionable boy as the need arises.

Of course the effect that a thoroughly manly, thoroughly straight and upright boy can have upon the companions of his own age, and upon those who are younger, is incalculable. If he is not thoroughly manly, then they will not respect him, and his good qualities will count for but little; while, of course, if he is mean, cruel, or wicked, then his physical strength and force of mind merely make him so much the more objectionable a member of society. He cannot do good work if he is not strong and does not try with his whole heart and soul to count in any contest; and his strength will be a curse to himself and to everyone else if he does not have thorough command over himself and over his own evil passions, and if he does not use his strength on the side of decency, justice, and fair dealing.

In short, in life, as in a football game, the principle to follow is:

Hit the line hard; don't foul and don't shirk, but hit the line hard!

•

THE STAG AT THE POOL

Aesop

**"Know thyself" was one of the most important dictates of the
ancient Greek philosophers. Take the time to learn your true
strengths and real weaknesses.**

A thirsty Stag came to a spring to drink. As he drank, he looked
into the pool of water and saw himself. He was very proud of his
horns when he saw how big they were and what branches they had.
But he looked at his feet, and took it hard that they should be so
thin and weak.

Now, while he was thinking about these things, a Lion sprang
out and began to chase him. The Stag turned and ran. As he was
very fleet, he outran the Lion so long as they were on the open
plain. But when they came to a wooded place, the Stag's horns
became caught in the branches of the trees. He could not run, and
the Lion caught up with him.

As the Lion fell upon him with his claws, the Stag cried out:
"What a wretch am I! I was made safe by the very parts I scorned,
and have come to my end by the parts I gloried in!"

•

THE ACHILLES HEEL

Adapted from a retelling by James Baldwin

**This famous story from Greek mythology reminds us that every
human being has a place where he can be hurt, and that even the
strongest need to be aware of their own vulnerability. We should
also remember that once we've seen someone else's soft spot, we
usually do not want to hit it. In battle, taking advantage of a
weakness is smart; in everyday living, it's often cruel.**

Mightiest of all the Greeks who went to fight the Trojans was Achilles. He was the son of King Peleus and the sea nymph Thetis, and when he was born a soothsayer predicted that his life, though glorious, would be short.

His mother determined to prove the prophecy wrong, and that her son would never die. With the child in her arms she went down to the gloomy kingdom of Hades. There around the underworld flowed the dark river Styx, the sacred stream by which the gods swore unbreakable oaths. If a mortal were dipped into its black waters, no sword or arrow or other weapon could ever injure him.

Thetis held the boy by the heel, between her thumb and forefinger, and gently lowered him into the stream. The mysterious river enveloped the infant hero, and hardened his flesh against all harm. In her haste to get out of that sunless world, however, the loving mother forgot that the waters had not touched the child's skin where she gripped him. And so in that heel, and only there, lay a tiny spot where he could be harmed.

She carried the babe back, and showed her work proudly to Peleus. The father's gray locks and wrinkled visage scared the child, and Peleus turned away, saying, "He is, after all, only a little whiner!" And they thereafter called him Ligyron, which means whining.

But soon Peleus sent the young Ligyron to live with the wise centaur Chiron, a creature half-man and half-horse, who had a famous school for heroes on the wooded slopes of Mount Pelion. Chiron changed the lad's name to Achilles and fed him with the hearts of lions and the marrow of bears and wild boars. The boy learned how to use the bow and manage horses, and how to take care of his own body that he might always be strong and brave. He slept in the open air, and chased wild boars through the forest, and overthrew savage robbers in mountain passes. And when he was finished at Chiron's school, he went back to his home a tall, yellow-haired youth, strong-limbed, and as graceful as he was brave. His mother wept when she saw him, for she remembered the soothsayer's prophecy. But his old father was proud of him, and took him out to show him the treasures of his palace.

"Here," said the king, "is the matchless armor of bronze which the gods gave me on my wedding day. No man has ever worn it, but soon you will be big enough for it to fit you. See this fair, round shield with many an image of beauty engraved upon it, and this helmet with its nodding horsehair plume—was ever anything so delightful to a young warrior's eye? And here is the ashen spear which your arms will soon be able to hurl. And, lastly, here are Swift and Old Gold, the noblest steeds that any mortal ever owned. All these things are yours, my son!"

And so Achilles grew up to be one of the greatest heroes. He sailed with the Greeks in the long war against Troy, and there proved himself to be the champion of his people. But as strong as he was, and as brave as he was, he was not perfect—as no mortal is. He wanted to make sure everyone knew he was the strongest and bravest. He thought and talked too much of his own glory. He had a hot temper. When he did not get his way, he sat in his tent and pouted. And his doom, which the soothsayer had foretold, came soon enough.

One day, while hard fighting was going on beneath the walls of Troy, Achilles drove his chariot close up to the famous gate and stopped to taunt the unhappy Trojans who stood upon the battlements. Vainly did the faithful steed Old Gold champ upon his foaming bit and rear in his traces and strain hard against his reins; for he knew of the fate that threatened his master and wanted to carry him away from the danger. But Achilles, standing high in the chariot, boasted of his great deeds: how from the sea he had laid waste twelve cities, and from the land eleven; how he had vanquished the queen of the Amazons, and had slain Hector, the hope of the Trojans; how he had taken great spoils and countless treasures from many lands; and how, in all the world, there was no name so terrible as his, no, not even the name of the sun-bright Apollo.

But scarcely had the last rash boast passed his lips when a gleaming spear circled down upon him from above. His armor could not ward off the swift death it brought. Some say the fatal weapon was hurled from the battlements by Paris, the perfidious prince who had caused all that sad war. Others assert it came from the hands of no mortal man, but was cast from the sky by great Apollo himself, offended beyond measure by the hero's boasting. I do not know which of these stories is true, nor does it matter now. All I need say is that the missile found the one mark on the heel where it could tear the flesh. The destroyer of three and twenty cities fell headlong and helpless in the dust, as many another boaster has done since his day, and the great world went on as before. And his wonderful war steeds, no longer restrained by his voice and hand, sprang wildly away and galloped with the speed of wind across the plain.

•

THE MAN, THE BOY, AND THE DONKEY

Retold by James Baldwin

Trying to please is fine, but even the art of pleasing requires some common sense, self-discipline, and the courage to say no when necessary. This tale has been told for centuries in Africa, Asia, and Europe.

Once upon a time a man and his son were going to market, and they were leading their donkey behind them. They had not gone far when they met a farmer, who said, "You are very foolish to walk all the way to town with that lazy donkey following behind you. What is a donkey good for, if not to ride upon?"

"Well, I never thought of that," said the man, "and I am very willing to please you." So he put the boy on the donkey, and they started again on their journey.

Soon they passed some men by the roadside. "See that lazy boy," said one of them. "He rides on the donkey, and makes his poor old father walk behind."

When the man heard this, he called to the boy and said, "Stop a minute! Let us see if we cannot please these men." Then he told the boy to get off, and mounted the donkey himself.

Two women next met them, and one said to the other, "Did you ever see so lazy a man? He rides and takes his ease, while his son walks behind."

The man did not know what to do. "My son," he said, "I think we should try to please everybody, but how can we please the women and the men at the same time?" After a while he thought of a plan. He took the boy up behind him, and the donkey went jogging along with both of them on his back.

When, at last, they came into the town, a crowd of men began to jeer and point at them. The man stopped and said, "What is the matter, my good friends?"

"Matter enough!" said the men. "You ought to be ashamed of yourself for being so cruel to that donkey. It is too much for so small an animal to carry so heavy a load."

"I had not thought of that," said the man. "It does seem hard for the donkey, but then we were only trying to please some of our friends." So he and his son got off and tried to think what to do next.

They thought and thought till at last a happy idea came into their minds. They found a long pole, and tied the donkey's feet to it. Then after a great deal of hard work, they raised the pole on their shoulders. The donkey did not like this, but he could not help himself.

It was as much as the man and boy could do to carry him. But they stood up very straight, while all the people laughed at the funny sight. "I think that we are pleasing everybody now," said the man.

When they came to Market Bridge, the donkey got one of his feet loose, and kicked out. This made the boy drop his end of the pole. The donkey fell on the bridge and rolled over into the river and was drowned.

"I think, my son," said the Man, "that we may learn a lesson from all this."

"What kind of a lesson, Father?"

"Try to please everybody, and you will please nobody."

•

THE SPIDER AND THE FLY

Mary Howitt

Unfortunately, as long as there is dishonesty in the world, there will be people ready to lay traps for us. We must learn to recognize them and guard against their wiles. Not everyone who talks sweetly offers sweets.

"Will you walk into my parlor?" said the spider to the fly,
" 'Tis the prettiest little parlor that ever you did spy.
The way into my parlor is up a winding stair,
And I have many curious things to show when you are there."
"Oh, no, no," said the little fly, "to ask me is in vain,
For who goes up your winding stair, can ne'er come down again."

"I'm sure you must be weary, dear, with soaring up so high;
Will you rest upon my little bed?" said the spider to the fly.
"There are pretty curtains drawn around; the sheets are fine and
    thin,
And if you'd like to rest awhile, I'll snugly tuck you in!"
"Oh, no, no," said the little fly, "for I've often heard it said,
They never, never wake again who sleep upon your bed!"

Said the cunning spider to the fly: "Dear friend, what can I do
To prove the warm affection I've always felt for you?
I have within my pantry good store of all that's nice;
I'm sure you're very welcome—will you please to take a slice?"
"Oh, no, no," said the little fly, "kind sir, that cannot be;
I've heard what's in your pantry, and I do not wish to see."

"Sweet creature," said the spider, "you're witty and you're wise;
How handsome are your gauzy wings, how brilliant are your eyes!
I have a little looking-glass upon my parlor shelf;
If you'll step in one moment, dear, you shall behold yourself."
"I thank you, gentle sir," he said, "for what you're pleased to say,
And bidding you good morning now, I'll call another day."

The spider turned her round about, and went into her den,
For well she knew the silly fly would soon come back again;
So she wove a subtle web in a little corner sly,
And set her table ready to dine upon the fly.
Then she came out to her door again, and merrily she sings:
"Come hither, hither, pretty fly, with the pearl and silver wings;
Your robes are green and purple; there's a crest upon your head;
Your eyes are like the diamond bright, but mine are dull as lead!"

Alas! alas! how very soon this silly little fly,
Hearing her wily, flattering words, came slowly flitting by.
With buzzing wings he hung aloft, then near and nearer drew,
Thinking only of his brilliant eyes, and his green and purple hue—
Thinking only of his crested head—poor foolish thing! At last

Up jumped the cunning spider, and fiercely held him fast.
She dragged him up her winding stair, into her dismal den,
Within her little parlor—but he ne'er came out again!

And now, dear little children, who may this story read,
To idle, silly, flattering words, I pray you ne'er give heed.
Unto an evil counselor close heart and ear and eye,
And take a lesson from this tale of the spider and the fly.

•

THE WOLF AND THE LAMB

Aesop

Here is wolfish behavior, the kind that no evidence, no argument, no plea will stop. When we go into the world, we have to watch out for people like this.

A Wolf saw a Lamb drinking at a brook and set about finding some good reason for catching him. He went to a place a little higher up the stream, and called out:

"How dare you muddy the water that I am drinking!"

"How can I," said the Lamb, humbly, "when I drink with the tips of my lips only? And, besides, the water runs from you to me, not from me to you."

"Well, last night, while I was trying to sleep, you kept me awake forever with your bleating."

"But how could that be?" asked the Lamb. "I slept on the other side of the hill, inside my master's barn, with my nose nestled into my mother's side."

"Well, you called my father names a year ago," growled the Wolf, finding another reason.

"I was not born a year ago," said the poor Lamb.

"You can make all the excuses you want," said the Wolf, "but I am hungry, and shall eat you just the same." And without further ado, he gobbled up the little lamb.

Some people, having made up their minds to do wrong, will not be stopped by the best of reasons.

•

HOW THE OSTRICH GOT HIS LONG NECK

This story from Africa reminds us that choosing the wrong friends against good advice can mean big trouble.

Long ago Ostrich had a short neck, just like all the other birds. In those days Ostrich wanted more than anything to be friends with Crocodile. All the other birds warned Ostrich he was making a mistake.

"You can't trust Crocodile," Monkey said. "He's mean, and has no manners, and scares all the other animals away from the river."

"He's lazy, too," Wildebeest warned. "All he does is lie around all day, basking in the sun and waiting for dinner."

"And he thinks only of himself," Elephant added. "He'll snap at you as soon as you turn your back. No, Crocodile can't be trusted."

But Ostrich paid no attention at all and insisted on playing with Crocodile.

One day Crocodile was quite hungry, for he had skipped breakfast that very morning. So he said to Ostrich: "My good friend, I have a terrible toothache today. Would you mind sticking your head into my mouth and seeing what's wrong with me?"

He opened his jaws wide, very wide.

"Why, of course, dear Crocodile," Ostrich said.

And he stuck his head inside.

"But you have so many teeth!" Ostrich called. "Which is the one that aches?"

"It's one in the back," Crocodile moaned. "Look in the back!"

So Ostrich stuck his head in further.

"It's awfully dark in here," he called out again. "And so many teeth! I'm still not sure which one aches."

"It's in the very, very back," Crocodile assured him. "Go back just a little more."

So Ostrich stuck his head in even further.

"Here?" he called.

"There!" Crocodile shouted. And he snapped his jaws shut on poor Ostrich's head!

"Help!" Ostrich yelled, and he pulled as hard as he could to get his head out. But Crocodile pulled right back.

They both pulled, and they pulled. Ostrich pulled one way, and Crocodile pulled the other. And as they pulled, Ostrich's neck began to stretch.

And s–t–r–e–t–c–h.

And S—T—R—E—T—C—H!

They pulled all day long, and Ostrich's neck grew longer and longer. It must have hurt quite a bit, but Ostrich kept pulling all the same, because of course he did not want to lose his head.

At last Crocodile got tired of pulling and let go. Ostrich jumped back and ran away from the river as fast as he could. And to this day he has a long neck to remind him to stay away from the likes of Crocodile.

•

A SOUND FOR A SMELL

The world is full of people who will try to get something they don't deserve—often, money they haven't earned. Here is wisdom that recognizes the false claims of greed. Various versions of this tale are told throughout Africa, Asia, and other parts of the world.

A poor traveler stopped at midday to rest in the shade of a spreading tree. He had journeyed far and had only a single piece of bread left for his lunch. But across the road stood a stall where a baker sold rich pastries and cakes, and the traveler enjoyed inhaling the fragrances wafting across the way while he munched on his thin, stale morsel.

When he rose to continue his journey, the baker suddenly ran across the road and seized him by the collar.

"Just a minute!" the baker cried. "You must pay me for my cakes!"

"What do you mean?" the startled traveler protested. "I haven't touched your cakes."

"You thief!" the baker shouted. "It's perfectly obvious you've enjoyed your own stale biscuit only by sniffing the pleasant odors of my bakery. You won't leave until you've paid me for what you've taken. I don't work for nothing, my friend."

A crowd gathered and urged the two to take their dispute before the local judge, who was a wise old man. The judge listened to their arguments, thought a long time, then rendered his judgment.

"You are right," he told the baker. "This traveler has savored the fruits of your labor. I rule the smell of your cakes is worth three gold coins."

"That's absurd!" the traveler objected. "Besides, I've spent all my money on my journey. I don't have a penny to pay."

"Ah," said the judge, "in that case I will help you." He pulled three gold coins from his own pocket, which the baker quickly reached to take.

"Not yet," said the judge. "You say this traveler merely smelled your cakes?"

"That's right," replied the baker.

"But he never swallowed a bite?"

"I told you he did not."

"He never tasted a pastry?"

"No!"

"And never touched your pies?"

"No!"

"Then since he has consumed only vapors, you must be paid with sound. Open your ears and receive what you deserve."

The wise judge let the gold coins tumble from one hand to the other so that their tingling entered the baker's greedy ears.

"If you had been kind enough to help this poor man along his way," the judge said, "then truly you would have found golden reward in Heaven."

•

PROCRUSTES THE PITILESS
Retold by James Baldwin

When we last saw Theseus in Chapter One, he had left home and set out to find his father in Athens. The road was long and full of surprises, even terror. Like most of us, Theseus soon learned that the world can be a dangerous place. Sometimes we meet those who would do us harm. It takes good judgment to recognize

**them, and courage and strength to overcome them. From the
villain Procrustes we get the expression "procrustean bed," meaning a situation into which we are violently or arbitrarily forced.**

Athens was now not more than twenty miles away, but the road
led through the Parnes Mountains, and was only a narrow path
winding among the rocks and up and down many a lonely wooded
glen. Theseus had seen worse and far more dangerous roads than
this, and so he strode bravely onward, happy in the thought that he
was so near the end of his long journey. But it was very slow
traveling through the mountains, and he was not always sure that
he was following the right path. The sun was almost down when he
came to a broad green valley where the trees had been cleared
away. A little river flowed through the middle of this valley, and on
either side were grassy meadows where cattle were grazing; and on
a hillside close by, half hidden among the trees, there was a great
stone house with vines running over its walls and roof.

While Theseus was wondering who it could be that lived in
this pretty but lonely place, a man came out of the house and
hurried down to the road to meet him. He was a well-dressed man,
and his face was wreathed with smiles. He bowed low to Theseus
and kindly invited him to come up to the house and be his guest
that night.

"This is a lonely place," he said, "and it is not often that travelers pass this way. But there is nothing that gives me so much joy as
to find strangers and feast them at my table and hear them tell of
the things they have seen and heard. Come up, and sup with me,
and lodge under my roof; and you shall sleep on a wonderful bed
which I have—a bed which fits every guest and cures him of every
ill."

Theseus was pleased with the man's ways, and as he was both
hungry and tired, he went up with him and sat down under the
vines by the door. The man said: "Now I will go in and make the
bed ready for you, and you can lie down upon it and rest. And later,
when you feel refreshed, you shall sit at my table and sup with
me, and I will listen to the pleasant tales which I know you will
tell."

When he had gone into the house, Theseus looked around
him to see what sort of a place it was. He was filled with surprise at
the richness of it—at the gold and silver and beautiful things with

which every room seemed to be adorned—for it was indeed a place fit for a prince. While he was looking and wondering, the vines before him were parted and the fair face of a young girl peeped out.

"Noble stranger," she whispered, "do not lie down on my master's bed, for those who do so never rise again. Fly down the glen and hide yourself in the deep woods ere he returns, or else there will be no escape for you."

"Who is your master, fair maiden, that I should be afraid of him?" asked Theseus.

"Men call him Procrustes, or the Stretcher," said the girl—and she talked low and fast. "He is a robber. He brings here all the strangers that he finds traveling through the mountains. He puts them on his iron bed. He robs them of all they have. No one who comes into his house ever goes out again."

"Why do they call him the Stretcher? And what is that iron bed of his?" asked Theseus, in no way alarmed.

"Did he not tell you that it fits all guests?" said the girl. "Most truly it does fit them. For if a traveler is too long, Procrustes hews off his legs until he is of the right length; but if he is too short, as is the case with most guests, then he stretches his limbs and body with ropes until he is long enough. It is for this reason that men call him the Stretcher."

"Methinks that I have heard of this Stretcher before," said Theseus. Then he remembered that someone had warned him to beware of the wily robber Procrustes, who lurked in the glens of the Parnes peaks and lured travelers into his den.

"Hark! hark!" whispered the girl. "I hear him coming!" And the vine leaves closed over her hiding place.

The very next moment Procrustes stood in the door, bowing and smiling as though he had never done any harm to his fellow men.

"My dear young friend," he said, "the bed is ready, and I will show you the way. After you have taken a pleasant little nap, we will sit down at table, and you may tell me of the wonderful things which you have seen in the course of your travels."

Theseus arose and followed his host. When they had come into an inner chamber, there, surely enough, was the bedstead of iron, very curiously wrought, and upon it a soft mattress which seemed to invite him to lie down and rest. But Theseus, peering about, saw the ax and the ropes with cunning pulleys lying hidden behind the curtains; and he saw, too, that the floor was covered with stains of blood.

"Now, my dear young friend," said Procrustes, "I pray you to lie down and take your ease, for I know that you have traveled far and are faint from want of rest and sleep. Lie down, and while sweet slumber overtakes you, I will have a care that no unseemly noise, or buzzing fly, or vexing gnat disturbs your dreams."

"Is this your wonderful bed?" asked Theseus.

"It is," answered Procrustes, "and you need but lie down upon it, and it will fit you perfectly."

"But you must lie upon it first," said Theseus, "and let me see how it will fit itself to your stature."

"Ah, no," said Procrustes, "for then the spell would be broken," and as he spoke his cheeks grew ashy pale.

"But I tell you, you must lie upon it," said Theseus, and he seized the trembling man around the waist and threw him by force upon the bed. No sooner was he prone upon the couch than curious iron arms reached out and clasped his body in their embrace and held him down so that he could not move hand or foot. The wretched man shrieked and cried for mercy, but Theseus stood over him and looked him straight in the eye.

"Is this the kind of bed on which you have your guests lie down?" he asked.

But Procrustes answered not a word. Then Theseus brought out the ax and the ropes and the pulleys, and asked him what they were for, and why they were hidden in the chamber. Procrustes was still silent, and could do nothing now but tremble and weep.

"Is it true," said Theseus, "that you have lured hundreds of travelers into your den only to rob them? Is it true that it is your wont to fasten them in this bed, and then chop off their legs or stretch them out until they fit the iron frame? Tell me, is this true?"

"It is true! it is true!" sobbed Procrustes. "Now kindly touch the spring above my head and let me go, and you shall have everything that I possess."

But Theseus turned away. "You are caught," he said, "in the trap which you set for others and for me. There is no mercy for the man who shows no mercy." And he went out of the room and left the wretch to perish by his own cruel device.

Theseus looked through the house and found there great wealth of gold and silver and costly things which Procrustes had taken from the strangers who had fallen into his hands. He went into the dining hall, and there indeed was the table spread with a rich feast of meats and drinks and delicacies such as no king would scorn, but there was a seat and a plate for only the host and none at all for guests.

Then the girl whose fair face Theseus had seen among the vines came running into the house. She seized the young hero's hands and blessed and thanked him because he had rid the world of the cruel Procrustes.

"Only a month ago," she said, "my father, a rich merchant of Athens, was traveling toward Eleusis, and I was with him, happy and carefree as any bird in the green woods. This robber lured us into his den, for we had much gold with us. My father he stretched upon his iron bed, but me he made his slave."

Then Theseus called together all the inmates of the house, poor wretches whom Procrustes had forced to serve him. He divided the robber's spoils among them and told them they were free to go wheresoever they wished. And on the next day he went on, through the narrow crooked ways among the mountains and hills, and came at last to the plain of Athens, and saw the noble city and, in its midst, the rocky height where the great Temple of Athena stood. And, a little way from the temple, he saw the white walls of the palace of the king.

•

ONE WORD AGAINST ANOTHER

Here's a real bold-faced lie. Some people act on the theory that if they hold their heads high enough, no one will question their lies. This Arab tale echoes a remark by Ralph Waldo Emerson: "The louder he talked of his honor, the faster we counted our spoons."

One day a neighbor knocked on the town mayor's door and asked, "Will you lend me your donkey for a while?"

"My good friend," the mayor replied, "you know there is nothing in the world I wouldn't do for you. I'd love to lend you my donkey. But I'm afraid he's away today."

Just then the donkey gave a bray loud enough to wake the dead.

"Well, this is my lucky day," said the neighbor. "It seems your donkey is here after all."

"How dare you!" protested the mayor, puffing up with shocked indignation. "Are you going to believe my donkey and doubt me, a man of distinction and status?"

•

FISH OR CAT?

This Arab tale reminds us that honesty is the best policy, if for no other reason than truth has a way of coming out in the end.

A man went at sunrise to his favorite spot on the river, cast his line, and pulled in a fat, shining fish. It weighed exactly six pounds.

He took it home and proudly showed it to his wife.

"Prettiest fish I ever caught," he said. "Six pounds of pure pleasure. I'll cook a grand feast tonight." Then he left the house and went to work.

His wife could not take her eyes off the fish. It made them water, it looked so tempting. At last she couldn't stand it any longer. She cooked it and sent for her brother, and they gorged themselves until there wasn't a morsel left.

That evening the man came home to find no fish.

"I'm so sorry," his wife cried, "but while I was in the garden the cat got into the kitchen and ate the whole thing, from head to tail!"

The man seized the cat and plopped it on a scale. It weighed exactly six pounds.

"If this is my fish, then where is the cat?" he asked. "And if this is the cat, then I wonder just where my fish might be."

•

THE THREE RIOTERS

Adapted from Geoffrey Chaucer

Unfortunately, there are some people (often young men) who go
into the world looking for trouble, and it usually finds them. This
famous story, "The Pardoner's Tale" from Chaucer's *Canterbury
Tales,* may help us choose the kind of people we want to be with
both in friendship and at work.

In Flanders there once lived a company of young men who
gave themselves over to folly and wrongdoing. They lounged about
the taverns all day, drinking, swearing, singing, dancing, and gam-
bling. And their gluttony and idleness made them so wicked that
when they heard of any other wrong thing, they not only laughed
at it but went straightway and sought out the sin for themselves.

Three of these rioters, of whom I have spoken, were sitting at
the tavern drinking, early one morning, when they chanced to hear
a bell ring. It was being carried at the head of a funeral procession
—as was the custom in those days. One of the rioters thereupon
called the tavern boy to him and said: "Go out and ask the name
of the dead man who passes by. And look you, report it to me
speedily."

"Sir," quoth the lad, "I do not need to ask, as the name was
told me here not two hours agone. He was, in sooth, a mate of
yours, and was slain only last night, while he sat here drinking, by
that prowling thief called Death who lays low all the people in this
country. With his spear he smote his heart in two and went his way
in silence. This very pestilence has slain thousands; and, master, ere
you come into his sight it were well that you be prepared to meet
him. For so my mother teaches me."

"By holy Mary, the child speaks truth," said the innkeeper, "for
Death hath slain both man and woman, child and page, to be found
in a large village within a mile of here. I think he must live there,
so many have met their end."

"Odds boddikins!" cried one of the rioters, springing up, "is
it then so great a peril to meet him? *I'll* seek him out, by hedge
and highway—and to this I make my vow! Hearken ye, my mates,
for we three are one in this. Let each of us hold up his hand and

swear to become the other's brother; and we will seek out and slay this traitor Death, who by stealth has slain so many of our friends."

The others loudly cheered him in their drunken way, and took the oath to stand together and make an end of Death before night-fall. So they started up at once and directed their steps toward the village of which the host had spoken; and many an oath they swore, on the way, of what they should accomplish.

They had not gone more than half a mile when they came to a stile, where they met a poor old man, who greeted them civilly enough with: "God be with you, my lordings."

But the proudest of these three rioters made answer: "Why, how now, churl! Why is your bag of bones so wrapped up, clear to your face? And how do you manage to hang on to life so long?"

The old man gave him a straight look and said: "I live thus because I cannot find—either in city or in village, though I walked to India—anyone who will change his youth for my age. And so I must still keep my age as long as it is God's will, for Death, alas! will not come and take me. Thus I go up and down, a restless wanderer."

Here the old man drew himself up with dignity and added: "But, sirs, it shows no courtesy in you to speak to one of my years so rudely, since he has done you no harm in word or deed. In Holy Writ you may read for yourselves that ye should respect the gray hairs of the aged. I have no more to say, but must go on my way."

"Nay, old churl, *that* you shall not do," said another of the gamesters with an oath. "You have just spoken of that arch traitor Death who has been slaying all our friends in the country round about. Belike you are his spy, so tell us where he is or it shall go hard with you!"

"Nay, sirs," replied graybeard, "speak not so rashly for your souls' good. But if you are so set upon finding Death, I can tell you which way to go. Turn up this crooked bypath; for in yonder grove I saw him sitting beneath a tree, and there he will abide for all your boasts. See ye that oak? Close by it ye shall find him. God save you, sirs, who would benefit mankind, and mend you all!"

But before the old man had quite finished his speech the three rioters turned and ran toward the oak he had shown them. There they saw no one; but on the ground they discovered a heap of golden coins, bright and round—well-nigh seven bushels of them, they thought. So delighted were they to see this great heap of glittering gold that they speedily forgot all about Death, whom they had been seeking. But Death was nearby, for all that, and did not forget them, as you shall see.

Down they squatted by this precious hoard and dug their fingers deep into it, and let the coins trickle through their fingers hungrily. The worst of the three was the first to speak a word.

"Brothers," said he, "take heed to what I say. This treasure will make our fortune, so that we may spend all the rest of our lives in mirth and jollity. Lightly as it comes we'll lightly spend. By heaven, who would have thought we should tumble into such luck!"

Thereupon he counseled them with rare cunning that they should not try to carry the treasure off in the daytime, lest they should be arrested for thieves. Instead, he advised that they draw lots, and the one chosen should go back to town for meat and drink, while the other two should remain in the grove and hide the gold until nightfall.

The counsel seemed good to the others, and they drew, and the lot fell to the youngest to go back for food. He therefore started without loss of time.

No sooner was he out of sight than the first speaker said to the other: "You know well that you are my sworn brother, so I will tell you something to your profit. Here is bright gold heaped up plentifully which is to be divided among three of us. But one of us is away, and if I can shape it so that the gold need only be divided between *two,* have I not done you a friendly turn?"

The other listened greedily but answered: "I know not how it can be done. Our mate knows all about the gold, and we couldn't fool him."

"Well, I can tell you how, and that in a few words, if you'll keep it dark," said the first one.

"Tell away," said the other. "I shall not betray you."

The first one tapped him on the shoulder and said in a low voice: "Look you, there are two of us, and two are stronger than one. When the youngster comes back we will make a game of him. You can pretend to wrestle with him while he is sitting down, and I will watch my chance and stab him. Then draw your dagger and do the same. After that, my dear friend, there will be only two of us to share the gold."

The other ruffian nodded his head at this, and so they plotted to murder the third in cold blood.

Meanwhile the young man who had gone to town was not idle

in wickedness, for all the way there he could not get his mind off the beauty of those new bright coins of gold.

"Oh Lord!" said he to himself, "if I could only devise a plan so that I might have all this treasure for myself, I should be the merriest fellow under the canopy of heaven!"

At last the fiend, our common enemy, put it into his head that he should buy poison and thus make an end of both his fellows. The fiend knew he would do this wicked thing for the sake of all the gold, and that he never would repent.

So the young man lost no time in going to an apothecary's shop, in the town, and he asked, plausibly enough, for some rat poison. He said there was a polecat roaming in his yard, which had carried off his fat geese, and he wanted some poison strong enough to kill the beast.

The apothecary answered: "You shall have something so strong that no living creature in this world could withstand it—even if he took an amount no greater than a grain of wheat."

The wretched plotter was secretly glad to hear this and bought the poison without delay. Then in the next street he bought three large bottles of wine. Into two of them he put the poison, while he kept the third pure for his own use. For he purposed to toil all night at carrying and hiding the gold away, after he had brought his comrades to a violent end.

When he had prepared his three bottles, he bought some meat also and went back to the other two rioters laden as if to dine.

What need is there of telling the rest? For as the other two had already planned, they slew the young man without delay.

When the bloody deed was done, the first one said: "Ha! now

that the young fool is out of the way, let us sit and drink and make us merry, and afterward we can bury the body."

And with the word he picked up one of the bottles which contained the poison. He drank deeply and gave it to his companion. The apothecary had told true. Within a little while the poison took effect and they both died in fearful agony.

Thus ended the two murderers, slain by the man they had murdered. And thus came Death—whom they had forgot—to seek his own at the last.

•

THE CAMEL'S NOSE

Sometimes trouble comes looking for us. This tale gives us some advice about how to keep trouble at bay.

One cold night, as a sheik lay in his tent, a camel thrust the flap aside and looked in.

"I pray thee, master," he said, "let me put my nose within the tent, for it is cold outside."

"By all means," yawned the sheik, who was bored and listless from having reposed on his pillows all day. "Do so if you wish."

The camel poked his nose into the tent.

"If I might but warm my neck also," he said presently.

"It's all the same to me," answered the sheik. So the beast stuck his neck inside, and contented itself for a while by looking about.

Soon the camel, who had been turning his head from side to side, spoke up again.

"It will take but little more room if I put my forelegs within the tent. I would feel a great deal better."

The sheik simply shrugged and rolled to one side to make a little more room.

The camel had hardly planted his forefeet within the tent when he said: "Master, I'm keeping the flap open by standing here like this. I think I ought to come all the way inside."

"Whatever you like," the sheik nodded, moving over some more so the beast might enter.

So the camel came forward and crowded into the tent. No sooner was he inside than he looked hard at the sheik.

"I think," he said, "that there is not enough room for both of us here. It will be best for you to stand outside, as you are the smaller. Then there will be room enough for me."

And with that he pushed the sheik out into the cold and darkness.

It is a wise rule to resist the beginnings of evil.

•

THE TWO TRAVELERS AND THE OYSTER

I include this old tale because it seems especially fit for modern times. It reminds us, as the English essayist Samuel Butler said, that in law nothing is certain but the expense. In the end, it's less costly simply to act honestly and responsibly.

As two men were walking by the seaside at low water they saw an oyster, and they both stooped at the same time to pick it up. One pushed the other away, and a dispute ensued.

A traveler was coming along at the time, and they determined to ask him which of the two had the better right to the oyster.

While each was telling his story, the traveler gravely took out his knife, opened the shell, and loosened the oyster. When they had finished, and were listening for his decision, he just as gravely swallowed the oyster, and offered them each a shell.

"The Court," said he, "awards you each a shell. The oyster will cover the costs."

•

HABIT

William James

The writer Flannery O'Connor once observed: "Time is very dangerous without a rigid routine.... Routine is a condition of survival." One of America's greatest philosophers concurs here. William James (1842–1910) reminds us that habits are forged, not inherited. And he asserts that the right kinds of habits are essential not only for survival in the world but also for the ability to do some good in the world.

No matter how full a reservoir of *maxims* one may possess, and no matter how good one's *sentiments* may be, if one has not taken advantage of every concrete opportunity to *act,* one's character may remain entirely unaffected for the better. With mere good intentions, hell is proverbially paved. And this is an obvious consequence of the principles we have laid down. A "character," as J. S. Mill says, "is a completely fashioned will"; and a will, in the sense in which he means it, is an aggregate of tendencies to act in a firm and prompt and definite way upon all the principal emergencies of life. A tendency to act becomes effectively ingrained in us only in proportion to the uninterrupted frequency with which the actions actually occur, and the brain "grows" to their use. Every time a resolve or a fine glow of feeling evaporates without bearing practical fruit is worse than a chance lost; it works so as positively to hinder future resolutions and emotions from taking the normal path of discharge. There is no more contemptible type of human character than that of the nerveless sentimentalist and dreamer, who spends his life in a weltering sea of sensibility and emotion, but who never does a manly concrete deed....

It is not simply *particular lines* of discharge, but also *general forms* of discharge, that seem to be grooved out by habit in the brain. Just as, if we let our emotions evaporate, they get into a way of evaporating; so there is reason to suppose that if we often flinch from making an effort, before we know it the effort-making capacity will be gone; and that, if we suffer the wandering of our attention, presently it will wander all the time. Attention and effort are ... but two names for the same psychic fact. To what brain processes they correspond we do not know. The strongest reason for believing that they do depend on brain processes at all, and are not pure acts of the spirit, is just this fact, that they seem in some degree subject to the law of habit, which is a material law. As a final practical maxim, relative to these habits of the will, we may, then, offer something like this: *Keep the faculty of effort alive in you by a little gratuitous exercise every day.* That is, be systematically ascetic or heroic in little unnecessary points, do every day or two something for no other reason than that you would rather not do it, so that when the hour of dire need draws nigh, it may find you not un-nerved and untrained to stand the test. Asceticism of this sort is like the insurance which a man pays on his house and goods. The tax does him no good at the time, and possibly may never bring him a return. But if the fire *does* come, his having paid it will be his salvation from ruin. So with the man who has daily inured himself to habits of concentrated attention, energetic volition, and self-denial in unnecessary things. He will stand like a tower when every-thing rocks around him, and when his softer fellow mortals are winnowed like chaff in the blast.

•

Is There a Santa Claus?

Francis P. Church

As we head further into the world, and gain more experience, we lose some of the fixtures of our childhood. But we also learn there are more things in life than we can see. This famous editorial appeared in *The New York Sun* on September 21, 1897. Many newspapers continue to reprint it around Christmastime.

We take pleasure in answering at once and thus prominently the communication below, expressing at the same time our great gratification that its faithful author is numbered among the friends of *The Sun:*

Dear Editor—I am 8 years old
Some of my little friends say there is no Santa Claus.
Papa says, "If you see it in *The Sun* it's so."
Please tell me the truth, is there a Santa Claus?
Virginia O'Hanlon
115 West 95th street.

Virginia, your little friends are wrong. They have been affected by the skepticism of a skeptical age. They do not believe except they see. They think that nothing can be which is not comprehensible by their little minds. All minds, Virginia, whether they be men's or children's, are little. In this great universe of ours man is a mere insect, an ant, in his intellect, as compared with the boundless world about him, as measured by the intelligence capable of grasping the whole of truth and knowledge.

Yes, Virginia, there is a Santa Claus. He exists as certainly as love and generosity and devotion exist, and you know that they abound and give to your life its highest beauty and joy. Alas! how dreary would be the world if there were no Santa Claus! It would be as dreary as if there were no Virginias. There would be no childlike faith then, no poetry, no romance to make tolerable this existence. We should have no enjoyment, except in sense and sight. The eternal light with which childhood fills the world would be extinguished.

Not believe in Santa Claus! You might as well not believe in fairies! You might get your papa to hire men to watch in all the chimneys on Christmas Eve to catch Santa Claus, but even if they did not see Santa Claus coming down, what would that prove? Nobody sees Santa Claus, but that is no sign there is no Santa Claus. The most real things in the world are those that neither children nor men can see. Did you ever see fairies dancing on the lawn? Of course not, but that's no proof that they are not there. Nobody can conceive or imagine all the wonders there are unseen and unseeable in the world.

You tear apart a baby's rattle and see what makes the noise inside, but there is a veil covering the unseen world which not the strongest man, nor even the united strength of all the strongest men that ever lived, could tear apart. Only faith, fancy, poetry, love, romance, can push aside that curtain and view and picture the supernal beauty and glory beyond. Is it all real? Ah, Virginia, in all this world there is nothing else real and abiding.

No Santa Claus! Thank God! he lives, and he lives forever. A thousand years from now, Virginia, nay, ten times ten thousand years from now, he will continue to make glad the heart of childhood.

Three

•

STANDING
FAST

"LOOK at a man in the midst of doubt and danger, and you will learn in his hour of adversity what he really is," wrote the Roman philosopher Lucretius. "It is then that true utterances are wrung from the recesses of his breast. The mask is torn off; the reality remains."

Some people's lives are filled with more hardship than others. But make no mistake—every life's journey has some tough stretches. Everyone is tested, everyone brought to the line. There will be occasional bumps in the road, unpleasant surprises, irritating delays, annoying mistakes and accidents. There will be days when everything seems to go wrong. ("When sorrows come, they come not single spies, but in battalions," Shakespeare observes in *Hamlet*.) And there will be those moments when our whole world seems to be falling apart. Adversity is a large part of life, and the sooner we learn to deal with it, the easier life will be for us.

This chapter helps us get ready for those times when the path suddenly gets steeper, the road rockier, when the wind and rain are at your face, and part of you wants more than anything else to turn back. At times like these, you may need almost every virtue in your arsenal to help you stand fast—perseverance, courage, self-discipline, responsibility, industry, integrity. And you may need the loyalty and friendship of one or two good companions, as well as faith in God to see you through the struggle.

We meet a few heroes in this chapter. Some are famous because of the way they stood fast in times of crisis. Others are ordinary people who stepped forward to take the tests of life we all must face. Here we find people standing firm at their posts and sticking to their assignments, even though temptation beckons them away. We witness people winning by small steps, tackling tasks piece by piece. We discover that sometimes the only way to get out of a tough spot is simply to buckle down and get to work. We see what it's like to blaze a rough trail where nobody has gone before. And we learn a few things about facing very bad situations, ones where certain pain and loss lie ahead.

Of course, virtues such as perseverance and courage must be informed by practical wisdom. You have to be able to recognize *when* the time is right to stand fast, and then you have to know *what* to do to hold your ground. The stories in this chapter, as in the last, help sharpen our intellectual virtues as well as our moral ones. We meet examples of reason giving direction to action. We learn the value of ingenuity in tough spots and fortitude under heavy fire. We see real concentration in action, a harnessing of thought and talent that brings the whole mind and whole heart to a task. And we witness the courage of imagination, the kind that dares to stick up for worthy ideas when everyone else shouts they're wrong.

If met correctly, of course, most of the troubles we encounter in life become opportunities to know and add to the strength of our virtues. The blows of adversity can be the best chances for improvement. "The gem cannot be polished without friction, nor man perfected without trials," a Chinese proverb says. Any real achievement, any worthwhile prize will probably come at the cost of a few failures. We set our sights and try and try again until we reach our goal.

The ultimate test, however, is not whether we finally reach that goal but how we conduct ourselves along the way. For sometimes the path is too steep to make it all the way to the top, and we must trust that the struggle itself was worth it and ready ourselves for new tests knowing, as the clergyman Henry Ward Beecher put it more than one hundred years ago, "We are always in the forge, or on the anvil; by trials God is shaping us for higher things."

•

THE HILL MOTHER

Adapted from a story by Katharine Pyle

**When it's time to do a daring deed, take on a tough task, or face
the unknown, there's no better ally than a loyal brother or sister.**

Once upon a time, a very, very long time ago, in a poor hut at
the edge of a forest, there lived a woodcutter and his wife and
their two little children, Peter and Roselein. The father and mother
worked hard, and Peter and Roselein helped them as best they
could by being good, and the little family was happy in their cottage
beside the woods.

One night while they were sitting in front of the fire, the father
stretched his weary back and sighed, " 'Tis a pity we should be so
poor for so long, when the gold of the Hill Mother lies somewhere
out there—piles of it to be found for the seeking."

"Who is the Hill Mother?" the children asked together.

"Don't be filling their heads full of nonsense!" cried their
mother. "The next thing you know, they'll be clambering all over
the countryside like fools, looking for pots of fool's gold."

"Tell us! Tell us!" the children begged.

So their father told them all about the Hill Mother, how she
was an old, old woman who lived under a hill, beyond the Desolate
Rocks. There she hoarded a treasure greater than anyone had ever
seen. All through the year she kept it hidden away under the hill,
but every midsummer night, when the moon was at the full, she
brought it out and counted it there by moonlight. Then, if anyone
found her, he might ask of her anything he wished, and she would
be obliged to grant it.

"But those who find her never come back," said their father.

"And why not?" cried the children.

"Well, first of all, because of her servants, the little hill men.
They will dance around you and bewitch you, so you can never
remember your way home again."

"Never?"

"Never. And on top of that, as soon as she grants your wish,
she has you in her power, and you must go down with her under
the hill."

"Forever?"

"Forever. Unless, of course, you trick her, and make her see the first morning light. Then she must let you go. But she's a crafty old hag, and no one's been able to trick her yet."

"Enough of your silly tales," scolded the mother. "Now off to bed with you two little ones, and no dreaming Hill Mothers and treasures, either."

But, of course, as soon as Peter and Roselein were in bed, they resolved to go in search of the Hill Mother's gold.

"This is midsummer, and the moon is full," whispered Peter. "We'll have to go tonight."

"But what about the little hill men?" asked Roselein. "What if they make us forget how to get home?"

"We must take something to mark the way," said Peter.

"Our pennies!" cried Roselein. She reached under the bed, and pulled out a little brown bag. It was their pennies they had saved for Christmas. "We'll take them and drop them as we go along. If we forget the way, we can follow them back."

So when the house was all dark, and their parents in bed, they opened a window and crawled out. They journeyed on and on through the forest, dropping pennies behind them, and Peter sang along the way:

> *Though forests be lonely,*
> *Though shadows be gray,*
> *A heart that is merry*
> *Will lighten the way.*

> *Though feet may be weary,*
> *And rough be the road,*
> *A heart that is merry*
> *Will lighten the load.*

And finally they came to a wide, gray country where there was nothing but rocks and twisted thorn bushes.

These were the Desolate Rocks.

And now the way grew so rough that they could hardly go on. One of Roselein's shoes was quite worn through, and great holes appeared in the sole. But she went on, singing to herself to keep up her spirits:

Past the Desolate Rocks,
  Over brier and stone,
Through mist and through moonlight
  We wander alone.

The moon's sinking low,
  And the bats are all out,
But brave heart and true heart
  Should never feel doubt.

Suddenly they saw before them the strangest-looking thorn-bush they had ever seen.

They stopped and looked at it. Soon it began to move, and they saw it was not thornbush after all, but an old woman, very gray and bent. It was the Hill Mother!

She sat in the moonlight, counting a great golden treasure that lay heaped all around her.

And in and out among the rocks shadowy figures were dancing and hopping. These were her servants, the little hill men.

As they danced, they were singing. Their voices were like the whistling of the wind through thorn branches.

The old Hill Mother paid no attention to them even when they brushed against her, but went on counting, counting her treasure.

Peter and Roselein, hidden among the rocks, lay watching and listening to the hill men's song:

As black as a thorn bush, and withered and old,
See the old Hill Mother counting her gold.
Old woman, old woman, is all of it thine?

The Hill Mother paid no heed to them, but counted on:

One hundred, twelve hundred, two thousand and nine—

Again the hill men sang:

> *Deep under the hills, with the rocks overhead,*
> *The hammers are beating, the fires burn red.*
> *Old Hill Mother, say, shall we never be free?*

Still the Hill Mother counted on:

A thousand, twelve thousand, a million and three—

The hill men sang and danced about:

> *See the old Hill Mother counting alone,*
> *As dry as a leaf and as cold as a stone!*
> *The moonlight is fading, the night has grown late.*

Two million, ten million, and thirty and eight!

counted the Hill Mother.

The hill men began calling to each other from among the rocks:

"Has a mist come over the moon, or is it sinking low?"
"It is sinking low."
"Has it yet touched the forest beyond the Desolate Rocks?"
"It still swings clear."
"Then there is time yet for the Old Hill Mother to count her treasure!" shouted all together.

But as they began dancing again, one of them spied Peter and Roselein, peering from behind their rock.

"Look, look, Long Nose," cried one to another, "there is something hiding behind a rock. Look and tell us what it is."

"I look through the moonlight," said Long Nose, "and I see what it is. It is two human beings, such as we used to be."

"How did they come here?"
"Even as we did, long ago."
"Why do they bend and stoop as they come?"

"They are looking for treasure, the Hill Mother's treasure, just as we once did!"

Shrilly the little men began singing again:

> *Who is it comes hither while dews are still cold?*
> *Two seeking the Hill Mother, seeking her gold.*
> *They have found her—have found her!*
> *Their journey is done.*
>
> *Ten billion, twelve billion, and twenty and one!*

counted the Hill Mother.

"Old Hill Mother, old Hill Mother, look up," shouted the hill men, "for someone is coming!"

Then the old Hill Mother raised her head and looked about her.

Her eyes were small and dim.

When she saw Peter and Roselein, she rose, and the gold pieces in her apron fell clinking among the rocks.

"Who are you, and what are you seeking here among the Desolate Rocks?" she croaked.

Peter told her they had come in search of the Hill Mother.

"Then you need look no further, for I am she. And now why have you come, and what would you have of me?"

"We would have you grant us a wish," answered Roselein.

"That I will," said the Hill Mother, "only you must make haste. For the moment yonder moon drops out of the sky, I must take my treasure and hide under the hill, ere the first morning light breaks overhead."

They had their wish ready, but there was one thing they wanted to know. If the Hill Mother granted it, would they have to go down under the hill with her and live there too?

"And what if you should?" cackled the Hill Mother. "Down under the hill it is wide and warm, and there you would find more treasure than you've seen in your dreams."

That might be true, but Peter and Roselein said they could not go down under the hill with her, for their parents would be waiting for them at home. If wishing a wish would make them go down under the hill, they would have to go home without it.

"Ask me your wish, ask me your wish!" cried the Hill Mother.

But they would not.

"Then come, my little hill men," cried the Hill Mother. "Weave about them in and out and round and round until they forget the way they came, for they shall never go home from the Desolate Rocks!"

And before they could escape, the little hill men had joined hands in a circle about them, and they began spinning round and round so fast that the children's heads spun, and they grew so dizzy they could hardly stand.

As they danced, the little men sang in their strange, windy voices:

> *Wing of bat and claw of beast,*
> *East be west and west be east.*
>
> *Eager hands and gaping mouth,*
> *South be north and north be south.*
>
> *Think not, children, to steal away.*
> *The Hill Mother speaks, and all obey.*

Then the hill men broke from the circle, each whirling away by himself.

Peter and Roselein stood with their hands to their heads. Think and think as they would, they could not remember the way home.

"Now you have forgotten the way you came," cried the Hill Mother, "so you had better ask me your wish, and then come down under the hill with me willingly, for come you must."

"Very well," said Roselein. "Then our wish is that you should fill my shoe with gold."

The old Hill Mother clapped her shadowy hands and laughed until the rocks echoed. The hill men, too, laughed shrilly and clapped.

"Hee-hee!" they cried. "They might have asked for half of her treasure, and now for as much as her shoe will hold, they'll go down and live with her under the hill forever!"

Roselein slipped off her worn-out shoe and held it out to the Hill Mother.

"There it is," she said. "Now fill it!"

Still chuckling, the Hill Mother picked up a double handful of gold and poured it into the shoe, thinking to fill it at once.

But the gold all ran through the hole in the sole, and left it as empty as ever.

"Look, look," cried the hill men, "the gold is running out!"

Then the Hill Mother knew she had been tricked.

"But I will fill it yet!" she shrieked.

With mad haste she poured more gold into the shoe, and more and more. But it was no use. The shoe was still empty.

Lower and lower sank the moon. More and more wildly the Hill Mother gathered her treasure and poured it into the shoe, crying as she poured:

> *A hole in the shoe! A hole in the shoe!*
> *Oh, what can the poor old Hill Mother do?*

Suddenly the moonlight was gone. The moon had sunk down behind the forest, and a cock crowed.

The Hill Mother gave a shrill cry—

> *The night has passed, and the cocks do crow.*
> *They have fooled the Hill Mother! Woe! Ah, woe!*

And just then the first morning light crept into the sky. Wailing and wringing her hands, the Hill Mother fled away into the hill, and it closed behind her with a boom.

But the little hill men jumped about among the rocks.

"Now Roselein, now Peter, the treasure is yours," they cried, "but what good will it do you? You have forgotten the way home, so you will have to stay here with us among the rocks forever."

But the children were not afraid. "We may have forgotten," they said, "but we can still find the way home. All we have to do is follow the pennies we dropped as we came."

When the hill men heard that, they gathered round, begging Peter and Roselein to take them home with them. They, too, had once lived in the world of boys and girls, but none of them knew the way back now. The Hill Mother had bewitched them and made them forget.

The children were willing, and in haste the hill men brought from among the rocks the bags they had brought with them when they came, long ago, in search of the Hill Mother's gold.

These they filled with treasure. Then, shouldering them as though they were packs, they followed Peter and Roselein as they traced their way among the rocks, following the pennies they had dropped, back toward the forest and home.

•

THE MOUSE WHO WAS AFRAID

Retold by Catherine T. Bryce

Sometimes the size and strength of a body mean less than the kind
of heart it carries inside. All the muscle in the world can't make
up for the heart that's not brave.

Once there was a little gray mouse. He lived in the same house
as an old gray cat. The little mouse was afraid of the cat.

"How happy I would be but for that old cat," he said. "I am
afraid of her all the time. I wish I were a cat."

A fairy heard the little mouse say this. She felt sorry for him.
So she turned him into a big gray cat.

At first he was very happy. But one day a dog ran after him.

"Oh dear!" he said. "It is not much fun to be a cat. I am afraid
of that dog all the time. I wish I were a big dog."

Again the fairy heard him. She felt sorry for the old gray cat.
So she turned him into a big dog.

Once more he felt happy. Then one day he heard a lion roar.

"Oh, just hear that lion!" he cried. "I am afraid when I hear
him. It is not so safe to be a dog after all. How I wish I were a lion.
Then I would be afraid of no one."

Off he ran to the fairy.

"Dear fairy," he said, "please turn me into a big, strong lion."

Again the fairy was sorry for him. She made him into a big,
strong lion.

One day a man tried to kill the lion. Once more he ran to the
fairy.

"What now?" asked the fairy.

"Make me into a man, dear fairy," he cried. "Then no one can
make me afraid."

"Make you into a man!" cried the fairy. "No, indeed, I will not.
A man must have a brave heart. You have only the heart of a mouse.
So a mouse you shall become again, and a mouse you shall stay."

So saying, she turned him back into a little gray mouse, and
away he ran to his old home.

•

THE KNIGHTS OF THE SILVER SHIELD
Raymond M. Alden

**Sometimes courage means resisting the call to action elsewhere
and standing fast at your post.**

There was once a splendid castle in a forest, with great stone
walls and a high gateway and turrets that rose way above the tallest
trees. The forest was dark and dangerous, and many cruel giants
lived in it, but in the castle was a company of knights, who were
kept there by the king of the country to help travelers who might
be in the forest and fight with the giants whenever they could.

Each of these knights wore a beautiful suit of armor and carried a long spear, while over his helmet there floated a great red
plume that could be seen a long way off by any one in distress. But
the most wonderful things about the knights' armor were their
shields. They were not like those of other knights, but had been
made by a great magician who had lived in the castle many years
before. They were made of silver and sometimes shone in the
sunlight with dazzling brightness. But at other times the surface of
the shields would be clouded as though by a mist, and one could
not see his face reflected there as he could when they shone
brightly.

Now, when each knight received his spurs and his armor, a
new shield was also given him from among those that the magician
had made; and when the shield was new its surface was always
cloudy and dull. But as the knight began to do service against the
giants or went on expeditions to help poor travelers in the forest,
his shield grew brighter and brighter, so that he could see his face
clearly reflected in it. But if he proved to be a lazy or cowardly
knight and let the giants get the better of him or did not care what
became of the travelers, then the shield grew more and more
cloudy, until the knight became ashamed to carry it.

But this was not all. When any one of the knights fought a
particularly hard battle and won the victory, or when he went on
some hard errand for the lord of the castle and was successful, not
only did his silver shield grow brighter, but anyone looking into
the center of it could see something like a golden star shining in its

very heart. This was the greatest honor that a knight could achieve, and the other knights always spoke of such a one as having "won his star." It was usually not till he was pretty old and tried as a soldier that he could win it. At the time when this story begins, the lord of the castle himself was the only one of the knights whose shield bore the golden star.

There came a time when the worst of the giants in the forest gathered themselves together to have a battle against the knights. They made a camp in a dark hollow not far from the castle and gathered all their best warriors together. All the knights made ready to fight them. The windows of the castle were closed and barred, the air was full of the noise of armor being made ready for use, and the knights were so excited that they could scarcely rest or eat.

Now there was a young knight in the castle named Sir Roland, who was among those most eager for the battle. He was a splendid warrior, with eyes that shone like stars whenever there was any-thing to do in the way of knightly deeds. And though he was still quite young, his shield had begun to shine enough to show plainly that he had done bravely in some of his errands through the forest. This battle, he thought, would be the great opportunity of his life. And on the morning of the day when they were to go forth to it, and all the knights assembled in the great hall of the castle to receive the commands of their leaders, Sir Roland hoped that he would be put in the most dangerous place of all, so that he could show what knightly stuff he was made of.

But when the lord of the castle came to him, as he went about in full armor giving his commands, he said: "One brave knight must stay behind and guard the gateway of the castle, and it is you, Sir Roland, being one of the youngest, whom I have chosen for this."

At these words Sir Roland was so disappointed that he bit his lip and closed his helmet over his face so that the other knights might not see it. For a moment he felt as if he must reply angrily to the commander, and tell him that it was not right to leave so sturdy a knight behind, when he was eager to fight. But he struggled against this feeling and went quietly to look after his duties at the gate. The gateway was high and narrow, and was reached from outside by a high, narrow bridge that crossed the moat which sur-rounded the castle on every side. When an enemy approached, the knight on guard rang a great bell just inside the gate, and the bridge was drawn up against the castle wall, so that no one could come across the moat. So the giants had long ago given up trying to attack the castle itself.

Today the battle was to be in the dark hollow in the forest, and it was not likely that there would be anything to do at the castle gate, except to watch it like a common doorkeeper. It was not strange that Sir Roland thought someone else might have done this.

Presently all the other knights marched out in their flashing armor, their red plumes waving over their heads, and their spears in their hands. The lord of the castle stopped only to tell Sir Roland to keep guard over the gate until they all returned, and to let no one enter. Then they went into the shadows of the forest, and were soon lost to sight.

Sir Roland stood looking after them long after they had gone, thinking how happy he would be if he were on the way to battle like them. But after a little he put this out of his mind, and tried to think of pleasanter things. It was a long time before anything happened, or any word came from the battle.

At last Sir Roland saw one of the knights come limping down the path to the castle, and he went out on the bridge to meet him. Now this knight was not a brave one, and he had been frightened away as soon as he was wounded.

"I have been hurt," he said, "so that I cannot fight anymore. But I could watch the gate for you, if you would like to go back in my place."

At first Sir Roland's heart leaped with joy at this, but then he remembered what the commander had told him on going away, and he said:

"I should like to go, but a knight belongs where his commander has put him. My place is here at the gate, and I cannot open it even for you. Your place is at the battle."

The knight was ashamed when he heard this, and he presently turned about and went into the forest again.

So Sir Roland kept guard silently for another hour. Then there came an old beggar-woman down the path to the castle, and asked Sir Roland if she might come in and have some food. He told her that no one could enter the castle that day, but that he would send a servant out to her with food, and that she might sit and rest as long as she would.

"I have been past the hollow in the forest where the battle is going on," said the old woman, while she was waiting for her food.

"And how do you think it is going?" asked Sir Roland.

"Badly for the knights, I am afraid," said the old woman. "The giants are fighting as they have never fought before. I should think you had better go and help your friends."

"I should like to, indeed," said Sir Roland. "But I am set to guard the gateway of the castle, and cannot leave."

"One fresh knight would make a great difference when they are all weary with fighting," said the old woman. "I should think that, while there are no enemies about, you would be much more useful there."

"You may well think so," said Sir Roland, "and so may I; but it is neither you nor I that is commander here."

"I suppose," said the old woman then, "that you are one of the kind of knights who like to keep out of fighting. You are lucky to have so good an excuse for staying at home." And she laughed a thin and taunting laugh.

Then Sir Roland was very angry, and thought that if it were only a man instead of an old woman, he would show whether he liked fighting or no. But as it was an old woman, he shut his lips and set his teeth hard together, and as the servant came just then with the food he had sent for, he gave it to the old woman quickly, and shut the gate that she might not talk to him anymore.

It was not very long before he heard some one calling outside. Sir Roland opened the gate, and saw standing at the other end of the drawbridge a little old man in a long black cloak.

"Why are you knocking here?" he said. "The castle is closed today."

"Are you Sir Roland?" said the little old man.

"Yes," said Sir Roland.

"Then you ought not to be staying here when your commander and his knights are having so hard a struggle with the giants and when you have the chance to make of yourself the greatest knight in this kingdom. Listen to me! I have brought you a magic sword."

As he said this, the old man drew from under his coat a wonderful sword that flashed in the sunlight as if it were covered with diamonds. "This is the sword of all swords," he said, "and it is for you, if you will leave your idling here by the castle gate and carry it to the battle. Nothing can stand before it. When you lift it, the giants will fall back, your master will be saved, and you will be crowned the victorious knight—the one who will soon take his commander's place as lord of the castle."

Now Sir Roland believed that it was a magician who was speaking to him, for it certainly appeared to be a magic sword. It seemed so wonderful that the sword should be brought to him that he reached out his hand as though he would take it, and the little old man came forward as though he would cross the drawbridge into the castle. But as he did so, it came to Sir Roland's mind again that that bridge and the gateway had been entrusted to him, and he called out, "No!" to the old man, so that he stopped where he was standing. But he waved the shining sword in the air again, and said: "It is for you! Take it, and win the victory!"

Sir Roland was really afraid that if he looked any longer at the sword, or listened to any more words of the old man, he would not be able to keep himself within the castle. For this reason he struck the great bell at the gateway, which was the signal for the servants inside to pull in the chains of the drawbridge, and instantly they began to pull, and the drawbridge came up, so that the old man could not cross it to enter the castle nor Sir Roland to go out.

Then, as he looked across the moat, Sir Roland saw a wonderful thing. The little old man threw off his black cloak, and as he did so he began to grow bigger and bigger, until in a minute more he was a giant as tall as any in the forest. At first Sir Roland could scarcely believe his eyes. Then he realized that this must be one of their giant enemies, who had changed himself to a little old man through some magic power, that he might make his way into the castle while all the knights were away. Sir Roland shuddered to think what might have happened if he had taken the sword and left the gate unguarded. The giant shook his fist across the moat that lay between them, and then, knowing that he could do nothing more, he went angrily back into the forest.

Sir Roland now resolved not to open the gate again and to pay no attention to any other visitor. But it was not long before he heard a sound that made him spring forward in joy. It was the bugle of the lord of the castle, and there came sounding after it the bugles of many of the knights that were with him, pealing so joyfully that Sir Roland was sure they were safe and happy. As they came nearer, he could hear their shouts of victory. So he gave the signal to let down the drawbridge again, and went out to meet them. They were dusty and bloodstained and weary, but they had won the battle with the giants; and it had been such a great victory that there had never been a happier homecoming.

Sir Roland greeted them all as they passed in over the bridge, and then, when he had closed the gate and fastened it, he followed them into the great hall of the castle. The lord of the castle took his place on the highest seat, with the other knights about him, and Sir Roland came forward with the key of the gate, to give his account of what he had done in the place to which the commander had appointed him. The lord of the castle bowed to him as a sign for him to begin, but, just as he opened his mouth to speak, one of the knights cried out:

"The shield! The shield! Sir Roland's shield!"

Everyone turned and looked at the shield which Sir Roland carried on his left arm. He himself could see only the top of it, and did not know what they could mean. But what they saw was the golden star of knighthood shining brightly from the center of Sir Roland's shield. There had never been such amazement in the castle before.

Sir Roland knelt before the lord of the castle to receive his commands. He still did not know why everyone was looking at him so excitedly and wondered if he had in some way done wrong.

"Speak, Sir Knight," said the commander, as soon as he could find his voice after his surprise, "and tell us all that has happened today at the castle. Have you been attacked? Have any giants come hither? Did you fight them alone?"

"No, my lord," said Sir Roland. "Only one giant has been here, and he went away silently when he found he could not enter."

Then he told all that had happened through the day.

When he had finished, the knights all looked at one another, but no one spoke a word. Then they looked again at Sir Roland's shield, to make sure that their eyes had not deceived them, and there the golden star was still shining.

After a little silence the lord of the castle spoke.

"Men make mistakes," he said, "but our silver shields are never mistaken. Sir Roland has fought and won the hardest battle of all today."

Then the others all rose and saluted Sir Roland, who was the youngest knight that ever carried the golden star.

•

Hans the Shepherd Boy

Retold by Ella Lyman Cabot

Hans was a little shepherd boy who lived in Germany. One day he was keeping his sheep near a great wood when a hunter rode up to him.

"How far is it to the nearest village, my boy?" asked the hunter.

"It is six miles, sir," said Hans. "But the road is only a sheep track. You might easily miss your way."

"My boy," said the hunter, "if you will show me the way, I will pay you well."

Hans shook his head. "I cannot leave the sheep, sir," he said. "They would stray into the wood and the wolves might kill them."

"But if one or two sheep are eaten by the wolves, I will pay you for them. I will give you more than you can earn in a year."

"Sir, I cannot go," said Hans. "These sheep are my master's. If they are lost, I should be to blame."

"If you cannot show me the way, will you get me a guide? I will take care of your sheep while you are gone."

"No," said Hans, "I cannot do that. The sheep do not know your voice, and—" Then he stopped.

"Can't you trust me?" asked the hunter.

"No," said Hans. "You have tried to make me break my word to my master. How do I know that you would keep your word?"

The hunter laughed. "You are right," said he. "I wish I could trust my servants as your master can trust you. Show me the path. I will try to get to the village alone."

Just then several men rode out of the wood. They shouted for joy.

"Oh, sir!" cried one. "We thought you were lost,"

Then Hans learned to his great surprise that the hunter was a prince. He was afraid that the great man would be angry with him. But the prince smiled and spoke in praise of him.

A few days later a servant came from the prince and took Hans to the palace.

"Hans," said the prince, "I want you to leave your sheep to come and serve me. I know you are a boy whom I can trust."

Hans was very happy over his good fortune. "If my master can find another shepherd to take my place, then I will come and serve you."

So Hans went back and tended the sheep until his master found another shepherd. After that he served the prince many years.

•

THE HONEST FARMER

Retold by Ella Lyman Cabot

The dictionary defines integrity as "an uncompromising adherence to a moral code" and says the word traces its origins to a Latin term meaning "untouched." Here is integrity, untouched and unshaken by altered circumstances.

There was a war in Germany long ago, and thousands of soldiers were scattered over the country. A captain of the cavalry, who had a great many men and horses to feed, was told by his colonel that he must get food from the farms nearby. The captain walked for some time through the lonely valley, and at last knocked at the door of a small cottage. The man who opened it looked old and lame. He leaned on a stick.

"Good day, sir," said the captain. "Will you kindly show me a field where my soldiers can cut the grain and carry it off for our army?" The old man led the soldiers through the valley for about a mile, and in the distance they saw a field of barley waving in the breeze.

"This is just what we want. We'll stop here," exclaimed the captain.

"No, not yet," said the old man. "You must follow me a little farther."

After another mile or two, they came to a second field of barley. The soldiers dismounted, cut down the grain, tied it in sheaves, and rode away with it.

Then the captain said to the old farmer: "Why did you make us walk so far? The first field of barley was better than this one."

"That is true, sir," answered the honest old man, "but it was not mine."

•

WHY THE THUMB STANDS ALONE

Sometimes standing fast means standing alone, as we see in this folktale from Africa.

Once five fingers stood side by side on a hand. They were all friends. Where one went, the others went. They worked together. They played together. They ate and washed and wrote and did their chores together.

One day the five fingers were resting on a table together when they spied a gold ring lying nearby.

"What a shiny ring!" exclaimed the First Finger.

"It would look good on me," declared the Second Finger.

"Let's take it," suggested the Third Finger.

"Quick! While nobody's looking!" whispered the Fourth Finger.

They started to reach for the ring when the Fifth Finger, the one named Thumb, spoke up.

"Wait! We shouldn't do that!" it cried.

"Why not?" demanded the other four fingers.

"Because that ring does not belong to us," said the Thumb. "It's wrong to take something that doesn't belong to you."

"But who is going to know?" asked the other fingers. "No one will see us. Come on!"

"No," said the Thumb. "It's stealing."

Then the other four fingers began to laugh and make fun of the Thumb.

"You're afraid!" said the First Finger.

"What a goody-goody," sang the Second Finger.

"You're just mad because the ring won't fit you," muttered the Third Finger.

"We thought you were more fun than that," said the Fourth Finger. "We thought you were our friend."

But the Thumb shook its head.

"I don't care what you say," it answered. "I won't steal."

"Then you can't hang around with us," shouted the other four fingers. "You can't be our friend."

So they went off in a group by themselves, and left the Thumb alone. At first they thought Thumb would follow them and beg them to take it back. But Thumb knew they were wrong and stood fast.

That is why today the thumb stands apart from the other four fingers.

•

LINCOLN LICKS THE BULLIES

This fight is famous not because it is a fight, but because it gives a glimpse of the fighter's character. Abraham Lincoln disliked quarrels, but he liked unfairness and bullying even less. As we see here, he acted according to the advice Polonius gave to his son Laertes in *Hamlet*: "Beware of entrance to a quarrel but, being in, bear't that th' opposed may beware of thee."

In the passage to adulthood, many boys and girls reach a time when they must face a bully. This story may help.

When Abraham Lincoln was still a young man, he went to work for a fellow named Denton Offutt in New Salem, Illinois. Offutt was impressed with Lincoln's six-foot-four, 185-pound frame; but he was even more impressed with the youngster's brains and ambition, so he offered him a job as a clerk in his general store.

Offutt's store was a favorite loafing place for the New Salem boys and young men. Among these were some of the roughest fellows in the settlement. They were known as the "Clary Grove Boys," and they were always ready for a fight, in which they would sometimes prove themselves to be bullies and tormentors. So when Offutt began to brag about his new clerk, the Clary Grove Boys made fun of him, whereupon the storekeeper cried:

"What's that? You can throw him? Well, I reckon not. Abe Lincoln can outrun, outwalk, outwrassle, knock out, and throw down any man in Sangamon County."

This was too much for the Clary Grove Boys. They took up Offutt's challenge and set up against Abe as their champion one Jack Armstrong.

All this was done without Lincoln's knowledge. He had no

desire to get into a row with anyone—least of all with the bullies who made up the Clary Grove Boys.

"I won't do it," he said, when Offutt told him of the proposed wrestling match. "I never tussle and scuffle, and I will not. I don't like this wooling and pulling."

"Don't let them call you a coward, Abe," said Offutt.

Of course, you know what the end would be to such an affair. Nobody likes to be called a coward—especially when he knows he is not one. So, at last, Lincoln consented to "rassle" with Jack Armstrong. They met, with all the boys as spectators. They wrestled, and tugged, and clenched, but without result. Both young fellows were equally matched in strength.

"It's no use, Jack," Lincoln at last declared. "Let's quit. You can't throw me, and I can't throw you. That's enough."

With that, all Jack's backers began to cry "coward!" and urged on the champion to another tussle. Jack Armstrong was now determined to win, by fair means or foul. He tried the latter and, contrary to all rules of wrestling, began to kick and trip, while his supporters stood ready to help, if need be, by breaking in with a regular free fight. This foul play roused the lion in Lincoln. He hated unfairness and at once resented it. He suddenly put forth his Samson-like strength, grabbed the champion of the Clary Grove Boys by the throat, and, lifting him from the ground, held him at arm's length and shook him as a dog shakes a rat. Then he flung him to the ground, and, facing the amazed and yelling crowd, he cried: "You cowards! You know I don't want to fight. But if you try any such games, I'll tackle the whole lot of you. I've won the fight."

He had. From that day, no man in all that region dared to tackle young Lincoln, or to taunt him with cowardice. And Jack Armstrong was his devoted friend and admirer.

●

GOD WILL PROVIDE

This Mexican folktale is an adaptation of Aesop's "Hercules and the Wagoner." It teaches the age-old moral that God helps those who help themselves. Good, hard work is often the best way out of a tough spot.

One sunrise two neighboring farmers set out for market in town. Their wagons were piled high with tomatoes that would ripen quickly in the hot noonday sun, so they pushed their horses steadily all morning, not wanting their precious cargoes to spoil on the way.

But the poor beasts were tired by the time they reached the steepest hill outside town, and strain as they might, they could not get up the slope. The wagons sat at the bottom of the hill, with the climbing sun beating down mercilessly.

"There's nothing to do but let them rest," said the first farmer, shrugging. "And come to think of it, I could use a little siesta myself. We've been on the road since sunup. I think I'll lie under this tree for a while."

"But you can't!" his companion exclaimed. "By the time you wake up, your load will be ruined."

"Don't worry, my friend. God will provide. He always does. I'll just say a few prayers before I doze off." He rolled over on his side with a yawn.

The second farmer, meanwhile, strode to the back of his wagon and, putting his shoulder to the rear, began to shove as hard as he could. He yelled at his horse to pull forward, but to no avail. He pushed till the veins stood out on his neck, and he cursed at the top of his lungs, but his cart ascended the hill not one inch.

Just then the Lord and Saint Peter passed along the road as they sometimes did, for often they walk abroad in order to look into men's hearts. The Lord saw the frantic, swearing farmer struggling with his load. He smiled and laid a kind hand on the wheel, and at once the cart rose to the top of the hill.

The Lord passed on with Saint Peter at his side. The Gatekeeper's gaze bent downward, as if he were pondering their every step.

"I don't understand," he said at last. "Why did you help that man? Even as we came upon him, we heard him cursing most irreverently. And yet you did not help his friend, who offered his prayers for your help."

The Lord smiled.

"The man I helped cursed, it's true, but not with his heart. That is just the way he talks to his horse. In his heart, he was thinking fondly of his wife and children and aged parents, who depend on his labor and need him to return with some profit for his toil. He would have stayed there pushing all day. His friend, on the other hand, calls on me only when he believes he needs me. What he thinks of is sleep. So let him have his nap."

•

THE HEEDLESS MAN AT THE GATES OF PARADISE

Shakespeare wrote that "readiness is all." Ancient dervish teachers used this tale to teach that lesson.

There was once a man who, like most of us, knew in his heart and mind the way to Heaven. He knew he should love his neighbor as himself, honor his parents, and deal with all men honestly. He knew to help the needy and defend the innocent. He knew humility and patience and self-restraint were the way of the wise.

And this man surely tried to do all these things—but only once in a while. He would help a friend if he happened to remember the friend was in need, or say a prayer of thanksgiving if convenient, or give money to the poor if stricken with a guilty conscience. But most of the time he was too busy with his own affairs.

The habits he practiced impressed themselves upon his soul. He developed the shortcoming of heedlessness. Opportunities for exemplary behavior came and went; occasionally he seized them, but usually he did not even notice the chance to do good.

Then one day he died. As he climbed the path toward Paradise, he looked back at his life. He recalled the times he had loved and aided his fellow creatures and judged them sufficient.

When he reached the towering gates of Heaven, though, he discovered they were locked.

A voice sounded from the air.

"Watch carefully," it warned. "The gates open only once every ten thousand years."

He stood wide-eyed and trembling in expectation. He resolved to stay alert. But, unaccustomed to practicing the virtue of mindfulness, he soon found his attention drifting away. After watching for what seemed an eternity, his shoulders slumped and his head began to nod. His eyelids fluttered, sank, and closed for a second in sleep.

At that instant the mighty gates swung open—and before he could open his eyes, crashed shut again with a thunder that tumbled the heedless from Paradise.

•

OPPORTUNITY

Edward Rowland Sill

It's not the sword—it's the man.

This I beheld, or dreamed it in a dream:
There spread a cloud of dust along the plain;
And underneath the cloud, or in it, raged
A furious battle, and men yelled, and swords
Shocked upon swords and shields. A prince's banner
Wavered, then staggered backward, hemmed by foes.
A craven hung along the battle's edge,
And thought: "Had I a sword of keener steel—
That blue blade that the King's son bears—but this
Blunt thing—!" he snapt and flung it from his hand,
And lowering crept away and left the field.
Then came the King's son, wounded, sore bestead,
And weaponless, and saw the broken sword,
Hilt-buried in the dry and trodden sand,
And ran and snatched it, and with battle shout
Lifted afresh he hewed his enemy down,
And saved a great cause that heroic day.

•

THE MAGIC SWORD

There is an old, old story from the days of knights in shining
armor, about a very ordinary youth who was afraid to test his skill
at arms on the tournament field. At length some of his friends,
thinking to have some fun with him, presented him with a sword
which they said possessed an ancient, magical power: The man who
wielded it could never meet defeat in battle.

To their amazement, the youth sprang to the field and quickly
put the gift to use, winning game after game. Never had anyone
witnessed such speed and daring at arms. With each tournament,

the news of his artistry spread, and before long he was hailed as the foremost knight of the realm.

At last, thinking it would now do no harm, one of his friends revealed the jest and confided that the instrument contained no magic at all, but was just an ordinary sword.

At once terror seized the young knight. When he stood at the edge of the field of combat, his legs shook beneath him, his breath caught in his throat, and his fingers lost all grip. No longer able to believe in his sword, he could not believe in himself. He never fought again.

●

THE GORGON'S HEAD

Adapted from a retelling by James Baldwin

Here is a great Greek hero who perseveres to overcome a series of obstacles, any one of which would deter a feeble heart.

Long ago on a distant island kingdom lived a beautiful woman named Danaë and her son, a brave and tall youth named Perseus. The king of this island was a man called Polydectes, and he was so pleased by Danaë's beauty that he wanted her to become his wife. But he was an evil, cruel man, and she did not like him at all, so she refused all of his offers. Polydectes thought Perseus was to blame for this and that if he could find some excuse to send the young man on a far journey, he might force Danaë to have him whether she wished or not.

To this end he gave a great feast, and announced that every guest was expected to bring a rich present. For he knew that Perseus, being poor, could not afford such a gift.

When the great banquet began, Perseus stood at the door, sorrowfully watching all the wealthy nobles go in, and his face grew red as they pointed at him and sneered, "What has Perseus to give?"

At last the lad grew mad with shame and, hardly knowing what he said, cried out, "See if I do not bring a better present than all of yours together!"

"Hear the boaster!" laughed Polydectes. "And what are you to bring—the head of Medusa?"

"Yes! I will bring that," swore Perseus, and he went away in anger while everyone laughed at him because of his foolish words.

And what was this Medusa's head which he had so rashly promised to bring?

Far, far away, on the very edge of the world, there lived three strange monsters, sisters, called the Gorgons. They had the bodies and faces of women, but they had wings of gold, and terrible claws of brass, and live serpents growing out of their heads instead of hair. They were so awful to look upon that no one could bear the sight of them. Whoever saw their faces was turned to stone. Two of these monsters had charmed lives, and no weapon could ever do them harm. But the youngest, whose name was Medusa, might be killed if indeed anybody could deliver the fatal stroke.

Perseus strode away from the king's palace, feeling sorry that he had ever spoken so rashly. He did not even know how to find the awful Gorgons. He went down to the shore and stood looking out over the sea while the sun went down and the moon rose. Then, all at once, two persons stood before him. Both were tall and noble. They were Hermes, the messenger of the gods, and Athena, the goddess of wisdom. They told Perseus they would help him.

"You must go first to the three Gray Sisters, who live beyond the frozen sea, in the far, far north," said Athena. "They have a secret which nobody knows, and you must force them to tell you. Ask them where you shall find the three Maidens who guard the golden apples of the West. When they have told you, go straight there. The Maidens will give you three things you will need to obtain the terrible head, and they will tell you how to find the home of the Gorgons."

"But I have no ship. How shall I go?" asked Perseus.

"You shall take my winged sandals," said Hermes. He took off the wonderful shoes, and put them on the youth's feet; and before Perseus could thank them for their kindness, he found himself speeding into the sky, swifter than any eagle.

The winged sandals bore him over the sea, straight toward the north. On and on he went, and soon the sea was passed. He flew over cities and towns and a range of snowy mountains covered with mighty forests, and then a vast plain where many rivers wandered, seeking the sea. Then came frozen marshes and a wilderness of snow, and finally an ocean of ice. On and on he winged his way, among toppling icebergs and over frozen billows and through air the sun never warmed, and at last he came to the cavern where the three Gray Sisters dwelled.

These creatures were so old they had forgotten their own age. The long hair that covered their heads had been gray since they were born. They had among them only a single eye and a single tooth, which they passed back and forth from one to another. Perseus heard them mumbling and crooning in their dreary home, and he stood very still and listened.

"We know a secret we will never tell, don't we, sisters?" said one.

"Ha! ha! That we do! That we do!" chattered the others.

"Give me the tooth, sister, that I may feel young and handsome again," said one.

"And give me the eye that I may look out and see the world," said another.

"Ah yes, yes, yes," mumbled the third, as she took both the tooth and the eye and held them out blindly toward the others.

Quick as thought, Perseus leaped forward and snatched both of the precious things from her hand.

"Where is the tooth? Where is the eye?" screamed the two, reaching out their long arms and groping here and there. "Have you dropped them, sister? Have you lost them?"

"I have your tooth and your eye," said Perseus, "and you shall not touch them again until you tell me your secret. Where are the Maidens who keep the golden apples of the Western Land?"

Then the Gray Sisters wept and coaxed and threatened. They moaned and mumbled and shrieked, but their words did not move him.

"Sisters, we must tell him," at last one said.

"Ah yes, we must part with the secret to save our eye," said the others.

Then they told him what road he should follow to find the Maidens; and when they had made everything plain to Perseus, he gave them back their eye and tooth.

"Ha! ha!" they laughed. "Now the golden days of youth have come again!" Perseus leaped into the air again. And from that day to this, though the winds still whistle through their cheerless cave, and the cold waves murmur on the shore of the wintry sea, and the ice mountains topple and crash, no other man has ever seen the three Gray Sisters.

The winged sandals now bore Perseus southward. He left the frozen wilderness behind and soon came to a sunny land, where there were green forests and flowery meadows and hills and valleys, and at last a pleasant garden with all kinds of fruits and blossoms. And here he found the three Maidens of the West dancing and singing around a tree of golden apples.

Perseus told them of his quest, and said he had come to ask them to give him three things to help him fight the Gorgons.

The Maidens answered they would give him not three things but four. One of them gave him a sharp sword, which she fastened to the belt at his waist. Another gave him a shield, which was brighter than any looking glass. The third gave him a magic pouch, which she hung by a long strap over his shoulder. Finally they all three gave him a magic helmet, the Helmet of Darkness; and when they had put it on his head, there was no creature on earth or in the sky that could see him.

Then they told him where he could find the Gorgons, and what he should do to obtain the terrible head and escape alive. Perseus donned the Helmet of Darkness, and sped away toward the farthest edge of the earth. And the three Maidens went back to their tree to sing and to dance and to guard the golden apples until the old world should become young again.

Perseus flew so swiftly it was not long until he had crossed the mighty ocean that encircles the earth and had come to the sunless land that lies beyond. He heard the sound of someone breathing heavily, and he looked around sharply to see where it came from. Among the foul weeds that grew close by the bank of a muddy river there was something glittering in the pale light.

He flew a little nearer, but he did not dare look straight forward, lest he should meet the gaze of a Gorgon, and be changed to stone. Instead, he turned around and held the shining shield before him in such a way that by looking into it he could see objects behind him as in a mirror.

Ah, what a dreadful sight it was! Half hidden among the weeds lay the three monsters, fast asleep, with their golden wings folded about them. Their brazen claws were stretched out as though ready to seize their prey, and their shoulders were covered with sleeping snakes. The two largest of the Gorgons lay with their heads tucked under their wings as birds hide their heads when they go to sleep. But the third, who lay between them, slept with her face turned up to the sky, and Perseus knew she was Medusa.

Very stealthily he went nearer and nearer, always with his back toward the monsters and always looking into his bright shield to see where to go. Then he drew his sharp sword and, dashing it quickly downward, struck a blow so sure, so swift, that the head of Medusa was severed from her shoulders and the black blood gushed like a river from her neck. Quick as thought he thrust the terrible head into his magic pouch, leaped into the air again, and flew away with the speed of wind.

Then the two older Gorgons awoke, and rose with dreadful screams, and spread their great wings to dash after him. They could not see him, for the Helmet of Darkness hid him from their eyes, but they scented the blood of their sister's head, and they followed him, sniffing the air. As he flew he could hear the clatter of their golden wings and the snapping of their horrible jaws. But the winged sandals were swift as the wind, and soon he had left the monsters far behind.

He flew on, toward home, until he passed over a country of sunshine and palm trees and a great river flowing from the south. Here, as he looked down, a strange sight met his eyes: He saw a beautiful girl chained to a rock by the seashore, and far away a huge beast swimming to devour her.

At once Perseus flew down, drew his sharp sword, and cut the chain which held her. By this time the monster was close at hand, lashing the water with its tale and opening its wide jaws so as to swallow both Perseus and the girl. But as it came roaring toward the shore, Perseus lifted the head of Medusa from its pouch and held it high. When the beast saw the dreadful face it stopped short and was turned into stone. And men say that the stone beast may be seen in that same spot today.

The girl told him her name was Andromeda, and that she was the princess of that land. She had been chained to the rock as an offering to the terrible beast, which was destroying the whole land. At once Perseus asked her to be his wife, and they were married with a great feast, and the two young people lived happily for some time in that sunny place.

But Perseus had not forgotten his mother, so one fine summer day he sailed home, taking Andromeda with him. He left his ship on the beach, and found his mother, and they wept over each other.

Then Perseus went up to the palace of Polydectes with the head of Medusa in his pouch. When he came to the great hall, the evil king sat at his table, with all his nobles on either side, feasting and drinking wine. Perseus stood upon the threshold and called Polydectes by name, but none of the guests knew the stranger, for he was changed by his long journey. He had gone out a boy, and he had come home a man and a great hero.

But Polydectes the Wicked knew him and scornfully called,

"Ah, foolish boaster! Have you found it easier to make a promise than to fulfill it?"

"When a promise is made to right a wrong, sometimes the gods help fulfill it," Perseus answered. And turning aside his own eyes, he drew open the pouch, held aloft the Gorgon's head, and cried, "Behold!"

Pale grew Polydectes and his guests as they looked upon the dreadful face. They tried to spring away, but they never rose from their seats. They stiffened, each man where he sat, into a ring of cold gray stones.

Then Perseus turned and left them, went down to his galley by the shore, and sailed away with his mother and his bride.

•

HEROES

William Canton

We all should have one or two heroes to help us stand fast and think right.

> For you who love heroic things
>   In summer dream or winter tale,
> I tell of warriors, saints, and kings,
>   In scarlet, sackcloth, glittering mail,
> And helmets peaked with iron wings.
>
> They beat down Wrong; they strove for Right.
>   In ringing fields, on grappled ships,
> Singing, they flung into the fight;
>   They fell with triumph on their lips,
> And in their eyes a glorious light.
>
> That light still gleams. From far away
>   Their brave song greets us like a cheer;
> We fight the same great fight as they,
>   Right against Wrong; we, now and here;
> They, in their fashion, yesterday.

•

PROTEUS

*Adapted from a retelling
by Elizabeth Harrison*

Here's a great story to remember when someone tells you to
"Hold on!" The tale, from *The Odyssey,* takes place on the island
of Pharos near Egypt. Menelaus was the king of Sparta and one of
the leaders of the Greeks in the Trojan War.

After the long and cruel Trojan War was over, King Menelaus
started in his good ship for his much loved home in Sparta. His
crew hoisted the sails, and they began the long voyage across the
dark, mysterious sea.

For a while the wind was favorable and helped them along
their journey. Then one evening they stopped for the night in a
sheltered bay on the coast of a little island. The next morning they
woke to find the wind blowing steadily in the opposite way from
the one they wished to sail. They waited all day, hoping the strong
breeze would die down, or at least change its direction. The next
day passed, and the next, and another, and still the wind blew
steadily away from their beloved homes.

Although it was invisible, it had more strength than all of them,
and they could make no headway against it. Day after day it blew a
fierce, wild gale over their heads, scattering the clouds across the
sky, dashing the waves against the shore, whirling the dust into
their faces, and hurriedly uttering hoarse whispering sounds as it
passed them. They knew it was warning them against daring to
continue their homeward journey.

Twenty days had come and gone, and still the wind kept up its
fierce, loud tone of command as it rushed from the faraway west,
shook the waters of the vast ocean, swept over the small, rocky
island, and sped on toward the east. The courage of the poor sailors
was almost exhausted. Their provisions were giving out. They tried
to catch fish to satisfy each day's hunger, but it was hard when the
surf was so wild.

Menelaus, their chief, went wandering alone on the seashore.
He was very unhappy, for he feared that all this trouble had come
because he and his comrades had done something to displease the

gods. So he was much distressed in mind as he walked along the sandy beach.

The sun was sinking to rest, the evening shadows were settling down between the rocky hills, the darkness of night was approaching, when suddenly there stood before him a beautiful being of so dazzling an appearance that he knew she could not be a woman, she must be an immortal. Her saffron robes gleamed with light as do the sunset clouds. Her face was as radiant as are the last rays of the departing sun. It was the beautiful goddess Idothea. Her face suddenly became stern as she looked at King Menelaus and asked him why he tarried idly upon the small, rocky island. He replied that he did not willingly remain, but that he must surely have sinned against the gods, as they had sent a strong, fierce wind to hinder his homeward voyage. Then he earnestly begged her to tell him what to do. The stern look left her face as she heard him confess that he had done wrong. She came nearer to him, and her glittering robes changed from saffron to pink, and blue, and even gray, and the lights played above, around, and about her in the most wonderful fashion, changing each moment as she spoke.

She told him that she was the daughter of Proteus, the Ancient of the Deep, who, living for thousands and thousands of years in the bottom of the great ocean, had gone wherever the restless waves of the sea had gone, and had learned the secrets of both land and water. He knew the song of the winds and could interpret every message they brought from the gods. Therefore he, and he alone, could tell Menelaus what it was that the strong, fierce wind had been crying out to him and his companions for the past twenty days.

This sea god, Proteus, was a most remarkable being. He had the power to change himself into whatever form he chose. The only way to get any secret from him was to catch him when he was asleep, and then to *hold on* to him, no matter what shape he might choose to take, until at last he returned to his original form of the old man of the sea.

Idothea told Menelaus that this strange father of hers would rise out of the sea at about noon the next day, and would walk over to a large cavern not far distant, where his sea calves took their daily sleep, and that when he had counted them to see if they were all there, he would lie down in the midst of them and go to sleep also. This, said she, would be the time for Menelaus and three of his trusted sailors to spring upon him and seize him firmly, and she added that they must *hold on to him, no matter what happened,* until he changed back into his own form, that of an old man. Then they could ask him any questions they wished and he would be compelled to answer them.

Having given Menelaus these instructions, the beautiful goddess suddenly plunged into the ocean and the green waves closed over her.

With bowed head and mind filled with anxious thought, Menelaus returned to his men. They gathered round their boats on the seashore and ate their scanty evening meal. Silently and solemnly the night settled down upon the landscape and made the trees look like dark, shadowy forms, and the outlines of the hills grew dim, and the ocean was covered by the hush of the darkness, and silence reigned over all.

The sailors threw themselves down upon the sand and were soon fast asleep. Menelaus lay beside them, but his mind was troubled. What would the next day bring forth? He was to meet the strange and terrible Ancient of the Deep, and was to struggle fiercely with him. Would he be able to cope with the monster? Would he have the courage to hold on to him? What awful and unknown shapes might not the creature take?

The night slowly wore away, and when the faint purplish light softened the eastern sky, he arose, and going apart from his sleeping comrades, he knelt down and prayed earnestly to the ever-living gods. Then, returning to his men, he awoke the three whom he could trust the most, and taking them with him, sought the spot where the goddess Idothea had promised to meet him. She, radiant as the dawn, was already there awaiting him.

Quickly digging four oblong holes in the wet sand, she commanded Menelaus and his three companions to lie down in them. This they did, and she skillfully spread over each of them a sealskin. Then the radiant goddess seated herself on a rock not far away, to await her father's coming.

After a while, the sea calves rose from the depths of the ocean and began crawling along the sand. They came in throngs and laid themselves down in rows upon the sandy shore beside the brave but anxious heroes. Soon the sunlit waves parted from right to left and slowly and solemnly Proteus, the Ancient of the Deep, appeared. His hair and beard and garments were covered with white foam. He walked over to where his sea calves lay basking in the sun and counted them. This was a trying time for Menelaus. His heart

beat loud and fast, so great was his fear that he and his companions might be discovered. But the goddess had done her work too well for that. Proteus did not notice any difference between them and the beasts which lay about them. Having finished his task, he stretched his body upon the sand beside his flock, ready for his afternoon nap.

Now was the critical moment! Menelaus and his men, throwing off the sealskins, sprang forward with loud shouts, and before the old sea god knew it, they had fast hold of his arms and legs.

Proteus, having the power to change his body into whatever shape he pleased, suddenly transformed himself into a roaring lion, so fierce and strong that it seemed as if he might crush anything that came in his way. Still Menelaus and his stouthearted men *held on*. Then, in an instant the lion became a fiery panther whose glaring eyes struck terror into their hearts, but still they *held on*. In a moment more a large snake was twisting and writhing in their hands, hissing and darting his forked tongue out as if he would gladly poison all of them, still they *held on*. Shape after shape the monster assumed, but still they *held on*. Now it was a clear, harmless stream of water flowing gently through their hands. Again it was a flame of fire darting here and there threatening to scorch their faces and even to burn out their eyes; still they *held on*. Then it became a beautiful tree, tall and stately, with broad spreading branches and shining green leaves, still they *held on*.

At last, finding that his enchantments were of no avail, he changed back into his real form and, turning to Menelaus, he said, "What wouldst thou have?" Menelaus begged him to tell why he and his faithful sailors were kept from crossing the dark waters of the sea to their distant homes. Then Proteus, the Ancient of the Deep, who knew all secrets of both gods and men, told him the cause of their troubles. In their impatience to get back to their homes, they had neglected to worship the gods and ask them for guidance to their journey's end. It was their own thoughtlessness that kept them prisoner.

Menelaus now understood what the wind had been trying to tell him. The very next day, he and his men paid due worship to the gods. Then right merrily the wind whistled and sang about their ears as it filled their white sails and helped them to speed across the blue water. In a few days they had reached their beloved homeland.

But never to the end of their lives did they forget the terrible struggle with the mighty Proteus, Ancient of the Deep, where by *holding on* they had won the silent battle. And oftentimes they told the story to their children and grandchildren, just as I am telling it to you today.

•

THE DOG OF MONTARGIS

Retold by James Baldwin

This unusual old story reminds us that loyalty is the virtue that helps us stand fast beside our friends—and our memories of our friends.

In the old castle of Montargis in France, there was once a stone mantelpiece of workmanship so rare that it was talked about by the whole country. And yet it was not altogether its beauty that caused people to speak of it and remember it. It was famous rather on account of the strange scene that was carved upon it. To those who asked about its meaning, the old custodian of the castle would sometimes tell the following story.

It happened more than five hundred years ago, when this castle was new and strong, and people lived and thought in very different ways than they do now. Among the young men of that time there was none more noble than Aubrey de Montdidier, the nephew of the Count of Montargis; and among all the knights who had favor at the royal court, there was none braver than the young Sieur de Narsac, captain of the king's men at arms.

Now these two men were devoted friends, and whenever their

other duties allowed them, they were sure to be in each other's company. Indeed, it was a rare thing to see either of them walking the streets of Paris alone.

"I will meet you at the tournament tomorrow," said Aubrey gaily, one evening, as he was parting from his friend.

"Yes, at the tournament tomorrow," said De Narsac, "and be sure that you come early."

The tournament was to be a grand affair. A gentleman from Provence was to run a tilt with a famous Burgundian knight. Both men were noted for their horsemanship and their skill with the lance. All Paris would be out to see them.

When the time came, De Narsac was at the place appointed. But Aubrey failed to appear. What could it mean? It was not at all like Aubrey to forget his promise; it was seldom that he allowed anything to keep him away from the tournament.

"Have you seen my friend Aubrey today?" De Narsac asked this question a hundred times. Everybody gave the same answer and wondered what had happened.

The day passed and another day came, and still there was no news from Aubrey. De Narsac had called at his friend's lodgings, but could learn nothing. The young man had not been seen since the morning before the tournament.

Three days passed, and still not a word. De Narsac was greatly troubled. He knew now that some accident must have happened to Aubrey. But what could it have been?

Early in the morning of the fourth day he was aroused by a strange noise at his door. He dressed himself in haste and opened it. A dog was crouching there. It was a greyhound, so thin that its ribs stuck out, so weak that it could hardly stand.

De Narsac knew the animal without looking at the collar on its neck. It was Dragon, his friend Aubrey's greyhound—the dog who went with him whenever he went out, the dog who was never seen save in its master's company.

The poor creature tried to stand. His legs trembled from weakness. He swayed from side to side. He wagged his tail feebly, and tried to put his nose in De Narsac's hand. De Narsac saw at once that he was half starved.

He led the dog into his room and fed him some warm milk. He bathed the poor fellow's nose and bloodshot eyes with cold water. "Tell me where your master is," he said. Then he set before him a full meal that would have tempted any dog.

The greyhound ate heartily, and seemed to be much stronger. He licked De Narsac's hands. Then he ran to the door and tried to make signs to his friend to follow him. He whined pitifully.

De Narsac understood. "You want to lead me to your master, I see." He put on his hat and went out with the dog.

Through the narrow lanes and crooked streets of the old city, Dragon led the way. At each corner he would stop and look back to make sure that De Narsac was following. He went over the long bridge—the only one that spanned the river in those days. Then he trotted out through the gate of St. Martin and into the open country beyond the walls.

In a little while the dog left the main road and took a bypath that led into the forest of Bondy. De Narsac kept his hand on his sword now, for they were on dangerous ground. The forest was a great hangout for robbers and lawless men, and more than one wild and wicked deed had been enacted there.

But Dragon did not go far into the woods. He stopped suddenly near a dense thicket of briers and tangled vines. He whined as though in great distress. Then he took hold of the sleeve of De Narsac's coat, and led him round to the other side of the thicket.

There under a low-spreading oak the grass had been trampled down. There were signs, too, of freshly turned-up earth. With moans of distress the dog stretched himself upon the ground, and with pleading eyes looked up into De Narsac's face.

"Ah, my poor fellow!" said De Narsac, "you have led me here to show me your master's grave." And with that he turned and hurried back to the city; but the dog would not stir from his place.

That afternoon a company of men, led by De Narsac, rode out to the forest. They found in the ground beneath the oak what they had expected—the murdered body of young Aubrey de Montdidier.

"Who could have done this foul deed?" they asked of one another. And then they wept, for they all loved Aubrey.

They made a litter of green branches, and laid the body upon it. Then, the dog following them, they carried it back to the city and buried it in the king's cemetery. And all Paris mourned the untimely end of the brave young knight.

After this, the greyhound went to live with the young Sieur de Narsac. He followed the knight wherever he went. He slept in his room and ate from his hand. He seemed to be as much devoted to his new master as he had been to the old.

One morning they went out for a stroll through the city. The streets were crowded, for it was a holiday and all the fine people of Paris were enjoying the sunlight and the fresh air. Dragon, as usual, kept close to the heels of his master.

De Narsac walked down one street and up another, meeting many of his friends, and now and then stopping to talk a little while. Suddenly, as they were passing a corner, the dog leaped forward and planted himself in front of his master. He growled fiercely and crouched as though ready for a spring. His eyes were fixed upon someone in the crowd.

Then, before De Narsac could speak, he leaped forward upon a young man whom he had singled out. The man threw up his arm to protect his throat, but the quickness of the attack and the weight of the dog caused him to fall to the ground. There is no telling what might have followed had not those who were with him beaten the dog with their canes, and driven him away.

De Narsac knew the man. His name was Richard Macaire, and he belonged to the king's bodyguard.

Never before had the greyhound been known to show anger toward any person. "What do you mean by such conduct?" asked his master as they walked homeward. Dragon's only answer was a low growl, but it was the best that he could give. The affair had put a thought into De Narsac's mind which he could not dismiss.

Within less than a week the thing happened again. This time Macaire was walking in the public garden. De Narsac and the dog were some distance away. But as soon as Dragon saw the man, he rushed at him. It was all that the bystanders could do to keep him from throttling Macaire. De Narsac hurried up and called him away; but the dog's anger was fearful to see.

It was well known in Paris that Macaire and young Aubrey had not been friends. It was remembered that they had had more than one quarrel. And now the people began to talk about the dog's strange actions, and some went so far as to put this and that together.

At last the matter reached the ears of the king. He sent for De Narsac and had a long talk with him. "Come back tomorrow and bring the dog with you," he said. "We must find out more about this strange affair."

The next day De Narsac, with Dragon at his heels, was admitted into the king's audience room. The king was seated in his great chair, and many knights and men at arms were standing around him. Hardly had De Narsac stepped inside when the dog leaped quickly forward. He had seen Macaire, and had singled him out from among all the rest. He sprang upon him. He would have torn him in pieces if no one had interfered.

There was now only one way to explain the matter.

"This greyhound," said De Narsac, "is here to denounce the Chevalier Macaire as the slayer of his master, young Aubrey de Montdidier. He demands that justice be done, and that the murderer be punished for his crime."

The Chevalier Macaire was pale and trembling. He stammered a denial of his guilt, and declared that the dog was a dangerous beast, and ought to be put out of the way. "Shall a soldier in the service of the king be accused by a dog?" he cried. "Shall he be condemned on such testimony as this? I, too, demand justice."

"Let the judgment of God decide!" cried the knights who were present.

And so the king declared that there should be a trial by the judgment of God. For in those rude times it was a very common thing to determine guilt or innocence in this way—that is, by a combat between the accuser and the accused. In such cases it was believed that God would always aid the cause of the innocent and bring about the defeat of the guilty.

The combat was to take place that very afternoon in the great common by the riverside. The king's herald made a public announcement of it, naming the dog as the accuser and the Chevalier Macaire as the accused. A great crowd of people assembled to see this strange trial by the judgment of God.

The king and his officers were there to make sure that no injustice was done to either the man or the dog. The man was allowed to defend himself with a short stick. The dog was given a barrel into which he might run if too closely pressed.

At a signal the combat began. Macaire stood on his guard while the dog darted swiftly around him, dodging the blows that were aimed at him, and trying to get at his enemy's throat. The man seemed to have lost all his courage. His breath came short and quick. He was trembling from head to foot.

Suddenly the dog leaped upon him and threw him to the ground. In great terror Macaire cried to the king for mercy, and acknowledged his guilt.

"It is the judgment of God!" cried the king.

The officers rushed in and dragged the dog away before he

could harm the guilty man. Macaire was hurried off to the punishment which his crimes deserved.

And this is the scene that was carved on the old mantelpiece in the castle of Montargis—this strange trial by the judgment of God. Is it not fitting that a dog so faithful, devoted, and brave should have his memory thus preserved in stone?

•

HERCULES KILLS THE HYDRA

The killing of the Hydra was the second of the famous twelve labors Hercules performed for his cousin Eurystheus, king of Mycenae. The myth reminds us that some battles require the help of good friends.

The second labor of Hercules was the killing of the Hydra, a terrible serpent that dwelled among the murky swamps. The murderous beast had nine heads on nine long necks, and the middle head was immortal. This gigantic water snake ravaged the herds and the flocks of the countryside; whenever any mortal came near its den, it rushed out, seized him, and tore him limb from limb with its nine dripping sets of fangs. And yet it was a confident Hercules who rode forth in a chariot with his friend Iolaus to face this demon of the bottomless swamps.

When the Hydra saw the hero approaching, it slunk away, and hid in its lair. It feared this man with arms as stout as limbs of oak, and a great lion's skin draped for a cloak over his shoulders. From the depths of its den, its eighteen slitted eyes peered out at the sword flashing like the fire of the sun and the huge, knotted club swinging at his side.

But Hercules soon devised a way to bring it out of hiding. He soaked an arrow in brimstone and pitch, set fire to it, and sent it winging its flaming way into the Hydra's den. Out came the serpent, wounded by the missile and choking from the smoke now pouring forth from the burning nest.

As soon as it crept out, Hercules attacked. His gleaming sword swept through the air and at once lopped off one of the heads. He told himself it was going to be an easy victory. But he was reckoning without knowing his enemy—for hardly had the head fallen than the startled hero saw two others spring up on the severed neck! He struck off one of these, and still two more living heads grew in its place!

This was indeed a problem, and at first Hercules did not know what to do. He fought the serpent valiantly, but what does valor count when, no matter how you wound your foe, it cannot be killed and never loses strength?

To make matters worse, a gigantic crab now crawled to the aid of the serpent. It was sent by Juno, the queen of the gods, who bore an ancient grudge against Hercules. This strange enemy tried to distract the hero so that the Hydra could deliver a fatal strike; it crawled about the ground while Hercules struggled with the snake, pinching and biting his feet. Hercules, however, soon put an end to the crab's attempts. He trod upon it and crushed it into the ground.

Now he turned all his strength to defeating the Hydra. It was no easy matter to fight a foe who had so many heads, every one with fangs that could inflict the death sting. Hercules knew he could not fight on to victory alone. So he called upon Iolaus to help him. His friend had really only come to watch the great fight, but he did not hesitate to take part when needed.

Battling fiercely, Hercules shouted out his instructions. Iolaus tore a limb from a tree, set the end on fire, and stood beside Hercules with the blazing torch. Then as soon as Hercules knocked off a head, Iolaus touched the fire to the severed neck, searing it closed and keeping new heads from springing up.

On and on the fighting went. Iolaus used up a whole forest of torches sealing the wounds of the dreaded snake. At last, however, the battle was won. The Hydra lay dead at the feet of the victors—all except the immortal middle head. But Hercules cut it off also, and buried it beneath a huge rock so it could never get free. Then, before leaving the scene, he dipped the tips of his arrows in the poisonous blood of his victim. Henceforth even the slightest scratch from these arrows would be fatal.

And so Hercules and Iolaus rode away to announce their victory. But the angry Juno raised the vanquished foes and placed them in the heavens. Even today, you can see them blazing overhead on a starry night—Hydra the Serpent, and Cancer the Crab.

•

FOR THE LOVE OF A MAN

Jack London

Friends pull each other through hard times. They bet on each
other. They do both—literally—in this excerpt from one of the
most popular American adventure stories, *The Call of the Wild.*
The book tells the story of a dog named Buck, who is adopted by
John Thornton, an Alaskan who is the first human being to show
him kindness.

For the most part, Buck's love was expressed in adoration.
While he went wild with happiness when Thornton touched him or
spoke to him, he did not seek these tokens. Buck was content to
adore at a distance. He would lie by the hour, eager, alert, at Thornton's feet, looking up into his face, dwelling upon it, studying it,
following with keenest interest each fleeting expression, every
movement or change of feature. Or, as chance might have it, he
would lie farther away, to the side or rear, watching the outlines of
the man and the occasional movements of his body. And often, such
was the communion in which they lived, the strength of Buck's gaze
would draw John Thornton's head around, and he would return
the gaze, without speech, his heart shining out of his eyes as Buck's
heart shone out.

But in spite of this great love he bore John Thornton, which
seemed to bespeak the soft civilizing influence, the strain of the
primitive, which the Northland had aroused in him, remained alive
and active. Faithfulness and devotion, things born of fire and roof,
were his; yet he retained his wildness and wiliness. He was a thing
of the wild, come in from the wild to sit by John Thornton's fire,
rather than a dog of the soft Southland stamped with the marks of
generations of civilization. Because of his very great love, he could
not steal from this man, but from any other man, in any other camp,
he did not hesitate an instant; while the cunning with which he
stole enabled him to escape detection.

He was older than the days he had seen and the breaths he
had drawn. He linked the past with the present, and the eternity
behind him throbbed through him in a mighty rhythm to which he
swayed as the tides and seasons swayed. He sat by John Thornton's

fire, a broad-breasted dog, white-fanged and long-furred; but behind him were the shades of all manner of dogs, half-wolves and wild wolves, urgent and prompting, tasting the savor of the meat he ate, thirsting for the water he drank, scenting the wind with him, listening with him and telling him the sounds made by the wild life in the forest; dictating his moods, directing his actions, lying down to sleep with him when he lay down, and dreaming with him and beyond him and becoming themselves the stuff of his dreams.

So peremptorily did these shades beckon him, that each day mankind and the claims of mankind slipped farther from him. Deep in the forest a call was sounding, and as often as he heard this call, mysteriously thrilling and luring, he felt compelled to turn his back upon the fire and the beaten earth around it, and to plunge into the forest, and on and on, he knew not where or why; nor did he wonder where or why, the call sounding imperiously, deep in the forest. But as often as he gained the soft unbroken earth and the green shade, the love for John Thornton drew him back to the fire again.

Thornton alone held him. The rest of mankind was as nothing. Chance travelers might praise or pet him; but he was cold under it all, and from a too demonstrative man he would get up and walk away. When Thornton's partners, Hans and Pete, arrived on the long-expected raft, Buck refused to notice them till he learned they were close to Thornton; after that he tolerated them in a passive sort of way, accepting favors from them as though he favored them by accepting. They were of the same large type as Thornton, living close to the earth, thinking simply and seeing clearly; and ere they swung the raft into the big eddy by the sawmill at Dawson, they understood Buck and his ways.

For Thornton, however, his love seemed to grow and grow. He, alone among men, could put a pack upon Buck's back in the summer traveling. Nothing was too great for Buck to do, when Thornton commanded. One day (they had grubstaked themselves from the proceeds of the raft and left Dawson for the headwaters of the Tanana) the men and dogs were sitting on the crest of a cliff which fell away, straight down, to naked bedrock three hundred feet below. John Thornton was sitting near the edge, Buck at his shoulder. A thoughtless whim seized Thornton, and he drew the attention of Hans and Pete to the experiment he had in mind. "Jump, Buck!" he commanded, sweeping his arm out and over the chasm. The next instant he was grappling with Buck on the extreme edge, while Hans and Pete were dragging them back into safety.

"It's uncanny," Pete said, after it was over and they had caught their speech.

Thornton shook his head. "No, it is splendid, and it is terrible, too. Do you know, it sometimes makes me afraid."

"I'm not hankering to be the man that lays hands on you while he's around," Pete announced conclusively, nodding his head toward Buck.

"Py Jingo!" was Hans's contribution. "Not mineself either."

Later on, in the fall of the year, Buck saved John Thornton's life. The three partners were lining a long and narrow poling-boat down a bad stretch of rapids on the Forty Mile Creek. Hans and Pete moved along the bank, snubbing with a thin Manila rope from tree to tree, while Thornton remained in the boat, helping its descent by means of a pole, and shouting directions to the shore. Buck, on the bank, worried and anxious, kept abreast of the boat, his eyes never off his master.

At a particularly bad spot, where a ledge of barely submerged rocks jutted out into the river, Hans cast off the rope, and, while Thornton poled the boat out into the stream, ran down the bank with the end in his hand to snub the boat when it had cleared the ledge. This it did, and was flying downstream in a current as swift as a millrace, when Hans checked it with the rope and checked too suddenly. The boat flirted over and snubbed in to the bank bottom up, while Thornton, flung sheer out of it, was carried downstream toward the worst part of the rapids, a stretch of wild water in which no swimmer could live.

Buck had sprung in on the instant, and at the end of three hundred yards, amid a mad swirl of water, he overhauled Thornton. When he felt him grasp his tail, Buck headed for the bank, swimming with all his splendid strength. But the progress shoreward was slow, the progress downstream amazingly rapid. From below came the fatal roaring where the wild current went wilder and was rent in shreds and spray by the rocks which thrust through like the teeth of an enormous comb. The suck of the water as it took the beginning of the last steep pitch was frightful, and Thornton knew that the shore was impossible. He scraped furiously over a rock, bruised across a second, and struck a third with crushing force. He clutched its slippery top with both hands, releasing Buck, and above the roar of the churning water shouted: "Go, Buck! Go!"

Buck could not hold his own, and swept on downstream, struggling desperately, but unable to win back. When he heard Thornton's command repeated, he partly reared out of the water, throwing his head high, as though for a last look, then turned obediently toward the bank. He swam powerfully and was dragged ashore by Pete and Hans at the very point where swimming ceased to be possible and destruction began.

They knew that the time a man could cling to a slippery rock in the face of that driving current was a matter of minutes, and they ran as fast as they could up the bank to a point far above where Thornton was hanging on. They attached the line with which they had been snubbing the boat to Buck's neck and shoulders, being careful that it should neither strangle him nor impede his swimming, and launched him into the stream. He struck out boldly, but not straight enough into the stream. He discovered the mistake too late, when Thornton was abreast of him and a bare half-dozen strokes away while he was being carried helplessly past.

Hans promptly snubbed with the rope, as though Buck were a boat. The rope thus tightening on him in the sweep of the current, he was jerked under the surface, and under the surface he remained till his body struck against the bank and he was hauled out. He was half-drowned, and Hans and Pete threw themselves upon him, pounding the breath into him and the water out of him. He staggered to his feet and fell down. The faint sound of Thornton's voice came to them, and though they could not make out the words of it, they knew that he was in his extremity. His master's voice acted on Buck like an electric shock. He sprang to his feet and ran up the bank ahead of the men to the point of his previous departure.

Again the rope was attached and he was launched, and again he struck out, but this time straight into the stream. He had miscalculated once, but he would not be guilty of it a second time. Hans paid out the rope, permitting no slack, while Pete kept it clear of coils. Buck held on till he was on a line straight above Thornton; then he turned, and with the speed of an express train headed down upon him. Thornton saw him coming, and, as Buck struck him like a battering ram, with the whole force of the current behind him, he reached up and closed with both arms around the shaggy neck. Hans snubbed the rope around the tree, and Buck and Thornton were jerked under the water. Strangling, suffocating, sometimes one uppermost and sometimes the other, dragging over the jagged bottom, smashing against rocks and snags, they veered in to the bank.

Thornton came to, belly downward and being violently propelled back and forth across a drift log by Hans and Pete. His first glance was for Buck. Thornton went carefully over Buck's body, when he had been brought around, finding three broken ribs.

"That settles it," he announced. "We camp right here." And camp they did, till Buck's ribs knitted and he was able to travel.

That winter, at Dawson, Buck performed another exploit, not so heroic, perhaps, but one that puts his name many notches higher on the totem pole of Alaskan fame. This exploit was particularly gratifying to the three men; for they stood in need of the outfit which it furnished, and were enabled to make a long-desired trip into the virgin East, where miners had not yet appeared. It was brought about by a conversation in the Eldorado Saloon, in which men waxed boastful of their favorite dogs. Buck, because of his record, was the target for these men, and Thornton was driven stoutly to defend him. At the end of half an hour one man stated that his dog could start a sled with five hundred pounds and walk off with it; a second bragged six hundred for his dog; and a third, seven hundred.

"Pooh! Pooh!" said John Thornton. "Buck can start a thousand pounds."

"And break it out, and walk off with it for a hundred yards?" demanded Matthewson, a Bonanza king, he of the seven hundred vaunt.

"And break it out, and walk off with it for a hundred yards," John Thornton said coolly.

"Well," Matthewson said, slowly and deliberately, so that all

could hear, "I've got a thousand dollars that says he can't. And there
it is." So saying, he slammed a sack of gold dust of the size of a
bologna sausage down upon the bar.

Nobody spoke. Thornton's bluff, if bluff it was, had been called.
He could feel a flush of warm blood creeping up his face. His
tongue had tricked him. He did not know whether Buck could start
a thousand pounds. Half a ton! The enormousness of it appalled
him. He had great faith in Buck's strength and had often thought
him capable of starting such a load; but never, as now, had he faced
the possibility of it, the eyes of a dozen men fixed upon him, silent
and waiting. Further, he had no thousand dollars; nor had Hans or
Pete.

"I've got a sled standing outside now, with twenty fifty-pound
sacks of flour on it," Matthewson went on with brutal directness,
"so don't let that hinder you."

Thornton did not reply. He did not know what to say. He
glanced from face to face in the absent way of a man who has lost
the power of thought and is seeking somewhere to find the thing
that will start it going again. The face of Jim O'Brien, a Mastodon
king and old-time comrade, caught his eyes. It was as a cue to him,
seeming to rouse him to do what he would never have dreamed of
doing.

"Can you lend me a thousand?" he asked, almost in a whisper.

"Sure," answered O'Brien, thumping down a plethoric sack by
the side of Matthewson's. "Though it's little faith I'm having, John,
that the beast can do the trick."

The Eldorado emptied its occupants into the street to see the
test. The tables were deserted, and the dealers and gamekeepers
came forth to see the outcome of the wager and to lay odds. Several
hundred men, furred and mittened, banked around the sled within
easy distance. Matthewson's sled, loaded with a thousand pounds
of flour, had been standing for a couple of hours, and in the intense
cold (it was sixty below zero) the runners had frozen fast to the
hard-packed snow. Men offered odds of two to one that Buck could
not budge the sled. A quibble arose concerning the phrase "break
out." O'Brien contended it was Thornton's privilege to knock the
runners loose, leaving Buck to "break it out" from a dead standstill.
Matthewson insisted that the phrase included breaking the runners
from the frozen grip of the snow. A majority of the men who had
witnessed the making of the bet decided in his favor, whereat the
odds went up to three to one against Buck.

There were no takers. Not a man believed him capable of the feat. Thornton had been hurried into the wager, heavy with doubt; and now that he looked at the sled itself, the concrete fact, with the regular team of ten dogs curled up in the snow before it, the more impossible the task appeared. Matthewson waxed jubilant.

"Three to one!" he proclaimed. "I'll lay you another thousand at that figure, Thornton. What d'ye say?"

Thornton's doubt was strong in his face, but his fighting spirit was aroused—the fighting spirit that soars above odds, fails to recognize the impossible, and is deaf to all save the clamor for battle. He called Hans and Pete to him. Their sacks were slim, and with his own the three partners could rake together only two hundred dollars. In the ebb of their fortunes, this sum was their total capital; yet they laid it unhesitatingly against Matthewson's six hundred.

The team of ten dogs was unhitched, and Buck, with his own harness, was put into the sled. He had caught the contagion of the excitement, and he felt that in some way he must do a great thing for John Thornton. Murmurs of admiration at his splendid appearance went up. He was in perfect condition, without an ounce of superfluous flesh, and the one hundred and fifty pounds that he weighed were so many pounds of grit and virility. His furry coat shone with the sheen of silk. Down the neck and across the shoulders, his mane, in repose as it was, half bristled and seemed to lift with every movement, as though excess of vigor made each particular hair alive and active. The great breast and heavy forelegs were no more than in proportion with the rest of the body, where the muscles showed in tight rolls underneath the skin. Men felt these muscles and proclaimed them hard as iron, and the odds went down to two to one.

"Gad, sir! Gad, sir!" stuttered a member of the latest dynasty, a king of the Skookum Benches. "I offer you eight hundred for him, sir, before the test, sir, eight hundred just as he stands."

Thornton shook his head and stepped over to Buck's side.

"You must stand off from him," Matthewson protested. "Free play and plenty of room."

The crowd fell silent; only could be heard the voices of the gamblers vainly offering two to one. Everybody acknowledged Buck a magnificent animal, but twenty fifty-pound sacks of flour bulked too large in their eyes for them to loosen their pouch-strings.

Thornton knelt down by Buck's side. He took his head in his two hands and rested cheek on cheek. He did not playfully shake him, as was his wont, or murmur soft love curses, but he whispered in his ear. "As you love me, Buck. As you love me," was what he whispered. Buck whined with suppressed eagerness.

The crowd was watching curiously. The affair was growing mysterious. It seemed like a conjuration. As Thornton got to his feet, Buck seized his mittened hand between his jaws, pressing in with his teeth and releasing slowly, half reluctantly. It was the answer, in terms not of speech but of love. Thornton stepped well back.

"Now, Buck," he said.

Buck tightened the traces, then slacked them for a matter of several inches. It was the way he had learned.

"Gee!" Thornton's voice rang out, sharp in the tense silence.

Buck swung to the right, ending the movement in a plunge that took up the slack and with a sudden jerk arrested his one hundred and fifty pounds. The load quivered, and from under the runners arose a crisp crackling.

"Haw!" Thornton commanded.

Buck duplicated the maneuver, this time to the left. The crackling turned into a snapping, the sled pivoting and the runners slipping and grating several inches to the side. The sled was broken out. Men were holding their breaths, intensely unconscious of the fact.

"Now, MUSH!"

Thornton's command cracked out like a pistol-shot. Buck threw himself forward, tightening the traces with a jarring lunge. His whole body was gathered compactly together in the tremendous effort, the muscles writhing and knotting like live things under the silky fur. His great chest was low to the ground, his head forward and down, while his feet were flying like mad, the claws scarring the hard-packed snow in parallel grooves. The sled swayed and trembled, half-started forward. One of his feet slipped, and one man groaned aloud. Then the sled lurched ahead in what appeared a rapid succession of jerks, though it never really came to a dead stop again . . . half an inch . . . an inch . . . two inches. . . . The jerks perceptibly diminished; as the sled gained momentum, he caught them up, till it was moving steadily along.

Men gasped and began to breathe again, unaware that for a moment they had ceased to breathe. Thornton was running behind, encouraging Buck with short, cheery words. The distance had been measured off, and as he neared the pile of firewood which marked the end of the hundred yards, a cheer began to grow and grow, which burst into a roar as he passed the firewood and halted at command. Every man was tearing himself loose, even Matthewson. Hats and mittens were flying in the air. Men were shaking hands, it did not matter with whom, and bubbling over in a general incoherent babel.

But Thornton fell on his knees beside Buck. Head was against head, and he was shaking him back and forth. Those who hurried up heard him cursing Buck, and he cursed him long and fervently, and softly and lovingly.

"Gad, sir! Gad, sir!" spluttered the Skookum Bench king. "I'll give you a thousand for him, sir, a thousand, sir—twelve hundred, sir."

Thornton rose to his feet. His eyes were wet. The tears were streaming frankly down his cheeks. "Sir," he said to the Skookum Bench king, "no, sir. You can go to hell, sir. It's the best I can do for you, sir."

Buck seized Thornton's hand in his teeth. Thornton shook him back and forth. As though animated by a common impulse, the onlookers drew back to a respectful distance, nor were they again indiscreet enough to interrupt.

●

The Mutiny

Alphonse de Lamartine

This crossing will stand forever as a triumph of unyielding courage and perseverance over fear of the unknown. It's a great episode to remember whenever we encounter rough passages in our own lives. The year, of course, is 1492.

When Columbus left the Canaries to pass with his three small ships into the unknown seas, the eruptions of Teneriffe illuminated the heavens and were reflected in the sea. This cast terror into the minds of his seamen. They thought that it was the flaming sword of the angel who expelled the first man from Eden, and who now was trying to drive back in anger those presumptuous ones who were seeking entrance to the forbidden and unknown seas and lands. But the admiral passed from ship to ship explaining to his men, in a simple way, the action of volcanoes, so that the sailors were no longer afraid.

But as the peak of Teneriffe sank below the horizon, a great sadness fell upon the men. It was their last beacon, the farthest sea-mark of the Old World. They were seized with a nameless terror and loneliness.

Then the admiral called them around him in his own ship, and told them many stories of the things they might hope to find in the wonderful new world to which they were going—of the lands, the islands, the seas, the kingdoms, the riches, the vegetation, the sunshine, the mines of gold, the sands covered with pearls, the mountains shining with precious stones, the plains loaded with spices. These stories, tinged with the brilliant colors of their leader's rich imagination, filled the discouraged sailors with hope and good spirits.

But as they passed over the trackless ocean, and saw day by day the great billows rolling between them and the mysterious horizon, the sailors were again filled with dread. They lacked the courage to sail onward into the unknown distance. The compass began to vacillate, and no longer pointed toward the north; this confused both Columbus and his pilots. The men fell into a panic, but the resolute and patient admiral encouraged them once more. So buoyed up by his faith and hope, they continued to sail onward over the pathless waters.

The next day a heron and a tropical bird flew about the masts of the ships, and these seemed to the wondering sailors as two witnesses come to confirm the reasoning of Columbus.

At eve and morning the distant waning clouds, like those that gather round the mountaintops, took the form of cliffs and hills skirting the horizon. The cry of "land" was on the tip of every tongue. Columbus by his reckoning knew that they must still be far from any land. But fearing to discourage his men he kept his thoughts to himself, for he found no trustworthy friend among his companions whose heart was firm enough to bear his secret.

During the long passage Columbus conversed with his own thoughts, with the stars, and with God, who he felt was his protector. He occupied his days in making notes of what he observed. The nights he passed on deck with his pilots, studying the stars and watching the seas. He withdrew into himself, and his thoughtful gravity impressed his companions sometimes with respect and sometimes with mistrust and awe.

Each morning the bows of the vessels plunged through the fantastic horizon which the evening mist had made the sailors mistake for a shore. They kept rolling on through the boundless and bottomless abyss. Gradually terror and discontent once more took possession of the crews. They began to imagine that the steadfast east wind that drove them westward prevailed eternally in this region, and that when the time came to sail homeward, the same wind would prevent their return. For surely their provisions and water could not hold out long enough for them to beat their way eastward over those wide waters!

Then the sailors began to murmur against the admiral and his seeming fruitless obstinacy, and they blamed themselves for obeying him, when it might mean the sacrifice of the lives of one hundred and twenty sailors.

But each time the murmurs threatened to break out into mutiny, Providence seemed to send more encouraging signs of land. And these for the time being changed the complaints to hopes. At evening little birds of the most delicate species, that build their nests in the shrubs of the garden and orchard, hovered warbling about the masts. Their delicate wings and joyous notes bore no signs of weariness or fright, as of birds swept far away to sea by a storm. These signs again aroused hope.

The green weeds on the surface of the ocean looked like waving corn before the ears are ripe. The vegetation beneath the water delighted the eyes of the sailors tired of the endless expanse of blue. But the seaweed soon became so thick that they were afraid of entangling their rudders and keels, and of remaining prisoners forever in the forests of the ocean, as ships of the northern seas are shut in by ice. Thus each joy soon turned to fear, so terrible to man is the unknown.

The wind ceased, the calms of the tropics alarmed the sailors. An immense whale was seen sleeping on the waters. They fancied there were monsters in the deep which would devour their ships. The roll of the waves drove them upon currents which they could not stem for want of wind. They imagined they were approaching the cataracts of the ocean, and that they were being hurried toward the abysses into which the deluge had poured its world of waters.

Fierce and angry faces crowded round the mast. The murmurs rose louder and louder. They talked of compelling the pilots to put about and of throwing the admiral into the sea. Columbus, to whom their looks and threats revealed these plans, defied them by his bold bearing or disconcerted them by his coolness.

Again nature came to his assistance, by giving him fresh breezes from the east, and a calm sea under his bows. Before the close of the day came the first cry of "Land ho!" from the lofty poop. All the crews, repeating this cry of safety, life, and triumph, fell on their knees on the decks, and struck up the hymn, "Glory be to God in heaven and upon earth." When it was over, all climbed as high as they could up the masts, yards, and rigging to see with their own eyes the new land that had been sighted.

But the sunrise destroyed this new hope all too quickly. The imaginary land disappeared with the morning mist, and once more the ships seemed to be sailing over a never-ending wilderness of waters.

Despair took possession of the crews. Again the cry of "Land ho!" was heard. But the sailors found as before that their hopes were but a passing cloud. Nothing wearies the heart so much as false hopes and bitter disappointments.

Loud reproaches against the admiral were heard from every quarter. Bread and water were beginning to fail. Despair changed to fury. The men decided to turn the heads of the vessels toward Europe, and to beat back against the winds that had favored the admiral, whom they intended to chain to the mast of his own vessel and to give up to the vengeance of Spain should they ever reach the port of their own country.

These complaints now became clamorous. The admiral restrained them by the calmness of his countenance. He called upon Heaven to decide between himself and the sailors. He flinched not. He offered his life as a pledge, if they would but trust and wait for three days more. He swore that, if, in the course of the third day, land was not visible on the horizon, he would yield to their wishes and steer for Europe.

The mutinous men reluctantly consented and allowed him three days of grace.

At sunrise on the second day rushes recently torn up were seen floating near the vessels. A plank hewn by an axe, a carved stick, a bough of hawthorn in blossom, and lastly a bird's nest built on a branch which the wind had broken, and full of eggs on which the parent-bird was sitting, were seen swimming past on the waters. The sailors brought on board these living witnesses of their approach to land. They were like a message from the shore, confirming the promises of Columbus.

The overjoyed and repentant mutineers fell on their knees before the admiral whom they had insulted but the day before, and craved pardon for their mistrust.

As the day and night advanced, many other sights and sounds showed that land was very near. Toward day delicious and unknown perfumes borne on a soft land breeze reached the vessels, and there was heard the roar of the waves upon the reefs.

The dawn, as it spread over the sky, gradually raised the shores of an island from the waves. Its distant extremities were lost in the morning mist. As the sun rose it shone on the land ascending from a low yellow beach to the summit of hills whose dark-green covering contrasted strongly with the clear blue of the heavens. The foam of the waves broke on the yellow sand, and forests of tall and unknown trees stretched away, one above another, over successive terraces of the island. Green valleys, and bright clefts in the hollows afforded a half glimpse into these mysterious wilds. And thus the land of golden promises, the land of future greatness, first appeared to Christopher Columbus, the Admiral of the Ocean.

•

THE CRISIS

Thomas Paine

These famous words by Thomas Paine appeared during the winter of 1776–1777, a time that may have been the gloomiest hour for the American revolutionary cause. The patriot forces seemed unable to win a battle. George Washington's army had been routed out of New York, driven across New Jersey, and lay shivering on the Pennsylvania side of the Delaware River. More and more men deserted every day. Racked by hunger, cold, and disease, those who remained simply waited in misery for their enlistments to expire so they could go home. Washington himself confided in a letter to a relative: "I think the game is pretty near up." Amid this crisis of morale, Paine implored the colonists not to give up the fight.

These are the times that try men's souls. The summer soldier and the sunshine patriot will, in this crisis, shrink from the service of their country; but he that stands it *now,* deserves the love and thanks of man and woman. Tyranny, like hell, is not easily conquered; yet we have this consolation with us, that the harder the conflict, the more glorious the triumph. What we obtain too cheap, we esteem too lightly: it is dearness only that gives every thing its value. Heaven knows how to put a proper price upon its goods; and it would be strange indeed if so celestial an article as FREEDOM should not be highly rated. . . .

I call not upon a few, but upon all: not on *this* state or *that* state, but on *every* state: up and help us; lay your shoulders to the wheel; better have too much force than too little, when so great an object is at stake. Let it be told to the future world, that in the depth of winter, when nothing but hope and virtue could survive, that the city and the country, alarmed at one common danger, came forth to meet and to repulse it. Say not that thousands are gone, turn out your tens of thousands; throw not the burden of the day upon Providence, but *"show your faith by your works,"* that God may bless you. It matters not where you live, or what rank of life you hold, the evil or the blessing will reach you all. The far and the near, the home counties and the back, the rich and the poor, will suffer or rejoice alike. The heart that feels not now, is dead: the blood of his children will curse his cowardice, who shrinks back at a time when a little might have saved the whole, and made *them* happy. I love the man that can smile in trouble, that can gather strength from distress, and grow brave by reflection. 'Tis the business of little minds to shrink; but he whose heart is firm, and whose conscience approves his conduct, will pursue his principles unto death.

•

A PRAYER AT VALLEY FORGE

Valley Forge has become a place forever linked in the American mind with the virtues of courage, perseverance, and loyalty to cause. Some 9,000 of George Washington's troops went into camp there in the late autumn of 1777. By the time the snows of winter

were gone, only 6,000 remained. Here is a story of heroic resolve
of ordinary men, as well as an example of how faith helped one
extraordinary man lead the rest through.

During the Revolutionary War the British army seized Philadelphia, the "rebel capital" where the Congress had been meeting.
They marched into the city with colors flying and bands playing,
and made themselves at home for the winter. George Washington
could do nothing to stop them. Once the British were in the city,
the only thing he could do was see that they did not get out into
the countryside to do any mischief. So he chose for his winter
quarters Valley Forge, a place only a few miles from Philadelphia.
There the American army could defend itself if attacked, and it
could keep close watch on the British.

It would have been easier to fight many battles than to spend
that winter in Valley Forge. It was December, and there was no
shelter of any kind. Men and officers bravely set to work con-
structing huts for themselves. They built some of heavy logs, with
roofs made of small trees wrapped with straw and laid side by side.
Clay was spread on top of that. The windows were simply holes cut
through the logs and covered with oiled paper.

Such a house was the height of luxury at Valley Forge. Most of
the huts were made of piled-up sod, or fence rails held together by
twisted twigs and daubed with clay. The snow sifted in at every
opening, the rain dripped through even the best of the roofs, and
the wind howled and roared and blew in at every crevice. There
were few blankets, and many brave defenders of their country lay
on the frozen ground because they had not even straw to put under
their heads. Sometimes they sat up all night, crowding up to the
fires to keep from freezing.

Their clothing was worse than their shelter. The whole army
was in rags. Many of the men had no shirts, even more were without
shoes. Wherever they walked, the snow was marked with blood.
Some cut strips from their precious blankets and wound them
about their feet to protect them from the freezing ground.

Food was scanty. Sometimes for several days the soldiers went
without meat, and some companies went without even bread. When
the word went around "no meat tonight," the soldiers groaned, but
they never yielded.

Here is an entry in the diary of one of the men:

"There comes a soldier—his bare feet peep through his worn-out shoes, his legs nearly naked from the tattered remains of an only pair of stockings . . . his shirt hanging in strings . . . his face meager—his whole appearance pictures a person forsaken and discouraged. He comes, and cries with an air of wretchedness and despair . . . I am sick, my feet lame, my legs are sore, my body covered with this tormenting itch. My clothes are worn out, my constitution is broken, my former activity is exhausted by fatigue. Hunger and cold. I fail fast. I shall soon be no more."

One cold day a Quaker farmer was walking along a creek at Valley Forge when he heard the murmur of a solemn voice. Creeping in its direction, he discovered a horse tied to a sapling, but no rider.

The farmer stole nearer, following the sound of the voice. There, through a thicket, he saw a lone man, on his knees in the snow.

It was General Washington. His cheeks were wet with tears as he prayed to the Almighty for help and guidance.

The farmer quietly slipped away. When he reached home, he said to his wife, "The Americans will win their independence! George Washington will succeed!"

"What makes thee think so, Isaac?" she asked.

"I have heard him pray, Hannah, out in the woods today," he said. "If there is anyone on this earth the Lord will listen to, it is this brave commander. He will listen, Hannah. Rest assured, He will."

•

MOLLY PITCHER

Here is an American "Horatius at the Bridge."

It was the twenty-eighth day of June, 1778. Two great armies, which were engaged in one of the world's most decisive struggles, were on the plains of Monmouth in New Jersey. Riding up and down the lines of the American forces was the great Washington, urging on the soldiers of freedom with words of encouragement and command.

The brilliant uniforms of the British glittered in the sunlight, and at their head rode the gallant General Clinton, whose military bravery had won for him the admiration of Europe.

The fighting was fierce and determined. Shell and shot mingled with the roar of cannon, and the beat of every instant left more wounded on the field.

The issue of the battle was doubtful. Neither side knew which was to be the victor, for triumph seemed within the grasp of either, at the instant.

In the midst of the conflict was a lad named William Hays. Not for an instant did he leave his post as artilleryman, even when it looked like the American forces might be thrown back.

"I'll not retreat," he muttered, "as long as there is another man on the field to fight."

By the side of this brave lad stood a young woman, scarcely out of her girlhood. It was Molly, his wife, and her face was set with determination.

"I will follow William through the army," she had said. "I can help the soldiers when they are in trouble, and I can stand it as well as he."

The laughing eyes and keen wit of Molly had brought cheer to many of the heartsick soldiers. Patiently she had ministered to their needs, and tenderly she had bound their bleeding wounds. The day was intensely hot; the temperature soared close to one hundred degrees. One by one, gasping soldiers began to drop from thirst and exhaustion, so Molly grabbed an artillery bucket and began carrying water from a cool spring to the troops. "Here comes Molly with her pitcher!" they would shout, and afterward she was known as Molly Pitcher.

But on one of her trips a deadly ball whizzed past her head— and William fell wounded. There was no one to take his place, and the cannon's crew prepared to abandon the field. But without a moment's hesitation, Molly grabbed the rammer staff from her fallen husband's hand and began swabbing and reloading the gun. Boom! Boom! It echoed across the battlefield, as she reloaded each time with the agility of a trained artilleryman.

"The enemy is almost upon us!" cried one of the soldiers.

"Stand fast," replied Molly.

The cheers of the soldiers rang down the line. The battle was turning, and there in the ranks stood Molly Pitcher—a cannoneer.

When the fighting was over, and the British were in retreat, the soldiers gathered about her to praise her courage, but she did not hear their words. She was bending over her husband, nursing his wounds.

The next day the story of Molly Pitcher passed through the camp. General Nathanael Greene heard it and strode straight to Molly's tent.

"Come, my brave girl," he said. "I want to take you to General Washington."

As they reached the tent of the great commander, he rose with his grave and stately manner, and with a courteous bow to the Irish girl, he extended his hand.

"You have made a brave stand," he said. "We will win our liberty, if we all stand fast like you."

It is said the young woman was awarded a warrant as a non-commissioned officer, and thereafter the admiring army called her "Sergeant Molly."

Such is the tale of Molly Pitcher, heroine of the American Revolution. The battlefield monuments tell of her courage, and an old rhyme recalls her deed:

> Moll Pitcher she stood by her gun
> And rammed the charges home, sir;
> And thus on Monmouth's bloody field
> A sergeant did become, sir.

•

THE STAR-SPANGLED BANNER
Adapted from Eva March Tappan

Many people sing the first verse of this song several times a year without knowing the context of its birth or the story of how our flag became the national symbol of perseverance through perilous times.

The year 1814 found the people of Maryland in trouble. A British fleet of some fifty ships had sailed into the Chesapeake Bay. Their cannon soon would be aimed at some town, but nobody knew which. The ships sailed up one river, came back down, and sailed up another, as if they had not decided which port would fall under their guns. All along the shores, people fired alarms and lit signal fires to let their neighbors know danger was near. The ships lingered, hesitated, then suddenly spread sails and ran to the north, up the bay.

"They will surely destroy us," thought the people of Annapolis. They crammed their household goods into wagons and carts, even into wheelbarrows, and hurried inland as fast as they could. But the ships sailed past Annapolis.

Suddenly there was no question which town they meant to attack. It was Baltimore. With forty-five thousand inhabitants, the port was the third-largest city in the country and a rich prize. To take it, however, the British fleet would have to get past Fort McHenry, which guarded Baltimore's harbor.

As the warships crept upstream toward the fort, the crews could see a gigantic flag with fifteen white stars and fifteen red and white stripes fluttering in the breeze above the ramparts. It was the work of widow Mary Young Pickersgill, a seamstress who specialized in making flags for Baltimore's merchant ships. Her own house wasn't large enough for the job of stitching the enormous banner together, so she and her thirteen-year-old daughter Caroline had worked on it in a Baltimore brewery. Now it flew as a proud, defiant symbol of an upstart country that was about to take on the most powerful nation in the world.

At 7 A.M. on the morning of September 13, the big British guns took aim at the flag and let loose a horrifying fire. They shot huge,

200-pound bombshells designed to explode on impact, scattering wreckage far and wide. Often, however, the erratic bombs blew up in midair. The shelling lasted nearly twenty-four hours. When dark fell the fleet used signal rockets, which traced fiery arcs across the night sky. It was a spectacular sight.

"If Fort McHenry can stand, the city is safe," Francis Scott Key muttered to himself, and he gazed anxiously through the smoke to see if the flag was still flying.

The Maryland lawyer had a particularly agonizing view of the battle—he watched from a little American vessel tied fast to the side of the British flagship. A friend had been seized as a prisoner by the British, and Key had gone out under a flag of truce to ask for his release. The British commander finally agreed to the request, but he had no intention of letting Key go back to the city with any information he might have picked up. "Until the battle is over, you and your boat stay here," he ordered.

Key had no choice but to wait it out, pacing the deck and hoping the fort could hold out. The firing went on. As long as daylight lasted, he could catch glimpses of the Stars and Stripes whenever the wind swayed the clouds of smoke. When night came, he could still see the banner now and then by the blaze of the cannon.

Finally the firing stopped. Key strained his eyes to see if the flag was still flying. "Could the fort have held out?" he wondered.

At last the faint gray of dawn appeared. He could see that some flag was flying, but it was too dark to tell whose. More and more eagerly he gazed. It grew lighter. A sudden breath of wind caught the banner, and it floated out on the breeze. It was no English flag. It was Mary Pickersgill's Stars and Stripes, still waving through the smoke and mist! Fort McHenry had stood, and the city was safe.

Overcome with emotion, Key took from his pocket an old letter and began scribbling on its back a few lines and phrases.

The British departed, and the little American boat sailed back to the city. Key gave a copy of the poem he had just written to his uncle, who had been helping defend the fort. His uncle sent it to a printer and had it struck off on some handbills. Before the ink was dry the printer snatched one up and hurried to a tavern where many patriots were assembling.

"Listen to this!" he cried, waving the paper, and he read:

O say, can you see by the dawn's early light,
What so proudly we hailed at the twilight's last gleaming,
Whose broad stripes and bright stars, through the perilous fight
O'er the ramparts we watch'd were so gallantly streaming?
And the rockets' red glare, the bombs bursting in air,
Gave proof through the night that our flag was still there.
O say, does that star-spangled banner yet wave
O'er the land of the free and the home of the brave?

"Sing it! Sing it!" the whole company cried. Someone mounted a chair and sang the poem to an old tune. The song caught on at once. Halls, theaters, and houses soon rang with its strains as the British fleet disappeared over the horizon.

Frances Scott Key's words never lost their popularity, and more than a century later, in 1931, Congress designated "The Star-Spangled Banner" as our national anthem.

•

The Marines' Hymn

There is an entire organization devoted to the ideal of fidelity to task. Its motto is a great one to adopt when seeing your way through a tough job: Semper Fidelis—Always Faithful.

From the Halls of Montezuma
To the shores of Tripoli
We fight our country's battles
On the land as on the sea.
First to fight for right and freedom
And to keep our honor clean;
We are proud to claim the title
Of United States Marines.

Our flag's unfurled to every breeze
From dawn to setting sun;
We have fought in every clime and place
Where we could take a gun.

In the snow of far-off Northern lands
And in sunny tropic scenes;
You will find us always on the job—
The United States Marines.

Here's health to you and to our Corps
Which we are proud to serve;
In many a strife we've fought for life
And never lost our nerve.
If the Army and the Navy
Ever look on Heaven's scenes,
They will find the streets are guarded
By United States Marines.

•

THE RACE FROM MARATHON

Here is the classic story of endurance, the tale which lends its
name to our popular modern contest. This original run, which
took place in 490 B.C., covered about twenty-five miles, the distance from Marathon to Athens. The current distance for modern
marathon races was established in 1908, when King Edward VII
of England wished to watch the start of the Olympic event from
his home at Windsor Castle. Thereafter, 26 miles 385 yards—the
distance from the castle to London's Olympic stadium—became
the official marathon distance.

Twenty-five hundred years ago, Darius I of Persia established
an empire that stretched across Asia and into Africa. Darius himself
was called "the Great King," or simply "the King," as if there were
no other ruler on the face of the earth. And he intended that there
should be no other if he should have his way. He made up his mind
to make himself master of the Greeks, known far and wide for their
skill in peace and courage in war.

Darius sent heralds to every state in Greece to demand tributes
of earth and water as symbols that the land and sea belonged to
him alone. Some of the states submitted, others proudly refused.

Athens was among the latter. The Athenians threw the Persian heralds into a muddy ditch. "There you will find both earth and water for your master," they cried.

When Darius heard of the rebuke he assembled his vast army, readied his fleet, and set sail over the Aegean Sea. The Athenians heard of his approach. Soon their city would be overrun. At once they thought of appealing to the famous Spartans, whose state lay 140 miles to the south, across the Isthmus of Corinth.

The rulers of Athens, seated in grave council on the Acropolis, sent for Pheidippides, their champion runner. They commanded him to hurry and urge Sparta to come to their aid.

Pheidippides ran. He scrambled up rocky paths, passed through shadowy gorges, crossed rivers that ran over slippery stones. For two days and two nights he ran, carrying the urgent plea. He reached Sparta hungry, dusty, and footsore.

But the Spartans, though fearless of Darius, were envious and mistrustful of Athens. They looked at Pheidippides in silence. They smiled darkly and murmured among themselves, while the messenger stood waiting.

"We must not act in haste," they said at last. "We must think it over. Besides, you know our custom; we never fight when the moon is at the half. Wait until the moon is full. Then perhaps we will come."

Pheidippides wanted to shout in anger and despair. But there was no time for bitterness—he had to let his countrymen know. He did not stop to trade insults with the Spartans. Back over the hills and plains he rushed, fording the streams, clambering over boulders, threading his way through forests. He arrived in Athens with the word: The Spartans will not help. The Athenians must depend on their own resources.

Now the Persians had landed on the Greek coast and gone into camp on the plain of Marathon, about twenty-five miles away. The Athenians resolved to oppose them at once. The weary but dauntless Pheidippides took his long spear and his heavy shield, and marched out with 10,000 men picked to meet the foe.

You can read in the history books how the outnumbered Greeks came down from the hills to meet the enemy. The Athenians charged courageously amid awful shouting and dreadful clash of arms. For a while the Persians stood fast, hurling their missiles, but at last the Greeks broke their line. When the day was over, Darius and his army were fleeing to their ships.

The Greek general called on Pheidippides.

"Take the news to Athens as fast as you can. Tell them of our victory."

Already exhausted from battle, Pheidippides flung down his shield and began to run as he had never run before. He thought only of his home and his worried people, waiting to know if they were destined to live or die. His heart pounded, his temples throbbed, the muscles in his legs trembled, but not once did he stop. One mile, five miles, ten, twenty, twenty-five miles back to the city. The anxious citizens made way as he staggered to the center and gasped:

"Rejoice! We conquer!"

The Athenians shouted for joy, but Pheidippides sank to the ground. And when the people raised him in their arms, they saw he was dead.

•

HENRY BOX BROWN'S ESCAPE

Henry Box Brown

Of all the stories of breathtaking escapes from slavery, Henry Box Brown's 1848 trip from Richmond to Philadelphia remains one of the most celebrated journeys to freedom on the Underground Railroad. Here are courage and ingenuity born of desperate circumstances.

At length, after praying earnestly to Him, who seeth afar off, for assistance, in my difficulty, suddenly, as if from above, there darted into my mind these words, "Go and get a box, and put yourself in it." I pondered the words over in my mind. "Get a box?" thought I. "What can this mean?" But I was not "disobedient unto the heavenly vision," and I determined to put into practice this direction, as I considered it, from my heavenly Father. I went to the depot, and there noticed the size of the largest boxes, which commonly were sent by the cars, and returned with their dimensions. I then repaired to a carpenter, and induced him to make me a box of such a description as I wished, informing him of the use I intended to make of it. He assured me I could not live in it; but as it was dear liberty I was in pursuit of, I thought it best to make the trial.

When the box was finished, I carried it, and placed it before my friend, who had promised to assist me, who asked me if that was to "put my clothes in." I replied that it was not, but to *"put Henry Brown in!"* He was astonished at my temerity; but I insisted upon his placing me in it, and nailing me up, and he finally consented.

After corresponding with a friend in Philadelphia, arrangements were made for my departure, and I took my place in this narrow prison, with a mind full of uncertainty. . . .

I laid me down in my darkened home of three feet by two, and like one about to be guillotined, resigned myself to my fate. My friend was to accompany me, but he failed to do so; and contented himself with sending a telegraph message to his correspondent in Philadelphia, that such a box was on its way to his care.

I took with me a bladder filled with water to bathe my neck with, in case of too great heat; and with no access to the fresh air, excepting three small gimblet holes, I started on my perilous cruise. I was first carried to the express office, the box being placed on its end, so that I started with my head downwards, although the box was directed, "this side up with care." From the express office, I was carried to the depot, and from thence tumbled roughly into the baggage car, where I *happened* to fall "right side up," but no thanks to my transporters. But after a while the cars stopped, and I was put aboard a steamboat, *and placed on my head.* In this dreadful position, I remained the space of an hour and a half, it seemed to me, when I began to feel of my eyes and head, and found to my dismay, that my eyes were almost swollen out of their sockets, and the veins on my temple seemed ready to burst. I made no noise, however, determining to obtain *"victory or death,"* but endured the terrible pain, as well as I could, sustained under the whole by the thoughts of sweet liberty.

About half an hour afterwards, I attempted again to lift my hands to my face, but I found I was not able to move them. A cold sweat now covered me from head to foot. Death seemed my inevitable fate, and every moment I expected to feel the blood flowing over me, which had burst from my veins. One half hour longer and my sufferings would have ended in that fate, which I preferred to slavery; but I lifted up my heart to God in prayer, believing that he would yet deliver me, when to my joy, I overheard two men say, "We have been here *two* hours and have travelled twenty miles, now let us sit down, and rest ourselves." They suited the action to the word, and turned the box over, containing my soul and body, thus delivering me from the power of the grim messenger of death, who a few moments previously, had aimed his fatal shaft at my head, and had placed his icy hands on my throbbing heart. . . .

Soon after this fortunate event, we arrived at Washington, where I was thrown from the wagon and again as my luck would have it, fell on my head. I was then rolled down a declivity, until I reached the platform from which the cars were to start. During this short but rapid journey, my neck came very near being dislocated, as I felt it crack, as if it had snapped asunder. Pretty soon, I heard someone say, "There is no room for this box, it will have to remain behind." I then again applied to the Lord, my help in all my difficulties, and in a few minutes I heard a gentleman direct the hands to place it aboard, as "it came with the mail and must go on with it." I was then tumbled into the car, my head downwards again, as I seemed to be destined to escape on my head; a sign probably, of the opinion of American people respecting such bold adventurers as myself; that our heads should be held downwards, whenever we attempt to benefit ourselves. Not the only instance of this propensity, on the part of the American people, towards the colored race. We had not proceeded far, however, before more baggage was placed in the car, at a stopping place, and I was again turned to my proper position.

No further difficulty occurred until my arrival at Philadelphia. I reached this place at three o'clock in the morning, and remained in the depot until six o'clock, A.M., at which time, a wagon drove up, and a person inquired for a box directed to such a place, "right side up." I was soon placed on this wagon, and carried to the house of my friend's correspondent, where quite a number of persons were waiting to receive me. They appeared to be some afraid to open the box at first, but at length one of them rapped upon it, and with a trembling voice, asked, "Is all right within?" to which I replied, "All right." The joy of these friends was excessive, and like the ancient Jews, who repaired to the rebuilding of Jerusalem, each one seized hold of some tool, and commenced opening my grave. At length the cover was removed, and I arose, and shook myself from the lethargy into which I had fallen; but exhausted nature proved too much for my frame, and I swooned away.

•

JINKYSWOITMAYA

C. H. Claudy

This story is from *The Youth's Companion,* a Boston magazine
that from 1827 until 1929 provided instructive and entertaining
reading for American children. Here's a great tale about putting
yourself on the line.

A proverb has it that "one man's meat is another man's poison," and true enough it is that what one assimilates with pleasure
another can only take with pain. The "water" was a terror to Jinks
for reasons which will appear anon; but he had resources of courage in other matters, which, for all they called him a coward, proved
him a hero after all.

"It was in the spring of 1897," says Mr. C. H. Claudy, writing in
The Youth's Companion, "while I was employed on botanical and
geological work in Alaska, that I made the acquaintance of 'Jinkyswoitmaya,' whom we called 'Jinks' for short. He was the son of a
Russian 'claim-jumper' and an Aleut Indian squaw, and he lived in
the little village of Nutchek, Hinchinbrook Island, Prince William
Sound.

"Jinks had had rather an unhappy life, for he was, in the estima-
tion of his companions, a coward; he had an innate fear of water.
Jinks could not be induced to enter a canoe for any purpose whatever, and on that account he was the scorn of the island, for the
Aleuts sport and hunt on the sea as if it were their natural element.
But Jinks is no physical coward, and this is the story of how I found
it out.

"I had been in the village just two days, when we had one of
those terrific rainstorms that occasionally visit the Alaskan coast late
in the spring. For three days and nights it rained in sheets. During
my enforced idleness I made the acquaintance of Jinks, who could
speak a little English, and speedily became fond of me, because I
never snubbed him nor spoke his name with the obnoxious Aleutian adjective which means 'one who is afraid' at the end of it.

"Jinks was then about fifteen years old, but strong and wiry,
and more than ordinarily bright.

"It was on the third day of our acquaintance, I think, that Jinks
told me of the wonderful view from a plateau of a mountain on the

island. He said it could be reached by about five hours' climbing. This view, I thought, must be remarkable indeed, and so it happened that, when Jinks shyly proffered his services as guide, I made ready to go as soon as the rain should cease.

"After waiting a day for the streams to subside and the wet ground to dry, we started. We carried a knapsack of food, a canteen of cold tea, a rifle, a sheath-knife apiece, forty feet of three-eighths rope, a hatchet, and a binocular.

"Tramping for an hour steadily west, we came to the foot of Mount Kenia, a hill some four thousand feet high, halfway up which was the wondrous view. Then our difficulties began. The way lay through dense woods for awhile, the ground getting steeper and steeper.

"Now and then a stone would start from our feet and go bounding down the mountain, smashing into trees, rebounding, going on again, until finally stopped by a tangle of underbrush; or, escaping that, it would go on and on until only the echoes of its crashing descent told that it was still on its way. The heavy rain had made the ground easy to our feet, but occasionally the foothold would prove treacherous, and we would slip down on our faces. Several times we came to banks so steep and slippery it seemed as if we were stalled; but Jinks could climb like a monkey, and would crawl up ahead somehow, fasten the rope to a tree and let it down to me, that I might haul myself bodily up after him. We finally reached the end of our climb, at a point about twenty-five hundred feet above the sea level.

"Here we turned to the right, on a natural road of rock, traversing a sort of miniature cañon.

"At the end of half an hour's walk we found ourselves at a standstill, brought up against a blank rock wall thirty feet in height. Nothing disconcerted, Jinks tied the rope about his waist, kicked off his disreputable footwear, and began to climb the wall. How he did it I don't know, for I found it difficult even with the help of the rope he let down to me.

"Once arrived on top, I soon forgot all my tribulations in the wonderful sight. We were on a narrow plateau, perhaps fifty feet wide—a rift in the mountain, which rose in sheer rock walls on each side of us at a distance of a quarter of a mile. A thin line of trees was ahead of me, and beyond them the ocean. Going through the trees, I found myself on the edge of a precipice, with the Pacific Ocean spread out before me.

"Directly in front the rock sloped away steeply for about forty feet, then took an abrupt dive downward, going sheer to the sea in a perpendicular line, about three thousand feet.

"The Alaskan gulf below looked like a huge panorama. Away off on the horizon I could see, with the aid of my glass, the white sails of a hull-down ship. On each side of me stretched away in limitless perspective the Alaskan continuation of the Rocky Mountains—snow-capped always. I will not attempt to describe the vast and desolate scene over which brooded such a silence, accentuated by the occasional single sad call of a gull.

"For perhaps the half of an hour we looked and said nothing. Jinks appeared quite satisfied with my first involuntary expression of delight at the picture, and I did not insult his perceptions by attempting to explain to him how fine I thought it.

"Then we lunched, and after that I walked a rod or two along the brink of the incline and sat down on a little knoll of grass-covered earth, letting my feet hang over on the rock slope below, and prepared to enjoy the changing lights and shadows of the clouds on the sunlit sea, while Jinks went to sleep reclining against a tree directly behind me.

"Then it happened! As I was sitting there peacefully, my thoughts on anything but the recent rainstorm, the little knoll, its cohesive force loosened by the water it contained, gently detached itself from the rock and slid, with me on it, swiftly down the forty feet of rock slope toward the brink beyond.

"As I went down that terrible slide, my first thought was to jump to safety, my next to spread out and attempt to catch on some projection of rock, and my last a prayer for help. Jinks says I screamed and woke him, but I have no recollection of it. In three or four seconds I had arrived at the edge, convinced that another instant would see me hurtling through the air to the rocks three thousand feet below. On the very edge I stopped, caught on a small uprising bit of rock. I was flat on my back, my arms extended on either side of me and above my head. I was bent in the form of a bow; my body from my waist down was over the brink.

"I did not faint and I was not frightened, which sounds absurd, I know; but it is true. Scientists will tell you that in moments of great and sudden danger, the instinct of self-preservation over-comes mere fear. Be that as it may, I was cool, calm, and much alive to my very slim chance of escape. I could not move. I don't mean that I was held, or that I was paralyzed, but I knew that if I should try to move I must fall over the brink.

"My senses were abnormally keen. I heard the cry of a gull so clearly that I thought it very close, but just then the bird came into my range of vision and I saw it was a long distance away. Jinks's shouting from forty feet above seemed right at my ear—by straining my eyes upward I could see the top of his head—but as he was excited and talked Aleutian, I could not understand him. Turning my eyes the other way and looking toward where my feet should have been, I could see a little strip of sea, the horizon, and the sails of a ship. I remembered I had seen a ship before; I tried to think when, but could not. It bothered my sense of location to see only the sails of a ship when it was between me and the horizon, but then I reflected that its hull was in the zone I could not see.

"I did not think of ways to extricate myself, because in one mental flash I knew my only hope was in Jinks and the rope, and I knew he had left it tied to the tree where he had fastened it for me to climb over the rocky wall at the end of the cañon. A little bit of earth, loosened from above in some way, struck me gently in the face. What if a large amount should come down on me before Jinks could get back with the rope?

" '*But it won't—I'm quite sure it won't—Jinks will be here in a minute now—and then—and then—I'll get out of this mess—the rope——*' and then a horrible thought: '*Suppose the rope is not long enough to reach?*'

"Hope is, in a way, the father of fear, and fear came to me now —with the nearness of relief. I was cold. I didn't tremble; I suppose I was too much afraid that if I did I must fall over the brink. But I was very much frightened by my thought that perhaps the rope would not be long enough to reach me.

"Although it seemed to me that I had been hanging a long time on the edge of the precipice, I realized that I thought so simply from the swiftness and number of my impressions. I tried really to calculate the time, and finally decided I had been there nearly twenty minutes; but that estimate was excessive.

"As the fright in a measure subsided, my body ached in protest against the strained position of the muscles; and then suddenly I forgot pain.

"I heard Jinks. 'Comin' now, misser. Got rope, get up minute now——' finishing off with a long string of Aleutian, which, although incomprehensible, was very comforting. I could not see anything of him, except once in a while the top of his head. It occurred to me, however, that there was really nothing to prevent my turning my head on one side. This I did, very slowly and carefully; and at last, by dint of much straining of eyes, I was able to see Jinks away above me, and in a curiously inverted and distorted perspective, working madly to get the rope untangled.

"In a moment he had finished, and then I had the impatient pleasure of seeing the rope coming slowly down the rock face, twisting and turning, like a thin, long snake. It was curious to watch, because it was all seen out of the corner of my eye—seen as one sees in a dream—shapeless, vague, and yet painfully real.

"Now I heard nothing, felt nothing, neither pain nor fright—saw nothing but this travesty of a snake coming slowly towards me. Slowly crawling, sliding, stopping and coming on down, catching on bits of rock and dropping again, it gradually came nearer. Of course it really came down in a few seconds—just as fast as Jinks could pay it out—but impatience and the abnormally acute state of my nerves made it seem a long time. And then it stopped—just six inches above my hand!

"My arms were stretched to their fullest extent, but the rope did not reach my hands. It did not seem to me to matter much; it must have been that I supposed Jinks had not finished paying out all the rope. Then, after a moment, the rope receded some four or five feet, underwent sundry gyrations, and Jinks disappeared from view. Then the rope descended again, this time with about a foot to spare.

"I held my breath, got a good firm grip with one hand, then with the other; and then, putting my weight on it slowly and timorously, afraid it might give in some way, I began to haul myself up. At last I got my feet on the rock, and the rest was easy. Turning on my face, I could help my arms in their task of hauling by sticking my toes into cracks and on projections, as I had seen Jinks do. Halfway up I had a terrible moment; the rope seemed to give a little, and at the same time I heard a smothered cry from Jinks.

"Now I was but ten feet from the top—now eight—now six— four—three feet—another haul and I was almost there—one foot —safety!

"And then I understood why Jinks was not in sight. He lay at full length on his face, his arms locked round the tree he had used as a pillow earlier in the day, the rope knotted around one ankle. The rope had not been long enough, and Jinks had lengthened it with his own body!

"Anyone who has ever attempted to remain suspended by the arms for more than a few seconds will have some faint idea of what poor Jinks must have suffered on that rack. I weigh one hundred and eighty pounds. The pain he endured without a murmur can be indicated by results. One of his arms was out of joint; that accounted for the sudden give in the rope and the smothered cry. The flesh on the ankle where the rope had been tied was cruelly crushed and bruised.

"Except for seeing him lying there suffering that I might live, I must have fainted away in reaction from the nervous strain. What I did do was perhaps as weak, but I trust excusable. I fell on my face beside Jinks, with one arm round his neck, and burst into sobs. In a moment he was sitting up, his dark face shining with joy, in spite of his pain, that he had saved 'misser' from death.

"I bound up his poor, crushed foot, pulled his arm back into place, and with infinite difficulty helped him home. We arrived just before midnight. We were nursed back to health and strength, and so loud were my praises of Jinks, he soon became the hero of the town. Through the aid of the missionary, I was enabled to make them all understand what a really brave fellow he was, and what an heroic thing he had done in risking his life and enduring pain that another might live.

"Jinks carries a wonderful watch now—and inside the cover is the inscription, 'From a grateful man to a brave one.' "

•

SCYLLA AND CHARYBDIS

Adapted from a retelling
by Edmund Carpenter

From *The Odyssey,* here is the classic rough passage, the kind
where you know there may be losses, where you gather your
courage, lower your head, and push through as best you can.

For ancient mariners there were countless terrors, both real
and imagined, on the rolling seas. But none was more dreaded than
a certain narrow passage of water said to be off the coast of southern Italy. It was a very treacherous strait, for there were two hideous
points, one on either side, that all sailors strived to shun. These
were called Scylla and Charybdis.

The first was a lofty crag, reaching even to the heavens with its
sharp peak. Dark clouds always hovered about its top, and perpetual darkness rested upon its summit. So steep was its face, and so
smooth, that no mortal could clamber up or down, though he might
have twenty hands and feet. Midway up the face of this great cliff
was a cave so high above the water no bowman, however strong,
could reach it with his arrow from a passing ship.

In this cave dwelt Scylla, the hideous monster who gave her
name to the crag itself. She had six long, scaly necks, and upon each
neck was a frightful, barking head. Each of these six heads had three
rows of sharp, greedy teeth, all set closely together. The story was
that Scylla hid herself within the cave, but every so often would
lean far out of the opening. The glaring eyes in her six heads would
scan the waters below. No passing fish or dolphin could escape her
dreadful vigilance, for when she saw one she would reach out and
catch it in her claws, draw it into her cave, and devour it. Seamen
were careful to avoid this crag, for if they allowed their vessel to go
too near, Scylla would suddenly reach down and snatch some poor,
unfortunate sailor from the deck and disappear with him into her
den.

On the other side of the strait was another crag, called
Charybdis. This peak was not so lofty as the other, and on its top
grew a tall, fine fig tree, always covered with leaves and fruit. But at
the foot of the cliff was a great gulf in the rock, down which the

water was sucked with great violence, forming a tremendous whirlpool. Then suddenly the water would come boiling back out, as powerfully as it had been sucked in, tossing onto the waves the planks of old ships and skeletons of hapless sailors. So fierce were these movements of the water that, if a passing vessel should chance to go too near, it would be either drawn into the vortex and sucked down out of sight, or else it would be tossed about, thrown against the rock, and crushed and all the crew drowned.

It was on the long voyage home, after the Trojan War, that Ulysses and his crew came to this horrible strait where they must pass between Scylla and Charybdis.

When the heroes came within sight and hearing of the place they were filled with fear. The oars fell from their hands, and the blood drained from their faces. The horrid murmur of the fiends cut into their very brains. The towering rocks seemed to threaten them with disaster; the boiling surf hid, they knew, treacherous spots.

Ulysses, seeing the state of his men, went up and down the deck encouraging them and reminding them that they had pulled through greater perils together. He begged that they give him the same trust they had offered before and assured them he would lead them through if only they would exert all the strength and wit they had. In particular he cheered up the pilot who sat at the helm, and told him he must now show more firmness than other men, as he had more responsibility committed to him. Ulysses ordered him to steer away from the whirlpool, as it would surely swallow them all, and set a course by the higher rock.

The crew heard him, and nerved again by their captain's gallant bearing, took to the oars. Ulysses, in his shining armor, stood on the prow of the vessel, two gleaming javelins in his hand, on guard, lest the six-mouthed Scylla should attack them as they swept by her rock.

The whirlpool of Charybdis swirled dark and cavernous before them as the ship entered the strait. The crew saw how horribly the black throat drew into her all the whirling deep, so that even the bone-strewn sands at the bottom of the sea lay bare. Then suddenly she disgorged the troubled waters again, in a great cloud of spray, so that all about her the ocean boiled as in a kettle.

The noise of the thundering waves, the roaring of Charybdis, the barking of the hideous Scylla, the howling of the wind, all these were deafening and terrifying. But, spurred on by Ulysses, the men toiled at the sweeps and as they gradually drew away from the whirlpool, it seemed that all might yet be well.

But it was not to be. From her black den, Scylla suddenly darted out her six long necks, and before Ulysses could strike, she seized half a dozen mariners! Ulysses heard their shrieks, coming from high in the air, and saw them with their heels turned up, and their hands thrown out to him for sweet life. He could do nothing. In all his sufferings he never had beheld a sight so full of miseries.

The remainder of the crew, terror-stricken at the fate of their companions, pulled frantically to get out of danger before the monster could make a second swoop. Angry at missing their prey, Charybdis boomed and Scylla barked. But the vessel shot through the roaring narrows and into the open sea. And the men, weary and heavy of heart, bent over their oars, and longed for rest.

•

THE SPHINX

*Adapted from a retelling
by Elsie F. Buckley*

Here is a famous Greek tale about that virtue we call fortitude, the firmness of mind that enables a person to face danger with courage and self-control. Here is someone who makes intelligence count in the nick of time.

It happened in times past that the gods, being angry with the inhabitants of Thebes, sent into their land a very troublesome beast called the Sphinx. This beast had the face and breast of a fair woman, but the claws of a lion and wings of an eagle. It lay crouched on top of a rock, halting all travelers who passed by and posing a riddle. Those who answered it could pass safely, but those who failed were killed. And no one had succeeded in solving the riddle.

One day a traveler named Oedipus came to the seven-gated Thebes, where he found all the people in deep distress and mourning because of the terrible monster. He stood in the marketplace and talked with the citizens.

"What is this famous riddle that none can solve?" he asked.

"No one can say," they answered. "For he who would solve the riddle must go up alone to the rock where the monster sits. There it chants the riddle, and if he cannot answer, it tears him from limb to limb. And if none go up to try the riddle, the monster swoops down on the city and carries off its victims. Our wisest and bravest have gone up, and our eyes have seen them no more. Now there is no one left courageous enough to face the terrible beast."

"I will go up and face this monster," Oedipus said. "It must be a tough riddle indeed if I cannot answer it."

"Oh, overbold and rash," they cried, "why do you think you can succeed, when so many have failed?"

"Better to try, and fail, than never to try at all."

"Yet, where failure is death, surely a man should think twice?"

"A man can die but once, and how better than in trying to save his fellows?"

They marveled at his answer, and seeing that nothing would turn him from his purpose, they showed him the path to the Sphinx's rock. All the people went with him to the edge of the city with their prayers and blessings. At the gate they left him, for he who goes up to face the Sphinx must go alone, and none can stand by to help him.

He crossed first a river and then a wide plain, where the mountain of the Sphinx stood dark and clear on the other side. Then he prayed to Pallas Athena, the gray-eyed goddess of wisdom, and she took all fear from his heart.

He went boldly up to the rock, where the monster sat waiting to spring on its prey, and for all his courage his heart beat fast as he looked upon it. For at first it appeared like a mighty bird, with great wings of bronze and gold. The glancing sunbeams played about them, casting a halo of light around, and in the midst of the halo the face shone out pale and beautiful as a star at dawn. But when it saw him coming near, a greedy fire lit up its eyes, and it put out its cruel claws and lashed its tail from side to side like an angry lion.

Nevertheless, Oedipus spoke steadily.

"I have come to hear your famous riddle, and answer it or die."

"Foolhardy manling, a dainty morsel the gods have sent this day, with your fair young face and fresh young limbs."

And it licked its cruel lips.

Then Oedipus felt his blood boil within him, and he wished to slay it then and there.

"Come, tell me your famous riddle, foul Fury that thou art, that I may answer it and rid the land of this curse."

And this is what the monster asked:

"At dawn it creeps on four legs. At noon it strides on two. At sunset and evening it totters on three. What is this thing, never the same, yet not many, but one?"

It chanted slowly, its eyes gleaming cruel and cold.

Oedipus thought within himself.

"Now or never must my learning and wit stand me in good stead, or in vain have I talked with the wisest men and learned the old secrets of Phoenicia and Greece."

The gods who had given him understanding sent light into his heart, and he boldly answered:

"What can this creature be but man, O Sphinx? For, a helpless babe at the dawn of life, he crawls on his hands and feet. At noon-time he walks erect in the strength of his youth. And at evening he supports his tottering limbs with a staff, the prop and stay of old age. Have I not guessed the answer to your famous riddle?"

With a loud cry of despair, and answering him never a word, the great beast sprang up from its seat on the rock and hurled itself over the precipice into the yawning gulf below.

Far away across the plain the people heard its cry, and they saw the flash of the sun on its brazen wings like a gleam of lightning in the summer sky. They sent up a great shout of joy to heaven, and poured out from every gate onto the open plain. Some raised Oedipus on their shoulders, and with shouts and songs bore him into the city. Then and there they made him their monarch, for who better to lead them than the slayer of the Sphinx and the savior of the city?

So Oedipus became king of Thebes, and wisely and well did he rule, and for many a long year the land prospered.

A TRUTH SPEAKER

Retold by Grace H. Kupfer

In this tale about the ancient writer Philoxenus (436–380 B.C.), we witness two important intellectual virtues in action: honesty and steadfastness. And we see the kind of courage it sometimes takes to speak the truth to power. In the end, the story speaks well of both Philoxenus and Dionysius.

There ruled in the city of Syracuse, in Sicily, many hundreds of years ago, a tyrant by the name of Dionysius. Not only was he sometimes ruthless in his actions, but he was vain of his own talents. His court was made up of flatterers, who were afraid to speak anything but praise to his face, though they spoke ill of him when there was no danger of being overheard.

Dionysius, among other vanities, considered himself a great poet. On all occasions he wrote verses. And when he had composed them, he would assemble all his courtiers and read the lines aloud. Then they would all lift their hands and exchange glances, as though in admiration of his genius, and exclaim over the beauty of the poetry, until even Dionysius was satisfied.

The most learned man in Syracuse at that time was a philosopher by the name of Philoxenus. Dionysius became so conceited, because of the flattery of all his courtiers, that he made up his mind to summon Philoxenus, so that he, too, might hear the poems and praise the poet.

Philoxenus came. The poems were read to him, and Dionysius eagerly awaited the critic's words of praise and admiration. But none came; for, instead, to the amazement of all, the philosopher, in disdain, said the verses were so bad that they did not deserve the name of poetry, nor did their author deserve the name of poet. Dionysius, almost beside himself with rage at this unexpected frankness, called his guards and ordered Philoxenus to be removed, in chains, to a deep, underground dungeon, where only the worst criminals were sent.

When the news of this action reached the ears of the friends of Philoxenus, they were very angry. As weeks passed, and still their friend was kept a prisoner in that underground dungeon, they became much excited, and at last sent to Dionysius a letter begging for the philosopher's release.

Perhaps Dionysius was afraid of rousing the anger of so many of his subjects, or possibly he had an entirely different reason, as you will presently see. At all events, he agreed to release the philosopher, provided he would come once more to dine with him.

Philoxenus came. After a great feast, at which all the courtiers were present, the king arose and read some new verses he had written. He wanted the truth-speaking Philoxenus to hear them, because he himself thought them uncommonly good. So, too, judging from their gestures and praises, did the fawning courtiers. Philoxenus alone sat silent, saying nothing and betraying nothing by the expression of his face.

This did not in the least suit Dionysius. He controlled his impatience as long as he could; but when Philoxenus continued silent, the king at length turned to him, and thinking he would not again dare to rouse his monarch's anger, said, "Tell me, Philoxenus, your opinion of this latest poem of mine."

You may be sure neither he nor his court expected the answer that was given. For, turning his back on the feast and the feasters, Philoxenus approached the guards of the banquet hall, and exclaimed, in a tone of disgust, "Take me back to my dungeon!" Nothing could more plainly have shown his opinion of the king's bad verses. He knew that by expressing his view honestly he would incur certain punishment; so he chose the simpler method of going back to prison of his own free will.

The courtiers were very much startled at this plain speaking, and looked in terror to see what Dionysius would do. But even this king, vain as he was, seems to have had a sense of humor, and a respect for real moral courage. For, turning with a smile from his trembling courtiers to the calm and untroubled Philoxenus, he bade him depart in peace.

•

THE SCULPTOR AND THE SISTINE CHAPEL

The question is not whether you will suffer disappointment in life —everyone does—but what it stirs inside you. As George Eliot wrote, everything depends not on the mere fact of disappointment, but on the nature affected.

One winter morning in 1494, young Michelangelo Buonarroti looked sadly out his window at a brilliant, white Florence. A heavy snow had fallen all night on the town. It lay now on the streets and plazas, churches and palaces, even the towers and spires—it had turned the whole place into a marble city. But that beauty only made Michelangelo forlorn. It reminded him that his friend and patron, the great Duke Lorenzo de' Medici, was gone forever. It was Lorenzo who had recognized the young sculptor's brilliance, who had taken him into his palace, and given him block after block of marble to carve.

But now the great Duke was dead, and in his place ruled his son, Piero. Piero was proud and foolish, and had no use for artists and their statues. Horses and games and feasts amused him; he bestowed more honor on his stableboy, because he could outrun a horse at full gallop, than he did on a mere sculptor. And so Michelangelo sat at his window, gazing down on the snow with his deep-set eyes, thinking of how it, too, would melt away to nothing, like his own talents and dreams.

He was shaken from his gloominess by a sudden knocking below. He leaned out the window. One of Piero's impudent messengers was beating on his door.

The page, looking up, caught sight of the boy.

"Come down, Michelangelo! This is your day. Piero has summoned his famous young sculptor. He wants you to carve a statue for him, at last!"

Michelangelo caught his breath. Had he heard right?

"What are you waiting for?" the messenger called. "Hurry up! His Magnificence won't wait forever, you know."

"Do you mean it?" Michelangelo asked. "Piero has never called me to the palace before."

"He is now, my young friend. He has much marble for you to work your magic with. Hurry!"

Michelangelo threw on a cloak and scurried down the stairs to the street. Silently he trudged at the messenger's side, but his heart leapt with every step.

"This is the day you've been waiting for, is it not?" his haughty companion laughed as they crossed the snow-covered plaza. "To sculpt again for the great Medici family—what could be more wonderful?"

A moment later they were in the palace. In an upper chamber they found Piero, surrounded by a crowd of his friends, standing at a long window that looked down on the gardens.

"He's here!" Piero shouted. "You probably thought we would never call upon you, young maestro. But today we have need for your talent. You do have great talent, do you not, my friend?"

Michelangelo clenched his fists. He met Piero's eyes.

"So your father used to think," he answered quietly.

Piero flushed, then turned to the window.

"You will go down to the gardens," he announced. "There you will find all the white marble your heart desires, lying heaped upon the ground. I am giving a dinner tonight, and I want my guests to be able to see one of your brilliant statues. Of course, tomorrow morning the sun will do away with all your hard labor. But nothing lasts forever, does it, young maestro?"

Michelangelo staggered back. He could not believe his ears. He, Michelangelo, the pride of Florence—must build a statue of snow!

A surge of anger welled up inside of him. It seemed to squeeze his chest, grip his breath, strangle his throat. He glared at the grinning expressions of Piero and his friends and wanted more than anything to strike out at them, to smash them, and make them feel his fury. But he knew he dared not. He felt a deep shame and longed to run and hide and never have to been seen by these arrogant fools again.

But something inside of him made him stand where he was. Michelangelo was young, and this was a cruel moment for a boy to face. But he was also confident. He knew he possessed a rare and wonderful talent, and that nothing could stand in its way. The waves of rage and humiliation passed over him, and he found an answer.

"I will do your bidding, O great Medici," he said quietly, and left them standing there.

A moment later he was in the gardens, relieved to be alone, his eyes fixed on the white, flawless blanket at his feet.

"I will show them what I can do," he muttered. "Even in snow, I will show them what I can do."

He began to work quickly. He stooped and gathered the snow, pushed it into a mound, packed it tight, and stooped for more. Hour after hour he gathered snow, building it into the kind of huge, hard block that always set his thoughts on fire.

Then he began to carve. He sculpted with all of his skill and power. A head emerged, then limbs, and hands and feet. The icy mass was coming to life. A huge figure was being born in the garden, full of vigor and strength. Every once in a while Michelangelo would stand back and look at his work. It needed more snow packed here, some scraped away there. The lips weren't quite right —they must be shaped again. Michelangelo labored in peace, mindless of everything except his art.

And at last the enormous man of snow was done.

It was finished, and it was good. It would be gone tomorrow. The sun would see to that. But for a few brief hours, it would make Florence a more beautiful and noble place.

A gasp brought Michelangelo back to the world of his troubles. He turned and found Piero standing behind him.

The Duke was gazing at the figure of snow. The proud sneer had melted away from the nobleman's mouth. A gleam of wonder showed in his eyes, and then a shadow of sorrow.

"Snow—not snow!" he murmured. "Something this beautiful should never pass away."

And so it was that Michelangelo proved his mettle. And with his chisel he proved his mastery over stone. The years passed. He won for himself all of Italy's praise. He was called to Rome, to carve statues for Pope Julius II. Full of excitement, he traveled to the famous marble quarries at Carrara to select gigantic blocks. He was overwhelmed by the sight of the great rocks; in every one he saw some figure waiting to be released from its slumber. He spent six happy months examining, choosing, buying, rejecting, his mind full of the images to come.

But when he finally got back to Rome with his marbles, he found the Pope had changed his mind. Julius led him into the Sistine Chapel, a huge, narrow box of a room with high walls and a huge, curved ceiling.

"I want it decorated," he said, pointing overhead. "I want you to paint it."

Michelangelo blanched.

"But I am a sculptor!" he protested. "I'm no painter."

"Did you not learn to mix colors in the studio of the master Ghirlandaio? You have only to remember the lessons he taught you."

"But I haven't painted in years! Get Raphael to do it. He is skillful with the brush."

"Nonsense. Raphael is busy. Besides, I have seen many of your drawings. No one can equal them."

Michelangelo looked up at the high ceiling. All of it—ten thousand square feet—would have to be filled with pictures. It would take months. He thought of his beautiful marbles and how they would lie useless while he wasted his time here. He shuddered.

This is not what I want to do! he thought. He choked back his rage and disappointment.

It is not easy to say no to a Pope, especially an insistent one. Michelangelo finally consented, but with a heavy heart.

Up the ladders, into the scaffolding went Michelangelo, to lie on his back and paint overhead. It was torturous work. The colors dripped onto his face and burned his eyes, and made him hate the job all the more.

"I'm a sculptor, not a painter!" he muttered.

It was many years since he had done any painting. He feared he could not do the work. He asked other artists to help him, but he found they were more a hindrance than a help. He sent them away and erased what they had done.

He worked alone, seeing nobody but his color-grinder and the Pope. If it had to be done, it would be done right, he told himself. In silence and solitude, he lay there painting.

Then, to his horror, the surfaces he had finished began to mold.

"I told your Holiness I was not painter!" he cried. "All I have done is destroyed." But it was soon found that he had made the plaster too wet, and no harm would result.

He kept going. He began his days at dawn. He did not stop until he could no longer see to paint. Many nights he did not leave the chapel at all. He lay on his back, and painted. He grew so used to his cramped position that whenever he received a letter during that period, he had to hold it over his head and bend backward to read it. He hardly took time for his meals, often contenting himself with a crust of bread. He became ill from exhaustion. But he kept going.

Sometimes the impatient Pope would climb the scaffolding and watch the work.

"When will you make an end?" was his constant cry.

"When I am done," answered the artist.

And gradually there emerged across the ceiling some of the most perfect and dignified scenes ever created by human hand: God the Father, separating light from dark; the creation of Adam and Eve; the fall of man; the great flood. They came one after another from the tips of Michelangelo's brushes, more than three hundred figures, every one sublime, every one possessing the same power and grandeur of the master's sculptures.

After four long years of enormous fatigue and sad isolation, the immense task was finished. The scaffolding was taken down, and the doors of the Sistine Chapel were thrown open. Great crowds came to look up and stand amazed. When Raphael came to see the work—the same Raphael that Michelangelo had begged the Pope to employ instead of himself—he thanked God that he had been born in the same century as Michelangelo.

The crowds still come to see the Sistine Chapel ceiling, to wonder at the physical performance of one man covering such a vast space alone, and the artistic achievement of bringing so many grand visions to life. They stand and gape at the power of a single man's determination and genius. If you go to Rome, you can join them and gaze up at one of the world's magnificent paintings, set forth by the hand of a sculptor.

•

THE MAN WHO MOVED THE EARTH

The Polish astronomer Nicolaus Copernicus (1473–1543) was not the first to assert that the earth moves, but he was the first to prove it. Here is the kind of courage willing to risk the scorn of public opinion for the sake of the truth, and the kind of perseverance willing to tackle a worthwhile job even if it takes a lifetime of lonely work.

It began with mathematics. At age twenty-one, Nicolaus Copernicus was dazzling the learned men of the university at Cracow with his extraordinary abilities. In fact, the college had grown a bit boastful of its star student, and whenever visiting dignitaries arrived, young Copernicus was given chalk and blackboard and put through the paces. He could work out problems involving a dozen figures and many fractions with a directness and precision that made him a wonder in that part of the world.

A college professor traveling through Poland invited the young genius to come to Italy with him and teach mathematics. Copernicus accepted and traveled to Bologna. There he heard a series of lectures on astronomy—lectures that changed not only his life but how men regarded their universe. For as Copernicus listened, his heart beat fast. At once he perceived how mathematics could be made valuable in calculating the movements of the stars.

For fourteen centuries, the best astronomers had based all of their science on the great book *The Almagest,* written by Ptolemy. It taught that the earth was the center of the universe, and that the sun and stars moved around it. To this theory, priests and astrologers gradually added their own explanations of the heavens. Most assumed that the earth was flat and had four corners. The stars were jewels hung in the sky and were moved about by angels. An angel looked after each star as well as all persons who were born under that star's influence, or else appointed some other angel for the purpose. Every person had a guardian angel to protect him from the evil spirits that occasionally broke out of Hell and came up to earth to tempt men.

In talking to astronomers, Copernicus perceived that very seldom did they know anything of mathematics. This ignorance on their part caused him to doubt them entirely. He sat up all night in the belfry of the cathedral and watched the stars. They moved steadily, surely, and without caprice. It was all natural, and could be reduced, Copernicus thought, to a mathematical system.

And so he began to study the matter. As he wondered and pondered, the truth began to dawn on him: The universe does not revolve around the earth. Indeed, the earth is a globe *revolving around the sun.* Like the other planets, it too is a heavenly body.

He began to teach what he was learning. In his lectures he made various references to Columbus's recent voyage, mentioning the obvious fact that in sailing westward he did not fall over the edge of the world into Hell itself, as it had been prophesied he would. He also explained that the red sky at sunset was not caused by reflections from Hell, nor was the sun moved behind a mountain by giant angels at night. He pointed out that to a man on a boat, the shores seemed to be moving past; could not the seeming movements of the stars likewise be caused by the moving of the earth?

Then, one day, a cardinal came from the Vatican to visit the young mathematician. In all kindness he cautioned him, and in love explained to him it was all right for a man to believe what he wished, but to teach others things that were not authorized was a mistake.

Copernicus was abashed. He was a deeply religious man. He only wanted to help men find the truth and understand the laws of God. He had thought his new ideas would add to the knowledge of Creation, and the beauty of the Church as well. It crushed him now to hear the rumors circulating—that he was trying to "dethrone God by a tape measure and a yardstick." Certain priests publicly denounced him. They declared he was guilty of heresy and accused him of stating things he could not prove. "You would have us believe the earth wobbles around the sun, like a moth around a lamp!" they sneered. "Outrageous!"

And so Copernicus packed his bags and went back to Poland. There he became a canon of the cathedral in the sleepy town of Frauenburg. And there he was a watched man. He lived in practical isolation and exile, for the Church had forbidden him to speak publicly on unauthorized themes. The universities and prominent churchmen were ordered to leave Copernicus and his theories alone.

Yet the humdrum duties of a country clergyman did not still his longing to know and understand the truth. He visited the sick, closed the eyes of the dying, kept his parish register. But his heart was in mathematics. In the back of the old church register he recorded long rows of figures as he worked at some astronomical problem. In the upper floor of the barn, in back of his old, dilapidated farmhouse, he cut holes in the roof to watch the stars. They came out for him nightly and moved in majesty across the sky. "They do me great honor," he said. "I am forbidden to converse with great men, but God has ordered for me a procession."

While the whole town slept, he watched the heavens and made minute records of his observations. He digested all that had been written on the subject of astronomy. Slowly and patiently he tested every hypothesis with his rude and improvised instruments. "Surely God will not damn me for wanting to know the truth about His glorious works," he used to say. "To look at the sky, and behold the wondrous works of God, must make a man bow his head and heart in silence. I have thought, and studied, and worked for years, and I know so little—all I can do is to adore when I behold this unfailing regularity, this miraculous balance and perfection of adaptation. The majesty of it all humbles me into the dust."

The exile in Frauenburg gave him leisure to pursue his theories in quiet. "God has set me apart," he wrote, "that I may study and make plain His works." But still that he could not make his discoveries known was a constant, bitter disappointment to him.

The simple, hard-working gardeners with whom he lived had a reverent awe for the great man. They guessed his worth, but still had suspicions of his sanity. They took his nightly vigils for a sort of religious ecstasy, and a wholesome fear made them quite unwilling to disturb him. So passed the days, and from a lighthearted, ambitious man, Copernicus had grown old and bowed, and nearly blind from continuously watching the stars at night.

But his work, *On the Revolutions,* was at last complete. For forty years he had worked at it, and for twenty-seven years, he himself said, not a day or night had passed without his having added something to it.

He felt that he had in this book told the truth. If men wanted to know the facts about the heavens they would find them here. He had built a science of astronomy he knew would stand secure.

But what should he do with all this mass of truth he had discovered? It was in his own brain, and it was in the hundreds and hundreds of pages of this book, which he had rewritten five times. In a few years at most his brain would be stilled in death. In five minutes, ignorance and malice might reduce the book to ashes and a lifetime of labor go for naught.

To send the book to Rome and ask for permission to publish it was out of the question. Too many people there would object. The request would be refused. The manuscript might even be destroyed.

To publish it at home without the consent of the Bishop would be equally dangerous. For in this volume, all that the priests taught of astronomy had been contradicted and refuted.

Copernicus waited, and worried, and pondered.

At last, at the urging of friends, he decided to send the manuscript to the city of Nuremberg to be printed. Hoping to free himself from accusations of heresy, he dedicated his work to Pope Paul III, who was a scholar and himself a lover of astronomy. "I am fully aware, Holy Father," he wrote, "that as soon as they hear that in these volumes of mine about the revolutions of the spheres of the universe I attribute some sort of motion to the Earth, some persons will immediately raise a cry of condemnation against me.... It will be a simple matter for you by your authority and your judgment to suppress attacks by slanderous tongues, although—as the proverb has it—there is no cure for the bite of a false accuser."

How would the world receive the book? Copernicus could only guess and wait.

The months went by, and fear, anxiety, and suspense had their sway. He was stricken with fever. In his delirium he called out, "The book—tell me—they surely have not burned it—you know I wrote no word but truth!"

On May 24, 1543, a messenger arrived from Nuremberg. He carried a copy of the printed book. He was admitted to the sick-room, where he placed the volume in the hands of the stricken man. It is said that a gleam of sanity came to Copernicus. He smiled and, taking the book, gazed upon it, stroked its cover as though caressing it, opened it, and turned the leaves. Then closing the volume and holding it to his heart, he closed his eyes, and sank to sleep, to wake no more.

•

GALILEO AND THE LEANING TOWER

Sometimes the most valuable kind of intellectual virtue is the courage to dispute "what everybody knows." It does not mean simply being disagreeable, or arguing just for the sake of being different. This kind of virtue is rooted in deep study, careful reflection, and a willingness to prove a claim, as we see in this famous story about the Italian astronomer, physicist, and mathematician Galileo (1564–1642).

In Italy some four hundred years ago there lived a young man named Galileo Galilei. He possessed an intensely inquiring spirit—that is to say, he was the kind of man who makes a point of seeing whatever he looks at, thinking about it afterward, and asking the question: "Why?" He started out as a student of medicine, but soon gave up that plan to spend time on what he really loved—physics and mathematics. He turned his whole mind to the pursuit, and by the time he was twenty-six years old, he became a professor of mathematics at the University of Pisa.

In those times, most people accepted without question the theories and statements inherited from the great thinkers of past ages. It did not enter their minds to test the truth of these statements for themselves. They regarded Aristotle, the ancient Greek philosopher, as the greatest of all authorities. "The master hath said it" was the motto in Galileo's day. Scholars committed Aristotle's doctrines to memory; doubting them was considered an act of blasphemy, if not a crime. Students were actually fined for disagreeing with the opinions of the ancients.

Now, one of the statements of Aristotle was this: The speed at which an object falls to earth depends upon its weight. A ten-pound weight, for example, will fall ten times faster than a one-pound weight.

But Galileo had noticed different objects falling to the ground, and he thought differently. He made a few experiments, and satisfied himself.

"Aristotle was wrong," he announced. "Weight has nothing to do with how fast objects fall. It is the resistance of air which affects the rate of the descent. As long as two objects can overcome the resistance of the air to the same extent, they will reach the ground at the same time, no matter how much they weigh. A heavy stone and a light stone will fall at exactly the same rate of speed."

The other professors at the university were shocked and angry. They declared that of course Aristotle had been right and that Galileo was making a fool of himself. He should be quiet and stop bothering them with his silly notions, if he wanted to keep his job.

"All right," said Galileo. "We'll have a little test—my theory against Aristotle's. If I'm wrong, I'll be quiet. Meet me at the tower."

The bell tower in Pisa is known the world over, of course, as the Leaning Tower, because it stands at an angle and looks as though it might topple to the ground at any time. Construction of the tower had begun in 1174; by the time the builders reached the third story, one side was sinking into the soft ground. They tried to compensate by making the remaining floors taller on the leaning side, but the settling continued. When it was finished, the 179-foot tower leaned so much that any object dropped from the top story on the lower side would land some fifteen or twenty feet from the building's base.

Up climbed Galileo. A crowd of scholars, students, and interested townspeople gathered on the lawn below. With every step, he could hear their snickers and jeers.

At the top, on the uppermost gallery, he placed two iron balls. One weighed ten pounds. The other weighed just one. And the question to be answered was this: When Galileo pushed them off, at exactly the same instant, would the heavier ball hit the ground first, as Aristotle had maintained, or . . . ?

Balancing the weights carefully on the balcony, Galileo rolled them over together.

From far below, the breathless crowd saw the two balls plunge over the edge. They came hurtling straight down. They fell at first side by side, then—side by side—and then finally—

There was a tremendous thud. One single thud. They had struck the ground together.

Galileo was right and Aristotle wrong.

Even then, some who had seen would not believe their own eyes. It is very difficult to let go of old ideas, especially ones that have persisted for centuries. Some of the professors made all sorts of excuses and continued to insist that Aristotle was correct. After all, if they were to admit that Galileo was right, how many more of the great Aristotle's principles might also be wrong? It was better, they thought, to silence this troublemaker. They booed and hissed Galileo at his lectures, and made his life as miserable as they could.

But Galileo was not one to be browbeaten. He said goodbye to Pisa, and took a job teaching at the University of Padua, where thoughts were given a bit more freedom. There he went on searching, questioning, and discovering, and showing the world what can be done when someone dares to think for himself.

•

ON HIS BLINDNESS

John Milton

In 1652, one of the world's greatest poets went blind. Yet during
the next several years of his life, John Milton composed in his
head and gradually dictated to his daughters, friends, and assis-
tants his epic *Paradise Lost,* perhaps the most profound poem
ever written in the English language. The sonnet below, one of
Milton's most popular pieces, gives some hint of the patience and
faith that turned years of affliction into a time of extraordinary
creation.

When I consider how my light is spent,
  Ere half my days in this dark world and wide,
  And that one talent which is death to hide
  Lodged with me useless, though my soul more bent
To serve therewith my Maker, and present
  My true account, lest he returning chide,
  "Doth God exact day-labor, light denied?"
  I fondly ask. But Patience, to prevent
That murmur, soon replies, "God doth not need
  Either man's work or his own gifts; who best
  Bear his mild yoke, they serve him best. His state
Is kingly: thousands at his bidding speed,
  And post o'er land and ocean without rest;
  They also serve who only stand and wait."

•

BEETHOVEN'S TRIUMPH

Ludwig van Beethoven (1770–1827) is one of the most beloved
composers of all times, not just because of the glory of his music,
but also because of the courage he brought to his life and his art.

As a child, Ludwig van Beethoven could play the piano better
than most adults. He gave his first public concert when he was only

seven years old; at age eleven, he worked as an organist at the Court of Cologne; at twelve he published his first significant composition. Four years later he visited Vienna and played for the great Mozart, who afterward left the room saying: "Watch that boy! Someday he will make the world talk about him."

Ludwig's father, who was a singer at Court, had visions of making piles of gold by charging people to hear his "wonder child." It seems he thought more about the money—and the drink it could buy—than he did about Ludwig's happiness. He used to reel into the house in the early hours of the morning, haul the sleepy boy from bed to piano, and conduct forced lessons until dawn, never sparing a few knocks and blows when the exhausted child missed a note.

It is a wonder that his father's harshness did not make Ludwig hate all music. Perhaps it was his gentle mother who helped him keep his courage through those troubling times. But when Ludwig was seventeen, his mother died. His father at once sold her clothes so he could buy more drink.

Ludwig felt the loss deeply. Now there was no one to take care of his two younger brothers. Taking matters into his own hands, he asked the prince to pay him half his father's salary so he could support his brothers. His request was granted, his father's career at the Court came to an end, and Ludwig became the head of the family. For the rest of his life he looked after his brothers, even though they often got into trouble and caused him more than enough anguish.

In 1792, when he was not quite twenty-two years old, Ludwig moved to Vienna to study under Joseph Haydn, the most famous living composer. Those years in Vienna were filled with hard work. He learned to play many instruments. He studied the horn, viola, violin, and clarinet, so he would better know how to write music for the orchestra. He labored over his scores, writing, correcting, revising, rejecting, and starting over again.

Gradually, the word of his genius spread. The citizens of Vienna were a music-loving people. Whenever they could, they flocked to hear Beethoven play. He gave a series of concerts in 1795, one of them for the benefit of Mozart's widow and children. From then on, his success seemed assured. For the next several years he wrote, and traveled, and performed, and made himself into a truly great musician.

Then, sometime before he was twenty-eight years old, he began to notice a humming in his ears. At first he tried to ignore it, but it only grew worse and worse. Finally, reluctantly, he consulted doctors. Their diagnosis was worse than a sentence of death: Beethoven was going deaf.

For a long time he could not bear to tell anyone. He shunned all company. "I confess I am living a wretched life," he wrote to a friend. "For two years I have avoided almost all social gatherings because it is impossible for me to say to people: 'I am deaf.' If I belonged to another profession, it would be easier. . . ."

He found refuge in the country, where he could take long walks alone through the woods. "My deafness troubles me less here than elsewhere," he wrote. "Every tree seems to speak to me of God."

Convinced he was going to die, Beethoven confessed his shame and despair in a testament he meant to leave behind for his brothers. "I could not bring myself to say to people, 'Speak louder, shout, for I am deaf,'" he wrote. "How should I bring myself to admit the weakness of a sense which ought to be more perfect in me than in others, a sense which I once possessed in the greatest perfection? . . . I must live like an exile. If I venture into company a burning dread falls on me, the dreadful risk of letting my condition be perceived. . . . What humiliation when someone stood by me and heard a flute in the distance, and *I* heard *nothing,* or when someone heard the herdboy singing, and I again heard nothing. Such occurrences brought me near to despair, a little more and I had put an end to my own life. . . ."

And yet Beethoven did something much more courageous than give up. He gave himself to his art. He went on writing music, even though what he wrote grew fainter and fainter in his own ears. As his hearing faded, his music began to take on a quality much different from the elegant compositions written by earlier composers. Many of Beethoven's works grew stormy and emotional and thrilling—much like his own courageous and turbulent life. Strange and wonderful to say, he wrote much of his best music, the music we remember him for, after he lost his ability to hear.

Eventually Beethoven went completely deaf. He was lonely and often unhappy, and yet he managed to compose uplifting music. His last symphony, the Ninth, concludes with the famous Ode to Joy. When the work was complete, Beethoven agreed to conduct an orchestra and choir in a concert in Vienna.

The hall was packed. Beethoven took his place in the center of the orchestra, with his back to the audience, and at a signal from him the music began. The magnificent strains entranced the audience. Yet Beethoven himself heard nothing. He followed the score only in his mind. The musicians had been directed to watch him, but to pay not a bit of attention to his beating of the time.

When it was over, the great master lowered his arms. He stood amid the silence, fumbling with his score. One of the singers tugged at his sleeve and motioned for him to look. Beethoven turned around.

He saw people on their feet, clapping their hands, waving their hats, throwing their arms into the air. The deaf musician bowed, and every eye in the audience held a tear.

The final years of this great soul's life were sad. During his last illness he found great comfort in reading music. A friend sent him some of Haydn's compositions, and he passed many pleasant hours gazing over the notes. He found much comfort, too, in Schubert's Songs. He died in 1827, and it is said that among his final words were these: "I shall hear in heaven."

•

THOMAS CARLYLE AND *THE FRENCH REVOLUTION*

Here is an extraordinary story of equanimity and determination in the midst of disaster. We all may not be able to maintain this kind of composure, but Carlyle's perseverance is a virtue we can all attain.

In the early part of 1835, Thomas Carlyle finally finished work on the first volume of his famous *French Revolution*. Writing it had been a terrific struggle. For almost two years he had read histories and made notes in preparation for the task, and then he had spent months painstakingly writing and revising his manuscript. It was a sleepless, exhilarating time for him. By the time the first volume was complete, his nerves were strained and his bank account almost empty. Yet he had confidence in his work—he thought it was going to be "a tolerable enough book."

He was delighted when his good friend the philosopher John

Stuart Mill offered to read the manuscript. Mill himself was a student of the Revolution and had long given his friend encouragement about the project. Carlyle tied the pages up in a neat bundle and handed it to him, hoping Mill could make some helpful suggestions.

One night, when Carlyle and his wife Jane were sitting before the fireplace, there came a knock at the door. Mill staggered in and collapsed in a chair. His hands trembled. His face was ashen.

"Why, Mill," gasped Carlyle, "what ails you, man? What is it?"

It was a moment before Mill could speak.

"It's about your manuscript," he stuttered. "An accident—it was wrapped in newspaper—the housekeeper—thought it was trash—put it into the fire. It's burned. All of it."

It was the only copy.

A deathly silence filled the room. Carlyle gaped at his friend, unable to comprehend the disastrous news. For what seemed an eternity, the three sat motionless, as if the tragedy had drained all life out of them.

Then Carlyle quietly put his hand on his friend's shoulder.

"Don't feel so bad, Mill," he said gently. "I'm sure it wasn't very good. Regardless, good or bad, it's gone now, and feeling guilty will not do a thing to bring it back. Accidents like this happen. Let's think no more about it."

Mrs. Carlyle turned her face away, unable to keep back the tears.

They talked a while longer. Carlyle steered the topic of conversation to other things. At length Mill left, still broken. As he closed the door behind his friend, Carlyle turned to his wife and said: "Well, Mill, poor fellow, is terribly cut up. We must endeavor to hide from him how very serious this business is to us."

And serious it was. Not only was the manuscript gone, so were the notes Carlyle had used to write it—he had thrown them away as he wrote. The book existed only in his memory. And he was down to the last penny of his savings. He did not know whether or not he should simply abandon the project. He went to bed that night full of utmost despair, feeling "something cutting or hard grasping me round the heart."

Yet the next morning he decided he would start over.

"I will not quit the game while the faculty is given me to try playing," he wrote in his journal. "Oh, that I had faith! Oh, that I had! Then were there nothing too hard or heavy for me. Cry silently to thy inmost heart to God for it. Surely He will give it thee. At all events, it is as if my invisible schoolmaster had torn my copybook when I showed it, and said, 'No, boy! Thou must write it better.' What can I, sorrowing, do but obey—obey and think it the best?"

And so he went back to his desk and began the daunting journey again. He wrote through the spring of that year, and into the hot summer, pushing "to be done with that burnt manuscript." By autumn he had succeeded in rewriting what was lost, and turned again to the work's second volume. He wrote on and on, feverishly, stubbornly. When volume two was complete, he plunged into volume three of the "wild, savage book" that "has come out of my own soul, born in blackness, whirl-wind and sorrow."

Almost two years after he had given his original manuscript to Mills, Thomas Carlyle finished his great *French Revolution,* "ready both to weep and pray." The work endures to this day as a classic of literature and a testament to one man's spirit of endurance.

•

THE TITANIC

From The Sun

The name *Titanic* has become synonymous with sea tragedy. It is worth knowing that even in the midst of such awful catastrophe, there were acts of heroism more moving than the disaster itself— such as the self-sacrifice of Mrs. Isador Straus, who sprang out of a lifeboat back onto the deck of the ship to stay behind with her husband. "We have been long together through a great many years," she told him. "We are old now. Where you go, I will go." They went down together. And there were acts of cowardice as well. These newspaper reports from the New York *Sun,* published just after the sinking, remind us that extreme conditions often bring out the best and the worst in the human character.

The 46-thousand-ton liner, the largest vessel that had ever put to sea, struck an iceberg late on the night of April 14–15, 1912. The supposedly unsinkable ship was on its maiden voyage from Southampton to New York. It went down with a loss of more than 1,500 lives.

The *Titanic* had been making good time and everyone aboard was happy in the hope of getting to New York in record time. The ship had worked beautifully. Sunday was calm and clear. There was no moon as the night fell, but it was perfectly clear. The sea was smooth. No icebergs had been sighted during the day or evening, at least none that were in a dangerous distance of the ship.

The *Titanic* was making twenty-two knots an hour as night fell upon the sea. The passengers promenaded the decks in the evening, gathered in the lounging rooms or smoking rooms. There was music in the music room and some singing. They had not begun to retire at 10 o'clock, except for a few women and children. The beautiful night kept many on deck.

There was a watch set forward and in the crow's nest. These men had powerful night glasses. They kept a careful watch on the sea ahead. So far as they could see there was no ice near the ship. But at 11:37 there loomed up directly in the path of the *Titanic* an enormous iceberg. It was of a color almost of the water itself. It could not be perceived one moment, but the next it was seen to be a mountain towering at least 100 feet above the sea and almost the area of a city block.

There was only time for the man in the crow's nest and the watch forward to shout "Ice ahead!" and for the quartermaster to bring his wheel down hard, when the *Titanic* smashed into a big berg. First came a smash on the port side forward, which split the berg and ran the *Titanic* into the berg itself, after which there was a heavy crash to the starboard. The *Titanic* had split off a part of the berg that was above water. Hundreds of tons of ice were in this way precipitated on the forward upper deck. The *Titanic,* it was afterward discovered, had literally climbed up on all of that part of the berg that was under water and below her keel.

Men came out of the smoking room asking: "What the devil was that? Did we hit something?" Women in the various lounging rooms, music room and grill room said: "Mercy! What could that have been?" There was no excitement. The electric lights did not even flicker at this time, and it was more in the perfunctory manner of people who were bored and wanted something to divert themselves that they arose in a leisurely way and walked out on the upper decks to see what it was. They could see stewards walking rapidly about and they stopped them and asked them what was the matter only to get the reply: "I don't know. We may have run into a little bit of ice, perhaps."

It was at 12:25 A.M. that Captain Smith, who had returned to the bridge, transmitted orders through Chief Officer Murdock that all persons should be assembled on the upper deck. Four hundred stewards and kitchen men immediately rushed through the ship, from lower to highest deck, summoning all persons on deck. There was yet no excitement. Women arose leisurely under orders to dress themselves in their warmest clothing. One woman who was rather indignant at being awakened was halfway to the deck when she remembered that she had not locked her trunk. She returned and performed this service and climbed leisurely to the upper deck.

Second Steward Dodd reported to Mr. Murdock, the first officer, fifteen minutes later that every person was on deck. Still there was no panic, no excitement or fear. The electric lights still burned and passengers all massed starboard and port on the upper deck. There was a little feeling of fear that ran through the crowd ten minutes later, however, when Chief Officer Murdock called sharply:

"Crews to the boats! Women and children first!"

At this time, although none yet believed that a tragedy was about to happen, little murmurs of dissent came, particularly from the women. Wives announced that they would not be separated from their husbands; mothers said they would not leave their sons; sisters their brothers. A few threw their arms around their menfolk and that sentiment showed itself among all classes of the ship.

"Come on," was the command from the officers, and there was a pause, no woman wishing to take the first step forward. Another moment's pause and the still more curt command: "Put them in."

The crew of the first boat simply grabbed the first woman they saw, hurled her up in the air, and dropped her into the boat. They turned again and grabbed another. Thereafter that was the general scene on both sides of the upper deck, members of the crew grabbing any woman who might have her arms around the neck of a man and passing her into the boat. In this the men were assisted by husbands, brothers, and sons.

Mrs. John Jacob Astor positively declined to leave her husband and he, with a steward, simply picked her up, carried her over and put her in boat No. 1. Every man, every crew seen that night remembered that during all this ordeal John Jacob Astor was not only cool but did valiant work in assisting the crew in getting the women into the boats.

It was then that the only display of cowardice was made. A

band of men from the steerage made for one of the boats. Murdock brought his revolver up to a level, with a curt declaration: "I'll kill the first man that rushes."

Three men rushed. There were two shots. Two men dropped, one shot through the head, the other with his jaw torn off. There was no use to shoot the third man. Quicker than a bullet could reach him a fist of the husky quartermaster landed on the point of the third man's jaw and he went down like a poleaxed ox. Then the work of filling the boats went on.

The boats swung from the davits after they were filled, one after another. Originally the rules called for six men of the crew and one person in command for each, but as the boats were filled, members of the crew in the boats obtained permission to get out.

"You can get along with four, sir," a steward would say. "I'll get out."

The order to lower the boats came from Captain Smith at 2 o'clock, and they all took the water. Members of the crew aboard each of the sixteen boats and the collapsibles got them away from the sides and rested on their oars fifty feet distant. "Go on!" was the command, and the crew obeying the orders began to pull their oars.

The eyes of all those in the little boats remained fixed on the *Titanic.* They could see that she had sunk about twenty-five feet at the head, raising her enormous stern high out of the water. But not a soul on those small boats thought even then that the great ship could sink. There was no moon, but still the night was clear. The light of the stars and the long rows of lights from the decks and portholes of the *Titanic* enabled them to see the men they had left moving along her deck further aft, but still showing no signs of excitement. Nobody in the small boats thought it possible that they were soon to see the greatest tragedy of the sea.

And then without warning, as the last boat got a mile away from the *Titanic,* the men and women in those small boats saw the bow of the *Titanic* dip down as if it had been pulled by a giant hand, while the last flicker of electric lights disclosed a great gap two-thirds aft. The big ship had split in two.

The forward part simply slipped into the water like a flash and as it swung down under the water there came a series of explosions. The forward boilers had blown up. That part of the boat carried with it hundreds of men in the engine room and stokehole.

The after part of the ship, upon which all the passengers and crew who were on deck had taken refuge, bobbed back from the spot, bent forward, and then a weak cheer came from the horror-stricken people in the boats as the hulk appeared to right itself, stood up on an even keel and floated. But prayers of thankfulness and cheer were changed almost in an instant.

There came from the front of the remaining hulk a great puff of steam as the roar of another great explosion came to them. The huge mass of steel was rent asunder. The fragment of ship suddenly choked up and the whole thing slid down under the water carrying with it the thousand or more men who had remained on it. As she went down her band was heard to play.

Not all of the last-minute actions aboard the Titanic *were heroic, as this further report from* The Sun *shows:*

A man in woman's clothes was among the survivors in lifeboat 10, according to Mrs. Mark Fortune of Winnipeg, who was rescued with her three daughters on that boat. Mrs. Fortune's husband, a Winnipeg real estate broker, and her son, Charles, were lost. Her daughters, Alice, Mabel, and Ethel, unite with her in saying that a man saved his life by his woman's dress, one of the daughters having the seat next to his in the lifeboat.

The lifeboat, said Mrs. Fortune, was greatly overcrowded. Four of the crew were in her and the rest were supposed to be women, with the exception of one stoker and a Chinese man. There was a figure dressed in a brown mackintosh with a shawl like that of a steerage passenger over its head. The face was completely hidden. Miss Alice Fortune sat directly beside the supposed woman.

Soon after the boat had left the ship the four sailors were transferred to another boat and at this time it was discovered that the figure was that of a man. When somebody asked who he was he refused to reply. The stoker and the Chinese man, who were the only men at the oars, demanded that the impostor bear a hand. He said that he did not know how to use an oar and the stoker struck him in the face.

The women then were put to the oars, rowing as best they could in the crowded condition of the boat. As sunrise came they saw the lights of the *Carpathia* in the west. They were the last boatload taken aboard that vessel. The women, in spite of their warm garments, were numb with cold. They were lifted aboard and heard and saw no more of the male impostor.

•

THE CONQUEST OF EVEREST

James Ramsey Ullman

To students of mountaineering such as myself, this story stands for the courage of explorers in all times. You may never have heard of George Herbert Leigh Mallory, but you have probably heard his famous answer when asked why he wanted to climb the world's highest mountain: "Because it is there." No one knows whether or not Mallory and Andrew Irvine became the first human beings to reach the top of Mount Everest in 1924. We only know they are heroes for trying to raise the human achievement to new heights. "Whether a man accepts from Fortune her spade and will look downward and dig," Justice Oliver Wendell Holmes wrote, "or from Aspiration her axe and cord, and will scale the ice, the one and only success which it is his to command is to bring to his work a mighty heart."

Bitterly chagrined at the failure of his first effort, Mallory was determined to have one last fling before the monsoon struck. Everest was *his* mountain, more than any other man's. He had pioneered the way to it and blazed the trail to its heights; his flaming spirit had been the principal driving force behind each assault; the conquest of the summit was the great dream of his life. His companions, watching him now, realized that he was preparing for his mightiest effort.

Mallory moved with characteristic speed. With young Andrew Irvine as partner he started upward from the col the day after Norton and Somervell descended. They spent the first night at Camp V and the second at Camp VI, at 26,800 feet. Unlike Norton and Somervell, they planned to use oxygen on the final dash and to follow the crest of the northeast ridge instead of traversing the north face to the couloir. The ridge appeared to present more formidable climbing difficulties than the lower route, particularly near the base of the summit pyramid where it buckled upward in two great rock towers which the Everesters called the First and Second Steps. Mallory, however, was all for the frontal attack and had frequently expressed the belief that the steps could be surmounted. The last Tigers descending that night from the highest camp to the col brought word that both climbers were in good condition and full of hope for success.

One man only was to have another glimpse of Mallory and Irvine.

On the morning of June eighth—the day set for the assault on the summit—Odell, the geologist, who had spent the night alone at Camp V, set out for VI with a rucksack of food. The day was as mild and windless as any the expedition had experienced, but a thin gray mist clung to the upper reaches of the mountain, and Odell could see little of what lay above him. Presently, however, he scaled the top of a small crag at about twenty-six thousand feet, and, standing there, he stopped and stared. For a moment the mist cleared. The whole summit ridge and final pyramid of Everest were unveiled, and high above him, on the very crest of the ridge, he saw two tiny figures outlined against the sky. They appeared to be at the base of one of the great steps, not more than seven or eight hundred feet below the final pinnacle. As Odell watched, the figures moved slowly upward. Then, as suddenly as it had parted, the mist closed in again, and they were gone.

The feats of endurance that Odell performed during the next forty-eight hours are unsurpassed by those of any mountaineer. That same day he went to Camp VI with his load of provisions, and then even higher, watching and waiting. But the mountaintop remained veiled in mist and there was no sign of the climbers returning. As night came on, he descended all the way to the col, only to start off again the following dawn. Camp V was empty. He spent a solitary night there in subzero cold and the next morning ascended again to Camp VI. It was empty too. With sinking heart he struggled upward for another thousand feet, searching and shouting, to the very limit of human endurance. The only answering sound was the deep moaning of the wind. The great peak above him loomed bleakly in the sky, wrapped in the loneliness and desolation of the ages. All hope was gone. Odell descended to the highest camp and signaled the tidings of tragedy to the watchers far below.

So ended the second attempt on Everest—and, with it, the lives of two brave men. The bodies of George Mallory and Andrew Irvine lie somewhere in the vast wilderness of rock and ice that guards the summit of the world. Where and how death overtook them no one knows. And whether victory came before the end no one knows either. Our last glimpse of them is through Odell's eyes —two tiny specks against the sky, fighting upward.

•

THE MAN WHO BROKE THE
COLOR BARRIER

Hal Butler

Jack Roosevelt Robinson (1919–1972) was playing baseball for
the Kansas City Monarchs in the Negro leagues in 1945 when
he learned that Branch Rickey, general manager of the Brooklyn
Dodgers, wanted to see him. Until that time, no black had ever
played major league baseball, and there seemed to be an unwrit-
ten rule among club owners to keep it that way. But Branch
Rickey was looking for a man to break the barrier.

The question he put to Jackie Robinson was this: "Do you
have the guts not to fight back?" Rickey knew the first black major
league player would suffer horrible abuse. But he also firmly believed that the only way to win public acceptance was for that
man to take every insult and threat and nasty name without showing anger—and play great baseball all the while. His plan was
for Robinson to spend one year with the Dodgers' farm team in
Montreal, then head for the majors. "You'll have to promise me
that for three years you will not answer back," he said. "You
cannot win this by a retaliation. You can't echo a curse with a
curse, a blow with a blow."

It was an incredibly daunting demand, but Jackie Robinson
stepped up to the plate without hesitation. Over the next several
years, he taught the nation that what mattered was not the color
of his skin, but his skill with the bat and ball—and the content of
his character. Here is an astounding story of self-control. Here is
the kind of courage and perseverance it takes to blaze a rough
trail so others can follow.

On October 23, 1945, Branch Rickey officially announced that
the Brooklyn Dodgers had signed Jackie Robinson to a contract and
assigned him to play with the Montreal Royals in the International
League. The unexpected announcement received a mixed reaction.
Some farsighted people were in favor of blacks playing in the
higher echelons of baseball; others were hostile and bitter. Even

those in favor, however, expressed doubt that it would work. The sports editor of the New York *Daily News* put it bluntly: "Robinson will not make the grade in the big league this year or next. He is a 1000-to-1 shot."

It didn't take long for the bigots to react to the appearance of Robinson on a baseball field occupied by white players. The Montreal team held spring training at Daytona Beach, Florida, but they allowed early comers to take drills at a nearby camp in Sanford. Jackie worked out for just two days in Sanford, and then the ax fell. Sanford's prejudiced civic leaders demanded that he get out of town.

The insolent demand infuriated Robinson, but he remembered Branch Rickey's words: *You will have to take everything they dish out and never strike back.* Without a word, he left town.

Two weeks later, another difficult situation arose. The Royals had an exhibition game scheduled with the Jacksonville team. When the team arrived at the Jacksonville park, they found the gate padlocked. The game had been called off because Robinson was on the team!

But it was when the Royals met Indianapolis in a spring training game at De Land, Florida, that Jackie suffered his most embarrassing moment. In the first inning Robinson tried to score from second base on a hit. He had to slide home to make it, stirring up a cloud of dust in the process. As the umpire called him safe, Jackie looked up through the dust to see a white policeman standing over him. The policeman had run onto the field and stood scowling down at him.

"Get off the field right now," he snarled, "or I'm putting you in jail!"

Clay Hopper, the Montreal manager, came bounding from the dugout.

"What's going on?" he demanded.

The policeman looked at him coldly. "We ain't havin' Nigras mix with white boys in this town," he said. "Now you tell that Nigra I said to git!"

Again, without a word, Robinson left.

Despite such unpleasant moments, Jackie Robinson established himself as Montreal's second baseman before spring training ended. Most of his teammates had by this time accepted him and recognized him as a talented ballplayer. But there were a few who would not. Robinson was aware of the resentment these few players had for him, and he knew he would simply have to overcome this dislike by his play on the field. He could do it by becoming the best second baseman Montreal had ever seen. That was his goal, his way of fighting back.

The Montreal Royals opened their season against Jersey City, and some 35,000 people were in the stands at Roosevelt Stadium. Jackie was understandably nervous in his first time at bat, and he grounded weakly to the infield. But on his second trip to the plate he hit a line drive into the left-field seats, and the crowd applauded him as he circled the bases.

His first hit for Montreal had been a home run, and the people in the stands had reacted warmly. Maybe, now that he had left the South, he would gain acceptance after all.

But acceptance did not come easily. Robinson found that rival players were violently hostile. As Branch Rickey had predicted, opposing pitchers threw at him continually, and time after time Jackie hit the dirt, got up, brushed himself off and said nothing. He was constantly insulted from the dugouts by opposing players who called him vile names that were unprintable—but he said nothing. One time in Syracuse a rival player held up a black cat and shouted, "Hey, Robinson! Here's one of your relatives!" Again, Jackie said nothing.

Once, during this trying season, Branch Rickey went to Montreal to talk to Robinson. "As long as you are in baseball," he told Jackie, "you will have to conduct yourself as you are doing now. That is the cross you must bear."

Robinson agreed. He was determined to take it all and fight back only on the diamond with base hits, stolen bases and great fielding plays.

He did this so well that he helped the Montreal Royals win the

International League pennant and the Little World Series in 1946. Jackie was the batting champion, with a .349 average, and was named Rookie of the Year. His performance made him a sure bet to be with the Brooklyn Dodgers the following year.

But when Branch Rickey announced that Robinson would play first base for Brooklyn (Eddie Stanky was a solid fixture at second base), the protests started. Some of the players took the news without complaint, but a dissident group signed a petition announcing that they would not play with a black player. Rickey called the protesting players into his office and told them bluntly that Robinson would play with the Dodgers whether they liked it or not. Some backed down and agreed to play. Others asked to be traded. Rickey obliged a few of them by shipping them to other clubs, but he was not able to rid himself of all of them.

If the 1946 season with Montreal was a bad dream, the 1947 season with the Dodgers turned out to be a nightmare for Robinson. Everything Branch Rickey had predicted would happen to him did—and more. Pitchers threw at him, making him hit the dirt in almost every game to escape injury. Efforts were made to spike him on the bases. Vicious insults flowed from the dugouts of opposing teams.

Even off the field, Robinson experienced troubles. In some cities where the Dodgers played, Robinson was not allowed to stay in the same hotel with the other players; there were restaurants he was forbidden to enter. But Robinson exhibited a courage few men have been called on to show. He took it all, never losing his temper, never striking back, even though many times he was tempted to hit back with his fists. Jackie Robinson was determined to follow to the letter the instructions of the man who had helped him break into the major leagues.

The hostility toward Jackie Robinson reached a high point on May 6, when the St. Louis Cardinals were scheduled to meet the Brooklyn Dodgers for the first time. A group of Cardinal players decided they would go on strike and refuse to play the game because of Robinson's presence. If that succeeded, they intended to mobilize players on other teams and call a general National League strike.

Fortunately, a sports writer on the New York *Herald Tribune* exposed the plot against Robinson before it happened, and Ford Frick, then president of the National League, took immediate and bold action. He sent a stinging ultimatum to the players planning to strike.

"If you do this," it warned, "you will be suspended from the league. You will find that the friends you think you have in the press box will not support you, that you will be the outcasts. I do not care if half the league strikes. All will be suspended. This is the United States of America, and one citizen has as much right to play as any other."

The Cardinal players had no recourse but to cancel the strike. But the insults and taunts continued with renewed vigor. One day, when they had reached new heights of viciousness, Pee Wee Reese, the Dodger shortstop who had been born in Ekron, Kentucky, jogged over from his position to talk to Robinson. He placed his hand gently on Jackie's shoulder as he talked, and a newspaper photographer shot the picture. The photograph appeared in newspapers across the country, and the fact became known that Reese, among all the Dodger players, was the most sympathetic toward Robinson's difficult problem. He saw in Robinson a superb ballplayer, and the color of his face mattered not.

By mid-season there were signs that most of the Dodgers were beginning to accept Robinson on an equal footing. The reason was obvious. Robinson, despite his troubles, was playing spectacular ball, and his play won him the respect that was due him. It required a superman to play good baseball under the tensions that gripped Robinson throughout this critical year, and Jackie proved himself to be a superman. In his first major-league season, he hit .297, batted in 18 runs, collected 12 home runs and stole 29 bases. In the World Series that followed against the New York Yankees, he contributed seven hits in 27 times up for a .259 batting average. And when the season ended, Jackie Robinson was named the National League Rookie of the Year.

•

THE PIONEER FAMILY

Alexis de Tocqueville

In 1831 the French government sent a young aristocrat named Alexis de Tocqueville to the United States to study its prison system. The observant Tocqueville saw much more than jail-

houses during his journey; his study of the democratic experiment unfolding in the New World resulted in his classic *Democ-
racy in America.* Less familiar to students of politics is
Tocqueville's *A Fortnight In the Wilderness,* also based on his
American notebooks, from which the selection below is ex-
cerpted. This wonderful portrait of a pioneer family tells us much
about the legacy of our American heritage. Goethe once said that
you must labor to possess what you have inherited. We must
practice that labor today.

The little bell which the pioneer takes care to hang round the
necks of his cattle, that he may find them in the dense forest, announces from a great distance the approach to the clearing. Soon
you hear the stroke of the axe. As you proceed traces of destruction
prove the presence of man. Lopped branches cover the road, trunks
half calcined by fire, or maimed by steel, are still standing in the
path. You go on, and reach a wood, which seems to have been
struck with sudden death. Even in the middle of summer the withered branches look wintry. On nearer examination a deep gash
is discovered round the bark of each tree, which, preventing the
circulation of sap, quickly kills it. This is generally the planter's first
measure. As he cannot in the first year cut down all the trees on his
new property, he kills them to prevent their leaves overshadowing
the Indian corn which he has sowed under their branches.

Next to this incomplete attempt at a field, the first step of
civilization in the wilderness, you come suddenly upon the owner's
dwelling. It stands in a plot more carefully cleared than the rest, but
in which man still sustains an unequal struggle with nature. Here
the trees have been cut down but not uprooted, and they still
encumber with their stumps the ground that they formerly shaded.
Round these withered remnants, corn, oak saplings, plants, and
weeds of every kind spring pell-mell, and grow side by side in the
stubborn and half-wild soil. In the centre of this strong and diversi-
fied vegetation, stands the planter's log-house. Like the field round
it, this rustic dwelling is evidently a new and hasty work. Its length
seldom exceeds thirty feet; its width twenty, and height fifteen. The
walls as well as the roof are composed of half-hewn trees; the cracks
are filled up with moss and mud. As the traveller advances the
scene becomes more animated. At the sound of his steps a group
of children who had been rolling in the dirt jump up hastily, and

fly towards the paternal roof, frightened at the sight of man, while two great half-wild dogs, with ears erect, and lengthened noses, come out of the hut and, growling, cover the retreat of their young masters.

At this moment the pioneer himself appears at his door. He casts a scrutinizing glance on the newcomer, bids his dogs go in, and himself sets immediately the example without exhibiting either uneasiness or curiosity.

On entering the loghouse the European looks around with wonder. In general there is but one window, before which sometimes hangs a muslin curtain; for here, in the absence of necessaries, you often meet with superfluities. On the hearth, made of hardened earth, a fire of resinous wood lights up the interior better than the sun. Over the rustic chimney are hung trophies of war or of the chase; a long rifle, a doeskin and eagles' feathers. On the right hangs a map of the United States, perpetually shaken by the wind which blows through the cracks of the wall. On a rough shelf near it are placed a few odd volumes, among them a Bible, the leaves and binding of which have been spoilt by the devotion of two generations, a Prayer-book, and sometimes one of Milton's poems, or Shakespeare's plays. With their backs to the wall are placed some rude seats, the product of the owner's industry; chests instead of wardrobes, agricultural tools, and specimens of the crop. In the middle of the room is an unsteady table, the legs of which, still covered with leaves, seem to have grown where they stand. Round this table the family assemble for their meals. On it is left an English china teapot, spoons, generally of wood, a few cracked cups, and some newspapers.

The appearance of the master of this dwelling is as remarkable as his abode. His sharp muscles and slender limbs show him at the first glance to be a native of New England; his make indicates that he was not born in the desert. His first years were passed in the heart of an intellectual and cultivated society. Choice impelled him to the toilsome and savage life for which he did not seem intended. But if his physical strength seems unequal to his undertaking, on his features, furrowed by care, is seated an expression of practical intelligence, and of cold and persevering energy. His step is slow and measured, his speech deliberate, and his appearance austere. Habit, and still more, pride, have given to his countenance a stoical rigidity, which was belied by his conduct. The pioneer despises (it is true) all that most violently agitates the hearts of men. His fortune or his life will never hang on the turn of a die, or the smiles of a woman. But to obtain competence he has braved exile, solitude, and the numberless ills of savage life; he has slept on the bare earth, he has exposed himself to the fever of the woods, and the Indian's tomahawk. Many years ago he took the first step. He has never gone back; perhaps twenty years hence he will still be going on without desponding or complaining. Can a man capable of such sacrifices be cold and insensible? Is he not influenced by a passion, not of the heart but of the brain, ardent, persevering, and indomitable?

His whole energies concentrated in the desire to make his fortune, the emigrant at length succeeds in making for himself an entirely independent existence, into which even his domestic affections are absorbed. He may be said to look on his wife and children only as detached parts of himself. Deprived of habitual intercourse with his equals, he has learnt to take pleasure in solitude. When you appear at the door of his lonely dwelling, the pioneer steps forward to meet you. He holds out his hand in compliance with custom, but his countenance expresses neither kindness nor joy. He speaks only to question you, to gratify his intelligence, not his heart; and as soon as he has obtained from you the news that he wanted to hear he relapses into silence. One would take him for a man who, having been all day wearied by applicants and by the noise of the world, has retired home at night to rest. If you question him in turn, he will give you in a clear manner all the information you require. He will even provide for your wants, and will watch over your safety as long as you are under his roof. But, in all that he does there is so much constraint and dryness; you perceive in him such utter indifference as to the result of your undertakings, that your gratitude cools.

Still the settler is hospitable in his own way, but there is nothing genial in his hospitality, because, while he exercises it, he seems to submit to one of the painful necessities of the wilderness. It is to him a duty of his position, not a pleasure. This unknown person is the representative of the race to which belongs the future of the New World; a restless, speculating, adventurous race, that performs coldly feats which are usually the result of passionate enthusiasm; a nation of conquerors, who endure savage life without feeling its peculiar charms, value in civilized life only its material comforts and advantages, and bury themselves in the wilds of America, provided only with an axe and a file of newspapers!

In describing the settler, one cannot forget the partner of his sufferings and perils. Look at the young woman who is sitting on the other side of the fire with her youngest child in her lap, superintending the preparations for supper. Like the emigrant, this woman is in the prime of life; she also recollects an early youth of comfort. The remains of taste are still to be observed in her dress. But time has pressed hardly upon her: in her faded features and attenuated limbs it is easy to see that life has to her been a heavy burden. And, indeed, this fragile creature has already been exposed to incredible suffering. At the very threshold of life she had to tear herself from the tender care of her mother, from the sweet fraternal ties that a young girl can never leave without tears, even when she quits her home to share the luxurious dwelling of a young husband. The wife of the settler, torn at once and forever from the cradle of her childhood, had to exchange the charms of society and of the domestic circle for the solitude of the forest. Her marriage bed was placed on the bare ground of the desert. To devote herself to austere duties, to submit to unknown privations, to enter upon an existence for which she was not fitted; such has been the employment of her best years; such have been the delights of her married life. Destitution, suffering, and lassitude have weakened her delicate frame, but have not dismayed her courage. While deep sadness is painted on her chiselled features, it is easy to descry religious resignation, peace, and a simple, quiet fortitude, enabling her to meet all the ills of life without fearing or defying them.

Round this woman crowd the half-clothed children, glowing with health, careless of the morrow, true children of the wilderness. Their mother turns on them from time to time a mingled look of sadness and of joy. Judging from their strength and her weakness, it would seem as if she had exhausted herself in giving them life, and without regretting the cost. The loghouse consists of a single room, which shelters the whole family at night; it is a little world, an ark of civilization in the midst of a green ocean. A few steps off the everlasting forest extends its shades, and solitude again reigns.

•

THE DEATH OF BECKET

Arthur Penrhyn Stanley

Here is one of the most famous martyrs in history. When Henry II
of England made Thomas Becket the archbishop of Canterbury in
1162, the king fully expected his friend to help him gain strict
control over the English clergy. But Becket, feeling his first duty
was to the church, resolved to defend its rights and privileges,
even at the cost of angering Henry. Relations between the king
and archbishop steadily deteriorated until one day in 1170, when
a bitter Henry uttered some violent words about the archbishop
in front of his followers. Four of his leading knights took the king's
remarks literally. On December 29 they rode toward Canterbury
and tragedy.

For hundreds of years after his death, Becket's tomb was a
destination of religious pilgrimages. The travelers of Chaucer's
Canterbury Tales told their stories en route to the shrine of the
"blisful martir" who considered his cause more vital than his life.

The vespers had already begun, and the monks were singing
the service in the choir, when two boys rushed up the nave, announcing, more by their terrified gestures than by their words, that
the soldiers were bursting into the palace and monastery. Instantly
the service was thrown into the utmost confusion; part remained at
prayer, part fled into the numerous hiding places the vast fabric
affords, and part went down the steps of the choir into the transept
to meet the little band at the door.

The Archbishop continued to stand outside, and said: "Go and
finish the service. So long as you keep in the entrance, I shall not
come in." They fell back a few paces, and he stepped within the
door, but, finding the whole place thronged with people, he paused
on the threshold, and asked, "What is it that these people fear?"
One general answer broke forth, "The armed men in the cloister."
As he turned and said, "I shall go out to them," he heard the clash
of arms behind. The knights had just forced their way into the
cloister, and were now (as would appear from their being thus seen
through the open door) advancing along its southern side.

They were in mail, which covered their faces up to their eyes, and carried their swords drawn. Three had hatchets. Fitzurse, with the ax he had taken from the carpenters, was foremost, shouting as he came, "Here, here, king's men!" Immediately behind him followed Robert Fitzranulph, with three other knights; and a motley group—some their own followers, some from the town—with weapons, though not in armor, brought up the rear.

At this sight, so unwonted in the peaceful cloisters of Canterbury, not probably beheld since the time when the monastery had been sacked by the Danes, the monks within, regardless of all remonstrances, shut the door of the cathedral, and proceeded to barricade it with iron bars. A loud knocking was heard from the band without, who, having vainly endeavored to prevent the entrance of the knights into the cloister, now rushed before them to take refuge in the church. Becket, who had stepped some paces into the cathedral, but was resisting the solicitations of those immediately about him to move up into the choir for safety, darted back, calling aloud as he went, "Away, you cowards! By virtue of your obedience I command you not to shut the door—the church must not be turned into a castle." With his own hands he thrust them away from the door, opened it himself, and catching hold of the excluded monks, dragged them into the building, exclaiming, "Come in, come in—faster, faster!"

The knights, who had been checked for a moment by the sight of the closed door, on seeing it unexpectedly thrown open, rushed into the church. It was, we must remember, about five o'clock in a winter evening; the shades of night were gathering, and were deepened into a still darker gloom within the high and massive walls of the vast cathedral, which was only illuminated here and there by the solitary lamps burning before the altars. The twilight, lengthening from the shortest day a fortnight before, was but just sufficient to reveal the outline of objects.

In the dim twilight they could just discern a group of figures mounting the steps of the eastern staircase. One of the knights called out to them, "Stay." Another, "Where is Thomas Becket, traitor to the king?" No answer was returned. Fitzurse rushed forward, and, stumbling against one of the monks on the lower step, still not able to distinguish clearly in the darkness, exclaimed, "Where is the Archbishop?"

Instantly the answer came: "Reginald, here I am, no traitor, but the archbishop and priest of God. What do you wish?" And from the fourth step, which he had reached in his ascent, with a slight motion of his head—noticed apparently as his peculiar manner in moments of excitement—Becket descended to the transept. Attired, we are told, in his white rochet, with a cloak and hood thrown over his shoulders, he thus suddenly confronted his assailants.

Fitzurse sprang back two or three paces, and Becket, passing by him, took up his station between the central pillar and the massive wall which still forms the southwest corner of what was then the chapel of St. Benedict. Here they gathered around him, with the cry, "Absolve the bishops whom you have excommunicated."

"I cannot do other than I have done," he replied, and turning to Fitzurse, he added, "Reginald, you have received many favors at my hands. Why do you come into my church armed?"

Fitzurse planted the ax against his breast, and returned for answer, "You shall die—I will tear out your heart." Another, perhaps in kindness, struck him between the shoulders with the flat of his sword, exclaiming, "Fly—you are a dead man."

"I am ready to die," replied the primate, "for God and the Church; but I warn you, I curse you in the name of God Almighty, if you do not let my men escape."

The well-known horror which in that age was felt at an act of sacrilege, together with the sight of the crowds who were rushing in from the town through the nave, turned their efforts for the next few moments to carrying him out of the church. Fitzurse threw down the ax, and tried to drag him out by the collar of his long cloak, calling, "Come with us—you are our prisoner."

"I will not fly, you detestable fellow," was Becket's reply, roused to his usual vehemence and wrenching the cloak out of Fitzurse's grasp. The three knights struggled violently to put him on Tracy's shoulders. Becket set his back against the pillar, and resisted with all his might, while Grim, vehemently remonstrating, threw his arms around him to aid his efforts. In the scuffle, Becket fastened upon Tracy, shook him by his coat of mail, and exerting his great strength, flung him down on the pavement. It was hopeless to carry on the attempt to remove him. And in the final struggle which now began, Fitzurse, as before, took the lead. He approached with his drawn sword, and waving it over his head, cried, "Strike, strike!" but merely dashed off his cap. Tracy sprang forward and struck a more decided blow.

The blood from the first blow was trickling down his face in a thin streak; he wiped it with his arm, and when he saw the stain, he said, "Into thy hands, O Lord, I commend my spirit." At the third blow, he sank on his knees—his arms falling, but his hands still joined as if in prayer. With his face turned toward the altar of St. Benedict, he murmured in a low voice, "For the name of Jesus, and the defense of the Church, I am willing to die." Without moving hand or foot, he fell flat on his face as he spoke. In this posture he received a tremendous blow, aimed with such violence that the scalp or crown of the head was severed from the skull.

"Let us go—let us go," said Hugh of Horsea. "The traitor is dead; he will rise no more."

THE LIFE HEROIC

I like the man who faces what he must
    With step triumphant and a heart of cheer;
    Who fights the daily battle without fear;
Sees his hopes fail, yet keeps unfaltering trust
That God is God; that somehow, true and just,
    His plans work out for mortals. Not a tear
    Is shed when fortune, which the world holds dear,
Falls from his grasp. Better with love a crust
Than living in dishonor; envies not,
    Nor loses faith in man, but does his best,
Nor ever murmurs at his humbler lot,
    But with a smile and words of hope gives zest
To every toiler. He alone is great
Who by a life heroic conquers fate.

Four

•

EASING THE PATH

" 'A man's true wealth hereafter, is the good he does in this world to his fellow man," Mohammed told us. "When he dies, people will say, 'What property has he left behind him?' but the angels will ask, 'What good deeds has he sent before him?' "

Virtues are not just about making our own journeys through life smoother and more successful. There is an abundance of literary, philosophical, and theological authority which reminds us that easing others' paths should be an equal—if not more important—concern. This chapter helps us examine the question: What do we owe to other people? These stories illustrate the meaning of words such as compassion, kindness, charity, generosity, beneficence, and sacrifice. We meet people who in one way or another seize opportunities to do good for their fellow travelers.

In Harper Lee's much-loved novel *To Kill a Mockingbird,* Atticus Finch offers his daughter some invaluable advice. "If you can learn a simple trick," he says, "you'll get along a lot better with all kinds of folks. You never really understand a person until you consider things from his point of view . . . until you climb into his skin and walk around in it." Trying to put yourself into another's place, to share for a moment his or her feelings, is often the starting point of compassion. But there's more to true compassion than just emotion. To help someone, you usually have to *do* something, not just *feel* something. Compassion takes the name of action. It means exerting yourself and bestowing some effort for someone else's sake.

Like anything else involving effort, compassion takes practice. We have to work at getting into the habit of standing with others in their distress. Sometimes offering help is a simple matter that does not take us far out of our way—remembering to speak a kind word to someone who is down, or spending an occasional Saturday morning volunteering for a favorite cause. At other times, helping involves some real sacrifice. "A bone to the dog is not charity," Jack London observed. "Charity is the bone shared with the dog, when you are just as hungry as the dog." If we practice taking the many small opportunities to help others, we'll be in shape to act when those times requiring real, hard sacrifice come along.

There is another reason for practicing helpfulness: We need to develop the ability to judge who truly needs aid and who doesn't. Not everyone who asks is really needy or deserving. Furthermore, we have to be able to discern what *kind* of help people need. Easing someone's path does not mean simply providing the path of least resistance. Sometimes the best way to help people is to hold them responsible; accepting no excuses can sometimes be the best kind of aid we can offer. And finally, the reality of life is that if we spend *all* of our time trying to help *everyone,* we will only end up neglecting our responsibilities to ourselves, our families, and to others who depend on us. So like all virtues, compassion must be tempered, and it must be informed by a good measure of reason.

Of all the virtues, when exercised properly with whole heart and discerning mind, compassion may bring the greatest degree of fulfillment. It enriches our lives with a sense of nobleness and purpose, makes us morally awake, and encourages us about life generally. Most people, thinking back over their lives, remember the times they spent giving and helping and loving as the very best moments. But feeling good in the future should not be the prime motivation for doing good. Sincerely helping others brings the real satisfaction. As Jeremy Bentham observed, the way to be comfortable is to make others comfortable; the way to make others comfortable is to appear to love them; the way to appear to love them—is to love them in reality.

THE PRINCESS WHO WANTED TO BE BEAUTIFUL

In the end, there are few things more beautiful than a kind heart.

Once upon a time there was a little Princess who was very unhappy because she was not as pretty to look at as she thought a little Princess should be.

She sat in the garden and was sorrowful and cried a great deal of the time, because she felt quite sure that no one would ever make her a queen.

One day she sat by the wall of the garden with her hands in her lap, and was looking very sad. An old woman, very bent and gray, and carrying a bundle, passed along the road outside and looked over the wall.

"Why do you cry, little Princess?" she asked.

"Because I am not beautiful," the little Princess replied, "and so I shall never be made a queen."

"Why do you not go out into the world and find someone who can make you beautiful?" asked the old woman as she started again on her way. And this seemed like such a new adventure that the little Princess went out through the garden gate and started down the road.

The old woman had disappeared as if the road had taken her into its gray dust, but before the little Princess had gone very far she overtook a boy. He was stumbling along the road as if it were hard for him to find his way. He put out his hand and touched the little Princess' silken sleeve.

"Where are you going?" he asked.

"I am going to find someone who will help to make me beautiful," the little Princess said. "I am not pretty enough to be a queen."

"Wait a while and help me," said the little boy. "I am blind, and I cannot find my way home."

So the little Princess took the blind boy's hand in hers and walked along with him, leading him very gently, until they came to the cottage by the side of the road where he lived.

Then the little Princess went on, hurrying, for she felt that she had lost a great deal of time. But before she had gone very far, she saw a little girl standing by the edge of the woods and crying. When the little girl saw the Princess, she looked up and asked, "Where are you going?"

"I am going to find someone who will help me to be beautiful," the little Princess said. "I am not pretty enough to be a queen."

"Wait awhile and help me," said the little girl. "My mother is ill, and I went to the dairy to fetch her some milk and eggs, but I have no money, and they say that I must pay."

The little Princess pulled from the silk bag at her side a bright gold piece. She had but two of them to buy herself food on her journey, but she gave one to the child. "This is to pay for the milk and eggs," she said. Then the little girl laughed with happiness. Her smile was as bright as the sunshine that came down through the trees and lighted them both.

"Now I must make great haste," thought the little Princess. "It is getting on in the day and I am no more beautiful than when I started." But she had gone only a little way when she came suddenly upon the same old woman, who had spoken to her in the morning.

"Did you do as I bade you?" asked the old woman.

"Yes," said the little Princess. "But I am still ugly to look at," she added, dropping her head.

"Oh no, you are not," said the old woman. "Look!" And she held a little mirror before the face of the Princess.

A strange thing had happened. The little Princess's eyes, in leading the little blind boy, had grown as bright as stars. Her hair was as shining as the gold piece which she had given away.

"Shall I ever be a queen!" asked the Princess.

The old woman took a small gold crown from the bundle she carried and set it upon the little Princess' head.

"You are a queen, my dear!" she said.

•

HOW THE ROBIN'S BREAST BECAME RED

Retold by Flora Cooke

This Native American tale shows us how someone very small can be a big help to others.

Long ago in the Far North, where it is very cold, there was only one fire. A hunter and his little son took care of this fire and kept it burning day and night. They knew that if the fire went out the people would freeze and the white bear would have the Northland all to himself.

One day the hunter became ill and his son had to do all the work. For many days and nights he bravely took care of his father and kept the fire burning.

The great white bear was always hiding near, watching the fire. He longed to put it out, but he did not dare, for he feared the hunter's arrows. When he saw how tired and sleepy the little boy was, he came closer to the fire and laughed wickedly to himself.

One night the poor boy grew so tired that he could keep awake no longer and fell fast asleep. Then the white bear ran as fast as he could and jumped upon the fire with his wet feet, and rolled upon it until he thought it was all out. Then he trotted happily away to his cave among the icebergs.

But a little gray robin had been flying near, and had seen what the white bear was doing.

She was greatly worried when she thought that the fire might be out, but she was so little that she could do nothing but wait until the bear was out of sight.

Then she darted down swiftly and searched with her sharp little eyes until she found a tiny live coal. This she fanned patiently with her wings for a long time.

Her little breast was scorched red, but she did not stop until a fine red flame blazed up from the ashes.

Then she flew away to every hut in the Northland. Wherever she touched the ground a fire began to burn.

Soon, instead of one little fire, the whole north country was lighted up, so that people far to the south wondered at the beautiful flames of red and yellow light in the northern sky.

But when the white bear saw the fires, he went farther back into his cave among the icebergs and growled terribly. He knew that now there was no hope that he would ever have the Northland all to himself.

This is the reason that the people in the north country love the robin, and never tire of telling their children how its breast became red.

THE STAR JEWELS

Adapted from the Brothers Grimm

This beautiful little story echoes the words we find in the gospel
of Matthew in the Bible: "I was hungry and you gave me food. . . .
I was naked and you clothed me."

A little girl once lived all alone with her old grandmother upon the borders of a forest. They were so poor that they were scarcely able to buy food to eat or clothes to cover them.

"Never mind, Granny," the little girl would say. "Some day I will be big enough to work, and then I will earn so much that I will be able to buy everything that we need, and to give something to other poor folk as well.

One day the child went off into the forest to gather sticks. These she hoped to sell for a few pennies in the town over beyond the hill. She was to be gone all day, so she took with her into the forest a bit of bread, which was all they had left to eat.

It was winter, and the air was bitterly cold. The child wrapped her little shawl about her, and ran on as fast as she could. She was hungry, but she intended to save her crust until after the sticks were gathered.

Just as she reached the edge of the forest she met a boy, even smaller than she herself, and he was crying bitterly.

The little girl had a tender heart. She stopped and asked the child why he was weeping.

"I am weeping," he answered, "because I am hungry."

"Have you had nothing to eat today?" she asked.

"I have had nothing, and I am starving, for I do not know where to go for food."

The little girl sighed. "You are probably hungrier than I am," she said, and she took the crust from her pocket and gave it to the boy. Then she again hurried on.

A little farther on, she met another child who was even more miserable-looking than the first, for this child seemed almost frozen with cold. Her clothing hung about her in rags, and her skin looked blue through the rents.

"Ah," cried she, "if I had but a warm little dress like yours! Help me, I pray you, or I will certainly die of cold."

The good little girl was filled with pity. "It is not right," thought she, "that I should have both a dress and a shawl. I will give one of them to this poor child."

She took off her dress and gave it to the child, and then wrapped the shawl closely about her shoulders. In spite of the shawl she felt very cold. Still she was near the place where the sticks were to be found, and as soon as she had gathered them she would run home again.

She hastened on, but when she reached the place where the sticks were she saw an old woman already there, gathering up the fallen wood. The old woman was so bent and poor and miserable-looking that the little girl's heart ached for her.

"Oh, oh!" groaned the old woman. "How my poor bones do ache. If I had but a shawl to wrap about my shoulders I would not suffer so."

The child thought of her own grandmother, and of how she sometimes suffered, and she had pity on the old woman.

"Here," said she, "take my shawl," and slipping it from her shoulders, she gave it to the old woman.

And now she stood there in the forest with her arms and shoulders bare, and with nothing on her but her little shift. The sharp wind blew about her, but she was not cold. She had eaten nothing, but she was not hungry. She was fed and warmed by her own kindness.

She gathered her sticks and started home again. It was growing dark and the stars shown through the bare branches of the trees. Suddenly an old man stood beside her. "Give me your sticks," said he, "for my hearth is cold, and I am too old to gather wood for myself."

The little girl sighed. If she gave him the sticks she would have to stop to gather more. Still she would not refuse him. "Take them," she said, "in heaven's name."

No sooner had she said this than she saw it was not an old man who stood before her, but a shining angel.

"You have fed the hungry," said the angel, "you have clothed the naked, and you have given help to those who asked it. You shall not go unrewarded. See!"

At once a light shone around the child, and it seemed to her that all the stars of heaven were falling through the bare branches of the trees, but these stars were diamonds and rubies and other precious stones. They lay thick upon the ground. "Gather them together," said the angel, "for they are yours."

Wondering, the child gathered them together—all that she could carry in the skirt of her little shift.

When she looked about her again the angel was gone, but the child hastened home with her treasure. It was enough to make her and her old grandmother rich. From then on they lacked for nothing. They were not only able to have all they wished for, but to give to many who were poor. So they were not only rich, but beloved by all who knew them.

•

MR. STRAW

It's interesting to compare this wonderful tale from Japan with the story of Mr. Vinegar (told in the Self-Discipline chapter of *The Book of Virtues*). Mr. Vinegar keeps trading down as he follows his foolish impulses. Mr. Straw, on the other hand, trades up; he quite unintentionally raises himself by lifting a hand to help others.

Once upon a time, long ago of course, for that's when most good stories take place, there lived a man named Mr. Straw. Mr. Straw had no home, he had no wife, he had no children, he had nothing but the shirt on his back, in fact. For Mr. Straw had no luck. He was always poor and had little to eat, so he was as thin as a piece of straw. That, you see, is why people called him Mr. Straw.

Every morning, Mr. Straw went to the temple to ask the Goddess of Fortune for better luck. One day he heard a voice.

"The first thing your hand touches when you leave the temple will bring you great fortune," it whispered.

Mr. Straw rubbed his eyes, pinched himself, and looked all around him. The temple was empty.

"Was I dreaming, or was that the Goddess of Fortune?" he wondered. He rushed out of the temple to find his new luck.

But poor Mr. Straw tripped on the temple steps and tumbled all the way down to the bottom, where he lay in the dirt. When he picked himself up, he found his hand was clutching a piece of straw.

"Well," he thought, "a piece of straw is a pretty worthless thing. But since the Goddess of Fortune meant me to pick it up, I'd better not throw it away."

So he walked along, holding the piece of straw.

Before long a dragonfly came and began to buzz around his head. Mr. Straw waved and shooed, but it wouldn't go away. It buzzed and whirred and flew circles around him.

"Very well," said Mr. Straw. "Since you won't go away, you must stay with me."

He caught the dragonfly and tied his straw to its tail, so it looked like a little kite on a tiny string. And he kept walking down the road.

Pretty soon he met the flower lady and her little boy coming the other way. They were going to the market to sell their flowers. They had been walking a long time, and the boy was hot and tired, and the dust brought tears to his eyes. But when he saw Mr. Straw's dragonfly buzzing on the end of the straw, his face lit up.

"Mother," he said, "can I have a dragonfly? Please?"

"Well," thought Mr. Straw, "the Goddess of Fortune told me this piece of straw would bring me luck. But this little boy is hot and tired, and it will make him happy."

So he gave the boy the dragonfly on the straw.

"You are very kind," the flower lady said. "I have nothing to give you in return except this rose. Will you take it?"

Mr. Straw thanked her and went on his way, holding his rose.

After a while he saw a young man sitting on a tree stump, holding his head in his hands. He looked so forlorn, Mr. Straw asked him what was the matter.

"This evening I'll ask my belle to marry me," the youth cried. "But I'm a poor man and have no gift to bring her."

"Well, I'm a poor man too," Mr. Straw said. "I have nothing valuable, but if you want to give her this rose, you are welcome to it."

The youth perked up when he saw the splendid rose.

"Please take these three oranges in return," he said. "It's all I have to offer."

So Mr. Straw set off again, carrying three plump, juicy oranges.

Soon he met a peddler pulling a little cart.

"Can you help me?" the peddler panted. "I've been pulling this cart all day, and I'm so thirsty I'm going to faint! I need a drink of water."

"I'm afraid there are no wells nearby," Mr. Straw said, "but you can have these oranges and drink the juice."

The peddler was so grateful he reached into his cart and pulled out his finest roll of silk.

"You're very, very kind," he said. "Please take this cloth in return."

So Mr. Straw set off once again, this time with his silk under his arm.

Before long, he met a princess in a golden carriage. She wore a worried look, but her face lit up when she saw Mr. Straw.

"Where did you get that silk?" she cried. "It's just what I've been looking for. Today is my father's birthday, and I want to make him a new royal robe."

"Well, since it's his birthday, you're welcome to have this silk," Mr. Straw said.

The princess couldn't believe her luck.

"You're very thoughtful and kind," she said with a smile. "Please take this jewel in return."

She rode away, leaving Mr. Straw holding a jewel that gleamed like the fire of the sun.

"Well, well," he told himself. "I started with a worthless piece of straw, and suddenly I find I have a jewel. Something tells me this has gone far enough."

He took the jewel straight to a merchant and sold it. Then he took the money and bought a great rice field. He worked hard in his field, and every year it grew more and more rice, and before too long he was a rich man.

But his wealth did not change him one bit. He always shared his rice with the hungry, and built a school for the village children, and helped anyone who needed a hand. And everyone said it all came from one little piece of straw, but Mr. Straw knew his luck really came from his kindness.

•

THE LINE OF GOLDEN LIGHT
Elizabeth Harrison

In this story, a brave girl's journey to make the path easier for her sister smooths the way for others as well.

Once upon a time there lived a child whose name was Avilla. She was sweet and loving, and fair to look upon, and had everything in the world to make her happy, but she had a little blind sister, and Avilla could not be perfectly happy as long as her sister's eyes were closed so that she could not see God's beautiful world, nor enjoy His bright sunshine. Little Avilla kept wondering if there was not something that she could do which would open this blind sister's eyes.

At last, one day, she heard of an old, old woman, nobody knew how old, who had lived for hundreds of years in a dark cave, not many miles away. This queer old woman knew a secret enchantment, by means of which the blind could receive their sight. The child, Avilla, asked her parents' permission to make a journey to the cave, in order that she might try to persuade the old woman to tell her this secret. "Then," she exclaimed joyfully, "my dear sister need sit no longer in darkness." Her parents gave a somewhat unwilling consent, as they had heard many strange stories about the old woman. At last, however, one fine spring morning, Avilla started on her journey. She had a long distance to walk, but the happy thoughts in her heart made the time pass quickly, and the soft, cool breeze seemed to be whispering a song to her all the way.

When she came to the mouth of the cave, it looked so dark and forbidding that she almost feared to enter it, but the thought of her little blind sister gave her courage, and she walked in. At first she could see nothing, for all the sunshine was shut out by the frowning rocks that guarded the entrance. Soon, however, she discerned the old woman sitting on a stone chair, spinning a pile of flax into a fine, fine thread. She seemed bent nearly double with age, and her face wore a look of worry and care, which made her appear still older.

The child Avilla came close to her side and thought, She is so aged that she must be hard of hearing. The old woman did not turn her head or stop her spinning. Avilla waited a moment and then took fresh courage and said, "I have come to ask you if you will tell me how I can cure my blind sister."

The strange creature turned and stared at her as if she were very much surprised. She then spoke in a deep, hollow voice, so hollow that it sounded as if she had not spoken for a very long time. "Oh," said she with a sneer, "I can tell you well enough, but you'll not do it. People who can see trouble themselves very little about those who are blind!" This last was said with a sigh, and then she scowled at Avilla until the child's heart began to beat very fast.

But the thought of her little blind sister made her brave again, and she cried out, "Oh, *please* tell me. I will do anything to help my dear sister!"

The old woman looked long and earnestly at her this time. She then stooped down and searched in the heap of the fine-spun thread which lay at her side until she found the end of it. This she held out to the child, saying, "Take this and carry it all around the world, and when you have done that, come to me and I will show you how your blind sister may be cured." Little Avilla thanked her and eagerly seized the tiny thread, and wrapping it carefully around her hand that she might not lose it, turned and hastened out of the close, damp cave.

She had not traveled far before she looked back to be sure the thread had not broken, it was so thin. Imagine her surprise to see that instead of its being a gray thread of spun flax, it was a thread of golden light, that glittered and shone in the sunlight, as if it were made of the most precious stuff on earth. She felt sure now that it must be a magic thread, and that it somehow would help her to cure her blind sister. So she hastened on, glad and happy.

Soon, however, she approached a dark, dense forest. No ray of sunlight seemed ever to have fallen on the trunks of its trees. In the distance she thought she could hear the growl of bears and the roar of lions. Her heart almost stopped beating. "Oh, I can never go through that gloomy forest," said she to herself, and her eyes filled with tears. She turned to retrace her steps, when the soft breeze which still accompanied her whispered, "Look at the thread you have been carrying! Look at the golden thread!" She looked back, and the bright, tiny line of light seemed to be actually smiling at her, as it stretched across the soft green grass, far into the distance, and, strange to say, each tiny blade of grass which it had touched, had blossomed into a flower. So, as the little girl looked back, she saw a flowery path with a glittering line of golden light running through it. "How beautiful!" she exclaimed. "I did not notice the flowers as I came along, but the enchanted thread will make the next traveler see them."

This thought filled her with such joy that she pushed forward into the dark woods. Sometimes she knocked her head against a tree which stood in her way, sometimes she almost feared she was lost, but every now and then she would look back and the sight of the tiny thread of golden light always renewed her courage. Once in a while she felt quite sure that she could see the nose of some wild beast poking out in front of her, but when she came nearer it proved to be the joint in a tree trunk, or some strange fungus which had grown on a low branch. Then she would laugh at her own fear and go on. One of the wonderful things about the mysterious little thread which she carried in her hand was, that it seemed to open a path behind it, so that one could easily follow in her footsteps without stumbling over fallen trees, or bumping against living ones. Every now and then a gray squirrel would frisk by her in a friendly fashion, as if to assure her that she was not alone, even in the twilight of the dark woods. By and by she came to the part of the forest where the trees were less dense, and soon she was out in the glad sunshine again.

But now a new difficulty faced her. As far as she could see stretched a low, swampy marsh of wet land. The mud and slime did not look very inviting, but the thought of her little blind sister came to her again, and she bravely plunged into the mire. The dirty, dripping mud clung to her dress and made her feet so heavy that she grew weary lifting them out of it. Sometimes she seemed to be stuck fast, and it was only with a great effort that she could pull out, first one foot, and then the other. A lively green frog hopped along beside her and seemed to say, in his funny, croaking voice, "Never mind the mud, you'll soon be through it." When she had at last reached the end of the slippery, sticky marsh, and stood once more on firm ground, she looked back at the tiny thread of golden light which trailed along after her. *What* do you think had happened? Wherever the mysterious and beautiful thread had touched the mud, the water had dried up, and the earth had become firm and hard, so that any other person who might wish to cross the swampy place could walk on firm ground. This made the child Avilla so happy, that she began to sing softly to herself.

Soon, however, her singing ceased. As the day advanced, the air grew hotter and hotter. The trees had long ago disappeared, and now the grass became parched and dry, until at last she found herself in the midst of a dreary desert. For miles and miles the scorching sand stretched on every side. She could not even find a friendly rock in whose shadow she might rest for a time. The blazing sun hurt her eyes and made her head ache, and the hot sand burned her feet. Still she toiled on, cheered by a swarm of yellow butterflies that fluttered just ahead of her. At last the end of the desert was reached, just as the sun disappeared behind a crimson cloud. Dusty and weary, the child Avilla was about to throw herself down on the ground to rest. As she did so, her eyes turned to look once more at the golden thread which had trailed behind her all day on the hot sand. Lo, and behold! What did she see? Tall shade trees had sprung up along the path she had traveled, and each tiny grain of sand that the wonderful thread had touched was now changed into a diamond, or ruby, or emerald, or some other precious stone. On one side the pathway across the desert shone and glittered, while on the other the graceful trees cast a cool and refreshing shade.

Little Avilla stood amazed as she looked at the beautiful trees and the sparkling gems. All feeling of weariness was gone. The air now seemed mild and refreshing, and she thought that she could hear in the distance some birds singing their evening songs. One by one the bright stars came out in the quiet sky above her head, as if to keep guard while she slept through the night.

The next morning she started forward on her long journey round the world. She traveled quite pleasantly for a while, thinking of how cool and shady the desert path would now be for anyone who might have to travel it, and of the precious jewels she had left for someone else to gather up. She could not stop for them herself, for she was too anxious to press forward and finish her task, in order that her little blind sister might the sooner see.

After a time she came to some rough rocks tumbled about in great confusion, as if angry giants had hurled them at each other. Soon the path grew steeper and steeper, and the rocks sharper and sharper, until they cut her feet. Before her she could see nothing but more rocks until they piled themselves into a great mountain, which frowned down upon her, as much as to say, "How dare you attempt to climb to my summit?" The brave child hesitated. Just then two strong eagles with outspread wings rose from their nest of sticks on the side of a steep cliff nearby and soared majestically and slowly aloft. As they passed far above her head they uttered a loud cry which seemed to say, "Be brave and strong and you shall meet us at the mountaintop."

Sometimes the ragged edges of the rocks tore her dress, and sometimes they caught the tiny golden thread, and tangled it so that she had to turn back and loosen it from their hold. The road was very steep and she was compelled to sit down every few minutes and get her breath. Still she climbed on, keeping the soaring eagles always in sight. As she neared the top, she turned and looked back at the enchanted thread of golden light which she had carried through all the long, strange journey. Another marvelous thing had happened! The rugged path of sharp, broken rocks had changed into broad and beautiful white marble steps, over which trailed the shining thread of light. She knew that she had made a pathway up this difficult mountain and her heart rejoiced.

She turned again to proceed on her journey, when, only a short distance in front of her, she saw the dark cave in which lived the strange old woman who had bidden her carry the line of light around the world. She hastened forward, and on entering the cave, she saw the old creature, almost bent double, still spinning the mysterious thread. Avilla ran forward and cried out, "I have done all you told me to do, now give sight to my sister!"

The old woman sprang to her feet, seized the thread of golden light and exclaimed, "At last! At last! I am freed!"

Then came so strange and wonderful a change that Avilla could hardly believe her own eyes. Instead of the ugly, cross-looking old crone, there stood a beautiful princess, with long golden hair and tender blue eyes, her face radiant with joy. Her story was soon told. Hundreds of years ago she had been changed into the bent old woman and shut up in the dark cave on the mountainside, be-

cause she, a daughter of the King, had been selfish and idle, thinking only of herself, and her punishment had been that she must
remain thus disguised and separated from all companions and
friends until she could find someone who would be generous and
brave enough to take the long, dangerous journey around the world
for the sake of others. Her mother had been a fairy princess and
had taught her many things which we mortals have yet to learn.
She showed the child Avilla how, by dipping the golden thread
into a spring of ordinary water, she could change the water into
golden water, which glittered and sparkled like liquid sunshine.
Filling a pitcher with this they hastened together to where the little
blind sister sat in darkness waiting for someone to come and lead
her home. The beautiful princess told Avilla to dip her hands
into the bowl of enchanted water, and then press them upon
the closed eyes of her sister. They opened! And the little blind girl
could see!

After that the fairy princess came and lived with little Avilla and
her sister, and taught them how to do many wonderful things, of
which I have no time to tell you today.

THE LAME BOY

Mrs. Charles A. Lane

By cheering on others, we encourage ourselves too.

He was little. He was lame. He was only six years old. His
mother was a poor washerwoman, and they lived in a tiny room on
a narrow street of a great city.

All day long he sat in his high chair, looking down into the
narrow street. He could see, by leaning forward, a bit of blue sky

over the tall warehouse opposite. Sometimes a white cloud would drift across the blue. Sometimes it was all dull gray.

But the street was more interesting. There were people down there. In the early morning men and women were hurrying to their work. Later the children came out and played on the pavement and in the gutters. Sometimes they danced and sang, but often they were quarrelsome. In the spring the street-organ man came, and then everybody seemed happy.

The boy's sad little face looked out all day long. Only when he saw his mother coming did he smile and wave his hand.

"I wish I could help you, Mother," he said one night. "You work so hard, and I can't do anything for you."

"Oh, but you do!" she cried quickly. "It helps me to see your face smiling down at me from the window. It helps me when you wave your hand. It makes my work lighter all day to think you will be there waving to me when I go home."

"Then I'll wave harder," said the little fellow.

And the next night a tired workman, seeing the mother look up and answer the signal, looked up too. Such a little, pinched face as he saw at the high window. But how cheery the smile was! The man laughed to himself and waved his cap, and the boy, a little shyly, returned the greeting.

So it went. The next evening the workman nudged his comrade to look up at the "poor little chap sitting, so patient, at the window," and again the smile shone out as two caps waved in the air below him.

Days came and passed, and the boy had more friends. Men and women went out of their way to send a greeting to him. Life didn't seem quite so hard to them when they thought how dreary it must be for him. Sometimes a flower found its way to him, or an orange, or a colored picture. The children stopped quarreling when they saw him watching them, and played games to amuse him. It pleased them to see how eager he was to share in their good times.

"Tell the lad we couldn't get on without him," said one of the weary laborers to the mother one night. " 'Tis a great thing to have a brave heart. It makes us all brave, too. Tell him that."

And you may be sure she did.

•

WAUKEWA'S EAGLE

James Buckham

Offer kindness, and you may be repaid in kind.

One day, when the Indian boy Waukewa was hunting along the mountainside, he found a young eagle with a broken wing lying at the base of a cliff. The bird had fallen from an aerie on a ledge high above, and being too young to fly, had fluttered down the cliff and injured itself so severely that it was likely to die. When Waukewa saw it he was about to drive one of his sharp arrows through its body, for the passion of the hunter was strong in him and the eagle plunders many a fine fish from the Indian's drying-frame. But a gentler impulse came to him as he saw the young bird quivering with pain and fright at his feet, and he slowly unbent his bow, put the arrow in his quiver, and stooped over the panting eaglet. For fully a minute the wild eyes of the wounded bird and the eyes of the Indian boy, growing gentler and softer as he gazed, looked into one another. Then the struggling and panting of the young eagle ceased. The wild, frightened look passed out of its eyes, and it suffered Waukewa to pass his hand gently over its ruffled and draggled feathers. The fierce instinct to fight, to defend its threatened life, yielded to the charm of the tenderness and pity expressed in the boy's eyes; and from that moment Waukewa and the eagle were friends.

Waukewa went slowly home to his father's lodge, bearing the wounded eaglet in his arms. He carried it so gently that the broken wing gave no twinge of pain, and the bird lay perfectly still, never attempting to strike with its sharp beak the hands that clasped it.

Warming some water over the fire at the lodge, Waukewa bathed the broken wing of the eagle, and bound it up with soft strips of skin. Then he made a nest of ferns and grass inside the lodge, and laid the bird in it. The boy's mother looked on with shining eyes. Her heart was very tender. From girlhood she had loved all the creatures of the woods, and it pleased her to see some of her own gentle spirit waking in the boy.

When Waukewa's father returned from hunting, he would have caught up the young eagle and wrung its neck. But the boy pleaded with him so eagerly, stooping over the captive and defending it with his small hands, that the stern warrior laughed. "Keep it, then," he said, "and nurse it until it is well. But then you must let it go, for we will not raise up a thief in the lodges." So Waukewa promised that when the eagle's wing was healed and grown so that it could fly, he would carry it forth and give it its freedom.

It was a month—or, as the Indians say, a moon—before the young eagle's wing had fully mended and the bird was old enough and strong enough to fly. And in the meantime Waukewa cared for it and fed it daily, and the friendship between the boy and the bird grew very strong.

But at last the time came when the willing captive must be freed. So Waukewa carried it far away from the Indian lodges, where none of the young braves might see it hovering overhead and be tempted to shoot their arrows at it, and there he let it go. The young eagle rose toward the sky in great circles, rejoicing in its freedom and its strange, new power of flight. But when Waukewa began to move away from the spot, it came swooping down again; and all day long it followed him through the woods as he hunted. At dusk, when Waukewa shaped his course for the Indian lodges, the eagle would have accompanied him. But the boy suddenly slipped into a hollow tree and hid, and after a long time the eagle stopped sweeping about in search of him and flew slowly and sadly away.

Summer passed, and then winter; and spring came again, with its flowers and birds and swarming fish in the lakes and streams. Then it was that all the Indians, old and young, braves and squaws, pushed their light canoes out from shore and with spear and hook waged pleasant war against the salmon and the red-spotted trout. After winter's long imprisonment, it was such joy to toss in the sunshine and the warm wind and catch savory fish to take the place of dried meats and corn!

Above the great falls of the Apahoqui the salmon sported in the cool, swinging current, darting under the lee of the rocks and leaping full length in the clear spring air. Nowhere else were such salmon to be speared as those which lay among the riffles at the head of the Apahoqui rapids. But only the most daring braves ventured to seek them there, for the current was strong, and should a light canoe once pass the danger point and get caught in the rush of the rapids, nothing could save it from going over the roaring falls.

Very early in the morning of a clear April day, just as the sun was rising splendidly over the mountains, Waukewa launched his canoe a half-mile above the rapids of the Apahoqui, and floated downward, spear in hand, among the salmon riffles. He was the only one of the Indian lads who dared fish above the falls. But he had been there often, and never yet had his watchful eye and his strong paddle suffered the current to carry his canoe beyond the danger point. This morning he was alone on the river, having risen long before daylight to be first at the sport.

The riffles were full of salmon, big, lusty fellows, who glided about the canoe on every side in an endless silver stream. Waukewa plunged his spear right and left, and tossed one glittering victim after another into the bark canoe. So absorbed in the sport was he that for once he did not notice when the canoe began to glide more swiftly among the rocks. But suddenly he looked up, caught his paddle, and dipped it wildly in the swirling water. The canoe swung sidewise, shivered, held its own against the torrent, and then slowly, inch by inch, began to creep upstream toward the shore. But suddenly there was a loud, cruel snap, and the paddle parted in the boy's hands, broken just above the blade! Waukewa gave a cry of despairing agony. Then he bent to the gunwale of his canoe and with the shattered blade fought desperately against the current. But it was useless. The racing torrent swept him downward; the hungry falls roared tauntingly in his ears.

Then the Indian boy knelt calmly upright in the canoe, facing the mist of the falls, and folded his arms. His young face was stern and lofty. He had lived like a brave hitherto—now he would die like one.

Faster and faster sped the doomed canoe toward the great cataract. The black rocks glided away on either side like phantoms. The roar of the terrible waters became like thunder in the boy's ears. But still he gazed calmly and sternly ahead, facing his fate as a brave Indian should. At last he began to chant the death-song, which he had learned from the older braves. In a few moments all would be over. But he would come before the Great Spirit with a fearless hymn upon his lips.

Suddenly a shadow fell across the canoe. Waukewa lifted his eyes and saw a great eagle hovering over, with dangling legs, and a spread of wings that blotted out the sun. Once more the eyes of the Indian boy and the eagle met; and now it was the eagle who was master!

With a glad cry the Indian boy stood up in his canoe, and the eagle hovered lower. Now the canoe tossed up on that great swelling wave that climbs to the cataract's edge, and the boy lifted his hands and caught the legs of the eagle. The next moment he looked down into the awful gulf of waters from its very verge. The canoe was snatched from beneath him and plunged down the black wall of the cataract; but he and the struggling eagle were floating outward and downward through the cloud of mist. The cataract roared terribly, like a wild beast robbed of its prey. The spray beat and blinded, the air rushed upward as they fell. But the eagle struggled on with his burden. He fought his way out of the mist and the flying spray. His great wings threshed the air with a whistling sound. Down, down they sank, the boy and the eagle, but ever farther from the precipice of water and the boiling whirlpool below. At length, with a fluttering plunge, the eagle dropped on a sand bar below the whirlpool, and he and the Indian boy lay there a minute, breathless and exhausted. Then the eagle slowly lifted himself, took the air under his free wings, and soared away, while the Indian boy knelt on the sand, with shining eyes following the great bird till he faded into the gray of the cliffs.

●

WHY THE WATER IN RIVERS IS NEVER STILL

*Adapted from a retelling
by Florence Holbrook*

Remember, really helping usually involves real work. If you take on the responsibility of helping others, stick to it—or you can end up doing more harm than good.

All kinds of strange things came to pass in the days of long ago, but perhaps the strangest of all was that brooks and rivers used to keep watch over little children. The children and brooks ran about together, through the fields and forests. Sometimes the brooks ran first and the children followed. Sometimes the children ran first and the brooks followed. Of course, if any animal came near that would hurt the children, a brook quickly flowed around them, so that they stood on an island and were safe from harm.

In those days lived a little boy and a little girl who were the son and daughter of the king. When the children were old enough to run about, the king called the rivers and brooks to come before him. They came gladly, for they felt sure that something pleasant would happen, and they waited so quietly that no one would have thought they were so full of frolic.

"I have called you," said the king, "to give you the care of my two little children. They like so well to run about, and of course it will be pleasant for them to have many playmates. So I felt that it would be better to ask every river and every brook to see that they are not hurt or lost."

"We shall have the king's own son and daughter for our playmates!" whispered the rivers. "Nothing so pleasant ever happened to us before."

But the king went on, "If you keep my children safe, and follow them so closely that they are not lost, then I will give you whatever gift you wish. But if I find that you have forgotten them one moment and they are lost or hurt, then you will be punished as no river was ever punished before."

The rivers and even the most frolicsome little brooks were again quiet for a moment. Then they all cried together, "O king, we will be good. There were never better friends than we will be to your children."

At first all went well, and the playmates had the merriest times that could be thought of. Then came a day when the sunshine was very warm, but the king's children ran faster and farther than boys and girls had ever run in the world before, and even the brooks could not keep up with them. The rivers had never been weary before, but when this warm day came, one river after another had some reason for being quiet.

One complained, "I have followed the children farther than any other river."

"Perhaps you have," said another, "but I have been up and down and round and round till I have forgotten how it seems to be quiet."

Another declared, "I have run about long enough, and I shall run no more."

A little brook said, "If I were a great river, perhaps I could run farther."

And a great river replied, "If I were a little brook, of course I could run farther."

So they talked, and the day passed. Night came before they knew it, and they could not find the king's little boy and girl.

"Where are my children?" cried the king.

"Indeed, we do not know," answered the brooks and rivers in great fear, and each one looked at the others.

"You have lost my children," said the king, "and if you do not find them, you shall be punished. Go and search for them."

"Please help us," the rivers begged of the trees and plants, and everything that had life began to search for the lost children.

"Perhaps they are underground," thought the trees, and they sent their roots down into the earth.

"Perhaps they are in the east," cried one animal, and he went to the east.

"They may be on the mountain," said one plant, and so it climbed to the very top of the mountain.

"They may be in the village," said another, and so that one crept up close to the homes of men.

Many years passed. The king was almost brokenhearted, but he knew it was of no use to search longer, so he called very sadly, "Search no longer. Let each plant and animal make its home where it is. The little plant that has crept up the mountain shall live on the mountaintop, and the roots of the trees shall stay underground. The rivers—" Then the king stopped, and the rivers trembled. They knew that they would be punished, but what would the punishment be?

The king looked at them. "As for you, rivers and brooks," he declared, "it was your work to watch my little boy and my little girl. The plants and trees shall find rest and live happily in their homes, but you shall ever search for my lost children, and you shall never have a home."

So from that day to this the rivers have gone on looking for the lost children. They never stop, and some of them are so troubled that they flow first one way and then the other.

•

Why Evergreen Trees Never Lose Their Leaves

Retold by Florence Holbrook

It's always easy to find a reason not to help another. This is perhaps the hardest part about learning compassion—fighting to
overcome our own excuses when they are merely selfish ones.

Winter was coming, and the birds had flown far to the south,
where the air was warm and they could find berries to eat. One
little bird had broken its wing and could not fly with the others. It
was alone in the cold world of frost and snow. The forest looked
warm, and it made its way to the trees as well as it could, to ask for
help.

First it came to a birch tree. "Beautiful birch tree," it said, "my
wing is broken, and my friends have flown away. May I live among
your branches till they come back to me?"

"No, indeed," answered the birch tree, drawing her fair green
leaves away. "We of the great forest have our own birds to help. I
can do nothing for you."

"The birch is not very strong," said the little bird to itself, "and
it might be that she could not hold me easily. I will ask the oak." So
the bird said: "Great oak tree, you are so strong, will you not let me
live on your boughs till my friends come back in the springtime?"

"In the springtime!" cried the oak. "That is a long way off. How
do I know what you might do in all that time? Birds are always
looking for something to eat, and you might even eat up some of
my acorns."

"It may be that the willow will be kind to me," thought the
bird, and it said: "Gentle willow, my wing is broken, and I could
not fly to the south with the other birds. May I live on your branches
till the springtime?"

The willow did not look gentle then, for she drew herself up
proudly and said: "Indeed, I do not know you, and we willows
never talk to people whom we do not know. Very likely there
are trees somewhere that will take in strange birds. Leave me at
once."

The poor little bird did not know what to do. Its wing was not yet strong, but it began to fly away as well as it could. Before it had gone far a voice was heard. "Little bird," it said, "where are you going?"

"Indeed, I do not know," answered the bird sadly. "I am very cold."

"Come right here, then," said the friendly spruce tree, for it was her voice that had called. "You shall live on my warmest branch all winter if you choose."

"Will you really let me?" asked the little bird eagerly.

"Indeed, I will," answered the kindhearted spruce tree. "If your friends have flown away, it is time for the trees to help you. Here is the branch where my leaves are thickest and softest."

"My branches are not very thick," said the friendly pine tree, "but I am big and strong, and I can keep the North Wind from you and the spruce."

"I can help, too," said a little juniper tree. "I can give you berries all winter long, and every bird knows that juniper berries are good."

So the spruce gave the lonely little bird a home. The pine kept the cold North Wind away from it. The juniper gave it berries to eat. The other trees looked on and talked together wisely.

"I would not have strange birds on my boughs," said the birch.

"I shall not give my acorns away for anyone," said the oak.

"I never have anything to do with strangers," said the willow, and the three trees drew their leaves closely about them.

In the morning all those shining, green leaves lay on the ground, for a cold North Wind had come in the night, and every leaf that it touched fell from the tree.

"May I touch every leaf in the forest?" asked the wind in its frolic.

"No," said the Frost King. "The trees that have been kind to the little bird with the broken wing may keep their leaves."

This is why the leaves of the spruce, the pine, and the juniper are always green.

•

SHELTERING WINGS

Harriet Louise Jerome

Love brings warmth and life.

It was intensely cold. Heavy sleds creaked as they scraped over the jeweled sounding board of dry, unyielding snow. The signs above shop doors shrieked and groaned as they swung helplessly to and fro. The clear, keen air seemed frozen into sharp little crystalline needles that stabbed every living thing that must be out in it. The streets were almost forsaken in mid-afternoon. Businessmen hurried from shelter to shelter. Every dog remained at home. Not a bird was to be seen or heard. The sparrows had been forced to hide themselves in crevices and holes. The doves found protected corners and huddled together as best they could. Many birds were frozen to death.

A dozen or more doves were gathered close under the cornice of the piazza of a certain house, trying with little success to keep warm. Some small sparrows, disturbed and driven from the cozy place they had chosen, saw the doves and came flying across the piazza.

"Dear doves," chirped the sparrows, "won't you let us nestle near you? Your bodies look so large and warm."

"But your coats are frosted with cold. We cannot let you come near us, for we are almost frozen now," murmured the doves sadly.

"But we are perishing."

"So are we."

"It looks so warm near your broad wings, gentle doves. Oh, let us come! We are so little, and so very, very cold!"

"Come," cooed a dove at last, and a trembling little sparrow fluttered close and nestled under the broad white wing.

"Come," cooed another dove, and another little sparrow found comfort.

"Come! Come!" echoed another warm-hearted bird, and another, until at last more than half the doves were sheltering small, shivering sparrows beneath their own half-frozen wings.

"My sisters, you are very foolish," said the other doves. "You mean well, but why do you risk your own beautiful lives to give life to worthless sparrows?"

"Ah! they are so small, and so very, very cold," murmured the doves. "Many of us will perish this cruel night. While we have life let us share its meager warmth with those in bitter need."

Colder and colder grew the day. The sun went down behind the clouds suffused with soft and radiant beauty, but more fiercely and relentlessly swept the wind around the house where the doves and sparrows waited for death.

An hour after sunset a man came up to the house and strode across the piazza. As the door of the house closed heavily behind him, a little child watching from the window saw something jarred from the cornice fall heavily to the piazza floor.

"Oh, Papa," she cried in surprise, "a poor frozen dove has fallen on our porch!"

When he stepped out to pick up the fallen dove the father saw the others under the cornice. They were no longer able to move or to utter a cry, so he brought them in and placed them in a room where they might slowly revive. Soon more than half of the doves could coo gratefully, and raise their stiffened wings. Then out from beneath the wing of each revived dove fluttered a living sparrow.

"Look, Papa!" cried the child. "Each dove that has come to life was holding a poor little sparrow close to her heart."

They gently raised the wings of the doves that could not be revived. Not one had a sparrow beneath it.

Colder and fiercer swept the wind without, cutting and more piercing grew the frozen, crystalline needles of air, but each dove that had sheltered a frost-coated sparrow beneath her own shivering wings lived to rejoice in the glowing gladsome sunshine of the days to come.

•

How the Animals Got Sunlight

Here's the kind of perseverance that tries against the odds, even when others before have tried and failed. It's also the kind of intellectual persistence that would learn from others' mistakes. Different versions of this enchanting tale were widespread among Native American peoples.

Once the world was continually dark, and all the animals kept fumbling around and knocking into each other, and they never knew where they were in such blackness. Finally they called a great council to decide how to solve the problem.

"What we need is light," the Owl said. The Owl presided over the meeting because he could see better in the dark than the other animals.

"That's right! We need light," everyone cried. "But where do we get it?"

"It's not an easy thing," the Owl warned. "They say there is light on the other side of the world. But that's a long way away. The journey will be dangerous. Whoever goes may well never come back."

"Then who should go?" everyone cried at once. "Who will risk the journey?"

There was a long silence. All the birds and beasts shuddered in the blackness.

At last they heard a lowly voice.

"I'll try," the Possum offered. "I have a long, bushy tail. I can wrap some light inside its fur and carry it home behind me."

So the Possum set out alone, traveling to the east. He walked for days and days across the black earth, never knowing where he really was, until finally he began to see a little glow in the sky.

He hurried toward it, and it grew lighter and lighter. Soon it was so bright it hurt his eyes, and he had to squint to keep it from blinding him. And even today, when you see a possum, you'll see how he keeps his eyes closed in narrow slits, so you'd almost think he was sleeping.

Finally, when he'd gone all the way to the other side of the world, the Possum found the sun. He grabbed a piece as fast as he could and wrapped it up in his long, bushy tail, and turned for home.

But the journey home was just as long, of course, and the piece of sun was too hot and bright for poor Possum. It burned all the fur off his tail and it fell onto the ground. That's why, today, Possum's tail is long and bare.

"Possum tried and failed," all the animals cried when he came home in darkness. "Now we'll never have any light."

"I'll try now," offered the Vulture. "Maybe this journey calls for someone with wings."

So the Vulture flew east, and finally he came to the sun. He dived and snatched a piece of it in his claws.

"Possum tried to carry the sun with his tail and dropped it," he told himself. "I'll try carrying it on my head."

Vulture set the piece of sun on his head and turned for home, but the sun was so hot that before long it had burned away all the feathers on his crown. He grew dizzy and lost his way, and began wandering around and around until the piece of sun tumbled to the ground. That is why today a vulture's head is bald, and you'll still see him drifting in circles high overhead.

"Now we're truly finished," the animals cried when Vulture returned in darkness. "Possum and Vulture tried as best they could, but it wasn't enough."

"Maybe we need to try one more time," a tiny voice rose from the weeds. "I'll go this time."

"Who is that?" the animals asked. "Who said that?"

"It's me, Old Lady Spider. I know I'm small and slow, but perhaps I'm the one who can make it."

Before she started, she gathered a bit of wet clay, and with her eight tiny hands she made a little pot.

"Possum and Vulture had nothing to carry the sun in," she said. "I'll put it in this pot."

Then she spun a thread and fastened the end to a rock.

"Possum and Vulture were blinded and lost from the sun's light on the way back," she said. "But I'll follow this thread home."

So she set out, traveling east, spinning her thread behind her as she walked. When she reached the sun, she pinched off a small piece and put it in her clay pot. It was still so bright she could hardly see, but she turned and followed her thread home.

She came walking out of the east all aglow, looking like the sun itself. And even today, when Old Lady Spider spins her web, it looks like the rays of the rising sun.

She reached home at last. All the animals could see for the first time. They saw how tiny and old Spider was, and they wondered that she could make the journey alone. Then they saw how she had carried the sun in the little pot, and that was when the world learned to make pots out of clay and set them in the sun to dry.

But Old Lady Spider had had enough of being so close to the sun. That is why, today, she spins her web in the early morning hours, before the sun is too high and hot.

•

WHY THE CHIMES RANG
Adapted from Raymond M. Alden

Little acts of kindness do not go unnoticed above, even if they go unseen by the crowd below.

There was once in a faraway country a wonderful church with a gray stone tower, with ivy growing over it as far up as one could see. In the tower was a chime of Christmas bells.

Every Christmas eve all the people of the city brought to the church their offerings to the Christ Child. When the greatest and best offering was laid on the altar, there would come sounding through the music of the choir the voices of the Christmas Chimes far up in the tower. Some said the wind rang them, and others that they were so high that the angels could set them swinging.

But the fact was that no one had heard the chimes for years and years. There was an old man living not far from the church, who said that his mother had spoken of hearing them when she was a little girl. But now it was said the people had been growing less careful of their gifts for the Christ Child, and that no offering was brought great enough to deserve the music of the chimes.

A number of miles from the city, in a little country village, lived a boy named Pedro and his little brother.

The day before Christmas was bitterly cold, but the two boys started on their way to the Christmas celebration. Before nightfall they had trudged so far, hand in hand, that they saw the lights of the big city just ahead of them. Indeed, they were about to enter one of the great gates in the wall that surrounded it when they saw something dark on the snow near their path, and stepped aside to look at it. It was a poor woman who had fallen just outside the city, too sick and tired and cold to get in where she might have found shelter. Pedro, finding that he could not rouse her, said, "It's no use, little brother. You will have to go alone to the church."

"Alone?" cried little brother. "And you will not see the Christmas Festival?"

"No," said Pedro, and he could not help a little choking sound of disappointment in his throat. "See this poor woman, her face looks like the Madonna in the chapel window, and she will freeze to death if nobody cares for her. If you get a chance, little brother, to slip up to the altar without getting in anyone's way, take this little silver piece of mine and lay it down for my offering, when no one is looking."

The great church was truly a wonderful place that night. After the service, the people took their gifts to the altar for the Christ Child. Some brought wonderful jewels; some baskets of gold so heavy that they could scarcely carry them down the aisle. A great writer laid down a book that he had been making for years and years. And last of all walked the king of the country, hoping with all the rest to win for himself the chime of the Christmas bells.

There was a great murmur through the church as the people saw the king take from his head the royal crown, all set with diamonds and other precious stones, and lay it gleaming on the altar as his offering to the Holy Child. "Surely," they said, "we shall hear the bells now." But the chimes did not ring.

The procession was over. The gifts were all on the altar, and the choir had begun the closing hymn. Suddenly the organist stopped playing, and everyone looked at the old minister, who was standing in his place and holding up his hand for silence. As the people strained their ears to listen, there came softly but distinctly, swinging through the air, the sound of the bells in the tower! So far away and yet so clear seemed the music, so much sweeter were the notes than anything else that had been heard before, rising and falling away up there in the sky, that the people in the church sat for a moment very still. Then they all stood up together and stared at the altar, to see what great gift had awakened the long-silent bells.

But all that the nearest of them saw was the childish figure of Pedro's brother, who had crept softly down the aisle when no one was looking, and had laid Pedro's little piece of silver on the altar.

•

PRINCE HARWEDA AND THE MAGIC PRISON

Elizabeth Harrison

In this imaginative and magical story, we witness the moral education of a selfish brat. Sometimes those who care about us—
whether they be fairy godparents or real parents—have to teach
tough lessons in order to ease our paths for the long run, the run
of a life.

Little Harweda was born a Prince. His father was King over all
the land and his mother was the most beautiful Queen the world
had ever seen and Prince Harweda was their only child. From the
day of his birth everything that love or money could do for him had
been done. The very wind of heaven was made to fan over an
aeolian harp that it might enter his room, not as a strong fresh
breeze, but as a breath of music. Reflectors were so arranged in the
windows that twice as much moonlight fell on his crib as on that of
any ordinary child. The pillow on which his head rested was made
out of the down from hummingbirds' breasts and the water in
which his face and hands were washed was always steeped in rose
leaves before being brought to the nursery. Everything that could
be done was done, and nothing which could add to his ease or
comfort was left undone.

But his parents, although they were King and Queen, were not
very wise, for they never thought of making the young Prince think
of anybody but himself and he had never in all his life given up any
one of his comforts that somebody else might have a pleasure. So,
of course, he grew to be selfish and peevish, and by the time he
was five years old he was so disagreeable that nobody loved him.
"Dear, dear what shall we do?" said the poor Queen mother and
the King only sighed and answered, "Ah, what indeed!" They were
both very much grieved at heart for they well knew that little
Harweda, although he was a Prince, would never grow up to be a
really great King unless he could make his people love him.

At last they decided to send for his fairy godmother and see if
she could suggest anything which would cure Prince Harweda of

always thinking about himself. "Well, well, well!" exclaimed the godmother when they had laid the case before her. "This is a pretty state of affairs and I his godmother too! Why wasn't I called in sooner?" She then told them that she would have to think a day and a night and a day again before she could offer them any assistance. "But," she added, "if I take the child in charge you must promise not to interfere for a whole year."

The King and Queen gladly promised that they would not speak to or even see their son for the required time if the fairy godmother would only cure him of his selfishness. "We'll see about that," said the godmother. "Humph, expecting to be a King some day and not caring for anybody but himself—a fine King he'll make!" With that, off she flew, and the King and Queen saw nothing more of her for a day and a night and another day. Then back she came in a great hurry. "Give me the Prince," said she. "I have his house all ready for him. One month from today I'll bring him back to you. Perhaps he'll be cured and perhaps he won't. If he is not cured then we shall try two months next time. We'll see, we'll see." Without any more ado, she picked up the astonished young prince and flew away with him as lightly as if he were nothing but a feather or a straw. In vain the poor Queen wept and begged for a last kiss. Before she had wiped her eyes, the fairy godmother and Prince Harweda were out of sight.

They flew a long distance until they reached a great forest. When they had come to the middle of it, down flew the fairy, and in a minute more the young Prince was standing on the green grass beside a beautiful pink marble palace that looked something like a good-sized summer house.

"This is your home," said the godmother, "In it you will find everything you need and you can do just as you choose with your time." Little Harweda was delighted at this, for there was nothing in the world he liked better than to do as he pleased, so he tossed his cap up into the air and ran into the lovely little house without so much as saying "Thank you" to his godmother.

"Humph," said she as he disappeared, "you'll have enough of it before you are through with it, my fine Prince." With that off she flew.

Prince Harweda had no sooner set his foot inside the small rose-colored palace than the iron door shut with a bang and locked itself. For you must know by this time that it was an enchanted house, as of course, all houses are that are built by fairies.

Prince Harweda did not mind being locked in, as he cared very little for the great beautiful outside world, and the new home which was to be *all his own* was very fine, and he was eager and impatient to examine it. Then too he thought that when he was tired of it, all he would have to do would be to kick on the door and a servant from somewhere would come and open it. He had always had a servant ready to obey his slightest command.

His fairy godmother had told him that it was *his* house. Therefore he was interested in looking at everything in it.

The floor was made of a beautiful red copper that shone in the sunlight like burnished gold and seemed almost a dark red in the shadow. He had never seen anything half so fine before. The ceiling was of mother-of-pearl and showed a constant changing of tints of red and blue and yellow and green, all blending into the gleaming white, as only mother-of-pearl can. From the middle of this handsome ceiling hung a large gilded bird cage containing a beautiful bird, which just at this moment was singing a glad song of welcome to the Prince. Harweda, however, cared very little about birds, so he took no notice of the songster.

Around on every side were costly divans covered with richly embroidered spreads and piled up with many sizes of soft down pillows. "Ah," thought the Prince, "here I can lounge at my case with no one to call me to stupid lessons!" Wonderfully carved jars and vases of wrought gold and silver stood about on the floor and each was filled with a different kind of perfume. "This is delicious," said Prince Harweda. "Now I can have all the sweet odors I want without the trouble of going out into the garden for roses or lilies."

In the center of the room was a fountain of sparkling water which leaped up and fell back into its marble basin with a kind of rhythmical sound that made a faint, dreamy music very pleasant to listen to.

On a table near at hand were various baskets of the most tempting pears and grapes and peaches, and near them were dishes of all kinds of sweetmeats. "Good," said the greedy young Prince, "that is what I like best of all," and therewith he fell to eating the fruit and sweetmeats as fast as he could cram them into his mouth. He ate so much he had a pain in his stomach, but strange to say, the table was just as full as when he began, for no sooner did he reach his hand out and take a soft mellow pear or a rich, juicy peach than another pear or peach took its place in the basket. The same thing occurred when he helped himself to chocolate drops or marshmallows or any of the other confectionery upon the table.

For, of course, if the little palace was enchanted, everything in it was enchanted also.

When Prince Harweda had eaten until he could eat no more he threw himself down upon one of the couches and an invisible hand gently stroked his hair until he fell asleep. When he awoke he noticed for the first time the walls, which, by the way, were really the strangest part of his new home. They had in them twelve long, checkered windows which reached from the ceiling to the floor. The spaces between the windows were filled in with mirrors exactly the same size as the windows, so that the whole room was walled in with windows and looking glasses. Through the three windows that looked to the north could be seen the far distant mountains Beautiful, as they were called, towering high above the surrounding country; sometimes their snow-covered tops were pink or creamy yellow as they caught the rays of the sunrise; sometimes they were dark purple or blue as they reflected a storm cloud. From the three windows that faced the south could be seen the great ocean, tossing and moving, constantly catching a thousand gleams of silver from the moonlight. Again and again, each little wave would be capped with white from its romp with the wind. Yet, as the huge mountains seemed to reach higher than man could climb, so the vast ocean seemed to stretch out farther than any ship could possibly carry him. The eastern windows gave each morning a glorious vision of sky as the darkness of the night slowly melted into the still gray dawn, and that changed into a golden glow and that in turn became a tender pink. It was really the most beautiful as well as the most mysterious sight on earth if one watched it closely. The windows on the west looked out upon a great forest of tall fir trees and at the time of sunset the glorious colors of the sunset sky could be seen between the dark green branches.

But little Prince Harweda cared for none of these beautiful views. In fact, he scarcely glanced out of the windows at all, he was so taken up with the broad handsome mirrors, for in each of them he could see himself reflected and he was very fond of looking at himself in a looking glass. He was much pleased when he noticed that the mirrors were so arranged that each one not only reflected his whole body, head, arms, feet and all, but that it also reflected his image as seen in several of the other mirrors. He could thus see his front and back and each side, all at the same time. As he was a handsome boy, he enjoyed these many views of himself immensely, and would stand and sit and lie down just for the fun of seeing the many images of himself do the same thing.

He spent so much time looking at and admiring himself in the wonderful looking glasses that he had very little time for the books and games which had been provided for his amusement. Hours were spent each day, first before one mirror and then another, and he did not notice that the windows were growing narrower and the mirrors wider until the former had become so small that they hardly admitted light enough for him to see himself in the looking glass. Still, this did not alarm him very much, as he cared nothing whatever for the outside world. It only made him spend more time before the mirror, as it was now getting quite difficult for him to see himself at all. The windows at last became mere slits in the wall and the mirrors grew so large that they not only reflected little Harweda but all of the room besides in a dim, indistinct kind of a way.

Finally, however, Prince Harweda awoke one morning and found himself in total darkness. Not a ray of light came from the outside and of course, not an object in the room could be seen. He rubbed his eyes and sat up to make sure that he was not dreaming. Then he called loudly for someone to come and open a window for him, but no one came. He got up and groped his way to the iron door and tried to open it, but it was, as you know, locked. He kicked it and beat upon it, but he only bruised his fists and hurt his toes. He grew quite angry now. How dare anyone shut him, a Prince, up in a dark prison like this! He yelled for his fairy god-mother, calling her all sorts of horrid names. Then he upbraided his father and mother, the King and Queen, for letting him go away with such a godmother. In fact, he blamed everybody and everything but himself for his present condition, but it was of no use. The sound of his own voice was his only answer. The whole of the outside world seemed to have forgotten him.

As he felt his way back to his couch he knocked over one of the golden jars which had held the liquid perfume, but the perfume was all gone now and only an empty jar rolled over the floor. He laid himself down on the divan but its soft pillows had been re-moved and a hard iron framework received him. He was dismayed and lay for a long time thinking of what he had best do with himself. All before him was blank darkness, as black as the darkest night you ever saw. He reached out his hand to get some fruit to eat, but only one or two withered apples remained on the table—was he to starve to death? Suddenly he noticed that the tinkling music of the fountain had ceased. He hastily groped his way over to it and he found in place of the dancing, running stream stood a silent pool of water. A hush had fallen upon everything about him. A dead silence was in the room. He threw himself down upon the floor and wished that he were dead also. He lay there for a long, long time.

At last he heard, or thought he heard, a faint sound. He listened eagerly. It seemed to be some tiny creature not far from him, trying to move about. For the first time for nearly a month he remembered the bird in its gilded cage. "Poor little thing," he cried as he sprang up, "you too are shut within this terrible prison. This thick darkness must be as hard for you to bear as it is for me." He went toward the cage and as he approached it the bird gave a sad little chirp.

"That's better than nothing," said the boy. "You must need some water to drink, poor thing," he continued as he filled its drinking cup. "This is all I have to give you."

Just then he heard a harsh, grating sound, as of rusty bolts sliding with difficulty out of their sockets, and then faint rays of light not wider than a hair began to shine between the heavy plate mirrors. Prince Harweda was filled with joy. "Perhaps, perhaps," said he softly, "I may yet see the light again. Ah, how beautiful the outside world would look to me now!"

The next day he was so hungry that he began to eat one of the old withered apples, and as he bit it he thought of the bird, his fellow-prisoner. "You. must be hungry, too, poor little thing," said he as he divided his miserable food and put part of it into the bird's cage. Again came the harsh, grating sound, and the boy noticed that the cracks of light were growing larger. Still, they were only cracks, nothing of the outside world could be seen. Still, it was a comfort not to have to grope about in total darkness. Prince Harweda felt quite sure that the cracks of light were a little wider, and on going up to one and putting his eye close to it as he would to a pinhole in a paper, he was rejoiced to find that he could tell the greenness of the grass from the blue of the sky. "Ah, my pretty bird, my pretty bird!" he cried joyfully. "I have had a glimpse of the great beautiful outside world and you shall have it too."

With these words, he climbed up into a chair and, loosening the cage from the golden chain by which it hung, he carried it carefully to the nearest crack of light and placed it close to the narrow opening. Again was heard the harsh, grating sound and the walls moved a bit and the windows were now at least an inch wide.

At this the poor Prince clasped his hands with delight. He sat himself down near the bird cage and gazed out of the narrow opening. Never before had the trees looked so tall and stately, or the white clouds floating through the sky so lovely. The next day as he was carefully cleaning the bird's cage so that the little creature might be somewhat more comfortable, the walls again creaked and groaned and the mirrors grew narrower by just so many inches as the windows widened. But Prince Harweda saw only the flood of sunshine that poured in, and the added beauty of the larger landscape. He cared nothing whatever now for the stupid mirrors, which could only reflect what was placed before them. Each day he found something new and beautiful in the view from the narrow windows. Now it was a squirrel frisking about and running up some tall tree trunk so rapidly that Prince Harweda could not follow it with his eyes. Again it was a mother bird feeding her young. By this time the windows were a foot wide or more.

One day as two white doves suddenly soared aloft in the blue sky the poor little canary who had now become the tenderly cared for comrade of the young Prince, gave a pitiful little trill. "Dear little fellow," cried Prince Harweda, "do you also long for your freedom? You shall at least be as free as I am." So saying, he opened the cage door and the bird flew out.

The Prince laughed as he watched it flutter about from chair to table and back to chair again. He was so much occupied with the bird that he did not notice that the walls had again shaken and the windows were now their full size, until the added light caused him to look around. He turned and saw the room looking almost exactly as it did the day he entered it with so much pride because it was all his own. Now it seemed close and stuffy and he would gladly have exchanged it for the humblest home in his father's kingdom where he could meet people and hear them talk and see them smile at each other, even if they should take no notice of him.

One day soon after this the little bird fluttered up against the windowpane and beat his wings against it in a vain effort to get out. A new idea seized the young Prince and, taking up one of the golden jars, he went to the window and struck on one of its checkered panes of glass with all his force. "You shall be free, even if I can not," said he to the bird. Two or three strong blows shivered the small pane and the bird swept out into the free open air beyond. "Ah, my pretty one, how glad I am that you are free at last," exclaimed the Prince as he stood watching the flight of his fellow prisoner. His face was bright with the glad, unselfish joy over the bird's liberty. The small pink marble palace shook from top to bottom, the iron door flew open and the fresh wind from the sea rushed in and seemed to catch the boy in its invisible arms. Prince Harweda could hardly believe his eyes as he sprang to the door. There stood his fairy godmother, smiling and with her hand reached out toward him.

"Come, my godchild," said she gently, "we shall now go back to your father and mother, the King and Queen, and they will rejoice with us that you have been cured of your terrible disease of selfishness."

Great indeed was the rejoicing in the palace when Prince Harweda was returned to them a sweet, loving boy, kind and thoughtful to all about him. Many a struggle he had with himself and many a conquest over the old habit of selfishness, but as time passed by he grew to be a great and wise King, loving and tenderly caring for all his people and loved by them in return.

•

JOHN SMITH AT JAMESTOWN

Like all pioneers, the first English colonists in America quickly discovered that survival meant self-reliance. It is doubtful the settlers at Jamestown, Virginia, would have lasted long enough to learn the lesson without the stern voice of John Smith, who bluntly warned that "idleness and sloth" would be the colonists' ruin, and that they "must be more industrious, or starve." Drawing from Saint Paul, Smith laid down his famous dictum: "He that will not work shall not eat." The settlers' sudden change of heart and habit provides us with one of the earliest lessons from American history. Sometimes the best way to ease the path is to accept no excuses, and to let it be known that people must pull their own weight.

One day in May in the year 1607, three small ships came sailing up a broad river. On the decks of the ships stood more than one hundred Englishmen, anxiously peering at the shores. They had spent many weeks crossing the ocean, and now they were looking toward a new home. Finally, at a place where a large piece of land jutted into the river, the ships stopped and the men stepped ashore.

The Indians called this river Powhatan, after their mighty chief. The Englishmen, however, named it the James River, after their own king.

Among the Englishmen was a sturdy young man with keen blue eyes and red hair and a big red beard. His name was Captain John Smith. He was a brave man and a good soldier, the kind of leader a small group of adventurers far from home could depend on.

Right away the Englishmen took out their sharp axes and began to chop at the thick, tall trees. They built huts where they could keep dry and sleep, a church where they could pray, and a fort where they could stay in times of danger. They named their little village Jamestown, and they called that part of the world Virginia.

When the excitement of reaching the New World wore off, however, many of the settlers at Jamestown began to shirk their duties. Some had been "gentlemen" in England and were not used to working hard with their hands. They did not know how to obey orders. They slipped away from their jobs, or slumped over their tasks. They were much better at quarreling among themselves and watching others do all the work.

Some of the settlers were quite willing to work, but only if it was the kind of work they wanted to do. They longed to search for treasure. They had heard the New World was full of silver and gold and precious pearls. They thought treasure hunting would be much easier work than clearing fields to grow food.

Others grew discouraged over the thought of being separated from home by the wide ocean. They were frightened by the Indians in the unknown forests. They feared the deadly diseases that seemed to strike so quickly in this new land. Brooding, they sat in their huts and complained about the heat in summer and the cold in winter.

But if some of the settlers were not good at working, they were very good at eating and drinking. When dinnertime came, they were just as hungry as those who labored, and expected to share in the fruits of that labor. The colonists at Jamestown put all the vegetables they grew and all the game they hunted into one collection called the common store. This common store supplied food for the whole village. And so those who were too lazy to do their duties could still eat as long as a few men worked to put food into the common store.

But before long supplies began to grow short. There were too many mouths wanting to be fed, and too few hands willing to do the work. Captain John Smith did his best to keep the colony from falling to pieces. He made many trips up the rivers and into the forests to trade with the Indians for food. He spoke to the men again and again about the need to grow crops. He warned them that disaster was near unless they changed their ways.

His arguments did little good. Too many settlers still spent their time arguing with each other and hiding from work. Some of them plotted to steal food from the rest. And still they dreamed of growing rich from treasure. One time, after a fire broke out and destroyed many of the cabins, Smith could barely get the colonists to rebuild the village. They were too busy digging yellow dirt which they thought held gold.

Finally Captain Smith gathered the settlers together and gave a stern speech. He told them the colony was on the verge of starvation because so many men refused to do any useful work. Up until then, about forty hard workers had been feeding one hundred and fifty idlers. But now things would have to change, or they would all die of hunger. No longer would the colony's common store be open to everyone, workers and idlers alike. In the future, there would be a new rule. "He that will not work shall not eat," Smith declared. Unless someone was sick, every man would have to pull his own weight.

Then Captain Smith began to give each one duties. To help everyone remember their tasks, he posted a chart in the fort for all to see. It listed the name of every man, his duties for the week, and those duties he had fulfilled. The chart made it plain who was working and, therefore, who would eat.

At once things changed. Men who had done nothing but argue and complain suddenly bent to their tasks. The colonists began planting more corn. They made fishnets out of vines. They caught crabs and gathered oysters. They picked wild berries, and hunted deer and wild turkeys in the forest.

Under Captain Smith's orders, they built more houses. They planted gardens, and went to work raising hogs and chickens. They put a sturdier roof on the church. They built up the wall around their fort to make it stronger, and dug a well inside so they would have plenty of water to drink in times of danger.

And so the Jamestown colony did not fall to pieces. Under Smith's firm hand, the settlers began to pull together.

One day in the autumn of 1609, Captain Smith and some of his men were sailing down the river when some gunpowder in their boat exploded, burning Smith terribly. He jumped into the water to put out the flames and nearly drowned before his men could pull him back into the boat. A short time later, Captain Smith returned to England to recover from his wounds. Jamestown had lost its best leader.

The colony faced many more years of hardship and hunger. Often the settlers were sick because the food they ate was spoiled, or because the water they drank was not pure. Sometimes they lived in peace with the Indians, but often there was bloodshed. The mosquitoes brought malaria, and always the sight of the empty, wide river brought loneliness. More than once the people of Jamestown thought of giving up and going back to England.

But most of them stayed, and labored, and against great odds made a home on the edge of the New World. John Smith had led them through the first hard months. He had shown them how to work for their own good. Now they struggled on, determined that their settlement would survive. And survive it did, for today we remember Jamestown as the first successful English colony in America.

•

POCAHONTAS

*Adapted from retellings by James Baldwin
and Grace Humphrey*

Historians have long debated the accuracy of Captain John Smith's
dramatic account of how Pocahontas saved his life. Whether the
incident was in fact a daring rescue or part of an orchestrated
ritual, the Indian princess's own life remains an example of courage, compassion, and friendship. She was no small player in the
destiny of the Jamestown colony in Virginia, the first successful
English settlement in America. As John Smith later wrote, 'She,
next under God, was still the instrument to preserve this colony
from death, famine, and utter destruction."

There was once a little Indian girl whose name was Pocahontas. Her father was a great chief, or Indian king, and his name was
Powhatan. Her home was not far from a broad river, in that part of
our country which is now called Virginia.

One summer when Pocahontas was about ten years old, some
white men came up the river and began to build a town on its
banks. They came in a great ship that was many times larger than
any canoe, and everything they did was so wonderful that the Indians were at first very much afraid of them.

At that time all this country was a wild land. There were no
pleasant farms or busy cities, but only woods and swamps and
lonely prairies. King Powhatan and his people had always lived in
the great forest. They spent their time in hunting and fishing. They
had never heard of any other way of living.

They watched the strange white men as they landed from the
ship. They watched them as they began to build queer houses of
logs on the shore. Then Powhatan grew bold, and asked them
where they came from, and what they were doing in his country.

The strangers pointed to the east, and said, "We came from
England, on the other side of the great sea. We are building homes
for ourselves here in this country, which does not belong to you,
but to our good King James."

"I do not see how that can be," said Powhatan. "My people

have always lived in this country, and it must be ours. Yet there is room here for you also."

Little by little the Indians made friends with their strange neighbors. On some days they brought them corn which they sold for beads and other trinkets; at other times they brought them game which they had killed in the woods.

Captain John Smith, the leader of the Englishmen, wanted to learn all about the country. So, one day, he started with two men to explore the rivers and the woods.

"The white men are looking at our lands," said the Indians. "Soon they will want to drive us away from them."

"We must not let them," said others. "We must drive them back to their own place."

One day some Indians lay in wait in the woods for Captain Smith and the two men. They killed the two men, and took Smith prisoner. They tied Smith's hands behind him, and led him from one Indian town to another. They did not know what to do with him. At last they took him to the great chief, King Powhatan.

Captain Smith was led into a long house built of the green boughs of trees. Two hundred Indians were there, and all wanted to see him put to death. King Powhatan stood at one end of the room. On his shoulders he wore a cape of raccoon skins, and around his neck hung chains of pearls.

The warriors stood in rows on each side, and they too were dressed in furs and feathers. Behind the warriors were the Indian women. Their necks were painted red; their heads were covered with the white down of birds; over their shoulders hung strings of beads.

All the Indians shouted when Smith was led into the room. The queen brought water for him to wash his hands. Another woman gave him a bundle of feathers to use as a towel. After this they brought him food. They gave him such a dinner as he had not had for many a day. And then the warriors and the king talked about what they should do with him.

At last it was agreed that Captain Smith should die. Two large stones were rolled into the room and placed in front of King Powhatan. Then Smith, with his arms tied behind him, was led to them. His head was laid on one of them.

All at once a cry was heard among the Indian women. The little maiden Pocahontas ran across the room, and threw herself at her father's feet. She asked him to spare the white man's life.

The king looked very cross, and did not seem to hear the child.

Two tall warriors stepped forward, each with a heavy club in his hand. Then Pocahontas threw herself down by the side of the prisoner. She took his head in her arms. "You cannot kill him without first killing me," she said.

The heart of the old king was touched, and he told his warriors to lay down their clubs. Smith was lifted from the ground, the cords were taken from his arms, and he was treated with great kindness. He was given some presents and sent back to his people.

After that, Pocahontas was always a good friend to the white people who made their homes in Virginia. Frequently she would go with her brothers or friends carrying corn or venison to the settlers, who were close to starving. Often at the risk of her own life she would let them know if there was danger. When her father wanted to make war upon them, she would say, "Let us live in peace with each other."

After she grew up, and Captain John Smith had gone back to England, Pocahontas fell in love with one of the settlers, a man named John Rolfe, and he fell in love with her. They were married in a log church, and a year later a son was born. The whole colony hoped the new little family would help bond the Indians and settlers in lasting friendship.

When they had been married two years, Pocahontas, John Rolfe, and their baby Thomas traveled to England. Everywhere she went there, Pocahontas was received with great honor as a foreign princess, and known as Lady Rebecca. She was entertained at banquets and receptions. She went to the theaters. Bishops and great lords and ladies drove in their coaches to call upon her.

She was presented to the king and the queen, who welcomed her with pomp and ceremony. She carried herself as the daughter of a king, and among all the ladies of the court, none was a greater favorite, for her beauty and gentle ways won all hearts.

John Smith had been away exploring again, but now, returning to England, he heard everyone talking of Pocahontas. Remembering old times and all he owed his little friend, he at once went to visit her. When Smith appeared she was greatly moved and for a long time could not speak. At last she said, "They told me you were dead!" Then the two good friends sat down for a long talk of the old days in Virginia, and all that had happened since their separation.

Though she was so admired in England, Pocahontas did not really belong there. More and more her thoughts turned toward home. She wearied of crowded London and longed for the forest again. Every day she would stand by the window, looking toward the west, where Virginia and her early life lay. She thought much of the old days, of the changes that had come to her and her people, and the appearance of the fair-haired stranger and his Englishmen.

John Rolfe worried about his wife's homesickness, and feared she would fall ill with longing. He wanted to get her back to Virginia, but first they must wait for their ship to be loaded with supplies. At last word came that all was ready, and sailors came to take them aboard.

But though she had set her face to the west, Pocahontas was not to return to her home. A sudden weakness overcame her, and she fell asleep. At age twenty-two, in a foreign land, she died and was buried in a little church.

The story of Pocahontas is full of romance, of adventure, of gentleness and daring courage. She did far more than save Smith's life, for it was through her friendship with the English that the colony was supplied with food. It was her marriage that made possible, at least for a brief time, peace between two peoples. It was she, said John Smith, who saved Virginia from famine, confusion, and death.

•

THE FIRE BEARER

Adapted from retellings by Fanny E. Coe and Flora Cooke

The ancient Greeks revered Prometheus as the earliest teacher and benefactor of mankind, a god who by a selfless act of compassion became the founder of human civilization. The tale recounted below contains an important, sobering lesson, however. Good acts are not always rewarded. Often those who make paths easier for others do so at the cost of making their own lives harder. This retelling of the myth is based on the account by the Greek playwright Aeschylus.

Ages ago, the Greeks believed that the world was ruled by many gods. Their chief god was named Zeus. Zeus lived on the top of a high mountain. Fleecy clouds hid his home from the sight of men.

There had once been giants in the world. These giants had fought with Zeus. They had piled the mountains one upon the other and had tried to climb to Zeus's palace. Zeus had fought them with fire. He had thrown thunderbolts into the faces of the giants. At last they were beaten and put into dark prisons underground.

There were only two sons of giants left on the earth. The name of one of these was Prometheus.

Prometheus had a kind heart. He longed to help those about him. Now, besides Prometheus and his brother, there were men dwelling upon the earth.

The men of those days were poor and unhappy. They lived in caves and holes in the earth. They were cold and often hungry. What food they had they ate raw. They had no dishes, no tools, no comforts.

Prometheus saw all this. "Poor man," he said, "how I pity him! If he only had fire! Then he would be happy."

Prometheus thought a long time. Then he said aloud, "I will do what I can."

He went to Zeus. "I have come to beg a gift for man. Give him fire. He needs it sorely."

Zeus frowned darkly. "Never," he cried. "Fire is not for man. If he had it he might grow wise; he might even grow to be as strong as the gods themselves. He must never have it."

Prometheus went away. He again saw little children freezing in the snows of winter. He saw hunger. He saw men living like beasts. Then he set his teeth together and clenched his fist. "Man shall have fire!" he cried. "Zeus may kill me, but man shall have fire."

He walked along the seashore searching for a certain reed. This reed was hollow. Then he set out on a long journey eastward.

One morning, he came to his journey's end. It was by the sea. As he stood there, a golden flush was in the sky. Then the great car of day, the golden sun itself, came slowly up out of the ocean.

Prometheus touched one of the blazing chariot-wheels with his reed. It caught fire. The fire was held in the hollow of the reed, and with this gift Prometheus went westward again.

It was midwinter. Snows were deep on the ground. Ice covered the rivers. Men were hiding in their holes in the earth.

Prometheus entered one of these caves. "See this wonder!" he said. He had two or three stones piled together. Then he had wood laid on this first hearth. Then a touch of the reed and lo! the first fire. Blue fingers were spread out to the wonderful warmth. Pinched faces smiled at each other in the lovely glow. "Summer is come again!" they cried.

Thus man came to know heat and light. The gift of fire turned the cave into a home.

Men from far and near came to wonder. Men from far and near wanted the gift of fire in their homes also. They gathered stones and wood, and Prometheus was glad to give them glowing coals. They called him the helper of mankind.

Prometheus was also the teacher of mankind. He showed men how to cook their food, how to make dishes, how to make tools, and how to dig metal from the earth.

Men learned quickly. In a very short time they grew busy and happy.

One day, Zeus happened to look down on the earth. It seemed strange to him. He saw towns and ships. He saw mines and forges. He saw a fire in every house.

"What!" he thundered. "Man has fire! Who has done this?"

Then someone said, "Prometheus!"

"He shall pay well for this," said Zeus.

He called to him two strong servants. "Seize Prometheus, and lead him to the top of yonder mountain. There Hephaestus will finish your work."

Hephaestus was Zeus's son. He was the blacksmith of the gods. Hephaestus was sorry for Prometheus, but he could not disobey Zeus.

Prometheus was forced to the top of the mountain by the strong servants. There Hephaestus loaded him with chains. These chains he fastened to a rock.

There Prometheus lay for ages. The suns of summer scorched him. The snows of winter fell upon his upturned face. Worst of all, Zeus sent a great vulture every day to tear his flesh and feed upon his liver, which then healed every night, so that the vulture preyed upon him again and again. Zeus said he must stay in this torment until he returned the fire to heaven.

So Prometheus stayed on the bleak mountaintop, bearing his pain in silence. Sometimes he grew so weary and faint-hearted that he was tempted to free himself and give back the fire to Zeus.

But when he looked down upon his people and saw smoke rising from their homes, he knew the fire was helping them, and how happy and contented they were. Always he grew strong and patient again to wait for the release which he knew would finally come to him.

And after many, many years a Greek hero who was coming over the mountains saw Prometheus. It was Hercules. He shot the vulture with a golden arrow, unbound the chains, and set the great-hearted giant free.

•

HOW THE INDIANS LEARNED TO HEAL

Retold by Mabel Powers

When we help each other, we often learn all sorts of things about our world and ourselves. Practicing compassion brings wisdom, this Iroquois tale reminds us.

A long, long time ago, some Indians were running along a trail that led to an Indian settlement. As they ran, a rabbit jumped from the bushes and sat before them.

The Indians stopped, for the rabbit still sat up before them and did not move from the trail. They shot their arrows at him, but the arrows came back unstained with blood.

A second time they drew their arrows. Now no rabbit was to be seen. Instead, an old man stood on the trail. He seemed to be weak and sick.

The old man asked them for food and a place to rest. They would not listen but went on to the settlement.

Slowly the old man followed them, down the trail to the wig-wam village. In front of each wigwam, he saw a skin placed on a pole. This he knew was the sign of the clan to which the dwellers in that wigwam belonged.

First he stopped at a wigwam where a wolf skin hung. He asked to enter, but they would not let him. They said, "We want no sick men here."

On he went toward another wigwam. Here a turtle's shell was hanging. But this family would not let him in.

He tried a wigwam where he saw a beaver skin. He was told to move on.

The Indians who lived in a wigwam where a deer skin was seen, were just as unkind. Nor was he permitted to enter wigwams where hung hawk, snipe, and heron skins.

At last he came to a wigwam where a bear skin hung.

"I will ask once more for a place to rest," he thought.

And here a kind old woman lived. She brought food for him to eat, and spread soft skins for him to lie upon.

The old man thanked her. He said that he was very sick. He told the woman what plants to gather in the wood, to make him well again.

This she did, and soon he was healed.

A few days later the old man was again taken sick. Again he told the woman what roots and leaves to gather. She did as she was told, and soon he was well.

Many times the old man fell sick. Each time he had a different sickness. Each time he told the woman what plants and herbs to find to cure him. Each time she remembered what she had been told.

Soon this woman of the Bear clan knew more about healing than all the other people.

One day, the old man told her that the Great Spirit had sent him to earth, to teach the Indian people the secrets of healing.

"I came, sick and hungry, to many a wigwam door. No blanket was drawn aside for me to pass in. You alone lifted the blanket from your wigwam door and bade me enter.

"You are of the Bear clan, therefore all other clans shall come to the Bear clan for help in sickness.

"You shall teach all the clans what plants, and roots, and leaves to gather, that the sick may be healed.

"And the Bear shall be the greatest and strongest of the clans."

The Indian woman lifted her face to the Great Spirit to thank him for this great gift and knowledge of healing. When she turned again to the man, he had disappeared.

No one was there, but a rabbit was running swiftly down the trail.

•

THE HAPPY PRINCE

Oscar Wilde

"There is no Mystery so great as Misery," the Happy Prince says in this tale. But the greatest mystery and miracle of the story is really his own charity.

High above the city, on a tall column, stood the statue of the Happy Prince. He was gilded all over with thin leaves of fine gold, for eyes he had two bright sapphires, and a large red ruby glowed on his sword hilt.

He was very much admired indeed. "He is as beautiful as a weathercock," remarked one of the Town Councillors who wished to gain a reputation for having artistic tastes, "only not quite so useful," he added, fearing lest people should think him unpractical, which he really was not.

"Why can't you be like the Happy Prince?" asked a sensible mother of her little boy who was crying for the moon. "The Happy Prince never dreams of crying for anything."

"I am glad there is someone in the world who is quite happy," muttered a disappointed man as he gazed at the wonderful statue.

"He looks just like an angel," said the Charity Children as they came out of the cathedral in their bright scarlet cloaks and their clean white pinafores.

"How do you know?" said the Mathematical Master. "You have never seen one."

"Ah! but we have, in our dreams," answered the children, and the Mathematical Master frowned and looked very severe, for he did not approve of children dreaming.

One night there flew over the city a little Swallow. His friends had gone away to Egypt six weeks before, but he had stayed behind, for he was in love with the most beautiful Reed. He had met her early in the spring as he was flying down the river after a big yellow moth, and had been so attracted by her slender waist that he had stopped to talk to her.

"Shall I love you?" said the Swallow, who liked to come to the point at once, and the Reed made him a low bow. So he flew round and round her, touching the water with his wings, and making

silver ripples. This was his courtship, and it lasted all through the summer.

"It is a ridiculous attachment," twittered the other Swallows, "she has no money, and far too many relations." And indeed the river was quite full of Reeds. Then, when the autumn came, they all flew away.

After they had gone he felt lonely and began to tire of his ladylove. "She has no conversation," he said, "and I am afraid that she is a coquette, for she is always flirting with the wind." And certainly, whenever the wind blew, the Reed made the most graceful curtsies. "I admit that she is domestic," he continued, "but I love traveling, and my wife, consequently, should love traveling also."

"Will you come away with me?" he said finally to her, but the Reed shook her head, she was so attached to her home.

"You have been trifling with me," he cried. "I am off to the Pyramids. Good-by!" and he flew away.

All day long he flew, and at nighttime he arrived at the city. "Where shall I put up?" he said; "I hope the town has made preparations."

Then he saw the statue on the tall column.

"I will put up there," he cried. "It is a fine position, with plenty of fresh air." So he alighted just between the feet of the Happy Prince.

"I have a golden bedroom," he said softly to himself as he looked round, and he prepared to go to sleep. But just as he was putting his head under his wing a large drop of water fell on him. "What a curious thing!" he cried. "There is not a single cloud in the sky, the stars are quite clear and bright, and yet it is raining. The climate in the north of Europe is really dreadful. The Reed used to like the rain, but that was merely her selfishness."

Then another drop fell.

"What is the use of a statue if it cannot keep the rain off?" he said. "I must look for a good chimney pot," and he determined to fly away.

But before he had opened his wings, a third drop fell, and he looked up, and saw—ah! what did he see?

The eyes of the Happy Prince were filled with tears, and tears were running down his golden cheeks. His face was so beautiful in the moonlight that the little Swallow was filled with pity.

"Who are you?" he said.

"I am the Happy Prince."

"Why are you weeping then?" asked the Swallow; "you have quite drenched me."

"When I was alive and had a human heart," answered the statue, "I did not know what tears were, for I lived in the Palace of Sans-Souci, where sorrow is not allowed to enter. In the daytime I played with my companions in the garden, and in the evening I led the dance in the Great Hall. Round the garden ran a very lofty wall, but I never cared to ask what lay beyond it, everything about me was so beautiful. My courtiers called me the Happy Prince, and happy indeed I was, if pleasure be happiness. So I lived, and so I died. And now that I am dead they have set me up here so high that I can see all the ugliness and all the misery of my city, and though my heart is made of lead yet I cannot choose but weep."

"What! Is he not solid gold?" said the Swallow to himself. He was too polite to make any personal remarks out loud.

"Far away," continued the statue in a low musical voice, "far away in a little street there is a poor house. One of the windows is open, and through it I can see a woman seated at a table. Her face is thin and worn, and she has coarse, red hands, all pricked by the needle, for she is a seamstress. She is embroidering passionflowers on a satin gown for the loveliest of the Queen's maids of honor to wear at the next Court ball. In a bed in the corner of the room her little boy is lying ill. He has a fever, and is asking for oranges. His mother has nothing to give him but river water, so he is crying. Swallow, Swallow, little Swallow, will you not bring her the ruby out of my sword hilt? My feet are fastened to this pedestal and I cannot move."

"I am waited for in Egypt," said the Swallow. "My friends are flying up and down the Nile, and talking to the large lotus flowers. Soon they will go to sleep in the tomb of the great King. The King is there himself in his painted coffin. He is wrapped in yellow linen, and embalmed with spices. Round his neck is a chain of pale green jade, and his hands are like withered leaves."

"Swallow, Swallow, little Swallow," said the Prince, "will you not stay with me for one night, and be my messenger? The boy is so thirsty, and the mother so sad."

"I don't think I like boys," answered the Swallow. "Last summer, when I was staying on the river, there were two rude boys, the miller's sons, who were always throwing stones at me. They never hit me, of course; we swallows fly far too well for that, and besides, I come of a family famous for its agility. But still, it was a mark of disrespect."

But the Happy Prince looked so sad that the little Swallow was sorry. "It is very cold here," he said, "but I will stay with you for one night, and be your messenger."

"Thank you, little Swallow," said the Prince.

So the Swallow picked out the great ruby from the Prince's sword, and flew away with it in his beak over the roofs of the town.

He passed by the cathedral tower, where the white marble angels were sculptured. He passed by the palace and heard the sound of dancing. A beautiful girl came out on the balcony with her lover. "How wonderful the stars are," he said to her, "and how wonderful is the power of love!"

"I hope my dress will be ready in time for the State ball," she answered. "I have ordered passionflowers to be embroidered on it: but the seamstresses are so lazy."

He passed over the river, and saw the lanterns hanging to the masts of the ships. At last he came to the poorhouse and looked in. The boy was tossing feverishly on his bed, and the mother had fallen asleep, she was so tired. In he hopped, and laid the great ruby on the table beside the woman's thimble. Then he flew gently round the bed, fanning the boy's forehead with his wings. "How cool I feel!" said the boy. "I must be getting better." And he sank into a delicious slumber.

Then the Swallow flew back to the Happy Prince, and told him what he had done. "It is curious," he remarked, "but I feel quite warm now, although it is so cold."

"That is because you have done a good action," said the Prince. And the little Swallow began to think, and then he fell asleep. Thinking always made him sleepy.

When day broke he flew down to the river and had a bath. "What a remarkable phenomenon!" said the Professor of Ornithology as he was passing over the bridge. "A swallow in winter!" And he wrote a long letter about it to the local newspaper. Everyone quoted it, it was full of so many words that they could not understand.

"Tonight I go to Egypt," said the Swallow, and he was in high spirits at the prospect. He visited all the public monuments, and sat a long time on top of the church steeple. Wherever he went the Sparrows chirruped, and said to each other, "What a distinguished stranger!" So he enjoyed himself very much.

When the moon rose he flew back to the Happy Prince. "Have you any commissions for Egypt?" he cried. "I am just starting."

"Swallow, Swallow, little Swallow," said the Prince, "will you not stay with me one night longer?"

"I am waited for in Egypt," answered the Swallow. "Tomorrow my friends will fly up to the Second Cataract. The river horse couches there among the bulrushes, and on a great granite throne sits the God Memnon. All night long he watches the stars, and when the morning star shines he utters one cry of joy, and then he is silent. At noon the yellow lions come down to the water's edge to drink. They have eyes like green beryls, and their roar is louder than the roar of the cataract."

"Swallow, Swallow, little Swallow," said the Prince, "far away across the city I see a young man in a garret. He is leaning over a desk covered with papers, and in a tumbler by his side there is a bunch of withered violets. His hair is brown and crisp, and his lips are red as a pomegranate, and he has large and dreamy eyes. He is trying to finish a play for the Director of the Theatre, but he is too cold to write anymore. There is no fire in the grate, and hunger has made him faint."

"I will wait with you one night longer," said the Swallow, who really had a good heart. "Shall I take him another ruby?"

"Alas! I have no ruby now," said the Prince. "My eyes are all that I have left. They are made of rare sapphires, which were brought out of India a thousand years ago. Pluck out one of them and take it to him. He will sell it to the jeweler, and buy firewood, and finish his play."

"Dear Prince," said the Swallow, "I cannot do that." And he began to weep.

"Swallow, Swallow, little Swallow," said the Prince, "do as I command you."

So the Swallow plucked out the Prince's eye, and flew away to the student's garret. It was easy enough to get in, as there was a hole in the roof. Through this he darted, and came into the room. The young man had his head buried in his hands, so he did not hear the flutter of the bird's wings, and when he looked up he found the beautiful sapphire lying on the withered violets.

"I am beginning to be appreciated," he cried. "This is from some great admirer. Now I can finish my play," and he looked quite happy.

The next day the Swallow flew down to the harbor. He sat on the mast of a large vessel and watched the sailors hauling big chests out of the hold with ropes. "Heave ahoy!" they shouted as each chest came up. "I am going to Egypt!" cried the Swallow, but nobody minded, and when the moon rose he flew back to the Happy Prince.

"I am come to bid you good-by," he cried.

"Swallow, Swallow, little Swallow," said the Prince, "will you not stay with me one night longer?"

"It is winter," answered the Swallow, "and the chill snow will soon be here. In Egypt the sun is warm on the green palm trees, and the crocodiles lie in the mud and look lazily about them. My companions are building a nest in the Temple of Baalbec, and the pink and white doves are watching them, and cooing to each other. Dear Prince, I must leave you, but I will never forget you, and next spring I will bring you back two beautiful jewels in place of those you have given away. The ruby shall be redder than a red rose, and the sapphire shall be as blue as the great sea."

"In the square below," said the Happy Prince, "there stands a little match girl. She has let her matches fall in the gutter, and they are all spoiled. Her father will beat her if she does not bring home some money, and she is crying. She has no shoes or stockings, and her little head is bare. Pluck out my other eye, and give it to her, and her father will not beat her."

"I will stay with you one night longer," said the Swallow, "but I cannot pluck out your eye. You would be quite blind then."

"Swallow, Swallow, little Swallow," said the Prince, "do as I command you."

So he plucked out the Prince's other eye, and darted down with it. He swooped past the match girl, and slipped the jewel into the palm of her hand. "What a lovely bit of glass!" cried the little girl. And she ran home, laughing.

Then the Swallow came back to the Prince. "You are blind now," he said, "so I will stay with you always."

"No, little Swallow," said the poor Prince, "you must go away to Egypt."

"I will stay with you always," said the Swallow, and he slept at the Prince's feet.

All the next day he sat on the Prince's shoulder, and told him stories of what he had seen in strange lands. He told him of the red ibises, who stand in long rows on the banks of the Nile, and catch goldfish in their beaks; of the Sphinx, who is as old as the world itself, and lives in the desert, and knows everything; of the merchants, who walk slowly by the side of their camels and carry amber beads in their hands; of the King of the Mountains of the Moon, who is as black as ebony, and worships a large crystal; of the great green snake that sleeps in a palm tree, and has twenty priests to feed it with honey cakes; and of the pygmies who sail over a big lake on large flat leaves, and are always at war with the butterflies.

"Dear little Swallow," said the Prince, "you tell me of marvelous things, but more marvelous than anything is the suffering of men and of women. There is no Mystery so great as Misery. Fly over my city, little Swallow, and tell me what you see there."

So the Swallow flew over the great city, and saw the rich making merry in their beautiful houses, while the beggars were sitting at the gates. He flew into dark lanes, and saw the white faces of starving children looking out listlessly at the black streets. Under the archway of a bridge two little boys were lying in one another's arms to try and keep themselves warm. "How hungry we are!" they said. "You must not lie here," shouted the watchman, and they wandered out into the rain.

Then he flew back and told the Prince what he had seen.

"I am covered with fine gold," said the Prince. "You must take it off, leaf by leaf, and give it to my poor. The living always think that gold can make them happy."

Leaf after leaf of the fine gold the Swallow picked off, till the Happy Prince looked quite dull and gray. Leaf after leaf of the fine gold he brought to the poor, and the children's faces grew rosier, and they laughed and played in the street. "We have bread now!" they cried.

Then the snow came, and after the snow came the frost. The streets looked as if they were made of silver, they were so bright and glistening; long icicles like crystal daggers hung down from the eaves of the houses, everybody went about in furs, and the little boys wore scarlet caps and skated on the ice.

The poor little Swallow grew colder and colder, but he would not leave the Prince, he loved him too well. He picked up crumbs outside the baker's door when the baker was not looking, and tried to keep himself warm by flapping his wings.

But at last he knew that he was going to die. He had just enough strength to fly up to the Prince's shoulder once more. "Good-by, dear Prince!" he murmured. "Will you let me kiss your hand?"

"I am glad that you are going to Egypt at last, little Swallow," said the Prince. "You have stayed too long here. But you must kiss me on the lips, for I love you."

"It is not to Egypt that I am going," said the Swallow. "I am going to the House of Death. Death is the brother of Sleep, is he not?"

And he kissed the Happy Prince on the lips, and fell down dead at his feet.

At that moment a curious crack sounded inside the statue, as if something had broken. The fact is that the leaden heart had snapped right in two. It certainly was a dreadfully hard frost.

Early the next morning the Mayor was walking in the square below in company with the Town Councillors. As they passed the column he looked up at the statue. "Dear me! How shabby the Happy Prince looks!" he said.

"How shabby, indeed!" cried the Town Councillors, who always agreed with the Mayor. And they went up to look at it.

"The ruby has fallen out of his sword, his eyes are gone, and he is golden no longer," said the Mayor. "In fact, he is little better than a beggar!"

"Little better than a beggar," said the Town Councillors.

"And here is actually a dead bird at his feet!" continued the Mayor. "We must really issue a proclamation that birds are not to be allowed to die here." And the Town Clerk made a note of the suggestion.

So they pulled down the statue of the Happy Prince. "As he is no longer beautiful he is no longer useful," said the Art Professor at the University.

Then they melted the statue in a furnace, and the Mayor held a meeting of the Corporation to decide what was to be done with the metal. "We must have another statue, of course," he said, "and it shall be a statue of myself."

"Of myself," said each of the Town Councillors, and they quarreled. When I last heard of them they were quarreling still.

"What a strange thing!" said the overseer of the workmen at the foundry. "This broken lead heart will not melt in the furnace. We must throw it away." So they threw it on a dustheap where the dead Swallow was also lying.

"Bring me the two most precious things in the city," said God to one of His Angels; and the Angel brought Him the leaden heart and the dead bird.

"You have rightly chosen," said God, "for in my garden of Paradise this little bird shall sing forevermore, and in my city of gold the Happy Prince shall praise me."

•

THE HERMIT OF THE HIMALAYAS
Retold by Frances Dadmun

One way or another, we all depend on the kindness of others— and sometimes, as we see in this tale from India, we depend on their courage as well. As Saint Paul wrote in his letter to the Romans, "none of us liveth to himself."

Once upon a time, and it may have been long ago, five hundred hermits lived together at the foot of the highest mountains in the world, the ridged and rocky, snow-capped Himalayas. But where the hermits lived, the land was not ridged and rocky; it was covered with a vast forest of banyan trees and thornbushes. The hermits lived on the edge of the forest because it was full of cool shadows when the sun was hot and because the banyan trees and thornbushes kept off the wind when the nights were cold. But the hermits did not spend their days lying under the banyan trees. They were not as lazy as all that. Indeed, they were most industrious hermits and worked hard raising rice on the flat ground on either side of the river. The hermits ate the rice—it was about all they had, except sometimes nuts and what honey the bees stored in the rocks and hollow trees. But the hermits liked rice and they liked nuts and honey, and the water of the river was cool and good to drink.

Then there came a time which they never forgot as long as

they lived, when the water of the river was so low that they could not drink it. There had been no rain for days and days. The rice fields dried up. The earth was like powder, and when the wind blew at all, it was a warm, choking wind which blew the powdery earth in the hermits' faces. So they stayed all the time under the banyan trees where it was shady, and they found a spring which did not dry up like the river, because it came from deep down under the highest mountains. The hermits drank of it and were not thirsty, but they were very hungry, for the rice had all dried up and there were not enough nuts and honey to last very long.

And then, when there was nothing they could do to help themselves, something very strange happened.

While the hermits were sitting near the spring, under the banyan trees, they heard the rustling of a thornbush and then a soft pitter-patter, and before they could catch their breath, a panther slipped silently from behind a bush. The hermits scrambled out of the way and hid behind trees—all but one. He sat still and watched, for he was sorry for the poor panther, whose tongue hung out of his mouth, he was so hot and thirsty.

The panther did not look at the hermit at all. He crawled up to the spring and tried to catch the drops of water as they trickled down the side of the rock.

"Oh, you poor beast!" exclaimed the hermit. "You can't get much that way. I will get a pail to catch the water."

The panther's big, velvety eyes looked as if he understood. The hermit brought a pail and the water soon filled it, so that the panther had all he needed. As he drank, he felt so much better that his legs grew stronger and quite soon he could walk off, almost as well as ever.

The next day, the hermit heard the pattering of feet again. Was it his friend the panther? He hoped so, for he already felt as fond of the great cat as you do of your dog or kitten. I think it was because he had helped him. Don't you?

Yes, it was the panther, but this time, he was not alone. He headed a long, long procession of beasts—the elephant and the lion, the deer and the fox, the wolf and the bear, the monkey and the buffalo, and last of all, a timid, little rabbit—all just as thirsty as they could be. The four hundred and ninety-nine hermits hid behind the trees again, but the one who was good and kind and not afraid was troubled only for fear there would not be enough water to go around. He was right. The water in the pail was gone in no time and the poor beasts were looking at him wistfully. There were so many of them, all looking at once, that he did not know what to do.

Just then, he noticed a fallen tree trunk nearby. It occurred to him that it would make a good trough, so he hollowed it out and dragged it under the spring. It was hard work, for he was weak from hunger, but when the trough began to fill with water so that more of the animals could drink at once, he felt that it had been worthwhile.

When the four hundred and ninety-nine hermits saw all the animals quietly drinking, they were so astonished that they forgot to be afraid, and they came crawling out from behind the trunks of the banyan trees very much as the panther had crawled out from behind the thornbush. Only *they* crawled because they were so hungry. All the animals noticed it, and they also saw how their good friend had staggered when he was dragging the tree trunk under the spring.

That night, the animals held a council in the forest when the moon was bright. They sat in a circle and the elephant spoke.

"Friends and enemies," he said, "we used to quarrel and kill each other, and sometimes we killed Man, but we are all friends now because we have all together nearly died of thirst. And Man is our friend because one hermit has saved our lives. But our friend Man will die soon if we do not bring him food. What can we do? I, for one, will strip the fruit from the banana trees with my trunk, for I have heard it said that bananas are good food for Man."

The other animals all agreed to help in any way they could. It was decided that the elephant, as well as any creatures which could climb, should gather fruit from the trees and that the others should carry it.

So next day, the hermits again heard the pattering of feet. They were no longer afraid. They supposed the animals were coming for water. But what was their surprise to see them come in sight loaded down with bananas and breadfruit, coconuts and mangoes and jambus and every fruit that grew far and wide throughout that land. Each dropped his gift before the hermits, drank from the trough, and went his way.

Every day after that, as long as the drought lasted, the animals brought fruit to the hermits and drank from the trough which the kindest hermit of them all had placed under the spring. Because each helped the other, the lives of all were saved, for the animals would have died without water and the hermits would have starved without food.

•

THE MOUSE TOWER

Adapted from retellings by Robert Southey
and Lilian Gask

This is a very scary story, and one that stays with you. Here is a
heartless man who heeds no injunction to help others. Though
there is justice in the end, it is very rough justice. The medieval
tale reminds us how deeply unsettling is the cruelty of one human
being to another.

Hatto, Bishop of Mayence, in Germany, was rich and greedy.
There was no doubt about that. Instead of devoting himself to
prayer and almsgiving, he thought only of increasing his great
wealth. His farms were the richest in the whole country, and his
granaries were stocked with wheat and corn. But that wasn't enough
for him. He raised taxes on the people over and over again. He
built a tall tower of stone on an island in the river Rhine and would
let no boat pass by without stopping and paying a toll in silver or
gold. His moneybags grew fat and burst at the seams. Whatever
might happen to other folk, Hatto would never suffer.

One spring the river overflowed, and the low-lying land was
flooded. The harvest failed, and famine descended upon the people. Finding themselves on the point of starvation, the villagers
went to beg Hatto's aid.

"Take pity, good Bishop, on our hungry children," they cried.
"They die while your granaries are full of wheat."

But Bishop Hatto only laughed.

"I cannot help that," he said. "If you want wheat, you'd better
buy it from me now. Tomorrow my prices will be higher."

But they were desperate, and every day they came crowding
around his house. However much he tried, he could not drive them
off. The little starving children scratched at his door, and the crying
mothers held their infants up to his windows.

Wearied, at last, by their begging, Hatto came out and faced
them.

"All right," he said, "you've convinced me. Meet me at my
largest barn, the empty one down by the river. I give you my word
that I'll bring an end to your suffering."

Now at last there was joy among the starving creatures. Their dim eyes brightened, and strength came back to their shrunken limbs as they dragged themselves to the barn and waited for the food to be distributed.

"You shall have bread tonight," they told their little ones, and the children ceased their wailing.

At the appointed time Bishop Hatto made his appearance. His cruel lips were pressed tightly together, and hatred burned in his deep-set eyes as he surveyed the hungry masses. He stood outside and watched the villagers limp into the barn.

As the last one filed inside, he closed the doors, and bolted them shut.

For a while the poor people could not fathom what was happening. Every moment they expected Hatto to enter and begin distributing food. But the minutes wore on, and he did not come. Instead, they heard his cruel voice laughing outside.

"You have pestered me like rats," he said, "and now you shall die like rats."

Then the people pounded on the walls, shrieked, and wept for mercy. But the doors stood fast, and the trapped victims were far too weak from hunger to break them down. Hours passed, and then days, and the poor villagers starved to death.

"I've done the country a great service," said Hatto, "ridding it of rats that only consumed the corn."

Weeks passed, and then months. The dead remained undisturbed. Finally, one of the bishop's servants opened the doors of the barn, intending to lay the bones to rest. The place was empty.

"Good riddance," said the bishop, shrugging. "Dust to dust."

But that night his sleep was broken by quick, little scratching sounds, as if something were scampering over the floor.

The next morning he was annoyed to find that a splendid portrait of himself in his bishop's robes, which had been painted by a famous artist at great expense, was lying on the ground, gnawed to shreds. He could see the marks of rats' sharp teeth on that part of the canvas where his face had been. He shuddered at the sight in spite of himself.

A few days later, one of his servants appeared before him, his face white with alarm.

"My lord," he whispered, "I opened one of your granaries this morning. The rats have eaten all the corn."

That very evening Hatto was sitting alone, eating his dinner, when he looked up and saw a mouse sitting at the other end of the table. It stared back at him with a hungry look in its eyes. He threw a fork at it, and it scampered away.

But after that, he noticed mice here and there all around his house. He saw their noses peeking out of cracks in the wall, and their tails hanging out of drawers and cupboards. He stepped on them in the stairway and sat on them in his favorite chair. They ran across his bedsheets, and even nested in his pillows.

He brought cats to keep them out. But the cats soon disappeared.

The rats swarmed all over the kitchen and pantry, devouring every last crumb. When the food was gone, they gnawed at the wood. He could hear them in the floors and walls. Hatto trembled, and knew fear for the first time.

And then one day a servant burst into his room.

"Fly, my lord bishop, fly!" he cried. "They are coming this way!"

Hatto looked out his window. Ten thousand rats covered the hillside where his old granary stood—and they were coming his way!

Panic seized the man who had committed so evil a crime. Mounting his horse, he went off at full gallop. Though his horse was fleet and he spurred him on unmercifully, the bishop found that the army of rats was gaining on him. Wild with terror, he reached the riverside, and jumping into a little boat, rowed with all his might to the middle of the stream, where his tall tower stood on its island.

He ran inside and barred the door. He was safe, he thought. The tower walls were high, and the island shores steep. The current in the river was strong, and the water deep.

He checked the cupboard—he had plenty of food stored there. That made him feel better. He counted the money he had hidden away. That made him feel even better. He could hold out until this invasion had passed. He climbed up and down the tower's stairs, barring every window, closing every door. Then he lay down and closed his eyes.

He woke in the middle of the night. Something made him go to the window and peep out. He could not believe what he saw.

The water was black and seething in the moonlight. Rats! It was full of them—thousands, millions of them—swimming straight for him! The river was choking with rats. He could hear them squeaking and squealing as they gained the shore.

Hatto ran up the stairs, as high as he could get, and locked himself in the uppermost room. He listened breathlessly. He could hear them whetting their teeth against the tower stones.

Desperately, he opened a window and began throwing out bread and corn and cheese, hoping to satisfy the ravenous horde. But that was not what they came for. Far below, he heard the scampering of thousands of tiny feet on the stairs.

He screamed. He dragged everything he could move—tables and chairs and heavy moneybags—against the door. He looked around him wildly. There was nothing left to push, nowhere else to go. He crouched in a dusty corner and waited.

The wait was not long. From within the walls, behind the door, down through the ceiling, up through the floor—came the sound of gnawing.

A few days later, some of the bishop's servants dared to enter the ruined tower. They found some bread and corn and cheese, and piles of moneybags lying about untouched. But they found no sign of Hatto.

●

KADDO'S WALL

Retold by Harold Courlander and George Herzog

In this story, Kaddo acts as though he could be a distant cousin of the Hatto of Mouse Tower fame. This remarkable tale comes from. west Africa.

In the town of Tendella in the Kingdom of Seno, north of the Gulf of Guinea, there was a rich man by the name of Kaddo. His fields spread out on every side of the town. At plowing time hundreds of men and boys hoed up his fields, and then hundreds of women and girls planted his corn seed in the ground for him. His grain bulged in his granary, because each season he harvested far more than he could use. The name of Kaddo was known far and wide throughout the Kingdom of Seno. Travelers who passed through the town carried tales of his wealth far beyond Seno's borders.

One day Kaddo called all of his people in the town of Tendella together for a big meeting in front of his house. They all came, for Kaddo was an important man, and they knew he was going to make an important announcement.

"There's something that bothers me," Kaddo said. "I've been thinking about it for a long time. I've lain awake worrying. I have so much corn in my granary that I don't know what to do with it."

The people listened attentively, and thought about Kaddo's words. Then a man said:

"Some of the people of the town have no corn at all. They are very poor and have nothing. Why don't you give some of your corn to them?"

Kaddo shook his head and said, "No, that isn't a very good idea. It doesn't satisfy me."

Another man said to Kaddo:

"Well, then, you could lend corn to the people who have had a bad harvest and have no seed for the spring planting. That would be very good for the town and would keep poverty away."

"No," Kaddo said, "that's no solution either."

"Well, then, why not sell some of your corn and buy cattle instead?" still another man said.

Kaddo shook his head.

"No, it's not very good advice. It's hard for people to advise a rich man with problems like mine."

Many people made suggestions, but nobody's advice suited Kaddo. He thought for a while, and at last he said:

"Send me as many young girls as you can find. I will have them grind the corn for me."

The people went away. They were angry with Kaddo. But the next day they sent a hundred girls to work for him as he had asked. On a hundred grindstones they began to grind Kaddo's corn into flour. All day long they put corn into the grindstones and took flour out. All day long the people of the town heard the sound of the grinding at Kaddo's house. A pile of corn flour began to grow. For seven days and seven nights the girls ground corn without a pause.

When the last grain of corn was ground into flour, Kaddo called the girls together and said:

"Now bring water from the spring. We shall mix it with the corn flour to make mortar out of it."

So the girls brought water in water pots and mixed it with the flour to make a thick mortar. Then Kaddo ordered them to make bricks out of the mortar.

"When the bricks are dry, then I shall make a wall of them around my house," he said.

Word went out that Kaddo was preparing to build a wall of flour around his house, and the people of the town came to his door and protested.

"You can't do a thing like this, it is against humanity!" they said.

"It's not right, people have no right to build walls with food!" a man said.

"Ah, what is right and what is wrong?" Kaddo said. "My right is different from yours, because I am so very rich. So leave me alone."

"Corn is to eat, so that you may keep alive," another said. "It's not meant to taunt those who are less fortunate."

"When people are hungry it is an affront to shut them out with a wall of flour," another man said.

"Stop your complaints," Kaddo said. "The corn is mine. It is my surplus. I can't eat it all. It comes from my own fields. I am rich. What good is it to be rich if you can't do what you want with your own property?"

The people of the town went away, shaking their heads in anger over Kaddo's madness. The hundred girls continued to make bricks of flour, which they dried in the sun. And when the bricks were dry, Kaddo had them begin building the wall around his house. They used wet dough for mortar to hold the bricks together, and slowly the wall grew. They stuck cowry shells into the wall to make beautiful designs, and when at last the wall was done, and the last corn flour used up, Kaddo was very proud. He walked back and forth and looked at his wall. He walked around it. He went in and out of the gate. He was very happy.

And now when people came to see him they had to stand by the gate until he asked them to enter. When the workers who plowed and planted for Kaddo wanted to talk to him, Kaddo sat on the wall by the gate and listened to them and gave them orders. And whenever the people of the town wanted his opinion on an important matter, he sat on his wall and gave it to them, while they stood and listened.

Things went on like this for a long time. Kaddo enjoyed his reputation as the richest man for miles around. The story of Kaddo's wall went to the farthest parts of the kingdom.

And then one year there was a bad harvest for Kaddo. There wasn't enough rain to grow the corn, and the earth dried up hard and dusty like the road. There wasn't a single ear of corn in all of Kaddo's fields or the fields of his relatives.

The next year it was the same. Kaddo had no seed corn left, so he sold his cattle and horses to buy corn for food and seed for a new planting. He sowed corn again, but the next harvest time it was the same, and there wasn't a single ear of corn on all his fields.

Year after year Kaddo's crops failed. Some of his relatives died of hunger, and others went away to other parts of the Kingdom of Seno, for they had no more seed corn to plant and they couldn't count on Kaddo's help. Kaddo's workers ran away, because he was unable to feed them. Gradually Kaddo's part of the town became deserted. All that he had left were a young daughter and a mangy donkey.

When his cattle and his money were all gone, Kaddo became very hungry. He scraped away a little bit of the flour wall and ate it. Next day he scraped away more of the flour wall and ate it. The wall got lower and lower. Little by little it disappeared. A day came when the wall was gone, when nothing was left of the elegant structure Kaddo had built around his house, and on which he had used to sit to listen to the people of the town when they came to ask him to lend them a little seed corn.

Then Kaddo realized that if he was to live any longer he must get help from somewhere. He wondered who would help him. Not the people of Tendella, for he had insulted and mistreated them and they would have nothing to do with him. There was only one man he could go to—Sogole, king of the Ganna people, who had the reputation of being very rich and generous.

So Kaddo and his daughter got on the mangy, underfed donkey and rode seven days until they arrived in the land of the Ganna.

Sogole sat before his royal house when Kaddo arrived. He had a soft skin put on the ground next to him for Kaddo to sit upon, and had millet beer brought for the two of them to drink.

"Well, stranger in the land of the Ganna, take a long drink, for you have a long trip behind you if you come from Tendella," Sogole said.

"Thank you, but I can't drink much," Kaddo said.

"Why is that?" Sogole said. "When people are thirsty they drink."

"That is true," Kaddo replied. "But I have been hungry too long, and my stomach is shrunk."

"Well, drink in peace then, because now that you are my guest you won't be hungry. You shall have whatever you need from me."

Kaddo nodded his head solemnly and drank a little of the millet beer.

"And now tell me," Sogole said. "You say you come from the town of Tendella in the Kingdom of Seno? I've heard many tales of that town. The famine came there and drove out many people, because they had no corn left."

"Yes," Kaddo said. "Hard times drove them out, and the corn was all gone."

"But tell me, there was a rich and powerful man in Tendella named Kaddo, wasn't there? What ever happened to him? Is he still alive?"

"Yes, he is still alive," Kaddo said.

"A fabulous man, this Kaddo," Sogole said. "They say he built a wall of flour around his house out of his surplus crops, and when he talked to his people he sat on the wall by his gate. Is this true?"

"Yes, it is true," Kaddo said sadly.

"Does he still have as many cattle as he used to?" Sogole asked.

"No, they are all gone."

"It is an unhappy thing for a man who owned so much to come to so little," Sogole said. "But doesn't he have many servants and workers still?"

"His workers and servants are all gone," Kaddo said. "Of all his great household he has only one daughter left. The rest went away because there was no money and no food."

Sogole looked melancholy.

"Ah, what is a rich man when his cattle are gone and his servants have left him? But tell me, what happened to the wall of flour that he built around his house?"

"He ate the wall," Kaddo said. "Each day he scraped a little of the flour from the wall, until it was all gone."

"A strange story," Sogole said. "But such is life."

And he thought quietly for a while about the way life goes for people sometimes, and then he asked:

"And were you, by any chance, one of Kaddo's family?"

"Indeed I was one of Kaddo's family. Once I was rich. Once I had more cattle than I could count. Once I had many cornfields. Once I had hundreds of workers cultivating my crops. Once I had a bursting granary. Once I was Kaddo, the great personage of Tendella."

"What! You yourself are Kaddo?"

"Yes, once I was proud and lordly, and now I sit in rags begging for help."

"What can I do for you?" Sogole asked.

"I have nothing left now. Give me some seed corn, so that I can go back and plant my fields again."

"Take what you need," Sogole said. He ordered his servants to bring bags of corn and to load them on Kaddo's donkey. Kaddo thanked him humbly, and he and his daughter started their return trip to Tendella. They traveled for seven days. On the way Kaddo became very hungry. He hadn't seen so much corn for a long time as he was bringing back from the Kingdom of the Ganna. He took a few grains and put them in his mouth and chewed them. Once more he put a few grains in his mouth. Then he put a whole handful in his mouth and swallowed. He couldn't stop. He ate and ate. He forgot that this was the corn with which he had to plant his fields. When he arrived in Tendella he went to his bed to sleep, and when he arose the next morning he ate again. He ate so much of the corn that he became sick. He went to his bed again and cried out in pain, because his stomach had forgotten what to do with food. And before long Kaddo died.

Kaddo's grandchildren and great-grandchildren in the Kingdom of Seno are poor to this day. And to the rich men of the country the common people sometimes say:

"Don't build a wall of flour around your house."

•

THE EMERALD LIZARD

Great hearts can help give rise to little miracles.

Brother Pedro lived in Guatemala long ago, hundreds of years ago, in fact, but all the good he did lives on in the stories of his work. He was a poor man and stayed poor all his life, for he gave whatever he had to those in need. He turned his own small, humble home into a place where the sick could find care. It is said that at night he walked the city streets ringing a little bell to remind people to thank God for their blessings and share those same gifts with others.

One day Brother Pedro was walking toward the city when he came upon a ragged man sitting beside the road. The man wiped away a tear as Brother Pedro approached.

"What ails you, my friend?" Brother Pedro asked, perceiving his despair.

"My troubles weigh heavily," the man sobbed. "My wife is sick and needs medicine. My children are hungry and want food. But I have no money and can find no work. I don't know what to do."

Brother Pedro looked at the suffering man's face and longed to help. But his own clothes were just as ragged, his own cupboard as bare, his own pockets as empty. He had nothing to give.

He turned his gaze upward, hoping for an answer. The sun's warm glow spread across his kind face. "Dear Lord," he whispered, "help me help this man."

There was a rustling at their feet, and from behind a gray rock, a bright green lizard crept into the sun. Brother Pedro stooped and gently caught it by the tail. With a smile he placed it into his companion's hands.

The poor man looked at Brother Pedro in bewilderment. Then he opened his hands and gasped. The lizard was suddenly rigid and heavy and hard. But it was still a rich green. The man peered closely, and beheld a miracle. The live creature had turned into an emerald lizard.

"Take this, and sell it," Brother Pedro said. "With the money it brings, you will be able to care for your wife and feed your children, and perhaps you will have enough left over to tend to others in need as well."

The grateful man did as he was told. He hurried to a jeweler, where he was able to sell the rare emerald for much gold. With medicine and food, his family grew healthy and strong again. The years passed. The man worked hard. His children grew up to be prosperous ranchers and farmers, and their wealth increased tenfold. But they lived quietly and sensibly, and took care of their aging parents, and gave much of their fortune to help the poor.

The day came when their father directed his footsteps back to the jeweler where he had sold the miraculous lizard. He bought the gem back and set out to find Brother Pedro.

The good Brother was much grayer now, and even poorer and more shabbily dressed than before. But his wrinkled face was every bit as kind.

"Do you remember me, Padre?" the visitor asked.

Brother Pedro looked at the stranger closely, searching his mind.

"I met you on the road one day long ago. My wife was sick, and my children were starving."

Brother Pedro shook his head. There had been so many!

"You gave me an emerald lizard, and told me to trade it for gold."

Brother Pedro's face brightened.

"Of course, of course. Now I remember. And how did things turn out? How is your wife? How are your children?"

"They are well," the man replied. "But now I've brought your emerald back. It has given my family health and wealth. You've worked hard all your life in the service of others. Take the gem, and rest from your labors. You can sell it for gold, as I did, and live your last days in ease."

He took the sparkling lizard from his pocket and placed it back in the good old man's hands.

Smiling gently, Brother Pedro stooped and set it on the ground. At once it turned into a live green lizard and disappeared under a rock.

•

MARGARET OF NEW ORLEANS

Sara Cone Bryant

Here is a true story of a real heroine. Born of Irish immigrant parents, Margaret Haughery moved to New Orleans from Baltimore in search of health for her husband. When both her husband and child died, she began helping the children of the Poydras Orphan Asylum. Most of the money she earned from her dairy and bakery went to the city's needy, and when Margaret died her life savings of $30,000 went to charity. The Margaret Statue, one of the earliest memorials erected to a woman in the United States, was dedicated in 1884. It still stands today, modest and compelling.

There is still work like this to be done in cities all over the country, and more Margarets needed to do it.

If you ever go to the beautiful city of New Orleans, somebody will be sure to take you down into the old business part of the city, where there are banks and shops and hotels, and show you a statue which stands in a little square there. It is the statue of a woman, sitting in a low chair, with her arms around a child, who leans against her. The woman is not at all pretty. She wears thick, common shoes, a plain dress, with a little shawl, and a sunbonnet. She is stout and short, and her face is a square-chinned Irish face. But her eyes look at you like your mother's.

Now there is something very surprising about this statue. It was one of the first that was ever made in this country in honor of a woman. Even in old Europe there are not many monuments to women, and most of the few are to great queens or princesses, very beautiful and very richly dressed. You see, this statue in New Orleans is not quite like anything else.

It is the statue of a woman named Margaret. Her whole name was Margaret Haughery, but no one in New Orleans remembers her by it, any more than you think of your dearest sister by her full name. She is just Margaret. This is her story, and it tells why people made a monument for her.

When Margaret was a tiny baby, her father and mother died,

and she was adopted by two young people as poor and as kind as her own parents. She lived with them until she grew up. Then she married, and had a little baby of her own. But very soon her husband died, and then the baby died, too, and Margaret was all alone in the world. She was poor, but she was strong, and knew how to work.

All day, from morning until evening, she ironed clothes in a laundry. And every day, as she worked by the window, she saw the little motherless children from the orphanage nearby working and playing about. After a while, a great sickness came upon the city, and so many mothers and fathers died that there were more orphans than the orphanage could possibly take care of. They needed a good friend now. You would hardly think, would you, that a poor woman who worked in a laundry could be much of a friend to them? But Margaret was. She went straight to the kind Sisters who ran the orphanage and told them she was going to give them part of her wages and was going to work for them, besides. Pretty soon she had worked so hard that she had some money saved from her wages. With this, she bought two cows and a little delivery cart. Then she carried her milk to her customers in the little cart every morning, and as she went, she begged the leftover food from the hotels and rich houses, and brought it back in the cart to the hungry children in the orphanage. In the very hardest times that was often all the food the children had.

A part of the money Margaret earned went every week to the orphanage, and after a few years it was made very much larger and better. And Margaret was so careful and so good at business that, in spite of her giving, she bought more cows and earned more money. With this, she built a home for orphan babies; she called it her baby house.

After a time, Margaret had a chance to get a bakery, and then she became a bread-woman instead of a milk-woman. She carried the bread just as she had carried the milk, in her cart. And still she kept giving money to the orphanage. Then the great war came, the Civil War. In all the trouble and sickness and fear of that time, Margaret drove her cart of bread, and somehow she had always enough to give the starving soldiers, and for her babies, besides what she sold. And despite all this, she earned enough so that when the war was over she built a big steam factory for her bread. By this time everybody in the city knew her. The children all over the city loved her. The businessmen were proud of her. The poor people all came to her for advice. She used to sit at the open door of her office, in a calico gown and a little shawl, and give a good word to everybody, rich or poor.

Then, by and by, one day, Margaret died. And when it was time to read her will, the people found that, with all her giving, she had still saved a great deal of money, and that she had left every cent of it to the different orphanages of the city—each one of them was given something. Whether they were for white children or black, for Jews, Catholics, or Protestants, made no difference; for Margaret always said, "They are all orphans alike." And just think, that splendid, wise will was signed with a cross instead of a name, for Margaret had never learned to read or write!

When the people of New Orleans knew that Margaret was dead, they said, "She was a mother to the motherless. She was a friend to those who had no friends. She had wisdom greater than schools can teach. We will not let her memory go from us." So they made a statute of her, just as she used to look, sitting in her own office door, or driving in her own little cart. And there it stands today, in memory of the great love and the great power of plain Margaret Haughery, of New Orleans.

•

THE BOY WHO BROUGHT LIGHT INTO A WORLD OF DARKNESS

It has been said that necessity is the mother of invention. As we learn from the remarkable life of Louis Braille (1809–1852), compassion can play a large role in invention too. Helen Keller wrote of Braille that "the unwearied activity of his clear, scientific mind, his calmness and forbearance, his inventive abilities as a teacher, the wealth of his heart expended in uncounted secret gifts out of his scanty savings to the needy, both blind and seeing, are a priceless legacy."

One day nearly two hundred years ago, a young French boy was standing in his father's workshop in the town of Coupvray, not far from Paris. Louis Braille was only three years old, but he loved to watch his father making saddles and harnesses out of tough leather hides. Sometimes his father gave him little scraps of leather to play with, and he pretended he was fitting them together into saddles too. Already, at that young age, he wanted to be just like his father.

Monsieur Braille sewed busily, smiling down at his son every once in a while. The harness-maker worked quickly and smoothly, cutting the leather with a sure hand and practiced eye. He held a piece up to the light, examined it closely, and saw he would need to use a different knife. Laying his work down, he crossed the room to search for the right tool.

Little Louis reached toward the workbench, picked up the awl his father had left behind, and began to poke at his own scrap of leather. He jabbed fiercely at the tough leather, trying make the point go all the way through. As he stabbed, his young fingers lost their grip. The sharp instrument sprang up and struck his left eye.

Monsieur Braille heard a scream and ran back to his bench, but it was too late. The damage was done.

The horrified parents took their young son to the doctor, hoping to save the eye, but the injury was too serious. And then, as time passed, the tragedy deepened. Infection spread to the other eye as well. Before long the boy could not see at all.

In those days people often treated the blind with great cruelty or neglect. Sometimes they were thrown out by their families to beg on the streets or sing for alms. Or they were hired out to do hard labor, like beasts of burden. In many places, blindness was viewed as the work of Satan or divine punishment for sin.

But it was different in the town of Coupvray, where everyone watched out for the little blind Louis. They listened for the tap of his cane, and smiled when they saw him coming. They stopped their own work to guide him across the street or around a corner. They helped him count how many taps it took to get to the market-place, or the edge of town, or school.

Louis and his father would walk together, and the boy would ask, "What color is the sky today?"

"As blue as can be, son," Monsieur Braille would say. "As blue as can be."

But although Louis struggled to recall a vision of blue, the pictures of his youth gradually faded from his mind, and he could no longer remember the beauty of such sights as colors.

He learned to help his father in his shop, handing him tools and pieces of leather. He went to school with his old friends, too, and everyone was surprised at the way he learned by listening and memorizing his lessons. He loved to spend his time talking to his teacher about history and geography, and to the town priest about music and Bible stories.

But in truth he was not happy with his studies, for he wanted to be able to read books and write letters like his classmates.

Then one day the schoolmaster told Louis about a school for the blind in Paris. It had a special kind of book that blind people could read, he said. Louis could hardly believe his ears. He begged his parents to send him to the wonderful school, and the village priest helped them find money to help pay the costs.

And so when he was ten years old, Louis and his father traveled to Paris, where the boy enrolled in the National Institute for the Young Blind. As soon as he arrived, he asked his new teachers the question that was burning in his mind: "Can you teach me to read?"

He learned that the school was experimenting with a new way of teaching the blind to read. The Institute's founder had printed some books with large, raised letters on the pages. By tracing the shape of the letters with their fingers, blind students could make out words and sentences.

It wasn't long, however, before Louis discovered the shortcomings of this method. The raised letters were so large that even a very short story filled many pages. A single book might weigh hundreds of pounds! Tracing the fingers over the print was a clumsy process, so it took a long time for a blind person to read just a few paragraphs. And since the books were expensive to make, the school could afford to print only a few. It wasn't long before Louis had read through its entire library.

Despite his disappointment in this cumbersome method, the boy from Coupvray studied hard and learned quickly. He especially loved music; with his keen hearing, quick fingers, and sharp memory he became a fine student of the piano and cello. He loved spending his free hours at the organ in the nearby church, and before long he began playing for the services there.

His love of music made him long more than ever for a better way to read. He wanted to be able to read not just words but musical notes as well. And he wanted to be able to write. Sometimes he lay awake at night thinking over the problem again and again.

"There must be a way," he kept telling himself. "If blind people are to learn as much as everyone else, they must be able to read and write. I must find a way."

Then one day he heard of an army captain named Charles Barbier who had invented a method to send messages in the dark. His "night writing" consisted of dots and dashes raised on paper; by running their fingers over the code, soldiers could read without using a light.

At once Louis recognized what such an idea meant. If a soldier could read and write messages in the dark, then a blind person could read and write too!

He went to question Monsieur Barbier. The captain was happy to demonstrate his system. He punched a few holes on a piece of paper with an awl, one similar to the very instrument that had destroyed Louis's own sight. He turned the paper over, and showed his visitor how the marks made little bumps. Louis ran his fingers over the raised dots. Barbier explained how certain combinations of dots and dashes could make words and sentences.

Louis hurried back to the Institute and set to work. Night after night, month after month he worked with Barbier's system, changing and refining. He knew the idea was sound, but he also knew the captain's arrangement of dots and dashes was too cumbersome to be truly useful to the blind.

Like many new ideas and inventions, Louis's work was viewed with suspicion. Some of the officials at the Institute resented his trying to change things. They had spent a small fortune printing their books with raised letters, and they saw no reason to change to a whole new system based on little bumps. They argued that a new writing invented solely for blind people would segregate them even more from the rest of society. They frowned on Louis's efforts.

When he was seventeen years old, Louis became a teacher at the Institute. By day he taught his students to read using the older method of large, raised letters, but at night he continued to develop his new system. He would work until the early morning hours, carefully punching holes, testing new patterns, searching for the right combinations, until he fell asleep in the midst of his tools and papers. Except for his beloved music, he gave all his spare time to the effort, always cheerful and brave and confident of success.

In 1829, by the time he was twenty years old, Louis arrived at his readable alphabet using various patterns of one to six raised dots. The Braille system was complete. He designed a little punch tool to write with, and after a while he could write almost as fast as someone could talk. He could even write and read music using his new system.

Word began to spread. Some of his students would come secretly to his room at night to learn the new method. Louis punched out his own books—Shakespeare and other classics—for them to read. After a while other blind people began to hear about the marvelous new method, and from all over the world they sent Louis letters asking about his invention.

And yet, sad to say, most people still could not see the importance of Braille's new system. Some saw its value, but did not care. Others were envious or resentful of the new method. Some of the teachers at the Institute, unwilling to try anything new, tried to make sure no one would ever learn to read using Louis Braille's dots.

But Louis went on refining and promoting his idea, hoping for the day when blind people all over the world would have the chance to read and write as he now could. He punched out more and more books, and taught any blind person who was interested how to read them. He talked to anyone who would listen about his method, demonstrating it again and again, trying to rouse public interest.

And through all the days and nights of work, he wore himself out. His health began to fail, and for a while it seemed as though the opportunity he had made for blind people might pass from the earth with him.

At last, however, his ideas found acceptance. Toward the end of his life, several places throughout Europe began to recognize the importance of Braille's work, and more blind people began to discover his raised dots. The light was dawning. As he lay in a hospital bed a few weeks before his death, Louis said to a friend, "Oh, unsearchable mystery of the human heart! I am convinced that my mission on earth is finished."

He died in 1852, just two days after his forty-third birthday.

In the years following Braille's death, more and more blind people turned to his raised-dot system. The Braille method spread from country to country, at last becoming the accepted method of reading and writing for those who cannot see. At last books could become a part of their lives, all because of a fifteen-year-old boy who devoted his own life to finding a better way.

•

BROTHER TO THE LEPERS

Charles Warren Stoddard

Here is an eyewitness account of the remarkable work of the
missionary Joseph Damien de Veuster, better known to the world
simply as Father Damien (1840–1888). The young Belgian
priest's offer to aid the leper colony on the Hawaiian island of
Molokai in 1873 was a complete act of self-sacrifice. He knew that
eventually he would almost certainly catch the dreaded disease
himself. Upon his arrival at Molokai, he discovered a community
of some six hundred lepers desperately in need of both spiritual
and physical care. He set to work without hesitation. The following description of Father Damien's work comes from Charles Warren Stoddard, a resident of the Hawaiian Islands who visited
Molokai with two government physicians in 1884.

The first glimpse of Kalawao might lead a stranger to pronounce it a thriving hamlet of perhaps five hundred inhabitants.
Its single street is bordered by neat whitewashed cottages, with
numerous little gardens of bright flowers, and clusters of graceful
and decorative tropical trees. It lies so near the base of the mountain that not a few of the huge stones that were loosened by the
rains have come thundering down the heights, and rolled almost to
the fences that enclose the village suburbs.

As we passed down the street, Dr. Fitch was greeted on every
hand. He had been expected, for it was his custom to visit the
settlement monthly; and many a shout of welcome was raised, and
many an *"Aloha!"*—the fond salutation of the race—rang from
doorway, window, and veranda. One group of stalwart fellows
swung their hats in air, and gave three lusty cheers for *"Kauka"*
(the doctor), topping them off with a burst of childish laughter.

Thus far, inasmuch as we had scarcely looked into the faces of
these villagers, they seemed to us the merriest and most contented
community in the world. But let it be remembered that we were all
in the deep afternoon shadow, and our arrival was the sensation of
the hour.

By the roadside, in the edge of the village, between it and the sea, stood a little chapel; the cross upon its low belfry, and the larger cross in the cemetery beyond, assured us that the poor villagers were not neglected in the hour of their extremity.

As we drew near, the churchyard gate was swung open for us by a troop of laughing urchins, who stood hat in hand to give us welcome. Now, for the first time, I noticed that they were all disfigured: that their faces were seared and scarred; their hands and feet maimed and sometimes bleeding; their eyes like the eyes of some half-tamed animal; their mouths shapeless; and their whole aspect in many cases repulsive.

These were lepers; so were they, each of them, that had greeted us as we passed through the village; so are they all, with a few privileged exceptions, who dwell in the two little villages under the cliffs by the sea.

Other lepers gathered about us as we entered the churchyard. The chapel steps were crowded with them—for a stranger is seldom seen at Kalawao—and as their number increased, it seemed as if each newcomer was more horrible than the last, until corruption could go no farther, and flesh suffer no deeper dishonor this side of the grave. They voluntarily drew aside as we advanced, closing in behind us, and encircling us at every step.

The chapel door stood ajar. In a moment it was thrown open, and a young priest paused upon the threshold to give us welcome. His cassock was worn and faded, his hair tumbled like a schoolboy's, his hands stained and hardened by toil. But the glow of health was in his face, the buoyancy of youth in his manner, while his ringing laugh, his ready sympathy, and his inspiring magnetism told of one who in any sphere might do a noble work, and who in that which he has chosen is doing the noblest of all works.

This was Father Damien, the self-exiled priest, the one clean man in the midst of his flock of lepers.

He was born in Louvain, Belgium, January 3, 1840. When he was but four and twenty, his brother, who had just entered the priesthood, was ordered to embark for Honolulu, but at the moment fell sick with typhoid fever. Young Damien, who was a theological student at the University, having received minor orders, and belonging to the same order—the Society of the Sacred Hearts of Jesus and Mary (commonly called Society of Picpus)—at once wrote to his superior, and begged that he might be sent upon the mission in his brother's stead. In one week he was on his way to that far country. He was ordained upon his arrival in Honolulu, and

for a few years led the life of toil and privation which invariably
falls to the lot of the Catholic missionary.

In 1873 he, in common with others of the clergy, was invited
to be present at the dedication of a beautiful chapel just completed
by Father Leonor at Wailuku, on the Island of Maui. There he met
the Bishop, who expressed regret that he was still unable to send a
priest to Molokai, for the demand was far in excess of the supply.
Father Damien at once said, "My Lord, I hear that a small vessel will
next week take cattle from Kawaihae to Kaulapapa. If you will permit me I will go there to help the lepers make their Easter duties."

His request was granted, and, in company with the Bishop and
the French Consul, he landed at the settlement, where he found a
colony of eight hundred lepers, of whom between four and five
hundred were Catholics. A public meeting was immediately called,
at which the Bishop and the Consul presided. His Grace arose to
address the singular gathering and said; "Since you have written
me so often that you have no priest, I leave you one for a little
time." And, imparting the benediction, he returned immediately to
the vessel which was to sail that very hour. Father Damien told him,
"As there is much to be done here, by your leave I will not even
accompany you to the shore."

Thus the good work was at once begun. It was high time.
The lepers were dying at the rate of from eight to twelve per
week. The priest had not time to build himself a hut—he had not
even the material with which to build it—and for a season he slept
in the open air, under a tree, exposed to the wind and the rain.

Soon after he received a letter of congratulation from the white
residents of Honolulu—chiefly Protestants—together with some
lumber, and a purse of $120. Then he put up his little house, and
began to feel at home.

After remaining some weeks at Kalawao, he was obliged to go
to Honolulu, there being no more convenient priest to whom he
could make his confession.

He naturally called upon the president of the Board of Health,
who seemed much surprised, but received the priest with frigid
politeness. He then asked leave to return to the settlement on Molokai and was curtly informed that he might indeed return, but that
in that case he must remain there for good.

Father Damien's duties were never-ending. From early Mass
till long after his flock was housed in sleep, he was busy. And when
at last he had sought his pillow, it was too often to lie awake plan-

ning for the future, and perhaps to be called again into the ward-rooms to ease the anguish of the sick or the dying.

The neat white cottages which have taken the place of the thatched huts of the natives were erected under his eye; and, furthermore, he personally assisted in the construction of most of them. The small chapel which he found at the settlement has become the transept of the present edifice; he, with the aid of a handful of lepers, enlarged the building, painted it without, decorated it within. There he daily offers the Holy Sacrifice of the Mass, preaches frequently, instructs the children, and fills all the offices of the Church.

He was indeed jack-of-all-trades: physician of the soul and of the body, magistrate, schoolteacher, carpenter, joiner, painter, gardener, housekeeper, cook, and even, in some cases, undertaker and gravedigger. Great was his need of help, and long was he in need of it before it came. More than 1,600 lepers had been buried under his administration, and a deathbed was always awaiting him—sometimes two or three of them.

I remember how, one day, as we were walking among the wards of the hospital at Kalawao, Father Damien turned suddenly to us, and said, "Ah, here is something dreadful I must show you!" We approached what seemed a little bundle of rags, or rubbish, half hidden under a soiled blanket. The curious doctors were about to examine it, when the good Father seized me, and cried, excitedly, "You must not look! You must not look!" I assured him that I was not at all afraid to see even the worst that could be shown me there, for my eyes had become accustomed to horrors, and the most sickening sights no longer affected me. A corner of the blanket was raised, cautiously. A breathing object lay beneath; a face, a human face, was turned slowly towards us—a face in which scarcely a trace of anything human remained. The dark skin was puffed out and blackened. A kind of moss, or mold, gummy and glistening, covered it. The muscles of the mouth, having contracted, laid bare the grinning teeth. The thickened tongue lay like a fig between them. The eyelids, curled tightly back, exposed the inner surface, and the protruding eyeballs, now shapeless and broken, looked not unlike bursted grapes. It was a leprous child, who within the last few days had assumed that horrible visage. Surely the grave knows nothing more frightful than this!

Once I wandered alone into the chapel. A small organ was standing near an open window; beyond the window was the very pandanus tree under which Father Damien found shelter when he first came to Kalawao. I sat at the instrument, dreaming over the keys, and thinking of the life one must lead in such a spot, of the need for and the lack of human sympathy, of the solitude of the soul destined to a communion with perpetual death—and, hearing a slight rustling near me, I turned, and found the chapel nearly filled with lepers, who had silently stolen in, one after another, at the sound of the organ. The situation was rather startling. But when I asked where Father Damien might be found, they directed me, and stood aside to let me pass.

I found him where I might have known he was likely to be found, working bravely among his men, he by far the most industrious of them all. As I approached them unobserved, the bell of the little chapel rang out the Angelus; on the instant they all knelt, uncovered, and in their midst the priest recited the beautiful prayer, to which they responded in soft, low voices—while the gentle breeze rustled the broad leaves about them, and the sun poured a flood of glory upon their bowed forms. Lepers all of them, save the good pastor, and soon to follow in the ghastly procession, whose motionless bodies he blesses in their peaceful sleep.

Angelus Domini! Was not that sight pleasing in the eyes of God?

Shortly after Stoddard's visit, Father Damien discovered he had caught leprosy. He lived for four more years, continuing his work almost to the end.

•

THE SHIPWRECK

Charles Dickens

Here is a glimpse of the kind of personal courage that sometimes rises in the human heart when others' lives are at stake—even strangers' lives. This is one of the finest descriptive passages from one of the finest novels in the English language, *David Copperfield.* The narrator, young David Copperfield, travels to Yarmouth to see his friend Ham Peggotty.

Having made up my mind to go down to Yarmouth, I went round to the coach office and took the box seat on the mail. In the evening I started, by that conveyance, down the road.

"Don't you think that a very remarkable sky?" I asked the coachman, in the first stage out of London. "I don't remember to have seen one like it."

"Nor I—not equal to it," he replied. "That's wind, sir; there'll be mischief done at sea, I expect before long."

It was a murky confusion—here and there blotted with a color like the color of the smoke from damp fuel—of flying clouds tossed up into most remarkable heaps, suggesting greater heights in the clouds than there were depths below them to the bottom of the deepest hollows in the earth, through which the wild moon seemed to plunge headlong, as if, in a dread disturbance of the laws of nature, she had lost her way and were frightened. There had been wind all day; and it was rising then, with an extraordinary great sound. In another hour it had much increased, and the sky was more overcast, and it blew harder. . . .

As we struggled on, nearer and nearer to the sea, from which the mighty wind was blowing dead on shore, its force became more and more terrific. Long before we saw the sea, its spray was on our lips, and showered salt rain upon us. The water was out, over miles and miles of the flat country adjacent to Yarmouth; and every sheet and puddle lashed its banks, and had its stress of little breakers setting heavily towards us. When we came within sight of the sea, the waves on the horizon, caught at intervals above the rolling abyss, were like glimpses of another shore with towers and buildings. When at last we got into the town, the people came out to their doors, all aslant, and with streaming hair, making a wonder of the mail that had come through such a night.

I put up at the old inn, and went down to look at the sea, staggering along the street, which was strewn with sand and sea-weed, and with flying blotches of sea foam. . . .

The tremendous sea itself, when I could find sufficient pause to look at it, in the agitation of the blinding wind, the flying stones and sand, and the awful noise, confounded me. As the high watery walls came rolling in, and, at their highest, tumbled into surf, they looked as if the least would engulf the town. As the receding wave swept back with a hoarse roar, it seemed to scoop out caves in the beach, as if its purpose were to undermine the earth. When some white-headed billows thundered on, and dashed themselves to pieces before they reached the land, every fragment of the late whole seemed possessed by the full might of its wrath, rushing to be gathered to the composition of another monster. Undulating hills were changed to valleys, undulating valleys (with a storm bird sometimes skimming through them) were lifted up to hills; masses of water shivered and shook the beach with a booming sound; every shape tumultuously rolled on, as soon as made, to change its shape and place, and beat another shape and place away; the ideal shore on the horizon, with its towers and buildings, rose and fell; the clouds flew fast and thick; I seemed to see a rending and up-heaving of all nature.

Not finding my old friend, Ham, among the people whom this memorable wind—for it is still remembered down there as the greatest ever known to blow upon that coast—had brought to-gether, I made my way to his house. It was shut; and as no one answered to my knocking, I went by back ways and bylanes to the yard where he worked. I learned there that he had gone to Lowes-toft, to meet some sudden exigency of ship repairing in which his skill was required; but that he would be back tomorrow morning in good time.

I went back to the inn; and when I had washed and dressed, and tried to sleep, but in vain, it was five o'clock in the afternoon. . . . I was very much depressed in spirits, very solitary, and felt an uneasiness in Ham's not being there, disproportionate to the occa-sion. . . . I was persuaded that possibly he would attempt to return from Lowestoft by sea, and be lost. This grew so strong with me, that I resolved to go back to the yard before I took my dinner, and ask the boat builder if he thought his attempting to return by sea at all likely. If he gave me the least reason to think so, I would go over to Lowestoft and prevent it by bringing him with me.

I hastily ordered my dinner, and went back to the yard. I was none too soon; for the boat builder, with a lantern in his hand, was locking the yard gate. He quite laughed when I asked him the question, and said there was no fear; no man in his senses, or out of them, would put off in such a gale of wind, least of all Ham Peggotty, who had been born to seafaring.

I went back to the inn. The howl and roar, the rattling of the doors and windows, the rumbling in the chimneys, the apparent rocking of the very house that sheltered me, and the prodigious tumult of the sea, were more fearful than in the morning. But there was now a great darkness besides; and that invested the storm with new terrors, real and fanciful.

I could not eat, I could not sit still, I could not continue steadfast in anything. Something within me, faintly answering to the storm without, tossed up the depths of my memory and made a tumult in them. Yet, in all the hurry of my thoughts, wild running with thundering sea, the storm and my uneasiness regarding Ham were always in the foreground.

My dinner went away almost untasted, and I tried to refresh myself with a glass or two of wine. In vain. I fell into a dull slumber before the fire, without losing my consciousness either of the uproar out of doors or of the place in which I was. Both became overshadowed by a new undefinable horror; and when I awoke— or rather when I shook off the lethargy that bound me in my chair —my whole frame thrilled with objectless and unintelligible fear.

I walked to and fro, tried to read an old gazetteer, listened to the awful noises; looked at faces, scenes, and figures in the fire. At length the steady ticking of the undisturbed clock on the wall tormented me to that degree that I resolved to go to bed. . . .

There was a dark gloom in my solitary chamber when I at length returned to it; but I was tired now, and, getting into bed again, fell off a tower and down a precipice into the depths of sleep. I have an impression that for a long time, though I dreamed of being elsewhere and in a variety of scenes, it was always blowing in my dream. At length I lost that feeble hold upon reality, and was engaged with two dear friends, but who they were I don't know, at the siege of some town in a roar of cannonading.

The thunder of the cannon was so loud and incessant, that I could not hear something I much desired to hear, until I made a great exertion, and awoke. It was broad day—eight or nine o'clock; the storm raging, in lieu of the batteries; and someone knocking and calling at my door.

"What is the matter?" I cried.

"A wreck! Close by!"

I sprang out of bed, and asked what wreck?

"A schooner, from Spain or Portugal, laden with fruit and wine. Make haste, sir, if you want to see her! It's thought she'll go to pieces every moment."

The excited voice went clamoring along the staircase; and I wrapped myself in my clothes as quickly as I could, and ran into the street. Numbers of people were there before us, all running in one direction, to the beach. I ran the same way, outstripping a good many, and soon came facing the wild sea.

The wind might by this time have lulled a little, though not more sensibly than if the cannonading I had dreamed of had been diminished by the silencing of half a dozen guns out of hundreds. But the sea, having upon it the additional agitation of the whole night, was infinitely more terrific than when I had seen it last. Every appearance it had then presented bore the expression of being *swelled;* and the height to which the breakers rose, and, looking over one another, bore one another down, and rolled in, in interminable hosts, was most appalling.

In the difficulty of hearing anything but wind and waves, and in the crowd, and the unspeakable confusion, and my first breathless attempts to stand against the weather, I was so confused that I looked out to sea for the wreck, and saw nothing but the foaming heads of the great waves. A half-dressed boatman standing next me pointed with his bare arm (a tattooed arrow on it, pointing in the same direction) to the left. Then, O great Heaven, I saw it, close in upon us!

One mast was broken short off, six or eight feet from the deck, and lay over the side, entangled in a maze of sail and rigging; and all that ruin, as the ship rolled and beat—which she did without a moment's pause, and with a violence quite inconceivable—beat the side as if it would stave it in. Some efforts were even then being made to cut this portion of the wreck away; for as the ship, which was broadside on, turned towards us in her rolling, I plainly descried her people at work with axes, especially one active figure, with long curling hair, conspicuous among the rest. But a great cry, which was audible even above the wind and water, rose from the shore at this moment: the sea, sweeping over the rolling wreck, made a clean breach, and carried men, spars, casks, planks, bulwarks, heaps of such toys, into the boiling surge.

The second mast was yet standing, with the rags of a rent sail, and a wild confusion of broken cordage, flapping to and fro. The ship had struck once, the same boatman hoarsely said in my ear, and then lifted in and struck again. I understood him to add that she was parting amidships, and I could readily suppose so, for the rolling and beating were too tremendous for any human work to suffer long. As he spoke, there was another great cry of pity from the beach: four men arose with the wreck out of the deep, clinging to the rigging of the remaining mast; uppermost, the active figure with the curling hair.

There was a bell on board; and as the ship rolled and dashed, like a desperate creature driven mad, now showing us the whole sweep of her deck, as she turned on her beam ends towards the shore, now nothing but her keel, as she sprung wildly over and turned towards the sea, the bell rang; and its sound, the knell of those unhappy men, was borne towards us on the wind. Again we lost her, and again she rose. Two men were gone. The agony on shore increased. Men groaned and clasped their hands; women shrieked, and turned away their faces. Some ran wildly up and down along the beach, crying for help where no help could be. I found myself one of these, frantically imploring a knot of sailors whom I knew, not to let those two lost creatures perish before our eyes.

They were making out to me, in an agitated way, that the lifeboat had been bravely manned an hour ago, and could do nothing; and that as no man would be so desperate as to attempt to wade off with a rope, and establish a communication with the shore, there was nothing left to try; when I noticed that some new sensation moved the people on the beach, and saw them part, and Ham come breaking through them to the front.

I ran to him, as well as I know, to repeat my appeal for help. But distracted though I was by a sight so new to me and terrible, the determination in his face, and his look out to sea, awoke me to a knowledge of his danger. I held him back with both arms, and implored the men with whom I had been speaking not to listen to him, not to do murder, not to let him stir from off that sand.

Another cry arose from the shore; and, looking towards the wreck, we saw the cruel sail, with blow on blow, beat off the lower of the two men, and fly up in triumph round the active figure left alone upon the mast.

Against such a sight, and against such determination as that of the calmly desperate man who was already accustomed to lead half the people present, I might as hopefully have intreated the wind. "Mas'r Davy," he said cheerily, grasping me by both hands, "if my time is come, 'tis come. If 't an't, I'll bide it. Lord above bless you, and bless all! Mates, make me ready! I'm a-going off!"

I was swept away, but not unkindly, to some distance, where the people around me made me stay; urging, as I confusedly perceived, that he was bent on going, with help or without, and that I should endanger the precautions for his safety by troubling those with whom they rested. I don't know what I answered, or what they rejoined, but I saw hurry on the beach, and men running with ropes from a capstan that was there, and penetrating into a circle of figures that hid him from me. Then I saw him standing alone, in a seaman's frock and trousers, a rope in his hand or slung to his wrist, another round his body; and several of the best men holding, at a little distance, to the latter, which he laid out himself, slack upon the shore, at his feet.

The wreck, even to my unpracticed eye, was breaking up. I saw that she was parting in the middle, and that the life of the solitary man upon the mast hung by a thread. Still he clung to it.

Ham watched the sea, standing alone, with the silence of suspended breath behind him, and the storm before, until there was a great retiring wave, when, with a backward glance at those who held the rope, which was made fast round his body, he dashed in after it, and in a moment was buffeting with the water—rising with the hills, falling with valleys, lost beneath the foam; then drawn again to land. They hauled in hastily.

He was hurt. I saw blood on his face from where I stood; but he took no thought of that. He seemed hurriedly to give them some directions for leaving him more free, or so I judged from the motion of his arm—and was gone, as before.

And now he made for the wreck—rising with the hills, falling with the valleys, lost beneath the rugged foam, borne in towards the shore, borne on towards the ship, striving hard and valiantly. The distance was nothing, but the power of the sea and wind made the strife deadly.

At length he neared the wreck. He was so near that with one more of his vigorous strokes he would be clinging to it—when a

high, green, vast hillside of water, moving on shoreward from beyond the ship, he seemed to leap up into it with a mighty bound,
and the ship was gone!

Some eddying fragments I saw in the sea, as if a mere cask had
been broken, in running to the spot where they were hauling in.
Consternation was in every face. They drew him to my very feet—
insensible, dead. He was carried to the nearest house; and, no one
preventing me now, I remained near him, busy, while every means
of restoration was tried; but he had been beaten to death by the
great wave, and his generous heart was stilled forever.

●

THE LAST FIGHT IN THE COLOSSEUM

Adapted from a retelling
by Charlotte Yonge

"Public sentiment" is always changing, sometimes for better,
sometimes for worse. The good changes often are brought about
through the tireless prodding of a relatively few voices. When the
Roman emperor Honorius closed the last of the infamous gladiator schools in 399, it was largely because of the vigorous writings
and preachings of Christian officials. And then, sometime around
the year 404, public outrage turned against the barbarous sport
following the remarkable incident described below. Here is a dramatic example of how even one determined person can help the
popular culture take a step forward.

The grandest and most renowned of all ancient amphitheaters
is the Colosseum, built by Vespasian and his son Titus in a valley
surrounded by the seven hills of Rome. The walls are so solid, and
so admirably put together, that still, after so many centuries, it
remains one of the greatest Roman wonders. Five acres of ground
were inclosed within the oval of its outer wall; altogether, when
full, the huge building held no fewer than 50,000 spectators!

Here the Romans came to see their famous games. When the
emperor had seated himself and given the signal, the sports began.

Sometimes a dancing elephant would begin the entertainment. Or a lion would come forth with a jeweled crown on his head, a diamond necklace around his neck, his mane plaited with gold, and his claws gilded, to play a hundred gentle antics with a little hare that danced fearlessly within his grasp.

Sometimes water was let into the arena, and then a ship sailed in and sent a crowd of strange animals swimming in all directions. Sometimes the ground opened, and trees came growing up through it, as if by magic, bearing golden fruit.

But these were only the opening spectacles, for the Colosseum had not been built for such harmless trifles. The fierce Romans wanted to be excited and to feel themselves strongly stirred. Soon the doors of the pits and dens around the arena were thrown open, and absolutely savage beasts were let loose upon one another— rhinoceroses and tigers, bulls and lions, leopards and wild boars— while the people watched with ferocious curiosity to see the various kinds of attack and defense, their ears at the same time being delighted, instead of horror-struck, by the roars and howls of the noble creatures whose courage was so misused.

Wild beasts tearing each other to pieces might, one would think, satisfy any taste for horror. But the spectators needed even nobler game to be set before their favorite monsters. Men were brought forward to confront them. Some of these were, at first, in full armor, and fought hard, generally with success. Or hunters came, almost unarmed, and gained the victory by swiftness and dexterity, throwing a piece of cloth over a lion's head, or disconcerting him by putting their fist down his throat. But it was not only skill, but death, that the Romans loved to see, and condemned criminals and deserters were reserved to feast the lions, and to entertain the populace with their various kinds of death. Among those condemned was many a Christian martyr, who witnessed a good confession before the savage-eyed multitude around the arena, and "met the lion's gory mane" with a calm resolution that the lookers-on could not understand. To see a Christian die with upward gaze was the most strange and unaccountable sight the Coliseum could offer and it was therefore the choicest, and reserved for the last of the spectacles in which the brute creation had a part.

The carcasses were dragged off with hooks, the bloodstained sand was covered with a fresh green layer, perfume was wafted in stronger clouds, and a procession come forward—tall, well-made men, in the prime of their strength. Some carried a sword and a lasso, others a trident and a net; some were in light armor, others in the full, heavy equipment of a soldier; some on horseback, some in chariots, some on foot. They marched in, made their obeisance to the emperor, and with one voice their greeting sounded through the building: "Hail, Caesar. Those about to die salute thee!" They were the gladiators—the swordsmen trained to fight to the death to amuse the populace.

Fights of all sorts took place—the light-armed soldier and the netsman—the lasso and the javelin—the two heavy-armed warriors —all combinations of single combat, and sometimes a general melee. When a gladiator wounded his adversary, he shouted to the spectators, "He has it!" and looked up to know whether he should kill or spare. When the people held down their thumbs, the conquered was left to recover, if he could; if they turned them up, he was to die; and if he showed any reluctance to present his throat for the deathblow, there was a scornful shout, "Receive the steel!"

Christianity, however, worked its way upward, and at last was professed by the emperor on his throne. Persecution came to an end, and no more martyrs fed the beasts in the Coliseum. The Christian emperors endeavored to prevent any more shows where cruelty and death formed the chief interest, and no truly religious person could endure the spectacle. But custom and love of excitement prevailed even against the emperor. They went on for fully a hundred years after Rome had, in name, become a Christian city.

Meantime the enemies of Rome were coming nearer and nearer. Alaric, the great chief of the Goths, led his forces into Italy, and threatened the city itself. Honorius, the emperor, was a cowardly, almost idiotic, boy, but his brave general, Stilicho, assembled his forces, met the Goths, and gave them a complete defeat, on Easter day of the year 403. He pursued them to the mountains, and for that time saved Rome.

In the joy of victory, the Roman Senate invited the conqueror and his ward Honorius to enter the city in triumph, at the opening of the new year, with the white steeds, purple robes, and vermilion cheeks with which, of old, victorious generals were welcomed at Rome. The churches were visited instead of the Temple of Jupiter, and there was no murder of the captives. But Roman bloodthirstiness was not yet allayed, and, after the procession had been completed, the Coliseum shows commenced, innocently at first, with races on foot, on horseback, and in chariots. Then followed a grand hunt of beasts turned loose in the arena, and next a sword dance. But after the sword dance came the arraying of swordsmen, with no blunted weapons, but with sharp spears and swords—a gladiator combat in full earnest. The people, enchanted, applauded with shouts of ecstasy this gratification of their savage tastes.

Suddenly, however, there was an interruption. A rude, roughly robed man, bareheaded and barefooted, had sprung into the arena, and, waving back the gladiators, began to call aloud upon the people to cease from the shedding of innocent blood, and not to requite God's mercy, in turning away the sword of the enemy, by encouraging murder. Shouts, howls, cries, broke in upon his words. This was no place for preachings—the old customs of Rome should be observed—"Back, old man!"—"On, gladiators!"

The gladiators thrust aside the meddler, and rushed to the attack. He still stood between, holding them apart, striving in vain to be heard. "Sedition! sedition!"—"Down with him!"—was the cry, and the prefect in authority himself added his voice. The gladiators, enraged at interference with their vocation, cut him down. Stones, or whatever came to hand, rained upon him from the furious people, and he perished in the midst of the arena! He lay dead.

And then the people began to reflect upon what had been done.

His dress showed that he was one of the hermits who had vowed themselves to a life of prayer and self-denial, and who were greatly reverenced, even by the most thoughtless. The few who had previously seen him told that he had come from the wilds of Asia on a pilgrimage, to visit the shrines and keep his Christmas at Rome. They knew that he was a holy man—no more. But his spirit had been stirred by the sight of thousands flocking to see men slaughter one another and in his simple-hearted zeal he had resolved to stop the cruelty, or die.

He had died, but not in vain. His work was done. The shock of such a death before their eyes turned the hearts of the people; they saw the wickedness and cruelty to which they had blindly surrendered themselves. And since the day when the hermit died in the Coliseum, there has never been another fight of gladiators. The custom was utterly abolished; and one habitual crime at least was wiped from the earth by the self-devotion of one humble, obscure, and nameless man.

GRIEF

Anton Chekhov

This story shows how very hard it is to suffer alone. True compassion joins in another's suffering to mitigate it.

It is twilight. A thick wet snow is slowly twirling around the newly lighted streetlamps, and lying in soft thin layers on the roofs, the horses' backs, people's shoulders and hats. The cab driver, Iona Potapov, is quite white, and looks like a phantom. He is bent double as far as a human body can bend double; he is seated on his box, and never makes a move. If a whole snowdrift fell on him, it seems as if he would not find it necessary to shake it off. His little horse is also quite white, and remains motionless. Its immobility, its angularity, and its straight wooden-looking legs, even close by give it the appearance of a gingerbread horse worth a kopeck. It is, no doubt, plunged in deep thought. If you were snatched from the plow, from your usual gray surroundings, and were thrown into this slough full of monstrous lights, unceasing noise and hurrying people, you too would find it difficult not to think.

Iona and his little horse have not moved from their place for a long while. They left their yard before dinner, and, up to now, have not had a single fare. The evening mist is descending over the town, the white lights of the lamps are replacing brighter rays, and the hubbub of the street is getting louder. "Cabby, for Viborg way!" suddenly hears Iona. "Cabby!"

Iona jumps, and through his snow-covered eyelashes, sees an officer in a greatcoat, with his hood over his head.

"Viborg way!" the officer repeats. "Are you asleep? Viborg way!"

With a nod of assent Iona picks up the reins, in consequence of which layers of snow slip off the horse's back and neck. The officer seats himself in the sleigh, the cabdriver smacks his lips to encourage his horse, stretches out his neck like a swan, sits up, and, more from habit than necessity, brandishes his whip. The little horse also stretches his neck, bends his wooden-looking legs, and makes a move undecidedly.

"What are you doing, werewolf!" is the exclamation Iona hears, from the dark mass moving to and fro as soon as they started.

"Where the devil are you going! To the r-r-right!"

"You do not know how to drive. Keep to the right!" calls the officer angrily.

A coachman from a private carriage swears at him. A passerby, who has run across the road and rubbed his shoulder against the horse's nose, looks at him furiously as he sweeps the snow from his sleeve. Iona shifts about on his seat as if he were on needles, moves his elbows as if he were trying to keep his equilibrium, and gapes about like someone suffocating, and who does not understand where he is or why he is there.

"What scoundrels they all are!" jokes the officer. "One would think they had all entered into an agreement to jostle you or fall under your horse."

Iona looks round at the officer, and moves his lips. He evidently wants to say something, but the only sound that issues is a snuffle.

"What?" asks the officer.

Iona twists his mouth into a smile, and with an effort says hoarsely:

"My son, sir, died this week."

"Hm! What did he die of?"

Iona turns with his whole body toward his fare, and says:

"And who knows! They say high fever. He was three days in hospital, and then died. . . . God's will be done."

"Turn round! The devil!" sounded from the darkness.

"Have you popped off, old doggie, eh? Use your eyes!"

"Go on, go on," said the officer, "otherwise we shall not get there by tomorrow. Hurry up a bit!"

The cab driver again stretches his neck, sits up, and, with a bad grace, brandishes his whip. Several times again he turns to look at his fare, but the latter had closed his eyes, and apparently is not disposed to listen. Having deposited the officer in the Viborg, he stops by the tavern, doubles himself up on his seat, and again remains motionless, while the snow once more begins to cover him and his horse. An hour, and another. . . . Then, along the foot path, with a squeak of galoshes, and quarreling, come three young men, two of them tall and lanky, the third one short and humpbacked.

"Cabby, to the Police Bridge!" in a cracked voice calls the humpback. "The three of us for twenty kopecks."

Iona picks up his reins, and clucks to his horse. Twenty kopecks is not a fair price, but he does not mind if it is a ruble or five kopecks —to him it is all the same now, so long as they are wayfarers. The young men, jostling each other and using bad language, approach the sleigh, and all three at once try to get on to the seat. Then begins a discussion about which two shall sit and who shall be the one to stand. After wrangling, abusing each other, and much petulance, it is at last decided that the humpback should stand, as he is the smallest.

"Now then, hurry up!" says the humpback in a twanging voice, as he takes his place, and breathes down Iona's neck. "Here, mate, what a cap you have got, there is not a worse one to be found in all Petersburg! . . ."

"Hi, hi, hi, hi," giggles Iona. "Such a. . . ."

"Now you, 'such a,' hurry up. Are you going the whole way at this pace? Are you? . . . Do you want it in the neck?"

"My head feels like bursting," says one of the lanky ones. "Last night at the Donkmasovs, Vaska and I drank the whole of four bottles of cognac."

"I don't understand what you lie for," said the other lanky one angrily. "You lie like a brute."

"God strike me, it's the truth!"

"It's as much a truth as that a louse coughs!"

"Hi, hi," grins Iona, "what merry young gentlemen!"

"Pshaw, go to the devil!" indignantly says the humpback.

"Are you going to get on or not, you old pest? Is that the way to drive? Use the whip a bit! Go on, devil, go on, give it to him!"

Iona feels at his back the little man wriggling, and the tremble in his voice. He listens to the insults hurled at him, sees the people; and little by little the feeling of loneliness leaves him. The humpback goes on swearing until he gets mixed up in some elaborate six-foot oath, or chokes with coughing. The lankies begin to talk about a certain Nadejda Petrovna. Iona looks round at them several times; he waits for a temporary silence, then, turning round again, he murmurs:

"My son . . . died this week."

"We must all die," sighs the humpback, wiping his lips after an attack of coughing. "Now, hurry up, hurry up! Gentlemen, I really cannot go any farther like this! When will he get us there?"

"Well, just you stimulate him a little in the neck!"

"You old pest, do you hear, I'll bone your neck for you! If one treated the like of you with ceremony one would have to go on foot! Do you hear, old serpent! Or do you not care a spit?"

Iona hears rather than feels the blows they deal him.

"Hi, hi," he laughs. "They are merry young gentlemen, God bless 'em!"

"Cabby, are you married?" asks a lanky one.

"I? Hi, hi, merry young gentlemen! Now I have only a wife: the moist ground. . . . Hi, ho, ho . . . that is to say, the grave! My son has died, and I am alive. . . . A wonderful thing, death mistook the door . . . instead of coming to me, it went to my son. . . ."

Iona turns round to tell them how his son died, but at this moment the humpback, giving a little sigh, announces that, thank God, they have at last reached their destination. Iona watches them disappear through the dark entrance. Once more he is alone, and again surrounded by silence. . . . His grief, which had abated for a short while, returns and rends his heart with greater force. With an anxious and a hurried look, he searches among the crowds passing on either side of the street to find if there is just one person who will listen to him. But the crowds hurry by without noticing him or his trouble. Yet it is such an immense, illimitable grief. Should his heart break and the grief pour out, it would flow over the whole earth it seems, and yet, no one sees it. It has managed to conceal itself in such an insignificant shell that no one can see it even by day and with a light.

Iona sees a hall porter with some sacking and decides to talk to him.

"Friend, what sort of time is it?" he asks.

"Past nine. What are you standing here for? Move on."

Iona moves on a few steps, doubles himself up, and abandons himself to his grief. He sees it is useless to turn to people for help. In less than five minutes he straightens himself, holds up his head as if he felt some sharp pain, and gives a tug at the reins. He can bear it no longer. "The stables," he thinks, and the little horse, as if he understood, starts off at a trot.

About an hour and a half later Iona is seated by a large dirty stove. Around the stove, on the floor, on the benches, people are snoring. The air is thick and suffocatingly hot. Iona looks at the sleepers, scratches himself, and regrets having returned so early.

"I have not even earned my fodder," he thinks. "That's what's my trouble. A man who knows his job, who has had enough to eat, and his horse too, can always sleep peacefully."

A young cab driver in one of the corners half gets up, grunts sleepily, and stretches toward a bucket of water.

"Do you want a drink?" Iona asks him.

"Don't I want a drink!"

"That's so? Your good health! But listen, mate—you know, my son is dead. . . . Did you hear? This week, in hospital. . . . It's a long story."

Iona looks to see what effect his words have, but sees none— the young man has hidden his face, and is fast asleep again. The old man sighs, and scratches his head. Just as much as the young one wanted to drink, the old man wanted to talk. It will soon be a week since his son died, and he has not been able to speak about it properly to anyone. One must tell it slowly and carefully; how his son fell ill, how he suffered, what he said before he died, how he died. One must describe every detail of the funeral, and the journey to the hospital to fetch his son's clothes. His daughter Anissia re- mained in the village—one must talk about her too. Was it nothing he had to tell? Surely the listener would gasp and sigh, and sympa- thize with him?

"I'll go and look at my horse," thinks Iona. "There's always time to sleep. No fear of that!"

He puts on his coat, and goes to the stables to his horse. He thinks of the corn, the hay, the weather. When he is alone, he dare not think of his son. He could speak about him to anyone, but to think of him, and picture him to himself, is unbearably painful.

"Are you tucking in?" Iona asks his horse, looking at his bright eyes. "Go on, tuck in, though we've not earned our corn, we can eat hay. Yes! I am too old to drive—my son could have, not I. He was a first-rate cab driver. If only he had lived!"

Iona is silent for a moment, then continues:

"That's how it is, my old horse. There's no more Kuzma Io- nitch. He has left us to live, and he went off. Now let's say, you had a foal, you were that foal's mother, and suddenly, let's say, that foal went and left you to live after him. It would be sad, wouldn't it?"

The little horse munches, listens, and breathes over his mas- ter's hand. . . .

Iona's feelings are too much for him, and he tells the little horse the whole story.

•

END OF THE TIGER

John D. MacDonald

This is a beautiful "tough love" story. Sometimes the best way to
help people find the right direction is to let them see for themselves just how rough and wrong the path they're taking is going
to be.

I saw Tiger Shaw the other day. He didn't recognize me.
There's no reason why he should. When he was going with my big
sister, Christine, I was just one of the swarm of little brothers and
sisters who knew enough not to get too close to him or you'd get a
Dutch rub with those big knuckles.

I saw him in a narrow street in town, unloading a truck into a
warehouse, tattoos on his big, meaty arms, his belly grown big as a
sack of cement, all of him looking sour and surly and dispirited. It
seemed too bad, because he was a beautiful young man back when
he was one of the best athletes they ever had in the high school. He
lasted a year in college before he got into a scandal about throwing
games, and they let him go into the army.

Christine and Tiger were a pair of beautiful people that summer.

There were seven of us children in all. Now there are six, and
when we all get together with all our wives and husbands and kids,
we think of Bunny and are saddened, because he was the littlest
one of all and dear to us. The times of getting together are rare
because we're scattered now. Christine's husband teaches at the
University of Toronto. Her eldest is twelve. All the marriages are
pretty good. Mine is fine.

And when we get together, one of the things we always do is
to tell grandfather stories. There are a lot of them. He raised us—
he and our mother. He was a big, wild, random old man, very
partial to dramatic scenes. At least half of the things he did made
absolutely no sense to us as children. He never explained. He just
lived according to his unpredictable instincts. But it is strange how,
as time goes by, we begin to see how some of the nonsense things
made sense.

Until the day he died, I don't think we all ever really forgave
him about the goose. Yesterday, when I saw Tiger Shaw, I wished

that my grandfather had at least tried to explain about Gretchen. That was the name of the goose.

That May, the summer Christine and Tiger were in love, Nan, the youngest sister, bought the baby goose from a farm up the road for ninety cents saved out of her allowance. For about three days it belonged to her, and then it belonged to all of us and owned the pond out in the side yard. We kids were all her fellow geese, and she plodded along behind us, making small nervous sounds about all the dangers the world holds for an unwary goose. She was blazing white and took excellent care of herself with that clever serrated bill. Anybody who rowed the skiff around the pond had Gretchen aboard before they could even launch it, standing in the bow, honking her pleasure.

By July, Gretchen was of pretty good size, and she was enchanted with Christine's long golden hair. Christine would sit, and Gretchen would preen that hair, never tugging or hurting, making little chortling sounds in her throat. We all learned Gretchen's likes and dislikes. She could be patted a little but not very much. She was nervous about night, ignored cats, despised dogs, and would bow very low in ceremonious oriental greeting when anyone approached.

Tiger was at our place a lot that summer. He was a hero, of course, huge and golden. But we quickly learned wariness. He was quick and he knew the places that hurt. And he would roar with laughter, and we, out of pride, would laugh with him, though eyes might be stinging.

I remember those long summer dusks after the evening meal before the littlest ones had to be shooed off to bed. We'd all be out in the side yard, and on the side porch, and Gretchen would come paddling up across the yard from the pond giving oriental greetings.

One of the grandfather stories we don't tell is about Tiger and the goose.

Gretchen was wary of Tiger Shaw, and it seemed to be a plausible instinct. As I remember that evening, Tiger was going to take Christine to some sort of barn dance just over the county line. Christine had on a blue dress with little white flowers. Her hair was brushed to a soft gleam. In the country fashion, Tiger had to stay around a little time before taking her away into the gathering dusk, going down the road with her in that car of his which made a snarling sound that faded into the distance, sounding as it died away like a bee buzzing nearby.

We kids were fooling around in the yard. Sheila was acting wistful. She was near to her dating time, when the young men would be coming for her. Our grandfather was on the porch in the rocker, and off in the east, by the far hills, there was darkness and a pink inaudible pulse of lightning.

Tiger and Christine were sitting a few feet apart, and Gretchen plodded up behind them, behind the low bench, and with a big whack of her white wings made an awkward hop up onto the bench, leaned the adoring curve of her neck toward Christine, and began with little chucklings, to preen the fine strands of the golden hair.

We were all watching it, thinking uneasily that Gretchen was uncommonly close to Tiger Shaw. He was very quick for such a big muscly person, quick without looking quick. And he was seldom without a cud of gum in his jaws. This is one of the memories of him, the knots working at the jaw corners and the smell of spearmint.

He reached and took Gretchen high on the neck with one hand, slipped the gum out of his mouth with the other, and when she opened her bill to yawp her protest, he thumbled the wad of gum up into the hollow of the top of her beak. He released her at once and began to roar with laughter.

We all laughed. It was so ridiculous. Gretchen closed her bill and it stuck. She looked astonished. She began to shake her head the way you shake your hand to shake moisture from your fingertips. She shook herself dizzy and fell sprawling off the bench. Then she began to run in circles in the yard, wings laboring, trying somehow to run away from this terrible impasse. Our nervous laughter turned shrill, climbing toward the edge of hysteria.

Above it all, above Tiger's laughter and our shrillness, I heard the grandfather laugh, the drumdeepbellowing of him as he came down off the porch. Soon, in terror Gretchen began driving that precious bill against things, against posts and stones, against places where the ground was hard. Then we were all howling in a shared panic, in heartbreak and concern. Because we all knew what that bill was to her—knife and fork, comb and brush, weapon, tool, sieve, bug-catcher.

So we tried to run to catch her, but my grandfather swept us back with his huge arms, laughing, bellowing at us that it was funny. I hated him then, I hated the three of them—my grandfather, Tiger, and Christine.

Because, you see, Christine was laughing, too. She stood up, hunched over, laughing. Grandfather and Tiger beat each other on the back and roared with delight at the deranged, scrabbling, terrorized creature, telling each other how funny it was. Christine moved slowly toward the steps, shrieking laughter, and as she hobbled up the steps it changed to a keening, wailing sound, the tears running down her face.

My grandfather's roaring laughter stopped abruptly as the screen door banged behind her, and he turned quickly away from the still hilarious Tiger.

Following grandfather's orders, we caught Gretchen, wrapped her firmly in burlap, and took her to the porch. Grandfather gently pried the bruised bill open and, holding Gretchen's head against his thigh, skillfully worked the sticky mass out of the concavity. Tiger stood watching, chuckling reminiscently, while we hiccuped in the aftermath of tears. When she was as clean as he could get her, my grandfather put her down and took the sacking off her. She scrambled to her feet and went headlong for the safety of her beloved pond, half running, half flying.

Tiger said it was time to go and sent Sheila in to get Christine. Sheila came out in a few moments and said Christine had a headache and couldn't go. Tiger hung around for a little while, acting sort of ugly. And then he went off, and the snarling drone of his car faded quickly. We went down to the pond. Gretchen was soiled and she had some broken feathers, but she looked unapproachably white there in the blue dusk, floating out in the middle, making no sound for us.

There were no more boat rides, no more preening the golden hair of the big sister, no more chuckling sound behind us when we walked across the yard, no more visits in the dusk. We told each other that if grandfather had let us help her before she became too terrified, it might have been all right, and we might have kept her trust.

We never quite forgave grandfather for that. Maybe he wasn't interested in our kind of forgiveness. He was a wild and random old man, and sometimes he made no sense at all. But when I saw Tiger the other day, I suddenly realized that if we'd helped Gretchen quickly, then it might have been just one of Tiger's little jokes, and Christine would have gone off with him that night and other nights, and the world might be quite different for her now. By delaying us, grandfather showed her Tiger's kind of laughter, of which there is often too much in the world.

But he never explained.

•

No Greater Love

John W. Mansur

This is a remarkable story of sacrifice born of deep friendship. The author says, "I heard this story when I was in Vietnam, and it was told to me as fact. I have no way of knowing for sure that it is true, but I do know that stranger things have happened in war."

Whatever their planned target, the mortar rounds landed in an orphanage run by a missionary group in the small Vietnamese village. The missionaries and one or two children were killed outright, and several more children were wounded, including one young girl, about eight years old.

People from the village requested medical help from a neighboring town that had radio contact with the American forces. Finally, an American Navy doctor and nurse arrived in a jeep with only their medical kits. They established that the girl was the most critically injured. Without quick action, she would die of shock and loss of blood.

A transfusion was imperative, and a donor with a matching blood type was required. A quick test showed that neither American had the correct type, but several of the uninjured orphans did.

The doctor spoke some pidgin Vietnamese, and the nurse a smattering of high school French. Using that combination, together with much impromptu sign language, they tried to explain to their young, frightened audience that unless they could replace some of the girl's lost blood, she would certainly die. Then they asked if anyone would be willing to give blood to help.

Their request was met with wide-eyed silence. After several long moments, a small hand slowly and waveringly went up, dropped back down, and then went up again.

"Oh, thank you," the nurse said in French. "What is your name?"

"Heng," came the reply.

Heng was quickly laid on a pallet, his arm swabbed with alcohol, and a needle inserted in his vein. Through this ordeal Heng lay stiff and silent.

After a moment, he let out a shuddering sob, quickly covering his face with his free hand.

"Is it hurting, Heng?" the doctor asked. Heng shook his head, but after a few moments another sob escaped, and once more he tried to cover up his crying. Again the doctor asked him if the needle hurt, and again Heng shook his head.

But now his occasional sobs gave way to a steady, silent crying, his eyes screwed tightly shut, his fist in his mouth to stifle his sobs.

The medical team was concerned. Something was obviously very wrong. At this point, a Vietnamese nurse arrived to help. Seeing the little one's distress, she spoke to him rapidly in Vietnamese, listened to his reply and answered him in a soothing voice.

After a moment, the patient stopped crying and looked questioningly at the Vietnamese nurse. When she nodded, a look of great relief spread over his face.

Glancing up, the nurse said quietly to the Americans, "He thought he was dying. He misunderstood you. He thought you had asked him to give all his blood so the little girl could live."

"But why would he be willing to do that?" asked the Navy nurse.

The Vietnamese nurse repeated the question to the little boy, who answered simply, "She's my friend."

Greater love has no man than this, that he lay down his life for a friend.

●

A PROBLEM

Anton Chekhov

This story carries a couple of important warnings about compassion. First, sometimes people are not at all grateful for help they receive. Second, true compassion does not mean giving people whatever they want. Sometimes it's easier to tell someone "Take this" or "It's O.K." in order to make yourself feel better or protect your own image. But that can be the kind of help that often does more harm than good.

The strictest measures were taken that the Uskovs' family secret might not leak out and become generally known. Half of the servants were sent off to the theatre or the circus. The other half were sitting in the kitchen and not allowed to leave it. Orders were given that no one was to be admitted. The wife of the Colonel, her sister, and the governess, though they had been initiated into the secret, kept up a pretense of knowing nothing; they sat in the dining room and did not show themselves in the drawing room or the hall.

Sasha Uskov, the young man of twenty-five who was the cause of all the commotion, had arrived some time before, and by the advice of kindhearted Ivan Markovitch, his uncle, who was taking his part, he sat meekly in the hall by the door leading to the study, and prepared himself to make an open, candid explanation.

The other side of the door, in the study, a family council was being held. The subject under discussion was an exceedingly disagreeable and delicate one. Sasha Uskov had cashed at one of the banks a false promissory note, and it had become due for payment three days before, and now his two paternal uncles and Ivan Markovitch, the brother of his dead mother, were deciding the question whether they should pay the money and save the family honor, or wash their hands of it and leave the case to go for trial.

To outsiders who have no personal interest in the matter such questions seem simple; for those who are so unfortunate as to have to decide them in earnest they are extremely difficult. The uncles had been talking for a long time, but the problem seemed no nearer decision.

"My friends!" said the uncle who was a colonel, and there was a note of exhaustion and bitterness in his voice. "Who says that family honor is a mere convention? I don't say that at all. I am only warning you against a false view. I am pointing out the possibility of an unpardonable mistake. How can you fail to see it? I am not speaking Chinese—I am speaking Russian!"

"My dear fellow, we do understand," Ivan Markovitch protested mildly.

"How can you understand if you say that I don't believe in family honor? I repeat once more: famil-y ho-nor fal-sely un-der-stood is a prejudice! Falsely understood! That's what I say: whatever may be the motives for screening a scoundrel, whoever he may be, and helping him to escape punishment, it is contrary to law and unworthy of a gentleman. It's not saving the family honor; it's civic cowardice! Take the army, for instance. . . . The honor of the army is more precious to us than any other honor, yet we don't screen our guilty members, but condemn them. And does the honor of the army suffer in consequence? Quite the opposite!"

The other paternal uncle, an official in the Treasury, a taciturn, dull-witted, and rheumatic man, sat silent, or spoke only of the fact that the Uskovs' name would get into the newspapers if the case went for trial. His opinion was that the case ought to be hushed up from the first and not become public property; but, apart from publicity in the newspapers, he advanced no other argument in support of this opinion.

The maternal uncle, kindhearted Ivan Markovitch, spoke smoothly, softly, and with a tremor in his voice. He began with saying that youth has its rights and its peculiar temptations. Which of us has not been young, and who has not been led astray? To say nothing of ordinary mortals, even great men have not escaped errors and mistakes in their youth. Take, for instance, the biography of great writers. Did not every one of them gamble, drink, and draw down upon himself the anger of right-thinking people in his young days? If Sasha's error bordered upon crime, they must remember that Sasha had received practically no education; he had been expelled from the high school in the fifth class; he had lost his parents in early childhood, and so had been left at the tenderest age without guidance and good, benevolent influences. He was nervous, excitable, had no firm ground under his feet, and, above all, he had been unlucky. Even if he were guilty, anyway he deserved indulgence and the sympathy of all compassionate souls. He ought, of course, to be punished, but he was punished as it was by his conscience and the agonies he was enduring now while awaiting the sentence of his relations. The comparison with the army made by the Colonel was delightful, and did credit to his lofty intelligence. His appeal to their feeling of public duty spoke for the chivalry of his soul, but they must not forget that in each individual the citizen is closely linked with the Christian. . . .

"Shall we be false to civic duty," Ivan Markovitch exclaimed passionately, "if instead of punishing an erring boy we hold out to him a helping hand?"

Ivan Markovitch talked further of family honor. He had not the honor to belong to the Uskov family himself, but he knew their distinguished family went back to the thirteenth century. He did not forget for a minute, either, that his precious, beloved sister had been the wife of one of the representatives of that name. In short, the family was dear to him for many reasons, and he refused to admit the idea that, for the sake of a paltry fifteen hundred rubles, a blot should be cast on the escutcheon that was beyond all price.

If all the motives he had brought forward were not sufficiently convincing, he, Ivan Markovitch, in conclusion, begged his listeners to ask themselves what was meant by crime? Crime is an immoral act founded upon ill will. But is the will of man free? Philosophy has not yet given a positive answer to that question. Different views were held by the learned. The latest school of Lombroso, for instance, denies the freedom of the will, and considers every crime as the product of the purely anatomical peculiarities of the individual.

"Ivan Markovitch," said the Colonel, in a voice of entreaty, "we are talking seriously about an important matter, and you bring in Lombroso, you clever fellow. Think a little, what are you saying all this for? Can you imagine that all your thunderings and rhetoric will furnish an answer to the question?"

Sasha Uskov sat at the door and listened. He felt neither terror, shame, nor depression, but only weariness and inward emptiness. It seemed to him that it made absolutely no difference to him whether they forgave him or not. He had come here to hear his sentence and to explain himself simply because kindhearted Ivan Markovitch had begged him to do so. He was not afraid of the future. It made no difference to him where he was: here in the hall, in prison, or in Siberia.

"If Siberia, then let it be Siberia, damn it all!"

He was sick of life and found it insufferably hard. He was inextricably involved in debt. He had not a farthing in his pocket. His family had become detestable to him. He would have to part from his friends and his women sooner or later, as they had begun to be too contemptuous of his sponging on them. The future looked black.

Sasha was indifferent, and was only disturbed by one circumstance; the other side of the door they were calling him a scoundrel and a criminal. Every minute he was on the point of jumping up, bursting into the study and shouting in answer to the detestable metallic voice of the Colonel:

"You are lying!"

"Criminal" is a dreadful word—that is what murderers, thieves, robbers are; in fact, wicked and morally hopeless people. And Sasha was very far from being all that. . . . It was true he owed a great deal and did not pay his debts. But debt is not a crime, and it is unusual for a man not to be in debt. The Colonel and Ivan Markovitch were both in debt. . . .

"What have I done wrong besides?" Sasha wondered.

He had discounted a forged note. But all the young men he

knew did the same. Handrikov and Von Burst always forged IOUs from their parents or friends when their allowances were not paid at the regular time, and then when they got their money from home they redeemed them before they became due. Sasha had done the same, but had not redeemed the IOU because he had not got the money which Handrikov had promised to lend him. He was not to blame. It was the fault of circumstances. It was true that the use of another person's signature was considered reprehensible, but, still, it was not a crime but a generally accepted dodge, an ugly formality which injured no one and was quite harmless, for in forging the Colonel's signature Sasha had had no intention of causing anybody damage or loss.

"No, it doesn't mean that I am a criminal ..." thought Sasha. "And it's not in my character to bring myself to commit a crime. I am soft, emotional. . . . When I have the money I help the poor. . . ."

Sasha was musing after this fashion while they went on talking the other side of the door.

"But, my friends, this is endless," the Colonel declared, getting excited. "Suppose we were to forgive him and pay the money. You know he would not give up leading a dissipated life, squandering money, making debts, going to our tailors and ordering suits in our names! Can you guarantee that this will be his last prank? As far as I am concerned, I have no faith whatever in his reforming!"

The official of the Treasury muttered something in reply. After him Ivan Markovitch began talking blandly and suavely again. The Colonel moved his chair impatiently and drowned the other's words with his detestable metallic voice. At last the door opened and Ivan Markovitch came out of the study. There were patches of red on his lean shaven face.

"Come along," he said, taking Sasha by the hand. "Come and speak frankly from your heart. Without pride, my dear boy, humbly and from your heart."

Sasha went into the study. The official of the Treasury was sitting down; the Colonel was standing before the table with one hand in his pocket and one knee on a chair. It was smoky and stifling in the study. Sasha did not look at the official or the Colonel; he felt suddenly ashamed and uncomfortable. He looked uneasily at Ivan Markovitch and muttered:

"I'll pay it . . . I'll give it back. . . ."

"What did you expect when you discounted the IOU?" he heard a metallic voice.

"I . . . Handrikov promised to lend me the money before now."

Sasha could say no more. He went out of the study and sat down again on the chair near the door. He would have been glad to go away altogether at once, but he was choking with hatred and he awfully wanted to remain, to tear the Colonel to pieces, to say something rude to him. He sat trying to think of something violent and effective to say to his hated uncle, and at that moment a woman's figure, shrouded in the twilight, appeared at the drawing-room door. It was the Colonel's wife. She beckoned Sasha to her, and, wringing her hands, said, weeping:

"*Alexandre,* I know you don't like me, but ... listen to me; listen, I beg you.... But, my dear, how can this have happened? Why, it's awful, awful! For goodness' sake, beg them, defend yourself, entreat them."

Sasha looked at her quivering shoulders, at the big tears that were rolling down her cheeks, heard behind his back the hollow, nervous voices of worried and exhausted people, and shrugged his shoulders. He had not in the least expected that his aristocratic relations would raise such a tempest over a paltry fifteen hundred rubles! He could not understand her tears nor the quiver of their voices.

An hour later he heard that the Colonel was getting the best of it; the uncles were finally inclining to let the case go for trial.

"The matter's settled," said the Colonel, sighing. "Enough."

After this decision all the uncles, even the emphatic Colonel, became noticeably depressed. A silence followed.

"Merciful Heavens!" sighed Ivan Markovitch. "My poor sister!"

And he began saying in a subdued voice that most likely his sister, Sasha's mother, was present unseen in the study at that moment. He felt in his soul how the unhappy, saintly woman was weeping, grieving, and begging for her boy. For the sake of her peace beyond the grave, they ought to spare Sasha.

The sound of a muffled sob was heard. Ivan Markovitch was weeping and muttering something which it was impossible to catch through the door. The Colonel got up and paced from corner to corner. The long conversation began over again.

But then the clock in the drawing room struck two. The family council was over. To avoid seeing the person who had moved him to such wrath, the Colonel went from the study, not into the hall, but into the vestibule.... Ivan Markovitch came out into the hall.... He was agitated and rubbing his hands joyfully. His tear-stained eyes looked good-humored and his mouth was twisted into a smile.

"Capital," he said to Sasha. "Thank God! You can go home, my dear, and sleep tranquilly. We have decided to pay the sum, but on condition that you repent and come with me tomorrow into the country and set to work."

A minute later Ivan Markovitch and Sasha in their greatcoats and caps were going down the stairs. The uncle was muttering something edifying. Sasha did not listen, but felt as though some uneasy weight were gradually slipping off his shoulders. They had forgiven him; he was free! A gust of joy sprang up within him and sent a sweet chill to his heart. He longed to breathe, to move swiftly, to live! Glancing at the street lamps and the black sky, he remembered that Von Burst was celebrating his name-day that evening at the "Bear," and again a rush of joy flooded his soul. . . .

"I am going!" he decided.

But then he remembered he had not a farthing, that the companions he was going to would despise him at once for his empty pockets. He must get hold of some money, come what may!

"Uncle, lend me a hundred rubles," he said to Ivan Markovitch.

His uncle, surprised, looked into his face and backed against a lamppost.

"Give it to me," said Sasha, shifting impatiently from one foot to the other and beginning to pant. "Uncle, I entreat you, give me a hundred rubles."

His face worked. He trembled, and seemed on the point of attacking his uncle. . . .

"Won't you?" he kept asking, seeing that his uncle was still amazed and did not understand. "Listen. If you don't, I'll give myself up tomorrow! I won't let you pay the IOU! I'll present another false note tomorrow!"

Petrified, muttering something incoherent in his horror, Ivan Markovitch took a hundred-ruble note out of his pocketbook and gave it to Sasha. The young man took it and walked rapidly away from him. . . .

Taking a sled, Sasha grew calmer, and felt a rush of joy within him again. The "rights of youth" of which kindhearted Ivan Markovitch had spoken at the family council woke up and asserted themselves. Sasha pictured the drinking party before him, and, among the bottles, the women, and his friends, the thought flashed through his mind:

"Now I see that I am a criminal. Yes, I am a criminal."

•

THE TWO GIFTS

Retold by Lilian Gask

This old tale asserts that it is not just the act of helping but the
motive for helping that counts.

A heavy snowstorm was raging, and great soft flakes fell
through the air like feathers shaken from the wings of an innumerable host of angels. By the side of the roadway sat a poor old woman,
her scanty clothing forming but a poor protection from the icy blast
of the wind. She was very hungry, for she had tasted no food that
day, but her faded eyes were calm and patient, telling of an unwa-
vering trust in Providence. Perhaps, she thought, some traveler
might come that way who would have compassion on her, and give
her alms; then she could return to the garret that she called
"home," with bread to eat, and fuel to kindle a fire.

The day drew in, and still she sat and waited. At last a traveler
approached. The thick snow muffled every sound and she was not
aware of his coming until his burly figure loomed before her. Her
plaintive voice made him turn with a start.

"Poor woman," he cried, pausing to look at her very pityingly.
"It is hard for you to be out in such weather as this." Then he
passed on, without giving her anything. His conscience told him
that he ought to have relieved her, but he did not feel inclined to
take off his thick gloves in that bitter cold, and without doing this
he could not have found a coin.

The poor woman was naturally disappointed, but she was
grateful for his kind words. By and by another traveler appeared.
This one was driving in a splendid carriage, warmly wrapped in a

great fur cloak. As he caught sight of the poor creature by the roadside, he felt vaguely touched by the contrast of his own comfort with her misery. Obeying a sudden impulse, with one hand he let down the carriage window and signed to his coachman to stop, and with the other felt in his pocket. The poor woman hurried up to the carriage, a thrill of hope bringing a tinge of color to her pale and withered cheeks.

"How terribly cold it is!" exclaimed the rich man, and as he took his hand from his pocket, and held out a coin to her, he noticed that instead of silver he was about to give her a piece of gold.

"Dear me! That is far too much," he cried, but before he could return it to his pocket, the coin slipped through his fingers, and fell into the snow. A rough blast of wind made his teeth chatter, and pulling up the window in a great hurry, with a little shiver he drew the fur rug around him.

"It certainly was too much," he murmured philosophically, as the carriage rolled on, "but then I am very rich, and can afford to do a generous action now and then."

When his comfortable dinner was over, and he was sitting in front of a blazing fire, he thought once more of the poor old woman.

"It is not nearly so cold as I thought," he remarked as he settled himself more comfortably in his deep armchair. "I certainly gave that old creature too much. However, what's done, is done, and I hope she will make good use of it. I was generous, very generous indeed, and no doubt God will reward me."

Meanwhile the other traveler had also reached his journey's end, and he too had found a blazing fire and a good dinner awaiting him. He could not enjoy it, however, for he was haunted by the remembrance of that bent and shrunken figure in the waste of snow, and felt very remorseful for not having stopped to help her. At last he could bear it no longer.

"Bring another plate," he said, calling the servant to him. "There will be two to dine instead of one. I shall be back soon."

Saying this, he hurried through the darkness to the spot where he had left the old woman. She was still there, feebly searching in the snow.

"What are you looking for?" he asked.

"I am trying to find a piece of money which a gentleman threw me from his carriage window," she told him falteringly, scarcely able to speak from cold and hunger. It was no wonder, he thought, that she had not found it, for her hands were numbed and half-frozen, and she was not only old, but nearly blind.

"I am afraid you will never find it now," he said. "But come with me," he added consolingly. "I will take you to my inn, where there is a bright fire and a good dinner waiting for both of us. You shall be my guest, and I will see that you have a comfortable night's lodging."

The poor woman could scarcely believe her good fortune. Trembling, she prepared to follow her new friend. Noticing that she was lame as well as nearly blind, he took her arm, and with slow and patient steps led her to the hotel.

When the recording angel wrote that night in the Book of Heaven, he made no mention of the piece of gold which the wealthy traveler had given by mistake, for only a worthy motive gains credit in that Book. But amidst the good deeds that had been wrought that day, he gave a foremost place to that of a man who had repented of his hardness, and faced once more the bitter cold that he might share his comforts with a fellow creature so much less fortunate than himself.

•

SAINT CATHERINE AND THE SILVER CRUCIFIX

Born in Sienna, Italy, in 1347 to well-to-do parents, Saint Catherine entered the Dominican sisterhood as a young woman, beginning a lifelong commitment to aiding the needy, nursing the sick, and making peace between different factions of the Catholic church. A patron saint of Italy, she is known as one of the greatest of the Christian mystics.

One early morning long ago, in the Italian town of Sienna, Saint Catherine was walking to mass at the church of Saint Dominic. The steep, narrow streets were still dark, but overhead the rising sun had touched the city's roofs and towers with gold, and Catherine's eyes were turned upward when she felt the touch of a hand at her cloak.

"Please help," a voice whispered, and nothing more.

Catherine turned and saw a man leaning against a wall, so thin and pale he could barely stand.

"What do you need of me?" Catherine asked kindly.

"Help for my journey," the man replied. "My home is far away, over the hills. I came here to work, and I have sent all that I earned home to my family, so my children may have bread. Now I've fallen ill, and I am too weak to start back. I need only a little money to buy something to eat and regain my strength."

"With all my heart, I would help," murmured Catherine, "but I am only a poor member of the Dominican sisterhood, and I have no money of my own to share with you."

She turned to move on, but once more the hand reached out and clasped her cloak.

"Please help me!" the man cried. "I ask for only a little."

Catherine gazed at him sorrowfully. She did not want to ignore his plea. But what could she do? She had already given away all she had. Her father and mother were kind, but she could not ask them to begin giving away their own things to perfect strangers. And there were so many, many more in need besides this one man. . . .

She prayed for help, closing her fingers upon the small silver crucifix she had worn since she was a young girl, the one she so often touched when she turned her thoughts to God. And, suddenly, the answer came to her.

True, it was just a tiny, child's cross, barely as big as a coin. And over the years it had worn thin and smooth in her hands. But it was silver, just the same, and this man could sell it and buy enough food to get him home.

She slipped it into the stranger's hand, and hastened on to church. Although she had just given away the thing she treasured most, her heart knew a gladness, as if she had just received the greatest of gifts.

And as she knelt a few moments later, she saw something wonderful and strange.

It seemed as though she stood in a great room with high, vaulted ceilings, a chamber filled with all sorts of glittering treasures, more beautiful than Catherine had ever imagined in her dreams. And in the midst stood Jesus, holding in his hand the most beautiful thing of all—a cross of gold set with so many gleaming jewels that their glory overwhelmed the eyes.

"Look upon these shining gifts," spoke the Lord. "These are the great and noble deeds done by men for my sake."

Catherine rejoiced at the sight, but a longing came over her heart, and she cried:

"O Lord, I am only one of your poor sisters. I can offer no service that would find a place among these precious gifts."

But she felt as though Jesus smiled upon her and, holding out the golden cross, he asked gently:

"Have you never seen this cross before, Catherine?"

"No, Lord," she answered meekly. "Never have I seen anything so wonderful."

Yet as she fixed her eyes upon it, she was filled with a sudden joy. For there, in the very midst of so many shining treasures of jewels and gold, in the heart of so much splendid light, she found her tiny, worn silver crucifix, the same one she had given away to the desperate man.

And soon the vision departed, but as it faded a voice sounded in her ears: "Inasmuch as ye did it unto one of these My brethren, even these least, ye did it unto Me."

•

SAINT MARTIN AND THE BEGGAR

Adapted from a retelling by Peggy Webling

Born around the year 316 in the Roman province of Pannonia (Hungary), Martin was forced into military service at the age of fifteen by his father, an army officer. It was in about 337 while he was stationed in Amiens, France, that the famous incident described below is said to have occurred. Martin converted to Christianity a short time later and began a long career of serving his God and fellow man, becoming Bishop of Tours and founding the renowned abbey of Marmoutier. Today he is a patron saint of France, and his symbol of a sword cutting a cloak in half is a widely loved reminder of the power of sharing.

It is a bright, frosty morning on a busy street in the old town of Amiens in France, hundreds of years ago. People are trudging to work or bustling to the marketplace. Here and there little crowds gather to talk together, while boys and girls run along, laughing, playing, behaving very much as they do today. A young scholar passes by, looking lost in thought, then a rich lady with a servant at her heels, then a prosperous merchant with his clerk beside him listening meekly to his master's orders.

In a shadow of the city wall, as unheeded as a mound of dust, stands a poor, ragged beggar, shivering with cold, one feeble hand stretched out for alms. The people pass him by, most of them ignoring him altogether, some with a glance of half-contemptuous pity, or even disgust.

His pleading voice is so weak that it fades away. He is utterly despised.

Suddenly there is the ring of horses' hooves on the hard road, and a little band of the Emperor's soldiers canter down the street. They are talking merrily among themselves. Their swords, their big spurs, and the trappings of their steeds glisten in the sunshine. They are leaving for a distant city, and carelessly glance at the people who stand still to watch them ride by, admiring their youth and gallant bearing.

As they pass by the shadow of the city wall, one of the young soldiers in the rear of the troop reins in his horse. His face changes when he notices something.

It is nothing to attract anyone's attention, only a shuddering beggar with outstretched hands and a haggard, starving face. But when Martin sees the other soldiers pass by the poor creature without a glance, he wonders if perhaps this man has been left for him to help.

There is no money in young Martin's purse—he has given it all away in charity or farewell gifts. But he feels he must do something.

Then an idea flashes into his head, suggested by the cold wind that whistles through the air. He loosens the great, warm military cloak hanging from his shoulders and holds it up with one hand. With the other hand he draws his sword, and cuts the cloth right down the middle. Then he leans from the saddle and with a word of sympathy drops one half of the garment over the shoulders of the wretched beggar. Then he sheaths his sword, tosses the rest of the cloak back over his own shoulders, and gallops after his companions.

Some of the other young officers break out in laughter and jests as Martin joins them, with his strip of torn cloak fluttering behind him. But others wish they had thought of doing what he has done.

And that night Martin had a dream in which he saw Jesus in heaven, surrounded by a company of angels. In this vision, the Lord was wearing one half of a cloak, and he showed it to the angels, saying, "See, here is the garment Martin gave to me."

Five

•

MOTHERS AND FATHERS, HUSBANDS AND WIVES

THERE are many obligations in life, but none are more important than the ones we accept when we become husbands and wives, mothers and fathers. In this chapter we find stories illustrating the virtues involved in those parts of life's journey.

In recent history, marriage has devolved from being a sacrament to a contract to a convention to, finally, a convenience. (I am told there is a modern wedding vow that states not "as long as we both shall live," but rather "as long as we both shall *love.*") Of course, some marriages simply will not work. But the enormous number of separations and divorces today suggests that we no longer believe what we say during the ceremony: that marriage is a serious, lifelong commitment made "in the presence of God," a commitment to give to each other as long as both shall live.

As Aristotle long ago pointed out, marriage is in fact a relationship based in no small part on virtues. The most basic of these is responsibility, for marriage is, after all, an arrangement held together by mutual dependence and reciprocal obligations. But successful marriages are about more than fulfilling the conditions of a contract. In good marriages, men and women seek to improve themselves for the sake of their loved one. They offer and draw moral strength, day in and day out, by sharing compassion, courage, honesty, self-discipline, and a host of other virtues. Thus the whole of the union becomes stronger and more wonderful than the sum of the parts. "What greater thing is there for human souls," asked George Eliot, "than to feel that they are joined for life—to strengthen each other in all labor, to rest on each other in all pain, to be one with each other in silent, unspeakable memories at the moment of the last parting?" The stories in this chapter inspire us in all of these endeavors.

For most of us, the obligations of parenthood eventually go hand in hand with those of marriage. No duty is more important than the nurture and protection of children, and if parents do not teach honesty, perseverance, self-discipline, a desire for excellence, and a host of basic skills, it is exceedingly difficult for any of society's institutions to teach those things in the parents' place. The philosopher John Stuart Mill summed up the fundamental responsibilities of adults toward their offspring: "The duties of parents to their children are those which are indissolubly attached to the fact of causing the existence of a human being. The parent owes to society to endeavor to make the child a good and valuable member of it, and owes to the children to provide, so far as depends on him, such education, and such appliances and means, as will enable them to start with a fair chance of achieving by their own exertions a successful life."

In this chapter we find mothers and fathers going about the business of fulfilling those basic obligations, and much more. We see parents putting aside their own wants in order to minister to their children's needs. We watch them resetting their priorities and reshaping their own behavior so that they may set good examples. We witness them devoting time and attention to the task of raising the young, and cherishing every moment. We see them committing acts of self-sacrifice, and literally going to the ends of the earth for the sake of their daughters and sons.

In *The Iliad,* the first of Homer's great epics, there is a moving scene in which the Trojan hero Hector says goodbye to his wife and infant son before leaving the city to battle the Greeks. Taking his boy in his arms, he prays to the gods, asking, "Some day let the Trojans say of him, 'He is better than his father.' " Surely this is the hope of every parent. As best we can, we set before our children the example of our own virtues and our own mistakes, and offer the wisdom learned from both, hoping to make our loved ones at least a little better than we were.

SLEEP BABY, SLEEP

We begin this chapter with lullabies that sum up what it means to be a parent: watching, guarding, guiding, loving.

> Sleep, baby, sleep.
> Thy father guards the sheep;
> Thy mother shakes the dreamland tree,
> Down falls a little dream for thee:
> Sleep, baby, sleep.
>
> Sleep, baby, sleep.
> The large stars are the sheep;
> The little stars are the lambs, I guess;
> And the gentle moon is the shepherdess:
> Sleep, baby, sleep.
>
> Sleep, baby, sleep.
> Our Savior loves His sheep;
> He is the Lamb of God on high,
> Who for our sakes came down to die:
> Sleep, baby, sleep.

●

ALL THE WORLD IS SLEEPING

> Go to sleep upon my breast,
> All the world is sleeping.
> Till the morning's light you'll rest,
> Mother watch is keeping.
>
> Birds and beasts have closed their eyes,
> All the world is sleeping.
> In the morn the sun will rise,
> Mother watch is keeping.

•

WHAT DOES LITTLE BIRDIE SAY?

Alfred Tennyson

What does little birdie say,
In her nest at peep of day?
  "Let me fly," says little birdie,
"Mother, let me fly away."

Birdie, rest a little longer,
Till the little wings are stronger.
So she rests a little longer,
  Then she flies away.

What does little baby say,
In her bed at peep of day?
  Baby says, like little birdie,
"Let me rise and fly away."

Baby, sleep a little longer,
Till the little limbs are stronger.
If she sleeps a little longer,
  Baby, too shall fly away.

•

THE SQUIRREL'S DEVOTION

Retold by Ella Lyman Cabot

The evidence of love is effort, the kind of effort that can bring even miracles.

Many ages ago, in the faraway land of India, a great tamarisk tree grew, with wide-spreading branches, far over the surface of a great lake, clear, shining, and still. Morning, midday, and evening shone with varying beauty in the lake where the green boughs of the tamarisk waved in the quiet air.

Far up in the very crown of the tamarisk, a mother squirrel built her home. Here the gentle swinging of the branches rocked the baby squirrel's cradle, so that the little one slept quietly, waiting for the glad day to come when he might frolic through the beautiful green bower as his mother did.

But one day a great storm arose. Away over the sky spread angry clouds. The lake shivered and the sunshine fled from its face. The big tamarisk trembled as the storm struck limb after limb from its strong trunk.

Suddenly the fierce wind hurled the squirrel's nest from its perch. The frail little home plunged through the air to the lake below. There it bobbed up and down on the storm-lashed waves, with the baby squirrel still inside. It was only a matter of moments before it would sink out of sight.

A great fear struck the heart of the mother squirrel, standing on the lake's edge, her pouches filled with milky nuts for her little one. No help was near. No great swan, on whose white back she might rescue her slowly sinking child. No kind, strong eagle was near to cleave the storm with his dark pinions to the little squirrel's side. No kind boy in a strong boat to come to the mother's aid. Must the mother stand still and see her baby drown? What could she do?

Suddenly the great fear was gone and a great joy took its place. There was just one thing to be done. Empty the lake of its water, and lead her little son to the safe shelter of the friendly bank.

Without an instant's delay, the mother squirrel set to work. Into the lake she plunged, soaked her long feathery tail in the water, climbed out, ran to the crest of a little hill, squeezed out the water on its further side, then back to repeat the work, over and over, and over.

But while the mother wrought thus with all her soul and with all her might, the great Father looked down with joy to see this faithful mother do all she could to save her child. Swift as a flash of lightning went forth the command to an angel to help the mother and save the child. Like a gleam of sunshine he flew to obey. Like a flash of light the little wet clinging squirrel was restored to its rejoicing mother, who had done everything in her little power to accomplish the miracle that the angel had been sent to assist in. But whether the angel was the white swan, or the black eagle, or a kindhearted lad with a friendly boat, I do not know.

•

THE STORY OF THE
SMALL GREEN CATERPILLAR

Elizabeth Harrison

There are two different words meaning "father" in Latin. "Genitor" means a biological father. "Pater" means a father who takes responsibility. The little caterpillar in this story is a foster-father who shows what "pater" is all about.

This story takes place in a quiet little garden of an old brick house in a sleepy country town. There, on the outside leaf of a large green cabbage-head, lived a little green caterpillar. He was not an inch long and not much bigger around than a good-sized broom straw, yet he was an honest little fellow in his way, and spent most of his time crawling about on his cabbage-leaf and nibbling holes in it, which you know, is about all a caterpillar can be expected to do. The great, beautiful sun, high up in the sky, sent his bright rays of light down to warm the little caterpillar just as regularly and with seemingly just as much love as he sent them to make the thousand wavelets of the swift-flowing river sparkle and gleam like diamonds, or as he sent them down to rest in calm, still sunshine on the quiet hilltops beyond.

The little green caterpillar's life was a very narrow one. He had never been away from his cabbage-leaf, in fact he did not know that there was anything else in the world except cabbage-leaves. He might have learned something of the beautiful silvery moon, or the shining stars, or of the glorious sun itself, if he had ever looked up, but he never did. Therefore the whole world was a big cabbage-leaf to him, and all of his life consisted in nibbling as much cabbage-leaf as possible.

So you can easily imagine his astonishment when one day a dainty, white butterfly settled down beside him and began laying small green eggs. The little caterpillar had never before seen anything half so beautiful as were the wings of the dainty, white butterfly, and when she had finished laying her eggs and flew off, he for the first time in his whole life, lifted his head toward the blue sky that he might watch the quick motion of her wings. She was soon beyond the tallest leaves of the tomato plants, above the feathery tips of the fine asparagus, even higher than the plum trees. He watched her until she became a mere speck in the air and at last vanished from his sight. He then sighed and turned again to his cabbage-leaf. As he did so his eyes rested on the twenty small green eggs which were no larger than pin heads.

"Did she leave these for me to care for?" said he to himself. Then came the perplexing question—how could he, a crawling caterpillar, take care of baby butterflies? He could not teach them anything except to crawl and nibble cabbage-leaves. If they were like their beautiful mother, would they not soon fly far beyond his reach? This last thought troubled him a great deal, still he watched over them tenderly until they should hatch. He could at least tell them of how beautiful their mother had been and could show them where to fly that they might find her.

He often pictured to himself how they would look, twenty dainty little butterflies fluttering about him on his cabbage-leaf for a time, and then flying off to the blue sky, for aught he knew, to visit the stars with their mother. He loved the great sun very dearly now, because it sent its rays down to warm the tiny eggs.

One day he awoke from his afternoon nap just in time to see a most remarkable sight! What do you think was happening? One after another of the small green eggs were breaking open, and out were crawling—what *do* you suppose! Little white butterflies? No, nothing of the kind—Little green caterpillars were creeping out of each shell. Their foster-father, as he had learned to call himself, could hardly believe his own eyes. Yet there they were, wriggling and squirming, very much like the young angleworms in the ground below.

"Well, well, well!" said he to himself, "who would ever dream that the children of that beautiful creature would be mere caterpillars?" Strange as it seemed to him, there was no denying the fact and his duty was to teach them how to crawl about and how to nibble cabbage-leaves. "Poor things," he used to say as he moved among them, "you will never know the world of beauty in which your mother lived, you will never be able to soar aloft in the free air, your lives must be spent in creeping about on a cabbage-leaf and filling yourselves full of it each day. Poor things! Poor things!"

The young caterpillars soon became so expert that they no longer needed his care. Feeling very tired and sleepy, he one day decided to make for himself a bed, or bag, and go to sleep, not caring much whether or not he ever awoke. He was soon softly wrapped from head to foot in the curious covering he had made, and then came a long, long sleep of three weeks or more. When at last he awakened, he began to work his head out of his covering. Soon his whole body was free and he began to breathe the fresh air and feel the warm sunshine. He was sure that something had happened to him though he could not tell what. He turned his head this way and that, and at last caught sight of his own sides. What do you think he saw? Wings! Beautiful white wings! And his body was white, too! The long sleep had changed him into a butterfly!

He began to slowly stretch his wings. They were so new he could hardly believe that they were part of himself. The more he stretched them the more beautiful they became, and soon they quivered and fluttered as gracefully as did other butterfly wings. Just at this moment a strong, fresh breeze swept over the garden, and before he had time to refuse, the new butterfly was lifted off the cabbage-leaf and was dancing through the air, settling down now on a bright flower, and now on a nodding blade of grass, then up and off again. He rejoiced gaily in his freedom for a time, but soon came the longing to try his wings in the upper sunshine.

Before attempting the unknown journey, however, he flew back to the round, green cabbage-head on which he had lived so long. There were the twenty, small, green caterpillars, still creeping slowly about and filling themselves with cabbage-leaf. This was all they knew how to do, and this they did faithfully. "Never mind, little caterpillars," said the new butterfly as he hovered over them, "keep on at your work; the cabbage-leaf gives you food, and the crawling makes you strong. By and by you, too, shall be butterflies and go forth free and glad into God's great upper world."

Having said this in so low a tone of voice that you would not have heard him had you been standing close by, he flew far away, so far that neither you nor I could have followed him with our eyes. But the small, green, caterpillars must have heard, for they went on crawling and nibbling cabbage-leaves quite contentedly, and not one of them was ever heard to complain of having to be a caterpillar, though occasionally one and then another of them would lift his head, and I doubt not he was thinking of the time when he, too, should become a beautiful white butterfly.

•

THE OWL AND THE PUSSY CAT

Edward Lear

Some say courting has gone out of style. If so, we need to bring it back. We should start by showing our children the civility, respect, and joy shared in courtships and marriages, as in these two poems, both famous in nurseryland.

The Owl and the Pussy Cat went to sea
    In a beautiful pea-green boat;
They took some honey, and plenty of money
    Wrapped up in a five-pound note.
The Owl looked up to the moon above,
    And sang to a small guitar,
"O lovely Pussy! O Pussy, my love,
    What a beautiful Pussy you are,
        You are,
What a beautiful Pussy you are!"

Pussy said to the Owl, "You elegant fowl!
    How wonderful sweet you sing!
Oh let us be married, too long we have tarried,
    But what shall we do for a ring?"
They sailed away for a year and a day
    To the land where the bong tree grows,
And there in a wood a Piggy-wig stood
    With a ring in the end of his nose,
        His nose,
With a ring in the end of his nose.

"Dear Pig, are you willing to sell for one shilling
    Your ring?" Said the Piggy, "I will."
So they took it away, and were married next day
    By the Turkey who lives on the hill.
They dined upon mince and slices of quince,
    Which they ate with a runcible spoon,
And hand in hand on the edge of the sand
    They danced by the light of the moon,
        The moon,
They danced by the light of the moon.

•

The Courtship and Marriage of Cock Robin and Jenny Wren

It was a merry time
    When Jenny Wren was young,
So neatly as she danced,
    And so sweetly as she sung,
Robin Redbreast lost his heart:
    He was a gallant bird;
He doft his hat to Jenny,
    And thus to her he said:

"My dearest Jenny Wren,
    If you will but be mine,
You shall dine on cherry pie,
    And drink nice currant wine.
I'll dress you like a Goldfinch,
    Or like a Peacock gay;
So if you'll have me, Jenny,
    Let us appoint the day."

Jenny blushed behind her fan,
    And thus declared her mind:
"Then let it be tomorrow, Bob,
    I take your offer kind—
Cherry pie is very good!
    So is currant wine!
But I will wear my brown gown.
    And never dress too fine."

Robin rose up early
    At the break of day;
He flew to Jenny Wren's house,
    To sing a roundelay.
He met the Cock and Hen,
    And bid the Cock declare,
This was his wedding day
    With Jenny Wren, the fair.

The Cock then blew his horn,
 To let the neighbors know,
This was Robin's wedding day,
 And they might see the show.
And first came parson Rook,
 With his spectacles and band,
And one of Mother Hubbard's books
 He held within his hand.

Then came the bride and bridegroom;
 Quite plainly was she dressed,
And blushed so much, her cheeks were
 As red as Robin's breast.
But Robin cheered her up;
 "My pretty Jen," said he,
"We're going to be married.
 And happy we shall be."

The Goldfinch came on next,
 To give away the bride;
The Linnet, being bride's maid,
 Walked by Jenny's side;
And, as she was a-walking,
 She said, "Upon my word,
I think that your Cock Robin
 Is a very pretty bird."

The Blackbird and the Thrush,
 And charming Nightingale,
Whose sweet jug sweetly echoes
 Through every grove and dale;
The Sparrow and Tom Tit,
 And many more, were there:
All came to see the wedding
 Of Jenny Wren, the fair.

"O then," says parson Rook,
   "Who gives this maid away?"
"I do," says the Goldfinch,
   "And her fortune I will pay:
Here's a bag of grain of many sorts,
   And other things beside;
Now happy be the bridegroom,
   And happy be the bride!"

"And will you have her, Robin,
   To be your wedded wife?"
"Yes, I will," says Robin,
   "And love her all my life."
"And will you have him, Jenny,
   Your husband now to be?"
"Yes, I will," says Jenny,
   "And love him heartily."

Then on her finger fair
   Cock Robin put the ring;
"You're married now," says parson Rook,
   While the Lark aloud did sing:
"Happy be the bridegroom,
   And happy be the bride!
And may not man, nor bird, nor beast,
   This happy pair divide."

The birds were asked to dine;
   Not Jenny's friends alone,
But every pretty songster
   That had Cock Robin known.
They had a cherry pie,
   Beside some currant wine,
And every guest brought something,
   That sumptuous they might dine.

The dinner things removed,
    They all began to sing;
And soon they made the place
    Near a mile round to ring.
The concert it was fine;
    And every bird tried
Who best could sing for Robin
    And Jenny Wren, the bride.

THE ROBIN TO HIS MATE

Love, union, work, children. This little poem has some of the really important ingredients of a blessed marriage.

Said Robin to his pretty mate,
    "Bring here a little hay;
Lay here a stick and there a straw,
    And bring a little clay.

"And we will build a little nest,
    Wherein you soon shall lay
Your little eggs, so smooth, so blue;
    Come, let us work away.

"And you shall keep them very warm;
    And only think, my dear,
'T will not be long before we see
    Four little robins here."

•

THE CHATTERING ASPEN

Adapted from a retelling by Mary Stewart

How does one look for a spouse? This Native-American tale suggests looking for virtue.

Listen! Do you hear the rustle, rustle of the leaves of that tree
over our heads? They are never still. They whisper and chatter all
the time, even when there is not wind enough to stir a leaf on one
of the other trees.

The Indians told a story about the first aspen tree. Come sit
nearer, and I will tell it to you.

Years and years ago there was a lake, *somewhere,* called Spirit
Lake, where the sun always shone and the winds were always soft.
Indian spirits lived there, and they were very wonderful to look
upon. They gleamed as though the never-failing sunshine of their
lake glowed within them. They wore golden tunics and mantles,
and the feathers in their headbands and on their arrows were
tipped with glimmering gold.

But, although they were so splendid and radiant, one of them,
Wahontas, longed for a human bride. Leaving Spirit Lake, he wandered through many Indian camps, looking for the most perfect
maiden.

At one tent he found two lovely sisters, Mistosis and Omemee.
Mistosis had eyes that gleamed like stars. Omemee had hair that
shone like the golden corn.

Wahontas went to their father, the old chief, and asked for the
hand of one of his daughters in marriage. The old chief was happy
to have such a suitor for his girls. But which one, he asked, did
Wahontas wish to marry?

Wahontas pondered the question. They were equally beautiful,
but which was the one for him? Then a plan came to him.

He disguised himself as an old, old Indian. Over his gold tunic
he threw a ragged cloak, and upon his feet he placed worn moccasins, full of holes. Then he went to the two sisters' tent, and found
them sitting outside.

A torrent of abuse greeted him as he approached.

"Away! Go away! There is no room for you here!" shouted
Mistosis. "Hurry, hurry, we have no time for strange beggars!"

"But I am aged, weary, and hungry," murmured Wahontas.

"Aged!" scolded Mistosis. "There should be no aged people in the world. We should not have to take care of them!" On and on went her tongue, scolding, scorning, gibing at the poor old man.

Then Omemee stepped forward. She said no word, but led the old man inside the tent, to a seat upon a soft deerskin. Quickly she lighted a fire and upon it she cooked her best venison and broth. As he ate she looked sadly at his torn shoes and, going to a corner, brought out her most beautiful moccasins, beaded with blue and gold. She put them on his feet, smiling sweetly at him as she did so, while all the time the tongue of Mistosis went on with its cruel scolding.

In broken words Wahontas thanked Omemee, and tottering to the flap of the tent, he lifted it painfully. Then in the golden light of the entrance, he paused and drew himself up to his full height. From his shoulders he tore the ragged cloak, from his head he pulled the long white hair which had covered his raven locks.

"I came to you as an old man, weary, hungry, and forlorn," he said. "I come again, not as a beggar, but as a suitor. I have made my choice. Only one of you is beautiful within. Will you have me, Omemee?

"No one should be forced to bear the ceaseless cruelty of Mistosis's tongue again," he went on. "She shall become the aspen tree, whose leaves are never silent."

As he spoke, Mistosis, amazed and furious, became rooted to the spot. Her arms changed to branches, her tongues to many chattering leaves!

Wahontas turned to Omemee and opened his arms. "Come, my bride, my dove," he cried. "Come with me to the golden Spirit Lake, where no cloud of sorrow or pain shall ever dim thy sweet life!"

For a moment Omemee rested in his arms. Then in the form of two doves they flew over the forests to the golden lake, where they dwelled blissfully for years and years. Perhaps they are there today, while in our forests and along our roadsides the leaves of the aspen tree still chatter, chatter without ceasing!

•

THE PLOWMAN
WHO FOUND CONTENT

Retold by Julia Darrow Cowles

Here are two old stories showing two different kinds of marriages.
Husbands and wives can raise each other up, as in the first tale, or
they can bring each other down, as in the second.

A plowman paused in his work one day to rest. As he sat on
the handle of his plow he fell a-thinking. The world had not been
going well with him of late, and he could not help feeling downhearted. Just then he saw an old woman looking at him over the
hedge.

"Good-morning!" she said. "If you are wise you will take my
advice."

"And what is your advice?" he asked.

"Leave your plow, and walk straight on for two days. At the end
of that time you will find yourself in the middle of a forest, and in
front of you there will be a tree towering high above the others.
Cut it down, and your fortune will be made."

With these words the old woman hobbled down the road,
leaving the plowman wondering. He unharnessed his horses, drove
them home, and said good-by to his wife; and then taking his ax,
started out.

At the end of two days he came to the tree, and set to work to
cut it down. As it crashed to the ground a nest containing two eggs
fell from its topmost branches. The shells of the eggs were smashed,
and out of one came a young eagle, while from the other rolled a
small gold ring.

The eagle rapidly became larger and larger, till it was of full
size; then, flapping its wings, it flew up.

"I thank you, honest man, for giving me my freedom," it called
out. "In token of my gratitude take the ring—it is a wishing ring. If
you wish anything as you turn it round on your finger, your wish
will be fulfilled. But remember this—the ring contains but one
wish, so think well before you use it."

The man put the ring on his finger, and set off on his homeward journey. Night was coming on when he entered a town. Almost the first person he saw was a goldsmith standing at the door of his shop. So he went up to him, and asked him what the ring was worth.

The goldsmith looked at it carefully, and handed it back to the man with a smile.

"It is of very little value," he said.

The plowman laughed.

"Ah, Mr. Goldsmith," he cried, "you have made a mistake this time. My ring is worth more than all you have in your shop. It's a wishing-ring, and will give me anything I care to wish for."

The goldsmith felt annoyed and asked to see it again.

"Well, my good man," he said, "never mind about the ring. I dare say you are far from home, and are in want of some supper and a bed for the night. Come in and spend the night in my house."

The man gladly accepted the offer, and was soon sound asleep. In the middle of the night the goldsmith took the ring from his finger, and put another just like it in its place without disturbing him in the least.

Next morning the countryman went on his way, all unconscious of the trick that had been played on him. When he had gone the goldsmith closed the shutters of his shop, and bolted the door. Then turning the ring on his finger he said, "I wish for a hundred thousand sovereigns!"

Scarcely had the sound of his voice died away than there fell about him a shower of hard, bright, golden sovereigns. They struck him on the head, on the shoulders, on the hands. They covered the floor. Presently the floor gave way beneath the weight, and the goldsmith and his gold fell into the cellar beneath.

Next morning, when the goldsmith did not open the shop as usual, the neighbors forced open the door, and found him buried beneath the pile.

Meanwhile the countryman reached his home, and told his wife of the ring.

"Now, good wife," said he, "here is the ring; our fortune is made. Of course we must consider the matter well; then, when we have made up our minds as to what is best, we can express some very big wish as I turn the ring on my finger."

"Suppose," said the woman, "we were to wish for a nice farm. The land we have now is so small as to be almost useless."

"Yes," said the husband, "but, on the other hand, if we work hard and spend little for a year or two we might be able to buy as much as we want. Then we could get something else with the wishing-ring."

So it was agreed. For a year the man and his wife worked hard. Harvest came, and the crops were splendid. At the end of the year they were able to buy a nice farm, and still had some money left.

"There," said the man, "we have the land, and we still have our wish."

"Well," said his wife, "we could do very well with a horse and a cow."

"They are not worth wishing for," said he. "We can get them as we got the land."

So they went on working steadily and spending wisely for another year. At the end of that time they bought both a horse and a cow. Husband and wife were greatly pleased with their good fortune, for, said they, "We have got the things we wanted and we have still our wish."

As time went on everything prospered with the worthy couple. They worked hard, and were happy.

"Let us work while we are young," they told each other. "Life is still before us, and who can say how badly we may need our wish some day?"

So the years passed away. Every season saw the bounds of the farm increase and the granaries grow fuller. All day long the farmer was about in the fields, while his wife looked after the dairy. Sometimes, as they sat alone of an evening, they would remember the unused wishing-ring, and would talk of things they would like to have for the house. But they always said that there was still plenty of time for that. And they smiled at each other, and were content.

The man and his wife grew old and gray. Then came a day when they both died—and the wishing-ring had not been used. It was still on his finger as he had worn it for forty years. One of his sons was going to take it off, but the oldest said:

"Do not disturb it; there has been some secret in connection with it. Perhaps our mother gave it to him, for I have often seen her look longingly at it."

Thus the old man was buried with the ring, which was supposed to be a wishing-ring, but which, as we know, was not, though it brought the old couple more good fortune and happiness than all the wishing in the world could ever have given them.

•

THE THREE WISHES

Retold by Katharine Pyle

Here's the wrong way to get along and get ahead. This tale comes
from Sweden.

Once upon a time a poor man took his ax and went out into
the forest to cut wood. He was a lazy fellow, so as soon as he was
in the forest he began to look about to see which tree would be the
easiest to cut down. At last he found one that was hollow inside, as
he could tell by knocking upon it with his ax. "It ought not to take
long to cut this down," said he to himself. He raised his ax and
struck the tree such a blow that the splinters flew.

At once the bark opened and a little old fairy with a long beard
came running out of the tree.

"What do you mean by chopping into my house?" he cried;
and his eyes shone like red hot sparks, he was so angry.

"I did not know it was your house," said the man.

"Well, it is my house, and I'll thank you to let it alone," cried
the fairy.

"Very well," said the man. "I'd just as soon cut down some
other tree. I'll chop down the one over yonder."

"That is well," said the fairy. "I see that you are an obliging
fellow, after all. I have it in my mind to reward you for sparing my
house, so the next three wishes you and your wife make shall come
true, whatever they are; and that is your reward."

Then the fairy went back into the tree again and pulled the
bark together behind him.

The man stood looking at the tree and scratching his head.
"Now that is a curious thing," said he. Then he sat down and began
to wonder what he should wish for. He thought and he thought,
but he could decide on nothing. "I'll just go home and talk it over
with my wife," said he. So he shouldered his ax, and set off for
home. As soon as he came in at the door he began to bawl for his
wife, and she came in a hurry, for she did not know what had
happened to him.

He told his story and his wife listened. "This is a fine thing to
have happen to us," said she. "Now we must be very careful what
we wish for."

They sat down one on each side of the fire to talk it over. They thought of ever so many things they would like to have—a bag of gold, and a coach and four, and a fine house to live in, and fine clothes to wear, but nothing seemed just the right thing to choose.

They talked so long that they grew hungry. "Well, here we sit," said the man, "and not a thing cooked for dinner. I wish we had one of those fine sausages you used to make."

No sooner had he spoken than there was a great thumping and bumping in the chimney and a great sausage fell down on the hearth before him.

"What is this?" cried the man staring.

"Oh, you oaf! you stupid!" shrieked his wife. "It's the sausage you wished for. There's one of our wishes wasted. I wish the sausage were stuck on the end of your nose! It would serve you right!"

The moment she said this, the sausage flew up and stuck to the man's nose, and there it was and he couldn't get it off. The man pulled and tugged, and his wife pulled and tugged, but it was all of no use.

"Well, there's no help for it," said the husband. "We'll have to wish it off again."

His wife begun to cry and bawl. "No, no," she cried. "We only have one wish left, and we can't waste it that way. Let's wish ourselves the richest people in the world."

But to this the man would not agree. He wanted the sausage off his nose whatever it cost. So at last the wife was obliged to let him have his own way. "I wish the sausage was off my nose again," said the man, and that was the third of their wishes. So all the good they had of the fairy's gift was a sausage for dinner; but then it was the best they had ever eaten. "And after all," said the man, "there's nothing much better in the world to wish for than a full stomach."

•

THE ROSES OF SAINT ELIZABETH

Saint Elizabeth was born in 1207 at Pressburg, the old capital of Hungary. She was the daughter of King Andrew II and Queen Gertrude, and at an early age she was betrothed to the Landgrave of Thuringia, an ancient kingdom lying in what is now Germany.

She became well known for her kindness and charity, building a
hospital at the foot of her castle. This legend of Elizabeth reminds
us that marriage means trust and tenderness, and it means respect
for the work each partner has to do.

Long ago, in the kingdom of Hungary, a beautiful daughter
named Elizabeth was born to the king and queen. The little princess
was so good and kind that all the people of Hungary loved her. She
always had a kind smile and gentle words for anyone she met, and
as she grew up, she spent her time trying to make life better for
those in need.

When Elizabeth was old enough, she married a nobleman
named Louis, and together they lived in a land called Thuringia.
Louis was a serious and quiet man who was several years older than
his young bride, and sometimes Elizabeth felt a little bit in awe of
him. But they loved each other very much, and before many years
passed they had four children, and their home was a happy place.

But even after she had a family of her own to look after, Elizabeth never stopped doing everything she could to help those who
were suffering in Thuringia. Sometimes she would send a little food
to a struggling family she knew was in need, or sometimes she
would go herself to visit and comfort the sick, and sit at their
bedsides.

Now, although Louis admired his wife's kindness and generosity, he had his own ideas about the way a princess should act, and
he did not like to see Elizabeth always walking among the common
people. He thought it did not look dignified for a noblewoman to
stand in the street talking to a peasant, and sometimes he frowned
upon his wife's frequent missions of charity.

One winter's day when Louis had ridden out to hunt with some
of his friends, Elizabeth left the castle and made her way down the
snow-covered path to visit a poor family. She carried several loaves
of bread in her cloak, as many as it would hold. The road grew icier
as she trudged along, and her load of bread made the walking
awkward. She dared not raise her eyes from the path, or she might
easily lose her balance. Finally, with a quiet sigh of relief, she
reached the bottom of the hill. When she looked up, to her dismay, she saw her husband and his friends returning early from the
hunt.

Elizabeth stopped in her tracks, suddenly flustered and embarrassed. She would have left the road and ducked into the woods

until the party had passed, but there was no time. In a moment the horses were clopping all around her, and the riders were peering down in amusement at the young princess standing alone in the snow, gathering her cloak about her.

Her husband smiled tenderly when he saw her. Riding to her side, he reached down and placed his hand on her shoulder.

"Where are you going, my dear?" he asked.

Elizabeth did not know what to do. She knew how Louis felt about her habit of walking out alone to visit poor people in wretched huts, and she did not want to shame him in front of all his high-born friends by telling him of her errand. She shrank from her husband and drew her bundle closer to her heart while she searched for something to say.

Louis saw her hesitation and gazed at her now with a clouded brow.

"What do you carry in your cloak that makes you stoop so with the weight of your load?" he asked. And as he spoke, all the courtiers and huntsmen drew about her to see.

Elizabeth looked up at her husband in confusion. She knew that all these knights and noblemen would smile with disdain if they saw what she carried, and she thought she might not be able to bear their scorn. Before she really knew what she was saying, she blurted out, "Roses!"

She blushed with shame the moment she spoke, for she knew what she had said was wrong. She would have given anything just then to be brave enough to admit she had lied, but the thought of the hunters' laughter kept her silent. She could only hang her head and clutch at her cloak with trembling hands.

Looking down at her, Louis could see that something was wrong, and he guessed the truth. Half of him felt compassion for his struggling wife, but the other half felt anger and dismay that she would embarrass him this way in front of his friends. Leaning from his saddle, he reached for her cloak.

"Let me see," he said firmly.

Taking a corner of the cloth, he drew it aside.

And then a marvelous thing happened. In the folds of the cloak he saw not the loaves of bread he had expected. He found roses—glowing red and white roses, as fresh and soft as only flowers can be, even though the season was midwinter. And the very sweetness of summertime arose and filled the air, like the richest fragrance.

For a moment nobody spoke. Louis looked wonderingly into Elizabeth's face for a while. Then he took one crimson rose from the cloak, placed it next to his own heart, and bent down to kiss his young wife.

"Go your way, my love," he said gently.

He turned his horse and rode with the others back toward the castle, leaving Elizabeth standing breathless and astonished in the frozen road, gazing down at her armful of roses.

•

"An Honorable Estate, Instituted of God"

For many of us, the vows we take on our wedding day are the most important promises we will ever make, or at least so we say. It is our responsibility to think hard about those promises long before and long after the ceremony, not just on the day we stand before the altar.

The language may be old-fashioned, but the ideas these words convey will always be crucial to the success of the marriage. It is worth lingering over the familiar phrases: "in sickness and in health," "in sorrow and in joy," "forsaking all others," "till death us do part." They remind us that the marriage ceremony is not only a time of joy, but it is also a commitment made reverently and soberly before God.

The Address

The persons to be married shall present themselves before the minister, the woman standing at the left hand of man. The minister shall then say,

Dearly beloved, we are gathered together here in the presence of God, and in the face of this congregation, to join together this man and this woman in holy matrimony; which is an honorable estate, instituted of God, and therefore is not by any to be enterprised or taken in hand lightly or unadvisedly; but reverently, discreetly, soberly, and in the fear of God.

If any man can show just cause why they may not lawfully be joined together, let him now speak, or else hereafter forever hold his peace.

The Charge

And then, speaking to the persons who are to be married, the minister shall say,

I require and charge you both, that if either of you know any impediment why ye may not be lawfully united in matrimony, ye do now confess it. For be ye well assured that so many as are joined together, otherwise than God's word doth allow, are not joined together by God, nor is their union blessed by him.

The Vows

There being no impediment, the minister shall then say to the man,

_____, Wilt thou have this woman to thy wedded wife, to live together after God's ordinance in the holy estate of matrimony? Wilt thou love her, comfort her, honor and keep her, in sickness and in health, in sorrow and in joy; and forsaking all others, keep thee only unto her so long as ye both shall live?

The man shall answer, I will.

The Minister shall then say to the woman,

_____, Wilt thou have this man to thy wedded husband to live together after God's ordinance in the holy estate of matrimony? Wilt thou love him, comfort him, honor and keep him, in sickness and in health, in sorrow and in joy; and, forsaking all others, keep thee only unto him so long as ye both shall live?

The Woman shall answer, I will.

Then the Minister shall say,

Who giveth this woman to be married to this man?

The minister, receiving the woman, at her father's or friend's hand, shall cause the man with his right hand to take the woman by her right hand, and to say after him,

I, _____, take thee, _____, to my wedded wife, to have and to hold from this day forward, for better, for worse, for richer, for poorer, in sickness and in health, to love and to cherish, till death us do part, according to God's holy ordinance, and thereto I give thee my troth.

Then the woman shall likewise say after the minister,

I, _____, take thee, _____, to my wedded husband, to have and to hold, from this day forward, for better, for worse, for richer or for poorer, in sickness and in health, to love and to cherish, till death us do part, according to God's holy ordinance, and thereto I give thee my troth.

The man and the woman shall then loose hands. The minister, receiving a ring from the best man, shall give it to the man, who shall in turn place it on the fourth finger of the woman's left hand. The man, holding the ring there, shall say after the minister,

With this Ring I thee wed; and to thee only do I promise to keep myself, so long as we both shall live. Amen.

If there are to be double rings used at the service, the minister shall receive a ring from the maid of honor, and give it to the woman, who shall place it upon the fourth finger of the man's left hand and say after the minister,

With this ring I thee wed; and to thee only do I promise to keep myself, so long as we both shall live. Amen.

The Prayer
The Minister shall then say,
Let us pray.

Eternal God, creator and preserver of all mankind, send thy blessing upon these thy servants, whom we bless in thy name. Enable them to perform through all their years the vows which they have made in thy presence.

May they seriously attend to the duties of the new relation into which they have now entered; that it may not be to them a state of temptation and discord, but of mutual love and peace. Grant them the virtues of trust and patience and undying affection. May they be blessings and comforts to each other, sharers of each other's joys and sorrows, loyal companions in the life and work of every day, and helpers, each to the other, in all the chances and changes of this mortal life.

Hallow to them the home which they are to make and share together. Give them a wise love for all who may be committed to their care, keeping them always mindful that in thee we live and move and have our being, and that thou art our dwelling place in all generations. Through Jesus Christ our Lord. Amen.

The Pronouncement of the Marriage
The minister shall then say,

Forasmuch as _____ and _____ have consented together in holy wedlock, and have witnessed the same before God and this company, and thereto have engaged and pledged themselves to each other, and have declared the same by joining hands and by giving and receiving a ring (rings), I pronounce that they are man and wife; and those whom God hath joined together, let no man put asunder.

•

AN EXCELLENT WIFE

My wife, Elayne, and I chose this passage from Chapter 31 of Proverbs as a reading at our wedding thirteen years ago. In describing my wife, I think this passage is even more accurate today.

An excellent wife, who can find?
For her worth is far above jewels.

The heart of her husband trusts in her,
And he will have no lack of gain.
She does him good and not evil
All the days of her life.
She looks for wool and flax,
And works with her hands in delight.
She is like merchant ships;
She brings her food from afar.
She rises also while it is still night,
And gives food to her household,
And portions to her maidens.
She considers a field and buys it;
From her earnings she plants a vineyard.
She girds herself with strength,
And makes her arms strong.
She senses that her gain is good;
Her lamp does not go out at night.
She stretches out her hands to the distaff,
And her hands grasp the spindle.
She extends her hand to the poor;
And she stretches out her hands to the needy.
She is not afraid of the snow for her household,
For all her household are clothed with scarlet.
She makes coverings for herself;
Her clothing is fine linen and purple.
Her husband is known in the gates,
When he sits among the elders of the land.
She makes linen garments and sells them,
And supplies belts to the tradesmen.
Strength and dignity are her clothing,
And she smiles at the future.
She opens her mouth in wisdom,
And the teaching of kindness is on her tongue.
She looks well to the ways of her household,
And does not eat the bread of idleness.
Her children rise up and bless her;
Her husband also, and he praises her, saying:
"Many daughters have done nobly,
But you excel them all."
Charm is deceitful and beauty is vain,
But a woman who fears the LORD, she shall be praised.

THE WIVES OF WEINSBERG

Adapted from a retelling
by Charlotte Yonge

Here are some heroines with quick wits and great hearts.

It happened in Germany, in the Middle Ages. The year was 1141. Wolf, the duke of Bavaria, sat trapped inside his castle of Weinsberg. Outside his walls lay the army of Frederick, the duke of Swabia, and his brother the emperor Konrad.

The siege had lasted long, and the time had come when Wolf knew he must surrender. Messengers rode back and forth, terms were proposed, conditions allowed, arrangements completed. Sadly, Wolf and his officers prepared to give themselves to their bitter enemy.

But the wives of Weinsberg were not ready to lose all. They sent a message to Konrad, asking the emperor to promise safe conduct for all the women in the garrison, that they might come out with as many of their valuables as they could carry.

The request was freely granted, and soon the castle gates opened. Out came the ladies—but in startling fashion. They carried not gold or jewels. Each one was bending under the weight of her husband, whom she hoped to save from the vengeance of the victorious host.

Konrad, who was really a generous and merciful man, is said to have been brought to tears by the extraordinary performance. He hastened to assure the women of their husbands' perfect safety and freedom. Then he invited them all to a banquet and made peace with the duke of Bavaria on terms much more favorable than expected.

The castle mount was afterwards known as the Hill of Weiber-treue, or woman's fidelity.

•

THE MOST PRECIOUS THING

This story of a young wife who matches words of love with a deed
of love echoes the stratagem of the wives of Weinsberg. Variations
of the tale are found in the folklore of eastern Europe.

It happened long ago that a young man and a young woman
fell in love with each other and decided to marry. They had almost
no money, but they did not hesitate over that. Their trust in each
other gave them faith that their future together must be a bright
one, as long as they had each other. They happily chose a date on
which they would join hearts and souls.

Before the wedding, the girl came to her fiancé with a request.

"I cannot imagine our ever wanting to be apart," she said. "But
it may be that, in time, we will tire of each other, or that you will
be angry with me, and want to send me back to my parents' house.
Promise me that if this should happen, you will allow me to carry
back with me the thing that has grown most precious to me."

Her fiancé laughed, and could see no sense in what she asked,
but the girl was not satisfied until he had written down his promise
and signed his name to it. Then the two were married and began
their life together.

They set their minds to improving their worldly position. They
were both willing to work hard at it, and soon their patient industry
found reward. Their first successes made them even more determined to put poverty behind them, and they worked harder than
ever before. Time passed, and their purses swelled. They became
comfortable, then well-to-do, and finally rich. They moved to a
bigger house, found a new set of friends, and surrounded themselves with all the trappings of fortune.

But in their single-minded pursuit of wealth, they began to
think more of their things than of each other. More and more, they
quarreled about what to buy, or how much to spend, or how they
should go about increasing their riches.

One afternoon, as they were preparing a feast for several important friends, they argued about some trifling matter—the flavor
of the gravy, or perhaps the order of seating at the table. They
began shouting and accusing each other.

"You care nothing for me!" cried the husband. "You think only of yourself, and the jewels and fine clothes you wear. Take those that are most precious to you, as I promised, and go back to your parents' house. There is no point in our going on together."

His wife went suddenly pale, and stared at him with a distracted look in her eyes, as if she had just seen something for the first time.

"Very well," she said quietly. "I am willing to go. But we must stay together one more night, and sit side by side at our table, for the sake of appearances in front of our friends."

The evening arrived. The feast began. It was as bountiful as their ample means allowed. When, one by one, the guests had succumbed to its influence, and her husband, too, had fallen asleep, the good woman had him carried to her parents' cottage and laid in bed there.

When he woke the next morning, he could not understand where he was. He raised himself up on his elbow to look about him, and at once his wife came to the bedside.

"My dear husband," she said softly, "your promise was that if you ever sent me away I might carry with me the thing that was most precious to me. You are that most precious thing. I care for you more than anything else, and nothing but death shall part us."

At once the man saw how selfishly they had both acted. He clasped his wife in his arms, and they kissed each other tenderly. That same day they returned home and began to devote themselves once again to each other.

●

FOR REMEMBRANCE

Adapted from Laura E. Richards

Words matter. In marriage, where there are so many words, they matter all the more.

A man sat by the coffin of the one who had been nearest to him, in black and bitter care. And as he sat, he saw passing beyond the coffin a troop of bright and lovely shapes, with clear eyes and faces full of rosy light.

"Who are you, fair creatures?" asked the man. And they answered:

"We are the words you might have spoken to her."

"Oh, stay with me!" cried the man. "Your sweet looks are a knife in my heart, yet still I would keep you, for she is cold and deaf, and I am alone."

But they answered: "Nay; we cannot stay, for we have no being, but are only a light that never shone."

And they passed on and were gone.

And still the man sat in black and bitter care.

And as he sat he saw rising up between him and the coffin a band of pale and terrible forms, with bloodless lips and hollow eyes of fire.

The man shuddered.

"What are you, dreadful shapes?" he asked. And they answered:

"We are the words she heard from you."

Then the man cried aloud in anguish:

"Depart from me, and leave me with my dead! Better solitude than such company."

But they, sitting down in silence, fixed their eyes upon him, and they stayed with him forever.

●

THE LION'S HAIR

In marriage, petty disagreements sometimes obscure and even overwhelm more important harmonies. This Ethiopian folktale reminds us that, as in so many facets of life, success in marriage is largely a result of the effort you put into it.

In a village in the mountains of Ethiopia, a young man and a young woman fell in love and became husband and wife. For a short while they were perfectly happy, but then trouble entered their house. They began to find fault with each other over little things—he blamed her for spending too much at the market, or she criticized him for always being late. It seemed not a day passed without some kind of quarrel about money or friends or household chores. Sometimes they grew so angry they shouted at each other, and yelled bitter curses, and then went to bed without speaking, but that only made things worse.

After a few months, when she thought she could stand it no longer, the young wife went to a wise old judge to ask for a divorce.

"Why?" asked the old man. "You've been married barely a year. Don't you love your husband?"

"Yes, we love each other. But it's just not working out."

"What do you mean, not working out?"

"We fight a lot. He does things that bother me. He leaves his clothes lying around the house. He drops his toenails on the floor. He stays out too late. When I want to do one thing, he wants to do another. We just can't live together."

"I see," said the old man. "Perhaps I can help you. I know of a magic medicine that will make the two of you get along much better. If I give it to you, will you put aside these thoughts of divorce?"

"Yes!" cried the woman. "Give it to me."

"Wait," replied the judge. "To make the medicine, I must have a single hair from the tail of a fierce lion that lives down by the river. You must bring it to me."

"But how can I get such a hair?" the woman cried. "The lion will surely kill me."

"There I cannot help you," the old man shook his head. "I know much about making medicines, but I know little of lions. You must discover a way yourself. Can you do it?"

The young wife thought long and hard. She loved her husband very much. The magic medicine might save their marriage. She resolved to get the hair, no matter what.

The very next morning she walked down to the river, hid behind some rocks, and waited. After a while, the lion came by to drink. When she saw his huge claws, she froze with fear. When he bared his sharp fangs, she nearly fainted. And when he gave his mighty roar, she turned and ran home.

But the next morning she came back, this time carrying a sack of fresh meat. She set the food on the ground, two hundred yards from the lion, and then hid behind the rocks while the lion ate.

The next day, she set the meat down one hundred yards away from the lion. And on the following morning, she put the food only fifty yards away, and stood nearby while he gulped it down.

And so every day she drew closer and closer to the fierce, wild beast. After a while she stood near enough to throw him the food, and finally came the day when she fed him right from her hand! She trembled as she watched the great teeth ripping and tearing the meat. But she loved her husband more than she feared the lion. Closing her eyes, she reached out and pulled a single hair from the tail.

Then she ran as fast as she could to the wise old judge.

"Look!" she cried. "I've brought a hair from the lion!"

The old man took the hair and looked at it closely.

"This is a brave thing you have done," he said. "It took a great deal of patience and resolve."

"Yes," said the woman. "Now give me the medicine to make my marriage better!"

The old man shook his head.

"I have nothing else to give you."

"But you promised!" the young wife cried.

"Don't you see?" asked the old man gently. "I have already given you all the medicine you need. You were determined to do whatever it took, however long it took, to gain a magic remedy for your problems. But there is no magic remedy. There is only your determination. You say you and your husband love each other. If you both give your marriage the same patience and resolve and courage you showed in getting this hair, you will be happy together for a long time. Think about it."

And so the woman went home with new resolutions.

•

THE BABY

George MacDonald

In most marriages, the blessing of children comes from the union of husband and wife. It has been said that every child born into the world is a new thought of God. This little poem suggests that when a baby is born, God is thinking of the parents, too.

> Where did you come from, baby dear?
> Out of the everywhere into the here.

Where did you get your eyes so blue?
Out of the sky as I came through.

What makes the light in them sparkle and spin?
Some of the starry spikes left in.

Where did you get that little tear?
I found it waiting when I got here.

What makes your forehead so smooth and high?
A soft hand stroked it as I went by.

What makes your cheek like a warm white rose?
Something better than any one knows.

Whence that three-cornered smile of bliss?
Three angels gave me at once a kiss.

Where did you get that pearly ear?
God spoke, and it came out to hear.

Where did you get those arms and hands?
Love made itself into hooks and bands.

Feet, whence did you come, you darling things?
From the same box as the cherub's wings.

How did they all just come to be you?
God thought about me, and so I grew.

But how did you come to us, you dear?
God thought of *you,* and so I am here.

•

WHY THE BABY SAYS "GOO"

Adapted from a retelling
by Gilbert L. Wilson

Here is one of the fundamental truths of family life: Baby changes everything.

In a village near the mountains lived an Indian chief. He was a brave man and had fought in many battles. No one in the tribe had won more battles than he.

Strange folk were then in the land. Fierce ice giants came out of the North and carried people away. Wicked witches dwelt in caves, and in the mountains lived the Mikumwess, magic little people.

But the chief feared none of them. He fought the ice giants and made them go back to their home in the North. Some of the witches he killed. Others he drove from the land.

Everybody loved the chief. He was so brave and good that the villagers thought there was no one like him anywhere.

But when he had driven out all the giants, the chief grew vain. He began to think he was the most important person in the world.

"I can conquer anyone," he boasted. "And no one tells me what to do."

When his wife heard how the great chief boasted, she smiled. "My husband *is* wonderful," she said, "but there is one who is mightier than he. There is one whom even he must obey."

When the chief heard her say this, he asked, "Who is this wonderful one? Where is he?"

His wife smiled again. "You already know him," she said. "His name is Wasis."

Now who do you think Wasis was? He was their own plump little Baby. In the middle of the floor he sat, crowing to himself and sucking a piece of maple sugar. He looked very sweet and contented.

Now the chief, like all vain people, thought he knew everything. He thought, of course, that the little Baby would obey him. So he smiled and said to little Wasis, "Baby, come to me!"

But the Baby smiled back and went on sucking his maple sugar.

The chief was surprised. The villagers always did what he bade them. He could not understand why the little Baby did not obey him, but he smiled and said again to little Wasis, *"Baby, come to me!"*

The little Baby smiled back and sucked his maple sugar as before.

The chief was astonished. No one had ever dared disobey him before. He grew angry. He frowned at little Wasis and roared out, "BABY, COME TO ME!"

But little Wasis opened his mouth and burst out crying and screaming. The chief had never heard such awful sounds. Even the ice giants did not scream so terribly.

The chief was more and more astonished. He could not think why such a little Baby would not obey him.

"Wonderful!" he said. "All other men fear me. But this little Baby shouts back war cries. Perhaps I can overcome him with my magic."

He took out his medicine bag and shook it at the little Baby. He danced magic dances. He sang wonderful songs.

Little Wasis smiled and watched the chief with big round eyes. He thought it all very funny. And all the time he sucked his maple sugar.

The chief danced until he was tired out. Sweat ran down his face. Red paint oozed over his cheeks and neck. The feathers in his headdress had fallen down.

At last he sat down. He was too tired to dance any longer.

"Did I not tell you that Wasis is mightier than you?" asked his wife. "No one is mightier than the Baby. He always rules the wigwam. Everybody loves him and obeys him."

"It is even so," sighed the chief, as he went out of the wigwam. But as he went he could hear little Wasis talking to himself on the floor.

"Goo, goo, goo!" he crowed, as he sucked his maple sugar.

Now, when you hear the Baby saying, "Goo, goo, goo," you will know what it means. It is his war cry. He is happy because he remembers the time when he made the great chief understand who really rules the wigwam.

•

THE COST OF ONE SEED

Here is a fine story for a discussion about the division of labor
between husbands and wives. It's also good reading for expectant
fathers in the waiting room. The tale comes from east Africa.

A husband decided he did not want to live with his wife any
longer and made up his mind to divorce her. But the couple had a
newborn son, and both father and mother wanted to keep the child,
so they went before a judge.

The woman spoke first.

"I bore this child for nine months," she pleaded. "I nurse him
at my breast, I sing to him in my lap, I rock him to sleep in my arms
every night. I hold him when he cries, and I tend him when he is
sick. I am with him night and day, and love him more than my own
life. Let me keep him."

Then the man spoke.

"I gave the seed that grew into this child," he said. "Therefore
the child is mine. I should be able to keep it if I want."

The judge looked at the man.

"So you gave the seed, you say" he asked.

"That's right," the man said proudly. "One little seed was all it
took."

"I see," said the judge. "So the father gives the seed, and the
mother carries and feeds the child. In that case, I think I can make
a ruling in this matter. But first we must have some scales."

He called for a pair of scales and ordered the infant to be
weighed.

"This child weighs nine pounds," the judge said to the father.
"If you gave just one seed to make him, it stands to reason your
wife has given nine pounds minus the weight of one grain of seed.
So if you want the child, you must pay your wife for nine pounds
worth of food."

The husband stared at the judge as if he were in the presence
of a lunatic.

"Wait, I'm not through," the judge said. "We also need to consult a baggage carrier."

A baggage carrier was summoned.

"How much do you charge to carry a burden for someone?" the judge asked.

"A coin a day for every pound I carry," he answered.

"Very good," the judge said. "We will figure that the woman carried one pound during the first month she was with child, ending with nine pounds by the ninth month she was with child. So for nine months' work of carrying the child, at a coin per pound every day, she earned nearly fourteen hundred coins. The husband must pay her fourteen hundred coins for carrying his burden for him."

The husband looked wide eyed at the judge.

"One other thing," the judge said. "If it took this much work just to bring the child into the world, think how much it will take to raise it."

The man stood silent, beginning to understand for the first time.

"I see now, Judge," he said at last. "Now I will start to take some of the burden from my wife, so that we might make the scales balance."

•

THE MAGIC CAVERN
Retold by Frances Jenkins Olcott

This is an old tale for the modern era. In today's parlance, it's a story of a parent who needs to get her priorities straight.

Once upon a time, a woman lived in a little hut near a mountain on which was a wide forest. She had one little child whom she loved dearly.

Now, in that forest grew many Strawberries very large and juicy, and one Midsummer Day the woman took the child to pick some. They climbed the mountainside, and presently lighted upon vines that were covered with berries larger, redder, and more luscious than any they had ever seen before.

These they picked. But no sooner had the woman put them in her basket than she saw the door of a large cavern open before her. Great heaps of gold lay glittering on the floor, while three White Maidens sat there guarding the treasure.

"Come in, good Woman," called the White Maidens. "Take as much gold as you can grasp at once."

The woman, holding her child by the hand, entered eagerly. She stooped and grasped a handful of gold and put it in her apron. But the touch of it filled her with greed, and, forgetting her child, she gathered up two more handfuls. Then she turned and ran out of the cave.

Instantly a loud rumbling sounded behind her, and a voice cried out:

"Unhappy Woman! You have lost your little one until next Midsummer Day."

The door of the cavern closed, and the child was shut inside.

Well, the poor woman wrung her hands and wept, but it was of no use, and she had to go home without her child. And though after that she often visited the place where the cavern had opened, she never could find the door.

Early on the next Midsummer Day she hurried to the spot; and what should she see but the door wide open! The great heaps of gold lay glittering on the floor, while the three White Maidens sat there guarding the treasure. And near them stood her little child holding a big red Apple.

"Come in, good Woman," called the White Maidens. "Take as much gold as you can grasp at once."

At that the woman ran eagerly in. She forgot all about the gold, and clasped her dear child in her arms.

"Good Woman," said the White Maidens, "take the little one home. We give it back to you, for now your love is greater than your greed."

So the woman took her child home with her, and loved it better than gold all the days of her life.

•

THE CRAB AND HIS MOTHER

Aesop

All parents are teachers, our first teachers, for better or worse.

A mother crab and her son went scurrying over the sand.

The mother chastised her child: "Stop walking sideways! It's much more becoming to stroll straightforward."

And the young crab replied: "I will, Mother dear, just as soon as I see how. Show me the straight way, and I'll walk in it behind you."

Words are important, but there is nothing like the power of example.

•

THE BABY

Laura E. Richards

The ancient Roman writer Juvenal gave us this advice: "When thou art contemplating some base deed, let thy infant son act as a check on thy headlong course to sin."

A man sat by the door of his house, smoking his pipe; and his neighbor (who was an enemy, though neither of them knew it) sat beside him and tempted him.

"You are poor and out of work," said the neighbor, "and here is a way of bettering yourself. It will be an easy job, and will bring you money; and it is no more dishonest than many things that are done every day by respectable people. You will be a fool to throw away such a chance as this. Come with me, and we will settle the matter."

And the man listened.

Just then his young wife came to the door of the cottage. She was warm and rosy, for she had been washing, and she had the baby in her arms.

"Will you hold Baby for a few minutes, John?" she asked. "He is fretful, and I must hang out the clothes."

The man took the baby and held it on his knees; and as he held it, the child looked up in his face and spoke.

"Flesh of your flesh!" said the baby. "Soul of your soul! What you sow I shall reap, and where you lead I shall follow. Lead the way, Father, for my feet come after yours."

Then the man said to the neighbor, "Go, and come here no more!"

He rocked the baby on his knees, and whistled a tune. Presently his wife came out and took the child.

"Baby, Baby," she said, "how could you cry when Father was holding you? Such a father as you have, too! Mind you grow up as good a man as he is!"

And she went into the house, singing to the child as she went.

•

LITTLE EYES UPON YOU

There are little eyes upon you
and they're watching night and day.
There are little ears that quickly
take in every word you say.
There are little hands all eager
to do anything you do;
And a little boy who's dreaming
of the day he'll be like you.

You're the little fellow's idol,
you're the wisest of the wise.
In his little mind about you
no suspicions ever rise.
He believes in you devoutly,
holds all that you say and do;
He will say and do, in your way,
when he's grown up like you.

There's a wide-eyed little fellow
who believes you're always right;
And his eyes are always opened,
and he watches day and night.
You are setting an example
every day in all you do,
For the little boy who's waiting
to grow up to be like you.

•

A FORTUNE

Laura E. Richards

Much of parenthood is about spending—spending time, effort, attention, money. It's about whom and what we spend on.

One day a man was walking along the street, and he was sad at heart. Business was dull; he had set his desire upon a horse that cost a thousand dollars, and he had only eight hundred to buy it with. There were other things, to be sure, that might be bought with eight hundred dollars, but he did not want those; so he was sorrowful, and thought the world a bad place.

As he walked, he saw a child running toward him. It was a strange child, but when he looked at it, its face lightened like sunshine, and broke into smiles. The child held out its closed hand.

"Guess what I have!" it cried gleefully.

"Something fine, I am sure!" said the man.

The child nodded and drew nearer, then opened its hand.

"Look!" it said, and the street rang with its happy laughter. The man looked, and in the child's hand lay a penny.

"Hurrah!" said the child.

"Hurrah!" said the man.

Then they parted, and the child went and bought a stick of candy, and saw all the world red and white in stripes.

The man went and put his eight hundred dollars in the savings bank, all but fifty cents, and with the fifty cents he bought a hobby-horse for his own little boy, and the little boy saw all the world brown, with white spots.

Is this the horse you wanted so to buy, Father?" asked the little boy.

"It is the horse I have bought!" said the man.

"Hurrah!" said the little boy.

"Hurrah!" said the man. And he saw that the world was a good place after all.

•

WHEN MOTHER READS ALOUD

Here is one of the greatest joys and responsibilities of parents, and an important aid in teaching children about virtue. There is nothing in the world like listening to a story read aloud by a loved one.

When Mother reads aloud, the past
    Seems real as every day;
I hear the tramp of armies vast,
I see the spears and lances cast,
    I join the thrilling fray.
Brave knights and ladies fair and proud
I meet when Mother reads aloud.

When Mother reads aloud, far lands
    Seem very near and true;
I cross the deserts' gleaming sands,
Or hunt the jungle's prowling bands,
    Or sail the ocean blue.
Far heights, whose peaks the cold mists shroud,
I scale, when Mother reads aloud.

When Mother reads aloud, I long
    For noble deeds to do—
To help the right, redress the wrong;
It seems so easy to be strong,
    So simple to be true.
Oh, thick and fast the visions crowd
My eyes, when Mother reads aloud.

•

THE CHARGE OF THE NIGHT BRIGADE

As every parent knows, bedtime can sometimes be a real chore.
But it can also be one of the best times in parenthood.

A scurry of feet on the bedroom stair,
   A titter along the hall—
And this is the charge of the night brigade,
   To capture me heart and all.
And there is the Captain, Sleepy Eyes,
   And there is Lieutenant Dream,
While the only arms of love are theirs
   As into my heart they stream.

A low, little laugh as they form in line
   Robed in their slumber gowns—
No armor rude with its harsh intrude,
   No helmets that clank and frown;
They come for the hug and the goodnight kiss,
   And unto my heart they bring
The song of the bedtime troops of love,
   With its old, ineffable ring.

I sigh as I think of the lonesome folk
   In their fortresses alone,
Where never the children charge with their cheer
   Where the bedtime song's unknown;
Who sit in their childless realm aloof
   Nor ever behold at all
The Sleepy Eyes and the Golden Dream
   Come marching down through the hall.

Who never have felt around their necks
   Nor ever upon their lips,
The soft caress of a little arm,
   Or a kiss with its sweet eclipse;
I do not know what I would do
   Were the bedtime troops away,
And I almost dread the time to come
   When they'll march to the grown-up fray.

In a single file, to a merry tune,
  Whispering, wild with glee,
They turn the knob and open the door
  And rush to the heart of me;
Retreat is vain, resist I won't,
  So on my lap they leap—
The troops of the night brigade that come
  For the kiss of the tender sleep.

•

PROSERPINA

Adapted from retellings by Flora Cooke, Frances Jenkins Olcott, and others

The next two myths associate the warmth of spring and summer with a mother's devotion. It is remarkable that ancient peoples linked something so encompassing and important as the seasons' cycles to the power of mother love.

The story of Proserpina (Persephone to the Greeks) is related by the Roman poet Ovid, among others. The image of Mother Ceres roaming the earth with her great torch in search of her lost daughter is one of the most stirring in classical mythology.

In olden days there lived—or so people believed—a goddess whose name was Ceres. People sometimes called her Mother Ceres, because she had power over all the earth. It was she who made the corn grow and the flowers spring up, who covered the trees with green leaves, who made the fruits ripen and brought the harvest to perfection. On her work and zeal depended all the life of all the people in the world.

Ceres loved all the beautiful ferns and grasses, loved all the trees and plants, but as much as she loved these, there was one thing she loved far more—her little daughter, Proserpina. And Proserpina loved her mother dearly in return, and played in the sunshine among the birds and flowers, and was as happy as the day was long.

One day the girl was playing in the meadow, making a wreath of delicate blossoms for her hair. She decided to take some flowers to her mother as well, so she began to gather as many as her arms could hold—violets and buttercups and daffodils and daisies.

Far away across the meadow she saw a white flower gleaming. She ran to it and found it was far more beautiful than any she had ever seen. On a single stem were a hundred blossoms. She tried to pick it, but the stem would not break. With all her strength she grasped it, and slowly it came up by the roots.

A low, rumbling sound began.

Proserpina stood still, listening. "Can that be thunder? There's not a cloud in the sky," she thought.

The rumbling grew louder, and she realized it came from beneath her feet. Suddenly, where she had pulled up the flower, the earth began to open, wider and wider. Out of the chasm sprang four coal black, fiery horses, and behind them came a chariot made of gold and rubies and other precious stones. In it sat King Pluto.

Pluto was king of the underground world. He lived and reigned alone in a dark, gloomy land, where the sun never shone and birds never sang and flowers never blossomed all the year round. When he saw Proserpina he thought how the presence of this beautiful little laughing child would brighten his gloomy palace. Springing down from his chariot, he strode into the meadow where Proserpina stood knee deep among the flowers. Seizing the frightened girl in his arms, he carried her back to his chariot, in spite of her cries and struggles, and the next minute he was driving away as fast as his steeds could gallop.

Poor Proserpina struggled and screamed, but it was all no use. And so fast did Pluto drive, lest Ceres should overtake him and snatch his newfound treasure from him, that very soon they reached the gate of his underground palace. In her despair, Proserpina snatched her wreath of flowers from her hair and flung it into a river that ran close by, begging the water nymphs to carry it to her mother. Then the gates swung to a crash behind the king's chariot, and Proserpina was a prisoner in the underground world.

Meanwhile, above the earth the sun had set, and Ceres returned to her home after her long day's work. As she came in sight of her dwelling place she looked up eagerly, expecting to see Proserpina come running out as usual to meet her. But tonight no Proserpina appeared. In vain did Ceres hunt for her among her usual haunts. In vain did she call her name in ever-increasing anxiety and alarm. And at last, in fear and distress, she lit a great torch and went out into the darkness searching far and wide, all through the hours of that long, sad night. And when morning dawned and still there was no sign of her dear child, the poor mother determined to leave her work and search through the wide world until she found Proserpina again.

Then began for poor Ceres a long, weary, hopeless search. All her daily duties were neglected. The corn died down, the flowers drooped and faded, and the grass withered away, for there was no one to look after them. The earth grew parched, the leaves fell off the trees, the plough broke in the furrow. The seed failed to come up, and the weeds grew rank and thick. Soon there arose a great famine all through the land. The people cried out to Mother Ceres to return and save them. But Ceres was far away and did not hear them; or if she heard, she did not heed, for she could think of nothing but her lost child.

"O Zephyr! Gentle Zephyr!" she asked the West Wind as he floated by, "have you seen my daughter?"

And when Zephyr whispered, "No," she hastened on.

"O Boreas! Strong Boreas!" she asked the North Wind as he rushed by, "have you seen my daughter?"

And when he roared, "No!" she hastened on.

At last, one day, as she sat beside the banks of a river, mourning and weeping, the waters suddenly flung a wreath of flowers into her lap. When she came to look at it, she knew it had been made by Proserpina's hands. As she gazed at it, longing to know the meaning of the message, she heard a fountain beside her speaking softly. And the fountain told her that, far down in the underground world from whence she had just come, Prosperina was seated on the throne by King Pluto's side.

"She is sad and sorrowful," gurgled the fountain. "Her cheeks are pale and her eyes are heavy with weeping. All King Pluto's wealth and riches cannot reconcile her to being separated from her dear mother."

When Ceres heard this she hurried to Jupiter, the great king of the gods. She told him she had found out where her daughter was hidden, and prayed him to command Pluto to give Proserpina back to her. At first Jupiter was very unwilling to interfere with the king of the underground world. But he saw the mother's tears, and they softened his heart. And the people of the earth joined their prayers to Ceres', and prayed that Jupiter grant her request, so that Ceres might attend to her duties once more and save them from the starvation that threatened them because of the terrible famine.

Then at last Jupiter gave way.

"Proserpina may return to you," he said, "as long as she has eaten no food while she has been in the underworld. Otherwise, she must stay with King Pluto, for that is the law. I will send my messenger Mercury to Pluto's palace right now."

Down in King Pluto's palace, Proserpina was weeping. She would take none of his gifts, and tasted none of his food. She longed only for her mother. Then Pluto remembered that Proserpina had told him that Mother Ceres always gave her fruit to eat, so calling one of his servants, he sent him up to the earth to fetch some.

The servant found the whole earth brown and dead—there was no fruit to be found on any of the trees. At last, however, he found one little withered pomegranate. Taking that, he hurried back to King Pluto's palace.

"Here, Proserpina, eat this," begged the king. "See, it is one of your own pomegranates. I had it brought from the earth for you."

Proserpina would not touch it, but King Pluto placed it near her and went away. It smelled so good that soon Proserpina took it in her hand. It had been so long since she had eaten, and she was so hungry. She lifted it to her lips.

Suddenly the door flew open, and there stood Mercury.

"Stop, Proserpina! Jupiter has sent me to take you home, but if you eat so much as one bite, I cannot take you with me. It is the law."

"I swallowed only six of the seeds!" cried Proserpina.

When Jupiter heard the sad news, he decreed that for each seed she had eaten, Proserpina must spend a month of every year in King Pluto's kingdom.

So for six months of every year Proserpina is obliged to go and live in the dark underground world, where she reigns as Pluto's queen, and while she is away the whole earth mourns for her. Flowers disappear; the leaves fall from the trees; even the skies weep at her departure. But when once more the gates of Pluto's kingdom fly open, and Proserpina comes back to spend six happy months with her mother, the whole earth breaks out into flower and song to greet her. The skies grow blue and smiling; the grass springs up fresh and green; the trees burst out into bud and blossom; and the birds pour out their gladdest, sweetest songs. And the time for the return of Proserpina is what we call spring.

While Ceres has her daughter beside her, she works cheerfully and diligently, and blesses the world with corn and wine, bringing forth an abundant harvest from the earth to provide for the needs of men. But when the time comes for Proserpina to go back to King Pluto, she grows sad and sorrowful, and leaves her work neglected while she mourns for her lost child. Then the people of the world have to live upon the grain and fruit they have garnered from the harvest, and manage for themselves as best they can while Proserpina is away. And the six months that Proserpina has to spend in her dark, gloomy kingdom are what we call winter.

And however long and cold and dreary the winter may be, yet we need never despair. The six months will be ended in good time, and then Proserpina will come back to earth, bringing springtime with her, and all will be sunshine and happiness once more.

THE DEATH OF BALDER

Adapted from a retelling by Anna McCaleb

In Norse mythology, Balder was a son of Odin, the chief of the gods, and Frigga, the goddess for whom some say the day Friday is named. It is thought that Balder represented the blessed, life-bringing influences of the short northern summer, and his death signified the coming of the long winter. Frigga's determination to protect her son, the ironic disaster that follows, and the gods' frantic attempts to bring their beloved friend and kinsman back to Asgard all combine to make this tragedy one of the most moving of the Norse tales.

Of all the gods in Asgard, Balder was the most beloved, for no one had ever seen him frown, and his smile made everyone happy. He was as good as he was beautiful, for he always offered a kind word, and he was forever ready to lift a strong arm to help any creature in need. Wherever he walked, light and warmth seemed to follow.

One morning the gods assembled in their great hall, called Valhalla, and they noticed that when Balder came among them, he looked less radiant than usual. They gathered about him, begging that he tell what troubled him. Balder only smiled and said, "It is nothing!" But it was not his old smile. It reminded the gods of the faint light the sun sheds when a thin cloud has drifted before it, and they knew something was wrong.

When, the next morning, Balder again came slowly into the great hall and showed a careworn face, Odin and Frigga, his father and mother, begged him to share the cause of his grief. At last Balder told them that for two nights he had had strange, haunting dreams. What they were he could not remember clearly when he woke, but he could not shake off their depressing effect.

"I only know," he said, "that there was a thick cloud that drifted between me and the sun, and there were confused sounds of woe, and travels in dark, difficult places."

Now, the gods knew well that their dreams were messages sent to them by the Fates. Frigga sensed that these visions were warnings of some danger that threatened her beloved son, and at once she busied herself with a plan which her mother love suggested.

She went all over the world, and made everything she met promise never to hurt Balder. Every bird, every beast, every creeping thing; all plants, stones, and metals; all diseases and poisons known to the gods and men; fire, water, earth, air—all things gladly took the oath to do Balder no harm, for everything in the world loved Balder for his brightness and kindness.

Gladly Frigga then took her way toward home, feeling certain she had saved Balder forever. As she was about to enter Valhalla, she noticed that on an oak branch grew a tiny, weak-looking shrub.

"That mistletoe is too young to promise, and too weak to do any harm," said Frigga, and she passed it by.

All the gods rejoiced when she told of her success. And when they discovered that nothing could harm Balder now, they invented a new game. Balder, smiling as of old, took his stand in their midst, and all the others hurled things at him, laughing to see how their missiles turned away from the bright young god. They threw stones and sticks, and even spears and swords and great battle-axes that would have killed anyone else on the instant. But all of their weapons fell short, or veered to one side, or floated harmlessly away as though they were blossoms on the wind. The gods grew merry over this pastime, Balder the most of all, and it soon became the favorite sport in Asgard.

But there was one who was jealous of Balder—Loki, the contriver of fraud and mischief, a giant who had forced himself into the company of the gods. When he saw that Balder was being used as a target but remained unhurt through all, he became angry—he could not bear this proof that all things loved Balder. And an evil thought came into his heart. He determined to find out if even one thing had failed to promise never to harm Balder.

And so Loki disguised himself as an old woman and hobbled off to find Frigga.

"Do you know," he croaked, "that the gods and heroes are playing a very dangerous game? They are hurling all sorts of things at your son, who stands in their midst."

"There is no danger," replied Frigga, smiling at the old woman. And she told how everything had sworn to do Balder no harm, everything except the tiny mistletoe, which was too young and feeble to bother.

That was enough for evil Loki. Once out of sight of Frigga, he moved rapidly. Soon he appeared in his own form among the gods, who were still shouting with joy over their game. In his hand he carried a dart; but who could have guessed, to look at it, that it had been fashioned from the mistletoe on the Valhalla oak?

Outside the circle of the gods stood Balder's brother Hoder, who was blind. Hoder was often forlorn, but he loved his young brother with a love that only siblings can share.

Crafty Loki approached him and asked, "Why do you not join the game?"

"Alas," said Hoder, "how can I, with my sightless eyes? And besides, I have nothing to throw."

"Here is a dart," said the wicked god. "Since you cannot direct your aim, I will guide your arm."

Eager to join in the game with his beloved brother, Hoder took the dart in his hand. With Loki's aid, he hurled it with all his might. And because the mistletoe, of all things in the world, had not taken Frigga's oath, it flew straight at Balder's chest, and lodged in his heart, and the young god fell dead on the grass.

Then, instead of the laughter that Hoder waited to hear, there rose a shuddering wail of terror. All the gods and goddesses gathered around Balder's lifeless body, unable to fathom the atrocious deed. The brokenhearted Hoder wept most of all, and begged that he might be allowed to take his brother's place in Death's dark realm.

But Frigga refused to give up hope. She called out to the gods for a volunteer to go down to Hela, the goddess of the dead, and beg her to send Balder back to Asgard. Another of Frigga's sons stepped forward—Hermod, the swiftest of the gods. Odin gave him his horse, a marvelous steed named Sleipner who could outrun the wind itself. At once Hermod mounted and set off on the perilous journey.

For nine days and nine nights Hermod rode through glens so dark he could see nothing, until he reached the river that runs between the upper and lower worlds. When he galloped across the golden bridge, it shook beneath his weight, and the guard of the bridge knew it was no shade but a living being that crossed. But when Hermod told his errand, he was allowed to go on. And at last he came into the presence of the queen of that pale realm. On his knees he begged her to allow Balder to return to the light and the upper air.

At first stern Hela sat unmoved by his pleas, but finally she gave this answer: "If, through all the earth, all things, living and dead, weep for Balder, then he shall return. But if one thing in all the world refuses to shed tears, here he shall stay."

Cheered by this promise, Hermod set out on his journey home. When he reached Asgard there was rejoicing among the gods. At once they set out upon their task, for all the gods wanted a part in the work of bringing Balder back to life. They rode throughout the world, begging everything they found to weep. Trees, stones, flowers, birds, and beasts all joined willingly in grief for Balder, for all knew of his goodness and beauty.

But as the joyful gods returned to Asgard, thinking they had accomplished their mission, they came to the mouth of a dark cave where sat an old woman, withered with age. They begged her to weep for Balder, as all things in heaven and earth had done. But in a shrill voice she mocked them and answered: "Why should I weep for him? Let Hela keep her own. You'll get nothing but dry tears from me."

Then with harsh laughteer she fled to the cave's dark depth. And as she fled, the gods knew that this old woman was none other than Loki himself, the evil Loki who could take any manner of disguise. For a second time he had stolen life from Balder.

And so because one thing in the world would not weep, Hela

kept the young god in her underground kingdom. Sadly the gods rode back to Asgard with grief in their hearts, for they knew that brightness was gone forever—that Balder the beautiful would return no more. And a time of darkness and silence fell over the world.

But the far-seeing Odin could look beyond that time of sorrow. Seated on his great throne in Valhalla, gazing over heaven and earth, the chief of the gods knew that this grief would not last forever. He could see a time coming when the clouds of desolation would part, the sun would shed its rays upon the world, and light would overcome shadows and confusion. The earth would rise green and fresh and smiling, the fields would bear ripened fruit, and Balder would be with his friends and kinsmen once more. And so Odin steeled his heart with courage to endure the dark times that were coming, looking past the long, cold night toward the glowing dawn.

•

"I KNOW OF A LOVELY GARDEN"

Martin Luther

John Donne said that letters mingle souls. Letters can be messages of love that draw parents and children toward each other.

Four-and-a-half centuries after his death, Martin Luther's deep affection for home and children still lives in his writings (including the one most familiar to children everywhere, the hymn beginning, "Away in a manger, no crib for a bed...."). In 1530 Martin Luther wrote the following letter to his son Hans, who was four years old.

To my little son, Hans Luther, grace and peace in Christ

My Heart-dear Little Son: I hear that you learn well and pray diligently. Continue to do so, my son. When I come home I will bring you a fine present from the fair.

I know of a lovely garden, full of joyful children, who wear little golden coats, and pick up beautiful apples, and pears, and cherries, and plums under the trees. They sing, and jump, and make merry. They have also beautiful little horses with golden saddles and silver bridles.

I asked the man that kept the garden who the children were. And he said to me, "The children are those who love to learn, and to pray, and to be good."

Then said I, "Dear sir, I have a little son, named Hans Luther. May he come into this garden, and have the same beautiful apples and pears to eat, and wonderful little horses to ride upon, and may he play about with these children?"

Then said he, "If he is willing to learn, and to pray, and to be good, he shall come into this garden; and his friends Lippus and Justus too. If they all come together, they shall have pipes, and little drums, and lutes, and music of stringed instruments. And they shall dance, and shoot with little crossbows."

Then he showed me a fine meadow in the garden, all laid out for dancing. There hung golden pipes and kettle-drums and fine silver crossbows; but it was too early to see the dancing, for the children had not had their dinner.

I said, "Ah, dear sir, I will instantly go and write to my little son Hans, so that he may study, and pray, and be good, and thus come into this garden. And he has a little cousin Lena, whom he must also bring with him."

Then he said to me: "So shall it be. Go home, and write to him."

Therefore, dear little son Hans, be diligent to learn and to pray; and tell Lippus and Justus to do so, too, that you may all meet together in that beautiful garden. Give cousin Lena a kiss from me. Herewith I recommend you all to the care of Almighty God.

•

"IN REGARD TO DUTY"

Robert E. Lee

Robert E. Lee (1807–1870) wrote this letter to his son, G. W. Custis Lee, who was in school at the time. Here is a father trying to impress his regard for virtue upon his own flesh and blood. There is no more important gift from parent to child. Would that we as parents be worthy to give it.

You must study to be frank with the world; frankness is the child of honesty and courage. Say just what you mean to do on every occasion, and take it for granted you mean to do right. If a friend asks a favor, you should grant it, if it is reasonable; if not, tell him plainly why you cannot; you will wrong him and wrong yourself by equivocation of any kind. Never do a wrong thing to make a friend or keep one; the man who requires you to do so, is dearly purchased at a sacrifice. Deal kindly but firmly, with all your classmates; you will find it the policy which wears best. Above all, do not appear to others what you are not. If you have any fault to find with anyone, tell him, not others, of what you complain; there is no more dangerous experiment than that of undertaking to be one thing before a man's face and another behind his back. We should live, act, and say, nothing to the injury of anyone. It is not only best as a matter of principle, but it is the path to peace and honor.

In regard to duty, let me, in conclusion of this hasty letter, inform you that, nearly a hundred years ago, there was a day of remarkable gloom and darkness—still known as "the dark day"— a day when the light of the sun was slowly extinguished, as if by eclipse. The Legislature of Connecticut was in session, and, as the members saw the unexpected and unaccountable darkness coming on, they shared in the general awe and terror. It was supposed by many that the last day—the day of judgment—had come. Someone, in the consternation of the hour, moved an adjournment. Then there arose an old Puritan legislator, Davenport, of Stamford, and said that, if the last day had come, he desired to be found at his place doing his duty, and, therefore, moved that candles be brought in, so that the House could proceed with its duty. There was quietness in that man's mind, the quietness of heavenly wisdom and inflexible willingness to obey present duty. Duty, then, is the sublimest word in our language. Do your duty in all things like the old Puritan. You cannot do more, you should never wish to do less. Never let me and your mother wear one gray hair for any lack of duty on your part.

•

"LIFT UP YOUR SOUL"

Amos Bronson and Abigail May Alcott

Louisa May Alcott (1832–1888), author of *Little Women,* one of the best-loved of all children's books, received almost all of her early education from her parents. The Alcott family was a remarkably close one despite frequent financial difficulties; as an educator, philosopher, and professional "conversationalist," Amos Bronson Alcott was a somewhat less than successful breadwinner. The success of *Little Women* brought Louisa May the cherished pleasure of being able to support her aging father.

Amos Bronson and Abigail May Alcott often gave their growing children little notes and letters of instruction, guidance, and encouragement. Here are two to Louisa May. Letter writing is a habit more parents should practice; with loving words like these, mothers and fathers not only raise little bodies but also lift little souls.

My Daughter,

You are Seven years old to-day and your Father is forty. You have learned a great many things, since you have lived in a Body, about things going on around you and within you. You know how to think, how to resolve, how to love, and how to obey. You feel your Conscience, and have no real pleasure unless you obey it. You cannot love yourself, or anyone else, when you do not mind its commandments. It asks you always to BE GOOD, and bears, O how gently! how patiently! with all endeavors to hate, and treat it cruelly. How kindly it bears with you all the while. How sweetly it whispers Happiness in your HEART when you Obey its soft words. How it smiles upon you, and makes you Glad when you Resolve to Obey it! How terrible its PUNISHMENTS. It is GOD trying in your soul to keep you always Good.

You begin, my dear daughter, another year this morning. Your Father, your Mother, and Sisters, with your little friends, show their love on this your Birthday, by giving you this BOX. Open it, and take what is in it, and the best wishes of

Your Father.

Beach Street,
Friday morning, Nov. 29, 1839.

15th Birthday,
Hillside.

Dearest,

Accept this pen from your mother and for her sake use it freely & worthily that each day of this your fifteenth year may testify to some good word or thought or work.

I know there will be born into your spirit new hopes, new gifts, for God helps the loving, trusting heart that turns to Him. Lift up your soul to meet the highest, for that alone will satisfy your yearning, aspiring nature.

Your temperament is a peculiar one, & there are few who can really help you. Set about the formation of character & believe me you are capable of obtaining a noble one. Industry, patience, love, creates, endures, gives all things, for these are the attributes of the Almighty, & they make us mighty in all things. May eternal love sustain you, infinite wisdom guide you, & the peace which passeth understanding reward you, my daughter.

Mother.

Nov. 29th, 1846.

•

TO HIS SON, VINCENT CORBET

ON HIS BIRTH-DAY, NOVEMBER 10, 1630,
BEING THEN THREE YEARS OLD.

Richard Corbett

Parents are there to protect their children from harm at the hands of the world—and the world from harm at the hands of their children. Richard Corbet, Bishop of Oxford and Norwich, was a popular poet during the reign of Charles I in the seventeenth century.

What I shall leave thee none can tell,
But all shall say I wish thee well;
I wish thee, Vin, before all wealth,
Both bodily and ghostly health:
Nor too much wealth, nor wit, come to thee,
So much of either may undo thee.

I wish thee learning, not for show,
Enough for to instruct, and know;
Not such as gentlemen require,
To prate at table, or at fire.
I wish thee all thy mother's graces,
Thy father's fortunes, and his places.
I wish thee friends, and one at court,
Not to build on, but support;
To keep thee, not in doing many
Oppressions, but from suffering any.
I wish thee peace in all thy ways,
Nor lazy nor contentious days;
And when thy soul and body part,
As innocent as now thou art.

•

MONICA, MOTHER OF AUGUSTINE

Laura M. Adams

For the discouraged mother, for the mother who has hoped and prayed, feared and wept over a wayward son, Monica, the mother of Saint Augustine, points the way to triumphant victory of mother love.

Early in the fourth century, Monica was born in Tagaste, North Africa. Her parents were Christians, and she was brought up to be a woman of strong, noble character. She seems, however, to have made a sad mistake in her marriage to Patricius, a pagan and a man of ungovernable temper.

Her life was made doubly miserable, because her mother-in-law, from whom Patricius must have inherited his disposition, lived with them, and it is believed aided and abetted him in ill-using Monica and mocking her religious life.

In the town where they lived, however, there were other unhappy wives whose lives would have been sadly embittered, had it not been for the patience and sweetness shown by Monica through all of her trials. In her sufferings she was on their level, but by her loftiness of spirit she helped them to climb with her the mountains of Hope and Courage.

Monica and Patricius had three children; but it was the famous Augustine who brought his mother's name into history, and made her known and loved down through the centuries.

As a little boy Augustine was very wayward. He seems to have inherited all of his father's—and doubtless some also of his grand-mother's—uneven temperament.

He was disobedient, lazy, and unfair in all of his dealings. He said himself, in later years, in his famous book of confessions, "I stole that of which I had enough, and much better. Nor cared I to enjoy what I stole, but joyed in the theft itself."

From boyhood to manhood he seemed to develop more and more into a lazy parasite, feeding upon the lusts of the world, and satisfying only his physical passions. At Carthage, where he studied rhetoric and public speaking for three years, he went often to the chariot races, the gladitorial fights and the theater. While at Carthage his father, who had finally become a Christain, died, and alone in her home Monica wept many a bitter tear over the sins of Augustine.

She prayed continually for him. Just as God's love broods over us in tenderness and love, so the heart of a true mother broods yearningly over the sins and mistakes of her boy, and she would die to save him from himself.

The years passed along and Monica's prayers began to bear fruit. Sick and disgusted with the sinful life he was leading, Augustine became morose and dissatisfied with everything.

His talent for rhetoric and public speaking were so pronounced that he finally took up the teaching of rhetoric in Milan, where he had passed a satisfactory examination.

To Milan the faithful mother followed Augustine, still hoping and praying for his sin-sick soul. Here the young man met a famous bishop by the name of Ambrose, who had a very strong influence for good upon his life.

Monica saw much in her boy's life at Milan to make her troubled, but she wisely refrained from "too much speaking," and contented herself with earnest prayer and Christian example. Little by little the study of the Bible, his mother's prayers, and Bishop Ambrose's sermons, melted the proud heart. Again and again he fought the tempter, and again and again he fell. At last a day came when he had his final battle, and alone in his garden he fought it out, and God triumphed. The *will* to sin was destroyed; and the little mother of many tears found her mourning turned to joy.

Seventeen years of wrestling with God for the soul of this boy. Was it worth it? Ask any mother who has gone through the same Gethsemane, and her face will shine as she answers, "This my son was lost and is found." It was worth any sacrifice.

Augustine now resigned his professorship in rhetoric and devoted his whole time to the service of God. For some time he and his mother lived quietly together while he wrote two books. In the evenings they would talk together about the beautiful things of God; and at the same time the son opened his heart to his mother, and told her of his longing to go back to Africa and preach to those whom in former years he may have led astray.

"It is well, my son; I will go with you," she said. No lagging behind for her own comfort, no diminishing of the ever brooding mother love. It was a wearisome journey over the Apennine Mountains, and the brave mother was pretty well exhausted by the time they reached the seaport of Ostia.

Before starting out on a sea voyage, they rested at Ostia in a house with a pretty garden overlooking the sea. Sitting quietly together in the twilight, evening after evening, Monica little by little revealed to her boy, perhaps unconsciously, the agony of the years through which she had passed, and Augustine was sorely smitten with remorse.

Here at Ostia Monica died; and bitter was the grief of her son. At last, however, a great peace filled his heart, and he resolved to live just as she would have wished him to live, in the love and service of God and his fellow-men.

He went on over to Africa, where he was ordained a priest, and finally became bishop of the town of Hippo. He wrote many books which have influenced the whole course of Christian thought even down to these days. He remained bishop of Hippo until his death, forty-three years after his baptism.

Forty-three years of rich service of God against seventeen years of a mother's prayers! Look up, weary little praying mother; look up, and be faint-hearted no longer. That wayward child of your earnest prayers may some day be an Augustine. Keep right on praying; dry your eyes and take fresh hope. With your hand in God's hand, with your hopes centered upon His glory alone, who knows how soon your boy or girl may come into the Kingdom?

•

THE BRAVEST MAN

Mickey Mantle

Here's a sports hero's hero.

When I was in high school we had to read a play once about a man who was sentenced to death. I don't remember too much about the play except that the man who was about to die was terribly scared and the chaplain of the prison—or somebody who had come to visit him in his cell—tried to comfort him by telling him a line of poetry from Shakespeare. I'm not much on poetry and I don't know very much about Shakespeare, but I have never forgotten the line because the prisoner on his way to his execution kept repeating it. It went, "Cowards die many times before their deaths; the valiant never taste of death but once."

The bravest man I ever knew was my father. He died the winter after my first year in the major leagues, when I was twenty and he was only forty-one. He died of Hodgkin's disease, a form of cancer like leukemia. He knew he had it. He knew it for a long time. He was a tremendously strong man but the disease weakened him so much that he was like a shell of what he used to be. He never told me he was sick, and I believe he never told anybody, until we found out about it by accident.

Here's how I learned about it. In the second game of the 1951 World Series, which was my first World Series, I fell chasing a fly ball in the outfield in Yankee Stadium, and I hurt my knee badly. I was taken home to the hotel I was living in in New York City, and then I had to go to the hospital. My father had come up from home to see the World Series and he had left the game with me and come to the hotel. Now he went with me in a taxi to the hospital. He got out of the cab first, outside the hospital, and then I got out. I was on crutches and I couldn't put any weight on the leg that was hurt, so as I got out of the cab I grabbed my father's shoulder to steady myself. He crumpled to the sidewalk. I couldn't understand it. He was a very strong man and I didn't think anything at all about putting my weight on him that way. He was always so strong. Well, the doctors took him into the hospital, too, and they examined him and then they told me how sick he was. It was incurable, they said, and he had only a few months to live.

After the Series was over and we had gone home to Commerce, Oklahoma, my wife Merlyn and I took my father up to the Mayo Clinic in Rochester, Minnesota, to see if they could do anything. They gave him treatments that eased his pain, but there was nothing anybody could do to cure him. He went home again to Commerce, but then during the winter he decided to go out to Denver. He said there was some hospital or other out there that said it could cure him and he said he thought he'd go out there and see.

He knew they couldn't cure him. But he went out to Denver so that the little kids in our family—I'm the oldest and my sister and three brothers were all just little kids at that time—wouldn't see him wasting away, getting thinner and thinner and sicker and sicker. So he went out to Denver, and he died there. He never complained, he never acted scared, and he died like a man. That line from that play fitted him for sure: "Cowards die many times before their deaths; the valiant never taste of death but once."

My father was brave in lots of ways. I was the oldest child and I was born in October of 1931, right in the middle of the Depression, in Spavinaw, Oklahoma. Kids nowadays don't have any idea of what the Depression was like—it's just a word in the history books —and that's great. But it was a hard time to bring up a family, especially where we lived, which was one of the poorest parts of the country. Even in wealthy parts of the country, people were standing in line for food. Finding work and earning money was the hardest thing in the world to do, and keeping a family alive and fed and happy at the same time was even harder. But he did both, he and my mother (she was pretty brave, too; she had to make do without very much—she did all our cooking on a wood stove, for one thing—but we never felt we were without anything). My father never quit, never admitted defeat.

One year he traded our house in Commerce, where he was working as a miner in the lead and zinc mines we have there, for a farm out in the country. It wasn't much of a farm—we lived in Dust Bowl country and a lot of people had quit and gone to California (you've heard of the Okies, haven't you?). But he thought maybe a farm might mean a better life for us kids. The very first year he had it, there was a flood and the river came up over the farm and ruined it. My father just picked up, went back into town, and down into the mines again.

The thing is, despite all the troubles he and my mother had

because of the Depression, we had a lot of fun growing up. I had a happy boyhood, and even though I probably make more money now in a year than my father made in his life, I don't know that my kids are any happier than we were. I didn't appreciate this as a boy, but as a man I am even more filled with admiration for my father —especially for his courage in the face of trouble.

He was a quiet man and even-tempered and he was well-liked, but he could get pretty mad in that quiet way of his. I remember once there was a dance that everybody went to, a country dance or whatever you want to call it, a barn dance, a square dance. All the families went to it, fathers and mothers and kids and everybody. A couple of wise guys started to make trouble for no reason at all, just to show how mean and stupid they could be, I guess. They made things real unpleasant and they were about to ruin the fine evening that everybody was having. It's funny, but I don't remember a fight or anything else, but all of a sudden there was no more trouble. My uncles told me later that my father took the two troublemakers outside and licked them both. Just like that. No fuss. No bother. He belted them, and they left, and he went back inside, and the dance went on. It got to be a story that people liked to tell when they were sitting around talking about the old days. But my father never talked about it.

He loved baseball and he always wanted me to be a ballplayer. He named me for Mickey Cochrane, the great catcher who was at his peak about the time I was born. Actually, Cochrane had a bad World Series the month I was born, when Pepper Martin and the St. Louis Cardinals were stealing bases on him and running wild. Cochrane was criticized, but baseball men said it wasn't his fault so much as it was his pitchers', who didn't hold the runners tight to their bases. Anyway, one bad Series couldn't affect my father's admiration for Cochrane, and maybe he named me Mickey just to show people that he was still loyal to the man he admired.

When I was growing up my father used to take me with him all the way to St. Louis to see major league games. That was the nearest big league town in those days, and he and friends of his would drive six hundred miles up and back on a weekend to take in a couple of games. My father always took me with him.

I guess my making the major leagues was one of the happiest things that ever happened to my father, and I often think how glad I am that I made it before he died. Though I almost didn't.

That first year I was with the Yankees, when I was nineteen, I

struck out an awful lot. Casey Stengel was the manager and he played me a good part of the time, but even though I got some hits now and then, I kept striking out. It was terrible. Finally, in July, the Yankees decided to send me down to the minors to get rid of the strikeout habit. It is a depressing thing being sent down to the minors, and I felt low. I thought I had missed my big chance. I figured they had looked at me and didn't want me.

The Yanks sent me to Kansas City, which at that time was a Yankee farm club in the American Association. There I got even worse. I believe I got one hit in my first twenty-two at bats, and that was a bunt. My father came up from home to Kansas City to see me play. I was living in a hotel there and, boy, was I glad to see him. I wanted him to pat me on the back and cheer me up and tell me how badly the Yankees had treated me and all that sort of stuff. I guess I was like a little boy, and I wanted him to comfort me.

He said, "How are things going?"

I said, "Awful. The Yankees sent me down to learn not to strike out, but now I can't even hit."

He said, "That so?"

I said, "I'm not good enough to play in the major leagues, and I'm not good enough to play here. I'll never make it. I think I'll quit and go home with you."

I guess I wanted him to say, Oh, don't be silly, you're just in a little slump, you'll be all right, you're great. But he just looked at me for a second and then in a quiet voice that cut me in two he said, "Well, Mick, if that's all the guts you have I think you better quit. You might as well come home right now."

I never felt as ashamed as I did then, to hear my father sound disappointed in me, ashamed of me. I shut my mouth. I didn't say anything more about quitting and going home. I kept playing. Things got better and a month later the Yankees called me back up to the majors, and I've been there ever since.

I have wondered sometimes exactly what it was. I know that I wanted my father to comfort me. He didn't. He didn't give me any advice. He didn't show me how to swing the bat any different. He didn't give me any inspiring speeches. I think that what happened was that he had so much plain ordinary courage that it spilled over, and I could feel it. All he did was show me that I was acting scared, and that you can't live scared.

A year later he was dead. I realized then that he was dying when he came to see me in Kansas City, though he never gave any sign to me. He didn't die scared, and he didn't live scared.

•

HIGH-WATER MARK

Bret Harte

The firm embrace of a parent's arms defines safety for a child. Bret Harte (1836–1902), the most influential writer of fiction about the American West of the Gold Rush era, depicts the courage that comes instinctively to parents when they act to protect their loved ones.

When the tide was out on the Dedlow Marsh, its extended dreariness was patent. Its spongy, low-lying surface, sluggish, inky pools, and tortuous sloughs, twisting their slimy way, eel-like, toward the open bay, were all hard facts. So were the few green tussocks, with their scant blades, their amphibious flavor, and unpleasant dampness.

And if you chose to indulge your fancy—although the flat monotony of the Dedlow Marsh was not inspiring—the wavy line of scattered drift gave an unpleasant consciousness of the spent waters, and made the dead certainty of the returning tide a gloomy reflection, which no present sunshine could dissipate. The greener meadowland seemed oppressed with this idea, and made no positive attempt at vegetation until the work of reclamation should be complete. In the bitter fruit of the low cranberry bushes one might fancy he detected a naturally sweet disposition curdled and soured by an injudicious course of too much regular cold water.

But if Dedlow Marsh was cheerless at the slack of the low tide, you should have seen it when the tide was strong and full. When the damp air blew chilly over the cold glittering expanse, and came to the faces of those who looked seaward like another tide; when a steel-like glint marked the low hollows and the sinuous line of slough; when the great shell-incrusted trunks of fallen trees arose again, and went forth on their dreary purposeless wanderings. When the glossy ducks swung silently, making neither ripple nor furrow on the shimmering surface; when the fog came in with the tide and shut out the blue above, even as the green below had been obliterated; when boatmen, lost in that fog, paddling about in a hopeless way, started at what seemed the brushing of mermen's fingers on the boat's keel, or shrank from the tufts of grass spreading around like the floating hair of a corpse, and knew by these signs that they were lost upon Dedlow Marsh, and must make a night of it, and a gloomy one at that—then you might know something of Dedlow Marsh at high water.

Let me recall a story connected with this latter view which never failed to recur to my mind in my long gunning excursions upon Dedlow Marsh. Although the event was briefly recorded in the county paper, I had the story, in all its eloquent detail, from the lips of the principal actor. I cannot hope to catch the varying emphasis and peculiar coloring of feminine delineation, for my narrator was a woman; but I'll try to give at least its substance.

She lived midway of the great slough of Dedlow Marsh and a good-sized river, which debouched four miles beyond into an estuary formed by the Pacific Ocean, on the long sandy peninsula which constituted the southwestern boundary of a noble bay. The house in which she lived was a small frame cabin raised from the marsh a few feet by stout piles, and was three miles distant from the settlements upon the river. Her husband was a logger—a profitable business in a country where the principal occupation was the manufacture of lumber.

It was the season of early spring, when her husband left on the ebb of a high tide with a raft of logs for the usual transportation to the lower end of the bay. As she stood by the door of the little cabin when the voyagers departed, she noticed a cold look in the southeastern sky, and she remembered hearing her husband say to his companions that they must endeavor to complete their voyage before the coming of the south-westerly gale which he saw brewing. And that night it began to storm and blow harder than she had ever before experienced, and some great trees fell in the forest by the river, and the house rocked like her baby's cradle.

But however the storm might roar about the little cabin, she knew that one she trusted had driven bolt and bar with his own strong hand, and that had he feared for her he would not have left her. This, and her domestic duties, and the care of her little sickly baby, helped to keep her mind from dwelling on the weather, except, of course, to hope that he was safely harbored with the logs at Utopia in the dreary distance. But she noticed that day, when she went out to feed the chickens and look after the cow, that the tide was up to the little fence of her garden patch, and the roar of the surf on the south beach, though miles away, she could hear distinctly.

And she began to think that she would like to have someone to talk with about matters, and she believed that if it had not been so far and so stormy, and the trail so impassable, she would have taken the baby and have gone over to Ryckman's, her nearest neighbor. But then, you see, he might have returned in the storm, all wet, with no one to see him; and it was a long exposure for baby, who was croupy and ailing.

But that night, she never could tell why, she didn't feel like sleeping or even lying down. The storm had somewhat abated, but she still "sat and sat," and even tried to read. I don't know whether it was a Bible or some profane magazine that this poor woman read, but most probably the latter, for the words all ran together and made such sad nonsense that she was forced at last to put the book down and turn to that dearer volume which lay before her in the cradle, with its white initial leaf as yet unsoiled, and try to look forward to its mysterious future. And, rocking the cradle, she thought of everything and everybody, but still was wide awake as ever.

It was nearly twelve o'clock when she at last lay down in her clothes. How long she slept she could not remember, but she awoke with a dreadful choking in her throat, and found herself standing, trembling all over, in the middle of the room, with her baby clasped to her breast, and she was "saying something." The baby cried and sobbed, and she walked up and down trying to hush it, when she heard a scratching at the door. She opened it fearfully, and was glad to see it was only old Pete, their dog, who crawled, dripping with water, into the room.

She would have liked to look out, not in the faint hope of her husband's coming, but to see how things looked; but the wind shook the door so savagely that she could hardly hold it. Then she sat down a little while, and then walked up and down a little while, and then she lay down again a little while. Lying close by the wall of the little cabin, she thought she heard once or twice something scrape slowly against the clapboards, like the scraping of branches.

Then there was a little gurgling sound, like the baby made when it was swallowing, then something went "click-click" and "cluck-cluck," so that she sat up in bed. When she did so she was attracted by something else that seemed creeping from the back door toward the center of the room. It wasn't much wider than her little finger, but soon it swelled to the width of her hand, and began spreading all over the floor. It was water!

She ran to the front door and threw it wide open, and saw nothing but water. She ran to the back door and threw it open, and saw nothing but water. She ran to the side window, and throwing that open, she saw nothing but water. Then she remembered hearing her husband once say that there was no danger in the tide, for that fell regularly, and people could calculate on it, and that he would rather live near the bay than the river, whose banks might overflow at any time. But was it the tide?

So she ran again to the back door, and threw out a stick of wood, It drifted away towards the bay. She scooped up some of the water and put it eagerly to her lips. It was fresh and sweet. It was the river, and not the tide!

It was then—oh, God be praised for his goodness! she did neither faint nor fall; it was then—blessed be the Saviour, for it was his merciful hand that touched and strengthened her in this awful moment—that fear dropped from her like a garment, and her trembling ceased. It was then and thereafter that she never lost her self-command, through all the trials of that gloomy night.

She drew the bedstead toward the middle of the room, and placed a table upon it, and on that she put the cradle. The water on the floor was already over her ankles, and the house once or twice moved so perceptibly, and seemed to be racked so, that the closet doors all flew open.

Then she heard the same rasping and thumping against the wall, and, looking out, saw that a large uprooted tree, which had lain near the road at the upper end of the pasture, had floated down to the house. Luckily its long roots dragged in the soil and kept it from moving as rapidly as the current, for had it struck the house in its full career, even the strong nails and bolts in the piles could not have withstood the shock. The hound had leaped upon its knotty surface, and crouched near the roots, shivering and whining.

A ray of hope flashed across her mind. She drew a heavy blanket from the bed, and, wrapping it about the babe, waded in the deepening waters to the door. As the tree swung again, broadside on, making the little cabin creak and tremble, she leaped on to its trunk. By God's mercy she succeeded in obtaining a footing on its slippery surface, and, twining an arm about its roots, she held in the other her moaning child.

Then something cracked near the front porch, and the whole front of the house she had just quitted fell forward—just as cattle fall on their knees before they lie down—and at the same moment the great redwood tree swung round and drifted away with its living cargo into the black night.

For all the excitement and danger, for all her soothing of her crying babe, for all the whistling of the wind, for all the uncertainty of her situation, she still turned to look at the deserted and water-swept cabin. She remembered even then, and she wondered how foolish she was to think of it at that time, that she wished she had put on another dress and the baby's best clothes; and she kept praying that the house would be spared so that he, when he returned, would have something to come to, and it wouldn't be quite so desolate and—how could he ever know what had become of her and baby? And at the thought she grew sick and faint. But she had something else to do besides worrying, for whenever the long roots of her ark struck an obstacle the whole trunk made half a revolution, and twice dipped her in the black water.

The hound, who kept distracting her by running up and down the tree and howling, at last fell off at one of these collisions. He swam for some time beside her, and she tried to get the poor beast upon the tree, but he "acted silly" and wild, and at last she lost sight of him forever. Then she and her baby were left alone.

The light which had burned for a few minutes in the deserted cabin was quenched suddenly. She could not then tell whither she was drifting. The outline of the white dunes on the peninsula showed dimly ahead, and she judged the tree was moving in a line with the river. It must be about slack water, and she had probably reached the eddy formed by the confluence of the tide and the overflowing waters of the river.

Unless the tide fell soon, there was present danger of her drifting to its channel, and being carried out to sea or crushed in the floating drift. That peril averted, if she were carried out on the ebb toward the bay, she might hope to strike one of the wooded promontories of the peninsula, and rest till daylight.

Sometimes she thought she heard voices and shouts from the river, and the bellowing of cattle and bleating of sheep. Then again it was only the ringing in her ears and throbbing of her heart. She found at about this time that she was so chilled and stiffened in her cramped position that she could scarcely move, and the baby cried so when she put it to her breast that she noticed the milk refused to flow; and she was so frightened at that that she put her head under her shawl, and for the first time cried bitterly.

When she raised her head again the boom of the surf was behind her, and she knew that her ark had again swung round. She dipped up the water to cool her parched throat, and found that it was salt as her tears. There was a relief, though, for by this sign she knew that she was drifting with the tide. It was then the wind went down, and the great and awful silence oppressed her. There was scarcely a ripple against the furrowed sides of the great trunk on which she rested, and around her all was black gloom and quiet.

She spoke to the baby just to hear herself speak, and to know that she had not lost her voice. She thought then—it was queer, but she could not help thinking it—how awful must have been the night when the great ship swung over the Asiatic peak, and the sounds of creation were blotted out from the world. She thought, too, of mariners clinging to spars, and of poor women who were lashed to rafts and beaten to death by the cruel sea. She tried to thank God that she was thus spared, and lifted her eyes from the baby who had fallen into a fretful sleep.

Suddenly, away to the southward, a great light lifted itself out of the gloom, and flashed and flickered, and flickered and flashed again. Her heart fluttered quickly against the baby's cold cheek. It was the lighthouse at the entrance of the bay. As she was yet wondering the tree suddenly rolled a little, dragged a little, and then seemed to lie quiet and still. She put out her hand and the current gurgled against it. The tree was aground, and, by the position of the light and the noise of the surf, aground upon the Dedlow Marsh.

Had it not been for her baby, who was ailing and croupy, had it not been for the sudden drying up of that sensitive fountain, she would have felt safe and relieved. Perhaps it was this which tended to make all her impressions mournful and gloomy. As the tide rapidly fell, a great flock of black brant fluttered by her, screaming and crying. Then the plover flew up and piped mournfully as they wheeled around the trunk, and at last fearlessly lit upon it like a gray cloud. Then the heron flew over and around her, shrieking and protesting, and at last dropped its gaunt legs only a few yards from her.

But, strangest of all, a pretty white bird, larger than a dove—like a pelican, but not a pelican—circled around and around her. At last it lit upon a rootlet of the tree quite over her shoulder. She put out her hand and stroked its beautiful white neck, and it never appeared to move. It stayed there so long that she thought she would lift up the baby to see it and try to attract her attention. But when she did so, the child was so chilled and cold, and had such a blue look under the little lashes, which it didn't raise at all, that she screamed aloud, and the bird flew away, and she fainted.

Well, that was the worst of it, and perhaps it was not so much, after all, to any but herself. For when she recovered her senses it was bright sunlight and dead low water. There was a confused noise of guttural voices about her, and an old squaw, singing an Indian "hushaby," and rocking herself from side to side before a fire built on the marsh, before which she, the recovered wife and mother, lay weak and weary.

Her first thought was for her baby, and she was about to speak when a young squaw, who must have been a mother herself, fathomed her thought and brought her the "mowitch," pale but living, in such a queer little willow cradle, all bound up, just like the squaw's own young one, that she laughed and cried together, and the young squaw and the old squaw showed their big white teeth and glinted their black eyes, and said, "Plenty get well, skeena mowitch," "Wagee man come plenty soon," and she could have kissed their brown faces in her joy.

And then she found that they had been gathering berries on the marsh in their queer comical baskets, and saw the skirt of her gown fluttering on the tree from afar, and the old squaw couldn't resist the temptation of procuring a new garment, and came down and discovered the "wagee" woman and child.

And of course she gave the garment to the old squaw, as you may imagine, and when *he* came at last and rushed up to her, looking about ten years older in his anxiety, she felt so faint again that they had to carry her to the canoe. For, you see, he knew nothing about the flood until he met the Indians at Utopia, and knew by the signs that the poor woman was his wife. And at the next high tide he towed the tree away back home, although it wasn't worth the trouble, and built another house, using the old tree for the foundation and props, and called it after her, "Mary's Ark!"

But you may guess the next house was built above highwater mark. And that's all.

Not much, perhaps, considering the malevolent capacity of the Dedlow Marsh. But you must tramp over it at low water, or paddle over it at high tide, or get lost upon it once or twice in the fog, as I have, to understand properly Mary's adventure, or to appreciate duly the blessings of living beyond high-water mark.

•

BEFORE HULL HOUSE

Jane Addams

In 1889 Jane Addams and Ellen Gates Starr turned a dilapidated Chicago mansion into a place where reform-minded people could live and work to improve neighborhood conditions. It was the beginning of Hull House, America's most famous settlement house. There, residents taught English to immigrants, established the first public playground in Chicago, promoted cleaner streets, pushed for child labor laws, organized civic groups, and pursued countless endeavors and reforms to improve living conditions in the city. By 1907 the settlement had grown to twelve buildings and covered a whole block.

The following excerpts come from the first chapter of Addams's *Twenty Years at Hull House.* In these recollections we discover one influence that engendered in this woman such a generous spirit—her father. Addams once wrote that "the child becomes largely what it is taught, hence we must watch what we teach it, and how we live before it." Here is a father living before his daughter in a great manner which helped shape her great character. That great manner was his example. Again, there is nothing like the moral power of example.

On the theory that our genuine impulses may be connected with our childish experiences, that one's bent may be tracked back to that "No-Man's Land" where character is formless but nevertheless settling into definite lines of future development, I begin this record with some impressions of my childhood.

All of these are directly connected with my father, although of course I recall many experiences apart from him. I was one of the younger members of a large family and an eager participant in the village life, but because my father was so distinctly the dominant influence and because it is quite impossible to set forth all of one's early impressions, it has seemed simpler to string these first memories on that single cord. Moreover, it was this cord which not only held fast my supreme affection, but also first drew me into the moral concerns of life, and later afforded a clew there to which I somewhat wistfully clung in the intricacy of its mazes.

It must have been from a very early period that I recall "horrid nights" when I tossed about in my bed because I had told a lie. I was held in the grip of a miserable dread of death, a double fear, first, that I myself should die in my sins and go straight to that fiery Hell which was never mentioned at home, but which I had heard all about from other children, and, second, that my father—representing the entire adult world which I had basely deceived—should himself die before I had time to tell him. My only method of obtaining relief was to go downstairs to my father's room and make full confession. The high resolve to do this would push me out of bed and carry me down the stairs without a touch of fear. But at the foot of the stairs I would be faced by the awful necessity of passing the front door—which my father, because of his Quaker tendencies, did not lock—and of crossing the wide and black expanse of the living room in order to reach his door. I would invariably cling to the newel post while I contemplated the perils of the situation, complicated by the fact that the literal first step meant putting my bare foot upon a piece of oilcloth in front of the door, only a few inches wide, but lying straight in my path. I would finally reach my father's bedside perfectly breathless and, having panted out the history of my sin, invariably received the same assurance that if he "had a little girl who told lies," he was very glad that she "felt too bad to go to sleep afterwards." No absolution was asked for nor received, but apparently the sense that the knowledge of my wickedness was shared, or an obscure understanding of the affection which underlay the grave statement, was sufficient, for I always went back to bed as bold as a lion, and slept, if not the sleep of the just, at least that of the comforted.

I recall an incident which must have occurred before I was seven years old, for the mill in which my father transacted his business that day was closed in 1867. The mill stood in the neighboring town adjacent to its poorest quarter. Before then I had always seen the little city of ten thousand people with the admiring eyes of a country child, and it had never occurred to me that all its streets were not as bewilderingly attractive as the one which contained the glittering toyshop and the confectioner. On that day I had my first sight of the poverty which implies squalor, and felt the curious distinction between the ruddy poverty of the country and that which even a small city presents in its shabbiest streets. I remember launching at my father the pertinent inquiry why people lived in such horrid little houses so close together, and that after receiving his explanation I declared with much firmness when I grew up I should, of course, have a large house, but it would not be built among the other large houses, but right in the midst of horrid little houses like these. . . .

An incident which stands out clearly in my mind as an exciting suggestion of the great world of moral enterprise and serious undertakings occurred in 1872, when I was not yet twelve years old. I came into my father's room one morning to find him sitting beside the fire with a newspaper in his hand, looking very solemn; and upon my eager inquiry what had happened, he told me that Joseph Mazzini was dead. I had never even heard Mazzini'a name, and after being told about him I was inclined to grow argumentative, asserting that my father did not know him, that he was not an American, and that I could not understand why we should be expected to feel badly about him. It is impossible to recall the conversation with the complete breakdown of my cheap arguments, but in the end I obtained that which I have ever regarded as a valuable possession, a sense of the genuine relationship which may exist between men who share large hopes and like desires, even though they differ in nationality, language, and creed; that those things count for absolutely nothing between groups of men who are trying to abolish slavery in America or to throw off Hapsburg oppression in Italy. At any rate, I was heartily ashamed of my meager notion of patriotism, and I came out of the room exhilarated with the consciousness that impersonal and international relations are actual facts and not mere phrases. I was filled with pride that I knew a man who held converse with great minds and who really sorrowed and rejoiced over happenings across the sea. I never recall those early conversations with my father, nor a score of others like them, but there comes into my mind a line from Mrs. Browning in which a daughter describes her relations with her father:—

> "He wrapt me in his large
> Man's doublet, careless did it fit or no."

•

DISTANCE

Raymond Carver

This is a story about a new father who must make a choice between pleasure and responsibility, and his discovery about which of the two brings the greater and firmer happiness. All fathers know this predicament.

She's in Milan for Christmas and wants to know what it was like when she was a kid. Always that on the rare occasions when he sees her.

Tell me, she says. Tell me what it was like then. She sips Strega, waits, eyes him closely.

She is a cool, slim, attractive girl, a survivor from top to bottom.

That was a long time ago. That was twenty years ago, he says. They're in his apartment on the Via Fabroni near the Cascina Gardens.

You can remember, she says. Go on, tell me.

What do you want to hear? he asks. What can I tell you? I could tell you about something that happened when you were a baby. It involves you, he says. But only in a minor way.

Tell me, she says. But first get us another drink, so you won't have to interrupt half way through.

He comes back from the kitchen with drinks, settles into his chair, begins.

They were kids themselves, but they were crazy in love, this eighteen-year-old boy and his seventeen-year-old girl friend when they married. Not all that long afterwards they had a daughter.

The baby came along in late November during a severe cold spell that just happened to coincide with the peak of the waterfowl season in that part of the country. The boy loved to hunt, you see, that's part of it.

The boy and girl, husband and wife now, father and mother, lived in a three-room apartment under a dentist's office. Each night they cleaned the upstairs office in exchange for their rent and utilities. In the summer they were expected to maintain the lawn and the flowers, and in winter the boy shoveled snow from the walks and spread rock salt on the pavement. The two kids, I'm telling you, were very much in love. On top of this they had great ambitions and they were wild dreamers. They were always talking about the things they were going to do and the places they were going to go.

He gets up from his chair and looks out the window for a minute over the tile rooftops at the snow that falls steadily through the late afternoon light.

Tell the story, she says.

The boy and girl slept in the bedroom, and the baby slept in a crib in the living room. You see, the baby was about three weeks old at this time and had only just begun to sleep through the night.

One Saturday night, after finishing his work upstairs, the boy went into the dentist's office, put his feet up on the desk, and called Carl Sutherland, an old hunting and fishing friend of his father's.

Carl, he said when the man picked up the receiver. I'm a father. We had a baby girl.

Congratulations, boy, Carl said. How is the wife?

She's fine, Carl. The baby's fine, too, the boy said. Everybody's fine.

That's good, Carl said. I'm glad to hear it. Well, you give my regards to the wife. If you called about going hunting, I'll tell you something. The geese are flying down there to beat the band. I don't think I've ever seen so many of them and I've been going for years. I shot five today. Two this morning and three this afternoon. I'm going back in the morning and you come along if you want to.

I want to, the boy said. That's why I called.

You be here at five-thirty sharp then and we'll go, Carl said. Bring lots of shells. We'll get some shooting in all right. I'll see you in the morning.

The boy liked Carl Sutherland. He'd been a friend of the boy's father, who was dead now. After the father's death, maybe trying to replace the loss they both felt, the boy and Sutherland had started hunting together. Sutherland was a heavy-set, balding man who lived alone and was not given to casual talk. Once in a while, when they were together, the boy felt uncomfortable, wondered if he had said or done something wrong because he was not used to being around people who kept still for long periods of time. But when he did talk the older man was often opinionated, and frequently the boy didn't agree with the opinions. Yet the man had a toughness and woods-savvy about him that the boy liked and admired.

The boy hung up the telephone and went downstairs to tell the girl. She watched while he laid out his things. Hunting coat, shell bag, boots, socks, hunting cap, long underwear, pump gun.

What time will you be back? the girl asked.

Probably around noon, he said. But maybe not until after five or six o'clock. Is that too late?

It's fine, she said. We'll get along just fine. You go and have some fun. You deserve it. Maybe tomorrow evening we'll dress Catherine up and go visit Sally.

Sure, that sounds like a good idea, he said. Let's plan on that.

Sally was the girl's sister. She was ten years older. The boy was a little in love with her, just as he was a little in love with Betsy, who was another sister the girl had. He'd said to the girl, If we weren't married I could go for Sally.

What about Betsy? the girl had said. I hate to admit it but I truly feel she's better looking than Sally or me. What about her?

Betsy too, the boy said and laughed. But not in the same way I could go for Sally. There's something about Sally you could fall for. No, I believe I'd prefer Sally over Betsy, if I had to make a choice.

But who do you really love? the girl asked. Who do you love most in all the world? Who's your wife?

You're my wife, the boy said.

And will we always love each other? the girl asked, enormously enjoying this conversation he could tell.

Always, the boy said. And we'll always be together. We're like the Canada geese, he said, taking the first comparison that came to mind, for they were often on his mind in those days. They only marry once. They choose a mate early in life, and they stay together always. If one of them dies or something, the other one will never remarry. It will live off by itself somewhere, or even continue to live with the flock, but it will stay single and alone amongst all the other geese.

That's sad, the girl said. It's sadder for it to live that way, I

think, alone but with all the others, than just to live off by itself
somewhere.

It is sad, the boy said. But it's Nature.

Have you ever killed one of those marriages? she asked. You
know what I mean.

He nodded. He said. Two or three times I've shot a goose, then
a minute or two later I'd see another goose turn back from the rest
and begin to circle and call over the goose that lay on the ground.

Did you shoot it too? she asked with concern.

If I could, he answered. Sometimes I missed.

And it didn't bother you? she said.

Never, he said. You can't think about it when you're doing it.
You see, I love everything there is about geese. I love to just watch
them even when I'm not hunting them. But there are all kinds of
contradictions in life. You can't think about the contradictions.

After dinner he turned up the furnace and helped her bathe
the baby. He marveled again at the infant who had half his features,
the eyes and mouth, and half the girl's, the chin and the nose. He
powdered the tiny body and then powdered in between the fingers
and toes. He watched the girl put the baby into its diaper and
pajamas.

He emptied the bath into the shower basin and then he went
upstairs. It was cold and overcast outside. His breath streamed in
the air. The grass, what there was of it, looked like canvas, stiff and
gray under the street light. Snow lay in piles beside the walk. A car
went by and he heard sand grinding under the tires. He let himself
imagine what it might be like tomorrow, geese milling in the air
over his head, the gun plunging against his shoulder.

Then he locked the door and went downstairs.

In bed they tried to read but both of them fell asleep, she first,
letting the magazine sink to the quilt. His eyes closed, but he roused
himself, checked the alarm, and turned off the lamp.

He woke to the baby's cries. The light was on out in the living
room. He could see the girl standing beside the crib rocking the
baby in her arms. In a minute she put the baby down, turned out
the light and came back to bed.

It was two o'clock in the morning and the boy fell asleep once
more.

The baby's cries woke him again. This time the girl continued
to sleep. The baby cried fitfully for a few minutes and stopped. The
boy listened, then began to doze.

He opened his eyes. The living room light was burning. He sat up and turned on the lamp.

I don't know what's wrong, the girl said, walking back and forth with the baby. I've changed her and given her something more to eat. But she keeps crying. She won't stop crying. I'm so tired I'm afraid I might drop her.

You come back to bed, the boy said. I'll hold her for a while.

He got up and took the baby while the girl went to lie down.

Just rock her for a few minutes, the girl said from the bedroom. Maybe she'll go back to sleep.

The boy sat on the sofa and held the baby. He jiggled it in his lap until its eyes closed. His own eyes were near closing. He rose carefully and put the baby back in the crib.

It was fifteen minutes to four and he still had forty-five minutes that he could sleep. He crawled into bed.

But a few minutes later the baby began to cry once more. This time they both got up, and the boy swore.

For God's sake what's the matter with you? the girl said to him. Maybe she's sick or something. Maybe we shouldn't have given her the bath.

The boy picked up the baby. The baby kicked its feet and was quiet. Look, the boy said, I really don't think there's anything wrong with her.

How do you know that? the girl said. Here, let me have her. I know that I ought to give her something, but I don't know what I should give her.

After a few minutes had passed and the baby had not cried, the girl put the baby down again. The boy and the girl looked at the baby, and then they looked at each other as the baby opened its eyes and began to cry.

The girl took the baby. Baby, baby, she said with tears in her eyes.

Probably it's something on her stomach, the boy said.

The girl didn't answer. She went on rocking the baby in her arms, paying no attention now to the boy.

The boy waited a minute longer, then went to the kitchen and put on water for coffee. He drew on his woolen underwear and buttoned up. Then he got into his clothes.

What are you doing? the girl said to him.

Going hunting, he said.

I don't think you should, she said. Maybe you could go later

on in the day if the baby is all right then. But I don't think you
should go hunting this morning. I don't want to be left alone with
the baby crying like this.

Carl's planning on me going, the boy said. We've planned it.

I don't give a damn about what you and Carl have planned, she
said. And I don't give a damn about Carl, either. I don't even know
the man. I don't want you to go is all. I don't think you should even
consider wanting to go under the circumstances.

You've met Carl before, you know him, the boy said. What do
you mean you don't know him?

That's not the point and you know it, the girl said. The point is
I don't intend to be left alone with a sick baby.

Wait a minute, the boy said. You don't understand.

No, you don't understand, she said. I'm your wife. This is your
baby. She's sick or something. Look at her. Why is she crying? You
can't leave us to go hunting.

Don't get hysterical, he said.

I'm saying you can go hunting any time, she said. Something's
wrong with this baby and you want to leave us to go hunting.

She began to cry. She put the baby back in the crib, but the
baby started up again. The girl dried her eyes hastily on the sleeve
of her nightgown and picked the baby up once more.

The boy laced his boots slowly, put on his shirt, sweater, and
his coat. The kettle whistled on the stove in the kitchen.

You're going to have to choose, the girl said. Carl or us, I mean
it, you've got to choose.

What do you mean? the boy said.

You heard what I said, the girl answered. If you want a family
you're going to have to choose.

They stared at each other. Then the boy took his hunting gear
and went upstairs. He started the car, went around to the windows
and, making a job of it, scraped away the ice.

The temperature had dropped during the night, but the
weather had cleared so that the stars had come out. The stars
gleamed in the sky over his head. Driving, the boy looked out at
the stars and was moved when he considered their distance.

Carl's porchlight was on, his station wagon parked in the drive
with the motor idling. Carl came outside as the boy pulled to the
curb. The boy had decided.

You might want to park off the street, Carl said as the boy came
up the walk. I'm ready, just let me hit the lights. I feel like hell, I

really do, he went on. I thought maybe you had overslept so I just this minute called your place. Your wife said you had left. I feel like hell.

It's okay, the boy said, trying to pick his words. He leaned his weight on one leg and turned up his collar. He put his hands in his coat pockets. She was already up, Carl. We've both been up for a while. I guess there's something wrong with the baby. I don't know. The baby keeps crying, I mean. The thing is, I guess I can't go this time, Carl.

You should have just stepped to the phone and called me, boy, Carl said. It's okay. You know you didn't have to come over here to tell me. What the hell, this hunting business you can take it or leave it. It's not important. You want a cup of coffee?

I'd better get back, the boy said.

Well, I expect I'll go ahead then, Carl said. He looked at the boy.

The boy kept standing on the porch, not saying anything.

It's cleared up, Carl said. I don't look for much action this morning. Probably you won't have missed anything anyway.

The boy nodded. I'll see you, Carl, he said.

So long, Carl said. Hey, don't let anybody ever tell you otherwise, Carl said. You're a lucky boy and I mean that.

The boy started his car and waited. He watched Carl go through the house and turn off all the lights. Then the boy put the car in gear and pulled away from the curb.

The living room light was on, but the girl was asleep on the bed and the baby was asleep beside her.

The boy took off his boots, pants and shirt. He was quiet about it. In his socks and woolen underwear, he sat on the sofa and read the morning paper.

Soon it began to turn light outside. The girl and the baby slept on. After a while the boy went to the kitchen and began to fry bacon.

The girl came out in her robe a few minutes later and put her arms around him without saying anything.

Hey, don't catch your robe on fire, the boy said. She was leaning against him but touching the stove, too.

I'm sorry about earlier, she said. I don't know what got into me. I don't know why I said those things.

It's all right, he said. Here, let me get this bacon.

I didn't mean to snap like that, she said. It was awful.

It was my fault, he said. How's Catherine?

She's fine now. I don't know what was the matter with her earlier. I changed her again after you left, and then she was fine. She was just fine and she went right off to sleep. I don't know what it was. Don't be mad with us.

The boy laughed. I'm not mad with you. Don't be silly, he said. Here, let me do something with this pan.

You sit down, the girl said. I'll fix this breakfast. How does a waffle sound with this bacon?

Sounds great, he said. I'm starved.

She took the bacon out of the pan and then she made waffle batter. He sat at the table, relaxed now, and watched her move around the kitchen.

She left to close their bedroom door. In the living room she put on a record that they both liked.

We don't want to wake that one up again, the girl said.

That's for sure, the boy said and laughed.

She put a plate in front of him with bacon, a fried egg, and a waffle. She put another plate on the table for herself. It's ready, she said.

It looks swell, he said. He spread butter and poured syrup over the waffle. But as he started to cut into the waffle, he turned the plate into his lap.

I don't believe it, he said jumping up from the table.

The girl looked at him and then at the expression on his face. She began to laugh.

If you could see yourself in the mirror, she said. She kept laughing.

He looked down at the syrup that covered the front of his woolen underwear, at the pieces of waffle, bacon, and egg that clung to the syrup. He began to laugh.

I was starved, he said, shaking his head.

You were starved, she said laughing.

He peeled off the woolen underwear and threw it at the bath-room door. Then he opened his arms and she moved into them.

We won't fight any more, she said. It's not worth it, is it?

That's right, he said.

We won't fight any more, she said.

The boy said, We won't. Then he kissed her.

He gets up from his chair and refills their glasses.

That's it, he says. End of story. I admit it's not much of one.

I was interested, she says. It was very interesting if you want to know. But what happened? she says. I mean later.

He shrugs and carries his drink over to the window. It's dark now but still snowing.

Things change, he says. I don't know how they do. But they do without your realizing it or wanting them to.

Yes, that's true, only—but she does not finish what she started.

She drops the subject then. In the window's reflection he sees her study her nails. Then she raises her head. Speaking brightly, she asks if he is going to show her the city, after all.

He says, Put your boots on and let's go.

But he stays by the window, remembering that life. They had laughed. They had leaned on each other and laughed until the tears had come, while everything else—the cold and where he'd go in it —was outside, for a while anyway.

•

ADMETUS AND ALCESTIS

Adapted from a retelling by James Baldwin

Stories of one spouse risking or even giving up life for the other appear over and over throughout the ages. The next four legends form a remarkable collection—two Greek, one Native American, and one Hindu—showing how love between husband and wife can challenge even death.

The first tale takes place in the region of classical Greece called Thessaly. The ancient writers Euripides and Apollodorus, among others, tell the story.

Admetus was the name of a Grecian king who ruled many, many years ago. He fell in love with a beautiful woman named Alcestis and asked if she would be his wife.

The wedding day arrived, and the guests came from far and wide. Apollo himself came down from Mount Olympus to join the feast, and he brought a present for the young bridegroom. It was a promise from the gods on the mountaintop that if Admetus should ever be sick and in danger of death, he might become well again if someone who loved him would die in his place.

Admetus and Alcestis lived together happily for a long time, and all the people in their little kingdom loved and blessed them. But at last Admetus fell sick, and, as he grew worse and worse every day, all hope that he would ever get well was lost. Then those who loved him remembered the wedding gift that Apollo had given him, and they began to ask who would be willing to die in his stead.

His father and mother were very old and could hope to live but a short time at best, and so it was thought that one of them would be glad to give up life for the sake of their son. But when someone asked them about it, they shook their heads and said that though life was short they would cling to it as long as they could.

Then his brothers and sisters were asked if they would die for Admetus, but they loved themselves better than their brother and turned away and left him. There were men in the town whom he had befriended and who owed their lives to him; they would have done everything else for him, but this thing they would not do.

Now while all were shaking their heads and saying "Not I," the beautiful Alcestis went into her own room and called to Apollo and asked that she might give up her life to save her husband. Then without a thought of fear she lay down upon her bed and closed her eyes; and a little while afterward, when her maidens came into the room they found her dead.

At the very same time Admetus felt his sickness leave him, and he sprang up as well and strong as he had ever been. Wondering how it was that he had been so quickly cured, he made haste to find Alcestis and tell her the good news. But when he went into her room, he saw her lying lifeless on her couch, and he knew at once that she had died for him. His grief was so great that he could not speak, and he wished that death had taken him and spared the one whom he loved.

In all the land every eye was wet with weeping for Alcestis, and the cries of the mourners were heard in every house. Admetus sat by the couch where his young queen lay, and held her cold hand in his own. The day passed and night came, but he would not leave her. All through the dark hours he sat there alone. The morning dawned, but he did not want to see the light.

At last the sun began to rise in the east, and then Admetus was surprised to feel the hand which he held growing warm. He saw a red tinge coming into the pale cheeks of Alcestis. A moment later the fair lady opened her eyes and sat up, alive and well and glad.

How was it that Alcestis had been given back to life?

When she died and left her body, the Shadow Leader, who knows no pity, led her, as he led all others, to the cheerless halls of Proserpina, the queen of the Lower World.

"Who is this who comes so willingly?" asked the pale-faced queen.

And when she was told how Alcestis, so young and beautiful, had given her life to save that of her husband, she was moved with pity; and she bade the Shadow Leader take her back again to the joy and sunlight of the Upper World.

So it was that Alcestis came to life, and for many years she and Admetus lived in their little kingdom not far from the sea. The Mighty Ones on the mountaintop blessed them; and, at last, when they became very old, the Shadow Leader led them both away together.

•

ORPHEUS AND EURYDICE

Retold by V. C. Turnbull

In Greek mythology, Orpheus was said to be the son of Calliope, the Muse of epic song. He was the most ancient of poets, living long before Homer. The story of his devotion to his wife, Euryd- ice, is one of the most famous of the classical myths.

Never was there a musician like Orpheus, who sang songs, inspired by the Muses, to a lyre that was given to him by Apollo. So mighty indeed was the magic of his music, that Nature herself owned his sway. Not only did rocks and rills repeat his lays, but the very trees uprooted themselves to follow in his train, and the savage beasts of the forest were tamed and fawned upon him as he played and sang.

But of all who hearkened enchanted to those matchless strains, none drew deeper delight than the singer's newly wed wife, the young and lovely Eurydice. Hour by hour she sat at his feet hear- kening to the music of his voice and lyre, and the gods themselves might have envied the happy pair.

And surely some god did look with envious eye upon those

two. For on an evil day, Eurydice, strolling with her maidens through a flowery meadow, was bitten on her foot by a viper and perished in all her beauty ere the sun went down.

Then Orpheus, terrible in his anguish, swore that death itself should not forever rob him of his love. His song, which could tame wild beasts and drag the ancient trees from their roots, should quell the powers of hell and snatch back Eurydice from their grasp.

Thus he swore, calling on the gods to help him; and taking his lyre in his hand he set forth on that fearful pilgrimage from which never man—unless, like Hercules, he was a hero, half man and half god—had returned alive.

And now he reaches the downward path, the end whereof is lost in gloom. Deeper and deeper he descended till the light of day was quite shut out, and with it all the sounds of the pleasant earth. Downward through the silence as of the grave, downward through darkness deeper than that of any earthly night. Then out of the darkness, faint at first, but louder as he went on, came sounds that chilled his blood—shrieks and groans of more than mortal anguish, and the terrible voices of the Furies, speaking words that cannot be uttered in any human tongue.

When Orpheus heard these things his knees shook and his feet paused as if rooted to the ground. But remembering once more his love and all his grief, he struck his lyre and sang, till his dirge, reverberating like a funeral march, drowned all the sounds of hell. And Charon, the old ferryman, subdued by the melody, ferried him over the ninefold Styx which none save the dead might cross. When Orpheus reached the other side great companies of pale ghosts flocked round him on that drear shore; for the singer was no shadowy ghost like themselves, but a mortal, beautiful though woebegone, and his song spoke to them as with a thousand voices of the sunlight and the familiar earth, and of those who were left behind in their well-loved homes.

But Orpheus, not finding Eurydice among these, made no tarrying. Onward he passed, over the flaming flood of Phlegethon, through the cloud-hung and adamantine portals of Tartarus. Here Pluto, lord of the underworld, sits enthroned, and round him sinners do penance for the evil that they wrought upon earth. There Ixion, murderer of his father-in-law, is racked upon the everturning wheel, and Tantalus, who slew his son, endures eternal hunger in sight of food and eternal fear from the stone ever ready to fall. There the daughters of Danaüs cease not to pour water into bottomless urns. There Sisyphus, who broke faith with the gods when they permitted him to return a little while to the upper world, evermore rolls up a steep hill a great stone that, falling back from the summit, crushes the wretch in its downward rush.

But now a great marvel was seen in hell. For as Orpheus entered singing, his melodies, the first that had ever sounded in that dread abode, caused all its terrors for a moment to cease. Tantalus caught no more at the fruits that slipped through his fingers, Ixion's wheel ceased to turn, the daughters of Danaüs paused at their urns, and Sisyphus rested on his rock. The very Furies themselves ceased to scourge their victims, and the snakes that mingled with their locks hung down, forgetting to hiss.

So came Orpheus to the throne of great Pluto, by whose side sat Proserpina, his queen. And the king of the infernal gods asked: "What wouldst thou, mortal, who darest to enter unbidden this our realm of death?"

Orpheus answered, touching his lyre the while: "Not as a spy or a foe have I come where no living wight hath ventured before, but I seek my wife, slain untimely by the fangs of a serpent. Such love as mine for a maiden such as she must melt the stoniest heart. Thy heart is not all of stone, and thou too didst once love an earthly maiden. By these places filled with horrors, and by the silence of these boundless realms, I entreat thee restore Eurydice to life."

He paused, and all Tartarus waited with him for a reply. The terrible eyes of Pluto were cast down, and to Proserpina came a memory of the far-off days when she too was a maid upon earth sporting in the flowery meads of Enna. Then Orpheus struck again his magic strings and sang: "To thee we all belong; to thee soon or late we all most come. It is but for a little space that I crave my Eurydice. Nay, without her I will not return. Grant, therefore, my prayer, O Pluto, or slay me here and now."

Then Pluto raised his head and spoke: "Bring hither Eurydice."

And Eurydice, still pale and limping from her mortal wound, was brought from among the shades of the newly dead.

And Pluto said: "Take back, Orpheus, thy wife Eurydice, and lead her to the upper world again. But go thou before and leave her to follow after. Look not once back till thou hast passed my borders and canst see the sun, for in the moment when thou turnest thy head, thy wife is lost to thee again and forever."

Then with great joy Orpheus turned and led Eurydice away. They left behind the tortured dead and the gibbering ghosts; they crossed the flaming Phlegethon, and Charon rowed them once more over the ninefold Styx; and up the dark path they went, the cries of Tartarus sounding ever fainter in their ears; and at last the light of the sun shone faint and far where the path returned to earth, and as they pressed forward the song of the little birds made answer to the lyre of Orpheus.

But the cup of happiness was dashed from the lips that touched its brim. For even as they stood upon the uttermost verge of the dark place, the light of the sun just dawning upon their faces and their feet within a pace of earthly soil, Eurydice stumbled and cried out in pain.

Without a thought Orpheus turned to see what ailed her, and in that moment she was caught from him. Far down the path he saw her, a ghost once more, fading from his sight like smoke as her faint form was lost in the gloom. Only for a moment could he see her white arms stretched toward him in vain. Only once could he hear her last heart-broken farewell.

Down the path rushed Orpheus, clamoring for his Eurydice lost a second time; but vain was all his grief, for not again would Charon row him across the Styx. So the singer returned to earth, his heart broken, and all joy gone from his life. Thenceforth his one consolation was to sit upon Mount Rhodope singing his love and his loss.

●

THE WHITE STONE CANOE

This beautiful story comes from the Chippewa Indians, who lived in the region of Lakes Huron and Superior. It bears a striking resemblance to the Greek tale of Orpheus and Eurydice.

There was once a very beautiful Indian maiden, who died suddenly on the day she was married to a handsome young warrior. He was also brave, but his heart was not proof against this loss. From the hour she was buried, there was no more joy or peace for him.

He went often to visit the spot where they had buried her, and sat musing there, when, it was thought by some of his friends, he would have done better to try to amuse himself in the chase, or by diverting his thoughts in the warpath. But war and hunting had both lost their charms for him. His heart was already dead within him. He pushed aside both his war-club and his bow and arrows.

He had heard the old people say, that there was a path that led to the land of souls, and he determined to follow it. He accordingly set out, one morning, after having completed his preparations for the journey. At first he hardly knew which way to go. He was only guided by the tradition that he must go south. For a while he could see no change in the face of the country. Forests, and hills, and valleys, and streams had the same looks which they wore in his native place.

There was snow on the ground when he set out, and it was sometimes piled and matted on the thick trees and bushes. At length it began to diminish, and finally disappeared. The forest assumed a more cheerful appearance, the leaves put forth their buds, and before he was aware of the completeness of the change, he found himself surrounded by spring.

He had left behind him the land of snow and ice. The air became mild, the dark clouds of winter had rolled away from the sky; a pure field of blue was above him, and as he went he saw flowers beside his path, and heard the songs of birds. By these signs he knew that he was going the right way, for they agreed with the traditions of his tribe. At length he spied a path. It led him through a grove, then up a long and elevated ridge, on the very top of which he came to a lodge. At the door stood an old man, with white hair, whose eyes, though deeply sunk, had a fiery brilliancy. He had a long robe of skins thrown loosely around his shoulders, and a staff in his hands.

The young Chippewayan began to tell his story; but the venerable chief arrested him before he had proceeded to speak ten words. "I have expected you," he replied, "and had just risen to bid you welcome to my abode. She whom you seek passed here but a few days since, and being fatigued with her journey, rested herself here. Enter my lodge and be seated, and I will then satisfy your inquiries, and give you directions for your journey from this point." Having done this, they both issued forth to the lodge door.

"You see yonder gulf," said he, "and the wide-stretching blue plains beyond. It is the land of the souls. You stand upon its borders, and my lodge is the gate of entrance. But you can not take your body along. Leave it here with your bow and arrows, your bundle, and your dog. You will find them safe on your return." So saying, he re-entered the lodge, and the freed traveler bounded forward as if his feet had suddenly been endowed with the power of wings.

But all things retained their natural colors and shapes. The woods and leaves, and streams and lakes, were only more bright and comely than he had ever witnessed. Animals bounded across his path, with a freedom and a confidence which seemed to tell him there was no blood shed here. Birds of beautiful plumage inhabited the groves, and sported in the waters. There was but one thing in which he saw a very unusual effect. He noticed that his passage was not stopped by trees or other objects. He appeared to walk directly through them. They were, in fact, but the souls or shadows of material trees. He became sensible that he was in a land of shadows.

When he had traveled half a day's journey, through a country which was continually becoming more attractive, he came to the banks of a broad lake, in the center of which was a large and beautiful island. He found a canoe of shining white stone, tied to the shore. He was now sure that he had taken the right path, for the aged man had told him this. There were also shining paddles. He immediately entered the canoe, and took the paddles in his hands, when, to his joy and surprise, on turning round he beheld the object of his search in another canoe, exactly its counterpart in everything. She had exactly imitated his motions, and they were side by side.

They at once pushed out from shore and began to cross the lake. Its waves seemed to be rising, and at a distance looked ready to swallow them up; but just as they entered the whitened edge of them they seemed to melt away, as if they were but the images of waves. But no sooner was one wreath of foam passed, than another, more threatening still, arose.

Thus they were in perpetual fear; and what added to it, was the *clearness of the water,* through which they could see heaps of beings who had perished before, and whose bones lay strewed on the bottom of the lake. The Master of Life had, however, decreed to let them pass, for the actions of neither of them had been bad. But they saw many others struggling and sinking in the waves. Old and young of all ages and ranks were there: some passed and some sank. It was only the little children whose canoes seemed to meet no waves.

At length every difficulty was gone, as in a moment, and they both leaped out on the happy island. They felt that the very air was food. It strengthened and nourished them. They wandered together over the blissful fields, where every thing was formed to please the eye and the ear. There were no tempests—there was no ice, no chilly winds—no one shivered for the want of warm clothes: no one suffered hunger—no one mourned for the dead. They saw no graves. They heard of no wars. There was no hunting of animals; for the air itself was their food. Gladly would the young warrior have remained there forever, but he was obliged to go back for his body. He did not see the Master of Life, but he heard his voice in a soft breeze.

"Go back," said the voice, "to the land from whence you came. Your time has not yet come. The duties for which I made you, and which you are to perform, are not yet finished. Return to your people, and accomplish the duties of a good man. You will be the ruler of your tribe for many days. The rules you must observe will be told you by my messenger, who keeps the gate. When he surrenders back your body, he will tell you what to do. Listen to him and you shall afterward rejoin the spirit, which you must now leave behind. She is accepted and will be ever here, as young and as happy as she was when I first called her from the land of snows." When this voice ceased, the narrator awoke. It was all the fabric of a dream, and he was still in the bitter land of snows, and hunger, and tears.

•

STRONGER THAN DEATH

Retold by Mary Stewart

This story of a Hindu princess was sung in India while the story of Orpheus and his heavenly music was being told in ancient Greece. All over the world we find marriages stronger than death.

Of all the beauteous princesses who ever lived and loved in India none compared with the perfect Savitri. As she grew from childhood to womanhood, her beauty seemed to glow around her in a golden radiance.

"Surely this princess was born to be a goddess!" strangers

would exclaim, and so dazzling was her beauty that no prince, however rich and powerful, dared ask her hand in marriage. This filled her father's heart with sadness. "Daughter," he whispered, "choose thyself a husband worthy of thy noble hand, and upon him who is thy heart's desire my richest blessings will I bestow."

So Savitri mounted her golden chariot, and surrounded by her faithful guard and aged courtiers she journeyed far and wide. Through deep jungles and pleasant forests she rode, in gorgeous palaces or simple hermitages she stopped to rest, and many princes and nobles and valiant soldiers bowed in reverence before her. Amongst them all whom did she choose?

One word of encouragement from her perfect lips would have made the most powerful king her ardent lover, the most splendid palace her home, the most gorgeous kingdom of her own. But Savitri was seeking something nobler than wealth, more enduring than earthly power. In the heart of a deep forest she found a king, old, exiled and blind. In his youth, when he lost his eyesight, enemies drove him from his kingdom, and with his wife and baby son he had sought refuge in the forest. There the little son grew to manhood, as free and fearless as a wild animal, loving the forest creatures as brothers, and caring more for the tall arching trees and glowing stars than for any splendid, scented palace chamber. Satyavan, Soul of Truth, he was called.

Thus the princess Savitri found him, and when, bowing before her father's throne on her return, the king questioned her of her choice she answered, "In the wild woods I have found Satyavan, Soul of Truth, and him alone I choose for my lord and husband!"

Beside the King sat his wisest adviser, an old, old man wrapped in a pink cloak, who could foretell the future. When he heard these words of the princess his face clouded with grief. "Sorrow and disaster alone will come to Savitri from such a choice!" he exclaimed.

"Wherefore?" questioned the King, "is the prince a coward, does he lack wisdom, is his heart dark with impure thoughts?"

"As his face is fair and radiant, so is his heart full of courage and truth and his mind of wisdom," answered the old man. "But although he knows it not, it is decreed by the heavens above that twelve months from to-day Satyavan shall see death!"

Trembling with horror, the startled King cried, "Never, never, Savitri, shall your life be thus clouded! Choose again, dear maiden, choose a happier fated lord!"

"Father," answered Savitri, and her words fell softly and slowly, "only once does a maiden give her heart, and may Satyavan's life be long or short, his virtues great or none, my heart and life are his forever."

Thus in the forest the wedding was celebrated, and when the last fervent blessing had been pronounced Savitri laid aside her royal robes and gleaming jewels, and clad herself, like her husband's mother, the aged Queen, in the bark of trees and flaming red cloth woven from the wool of wild sheep. Then with her fair white hands, unused to any toil, she served her husband's parents, and all with such grace and sweetness that she was like a torch of golden light in that dark place, and Satyavan loved her with a love unspeakable.

But although her lips smiled and her eyes were serene, in her heart was hidden always the bitter secret of her husband's approaching death, a secret undreamed of by Satyavan and his parents. No word of it she spoke, but she counted the days one after another, and one morning her heart grew cold, for there were but three days left—three days, and her beloved husband, now so full of life and strength, would be lying still and lifeless at her feet. Filled with desperate dread, she made a vow to spend those three days standing without food or sleep, praying always to the gods to heed her.

Motionless and silent, her great dark eyes shining with unshed tears, Savitri stood for three sunlit days and three gloomsome nights, her lips moving ceaselessly in silent prayer. The dawn of the third day broke, the fated morning, and the Princess prayed her last desperate prayer before the fire kindled in honor of the gods. Then, exhausted as she was, she gently refused the food offered her by her loving parents. One more day she must fast, she said, and now her one desire was to go with her husband into the dark jungle, where, still full of life and vigor, he was going to hew trees for firewood. At first Satyavan was afraid to take her, she looked so weak and pale, although as lovely as a lotus blossom, but he could not withstand her urgent entreaty and together they wandered out into the deep forest.

The morning sun glistened on the gay flowers and bright plumage of the birds, the silver streams rippled, the trees rustled softly, and sweeter even than the songs of the birds were the words of love and tenderness Satyavan spoke to his young wife. Savitri smiled back at him, showing by no word or sign the anguish within her heart.

Gaily Satyavan filled the great basket with wild fruit. With his splendid strength he swung his axe, hewing many a sturdy tree. And then, suddenly, he grew faint and weary and murmuring, "A hundred needles pierce me, my aching head grows numb, let me rest here!" he fell upon the ground beside Savitri. Filled with a wild and speechless terror she clasped him to her, kissing his lips with desperate longing, while the forest grew darker around them and he slept, she knew, the sleep of death!

Then through the gloom Savitri saw approaching a black and terrible figure. His inky robes floated back among the shadows, a dark crown was upon his head, his eyes were blood red, and in his hand he carried a silken cord. In solemn silence he stood and looked upon Satyavan, and Savitri grew cold with terror. But her love was stronger than her fear and with quivering tongue she asked faintly, "Who art thou?"

"I am Yama, mighty Monarch of the Dead," answered the dark form. "Thy husband's days and loves are ended. With this noose I shall bind and carry away the spark of his immortal life. Princess, let thy husband depart!"

Then from Satyavan's body, cold and bloodless, Yama drew the vital spark—smaller than a man's thumb it is—with his silken cord he bound it, and turning silently passed his darksome way into the realm of shadows.

Southward he went and swiftly, but not alone; by his side into the dark and cold walked Savitri.

"Turn, Princess!" commanded Yama, "no living creature may go further with Death's Monarch."

"Where my husband's life leads I may not choose but follow," answered Savitri. "No law can divide us. A woman's life is filled with duty to the poor and suffering, with pity and with wisdom, but the crown of all is truth and deathless love. Bid me not turn back! Grant me one boon!"

"True and holy are thy words, fair Princess," answered Yama. "I would bless thee if I could, but I know the boon which thou desirest, and the dead come not to life. Ask another boon and I will grant it."

"For my husband's banished father, then, let me beg," said Savitri; "grant him eyesight and strength through thy mercy."

"Thy prayer is granted," answered Yama, "and now, Savitri, turn back; no mortal may pass further within the realms of Death."

Around them the night was terrible, shades and darksome creatures flitted among the shadows, strange sounds of beating wings and wailing came nearer and nearer.

Then in that horrible spot Savitri began to sing. She sang of the morning hours when she and her husband had passed so gaily through the forest, of the caroling birds and fragrant flowers, the sparkling brooks and the blue sky. Yama listened and his heart grew soft and tender.

"Blessed art thou, brave Savitri!" he cried. "I would grant thy desire, but the dead come not to life; ask another boon."

"Once again for my husband's father I beg. Give him back his wealth and kingdom, in thy mercy."

"Loving daughter," replied Yama, "wealth and kingdom I bestow, and now I command thee to turn back. No power can save thee within this abode of the Monarch of the Dead."

About them the black terror was closing in, breathless, remorseless, terrible. And Savitri—only sang again. This time her song was not of birds or flowers or spring time, it was of love, love stronger than life, love stronger than death!

Then the Black King turned upon her and his words were like cooling summer rain.

"Noble woman, ask thy boon! No god can listen in vain to such pleading."

"Grant me my husband's life!" begged Savitri. "May he live to be a father, the father of princes as brave and noble as himself!"

"Thy desire is granted," answered Yama, "for thou has taught me the strength of a woman's love; it abideth stronger even than the doom of Death!"

Back to the forest where her husband's body lay hastened Savitri. As she raised his unconscious head her touch thrilled him back to waking life.

"Did I dream, sweet Savitri," he asked faintly, opening his eyes, "of a dark and fearful monarch who captured me?"

"The Black King has come and gone," answered Savitri. "Tomorrow I will tell you all. But see, the night is about us, wild

beasts approach through the jungle, and a forest fire blazes in the darkness. Let us hasten homeward where thy parents await us, happier and more blessed than in many a long year."

Satyavan looked at his wife in astonishment; her face was radiant, a glorious joy shone about her. Then blissful and in silence, with his strong arm around her, Satyavan and his wife walked back through the jungle, while the hushed and throbbing midnight looked down upon the deathless love of Savitri.

•

MY VERY DEAR SARAH ...

Sullivan Ballou

A young Providence lawyer and former Speaker of the Rhode Island House of Representatives, Major Sullivan Ballou interrupted a promising political career to join the 2nd Rhode Island Volunteers at the outbreak of the Civil War. He wrote home to his wife from a camp near Washington one week before the First Battle of Bull Run, the first major land battle of the war.

Camp Clark, Washington
July 14, 1861

My very dear Sarah,

The indications are very strong that we shall move in a few days—perhaps tomorrow. Lest I should not be able to write again, I feel impelled to write a few lines that may fall under your eye when I shall be no more. Our movements may be of a few days' duration and full of pleasure—and it may be one of some conflict and death to me. "Not my will, but thine, O God be done." If it is necessary that I should fall on the battlefield for my Country, I am ready.

I have no misgivings about, or lack of confidence in, the cause in which I am engaged, and my courage does not halt or falter. I know how strongly American Civilization now leans on the triumph of the Government, and how great a debt we owe to those who went before us through the blood and sufferings of the Revolution. And I am willing—perfectly willing—to lay down all my joys in this life, to help maintain this Government, and to pay that debt. . . .

Sarah, my love for you is deathless. It seems to bind me with mighty cables that nothing but Omnipotence could break; and yet my love of Country comes over me like a strong wind and burns me unresistibly on with all these chains to the battlefield.

The memories of the blissful moments I have spent with you come creeping over me, and I feel most gratified to God and to you that I have enjoyed them so long. And hard it is for me to give them up and burn to ashes the hopes of future years, when, God willing, we might still have lived and loved together, and seen our sons grown up to honorable manhood around us. I have, I know, but few and small claims upon Divine Providence, but something whispers to me—perhaps it is the wafted prayer of my little Edgar—that I shall return to my loved ones unharmed. If I do not, my dear Sarah, never forget how much I love you, and when my last breath escapes me on the battlefield, it will whisper your name. Forgive my many faults, and the many pains I have caused you. How thoughtless and foolish I have often times been! How gladly would I wash out with my tears every little spot upon your happiness, and struggle with all the misfortunes of this world to shield you and your children from harm. But I cannot. I must watch you from the Spirit-land and hover near you, while you buffet the storm, with your precious little freight, and wait with sad patience till we meet to part no more.

But, O Sarah! If the dead can come back to this earth and flit unseen around those they loved, I shall always be near you; in the gladdest days and in the darkest nights, advised to your happiest scenes and gloomiest hours, *always, always,* and if there be a soft breeze upon your cheek, it shall be my breath; as the cool air fans your throbbing temple, it shall be my spirit passing by. Sarah, do not mourn me dead; think I am gone and wait for thee, for we shall meet again.

As for my little boys—they will grow up as I have done, and never know a father's love and care. Little Willie is too young to remember me long, and my blue-eyed Edgar will keep my frolics with him among the dim memories of childhood. Sarah, I have unlimited confidence in your maternal care and your development of their character, and feel that God will bless you in your holy work.

Tell my two Mothers I call God's blessing upon them. O! Sarah. I wait for you there; come to me and lead thither my children.

Sullivan

A week later, Sullivan Ballou was killed at Bull Run.

•

ON MY FIRST DAUGHTER

Ben Jonson

I have read and have been told that the death of a child is the hardest thing for a human being to endure. The ancient Greek playwright Euripides called it the "grief surpassing all." Here is the poet Ben Jonson (1572–1637) on the deaths of his own daughter and son.

The word "ruth" in the first line means grief. The date of Mary's death is unknown.

Here lies, to each her parents' ruth,
Mary, the daughter of their youth;
Yet all heaven's gifts being heaven's due,
It makes the father less to rue.
At six months' end she parted hence
With safety of her innocence;
Whose soul heaven's queen, whose name she bears,
In comfort of her mother's tears,
Hath placed amongst her virgin-train:
Where, while that severed doth remain,
This grave partakes the fleshly birth;
Which cover lightly, gentle earth!

•

ON MY FIRST SON

Ben Jonson

Benjamin Jonson died in 1603 on his birthday. The first line of
this poem refers to the fact that the name Benjamin means "child
of the right hand" in Hebrew.

> Farewell, thou child of my right hand, and joy;
> My sin was too much hope of thee, loved boy:
> Seven years thou wert lent to me, and I thee pay,
> Exacted by thy fate, on the just day.
> O could I lose all father now! for why
> Will man lament the state he should envy,
> To have so soon 'scaped world's and flesh's rage,
> And, if no other misery, yet age?
> Rest in soft peace, and asked, say, "Here doth lie
> Ben Jonson his best piece of poetry."
> For whose sake henceforth all his vows be such
> As what he loves may never like too much.

•

THE WATER OF YOUTH

Rudolf Baumbach

This beautiful and unusual story of a husband and wife growing
old together perfectly illustrates George Eliot's definition of love
—"an enfolding of immeasurable cares which yet are better than
any joys outside our love."

It was Midsummer Day, and the heat of noon brooded over
the cornfields. Now and then a fresh breeze blew down from the
wooded hill, bending the stalks of corn and scattering the scarlet
petals of the poppies. The air was full of the chirping of grasshop-

pers, and from the hawthorn tree at the edge of the field came the low call of the yellow-hammer.

Along the path which crossed the broad cornfield came a slim, strong figure—a young woman in peasant dress, with a red kerchief on her head, a basket on her arm, and a jug in her hand.

When the yellow-hammer caught sight of her he flew to the topmost bough of his hawthorn tree and twittered a greeting to her: "Pretty maid, pretty maid, how's the world using you?" But he was making a mistake, for golden-haired Greta was not a maid, but a young bride, and she was on her way to her husband, who was cutting wood in the forest.

At the edge of the wood she stood still to listen. Following the sound of the ax, she soon came in sight of her husband, who was felling a fir tree with strong strokes, and she hailed him gaily.

"Stand still!" he shouted back. "The tree is falling!" And the great fir tree groaned deeply, bent its head, and came crashing to the ground.

Then Greta walked on, and the brown-faced woodcutter took his young wife in his arms and kissed her tenderly. They sat down and unpacked the basket of food which she had brought, but as Hans was beginning to eat he laid down his bread, seized his ax, and cut three crosses on the stump of the tree that he had just felled.

"What is that for?" asked his wife.

"For the sake of the little old women of the wood," he answered. "Their enemy, the wild huntsman, lies in wait for them day and night, and sets his dogs on them. But if the poor little things can reach a tree trunk like that, the wild huntsman cannot touch them, because of the three crosses."

Greta opened her eyes wide. "Have you ever seen one of the little folk?"

"No; they seldom show themselves. But this is Midsummer Day, so perhaps we might see one." And he called into the forest in his ringing voice, "Little woman of the woods, come forth!" He only meant to tease his wife, but on St. John's Day it is not safe to make jokes like that.

Instantly there stood before them a lovely little lady, about an ell high. She wore trailing white robes, and in her hair there were sprays of mistletoe. The two young people jumped up in astonishment, and Greta made her best curtsy.

"You called me just at the right moment," said the little woman, pointing to the sun, which stood exactly over her head. "And one good turn"—here she looked toward the stump with the three crosses—"deserves another. Silver and gold have I none, but I have better things to give you. Come with me without fear, and bring your jug; it will be useful."

So saying, she turned toward the forest, followed by Hans, ax on shoulder, and Greta, jug in hand. She walked just like a duck, and Greta touched her husband on the arm, pointing to the little waddling figure, and was going to whisper something to him, but he laid his finger on his lips.

Nothing hurts the little good folk so much as being made fun of. They have feet like geese, and that is why they wear long trailing skirts.

They walked on until they came to an open space in the wood. Hoary trees stood in a circle round a green meadow; the grass was gay with lilies and bluebells and the fluttering wings of the butterflies.

Hans thought that he knew every inch of the forest, but he had never seen this lovely spot before. In the meadow there was a tiny house; the walls were of bark, the roof of the scales of fir-cones, every scale pinned down with a rose-thorn. This was the home of the little woman of the woods.

She led her guests round to the back of the house and showed them a well, whose waters rose noiselessly out of the dark earth. Iris and coltsfoot grew on the brink, and gold and green dragonflies danced over it.

"That is the well of youth," she said. "A dip in it will turn an old man into a boy again, and an old woman into a blooming girl. To drink the water keeps one young and fresh till one's dying day. Fill your jug and carry it home. But be very careful of the precious water: one drop every Sunday will be enough to keep you young.

"One thing more. When you cease to love each other the magic power of the water will be gone. Remember that. Now fill your jug, and fare-you-well." Before they could thank her the little woman had vanished into her house.

Greta filled her jug with the water of youth, and they hurried home to their cottage. When they got there, Hans poured the water into a bottle and sealed it with fir resin.

"Just now we have no use for the water of youth," he said, "so we can save it up till we do need it."

He put the bottle in the cupboard where they stored their treasures—a couple of old coins, a string of garnet beads with a golden penny hung on it, and two real silver spoons—and he said: "Now, Greta, we must be very, very careful not to make the water lose its power."

A year went by, full of love and happiness for the young pair. And then there was a rosy little baby boy, who kicked and crowed till his father's heart overflowed with pride.

"Now is the time," he said, "for opening our bottle. Don't you think, Greta, that a drop of the water of youth would do you good?"

The young mother thought it would, so he went to fetch it from the next room. His hands trembled with joy as he broke the seal, and so the bottle slipped out of his grasp, and the water of youth was spilled on the floor. Hans nearly fell on the floor, too, in his horror at the mischance. What could he do?

He dared not tell his wife, lest she should die of fright. Later on perhaps he could tell her, or one day he might find again the well of youth, which he had often looked for in vain, and get a fresh supply. Hurriedly he got another bottle exactly like the first, filled it with spring water, and brought it to his wife.

"Ah!" said Greta. "How that gives me new life and strength! Take a drop yourself, my dear."

Hans obeyed her, and said what a wonderful drink it was; and after that they each took a drop every Sunday when the bells were calling them to church.

Greta bloomed like a rose, and Hans was a perfect picture of vigorous manhood. But day after day he put off confessing his misdeed, in the hope of finding the well of youth. Roam through the woods as he might, he could never get a glimpse of that meadow again.

Thus two years went by. A little girl had come to keep the little boy company, and Greta's round chin had grown double, but she never noticed it; there were no looking-glasses in those days. Hans did notice it, but he took care not to say anything, and he loved his fat wife more than ever. Then a misfortune befell them.

One day when Greta was busy housecleaning, little Peter, her eldest, got into the cupboard where the water of youth was kept, and knocked over the bottle, which broke and spilled its contents on the floor.

"Oh, merciful Powers!" cried the mother. "But what a blessing Hans is not at home!" With trembling fingers she picked up the pieces of glass, and replaced the bottle by another, which she filled from the spring.

"I shall soon be found out, for there's an end of our eternal youth. Alas!" But she made up her mind not to let her husband suspect that there was anything wrong.

Time passed by, and Hans and Greta lived and loved together. Each of them took care not to let the other think that youth was gone, and every Sunday they took the magic drop.

One morning when Hans was combing his hair, a gray hair fell on his sleeve. And he said to himself, "Now I must confess to my wife."

Heavy at heart he began: "Greta, it seems to me that the magic water must have lost its power. Look! I have found a gray hair! I am getting old."

Greta was startled, but she recovered herself and laughed, though not quite naturally, as she answered: "A gray hair! Why, when I was only ten I had a gray lock in my hair. That is quite a common thing. You have just been skinning a badger, and very likely you got some of the fat on your hair. You know that badger's fat does turn hair gray. No, dear Hans, the water keeps its magic power, or"—she glanced at him anxiously—"do you think that I am growing old, too?"

Hans laughed loudly at that. "You—old? You are as blooming as a peony!" And he threw his arms round her portly figure and kissed her.

But when he was alone he said joyfully. "She has no idea that we are growing old. So what I did must have been the right thing." And his wife said just the same to herself.

That evening the lads and lasses of the village danced to the music of a strolling fiddler, and no couple footed it under the lime trees more merrily than Hans and Greta. The peasants made some jokes at their expense, but the two happy people did not hear them.

The following autumn, while they and their children were eating their Martinmas goose, Greta broke a front tooth. There was great woe, for she had always been proud of her pretty white teeth.

When husband and wife were alone together, Greta said in a faltering voice, "A misfortune like that could never have happened if the water—" But Hans scolded her.

"You think the water can keep off all bad luck? Does not a child often break a tooth in cracking nuts? How can you grumble? Has not the water kept you as fresh and healthy as a spring lettuce?"

At that his wife laughed, dried her tears, and kissed her old man till he was almost out of breath. Then they sat down together on the stone seat in front of their house, and sang little songs about true love. The passersby said, "What silly old folk!" But the happy couple did not hear them.

Many years went past. The house had grown too small for the children, and they had married and gone away, and had children of their own. The two old people were alone together once more.

They were as much in love with each other as on their wedding day, and every Sunday, when the church bells were ringing, they each took one drop out of the bottle.

Midsummer Day came round again. On the eve of it, Hans and Greta were sitting in front of their house, looking toward the hill, where the bonfire was blazing, and the young men and maidens were shouting as they jumped through the flames hand-in-hand.

Greta turned to her husband: "Dear Hans, I should like to go into the forest again. Would you start early tomorrow morning? Only you must waken me, for when the elderberry is in bloom young women are apt to sleep long after daylight."

Hans agreed. Next morning he awoke his wife, and together they set out for the forest. They walked arm-in-arm like lovers, and each kept a watchful eye on the other's steps. When Hans lifted one foot cautiously over the root of a tree, his wife would say, "Why, Hans, you are skipping like a kid!"

And when Greta timidly crossed a little hole in the path, her husband cried laughingly, "Hold up your skirts, wife! Jump!" After a while they came to an old fir tree, and in its shade they spread a little feast out of Greta's basket.

"It was just here," said Hans, "that the little old woman of the woods appeared to us that day, and over there must lie the meadow with the well of youth. But I have never been able to find it again."

"And, mercifully, there was no need of your finding it," put in Greta hurriedly, "for our bottle is by no means empty yet."

"That is quite true," Hans agreed, "but all the same, I should like to see the good little woman again, and to thank her for the gift she gave us. Come and look for her. Perhaps we shall be as lucky as we were before."

So they rose and went into the heart of the forest. They had walked but a little way when lo! the sunny meadow lay before them. Lilies and bluebells were blooming in the grass, gay butterflies flitted to and fro, and the little house stood there just as of yore.

With fast-beating hearts they walked round the house, and there was the well of youth with the gold and green dragonflies hovering over it. Hans and Greta stepped up to the brink. Hand-in-hand they bent over the water, and out of its clear depths two gray heads with kindly, wrinkled faces gazed back at them.

Hot tears rushed to their eyes, with broken words and sobs they confessed their misdeeds, and it was some time before they could understand that all these years each of them had been deceiving the other for love's sake.

"Then you knew that we were both growing old?" said Hans.

"Of course I did!" his wife laughed through her tears.

"So did I! So did I!" cried Hans, and he tried to leap for joy. And he took Greta's head between his hands and kissed her, just as when she had plighted her troth to him.

Then, as if she had sprung out of the earth, the little old woman of the woods stood before the old couple.

"Welcome!" she said. "It is long since you came to visit me. But what is this?" She shook her finger at them. "You have not taken care of the water of youth. Wrinkles and gray hairs! This will never do.

"However, I can soon cure that. You have come just at the right moment. Quick! Jump into the well—it is not deep—plunge your gray heads under, and you will see a miracle. All the strength and beauty of youth will be given back to you. But be quick, or the sun will have gone down."

Hans and Greta looked questioningly at each other.

"Will you?" he asked in a voice that shook.

"Never!" answered Greta promptly. "I can't tell you what bliss it is that at last I can be old. Then think of our children and grandchildren. No, dear little woman, we thank you with all our hearts, but we will stay old. Won't we, Hans?"

"Yes, yes," said Hans, "we will stay old. Hurrah! Greta, if you only knew how well your gray hair suits you!"

"As you will," said the little woman of the woods. "I do not insist on it." And with rather an offended air she went into her house and shut the door.

The old folk kissed each other once more and turned homeward. Arm in arm they went through the forest, and the midsummer sun set a crown of gold upon their gray heads.

•

BELIEVE ME, IF ALL THOSE
ENDEARING YOUNG CHARMS

Thomas Moore

Good marriages grow better as they grow older. Fidelity ages well.
The next two poems echo the sentiment of Robert Browning's
famous call: "Grow old along with me, the best is yet to be."

Believe me, if all those endearing young charms,
    Which I gaze on so fondly today,
Were to change by tomorrow, and fleet in my arms,
    Like fairy gifts, fading away,
Thou wouldst still be adored, as this moment thou art,
    Let thy loveliness fade as it will,
And around the dear ruin each wish of my heart
    Would entwine itself verdantly still.

It is not while beauty and youth are thine own,
    And thy cheeks unprofaned by a tear,
That the fervor and faith of a soul can be known,
    To which time will but make thee more dear.
No, the heart that has truly loved never forgets,
    But as truly loves on to the close,
As the sunflower turns on her god, when he sets,
    The same look which she turned when he rose.

•

WE HAVE LIVED AND LOVED TOGETHER

Charles Jeffreys

We have lived and loved together
　　Through many changing years;
We have shared each other's gladness
　　And wept each other's tears;
I have known ne'er a sorrow
　　That was long unsoothed by thee;
For thy smiles can make a summer
　　Where darkness else would be.

Like the leaves that fall around us
　　In autumn's fading hours,
Are the traitor's smiles, that darken
　　When the cloud of sorrow lowers;
And though many such we've known, love,
　　Too prone, alas, to range,
We both can speak of one love
　　Which time can never change.

We have lived and loved together
　　Through many changing years;
We have shared each other's gladness
　　And wept each other's tears.
And let us hope the future
　　As the past has been will be:
I will share with thee my sorrows,
　　And thou thy joys with me.

•

THE GREATEST OF THESE IS LOVE

The Apostle Paul

The kind of love described here is an embodiment of all the
virtues, the kind of love all husbands and wives should give to
each other, and the kind both should give to their children. These
verses so often and appropriately read at weddings come from
Paul's first letter to the Corinthians.

Though I speak with the tongues of men and of angels, and
have not love, I am become as sounding brass, or a tinkling cymbal.

And though I have the gift of prophecy, and understand all
mysteries, and all knowledge; and though I have all faith so that I
could remove mountains and have not love, I am nothing.

And though I bestow all my goods to feed the poor, and though
I give my body to be burned, and have not love, it profiteth me
nothing.

Love suffereth long and is kind; love envieth not, love vaunteth
not itself, is not puffed up,

Doth not behave itself unseemly, seeketh not her own, is not
easily provoked, thinketh no evil,

Rejoiceth not in iniquity, but rejoiceth in the truth.

Beareth all things, believeth all things, hopeth all things, en-
dureth all things.

Love never faileth; but whether there be prophecies, they shall
fail; whether there be tongues, they shall cease; whether there be
knowledge, it shall vanish away.

For we know in part, and we prophesy in part.

But when that which is perfect is come, then that which is in
part shall be done away.

When I was a child, I spake as a child, I understood as a child,
I thought as a child, but when I became a man I put away childish
things.

For now we see through a glass darkly; but then face to face:
now I know in part; but then shall I know even as also I am known.

And now abideth faith, hope, love, these three; but the greatest
of these is LOVE.

Six

CITIZENSHIP
AND
LEADERSHIP

"MAN is by nature an animal intended to live in a polis," Aristotle wrote more than two thousand years ago. Human beings are social and political beings. We can apply Aristotle's observation about the polis, or Greek city-state, not only to our modern concept of town, state, and country but also to any number of associations. We are all members of groups. We join clubs, churches, school organizations, civic associations, and political parties in order to better ourselves and the condition of others.

The success of any organization depends on the character of its citizens. Good citizens are those who know and live up to their duties by exercising virtues such as responsibility, loyalty, self-discipline, work, and friendship. In this chapter we find examples of individuals ready and willing to do their parts. We encounter people laboring together cheerfully toward common goals. We see them keeping their promises and accepting responsibility for their own mistakes. We come across those who stand fast beside their comrades—as well as those who do not. And we meet those who are willing to sacrifice their own interests, even their own lives, for the good of the rest.

At certain times in our lives, most of us are called to lead in some capacity: as team captain, club president, state representative, or member of a student council, vestry, or board of directors. This chapter also reminds us of the virtues required to hold these positions, virtues such as compassion, courage, perseverance, wisdom, and sometimes faith. In these stories, we see that leaders are ultimately judged in terms of how well they serve their followers and by the examples they set. They lead not just by command but by the force of good character. And we notice that before they lead, they learn to be good followers—they know how to help shoulder a load and share hardships.

Finally, I have included a number of selections about a virtue too often overlooked today—gratitude. If we are not grateful for our gifts and opportunities, we are not likely to value them, and if we do not value them, we are not likely to work hard to preserve and improve them. Gratitude is an important attribute of good citizenship, especially among a people blessed with an inheritance of political freedom and material wealth unmatched in the history of mankind. Disposition counts. Good citizenship and good leadership usually require a certain degree of cheerfulness. The chronic complainer, on the other hand, not only fails to contribute but he often threatens to become the one who dooms the common enterprise. He is the man described by Joseph Conrad:

> They all knew him! He was the man that cannot steer, that cannot splice, that dodges the work on dark nights; that, aloft, holds on frantically with both arms and legs, and swears at the wind, the sleet, the darkness; the man who curses the sea while others work. The man who is the last out and the first in when all hands are called. The man who can't do most things and won't do the rest. The pet of philanthropists and self-seeking landlubbers. The sympathetic and deserving creature that knows all about his rights, but knows nothing of courage, of endurance, and of the unexpressed faith, of the unspoken loyalty that knits together a ship's company.

Whining, grumbling, and complaining are not simply unattractive; they are symptoms of selfishness. And an overriding concern with the self is not the business of citizenship. Among good citizens, Aristotle told us, "the salvation of the community is the common business of them all."

THE QUAILS

Here is one of the basic truths of citizenship: In our common affairs we pull and lift together, or we perish. This ancient fable is from the group of Buddhist stories known as the *Jataka* tales.

Ages ago a flock of more than a thousand quails lived together in a forest in India. They would have been happy, but that they were in great dread of their enemy, the quail catcher. He used to imitate the call of the quail; and when they gathered together in answer to it, he would throw a great net over them, stuff them into his basket, and carry them away to be sold.

Now, one of the quails was very wise, and he said: "Brothers! I've thought of a good plan. In the future, as soon as the fowler throws his net over us, let each one put his head through a mesh in the net and then all lift it up together and fly away with it. When we have flown far enough, we can let the net drop on a thorn bush and escape."

All agreed to the plan. The next day when the fowler threw his net, the birds all lifted it together in the very way that the wise quail had told them, threw it on a thorn bush and escaped. While the fowler tried to free his net from the thorns, it grew dark, and he had to go home.

This happened many days, till at last the fowler's wife grew angry and asked her husband: "Why is it that you never catch any more quail?"

Then the fowler said: "The trouble is that all the birds work together and help one another. If they would only quarrel, I could catch them fast enough."

A few days later, one of the quails accidentally trod on the head of one of his brothers, as they alighted on the feeding ground.

"Who trod on my head?" angrily inquired the quail who was hurt.

"Don't be angry, I didn't mean to tread on you," said the first quail.

But the brother quail went on quarreling.

"I lifted all the weight of the net! You didn't help at all!" he cried.

That made the first quail angry, and before long all were drawn into the dispute. Then the fowler saw his chance. He imitated the cry of the quail and cast his net over those who came together. They were still boasting and quarreling, and they did not help one another lift the net. So the hunter lifted the net himself and crammed them into his basket. But the wise quail gathered his friends together and flew far away, for he knew that quarrels are the root of misfortune.

WHEN MR. BLUEBIRD WON HIS COAT

Thornton W. Burgess

Sometimes leaders are born when one in the crowd steps forward to try.

It happened a great while ago when the world was young. Mr. Bluebird was one of the quietest and most modest of all the birds. He wore just a modest gray coat, and no one took any particular notice of him. In fact, he didn't even have a name. He never quarreled with his neighbors. He never was envious of those to whom Old Mother Nature had given beautiful coats, or if he was, he never showed it. He just minded his own affairs and did his best to do his share of the work of the Great World, for even in the beginning of things there was something for each one to do.

Old Mother Nature was very busy those days making the Great World a fit place in which to live, and as soon as she had started a new family of birds or animals she had to leave them to take care of themselves and get along as best they could. Those who were too lazy or too stupid to take care of themselves disappeared, and others took their places. There was nothing lazy or stupid about Mr. Bluebird, and he quickly learned how to take care of himself and at the same time to keep on the best of terms with his neighbors.

When the place where the first birds lived became too crowded and old King Eagle led them out into the new land Old Mother Nature had been preparing for them, Mr. Bluebird was one of the first to follow him. The new land was very beautiful, and there was plenty of room and plenty to eat for all. Then came Jack Frost with snow and ice and drove all the birds back to the place they had come from. They made up their minds that they would stay there even if it was crowded. But after a while Old Mother Nature came to tell them that soon Jack Frost would be driven back from that wonderful new land, and sweet Mistress Spring would waken all the sleeping plants and all the sleeping insects up there so that it would be as beautiful as it was before, even more beautiful than the place where they were now. She said that she would expect them to go to the new land and make it joyous with their songs and build their homes there and help her to keep the insects and worms from eating all the green things.

"But first I want a herald to go before Mistress Spring to tell those who have lived there all through the time of snow and ice that Mistress Spring is coming. Who will go as the herald of sweet Mistress Spring?" asked Old Mother Nature.

All the birds looked at one another and shivered, and then one by one they tried to slip out of sight. Now Mr. Bluebird had modestly waited for some of his big, strong neighbors to offer to take the message of gladness up into that frozen land, but when he saw them slip away one by one, his heart grew hot with shame for them, and he flew out before Old Mother Nature. "I'll go," said he, bobbing his head respectfully.

Old Mother Nature just had to smile, because compared with some of his neighbors Mr. Bluebird was so very small. "What can such a little fellow as you do?" she asked. "You will freeze to death up there, for it is still very cold."

"If you please, I can at least try," replied Mr. Bluebird modestly. "If I find I can't go on, I can come back."

"And what reward do you expect?" asked Old Mother Nature.

"The joy of spreading such good news as the coming of Mistress Spring will be is all the reward I want," replied Mr. Bluebird.

This reply so pleased Old Mother Nature that she then and there made Mr. Bluebird the herald of Mistress Spring and started him on his long journey. It *was* a long journey and a hard journey. You see, everything was new to him. And then it was so cold! He couldn't get used to the cold. It seemed sometimes as if he certainly would freeze to death. At these times, when he sat shivering and shaking, he would remember that sweet Mistress Spring was not very far behind and that he was her herald. This would give him courage, and he would bravely keep on. Whenever he stopped to rest, he would whistle the news that Mistress Spring was coming, and sometimes, just to keep up his own courage, he would whistle while he was flying, and he found it helped. To keep warm at night he crept into hollow trees, and it was thus he learned how snug and safe and comfortable such places were, and he made up his mind that in just such a place he would build his nest when the time came.

As he passed on he left behind him great joy, and Mistress Spring found as she journeyed north that all in the forests and on the meadows were eagerly awaiting her, for they had heard the message of her coming; and she was glad and told Old Mother Nature how well her herald had done his work. When he had completed his errand, Mr. Bluebird built a home and was as modest and retiring as ever. He didn't seem to think that he had done anything out of the usual. He simply rejoiced in his heart that he. had been able to do what Old Mother Nature had requested, and it never entered his head that he should have any other reward than the knowledge that he had done his best and that he had brought cheer and hope to many.

When Jack Frost moved down from the far North in the fall, all the birds journeyed south again, and of course Mr. Bluebird went with them. The next season when it was time for Mistress Spring to start north, Old Mother Nature assembled all the birds, and this time, instead of asking who would carry the message, she called Mr. Bluebird out before them and asked if he was willing to be the herald once more. Mr. Bluebird said that he would be glad to be the herald if she wished it. Then Old Mother Nature told all the birds how brave Mr. Bluebird was and how faithful and true, and she made all the other birds feel ashamed, especially those bigger and stronger than Mr. Bluebird. Then she said: "Bluebird, I here and now appoint you the herald of Mistress Spring, and the honor shall descend to your children and your children's children forever and ever, and you shall be one of the most loved of all the birds. And because you are a herald, you shall have a bright coat, as all heralds should have; and because you are true and faithful, your coat shall be blue, as blue as the blue of the sky."

She reached out and touched Mr. Bluebird, and sure enough his sober gray coat turned the most wonderful blue. Then once more he started on his long journey and he whistled his message more joyously than before. And because his whistle brought joy and gladness, and because he was beautiful to see, it came about just as Old Mother Nature had said it would, that he was one of the most loved of all the birds, even as his great-great-ever-so-great-grandson is today.

•

THE TOWER TO THE MOON

Sometimes people with high titles get high notions of themselves, as we see in this tale from the Dominican Republic. But a title is no guarantee of real leadership, even if your name is "king." Serving the interests of those who follow is the true crown of leadership.

Long ago there lived an island king who one night, letting his thoughts drift beyond the sandy shores of his kingdom, got it into his head that he would like to touch the moon.

"Why not?" he asked himself. "I am king. What I want, I get. I want to touch the moon."

The next morning he called the chief carpenter in the land to his court.

"I want you to build me a tower," he commanded, "one tall enough to reach the moon."

The carpenter's eyes bulged.

"The moon? Did you say the moon?"

"You heard me. The moon. I want to touch the moon. Now go do it."

The carpenter went and talked it over with all the other carpenters. They scratched their heads and decided his majesty must have been joking, and built nothing at all.

A few days later the king summoned the chief carpenter back to court.

"I don't see my tower," he barked. "What's taking so long?"

"But Your Majesty," the carpenter cried, "you can't be serious. A tower to the moon? We don't know how."

"I don't care how!" the king yelled. "Just get it done. You have three days. If by that time I have not touched the moon, I hate to think what will happen to you."

The shaken carpenter went back to his friends, and they scratched their heads some more, and drew lines on paper, and racked their brains for an answer. Finally they came up with a plan.

The chief carpenter went back to the king.

"We have an idea that just might work," he said. "But we'll need every box in the kingdom."

"Excellent!" cried the king. "Let it be done!"

He sent out a royal decree that every box on the island be carried to the palace. The people brought them in every shape and size—crates and chests and cases and cartons, shoe boxes, hat boxes, flower boxes, even bread boxes.

Then the carpenter ordered that all the boxes be piled one on top of the other, until there wasn't a single box left. But the tower wasn't high enough to reach the moon.

"We'll have to make more," he told the king.

So another royal decree went out. His majesty ordered all the trees on the island to be chopped down and the timber brought to the palace. The carpenters made more boxes, and stacked them on top of the tower.

"I think it's high enough," the king announced.

The carpenters looked up nervously.

"Perhaps I should go up first," the chief carpenter suggested. "Just to be on the safe side."

"Don't be silly!" the king barked. "This was my idea. I will be the first one to touch the moon. The honor belongs to me."

He started to climb. Higher and higher he mounted. He left the birds far below, and broke through the clouds. When he got to the top, he stretched out his arms—but he was just barely short! A few more inches, and he would be able to touch the moon! Or at least that's the way it looked to him.

"One more box!" he yelled down. "I need just one more box!"

The carpenters shook their heads. They had already used every stick of wood on the island.

"We don't have any more!" they yelled at the top of their lungs. "No more boxes! You'll have to come down!"

The king stamped his foot and jumped up and down, and the whole tower trembled.

"I won't come down! I won't!" he yelled. "I want to touch the moon, and no one's going to stop me!"

Then his majesty had his brilliant idea.

"Listen here," he called. "I know what to do. Take the first box from the bottom and bring it to the top."

The carpenters stared at each other.

"You fools!" the king yelled. "You're wasting my time! Take out the first box and bring it up now!"

The carpenters shrugged.

"This is a very stubborn king," the chief carpenter said. "I suppose we must obey his command."

So they pulled out the bottom box. You don't need to be told the end of the story.

•

THE GORDIAN KNOT
Adapted from a retelling by James Baldwin

Often, leaders are people who aren't discouraged by the odds, who find a way through no matter what. This old story of determination and decisiveness is great to remember at times when you need to cut through red tape.

In the western part of Asia there is a rich and beautiful region which in olden times was called Phrygia. The people of that place once had a king named Gordius, a man who brought peace to the land by ruling wisely, righting old wrongs, and making laws for the good of all.

Now, when he became king, Gordius did something very

strange and marvelous. In the temple of Jupiter overlooking the town, he tied a great knot of rope. So intricate were its twists and turns, and so deftly did Gordius hide the ends of the rope, that no one could see how to untie it.

After years of ruling wisely, Gordius died. But the knot remained, and all strangers who came to the temple of Jupiter admired its design and strength.

"Only a very great man could have tied such a knot as that," said some.

"You have spoken truly," said the oracle of the temple. "But the man who undoes it will be much greater."

"What do you mean?" asked the visitors.

"The man who undoes this wonderful knot shall have the world for his kingdom," came the answer.

After that a great many people came every year to see the Gordian knot. Princes and warriors from every land tried to untie it. But the ends of the rope remained hidden, and they could not even make a beginning of the task.

Hundreds of years passed. King Gordius had been dead for so long that people remembered him only as the man who tied the wonderful knot, the knot that could not be undone.

Then there came into Phrygia a young king from Macedonia, far across the sea. The name of this young king was Alexander. He had conquered all of Greece, and now he had set his sights on Asia.

"Where is the fabled Gordian knot?" he asked.

The people led him into the temple of Jupiter and showed him the knot where Gordius had left it.

"What is it the oracle said about this knot?" Alexander asked.

"It said that the man who undoes it will have the world for his kingdom. But many have tried, and all have failed."

Alexander looked at the knot carefully. He could not find the ends, but what did that matter? He raised his sword and, with one stroke, cut it into so many pieces that the rope dropped to the ground.

"It is thus," said the young king, "that I cut all Gordian knots."

And then he went on with his little army to conquer Asia.

"The world is my kingdom," he said.

•

THE PEDDLER'S PACK

Retold by Mary De Morgan

This old English folktale has a couple of timely lessons for an age
of growing credit card use and national debt: Don't promise what
you don't have, and don't live off the promises of others. The state
of the economy has a great deal to do with the state of responsibility and honesty in the dealings of citizens.

A peddler was toiling along a dusty road carrying his pack on
his back, when he saw a donkey grazing by the wayside.

"Good day, friend," said he. "If you have nothing to do, perhaps you would not mind carrying my load for me for a little."

"If I do so, what will you give me?" said the donkey.

"I will give you two pieces of gold," said the peddler, but he
did not speak the truth, for he knew he had no gold to give.

"Agreed," said the donkey. So they journeyed on together in a
very friendly manner, the donkey carrying the peddler's pack, and
the peddler walking by his side. After a time they met a raven, who
was looking for worms in the roadside, and the donkey called out
to him: "Good morrow, black friend. If you are going our way, you
would do well to sit upon my back and drive away the flies, which
worry me sadly."

"And what will you pay me to do this?" asked the raven.

"Money is no object to me," said the donkey, "so I will give
you three pieces of gold." And he too knew he was making a false
promise, for he had no gold at all to give.

"Agreed," said the raven. So they went on in high good humor,
the donkey carrying the peddler's wares, and the raven sitting on
the donkey's back driving away the flies.

After a time they met a hedge sparrow, and the raven called
out to him: "Good day, little cousin. Do you want to earn a little
money? If so, bring me some worms from the bank as we go along,
for I had no breakfast, and am very hungry."

"What will you give me for it?" asked the hedge sparrow.

"Let us say four pieces of gold," said the raven grandly, "for I
know how to spend." But he knew this was not true, for he had not
saved any gold at all.

"Very well," said the hedge sparrow, and so on they went, the donkey carrying the peddler's pack, the raven keeping the flies away from the donkey, and the hedge sparrow bringing worms to the raven.

Presently they saw in the distance a good-sized town, and the peddler took out from his pack some shawls and shirts and hung them over the donkey's back that the passersby might see, and buy if they were so disposed. On the top of the other goods lay a small scarlet blanket, and when he saw it the hedge sparrow said to the peddler, "What will you take for that little blanket? It seems to be a good one. Name your price and you shall have it whatever it is, for I am badly in want of a blanket just now." But as the hedge sparrow had not a penny in the world, he knew he could not pay for it.

"The price of the blanket is five pieces of gold," said the peddler.

"That seems to me to be very dear," said the hedge sparrow. "I don't mind giving you four pieces of gold for it, but five is too much."

"Agreed," said the peddler, and he chuckled to himself and thought, "Now I shall be able to pay the donkey, otherwise I might have had some trouble in getting rid of him."

The hedge sparrow flew to the raven's side and whispered in his ear, "Please to pay me the four pieces of gold you owe me, for we are coming to a town, and I must be turning back."

"Four pieces of gold is really too much for bringing a few worms," said the raven. "It is absurd to expect such payment, but I will give you three, and you shall have them almost immediately." He bent down over the donkey's ear and whispered, "My friend, it is time you paid me the three pieces of gold which you promised, for the peddler will stop at this town, and you will not have to go farther with him."

"On thinking it over," said the donkey, "I have come to the conclusion that three pieces of gold are really a great deal too much to give for having a few flies driven away. You must have known that I was only joking when I said it, but I will let you have two, though I consider that it is much more than the job was worth. And the donkey turned again to the peddler, saying, "Now, good sir, your two pieces of gold, if you please."

"In a moment," said the peddler, and turning to the hedge sparrow, he said, "I really must have the money for the blanket at once."

"So you shall," answered the hedge sparrow, and cried angrily to the raven, "I want my money now, and cannot wait."

"In an instant," answered the raven, and again whispered to the donkey, "Why can't you pay me honestly? I should be ashamed of trying to slip out of my debts in such a way."

"I won't keep you waiting a second," said the donkey, and he turned once more to the peddler and cried, "Come, give me my money. For shame! A man like you trying to cheat a poor beast like me."

Then the peddler said to the hedge sparrow, "Pay me for my blanket, or I'll wring your neck."

And the hedge sparrow cried to the raven, "Give me my money or I'll peck out your eyes."

And the raven croaked to the donkey, "If you don't pay me, I'll bite off your tail."

And the donkey again cried to the peddler, "You dishonest wretch, pay me my money or I'll kick you soundly."

And they made such an uproar outside the walls of the town that the sheriff came out to see what it was all about. Each turned to him and began to complain of the other loudly.

"You are a set of rogues and vagabonds," said the sheriff, "and you shall all come before the mayor, and he'll settle your quarrels pretty quickly, and treat you as you deserve."

At this they all begged to be allowed to go away, each one saying he did not care about being paid at all. But the sheriff would not listen to them, and led them straightaway to the marketplace, where the mayor sat judging the people.

"Now, whom have we here?" cried he. "A peddler, a donkey, a raven, and a hedge sparrow. A set of worthless vagabonds, I'll be bound! Let us hear what they have to say for themselves."

On this the pedlar began to complain of the hedge sparrow, and the hedge sparrow of the raven, and the raven of the donkey, and the donkey of the peddler.

The mayor did not heed them much, but he eyed the peddler's pack, and at length interrupted them, and said, "I am convinced that you are a set if good-for-nothing fellows, and one is quite as bad as the other, so I order that the peddler be locked up in the prison, that the donkey be soundly well thrashed, and that the raven and the hedge sparrow both have their tail feathers pulled out, and then be turned out of the town. As for the blanket, it seems to me to be the only good thing in the whole matter, and as I cannot allow you to keep the cause of such a disturbance, I will take it for myself. Sheriff, lead the prisoners away."

So the sheriff did as he was told, and the peddler was locked up for many days in the prison.

"It is very sad to think to what straits an honest man may be brought," he sighed to himself as he sat lamenting his hard fate. "In the future this will be a warning to me to keep clear of hedge sparrows. If the hedge sparrow had paid me as he ought, I should not be here now."

Meantime the donkey was being soundly well thrashed, and after each blow he cried, "Alas! alas! See what comes to an innocent quadruped for having to do with human beings. Had the peddler given me the money he owed, I should not now be beaten thus. In the future I will never make a bargain with men."

The raven and the hedge sparrow hopped out of the town by different roads, and both were very sad, for they had lost all their tail feathers, which the sheriff had pulled out.

"Alas!" croaked the raven, "my fate is indeed a hard one. But it serves me right for trusting a donkey, who goes on his feet and cannot fly. It is truly a warning to me never again to trust anything without a beak."

The hedge sparrow was quite crestfallen, and could scarcely keep from tears. "It all comes of my being so taken in by that raven," he sighed. "But I should have known that these large birds are never honest. In the future I will be wise, and never make a bargain with anything bigger or stronger than myself."

•

SOMEONE MUST PAY

One good measure of a nation's spirit—and its citizens' sense of responsibility—is how many times you hear the phrase "it wasn't my fault" or "someone *else* must pay." This old Arab tale makes great reading for our times.

One morning a well-known thief with a splint on his leg hobbled into a courtroom and approached the bench.

"Your Honor," he began, bowing the best he could, "I have a complaint. Yesterday I was walking down the street, minding my own business, when I noticed a house with a window that was clearly unlocked. Now, who could pass by an invitation like that? Of course I had to investigate. I climbed over the fence, made my way through the yard, and opened the window. But I was only halfway inside when the sill gave way. I tumbled to the ground and, as you can plainly see, broke my leg. Now I demand justice."

The judge nodded, stroked his beard, and ordered the owner of the house to be summoned at once.

"Now, see here," he barked when the owner arrived, "your window broke this man's leg as he tried to enter your house. Just what makes you think you can expose the public to a dangerous, faulty window?"

Well, the poor homeowner had never stood before a judge in his life, and he was frightened out of his wits. He searched his brain for an answer.

"Your Honor," he pleaded, "it's not my fault. I paid the carpenter good money to build my window. He should have built it so it wouldn't fall apart."

"You're right! Bring me the carpenter!" the judge roared from the bench.

The bailiff rounded up the carpenter.

"How dare you build a window that would break a man's leg!" the judge thundered. "What's wrong with you?"

The carpenter trembled and shifted from foot to foot.

"Your Honor," he faltered, "perhaps I did not build the window quite as well as I should. But it wasn't my fault. The truth is, I was feeling ill the day I nailed it together. I had eaten a pie from a baker's shop, and it upset my stomach."

The judge slammed down his fist.

"We'll get to the bottom of this," he promised. "Bring me the baker!"

The baker found himself dragged into court.

"I hear you're baking bad pies," the judge said. "The carpenter says you sold him a pie which made him sick, which made his window bad, which broke this man's leg."

The baker shook his head.

"I remember the day I sold him the pie," he said. "It's true, Your Honor, that perhaps the pie was only half-baked. Perhaps I put in a pinch too much of this, or a smidgen too much of that. But that's because, when I was making it, a beautiful woman came into my shop to buy pastries. And you should have seen the dress she had on! I've never seen such a dress—they shouldn't be allowed to wear them like that in public! So, of course, Your Honor, I may not have paid quite enough attention to my pies."

"We'll see about this!" shouted the judge. "Find that woman!"

The woman was located. The judge told her how she had broken a man's leg.

"But, Your Honor," she protested, "as the baker himself admitted, the dress caught his eye, not me. The dressmaker is the one to blame."

"Arrest the dressmaker!" the judge ordered.

The dressmaker was hauled before the bench.

"What do you mean by corrupting the public this way?" the judge demanded. "Your dress has made this woman turn this baker's head, which made his pies bad, which made the carpenter ill, which made his window frame bad, which broke this poor man's leg. What do you have to say for yourself?"

But the dressmaker was not a speechmaker. He stammered and stuttered, and could think of nothing at all to say. The judge ordered him hanged.

The bailiff looked the condemned man up and down.

"He's a big one, Your Honor," he suggested. "I'm afraid he'll be too tall for our gallows. His feet will just land on the ground."

"So find a shorter dressmaker, and hang him instead," the judge stormed. "Someone must pay, after all."

Then he ordered the woman to wear something else, and the baker to pay attention to his pies, and the carpenter to fix the window, and the owner to keep it locked.

But a lock is nothing to a thief. As soon as his leg healed, the plaintiff went back to the house and, knowing the window was safe now, broke in and took whatever he wanted.

•

GRUMBLE TOWN

There is nothing more unattractive than the sound of whining in the midst of plenty. It is not a good sign of character at any level —in individuals, families, communities, or nations as a whole.

There was once a place called Grumble Town where everybody grumbled, grumbled, grumbled. In summer, the people grumbled that it was too hot. In winter, it was too cold. When it rained, the children whimpered because they couldn't go outside. When the sun came out, they complained that they had nothing to do. Neighbors griped and groaned about neighbors, parents about children, brothers about sisters. Everybody had a problem, and everyone whined that *someone* should come do something about it.

One day a peddler trudged into town, carrying a big basket on his back. When he heard all the fussing and sighing and moaning, he put his basket down and cried: "O citizens of this town! Your fields are ripe with grain, your orchards heavy with fruit. Your mountains are covered by good, thick forests, and your valleys watered by deep, wide rivers. Never have I seen a place blessed by such opportunity and abundance. Why are you so dissatisfied? Gather around me, and I will show you the way to contentment."

Now this peddler's shirt was tattered and torn. His pants showed patches, his shoes had holes. The people laughed to think that someone like him could show them how to be content. But while they snickered, he pulled a long rope from his basket and strung it between two poles in the town square. Then, holding his basket before him, he cried: "People of Grumble Town! Whoever is dissatisfied, write your trouble on a piece of paper, and bring it and put it in this basket. I will exchange your problem for happiness!"

The crowd swarmed around him. No one hesitated at the chance to get rid of his trouble. Every man, woman, and child in the village scribbled a grumble onto a scrap of paper and dropped it into the basket.

They watched as the peddler took each trouble and hung it on the line. By the time he was through, troubles fluttered on every inch of rope, from end to end. Then he said: "Now each one of you should take from this magic line the smallest trouble you can find."

They all rushed forward to examine all the troubles. They hunted and fingered and pondered, each trying to pick the very smallest trouble. After a while the magic line was empty.

And behold! Each held in his hand the very same trouble he had put into the basket. Each had chosen his own trouble, thinking it was the smallest of all on the line.

From that day, the people of Grumble Town stopped grumbling all the time. And whenever anyone had the urge to whimper or whine, he thought of the peddler and his magic line.

•

THE GRUMBLE FAMILY

There's a family nobody likes to meet,
They live, it is said, on Complaining Street,
In the city of Never-Are-Satisfied,
The river of Discontent beside.
They growl at that and they growl at this,
Whatever comes there is something amiss;
And whether their station be high or humble,
They are known by the name of Grumble.

The weather is always too hot or cold,
Summer and winter alike they scold;
Nothing goes right with the folks you meet
Down on that gloomy Complaining Street.
They growl at the rain and they growl at the sun,
In fact, their growling is never done.
And if everything pleased them, there isn't a doubt
They'd growl that they'd nothing to grumble about!

But the queerest thing is that not one of the same
Can be brought to acknowledge his family name,
For never a Grumbler will own that he
Is connected with it at all, you see.
And the worst thing is that if anyone stays
Among them too long he will learn their ways,
And before he dreams of the terrible jumble
He's adopted into the family of Grumble.

So it were wisest to keep our feet
From wandering into Complaining Street;
And never to growl, whatever we do,
Lest we be mistaken for Grumblers, too.
Let us learn to walk with a smile and song,
No matter if things do sometimes go wrong,
And then, be our station high or humble,
We'll never belong to the family of Grumble!

•

THE KING AND THE SHIRT

**Learning how to work and learning how to be satisfied often seem
to go hand in hand.**

A king once fell gravely ill. As each day passed he grew worse
and worse. His doctors and wise men tried cure after cure, but
nothing worked. They were ready to give up hope when the king's
old nursemaid spoke up.

"I will tell you how to save the king," she said. "If you can find
a happy man, and take the shirt from his back, and put it on the
king—then he will recover."

So the king sent forth his messengers. They rode far and wide
throughout the kingdom, and yet nowhere could they find a happy
man. No one seemed content; everyone had some complaint.

"That stupid tailor!" they heard a rich man say. "He's made
these pants too short! And by the way, this food is terrible! Can't
that cook do anything right?"

"What's wrong with our children?" the miller grumbled to his
wife. "They never do what we say! Can't they teach them manners
at school? And they make so much noise—tell them to go outside
and play."

"My roof is leaking," the candle maker groaned. "This ought
not to happen! Can't the government do something about it?"

Everywhere they went, the king's messengers heard nothing
but whining and griping. If a man was rich, he never had enough.
If he was not rich, it was someone else's fault. If he was healthy, he
had a bad mother-in-law. If he had a good mother-in-law, he was
catching a cold. Everyone had *something* to complain about.

Finally one night the king's own son was passing a small cottage when he heard someone say: "Thank you, Lord. I've finished
my daily labor, and helped my fellow man. I've eaten my fill, and
now I can lie down and sleep in peace. What more could I want?"

The prince rejoiced to have found a happy man at last. He gave
orders to take the fellow's shirt to the king, and pay the owner as
much money as he wished.

But when the king's messengers went into the cottage to take
the happy man's shirt off his back, they found he was so poor he
had no shirt at all.

•

Two Surprises

A workman plied his clumsy spade
  As the sun was going down;
The German king with his cavalcade
  Was coming into town.

The king stopped short when he saw the man.
  "My worthy friend," said he,
"Why not cease work at eventide,
  When the laborer should be free?"

"I do not slave," the old man said,
  "And I am always free;
Though I work from the time I leave my bed
  Till I can hardly see."

"How much," said the king, "is thy gain in a day?"
  "Eight groschen," the man replied.
"And canst thou live on this meager pay?"
  "Like a king," he said with pride.

"Two groschen for me and my wife, good friend,
  And two for a debt I owe;
Two groschen to lend and two to spend
  For those who can't labor, you know."

"Thy debt?" said the king. Said the toiler, "Yea,
  To my mother with age oppressed,
Who cared for me, toiled for me, many a day,
  And now hath need of rest."

"To whom dost lend of thy daily store?"
  "To my three boys at school. You see,
When I am too feeble to toil anymore,
  They will care for their mother and me."

"And thy last two groschen?" the monarch said.
  "My sisters are old and lame;
I give them two groschen for raiment and bread,
  All in the Father's name."

Tears welled up in the good king's eyes.
"Thou knowest me not," said he;
"As thou hast given me one surprise,
Here is another for thee.

"I am thy king; give me thy hand."
And he heaped it high with gold.
"When more thou needest, I command
That I at once be told.

"For I would bless with rich reward
The man who can proudly say,
That eight souls he doth keep and guard
On eight poor groschen a day."

•

THE STONE IN THE ROAD

Civic responsibility means doing something, not complaining that something ought to be done.

There is a story told of a king who lived long ago in a country across the sea. He was a very wise king, and spared no effort to teach his people good habits. Often he did things which seemed to them strange and useless; but all that he did, he did to teach his people to be industrious and careful.

"Nothing good can come to a nation," he said, "whose people complain and expect others to fix their problems for them. God gives the good things of life to those who take matters into their own hands."

One night, while everyone else slept, he placed a large stone in the road that led past his palace. Then he hid behind a hedge, and waited to see what would happen.

First came a farmer with his wagon heavily loaded with grain, which he was taking to the mill to be ground.

"Well, whoever saw such carelessness?" he said crossly, as he turned his team and drove around the stone. "Why don't these lazy people have that rock taken from the road?" And so he went on complaining of the uselessness of others, but not touching the stone himself.

Soon afterward, a young soldier came singing along the road. The long plume of his cap waved in the breeze, and a bright sword hung at his side. He was thinking of the wonderful bravery he would show in the war.

The soldier did not see the stone, but struck his foot against it and went sprawling in the dust. He rose to his feet, shook the dust from his clothes, picked up his sword, and stormed angrily about the lazy people who had no more sense than to leave such a huge rock in the road. Then he, too, walked away, not once thinking that he might move it himself.

So the day passed. Everyone who came by complained and whined because the stone lay in the road, but no one touched it.

At last, just at nightfall, the miller's daughter came past. She was a hard-working girl, and was very tired, because she had been busy since early morning at the mill.

But she said to herself, "It is almost dark. Somebody may fall over this stone in the night, and perhaps he could be badly hurt. I will move it out of the way."

So she tugged at the heavy stone. It was hard to move, but she pulled and pulled, and pushed, and lifted until at last she moved it from its place. To her surprise, she found a box underneath.

She lifted the box. It was heavy, for it was filled with something. Upon it was written: "This box belongs to the one who moves the stone."

She opened the lid, and found it was full of gold!

The miller's daughter went home with a happy heart. When the farmer and the soldier and all the others heard what had happened, they gathered around the spot in the road where the stone had been. They scratched at the dust with their feet, hoping to turn up a piece of gold.

"My friends," said the king, "we often find obstacles and burdens in our way. We may complain out loud while we walk around them if we choose, or we can lift them and find out what they mean. Disappointment is usually the price of laziness."

Then the wise king mounted his horse and, with a polite "Good evening," rode away.

THE BUSY MAN

Hard work is a good sign of a willingness to be responsible. People who are doing things are usually getting things done for other people as well as for themselves.

If you want to get a favor done
    By some obliging friend,
And want a promise, safe and sure,
    On which you may depend,
Don't go to him who always has
    Much leisure time to plan,
But if you want your favor done,
    Just ask the busy man.

The man with leisure never has
    A moment he can spare,
He's always "putting off" until
    His friends are in despair.
But he whose every waking hour
    Is crowded full of work
Forgets the art of wasting time,
    He cannot stop to shirk.

So when you want a favor done,
    And want it right away,
Go to the man who constantly
    Works twenty hours a day.
He'll find a moment, sure, somewhere,
    That has no other use.
And help you, while the idle man
    Is framing an excuse.

•

THE OLD MAN AND DEATH

Aesop

**Every life has its share of struggles of one kind or another. We are
not so quick to complain when we consider the alternative.**

An old man, bent with years and groaning beneath the weight
of a heavy load of firewood which he carried, sought, weary and
sore-footed on a long and dusty road, to gain his distant cottage.
Unable to bear the weight of his burden any longer, he let it fall by
the roadside, and lamented his hard fate.

"What pleasure have I known since I first drew breath in this
sad world? From dawn to dusk it has been hard work and little pay!
At home is an empty cupboard, a discontented wife, and lazy and
disobedient children! O Death! O Death! come and free me from
my troubles!"

At once the ghostly King of Terrors stood before him. "What
do you want with me?" Death queried in hollow tones.

"Noth—nothing," stammered the awed and frightened peasant,
"nothing except for you to help me put again upon my shoulders
the bundle of sticks I have let fall!"

•

GRATEFULNESS

George Herbert

Gratitude is better than grumbling.

Thou that hast given so much to me,
Give one thing more—a grateful heart;
Not thankful when it pleaseth me,
As if thy blessings had spare days,
But such a heart whose pulse may be.
Thy praise.

•

SAINT FRANCIS AND THE WOLF

Retold by Frances Dadmun

Sometimes the courage to lead comes from deep faith.

Saint Francis lived several hundred years ago in Italy. All the clothes he owned were a brown robe with a rope for a belt, and leather sandals. He generally went bareheaded unless the sun was hot or the rain heavy, and then he drew the hood of his robe over his head and went his way very comfortably. There were years when he had no home, but it made no difference, for he was happy anywhere. Every man was his friend and even the wild beasts trusted him.

One day, when Saint Francis was out for a walk, he saw a little town perched on a hill.

"There is Gubbio," he said to some friends who were walking with him. "I have good friends there. We must go up and make them a visit."

There was a high stone wall all about Gubbio which you couldn't possibly have climbed because it was higher than a house and very steep. People went in and out of a great gate which was locked every night to keep out robbers, but in the daytime it was generally wide open.

This morning, when Saint Francis and his friends came to the gate, they were surprised to find it closed. They had to knock several times before anyone opened it.

"What is the trouble, good brother, that the gate is shut?" asked Saint Francis.

"It's a great Wolf!" said the man, who was a peasant. "A huge fierce fellow he is, too. He eats men. He is so bold that we have seen him at this very gate where you came in, just now. It's a mercy that he didn't eat you."

"And no one dares go outside?" said Saint Francis.

"No one," said the peasant.

By this time, the street was full of people who had heard the knocking at the gate. They looked so frightened and wild-eyed that Saint Francis was sorry for them.

"Come, brothers," he said to his companions, "we will go out and see this Wolf."

The people cried out, "No, no!" until the narrow street echoed. Those who were nearest clutched the skirts of Saint Francis's brown robe.

"Yes, yes!" said St. Francis, "I am not afraid of the Wolf. He will be my friend."

The people knew that Saint Francis meant what he said and opened the gates, but their fingers trembled as they drew back the bolts.

Saint Francis and his companions went straight to the hills where the Wolf was hiding and the people of Gubbio followed at a safe distance. But Saint Francis was fearless. He put his trust in God.

So he left even his faithful companions and went on alone. And then he saw the Wolf, running swiftly with head low and mouth partly open. Saint Francis stood still.

"Come here, Brother Wolf," said Saint Francis. "In the name of Jesus, do not hurt anybody."

The Wolf closed his mouth, stopped running. He crept forward and lay down at the feet of Saint Francis.

"Brother Wolf," said Saint Francis, "you have done great harm in these parts, killing God's creatures—not only beasts but people, whom God made in his image! All people cry against you and all this land hates you. But I, Brother Wolf, would make peace between you and the people. Do no more harm and they will forgive you, and neither people nor dogs shall torment you anymore."

The Wolf wagged his tail and his head drooped. He knew what it was to be tormented by people and dogs. He, as well as the people, had had a hard time.

"Brother Wolf," said Saint Francis, and he looked at the poor, lean sides where every rib showed, "if you are willing to be peaceable, I promise you that you will be fed as long as you live; for I know well that you have done all this harm because you were hungry. But since I do this for you, Brother Wolf, will you promise me that you will never again hurt either an animal or a human being?"

The Wolf bowed his head, but Saint Francis wanted more.

"Brother Wolf, you must give a pledge for your promise, that I may surely trust you."

Saint Francis stretched forth his right hand. The people gave a great cry of wonder, for the Wolf lifted his right paw and meekly placed it in the hand of Saint Francis, giving all the promise he could.

"Brother Wolf," said Saint Francis, "come with me and let us repeat this promise before all the people."

The Wolf followed Saint Francis back to the town, and as the news spread, men and women, young and old, big and little, trooped to the marketplace to see the Wolf with Saint Francis. When everybody in town was surely there, Saint Francis—and you know by this time that he was a real saint—spoke to the people.

"Listen, my brothers. Brother Wolf, here before you, has promised me to make peace with you and not to trouble you again in any way; and you are to promise him that you will give him all he needs to eat."

The people all shouted at once that they would feed their new friend regularly.

"And you, Brother Wolf," said Saint Francis, "do you promise to observe this treaty of peace that you will harm neither people nor animals nor any creature?"

The Wolf kneeled and bowed his head. He wriggled gently, he wagged his tail and lifted his ears, showing as plainly as a wolf could that he would keep the treaty.

"But, Brother Wolf," urged Saint Francis, "I wish you to promise me before all these people as you did outside the gate, and let me promise in turn never to break my word to you."

The Wolf understood, for he lifted his paw and placed it in the hand of Saint Francis. Once more the people cried out, this time with joy, and they thanked God for sending them Saint Francis, who had saved them from the mouth of the Wolf. No one knows what the Wolf thought, but we can guess that he was thankful too; for he would never have been so fierce if he had not nearly starved to death in the first place.

He lived two years in Gubbio and went among the houses from door to door, without hurting anyone. He was fed by the people most politely, and not even a dog barked at him. After two years, Brother Wolf died of old age, and everyone was sorry. He was not only loved for his own sake but was always reminding the people of their dear friend, Saint Francis.

•

THE MAID OF ORLÉANS

Adapted from
Louis Maurice Boutet de Monvel

Here is one of the most famous heroines of all time, a sweet peasant girl who challenged kings, led her troops, and died for love of God and country.

She was born Joan d'Arc in 1412, in the little French village of Domrémy. Her parents were honest laboring folk who lived by their toil. Their little house stood so close to the church that its garden touched the graveyard.

The child grew up there, under the eye of God.

She was a sweet, upright girl. Everyone loved her, for all knew her kind heart. A brave worker, she aided her family in their labors. By day she led the beasts to pasture, and in the evening she sat spinning by her mother's side.

She loved God, and often prayed to Him.

Now, in those days, France and England were at war. France had no real ruler. The English king had invaded the land, determined to make it his own. The French did not want to be ruled by the English, and they fought to put Charles the Dauphin, the son of their last king, on the throne.

But the Dauphin had no army, no money, and no will to fight. Day by day, pieces of his kingdom fell away to the enemy. Famine and anarchy reigned across the land.

One summer day, when she was thirteen years old, Joan heard a voice at midday in her father's garden. It told her to be a good girl and go to church. Then it told her that she was to save all of France, and that she must go to help the Dauphin.

"But I am only a poor girl," cried Joan.

"God will help thee," answered the voice.

And the child, overcome, was left weeping.

From that day she began to spend more and more time away from her playmates, listening to heavenly voices. As time passed, they became more urgent. The peril was great, they said; she must go help the king and save the kingdom.

And, of course, when Joan began to speak of her mission, many people laughed, and called her crazy. But the simple-hearted folk, moved by her faith, believed in her. A kind squire offered to take her to see the Dauphin. The poor folk, adding their mites together, raised the money to clothe and arm the little peasant girl. They bought her a horse, and on the appointed day she set out with a small escort.

"God keep you!" cried the multitude, and they wept.

The enemy held the country through which the little party was to pass. They had to travel at night and hide through the day. Joan's companions, alarmed, spoke of turning back.

"Fear nothing," said she. "God is leading us."

On the twelfth day they arrived at the court of the Dauphin. At first it looked as if he would not receive the inspired girl. But at last an interview was granted. One evening, by the light of fifty torches, Joan was brought into the great hall of the castle, crowded with all the nobles of the court. She had never seen the Dauphin.

To see if God were really guiding her, as she claimed, the Dauphin changed places with one of noblemen in the court, and disguised himself in plain clothes. But Joan singled him out among the multitude at once, and knelt before him.

"God give you a happy life, gentle Dauphin," she said.

"I am not the king," he answered. "Yonder is the king."

"You are he, gentle prince, and no other," she replied with perfect confidence. Then she told him that God had sent her to aid him, and asked for troops to save the city of Orléans, which lay under siege by the English troops. Everyone knew that if Orléans fell, France would be lost.

The king hesitated. The girl might be a sorceress. He sent her to be examined by learned men. For three weeks they tormented her with their questions. When they told her that God should have no need of men-at-arms to deliver France, she drew herself up quickly. "The soldiers will fight, but God will give the victory," she said.

The people declared that the maid was indeed inspired, and the learned and powerful were forced to yield to the multitude.

The French troops assembled. On Thursday, the 28th of April, 1429, the little army moved forward, led by Joan. She was clad in glistening armor, and carried a white banner embroidered with the lilies of France. When she entered Orléans, the people crowded to meet her. She passed by torchlight through the city; men, women, and children thronged to get near her, stretching forth their hands to touch the inspired maiden's horse.

Joan spoke kindly to them, promising to deliver the city. Her confidence influenced everyone around her. The people of Orléans, so lately timid and discouraged, now wished to hurl themselves at the enemy. Joan, meanwhile, had letters thrown over the walls of the city, ordering the besieging English to depart and return to their own country. They answered her with insults. So Joan mounted her warhorse and led her soldiers into battle.

Around Orléans stood the forts which the English held. The French now captured them one by one. Soon all but the last was taken from the enemy. Its walls were forbidding, and the French generals wanted to wait for more soldiers before making an attack. But Joan pushed them on.

The fighting was fierce. At one point Joan descended into a moat, and was raising a ladder against a parapet when an English arrow struck her between her neck and shoulder. She fell backward into the trench and, thinking her killed, the English rallied. But the brave girl pulled the arrow out of the wound, and was soon foremost in the fight again.

"Forward!" she cried. "All is yours!"

The English were routed. And Orléans, which had been besieged for eight months, was delivered in only four days.

The Maid of Orléans, as she was now called, hastened to the court of the Dauphin. She desired at once to take him to Rheims, where he could be crowned. He received her with great honors, but refused to follow her. He accepted the devotion of the heroic girl, but did not want her generous efforts to disturb his easy life. Instead, he sent her to attack the places still held by the English on the banks of the river Loire.

In battle after battle, the French were victorious. Joan was always in the front of the ranks. She constantly exposed herself to blows and was often wounded, but would never use her sword. Her only weapon was her banner painted with the lilies of France.

At last the Dauphin agreed to proceed to Rheims. On the 16th of July he entered the town at the head of his troops. The next day in the cathedral, with Joan standing at his side, he was crowned Charles VII of France.

But after the coronation, Joan seemed to lose her power. She began to lose battles. While defending the town of Compiègne, her army was driven back. During the retreat, Joan, deserted by all, found herself nearly surrounded by the enemy. She parried the blows of her assailants, steadily retreating until she reached the walls of the city. A step more and she would have been safe inside; but through either jealousy, imprudence, or treason, those who were defending the entrance to the city closed the gates and raised the bridge, leaving Joan outside. She fell into the hands of the English.

Ashamed at having been beaten so many times by a mere girl, her captors accused her of sorcery. They dragged her from prison to prison, and finally shut her up in a dungeon at Rouen. They brought her out for examination as many as sixteen times, worried her with all sorts of perplexing questions, then shut her up again. They used torture to make her confess that heaven had not sent her.

Many of the English believed that while Joan lived they would be defeated, so they clamored for her death. A tribunal composed of bribed French priests was given the power to try her as a witch and a heretic. The unhappy maiden could oppose the insidious questions of her judges only with the uprightness and simplicity of her heart. "I have nothing more to do here," she said. "Send me back to God, from whom I came." After a long trial and painful imprisonment, Joan was condemned and sentenced to be burned at the stake.

And throughout her ordeal, King Charles of France, who owed her so much, made no attempt to help her.

On the morning of May 30, 1431, at nine o'clock, Joan rode through the streets of Rouen in the executioner's cart. On seeing the pile placed in front of the old marketplace, a cry escaped her.

"Ah, Rouen, Rouen, are you then to be my last home?" she exclaimed.

She knelt and prayed. Then, turning to her judges and enemies, she begged them to have a Mass said for her soul. She mounted the pile, and while they bound her hands, she asked to be shown a crucifix. Then they lit the fire. In the midst of the clouds of smoke and lurid gleam of flames, she forgave all, and said her last prayer.

Everyone present wept, even the executioners and judges. It is said that many turned away, unable to bear the sight, and as they fled cried: "We are lost! We have burned a saint!"

•

GIDEON AND HIS BRAVE THREE HUNDRED

Adapted from retellings by
Frances Dadmun and Jesse Lyman Hurlbut

As this story from the book of Judges in the Bible reminds us, an important part of leadership is knowing how to choose the right people to lead. The story shows us how to look for courage and resolution, and reminds us that it's not the size of the dog in the fight that counts, but the size of the fight in the dog.

Long ago, a young man lived in Israel whose name was Gideon. He was the only son his father had left. His brothers, older than he, had died in battle. For Israel was hard-pressed by the tribe of Midianites, who lived across the River Jordan. For a time they would lie quiet and Israel would think all was well; but as soon as the wheat fields of Israel were yellow and ripe for harvest, the Midianites would cross the river, fight with Israel, and carry off the wheat. Israel had been beaten so many times that now she dared not stir. Her men lived in caves, just as animals creep into holes in the earth to protect themselves.

Gideon thought it a shame. He was brave, too brave to hide in the earth and let the Midianites carry off his father's wheat. Then God put the thought in his heart to save his people. So it happened that one morning, when a frightened messenger came running to say that the Midianites had crossed the river again, Gideon stood on a hilltop and blew a trumpet.

The Israelites ran from their caves at the sound of the trumpet blast, and gathered around Gideon. Then he sent messengers throughout the land to call the fighting men together. The Israelites were so glad to have a brave leader that Gideon soon had an army of thirty-two thousand men.

Early in the morning they pitched their tents south of the

enemy. When the Midianites woke and came out of their own tents, they stared in surprise. There was Israel just opposite, and from the number of tents, it looked like a great host!

But Gideon was not sure of his army. The men had been brave enough at the call of the trumpet, but when they faced the camp of the Midianites, extending up and down the valley as far as they could see, they began to wish they had stayed hidden in their own caves. They were not as sure as Gideon was that God would give them the victory. After all, they said to one another, what sort of captain was Gideon? He was little more than a boy.

But God said to Gideon: "Your army is too large. Send home all those who are afraid to fight."

And Gideon saw that a small army of brave men would be better than a multitude of cowards. So he sent word through the camp that whoever was afraid of the enemy should go home. Twenty-two thousand people went away, leaving only ten thousand in Gideon's army.

But God said to Gideon: "The people are yet too many. You need only a few of the bravest and best men to fight in this battle. Bring the men down the mountain, beside the water, and there I will show you how to find the ones you need."

So in the morning, by God's command, Gideon called his ten thousand men out and made them march down the hill, just as though they were going to attack the enemy. And when they were beside the water, he noticed how they drank, and set them apart into two companies.

As they came to the water, most of the men threw aside their shields and spears and knelt down to scoop up a drink with both hands together like a cup. If there had been any Midianites hidden in the bushes they could have shot the drinkers with arrows, for they were off their guard. These men Gideon commanded to stand in one company.

But there were a few men who did not stop to take a long drink of water. Holding spear and shield in one hand, with eyes wide open in case the enemy should suddenly appear, they merely caught up a handful of water in passing and marched on, lapping the water from the other hand.

God said to Gideon: "Set by themselves these men who have lapped up each a handful of water. These are the ones I have chosen to set Israel free."

Gideon counted these men and found there were only three hundred. But they were three hundred earnest men, of one purpose, who would not turn aside from their aim, even to drink.

Gideon waited for the sun to go down. When it was dark, he crept into the camp of the Midianites, and listened. When he heard them talking, he was glad, for he could tell that the Midianites, for all their number, were afraid of the Israelites. So he hurried back to his own camp.

Gideon's plan did not need a large army, but it did need a few careful, bold men who would do exactly as their leader commanded. He gave to each of his three hundred soldiers a lamp, a pitcher, and a trumpet, and told the men what to do with them. The lamps were lighted, but were placed inside the pitchers, so they could not be seen. He divided his men into three companies, and very quietly led them down the mountain in the middle of the night, and arranged them all around the Midianite camp.

Then at once a great shout rang out in the darkness, and after it came a crash of breaking pitchers and then a flash of light in every direction. The men blew their trumpets with a mighty noise. The Midianites were startled from their sleep to see enemies all around them, lights beaming and swords flashing in the darkness, and everywhere the sharp blaring of horns.

They were filled with sudden terror and thought only of escape, not of fighting. But wherever they turned, their enemies seemed to be standing with swords drawn. Their own land was east, across the river Jordan, and they fled in that direction, down a valley between the mountains, and they never came back again.

And so Israel was free, all because Gideon was brave and found three hundred men who stood with him.

•

How They Built the Walls

Retold by Henry Hallam Tweedy

Any people who would build or preserve a nation should remember the courage, perseverance, vigilance, hard work, and faith of Nehemiah. Here are some of the virtues needed to make a country safe and strong. The story is from the book of Nehemiah in the Bible.

About four hundred and fifty years before Jesus was born, there lived in the palace of the king of Persia a young Jew, whose name was Nehemiah. He seemed to have everything to make him happy. He had clothes of silk, and plenty of food, and could enjoy the fine things in the palace. Moreover, the king loved him and trusted him, so much so that he made Nehemiah his cupbearer. This meant a great deal in those days. For when wicked men wished to kill the king they used to try to put poison in his cup. Only a true friend might fill and bring it, and he would taste it before he gave it to the king to show that the king need not be afraid.

But with all this Nehemiah was not happy. For he was far from the city where his fathers had lived and now were buried. He had friends there, whom he longed to see, and he was eager to make his home in the land of his people, and to serve it, and make it beautiful, and protect it against its foes.

One day his brother came to him with some men from Jerusalem, who brought bad news. They told him that his friends were poor, and that they were having a great deal of sorrow and trouble. As for the city, which he loved, its great wall, built to guard it from its enemies, was broken down, while the great gates, through which people might enter by day but which were closed to keep out foes and robbers at night, had been burned.

When Nehemiah heard this, he was very sad. He knew that wild animals could creep in and prowl around its streets at night. Worse yet, wild men could steal in under the cover of darkness, and rob his friends, and even kill them. Perhaps some cruel king would march against it with his soldiers, and burn all the homes and make the people his slaves. No wonder that Nehemiah was unhappy. He felt so bad that he sat down and cried, and for days and days he could not even bear to eat.

But there was no use in crying. He knew that. And to go without food would only make him weak and unable to work, while it would not build the walls of his city or bring aid to his friends. So he made up his mind to do something, and the first thing that he did was to ask God to help him and to guide him, so that he might go back home and serve his city and his friends. Then he arose, and made himself ready to act as cupbearer, and went in to wait on the king.

The king saw at once that his cupbearer's heart was full of sorrow. "Why are you sad," he asked, "inasmuch as you are not sick?"

At first Nehemiah was almost afraid to tell him, for while he knew that his city needed him, he feared that the king would not let him go. But at last he plucked up courage, and with a prayer in his heart that God would cause the king to be gracious, he made answer. "Why should I not be sad," he said, "when the city where my fathers are buried lies waste, and its walls are broken down, and its gates are burned?"

Then the king was sorry for him, and said, "What can I do for you? Come, tell me!"

Nehemiah bowed himself before the king, and said, "If I have pleased you and you really love me, send me to Jerusalem, that I may build its walls."

To his great joy, the king said that he might go. He even sent soldiers with him to guard him and help him. He also gave Nehemiah letters to his servants, who ruled for him in the land lying between Persia and Judah, bidding these men to give him wood with which to make the gates. So Nehemiah started out on his long journey, and at last found himself safe in Jerusalem among his friends.

It seemed wise not to tell them why he had come until he knew just what needed to be done. So one night Nehemiah and a few of his men walked around the city and looked at the walls. He soon saw that these were badly broken and quite useless, as the men had told him. Before the people were awake, he and his friends were back in their homes.

The next morning, he called the people together and said, "Come, and let us build the walls of our city! The king, my master, says that we may do so. God will help us, and if we love Him and obey Him, He will give us strength to drive away our foes."

Now, the wall was a very, very long one, and it had to be very thick and very high. It seemed as if they never would be able to finish it, and they could not have done so if they had not all worked, and worked hard. There were doubtless some lazy men, who did not want to work, and some cowards who were afraid that foes would come and hurt them while they were at work and some greedy, selfish men, who did not love their city very much, and said that unless Nehemiah paid them money they would not work. But Nehemiah made the lazy men ashamed of themselves, and cheered those who were afraid, and told the selfish ones that if they did not work, their foes and robbers would come and take away the money that they had already.

Most of the people worked with a will gladly, and began at once to build next to their own homes. Some said that they would build one gate, and some another. Both men and women worked on the walls. The boys and girls were busy, too. Everybody worked and sang and pounded and shouted as the great stones were put into place. It was very hard labor. Their hands were bruised and torn, and their arms ached, and their backs were weary. But they loved their city dearly, and when people work for somebody or something that they love, the hardest toil is done gladly and often seems light.

Round about the country were men who hated Nehemiah and his people. They did not want to have the walls built, for then it would be harder to take the city, and they could not break into it and make the people slaves. Some of them used to stand near the men while they were at work, and laugh at them. "You can never build such great walls," they cried. "What is the use of trying!" When the people kept right on, they sent word, saying that if the work was not stopped, they would come and fight. But Nehemiah told the people not to be afraid. "Trust God," he said, "and work with your trowel in one hand and your sword in the other."

Every day saw fewer holes in the walls of the city. One by one the big gates were made and swung into place. At last the great work was done, and Nehemiah and his friends were as happy as they were weary. No robbers could creep into their homes now. There would be no more wild beasts prowling around their streets at night. As for the men who had jeered at them and tried to stop the work, the workers could laugh at them now. The people had loved their city enough to labor for it, and to suffer hardship, and endure danger. But as the result of their work, it was now a strong fort, and their lives and their homes were safe once more. And the men and women and boys and girls who had helped Nehemiah were happy and loved the city better and were prouder of it because each had worked and done a full share in building the great wall.

Nehemiah did many other things to make his city better and more beautiful, and all men loved him and honored him, because he had served his country so well.

•

BETSY ROSS AND THE FIRST FLAG

*Adapted from a retelling
by Grace Humphrey*

Historians don't know if Betsy Ross actually made the very first American flag. But whether legend or fact, the incident has become one of our most beloved portraits of the patriotic citizen ready to do his or her part.

In 1752 the eighth child was born in the Quaker family of Griscom in Philadelphia, and was named Elizabeth. Nine other children came after her, so with a total of sixteen brothers and sisters you may be sure she never had much opportunity to be lonely. Perhaps the large number of children is the explanation for her being apprenticed at Webster's, the leading upholstery establishment in the city. There Elizabeth became acquainted with John Ross, one of her fellow apprentices. Their friendship grew to love, and when she was twenty-one they were married.

Soon afterward they left Webster's and opened a little upholstery shop of their own, in a two-story house on Arch Street—a quaint little house that was old then, for it was built of bricks that came over to America as ballast in one of William Penn's vessels. It is still standing, in a good state of preservation, and very little changed from the old days, with its wide doors, big cupboards, narrow stairs, and tiny windowpanes. The front room was the shop, where Elizabeth and John waited on customers.

The happiness of the Ross family was not to last long. The spirit of liberty was awakening among the colonists, the spirit of resistance to the demands of the mother country. In common with many patriotic women, Betsy Ross saw her husband march away for military service. With several other young men he was guarding cannonballs and artillery stores on one of the city wharves along the Delaware River, when he received a serious injury. He died in January 1776, after long and anxious nursing on the part of his young wife.

There was Betsy Ross, a widow at twenty-four. She determined to maintain herself independently, if possible, and to continue alone the upholstery business they had developed together. About five months after her husband's death, sometime between the twenty-second of May and the fifth of June, she was one day working in the shop when three gentlemen called.

The first was General Washington, in Philadelphia for a few days to consult the Continental Congress. Mistress Ross had frequently seen him, for the story is that he had visited her shop more than once, to have her embroider the ruffles for his shirts. With him was Robert Morris, who would go down in history as the treasurer and financier of the Revolution, and her husband's uncle, Colonel George Ross, a signer of the Declaration of Independence.

These gentlemen had come to consult her. She knew, of course, how the various banners carried by troops from the different colonies, as well as by different regiments, had caused confusion and might mean danger. It was time to do away with the pine tree flag, the beaver flag, the rattlesnake flag, the hope flag, the silver crescent flag, the anchor flag, the liberty tree flag, and all the rest of them, and have a single standard for the American army. Betsy Ross had heard, too, of the Cambridge flag, often called the grand union flag, which Washington had raised the New Year's Day before, a flag half English, half American, with thirteen red and white stripes, and the crosses of St. George and St. Andrew. But since the first of the year events had moved rapidly and the desire for separation from England had become steadily stronger. A new flag was needed, to show the growing spirit of Americanism—which was soon to crystallize on the Fourth of July.

All this Betsy Ross knew, as a good patriot would. And she could not have been greatly surprised when General Washington said they had come to consult her about a national flag.

"Can you make a flag?" he asked.

Modestly and with some diffidence she replied, "I don't know, sir, but I can try."

Then in the little back parlor Washington showed her a rough sketch he had made—a square flag with thirteen stripes of red and white, and thirteen stars in the blue canton. He asked her opinion of the design. With unerring accuracy of eye she saw at once what was needed to make the flag more beautiful. She suggested that the proportions be changed, so that the length would be a third more than the width. She proposed that the thirteen stars be grouped to form some design, say a circle or a star, or placed in parallel rows. And last she remarked that a five-pointed star was more symmetrical than one with six points.

"But," ask Washington, "isn't it more difficult to make?"

In answer practical Betsy Ross took up a piece of paper, folded it over, and with one clip of her scissors cleverly made a perfect star with five even points.

That was sufficient, and the general drew up his chair to her table and made another pencil sketch, embodying her three suggestions. The second sketch was copied and colored by a Philadelphia artist, William Barrett, a painter of some note, who returned it to Mistress Ross. Meantime, not knowing just how to make a flag, for it must be sewed in a particular way, she went to a shipping merchant, an old Scotchman who was a friend of Robert Morris, to borrow a ship's flag as a guide.

And in that way Betsy Ross made the first Stars and Stripes. To try the effect, the story goes, the new banner was run up to the peak of a vessel in the Delaware River. Several months later, the Continental Congress passed a resolution formally adopting the flag as the national standard.

This is the story Betsy told over and over, to her daughters and grandchildren, and in later years they wrote the account down, just as they had heard it, and as you have read it here. It was George Washington, more than any other, who seems to have been most interested in the question of a national flag. But it was the skilled seamstress to whom he took his first, rough design, to have her opinion of its worth. Much of the flag's beauty is due to the keen eye, confident hand, and ready heart of patriot Betsy Ross.

•

HE GAVE HIS LIFE FOR HIS COUNTRY

Brave citizens come in all ages. Here are two tales of young heroes
who thought of their country before themselves. The first story
takes place in Tyrol, now a province of Austria.

Some years ago there was war between the French and the
people who lived in a little country to the northeast of Italy called
Tyrol. I suppose most people love their native land, but at this
particular time the Tyrolese were so anxious to save their country
that even the women and children followed the soldiers to battle,
in hopes of being of some use to them.

One of the boys who thus followed his father was called Albert
Speckbacher. He was only ten years old, but his father was one of
the bravest leaders of the Tyrolese, and, young as he was, Albert
was determined that he would help him somehow.

One day the French went to attack a village. They came to a
deep ravine, at the bottom of which the river Ard dashed along at
a terrific pace. The only way to reach the village was by crossing a
bridge. A strange sort of bridge it was, too, just the kind to keep
a village free from any enemies. It was simply a great tree, which
had been felled from the mountainside and allowed to fall right
across the ravine, so that its topmost boughs caught on the opposite
rocks—a dangerous crossing place, and one on which only one
person could go at a time.

The Tyrolese knew what the French were doing, and a party of
three hundred men, with Speckbacher as their leader, was sent
down to defend this bridge. For an hour the battle raged on each
side of the ravine, and the Tyrolese seemed to be getting the best
of it. Then the French general ordered two cannon to be dragged
up the rocks, and in a very short time more than half the brave
Tyrolese were killed, Speckbacher amongst the number.

Little Albert knelt beside his father's dead body, and wondered
what he could do to save his country. He saw that the Tyrolese were
going to try to destroy the bridge. If that could be done, the French
could not possibly enter the village. He watched them get their axes
and begin cutting through the roots and trunk of the tree.

But as they boldly worked, the French rifles killed one after another of them, till at last their courage failed, and no one came forward to take his place at the task which had proved fatal to so many. A great part of the tree had been cut through, but there still remained enough to hold it firm.

Albert looked down at his father's white face, then up to the bright heaven for a moment. Then he seized the axe and worked with all his strength. A shower of bullets fell round him, but none touched him. The tree was cut through at last, excepting at one point, which was quite out of his reach. It was only a small piece of the inner bark, but he could not get at it. Albert saw in a moment there was only one way in which he could break the tree away from this point. He must put a weight on the top of it, and so snap it off.

He waited till the French had fired their rifles once more; then, while they stopped to reload, he sprang upon the tree, jumping with all his might. His weight, light as it was, snapped the little piece by which it was held, and he and the bridge went tumbling into the ravine below.

Thus did the brave boy of ten sacrifice his life to save his native village.

The French retired when they saw the bridge fall, and the next day they found the body of the poor lad floating in the stream at the foot of the mountain. Enemies though they were, they could admire such a noble deed as his. They buried the hero on the mountainside, and put up a stone telling the story of his bravery.

●

An American Army of Two

*Adapted from a retelling
by Florence Farmer*

Here are quick wits and courage—the best kinds of weapons.

If you have ever wondered if just one or two people can make a difference, just remember the "American Army of Two."

Rebecca and Abigail Bates lived on the coast of Massachusetts, near a little village named Scituate. Their father was the keeper of the lighthouse, which stood at the entrance of the harbor and warned ships away from the rocky coast.

One day Rebecca and Abigail were up in the tower, polishing the great glass that sent the light far over the sea. Their father and mother had rowed across the bay to the village, leaving the lighthouse in their daughters' care. As they polished away with all their might, they noticed a strange ship creeping around a point. It stopped and lowered two little boats, which turned and started toward land.

At that time people feared every ship they did not know, for the year was 1814, and America and England were at war. British ships often sailed right into harbors and sent their soldiers ashore to attack the villages. The British had already made one raid on Scituate's harbor, and had burned ten vessels before putting back to sea.

Now Rebecca and Abigail stood frozen in the lighthouse, peering down and holding their breath while they waited to see what these two strange boats would do. Closer and closer they crept, until finally they entered the harbor. They were full of British soldiers!

The girls looked along the shore. No help was to be seen. What could they do? If they could only warn the townspeople! But they had no boat, and there would be no time to run to the village, for it was a long way around the bay.

Rebecca grabbed her sister by the sleeve.

"Listen, Abigail," she cried. "Here's what we two girls are going to do." And she began whispering into her ear, as if the British might hear her plan as they rowed swiftly across the water.

The sisters raced down the winding staircase and across the lawn to their house. Abigail snatched up a drum, which her father had brought home to mend just the other day. Rebecca grabbed a fife, and they slipped out of the house toward the beach, crouching behind bushes and sandhills to keep out of sight.

The British boats were now quite close, and the soldiers were preparing to leap ashore. Suddenly the order was given to halt. The soldiers listened closely.

From behind a clump of cedar trees came the beating of a drum, and then the squeak of a fife. It was not skillful, but it was loud and clear—the strains of "Yankee Doodle" floated over the sands.

"The militia has seen us coming!" cried the British soldiers. "They will attack us as soon as we land!" They turned their boats around and rowed for their lives, back to their ship.

A moment later the villagers spotted the British boats. They raised a great alarm, and all hurried toward the lighthouse.

When they reached the point, they found only Rebecca and Abigail Bates, sitting on a rock, watching a faraway ship put to sea. A drum and fife lay beside them.

The "American Army of Two" had won the day.

•

A LEGEND OF THE ROMAN FORUM

This story was a favorite Roman legend of patriotism and self-sacrifice. The Forum in Rome was the center of civic life, an open area surrounded by temples, legislative chambers, markets, and other public buildings.

In the year 362 B.C. Rome was shaken by an awful earthquake, and a huge chasm suddenly opened in the middle of the Forum, so deep that no one could see the bottom. The citizens brought stones and earth to fill it up, but no matter how much they threw in, the yawning gulf seemed as terrible as before.

The Senate then consulted the soothsayers, who announced that the crater could not be filled up until what was most valuable in Rome was cast into it.

"Heed this," said the augurs. "Your most sacred treasure must be dedicated to the Gods in this place if Rome is to stand fast."

The horrified people rushed to the edge of the pit and began throwing in their most valuable possessions—gold and silver and jewelry—but still the hole was as deep as ever. As they stood agonizing over what to do next, a noble youth named Marcus Curtius rode forward, armed as though for battle.

"What is more valuable to Rome than courage?" he cried. "What is more valuable than a citizen who is willing to give himself for his country?"

All the people stood silent. Curtius gazed at the temples of the immortal gods lining the Forum and stretched forth his arms to heaven above. Then, sword in hand, he spurred his horse and leapt into the great pit.

Immediately the ground closed behind him, and neither he nor his horse was ever seen again. All was as it had been before the earthquake.

•

GOD AND THE SOLDIER

This inscription was reportedly discovered on an old stone sentry box on the island of Gibraltar. Nations last when citizens remember the important things in times of difficulty *and* in times of ease.

> God and the soldier
> All men adore
> In time of trouble,
> And no more;
> For when war is over
> And all things righted,
> God is neglected—
> The old soldier slighted.

•

THE CHEVALIER D'ASSAS

Here is the sound of courage.

Long ago, a war was going on between the French and the Germans. A French army in the south of Germany was retreating before the enemy and had encamped for the night after a long day's march. The regiment of Auvergne was on the side of the French nearest the enemy, and the most advanced outpost of that regiment was a company that had for its captain a very brave young officer, the Chevalier D'Assas.

The French general thought that the enemy would try to attack his army the next day. He did not think that they were near enough to be dangerous for that night, but he wanted to know just where they were. The colonel of the regiment of Auvergne ordered the Chevalier D'Assas to find out if there were any of the enemy near the camp.

It was a dark, black night. D'Assas went out all alone and pushed his way cautiously through the thickets and woods that lay all around. There was no moon to help, and he had to feel his way along.

At first he found no sign of the enemy, nor did he hear any sound. The woods were completely quiet as he slowly, and as noise-lessly as possible, crept through them.

He had only gone a very short distance when he pushed past some low bushes and stepped out into what seemed like an open space.

Instantly a number of dim forms closed in around him. He felt bayonets pressed against his body on every side, and a voice whispered in his ear: "If you make a sound, you die!"

D'Assas realized in a flash that the enemy had managed to get close to the camp, and were trying to take the French army by surprise. If he could warn his regiment they could be ready in time to hold the enemy off and to save the rest of the army. He knew, too, that if he made a sound, he would pay the price.

He did not hesitate a second.

He drew back, but only to get a full breath, and then, with all the power he had, he shouted: "Auvergne! Auvergne! The enemy! The enemy are here!"

Instantly twenty bayonets were plunged into his body, and he fell dead to the ground.

His company and the rest of the regiment were roused by his cry. They came as quickly as they could to his rescue but they were too late to save him. They were in time, though, to hold off the attack until the rest of the French army was ready to meet it. When the Germans found that their surprise had failed, they retreated.

The name of D'Assas was honored and admired by the whole nation for his heroic sacrifice. The story reminds us that the fate of an army sometimes depends on the deed of one brave soul.

•

THE KEYS OF CALAIS

Adapted from a retelling
by Charlotte Yonge

This story reminds us that those of high rank and achievement sometimes step forward to make the greatest sacrifices. Here are some noblemen who truly acted nobly.

In 1346, at the outset of the Hundred Years War, King Edward III of England marched upon Calais, the most important town in northern France. He arrived before the town in early August, his good knights and squires arrayed in flashing armor, his stout archers wielding their deadly long-bows, his royal standards floating in the breeze above the whole glittering army. The walls of the city were of huge thickness, with towers raised to a great height, and the king knew it would be useless to attempt a direct assault.

A herald, in a rich, long robe embroidered with the arms of England, rode up to the gate, a trumpet sounding before him, and called upon Sir Jean de Vienne, the governor of Calais, to surrender the place to Edward. Sir Jean made answer that he held the town for Philip, King of France, and that he would defend it to the last. The herald rode back again, and the English began the siege of the city. At first they covered the whole plain with their white canvas tents. Then, as time passed, they erected a little wooden town, with streets and a market and even a wooden palace for the king's comfort.

After a while a large and colorful fleet came crossing the waters from the white cliffs of Dover. King Edward and his knights rode down to the landing place to welcome the fair-haired Queen Philippa, and all her train of ladies. They had come from England in great numbers to visit their husbands, fathers, and brothers in their camp. Then there was a great court, and numerous feasts and dances, and the knights and squires were constantly striving to see who could do the bravest deed to please the ladies.

While this high merriment was going on outside their walls, the people of Calais were growing lean in the cheeks. At first a few brave French sailors, who knew the coast thoroughly, managed to guide little fleets of boats loaded with bread and meat into the city.

They were often chased by Edward's vessels, and sometimes nearly taken, but they always managed to escape. So at last Edward, growing wrathful, built a great wooden castle on the seashore and filled it with archers and machines that tossed huge, ship-crushing stones. They kept such a watch upon the harbor that the French sailors dared not enter it. Then the townspeople began to feel what hunger really was.

One night the forlorn citizens looked down from their high walls and spied the thing they had been desperately awaiting—a great and noble French army spreading across the hillsides! It was a beautiful sight to the starving garrison to watch their countrymen pitching their white tents right behind the English forces, the knights' armor glancing and banners flying in the moonlight. King Philip had arrived to drive the invaders away!

But soon their hopes were dashed. King Philip was not eager to risk a defeat at the hands of the English. There were a few skirmishes. The armies traded insults and challenges. Three days of parleys ensued. Then, without the slightest real effort to rescue the brave, patient townspeople, away went King Philip of France with all his men. The people of Calais saw the French host that had crowded the hillside melt away like a summer cloud.

August had come again, and they had suffered privation for a whole year for the sake of a king who deserted them at their utmost need. They were in so grievous a state of hunger and distress that the hardiest could endure no more. The governor, Sir Jean de Vienne, went to the battlements and made signs he wished to hold a parley. He owned that the garrison was reduced to the greatest extremity of distress, and requested King Edward to be content with obtaining the city and its fortress, leaving the citizens and soldiers to depart in peace.

But Edward was so enraged at the delay and expense the siege had cost him, he would consent to receive the town only on unconditional terms. He would slay, or ransom, or make prisoner whomever he pleased, and he let it be known that there was a heavy reckoning to pay.

The town's brave answer was: "These conditions are too heavy for us. We are but a small number of knights and squires, who have loyally served our king, as you would have done. We have suffered greatly, but we will endure far more before we consent to endanger the children of our town. We therefore entreat you to reconsider."

The king was in a stern mood, and he answered that he would

pardon the townspeople only on one condition. Six of the chief citizens of Calais must come forward with halters around their necks, carrying the keys to the town. These six the king would punish as he saw fit. The remainder of the inhabitants could go free.

On hearing this, Sir Jean de Vienne begged that he be allowed to consult the citizens. He went to the marketplace and rang a great bell, upon which all the townspeople assembled. As he told them the hard terms, he could not keep them from weeping bitterly. Should all starve together, or should they sacrifice their most honored comrades?

Then a voice was heard. It was that of the richest citizen in the town, Eustache de St. Pierre.

"Ladies and gentlemen, high and low," he said, "it would be a pity to cause so many people to die through hunger, if it could be prevented. To hinder it would be meritorious in the eyes of our Savior. I have such faith and trust in finding grace before God, if I die to save my townspeople, that I name myself as first of the six."

As he ceased, his fellow townspeople wept aloud.

Another citizen, very rich and respected, rose and said: "I will be the second to my comrade Eustache," His name was Jean Daire. After him, Jacques Wistant, another very rich man, offered himself as companion to these, who were both his cousins. His brother Pierre would not be left behind. Two others then named themselves to the gallant band, and the number demanded by Edward was complete.

The gates were opened, the governor and the six passed through, and the gates were again shut behind them. Sir Jean then rode out to the English representatives and told them how these six burghers had offered themselves up, and begged them to do all in their power to save them. The governor then went back to the town, full of grief.

The six citizens were led to the presence of the king in his full court. They all knelt down, and the foremost said: "Most gallant king, you see before you six citizens of Calais, who have been important merchants, and who bring to you the keys of the castle and the town. We yield ourselves to your absolute will and pleasure, in order to save the remainder of the inhabitants of Calais, who have suffered much distress and misery. Condescend, therefore, out of your nobleness of mind, to have mercy on us."

Pity stirred among all the English barons, knights, and squires assembled there. They saw the resigned faces, pale and thin with patiently endured hunger, of those venerable men, offering themselves in the cause of their fellow townspeople. They wept at the sight. But the king was unmoved. He cast angry glances at the six, and ordered their heads struck off.

The English knights begged the king to be more merciful. They told him that such an execution would tarnish his honor. They warned that reprisals would be made against his own garrisons. They pointed to the selflessness and nobility of the six. But the king would not listen. He sent for the headsman and his great ax.

Then suddenly the Queen of England, her eyes streaming with tears, threw herself on her knees among the captives and cried: "Ah, gentle sir, I have crossed the sea, with so much danger, to be with you. I have never asked you one favor. But now I ask as a gift, for the sake of the Son of the Blessed Mary, and for your love to me, that you will spare these six men!"

For some time the king looked at her in silence. Then he exclaimed: "Dame, dame, I wish you had been anywhere else but here! You have entreated in such a manner that I cannot refuse you. I therefore give you these men, to do as you please with them."

The queen conducted the six citizens to her own chambers, where she made them welcome and had the halters taken from their necks. She clothed them, and fed them, and gave them gifts to remember her by. Then she saw them safely escorted out of the English camp. Such is the story of six brave and patient men who went forth, by their own free will, to meet what might have been a cruel death, in order to obtain the safety of their fellow townspeople.

•

Bat

At some point, you have to say where you stand, or risk the fate
of the Bat. This tale about honesty, loyalty, and courage appears
in Aesop's fables, in Native American lore, and in other folk traditions around the world. It's a good story for students and prac-
titioners of politics.

Once there was a war between the birds and the beasts. The
Bat was on the birds' side. But in the first battle, the birds were
badly beaten. As soon as Bat saw it was going against them, he crept
away, hid under a log, and stayed there until the fight was over.

When the victorious beasts were going home, Bat slipped in
among them.

After they had gone some distance, the beasts noticed him and
said: "Wait a minute. Aren't you one of the ones who fought against
us?"

Bat replied, "Oh, no! I'm one of you; I don't belong to the
birds. Don't you see my ears, and my claws? And look at my teeth.
Did you ever see a bird with fangs like these? Of course not. No,
I'm one of the beasts."

They said nothing more, and let Bat stay with them.

Soon after, there was another battle, and this time the birds
won. As soon as Bat saw his side was beaten, he slipped away and
hid under a log. When the battle was over and the birds were going
home, Bat went in among them.

When they noticed him, they said, "You are our enemy. We
saw you fighting against us."

"Oh, no," said Bat, "I'm one of you. I don't belong to those
beasts. Did you ever see one of them with wings?"

They said nothing more, and let him stay with them.

So Bat went back and forth as long as the war lasted. But finally,
tired of fighting, the birds and beasts decided to make peace. They
held a council to decide what to do with Bat.

"You fought with the birds, so go live with them," the beasts
cried.

"We don't want you!" shouted the birds. "You fought with the
beasts. Go live with them."

They decided to cast him out, saying: "Hereafter, you will fly alone at night, and will never have any friends, among either those that fly, or those that walk."

So now the Bat sneaks around in the dark, and lives in black caves. He flies like a bird, but never perches in treetops. And nobody cares what kind of creature he is.

•

THE MAN WITHOUT A COUNTRY

Here is the most despised name in American history. Benedict Arnold (1741–1801) was a descendant of a distinguished New England family and an American hero in the early part of the Revolutionary War. But he grew to love luxury, and he lusted after glory. In 1779, he began selling military information to the British, and in the summer of 1780, while in command of West Point in New York, Arnold secretly offered to surrender the fort and its garrison to the British for £20,000. The American forces discovered the plot, but Arnold managed to escape. For the rest of the war he served as a British brigadier, further blackening his name by conducting destructive raids in Virginia and his own native Connecticut.

After the war, Arnold and his family sailed to England, where he gradually discovered that the disgrace of a traitor knows no national boundaries.

Benedict Arnold sailed from his native land and returned no more. From that time forth, wherever he went, three whispered words followed him, singing through his ears into his heart—*Arnold the Traitor.*

When he stood beside the King in the House of Lords, a whisper crept through the thronged House, and as the whisper deepened into a murmur, one venerable lord arose and said he loved his sovereign, but could not speak to him while by his side stood —*Arnold the Traitor.*

He went to the theater, parading his warrior form amid the fairest flowers of British nobility and beauty; but no sooner was his face seen than the whole audience rose—the lord in his cushioned seat, the vagrant in the gallery. They rose together, while from the pit to the dome echoed the cry—*"Arnold the Traitor."*

When he issued from his gorgeous mansion, the liveried servant who ate his bread whispered in contempt to his fellow lackey, as he took his position in his master's carriage—*"Arnold the Traitor."*

Grossly insulted in a public place, he appealed to the company, and scowling at his antagonist with his fierce brow, he spat full in his face. His antagonist was a man of courage, and he said: "Time may scorn me, but I never can stain my sword by killing—*Arnold the Traitor."*

He left London. He engaged in commerce. His ships were on the ocean, his warehouses in Nova Scotia, his plantations in the West Indies. One night his warehouses were burned to ashes. The entire population of St. John's—accusing the owner of burning his own property, to defraud the insurance companies—assembled in that British town, and in sight of his very window they hanged an effigy, which bore a huge placard, inscribed—*"Arnold the Traitor."*

There was a day when Talleyrand arrived in Le Havre, hotfoot from Paris. It was in the darkest hour of the French Revolution. All who belonged to the ranks of the aristocracy were fleeing. Pursued by the bloodhounds of the Reign of Terror, stripped of his property and power, Talleyrand secured a passage to America in a ship about to sail. He was going, a beggar and a wanderer, to a strange land to earn his bread by daily labor. "Is there any American gentleman staying at your house?" he asked the landlord of his hotel. "I am about to cross the water, and would like a letter to some person of influence in the New World."

The landlord hesitated, and then said: "There is a gentleman upstairs, from either America or Britain, but whether American or Englishman I cannot tell."

He pointed the way, and Talleyrand, who during his life was bishop, prince, prime minister, ascended the stairs, knocked at the stranger's door, and entered.

In the far corner of a dimly lighted room sat a gentleman of some fifty years, his arms folded and his head bowed on his breast. From a window directly opposite, a flood of light poured over his forehead. His eyes, looking from beneath the downcast brows, gazed in Talleyrand's face with a peculiar and searching expression. His face was striking in its outline; his mouth and chin indicative of an iron will. His form was clad in a dark but rich and distinguished costume. Talleyrand advanced, stated that he was a fugitive, and, under the impression that the gentleman who sat before him was an American, he solicited his kind offices.

"I am a wanderer—an exile. I am forced to fly to the New World, without a friend or a hope. You are an American? Give me, then, I beseech you, a letter of introduction to some friend of yours, so that I may earn my bread. A gentleman like you has doubtless many friends."

The strange gentleman rose. With a look that Talleyrand never forgot, he retreated toward the door of the next chamber, saying: *"I am the only man born in the New World that can raise his hand and say I have not one friend—not one—in all America!"*

"Who are you?" cried the exile, as the strange man retreated. "Your name?"

"My name is *Benedict Arnold.*"

He was gone. Talleyrand sank into a chair, gasping the words —*"Arnold the Traitor!"*

Thus he wandered over the earth, another Cain, with the murderer's mark upon his brow. We cannot doubt that he died friendless, and that the memory of his treachery to his native land gnawed like a cancer at his heart, murmuring: "True to your country, what might you not have been, *O Arnold the Traitor!"*

•

My Native Land

Sir Walter Scott

Breathes there the man, with soul so dead,
Who never to himself hath said,
    This is my own, my native land?
Whose heart hath ne'er within him burned,
As home his footsteps he hath turned
    From wandering on a foreign strand?
If such there breathe, go, mark him well;
For him no minstrel raptures swell;
High though his titles, proud his name,
Boundless his wealth as wish can claim—

Despite those titles, power, and pelf,
The wretch, concentered all in self,
Living, shall forfeit far renown,
And, doubly dying, shall go down
To the vile dust from whence he sprung,
Unwept, unhonored, and unsung.

•

TARPEIA

Retold by Sara Cone Bryant

Here is another famous story of treason. This ancient Roman legend reminds us that traitors usually act for one reason: greed. This legend was used to explain the name of a famous cliff overhanging Rome called the Tarpeian Rock, from which traitors were thrown.

There was once a girl named Tarpeia, whose father was guard of the outer gate of the citadel of Rome. It was a time of war—the Sabines were besieging the city. Their camp was close outside the city wall.

Tarpeia used to see the Sabine soldiers when she went to draw water from the public well, for that was outside the gate. And sometimes she stayed about and let the strange men talk with her, because she liked to look at their bright silver ornaments. The Sabine soldiers wore heavy silver rings and bracelets on their left arms—some wore as many as four or five.

The soldiers knew she was the daughter of the keeper of the citadel, and they saw that she had greedy eyes for their ornaments. So day by day they talked with her, and showed her their silver rings, and tempted her. And at last Tarpeia made a bargain, to betray her city to them. She said she would unlock the great gate and let them in, *if they would give her what they wore on their left arms.*

The night came. When it was perfectly dark and still, Tarpeia stole from her bed, took the great key from its place, and silently unlocked the gate which protected the city. Outside, in the dark, stood the soldiers of the enemy, waiting. As she opened the gate, the long shadowy files pressed forward silently, and the Sabines entered the citadel.

As the first man came inside, Tarpeia stretched forth her hand for her price. The soldier lifted high his left arm. "Take thy reward!" he said, and as he spoke he hurled upon her that which he wore upon it. Down upon her head crashed—not the silver rings of the soldier, but the great brass shield he carried in battle!

She sank beneath it, to the ground.

"Take thy reward," said the next, and his shield rang against the first.

"Thy reward," said the next—and the next—and the next—and the next; every man wore his shield on his left arm.

So Tarpeia lay buried beneath the reward she had claimed, and the Sabines marched past her dead body, into the city she had betrayed.

•

THE MAN WHO DINED ON TURNIPS

The French writer La Rochefoucauld noted that "more men are guilty of treachery through weakness than through any studied design to betray." Here is a man who strengthened himself against temptation and demonstrated that self-discipline is one proof against the old adage that power corrupts. Manius Curius, who lived in the early part of the third century B.C., was a famous example of a life lived according to steadfast Roman virtue.

In ancient Rome there lived a consul named Manius Curius. He was a peerless general in time of war, and a great statesman in time of peace. Yet he lived in a little cottage. His food and clothing were plain, his possessions few, his needs simple.

His honor shined like the richest jewel.

One time the Samnites, enemies of Rome, were planning to make war. In secret they sent ambassadors to Manius Curius to persuade him to stay away from the Roman army.

The ambassadors found him in his cottage, sitting in the chimney corner peeling turnips for his supper. They laid gold at his feet, hoping to tempt their foe.

Manius Curius smiled when he saw their offers.

"Do you think a man who is content with turnips for dinner has any need for gold?" he asked. "I think it would be better to conquer the Samnites than take their bribes."

The ambassadors left looking foolish.

For many years afterward, the Romans pointed to the little hut and said: "There is the cottage that belonged to the consul who dined on turnips."

•

GOOD KING WENCESLAS

Saint Wencelas was a tenth-century duke of Bohemia. This old carol about him tells a beautiful legend that has come down to us from the Middle Ages. The incident is said to have taken place on St. Stephen's Day, the day after Christmas. Wenceslas was standing at his castle window when he saw a figure struggling through the snow. The king and his young page set out to aid the man, but the boy's courage began to fail in the fierce blizzard. Wenceslas gently told him to walk close behind him, and it was then that the miracle occurred: The page found that green grass sprang up in the kindhearted monarch's footprints, and that as long as he placed his feet in the track, he seemed to be walking in the warmth of a summer's afternoon.

Good leaders bring others along in their footsteps, teaching by example.

> Good King Wenceslas looked out
> On the Feast of Stephen,
> When the snow lay round about,
> Deep, and crisp, and even.
> Brightly shone the moon that night,
> Though the frost was cruel,
> When a poor man came in sight,
> Gath'ring winter fuel.

"Hither, page, and stand by me,
    If thou know'st it, telling,
Yonder peasant, who is he?
    Where and what his dwelling?"
"Sire, he lives a good league hence,
    Underneath the mountain;
Right against the forest fence,
    By Saint Agnes' fountain."

"Bring me flesh, and bring me wine,
    Bring me pine-logs hither:
Thou and I will see him dine,
    When we bear them thither."
Page and monarch forth they went,
    Forth they went together;
Through the rude wind's wild lament
    And the bitter weather.

"Sire, the night is darker now,
    And the wind blows stronger;
Fails my heart, I know not how,
    I can go no longer."
"Mark my footsteps, my good page;
    Tread thou in them boldly:
Thou shalt find the winter's rage
    Freeze thy blood less coldly."

In his master's steps he trod,
    Where the snow lay dinted;
Heat was in the very sod
    Which the saint had printed.
Therefore, Christian man, be sure,
    Wealth or rank possessing,
Ye who now will bless the poor,
    Shall yourselves find blessing.

•

THE SLEEPING SENTINEL

Adapted from Albert Blaisdell
and Francis Ball

This story, based on an incident that occurred early in the Civil War, entered the corpus of Lincoln lore when it was set to verse and read in the U.S. Senate chamber before an audience that included President Lincoln himself. It reminds us that good leaders set high but reasonable expectations for those who would follow.

On a rainy morning in September 1861, during the first year of the Civil War, a group of Union soldiers came to the White House to plead for the life of one of their friends. They were granted an audience with President Lincoln himself, and in faltering words they told why they had come.

The soldiers were part of the 3rd Vermont Regiment, which was made up mostly of farm boys from the Green Mountains. Since their arrival in Washington they had been stationed at Chain Bridge, a few miles above the city. The bridge was of vital importance since Confederate forces occupied the hills on the opposite side of the Potomac River. The soldiers' orders were strict: Any sentinel caught sleeping at his post was to be shot within twenty-four hours.

According to the soldiers' story, a boy named William Scott had enlisted in Company K. He had been on duty one night, and the following night had taken the place of a comrade too sick to stand guard. The third night he had been called out on guard duty yet again. The young fellow could not keep awake for three nights in a row. When the relief guard came around, he was found asleep. Arrested, tried, and found guilty, he was sentenced to be shot.

"William Scott, sir, is as brave a soldier as there is in your army," the Green Mountain Boys told Lincoln. "He is no coward. It's not right to shoot him like a traitor and bury him like a dog."

Later in the day President Lincoln rode from the White House in the direction of Chain Bridge. Within a day or so the newspapers reported that a soldier sentenced to death for sleeping at his post had been pardoned by the president, and had returned to his regiment.

It was a long time before Scott would speak of his interview with President Lincoln. One day he told a comrade the whole story.

"I knew the president at once," he said, "by a Lincoln medal I had long worn. I was scared at first, for I had never talked with a great man before. He asked me all about the folks at home, my brothers and sisters, and where I went to school, and how I liked it. Then he asked me about my mother. I showed him her picture. He said that if he were in my place he would try to make a fond mother happy, and never cause her a sorrow or a tear.

" 'My boy,' he said, 'you are not going to be shot. You are going back to your regiment. I have been put to a good deal of trouble on your account. Now what I want to know is how you are going to pay me back. My bill is a large one, and there is only one man in all the world who can pay it. His name is William Scott. If from this day you will promise to do your whole duty as a soldier, then the debt will be paid. Will you make that promise and try to keep it?' "

Gladly the young Vermont soldier made the promise, and well did he keep it. From that day William Scott became a model man of his regiment. He was never absent from a roll call. He was always on hand if there was any hard work to do. He worked nights in the hospital, nursing the sick and wounded, because it trained him to keep awake. He made a record for himself on picket duty, and distinguished himself as a scout.

Sometime after this the 3rd Vermont went into one of its many hard battles. They were ordered to attack the Confederate lines, and William Scott fell in the enemy volley.

His comrades caught him up, carried him bleeding and dying from the field, and laid him on a cot.

"Tell the president I have tried to be a good soldier, and true to the flag," he said.

Then, making a last effort, with his dying breath he prayed for Abraham Lincoln.

Company K buried William Scott in a grove just in the rear of the camp, at the foot of a big oak tree. Deep into the oak they cut the initials "W.S." and under it the words "A Brave Soldier."

•

CHARLEMAGNE AND THE
ROBBER KNIGHT

Adapted from a retelling by Marie Frary
and Charles Stebbins

In this old German legend we find true force of character—the kind that leads by example, pulling others upward. Charlemagne (742–814), also known as Charles the First, king of France and emperor of the Holy Roman Empire, established a cultural revival that laid the foundation of European civilization in the late Middle Ages.

Once the great King Charlemagne built a magnificent palace on the river Rhine, where he could watch the waters slip past, and gaze on the distant hills, and hunt with his friends in the deep, green forests. When the castle was completed he went to visit it. The very first night he slept there, an angel appeared in his dreams. It stood by his bed, clothed in splendid light, and said: "Arise, good Emperor. Arise, go forth secretly, and steal."

Charlemagne woke, much puzzled at the dream. It seemed impossible that an emperor should be ordered to become a robber. So he lay down and went back to sleep.

But the angel reappeared again. "Arise, Emperor," it said. "Go forth, and steal from your own people."

Again Charlemagne woke, aghast at the command. He still could not believe such an order could come from an angel, so he did not move. Once more the angel appeared by the side of his bed. It stretched forth its hand, saying: "Arise! Do not tarry. Go into the forest and steal, or repent forever."

Charlemagne rose and passed quietly through the halls of his castle. His knights were fast asleep. He went to his stable, saddled his horse, armed himself, and rode silently into the depths of the forest.

As he was going along the dark way thoughtfully, he heard someone approaching, and he soon perceived it was a knight clad in black armor. Charlemagne could think of no good reason why a knight should be riding at such an hour, so he challenged the man.

"Where are you riding, and upon what mission, at this time of the night?" he demanded.

The knight did not answer, but put spurs to his horse and charged the Emperor. Seeing his movement, the Emperor did likewise, and the two met with a violent shock. Both were unhorsed, and in the hand-to-hand conflict which followed, the Emperor got the better of the unknown knight and brought him to the ground. With his sword at the stranger's throat, he demanded his name.

"I am Elbegast," he replied, "the robber knight, who has committed many a bold deed. You are the first who has had the power to overcome me."

"Arise," said the Emperor, without revealing who he was, "and come with me. I am on a mission like thine own."

Without hesitating, the robber knight joined his conqueror. They rode through the forest until they reached a stately house. It was the home of Arnot, one of the Emperor's most trusted ministers.

Elbegast was not long in gaining entrance. Bidding his companion to wait for him outside, he stole noiselessly into the house.

As he approached the minister's bedroom, the sound of voices in earnest conversation came to his ears. He listened, and heard Arnot disclose to his wife a plan for the murder of the Emperor himself on the following day.

Forgetting his purpose for breaking into the house, the knight made his way hastily back to his companion, and begged him to go at once to Charlemagne and inform him of the coming danger.

"Why not go yourself and tell him?" asked the Emperor.

Elbegast hung his head.

"I would gladly do it, if I could. A man like me, who has committed evil deeds, dares not seek out the Emperor. I would risk imprisonment to save his life, but it would do no good—the Emperor would scarcely believe a man with my reputation. But I tell you this: Whatever I have done, I hold great admiration for the man who has never been conquered in battle, and who has always worked for the good of his people. He rules wisely and kindly, and I would keep him from harm."

Then Charlemagne and Elbegast parted, one returning to his stronghold in the mountains and the other retracing his steps slowly and thoughtfully to his palace.

On the morrow Arnot and his conspirators attempted to carry out their plans, but the Emperor was ready for them. As they came riding into the castle courtyard, the gates slammed shut behind them, and a dozen guards sprang forth.

"What kind of greeting is this for someone who has come to pay his respects to his emperor?" Arnot demanded, with pretended indignation.

"What kind of greeting do you bring, when you come to pay your respects this way?" asked one of the guards. As he spoke, he tore the clothes of Arnot and his companions, disclosing their hidden daggers.

Charlemagne took all of them into custody, and they confessed their plot against him.

The Emperor then set his mind upon Elbegast. He sent a messenger to him, requesting him to come to the palace.

"I, Charlemagne, Emperor of Germany," his message ran, "would speak privately with Elbegast, the robber knight, and promise him safe conduct to and from my castle."

Elbegast rode to the palace and was admitted to the private council chamber. Soon a man entered, clad in armor, and Elbegast recognized the knight who had been his companion the night before.

"Elbegast," said Charlemagne, "you recognize me and yet you do not know me."

Then Charlemagne raised his visor, and the robber knight saw that he was standing in the presence of the Emperor.

"You have done wrong in the past," said Charlemagne. "But now you have done me faithful duty. Here is your chance to begin your life anew. I offer you a place among my retainers. A man of your courage and loyalty is worthy of a place in the Emperor's service."

Elbegast was so moved that he could hardly speak. Charlemagne was the only man who had ever been able to defeat him in battle, and for this he admired him greatly. But more than this, he stood in awe of the Emperor's reputation for kindness and wisdom. And so Elbegast, the robber knight, was disarmed by Charlemagne's own character. He willingly forsook his evil life in the forest and became a devoted friend to the end of his days.

And in commemoration of the angel's visit, which had caused him to find this loyal knight, Charlemagne named his new castle Ingelheim, meaning "angel's home."

•

GEORGE PICKETT'S FRIEND

Charles W. Moores

Great people are capable of small acts of friendship and kindness.
Abraham Lincoln is famous for moments like this one. His friend
George Pickett led the Confederate troops that made the famous
attack at Gettysburg in 1863, now known as Pickett's Charge.

George Pickett, who had known Lincoln in Illinois, years before, joined the Southern army, and by his conspicuous bravery and
ability had become one of the great generals of the Confederacy.
Toward the close of the war, when a large part of Virginia had
fallen into the possession of the Union army, the President called at
General Pickett's Virginia home.

The general's wife, with her baby on her arm, met him at the
door. She herself has told the story for us.

" 'Is this George Pickett's home?' he asked.

"With all the courage and dignity I could muster, I replied:
'Yes, and I am his wife, and this is his baby.'

" 'I am Abraham Lincoln.'

" 'The President!' I gasped. I had never seen him, but I knew
the intense love and reverence with which my soldier always spoke
of him.

"The stranger shook his head and replied: 'No; Abraham Lincoln, George's old friend.'

"The baby pushed away from me and reached out his hands to
Mr. Lincoln, who took him in his arms. As he did so an expression
of rapt, almost divine tenderness and love lighted up the sad face.
It was a look that I have never seen on any other face. The baby
opened his mouth wide and insisted upon giving his father's friend
a dewy kiss.

"As Mr. Lincoln gave the little one back to me he said: 'Tell
your father, the rascal, that I forgive him for the sake of your bright
eyes.' "

•

MAN ENOUGH FOR THE JOB
Retold by Ella Lyman Cabot

Great men do not disdain small duties.

An incident is told of the first American war, about an officer who set his men to fell some trees which were needed to make a bridge. There were not nearly enough men, and work was getting on very slowly. Up rode a commanding-looking man and spoke to the officer in charge, who was urging on his men but doing nothing himself. "You haven't enough men for the job, have you?"

"No, sir. we need some help."

"Why don't you lend a hand yourself?" asked the man on horseback.

"Me, sir? Why, I am a corporal," replied the officer, looking rather affronted at the suggestion.

"Ah, true," quietly replied the other, and getting off his horse he labored with the men until the job was done. Then he mounted again, and as he rode off he said to the officer, "Corporal, the next time you have a job to put through and too few men to do it you had better send for the Commander-in-Chief, and I will come again."

It was General Washington.

•

THE MAN WHO WOULD NOT
DRINK ALONE
Adapted from a retelling
by Rosalie Kaufman

Loyalty is a two-way street; sharing hardship is the mark of a loyal leader. The ancient historian Plutarch recounts this tale about Alexander the Great (356–323 B.C.).

Alexander the Great was leading his army homeward after his great victory against Porus in India. The country through which they now marched was bare and desert, and his army suffered dreadfully from heat, hunger, and, most of all, thirst. The soldiers' lips cracked and their throats burned from want of water, and many were ready to lie down and give up.

About noon one day the army met a party of Greek travelers. They were on mules, and carried with them a few vessels filled with water. One of them, seeing the king almost choking from thirst, filled a helmet and offered it to him.

Alexander took it into his hands, then looked around at the faces of his suffering soldiers, who craved refreshment just as much as he did.

"Take it away," he said, "for if I drink alone, the rest will be out of heart, and you have not enough for all."

So he handed the water back without touching a drop of it. And the soldiers, cheering their king, leaped to their feet, and demanded to be led forward.

•

BROTHERHOOD OF LONG AGO

Fanny E. Coe

Here is another story of perseverance winning the day because a leader knew how to help shoulder the load. This act of encouragement and compassion by the Marquis de Lafayette (1757–1834) reminds us of the story of Saint Martin in Chapter 4.

More than two hundred years ago, when our country was fighting against England, there came to help us a young French nobleman named Lafayette. Although only a boy of nineteen years, he had run away from his country because he longed to fight for liberty. He said that he came to learn, not to teach, and, from the first, he took George Washington for an ideal.

Lafayette and Washington became lifelong friends. Lafayette named his son for Washington and, on his return to America in 1787, he paid a delightful visit to Washington at Mount Vernon. He promised soon to return, but almost forty years passed by before he kept his word.

He came at last, in 1824, a bent old man, with a heart loyal as ever to his adopted country. He visited every state and territory in the Union and was welcomed everywhere with the warmest enthusiasm. Receptions, dinner parties, and balls followed each other in brilliant succession, always with Lafayette the chief figure. The welcome of the people was voiced in a song of the time:

> "We bow not the neck,
> We bend not the knee,
> But our hearts, Lafayette,
> We surrender to thee."

The following incident occurred during the visit of 1824.

A brilliant reception was under way. A slowly moving line of stately guests passed by the noble old marquis, who greeted each with courtly grace. Presently there approached an old soldier clad in a worn Continental uniform. In his hand was an ancient musket, and across his shoulder was thrown a small blanket, or rather a piece of blanket. On reaching the marquis, the veteran drew himself up in the stiff fashion of the old-time drill and gave the military salute. As Lafayette returned the salute, tears sprang to his eyes. The tattered uniform, the ancient flintlock, the silver-haired veteran, even older than himself, recalled the dear past.

"Do you know me?" asked the soldier. Lafayette's manner had led him to think himself personally remembered.

"Indeed, I cannot say that I do," was the frank reply.

"Do you remember the frosts and snows of Valley Forge?"

"I shall never forget them," answered Lafayette.

"One bitter night, General Lafayette, you were going the rounds at Valley Forge. You came upon a sentry in thin clothing and without stockings. He was slowly freezing to death. You took his musket, saying, 'Go to my hut. There you will find stockings, a blanket, and a fire. After warming yourself, bring the blanket to me. Meanwhile I will keep guard.'

"The soldier obeyed directions. When he returned to his post, you, General Lafayette, cut the blanket in two. One half you kept, the other you presented to the sentry. Here, General, is one half of that blanket, for I am the sentry whose life you saved."

•

THE LADY WITH THE LAMP

Elmer Adams and Warren Foster

Born in 1820 to wealthy parents, Florence Nightingale spent her childhood on comfortable family estates in England. When she was sixteen years old, she thought she heard the voice of God informing her that she had a specific mission in life. For the next few years she spent more and more of her time studying public health and reforms to aid the suffering. In 1850, against her family's wishes, she attended a training school for nurses, and at age thirty-three she became superintendent of a women's hospital in London.

In 1854, when England and France went to war with Russia in the Crimea, the British people grew outraged over reports of sick and wounded soldiers dying in disgraceful conditions. At the appeal of the minister of war, Nightingale traveled to Scutari, Turkey, to take charge of the military hospital there. She stepped ashore to discover scores of maimed troops just arrived from the Battle of Balaklava, where the disastrous Charge of the Light Brigade had occurred. The story of how this heroine rescued Scutari and founded the modern nursing profession is the stuff of legend. It was not only Florence Nightingale's remarkable organizational and administrative skills that saved the day. It was the force of her remarkable character—her compassion, her courage, her perseverance.

The Crimean War was in progress, France and England being allied to defend Turkey against Russian aggression. The British army had sailed to a strange climate with shamefully poor commissary and medical staffs. The weather was stormy and the soldiers had little shelter against it. Said a correspondent of the *London Times,* "It is now pouring rain, the skies are black as ink, the wind is howling over the staggering tents, the trenches are turned into dikes; in the tents the water is sometimes a foot deep; our men have not either warm or waterproof clothing; they are out for twelve hours at a time in the trenches"—and so on without end.

Plenty of food and clothing had been shipped from England,

but they never reached their destination. Some vessels were delayed; in some the stores were packed at the bottom of the hold and could not be raised; some hove in with the wrong goods at the wrong port—and, on one, the consignment of boots proved to be all for the left foot! But the most criminal point of mismanagement was this: food, clothing and medicine might be stored in a warehouse within easy reach of the army, but the official with authority to deal them out would be absent, and so stringent were the army rules that no one dared so much as point at them! The rigid system was infinitely worse than no system. And the soldiers were starving in the midst of plenty, and freezing under the shadow of mountains of good woolen clothing.

Now, to come at once to the worst, imagine these conditions transferred to the military hospitals. In the great Barrack Hospital at Scutari lay two thousand sorely wounded men, and hundreds more were coming in every day. The wards were crowded to twice their capacity—the sick lay side by side on mattresses that touched each other. The floors and walls and ceilings were wet and filthy. There was no ventilation. Rats and vermin swarmed everywhere. The men lay "in their uniforms, stiff with gore and covered with filth to a degree and of a kind no one could write about." It was a "dreadful den of dirt, pestilence, and death."

It is difficult to imagine a scene of worse disorder and misery. The proportion of deaths to the whole army, from disease alone— malaria and cholera—was sixty percent. Seventy died in the hospital in one night. There was danger that the entire army would be wiped out—most of it without ever receiving a scratch from the enemy's weapons.

It was in this extremity that the British nation appealed to Florence Nightingale to save the sick and wounded men—an army of twenty-eight thousand as helpless as children before the ravages of disease—and to save the war. The minister of war requested her to organize a band of nurses for Scutari and gave her power to draw upon the government to any extent.

Miss Nightingale at the time was thirty-four years old. An acquaintance described her thus: "Simple, intellectual, sweet, full of love and benevolence, she is a fascinating and perfect woman. She is tall and pale. Her face is exceedingly lovely. But better than all is the soul's glory that shines through every feature so exultingly. Nothing can be sweeter than her smile. It is like a sunny day in summer."

Within six days from the time she accepted the post, Miss

Nightingale had selected thirty-eight nurses, and departed for the
seat of war. She arrived at Scutari November 4, 1854, and walked
the length of the barracks, viewing her two miles of patients. And
next day before she could form any plans, the fresh victims of
another battle began to arrive. There was not space for them within
the walls and hundreds had to repose, with what comfort they
could, in the mud outside. One of the nurses wrote, "Many died
immediately after being brought in—their moans would pierce the
heart—and the look of agony on those poor dying faces will never
leave my heart."

But the nurse did not hesitate. She ordered the patients
brought in, and directed where to lay them, and what attention they
should have. She was up and around twenty hours that day, and as
many the next, until a place had been found for every man, even in
the corridors and on the landings of the stair. As leader of the
nurses she might have confined herself to administrative tasks—of
which there were enough for any woman—and stayed in the office.
But no. She shrank from the sight of no operation. Many men,
indeed, whose cases the surgeons thought hopeless, she nursed
back to health. A visitor saw her one morning at two o'clock at the
bedside of a dying soldier, lamp in hand. She was writing down his
last message to the home folks; and for them, too, she took in
charge his watch and trinkets—and then soothed him in his last
moments. And this was but one case in thousands. "She is a minis-
tering angel, without any exaggeration, in these hospitals," wrote a
correspondent of the *London Times,* "and as the slender form
glides quietly along each corridor, every poor fellow's face softens
with gratitude at the sight of her. When all the medical officers have
retired for the night, and silence and darkness have settled down
upon the miles of prostrate sick, she may be observed alone, with
lamp in hand, making her solitary rounds."

In a place like Scutari, however, this kind of feminine tenderness alone would avail little. Science was needed, the most perfect
skill in scientific nursing. The windows were few, and the few were
mostly locked; and where one was opened the odors of decaying
animals came in to pollute still more the foul air of the wards.

The food for the whole hospital—for those sick of fever, cholera, wounds, and what not, as well as for those in health—was
cooked, like an "Irish stew," in big kettles. Vegetables and meats
were dumped in together, and when anyone felt hungry he could
dip for himself. Naturally some got food overdone, and some got it
raw; the luckiest got a mess that was scarcely palatable; and the sick

could generally not eat at all. As for other matters, it has been shown how unclean the barrack wards were, how "only seven shirts" had been laundered in all those wretched weeks, and how the infected bed linen of all classes of patients was thrown, unsorted, into one general wash.

But Florence Nightingale had spent twelve years in the hospitals of Europe to learn how to conquer just such situations as this. She had the waste and pollution outside the walls cleared away. Then she threw up the windows, and set a carpenter to make more. Within ten days she had established a diet kitchen and was feeding the men each on the food his particular case demanded. She set up a laundry, too, where the garments of the sick could be cleansed in a sanitary way. All this was the easier to do because with wise foresight she had brought the necessary articles with her on the *Victus* from England. The ship gave up chicken, jelly, and all manner of delicacies; and, on a single day, "a thousand shirts, besides other clothing." In two weeks that "dreadful den of dirt, pestilence, and death" had vanished; and in its place stood a building, light and well aired throughout, where patients lay on spotless cots, ate appetizing food from clean dishes, had their baths and their medicine at regular intervals, and never for an hour lacked any attention that would help their recovery.

But after all is said of Florence Nightingale's sympathy and her science, she owed her final triumph in the Crimea to a rarer talent, that of tactful organizing and executive power. Why was she not tethered by the system and the red tape that rendered ineffectual the best efforts of the medical men? Most things needful were in store not far from the barracks hospital. But the regular physicians could not get at them. Why could she?

In the first place she had tact enough not to offend the system. The minister of war had warned her, "A number of sentimental, enthusiastic ladies turned loose into the hospital at Scutari would probably after a few days be '*mises à la porte*' by those whose business they would interrupt and whose authority they would dispute." Florence Nightingale did not at first interrupt or dispute anybody. She began by doing the neglected minor things, the things that no one else had time for. She opened windows. She scrubbed floors and walls. She laundered shirts. She peeled potatoes and boiled soup. She bathed the patients, dosed them with medicine while the worn-out surgeons were asleep, read to them, and wrote letters for them. In these activities she asked not even supplies from the system, but procured them from her own ship.

The hidebound officials were even then slow to concur. Per-haps they were jealous to see their own incompetence exposed. And there was one case—just one—where she came to blows with them. The hospital inmates were in desperate want, and the articles for their relief were nearby in a warehouse, but the stores could not be disturbed until after inspection. Miss Nightingale tried to hasten the inspection. Failing of that, she tried to get them distrib-uted without inspection. That also failed. "My soldiers are dying," she said. "I must have those stores." Whereupon, she called two soldiers, marched them to the warehouse, and bade them burst open the doors!

That was the kind of firm hand she could use. More often, though, she attained her ends in a peaceful way. Only a little femi-nine tact was necessary to bring together the dilatory members of a board and get them to unlock a storehouse. She was soon able to lay her hands on an abundance of anything the situation demanded. Then, besides her own small band of nurses, a large number of orderlies and common soldiers were, after a time, detailed to work under her direction. "Never," she says, "came from them one word or one look which a gentleman would not have used;" and many of them became attached to her with an almost slavish affection.

And the result of her efforts justified this faith. When she ar-rived the death rate was sixty percent. She reduced it in a few weeks to one percent. Nine of her nurses died on duty; others were invalided home; she herself was long fever sick and near to death. But for two years she battled against disease, always in a winning fight. She conquered disease. And it is not too much to say that she conquered the Russian army, and saved the war for the allies. No wonder England welcomed her home as one of the greatest hero-ines in all its history.

●

Santa Filomena

Henry Wadsworth Longfellow

Florence Nightingale was born in and named after the city of Florence, Italy. "Santa Filomena" is Italian for "Saint Nightingale."

Whene'er a noble deed is wrought,
Whene'er is spoken a noble thought,
   Our hearts, in glad surprise,
   To higher levels rise.

The tidal wave of deeper souls
Into our inmost being rolls,
   And lifts us unawares
   Out of all meaner cares.

Honor to those whose words or deeds
Thus help us in our daily needs,
   And by their overflow
   Raise us from what is low!

Thus thought I, as by night I read
Of the great army of the dead,
   The trenches cold and damp,
   The starved and frozen camp—

The wounded from the battle-plain,
In dreary hospitals of pain,
   The cheerless corridors,
   The cold and stony floors.

Lo! in that house of misery
A lady with a lamp I see
   Pass through the glimmering gloom,
   And flit from room to room.

And slow, as in a dream of bliss,
The speechless sufferer turns to kiss
   Her shadow, as it falls
   Upon the darkening walls.

As if a door in heaven should be
Opened and then closed suddenly,
   The vision came and went,
   The light shone and was spent.

On England's annals, through the long
Hereafter of her speech and song,
    That light its rays shall cast
    From portals of the past.

A Lady with a Lamp shall stand
In the great history of the land,
    A noble type of good,
    Heroic womanhood.

Not even shall be wanting here
The palm, the lily, and the spear,
    The symbols that of yore
    Saint Filomena bore.

•

THE BIRDS WHO BEFRIENDED A KING

*Adapted from a retelling
by Constance Armfield*

"And men came from all peoples to hear the wisdom of Solomon,"
the first book of Kings in the Bible tells us. No leader in history
has been more renowned for learning and judgment than the
tenth-century B.C. ruler of Israel and Judah. Every boy or girl who
hopes someday to lead a company, community, or country would
do well to learn the lesson Solomon offers in the next two stories:
To lead is to serve.

The hoopoes in the story below are jay-sized birds living in
Africa, in India, and in warm, dry regions of southern Europe.
Because of its striking plumage, including a showy crown of feath-
ers, the hoopoe is a favorite bird of legend and folklore.

Once the great King Solomon was journeying in the desert.
Across the sand the king's caravan made its way, the camels' embroidered saddle cloths as bright as flowers, and their jeweled bridles
flashing as brightly as the sun itself. But the heat smote down on
the king's head, and Solomon yearned for shade. As if in answer to

his longing, who should appear but a flock of Hoopoes? Being curious by nature, they circled around until they reached the king's camel and kept just overhead, so that they might watch this most famous of all monarchs and perhaps overhear some word of wisdom.

Thus the little birds cast a grateful shadow over the king for his whole journey. And richly repaid they were. For Solomon, who was always polite to the humblest creature in his kingdom, conversed freely with them the whole time, bestowing upon them many wise words. When they reached his palace, he thanked them for providing the shade, and asked what he could do in return.

Now the Hoopoes had begun their conversation with Solomon modestly enough; in fact, they had been very surprised that he had spoken to them at all. But he had questioned them so kindly about their way of living, and their likes and preferences and relations, that they lost their fear of him. They came into his wonderful palace and saw all the servants in their shining robes standing behind the king's throne, and waiting on his table, and lining the great courtyard. They beheld the walls of ivory inlaid with gold, and the golden lions guarding the steps, and the white peacocks on their silver terraces. And it quite turned the little birds' heads to think they had journeyed right across the desert with the owner of all these riches.

So instead of answering Solomon with thanks on their part and telling him his words of wisdom were rich reward for any shelter they had given, the Hoopoes begged leave to consult together and withdrew to the palace roof, where they discussed what they would ask for.

Finally they decided they would like golden crowns such as the king himself wore; then they could return to the other birds and reign over them. At once the little birds flew down with a rush and made their request to the king as he walked in his wonderful garden.

"What the king has said, the king has said," Solomon replied. "The gift you desire shall be granted. Yet, because you rendered me true service, when you wish to get rid of your crowns, you may return and exchange them for wisdom."

"Nay, King," said the Hoopoes. "Well we know that wisdom has brought you great renown, but no one would bow down to you or give attention to your words, unless you wore your golden crown. We shall be able to repeat your wise words profitably now, for all will listen when they see gold crowns on our heads, too."

"All the same, return to me without fear or shame, if your crowns do not satisfy," said King Solomon kindly. Then he ordered his goldsmiths to supply the Hoopoes with crowns of the finest gold. Off flew the silly birds, with the shining crowns upon their heads, prouder than peacocks and chattering more loudly than parrots.

They could scarcely wait to get back to their friends and hear their exclamations. But when the Hoopoes announced they were now Kings of the Bird World, their friends only laughed and said they were quite satisfied with Solomon, and he was the only king they wished or needed. Then they drove the Hoopoes from the trees, for their golden crowns were always catching in the branches, and the other birds grew tired of freeing them. But the Hoopoes decided the other birds were only jealous and, rather flattered, gathered around the pools so they could admire themselves in the water.

Very soon people began to notice the antics of the silly little things as they strutted up and down, cocking their heads first this way, then that. Finally a man caught one and discovered the wonderful gold crown it wore. He hurried off to a goldsmith, who gave him a high price for it. The man rushed back to the pool and laid snares for the Hoopoes, who were so taken up with admiring themselves that they walked straight into the traps.

Then came the saddest time for the Hoopoes. Everyone began to hunt them. The poor little birds could not go to the wells and the pools, for they were thick with nets. They could not go into the gardens, for fowlers lurked behind the flowers. They could not fly up onto the housetops, for even there the people had set traps for them. There was not a spot on earth where they could rest. At last the wretched little birds flew back to the palace and waited until they beheld the great King Solomon coming along his terrace, listening to his singers as they performed in the cool of the evening.

"O king," they said, "we have found that golden crowns are vanity. We know not what you do to keep yourself from being chased about and hunted, and so we have come to ask you to remove ours from us."

"Beloved Hoopoes," said the king, "a crown that people are expected to bow down to always sits heavy on the head, and a crown that excites envy is a net for the feet. The only crown that can be worn with comfort is the crown of service, and that crown should spring up naturally so that no one takes any particular notice of it."

"Give us that crown of service, O wise king," said the poor little Hoopoes very humbly, for they now wanted nothing better than to live without notice.

"May it shelter you even as it sheltered me," said the great king; and on their heads, the Hoopoes beheld crowns of feathers. But with these crowns came quite a new feeling to the Hoopoes. They no longer wished to rule, but to serve.

•

KING SOLOMON AND THE ANTS
John Greenleaf Whittier

This poem is based on an old story found in the Koran, the sacred book of Islam.

Out from Jerusalem
   The king rode with his great
   War chiefs and lords of state,
And Sheba's queen with them.

Proud in the Syrian sun,
   In gold and purple sheen,
   The dusky Ethiop queen
Smiled on King Solomon.

Wisest of men, he knew
   The languages of all
   The creatures great or small
That trod the earth or flew.

Across an ant-hill led
   The king's path, and he heard
   Its small folk, and their word
He thus interpreted:

"Here comes the king men greet
   As wise and good and just,
   To crush us in the dust
Under his heedless feet."

The great king bowed his head,
  And saw the wide surprise
  Of the Queen of Sheba's eyes
As he told her what they said.

"O king!" she whispered sweet,
  "Too happy fate have they
  Who perish in thy way
Beneath thy gracious feet!

"Thou of the God-lent crown,
  Shall these vile creatures dare
  Murmur against thee where
The knees of kings kneel down?"

"Nay," Solomon replied,
  "The wise and strong should seek
  The welfare of the weak;"
And turned his horse aside.

His train, with quick alarm,
  Curved with their leader round
  The ant-hill's peopled mound,
And left it free from harm.

The jeweled head bent low;
  "O king!" she said, "henceforth
  The secret of thy worth
And wisdom well I know.

"Happy must be the State
  Whose ruler heedeth more
  The murmurs of the poor
Than flatteries of the great."

•

A PIONEER OF COMPASSION

Francis T. Miller

Matthew Arnold wrote that "the world is forwarded by having its
attention fixed on the best things." Dorothea Dix (1802–1887)
lived to fix the world's attention on her crusade to help the suffering, and so led civilization forward. Here is leadership and citizenship born of compassion.

A girl of fourteen years, she found herself facing one of the
world's greatest problems—self-support. In addition, she must also
support two younger brothers.

"I know I can earn a living," she said. "I can teach the children
who are younger than I. I will open a private school."

The child schoolteacher stood before her little pupils with a
resoluteness of purpose that inspired them. To give herself an older
appearance, she lengthened her skirts and her sleeves. Although
scarcely older than the children she taught, her seriousness commanded their respect and affection.

At nineteen, this child teacher was the principal of a boarding
school for the daughters of many prominent men of the time. Her
strong moral influence had brought her reputation and success.

The early burdens of life wore upon her. Her blue eyes, their
warmth chilled by gray, as though sorrow had early crept into her
sunny skies, showed failing health, and those about her became
greatly worried.

"I do not fear to die," she said, "but I cannot bear the thought
of leaving my little brothers. While I live," she added, "I will make
myself useful to humanity."

As she looked about her, she found many who were in deeper
trouble than herself, some of them with burdens almost too great
to bear. She found that there were afflictions in the world as great
as physical sickness. There was mental sickness—as hideous in its
torment and suffering as any bodily disease.

It was in the year 1841. This young woman was visiting the
unfortunate in the House of Correction at East Cambridge, in Massachusetts, when the moans of the wretched came to her ears. Imprisoned in a room, in filth and unspeakable horror, were human

beings who had lost their reason, many of them through way-wardness and dissipation. Her young heart went out in compassion for them in their misery, and in that compassion burned the fires of justice.

"It is true that they have lost their reason," she admitted, "but they are human beings, they are our fellow men, and we must protect them."

"This is my mission in life," she decided, and with that decision, she began an investigation of the treatment of the mentally afflicted. She found that civilization looked upon the loss of reason as a curse, and upon its victims as wild beasts, to be chained and bound in irons. Her eyes rested upon sights which she did not know existed in a Christian world. She saw men and women in cages, closets, stalls, and pens. Sometimes they were naked. Often they were cruelly beaten into submission. The gentle voice of this woman cried out in protest.

Hostility and abuse were the response that came back to her.

"It is all humbug," declared the political leaders.

A legislator, after attacking her statements on the floor of the House, declared that he and some of his committee would go to her and refute her allegations. As they entered her home, they were met by the gentle face and voice of this woman.

"We came to inquire about these allegations against our institutions," the leader said coldly.

The woman, smiling, told him of her experiences. She described the misery and fearful sufferings that she had witnessed. As she appealed to the hearts of her visitors, the legislator, after sitting spellbound for an hour and a half, arose and stepping to her side, exclaimed: "Madam, I bid you good night. I do not want, for my part, to hear anything more. The others can stay if they wish to. *I am convinced.* You have conquered me out and out. If you'll come to the House and talk there as you've done here, no man who isn't a brute can withstand you. When a man's convinced, that's enough. The Lord bless you."

The heart of the nation was aroused. Thousands came to her support, while countless others denounced her. She became a political issue in Massachusetts, and the legislature, after a heated discussion, passed an appropriation to remove the insane from the jails to institutions where they could receive mental treatment.

The life work of the woman had now just begun. She went from Massachusetts to Rhode Island, and on and on until she had visited all the states east of the Rocky Mountains. Everywhere her eyes rested upon the same inhuman conditions that she had found in Massachusetts. In the treatment of its mental unfortunates, civilization had become savage. She visited the prisons and almshouses. Her appeals to humanity were overpowering. As she journeyed through the country, she wore a simple dress of plain gray for traveling, and appeared in severe black on public occasions, frequently wearing a shawl about her shoulders.

One day, while in Rhode Island, she went to see a millionaire who had no special fondness for benevolence. He tried to baffle her with commonplace generalities, which she met with kindness. At last, rising with commanding dignity, she announced the purpose of her interview.

The financier, hardened though he was by a life devoted to mere money-making, listened. Her low-voiced eloquence appealed to him.

"God will not hold us guiltless for the neglect of one of the least of His Creatures," she declared.

"But what would you have me do?" inquired the rich man.

"Give fifty thousand dollars toward a new asylum for the insane," she answered.

"I will do it," he replied.

Some months later this woman, now a broken-down invalid, weakened by her travels and labors, stood before Congress. For six years she pleaded with the government for better laws for the insane, and at last her wisdom and humanity conquered the hearts and minds of the statesmen.

It was 1854. A bill before Congress was for an appropriation of 12,225,000 acres of public lands—about 20,000 square miles—to be apportioned among the states for the care of the insane, allowing the odd 225,000 acres for the deaf. The bill swept the Senate by more than a two-thirds majority, and passed the House by a plurality of fourteen.

The woman wept with thanksgiving.

"I must resist the deep sympathies of my heart," said President Pierce, as he returned the bill to the Senate without his signature and bearing his veto.

The worn woman was crushed by this defeat, and she was taken across the seas to recover her lost energy and strength. But her life mission weighed upon her, and, immediately upon her arrival in Scotland, she began to work for the remodeling of its lunacy laws. Some officials resented the intrusion, and moved to oppose her. Refusing to give up, she turned toward London for help, and her efforts led Parliament to rise to the defense of mental sufferers and revise its laws on principles of Christian brotherhood.

The conquest of civilization by an invalid American woman was now well begun. When she entered Italy, in 1856, she found the prisons and hospitals of ancient Rome in confusion and disorder. A few days later she stood before Pope Pius IX, and appealed to his beneficence. He expressed himself surprised and shocked at the details of her recital, and, on the following day he fell unawares on the officials and personally investigated the conditions in the prisons, which he found to be only too true. The result was the purchase of land and the establishment of a retreat for the mentally afflicted of the great metropolis of the ancient civilization.

Cries of distress from all parts of Europe called this American woman from Rome. In Athens, Constantinople, Moscow, St. Petersburg, Vienna, Paris, Florence—everywhere she carried the new light of science to those who were suffering under the shadow of a great affliction.

The gloom of a great civil war fell upon her beloved America. And as the cannon boomed, under the flag that she loved, she carried the compassion of her heart to the wounded and dying and offered her life to her country as a superintendent of nurses. It was through her efforts that many monuments were erected to the Union soldiers who had fallen on the field or perished in the prison pens or hospital wards. It was this woman who brought to the army and navy compassion for the heroes who had become insane in the service. It was this good Samaritan whose name ran through every state in the Union, across Canada, and around the world—appealing to the universal heart of humanity.

And yet, this great woman, whose soul was overflowing with

love for all humanity, was herself a homeless wanderer. This life spent for the happiness of others was poured out in loneliness and suffering.

One day a white-haired lady of about eighty years of age, plainly dressed, and bent by the weight of years, retired to the mental hospital at Trenton, New Jersey.

"This is my first-born child," she said. "It is here that I want to die."

Five years later this beneficent life passed away so quietly that the world hardly knew she was gone. Those for whom she had labored did not know, and could not love. Over her lifeless form they could not grieve; they were in darkness that knows no grief.

But there is One who knows and One who loves, and to those all-embracing arms she passed with the tender words: "Come, ye blessed of my Father, inherit the kingdom prepared for you from the foundation of the world, for I was hungry and ye gave me meat; I was thirsty and ye gave me drink; I was a stranger and ye took me in; naked and ye clothed me; sick and in prison and ye visited me."

And as the light of His face falls upon her, we can hear the echo of the voice of Him who gave his life to save humanity: "Inasmuch as ye have done it unto one of the least of these my brethren, ye have done it unto me."

This is a story of the heroism of peace—the story of Dorothea Lynde Dix, one of the noblest of American women.

•

SOJOURNER TRUTH

From *The Narrative of Sojourner Truth*

In 1843, a former slave born with the name Isabella left New York City with a bag of clothes, twenty-five cents, and a new name— Sojourner Truth—a name she chose, she said, because God had told her to travel the land, declaring the truth. For the remainder of her life, she spoke out loudly and fearlessly on behalf of her causes, which included the abolition of slavery, equal rights for women, and education for freed slaves. Here is someone born into the worst of conditions who nonetheless rose to lead others to better lives. The passage below comes from *The Narrative of Sojourner Truth,* published in 1875. The incident described here took place in Washington, D.C., shortly after the Civil War.

While Sojourner was engaged in the hospital, she often had occasion to procure articles from various parts of the city for the sick soldiers, and would sometimes be obliged to walk a long distance, carrying her burdens upon her arm. She would gladly have availed herself of the street cars; but, although there was on each track one car called the Jim Crow car, nominally for the accommodation of colored people, yet should they succeed in getting on at all they would seldom have more than the privilege of standing, as the seats were usually filled with white folks. Unwilling to submit to this state of things, she complained to the president of the street railroad, who ordered the Jim Crow car to be taken off. A law was now passed giving the colored people equal car privileges with the white.

Not long after this, Sojourner, having occasion to ride, signaled the car, but neither conductor nor driver noticed her. Soon another followed, and she raised her hand again, but they also turned away. She then gave three tremendous yelps, "I want to ride! *I want to ride!* I WANT TO RIDE!!!" Consternation seized the passing crowd— people, carriages, go-carts of every description stood still. The car was effectually blocked up, and before it could move on, Sojourner had jumped aboard. Then there arose a great shout from the crowd, "Ha! ha! ha!! She has beaten him," &c. The angry conductor told her to go forward where the horses were, or he would put her out. Quietly seating herself, she informed him that she was a passenger. "Go forward where the horses are, or I will throw you out," said he in a menacing voice. She told him that she was neither a Marylander nor a Virginian to fear his threats; but was from the Empire State of New York, and knew the laws as well as he did.

Several soldiers were in the car, and when other passengers came in, they related the circumstance and said, "You ought to have heard that old woman talk to the conductor." Sojourner rode farther than she needed to go; for a ride was so rare a privilege that she determined to make the most of it. She left the car feeling very happy, and said, "Bless God! I have had a ride."

Returning one day from the Orphans' Home at Georgetown, she hastened to reach a car; but they paid no attention to her signal, and kept ringing a bell that they might not hear her. She ran after it, and when it stopped to take other passengers, she succeeded in overtaking it and, getting in, said to the conductor, "It is a shame to make a lady run so." He told her if she said another word, he would put her off the car, and came forward as if to execute his threat. She replied, "If you attempt that, it will cost you more than your car and horses are worth." A gentleman of dignified and commanding manner, wearing a general's uniform, interfered in her behalf, and the conductor gave her no further trouble.

•

KING JOHN AND THE MAGNA CARTA
Retold by James Baldwin

Here is a leader of the church doing his part to establish the rights of Englishmen, which in time would come to mean human rights. More than once in the course of Western civilization has the courage of religious leaders become the seed of political achievement. The Magna Carta was signed in 1215.

King John was so selfish and cruel that all the people in his kingdom both feared and hated him.

One by one he lost the dominions in France which the former kings of England had held. Men called him Lackland, because in the end he had neither lands nor castles that he could rightfully call his own.

He robbed his people. He quarreled with his knights and barons. He offended all good men. He formed a plan for making war against King Philip of France, and called upon his barons to join him. When some of them refused, he burned their castles and destroyed their fields.

At last the barons met together at a place called St. Edmundsbury to talk about their grievances. "Why should we submit to be ruled by such a king?" said some of the boldest. But most of them were afraid to speak their minds.

Stephen Langton, the Archbishop of Canterbury, was with them, and there was no bolder friend of liberty than he. He made a stirring speech that gave courage even to the most cowardly.

"Are you men?" he said. "Why then do you submit to this false-hearted king? Stand up and declare your freedom. Refuse to be the slaves of this man. Demand the rights and privileges that belong to you as free men. Put this demand in writing—in the form of a great charter—and require the king to sign it. So shall it be to you and your children a safeguard forever against the injustice of unworthy rulers."

The barons were astonished at the boldness of this speech. Some of them shrank back in fear, but the bravest among them showed by their looks and gestures that they were ready to make a bold stand for liberty.

"Come forward!" cried Stephen Langton. "Come, and swear that you will never rest until King John has given you the rights that are yours. Swear that you will have the charter from his hand, or that you will wage war upon him to the very death."

Never before had Englishmen heard such a speech. The barons took the oath which Stephen Langton prescribed. Then they gathered their fighting men together and marched upon London. The cowardly king was frightened.

"What do these men want?" he asked.

They sent him word that they wanted their rights as Englishmen, and that they would never rest until he had given them a charter of liberties signed by his own hand.

"Oh, well! If that is all, you shall surely have it," he said.

But he put them off with one excuse and another. He sent a messenger to Rome to ask the Pope to help him. He tried, by fine promises, to persuade Stephen Langton to abandon the cause he had undertaken. But no one knew the falseness of his heart better than the Pope and the Archbishop of Canterbury.

The people from all parts of the country now came and joined the army of the barons. Of all the knights in England, only seven remained true to the king.

The barons made out a list of their demands, and Stephen Langton carried it to the king. "These things we will have," they said, "and there shall be no peace until you grant them."

Oh, how angry was King John! He raved like a wild beast; he clenched his fists; he stamped upon the floor. But he saw that he was helpless. At last he said that he would sign the charter at such time and place as the barons might name.

"Let the time be the fifteenth of June," they said, "and let the place be Runnymede."

Now, Runnymede was a green meadow not far from the city of

London, and there the king went with his few followers. He was met by the barons, with an army of determined men behind them.

The charter which Stephen Langton and his friends had drawn up was spread out before the king. He was not a scholar, and so it was read to him, line by line. It was a promise that the people should not be oppressed; that the rights of the cities and boroughs should be respected; that no man should be imprisoned without a fair trial; that justice should not be delayed or denied to anyone.

Pale with anger, the king signed the charter, and then rode back to his castle at Windsor. As soon as he was in his own chamber he began to rave like a madman. He rolled on the floor. He beat the air with his fists. He gnawed sticks and straws. He foamed at the mouth. He cursed the barons and the people for treating their king so badly.

But he was helpless. The charter was signed—the Magna Carta, to which Englishmen still point as the first safeguard of their rights and liberties.

As might have been expected, it was not long before John tried to break all his promises. The barons made war upon him, and never again did he see a peaceful day. His anger and anxiety caused him to fall into a fever which nothing could cure. At last, despised and shunned as he deserved to be, he died. I doubt if there was an eye in England that wept for him.

●

SACAJAWEA

Francis T. Miller

Sacajawea (whose name means "bird woman") helped lead the way on one of the greatest overland adventures in American history. Here is the kind of courage and perseverance that moves the world along.

It was a full hundred years ago that the tribe of Indians known to history as the Shoshones made their home a little west of the Rocky Mountains, or, as the range was called by them, the "Bitter Root Mountains." Here it was that Sacajawea and her little friends played their childish games, with no thought of anything outside of their own lives. It was not always play time among the children; from infancy they were taught to labor with their hands, and their education in other respects was not neglected. At a surprisingly early age, they became skilled in the use of the bow, and they were sent into the forest to gather herbs and roots, for medicine and food.

One day, into this peaceful valley, without warning, the powerful Minnetarees, or Blackfeet, tribe swept down in battle array. Devastation followed in their wake. Many of the Shoshones were killed and many were carried away into captivity. Among the captives was little Sacajawea. Away over the mountains she was borne into the far, far east. Naturally alert and observing, the little maid absorbed every incident of this new experience, so that in after years, when traveling back over this same country, she was able to recognize most of the landmarks on the way.

Sacajawea was sold as a slave when she reached the east. A French Canadian, named Charboneau, who was an Indian interpreter, bought her when she was only five years old. When she was fourteen he made her his wife, and a year later a son was born to her.

It was about this time that American explorers were looking toward the great, mysterious region in the Far West. They believed that it was a land of great wealth, and they longed to plant the American flag on its mountains. Men called them foolhardy and said that it was a worthless jungle of forests and rocks and beasts, that it was not worth the risk of life it would take to survey it.

But there were two explorers—Lewis and Clark—who were willing to undertake it. Shortly after starting on their hazardous journey, they entered the little Indian village of Mandan. There they found Charboneau, who could talk many tongues. Their eyes fell also upon the little Indian mother, Sacajawea. Charboneau told them that his Indian wife knew the whole country, and was a natural guide. Sacajawea, in her native tongue, told them how she knew the trails; how she could take them through country never before traveled by the feet of white men; and how she could show them the beauties of the land of her birth, with its towering blue mountains, capped with snow, and its golden valleys, its gorges and rivers, its glittering sands, and its thousand and one beauties that have since given it the name of the "Garden of the Gods."

"We will go with you," said Charboneau and Sacajawea.

And so it was that when that expedition, which opened up the western domain of America, started on the most perilous portion of its journey, Sacajawea was a guide and Charboneau an interpreter. Sacajawea strapped her two-month-old baby on her shoulders, and carried him in this snug pocket throughout the entire journey. She was the only woman in the party and she rendered vital service to the explorers.

Into the heart of the wilderness they plunged. When all signs of human life were left far behind them, and there were none to beckon them onward, then it was that the native instinct of this woman came to their assistance. At times sickness or starvation seemed imminent. Then Sacajawea would go into the woods, where in secret she gathered herbs to cure each ailment, or dug roots, from which she prepared savory dishes for their meals.

The men marveled at the courage and ingenuity of this faithful pilot. Burdened though she was with the care of the young child, she never seemed to feel fatigue. No complaint ever escaped her lips. Patient, plucky, and determined, she was a constant source of inspiration to the explorers.

The baby laughed and cooed as the wonders of the world were revealed to it. With all its mother's fearlessness, it swung calmly on her faithful back while she climbed over jagged precipices and forded swiftly running rivers.

One day a little incident occurred, which illustrates the true character of this woman. While making their way along one of the rivers, her husband, in a clumsy attempt to readjust things, over-turned the canoe containing every article necessary for the journey. Without a moment's hesitation Sacajawea plunged into the river, risking her own life and that of the infant strapped to her. Clothing, bundles, and many valuable documents of the expedition were thus rescued. If these things had been lost, the party would have been obliged to retrace its steps hundreds of miles, in order to replace them. This is, indeed, the heroism that makes history. The alertness of Sacajawea's native instinct and her faithful kindness worked ines-timable benefit to our nation. In gratitude for her great services, the explorers named after her the next river that they discovered.

Some months later, scenes began to take on a familiar aspect to Sacajawea, and she showed signs of elation. She pointed out old landmarks which indicated that she was nearing her old home. They at last pitched their camp where years before, as a little child, she had been taken captive. Here she soon found old friends, and to her unspeakable delight she discovered among them her own brother. Wrapped closely in his arms, she sobbed out all the sorrow which had been bound up in her heart for so many years. From him she learned that all of her family had died, except two of her brothers and a son of her eldest sister.

Sacajawea was at home again. Now and then little snatches of songs of contentment reached the ears of the members of the great expedition. They might naturally have thought that now it would not be easy for the girl to attend them on their westward journey. But if they entertained this fear, they misjudged Sacajawea. She never flinched from her first intention, and cheerfully left her long-lost friends to plunge once more into the unbroken and unknown forests beyond the Rockies. The solitude was enough to shake a strong man's courage. Never a sound was to be heard except the dismal, distant howl of wild beasts and occasionally the war cry of savages, but Sacajawea did not falter.

Thus they plodded overland, ever westward, until the end of the journey drew near. They made a camp inland, leaving Sacajawea in its protection, and then pushed to the coast.

"It is the Pacific!" they cried at last.

In their enthusiasm, the explorers forgot the brave Sacajawea. They talked of the Pacific in the camp, but did not allow her to go to the coast until she pleaded with them to let her gaze upon the waters.

Then she was satisfied. She had seen the "great waters" and the "fish," as she called the whale which spouted on its surface.

It was an epoch-making journey, in which the path was blazed  by a woman. It rivaled the great explorations of Stanley and Livingstone in daring, and far exceeded them in importance. It was an expedition that moved the world along; that pushed the boundary of the United States from the Mississippi to the Pacific; that gave us the breadth of the continent from ocean to ocean; that led to the command of its rivers and harbors, the wealth of its mountains, plains and valleys—a dominion vast enough for the ambitions of kings.

•

WASHINGTON'S GLASSES

This is one of my favorite stories from American history. I taught
it in classrooms across the country when I was the U.S. secretary
of education. This moment of recognition of George Washington's
greatness in leadership came not in the noise of battle, but in the
quiet of reflection.

At the end of the Revolutionary War, the new United States
came close to disaster. The government owed back pay to many
officers in the army, men who had fought long and hard for the
nation's freedom. But Congress had no money, and rumors
abounded that it intended to disband the armed forces and send
them home without pay.

As the weeks passed, the army's cry for pay grew louder. The
soldiers insisted that they had performed their duty faithfully, and
now the government should do the same. They sent appeals to
Congress, with no effect. Patience began to wear thin. Tempers
smoldered. At last some of the officers, encamped at Newburgh,
New York, issued what amounted to a threat. The army would not
disband until paid; if necessary, it would march on Congress. Mutiny was close at hand.

There was no doubt in anyone's mind that one man alone
could persuade the army to give the government more time.

On March 15, 1783, George Washington strode into the Temple of Virtue, a large wooden hall built by the soldiers as a chapel
and dance hall. A hush fell over the gathered officers as the tall
figure took to the lectern at the front of the room. These men had
come to love their commander-in-chief during the lean, hard years
of fighting; now, for the first time, they glared at him with restless
and resentful eyes. A deathlike stillness filled the room.

Washington began to speak. He talked of his own dedicated
service, and reminded the group that he himself had served without
pay. He spoke of his love for his soldiers. He urged them to have
patience, and pointed out that Congress in the past had acted
slowly, but in the end would act justly. He promised he would do
everything in his power to see that the men received what they
deserved.

He asked them to consider the safety and security of their new country, begging them not to "open the flood gates of civil discord, and deluge our rising empire in blood." He appealed to their honor. "Let me entreat you, gentlemen, on your part," he said, "not to take any measures which, viewed in the calm light of reason, will lessen the dignity and sully the glory you have hitherto maintained."

He paused. A restlessness pervaded the air. His audience did not seem moved. The men stared at him tensely.

Washington produced a letter from a congressman explaining the difficulties the government now faced. He would read it to them. It would help them comprehend the new government's difficulties. He unfolded the paper. He started to read, slowly. He stumbled over some of the words, then stopped. Something was wrong. The general seemed lost, slightly confused. The officers leaned forward.

Then Washington pulled from his pocket something the men had never seen their commander-in-chief use before—spectacles.

"Gentlemen, you must pardon me," he said quietly. "I have grown gray in your service, and now find myself growing blind."

It was not merely what the beloved general said, but the way he spoke the few, simple words. The humble act of this majestic man touched the soldiers in a way his arguments had failed to do. There were lumps in many throats, tears in every eye. The general quietly left the hall, and the officers voted to give the Congress more time.

George Washington had saved his new country from armed rebellion. As Thomas Jefferson later said, "The moderation and virtue of a single character probably prevented this Revolution from being closed, as most others have been, by a subversion of that liberty it was intended to establish."

•

THE CHARACTER OF LEADERSHIP

Thomas Jefferson

Here is one great American leader writing honestly and unselfishly about another. Here is a true portrait of the character of leadership. Jefferson wrote this probing, candid assessment at Monticello in a letter to Dr. Walter Jones dated January 2, 1814.

I think I knew General Washington intimately and thoroughly; and were I called on to delineate his character, it should be in terms like these.

His mind was great and powerful, without being of the very first order; his penetration strong, though not so acute as that of a Newton, Bacon, or Locke; and as far as he saw, no judgment was ever sounder. It was slow in operation, being little aided by invention or imagination, but sure in conclusion. Hence the common remark of his officers, of the advantage he derived from councils of war, where hearing all suggestions, he selected whatever was best; and certainly no general ever planned his battles more judiciously. But if deranged during the course of the action, if any member of his plan was dislocated by sudden circumstances, he was slow in readjustment. The consequence was, that he often failed in the field, and rarely against an enemy in station, as at Boston and York. He was incapable of fear, meeting personal dangers with the calmest unconcern. Perhaps the strongest feature in his character was prudence, never acting until every circumstance, every consideration, was maturely weighed; refraining if he saw a doubt, but, when once decided, going through with his purpose, whatever obstacles opposed. His integrity was most pure, his justice the most inflexible I have ever known, no motives of interest or consanguinity, of friendship or hatred, being able to bias his decision. He was, indeed, in every sense of the words, a wise, a good, and a great man. His temper was naturally irritable and high toned; but reflection and resolution had obtained a firm and habitual ascendancy over it. If ever, however, it broke its bonds, he was most tremendous in his wrath. In his expenses he was honorable, but exact; liberal in contributions to whatever promised utility; but frowning and unyielding on all visionary projects, and all unworthy calls on his charity. His heart was not warm in its affections; but he exactly calculated every man's value, and gave him a solid esteem proportioned to it. His person, you know, was fine, his stature exactly what one would wish, his deportment easy, erect and noble; the best horseman of his age, and the most graceful figure that could be seen on horseback. Although in the circle of his friends, where he might be unreserved with safety, he took a free share in conversation, his colloquial talents were not above mediocrity, possessing neither copiousness of ideas, nor fluency of words. In public, when called on for a sudden opinion, he was unready, short and embarrassed. Yet he wrote readily, rather diffusely, in an easy and correct style. This he had acquired by conversation with the world, for his education was merely reading, writing and common arithmetic, to which he added surveying at a later day. His time was employed in action chiefly, reading little, and that only in agriculture and English history. His correspondence became necessarily extensive, and, with journalizing his agricultural proceedings, occupied most of his leisure hours within doors. On the whole, his character was, in its mass, perfect, in nothing bad, in few points indifferent; and it may truly be said, that never did nature and fortune combine more perfectly to make a man great, and to place him in the same constellation with whatever worthies have merited from man an everlasting remembrance. For his was the singular destiny and merit, of leading the armies of his country successfully through an arduous war, for the establishment of its independence; of conducting its councils through the birth of a government, new in its forms and principles, until it had settled down into a quiet and orderly train; and of scrupulously obeying the laws through the whole of his career, civil and military, of which the history of the world furnishes no other example.

•

A VICE GROWN INTO FASHION

George Washington

Ralph Waldo Emerson once observed that "we infer the spirit of the nation in great measure from the language." George Washington issued this general order to his troops in New York in July 1776. Do we the American people hold ourselves to this standard today? No, we do not.

GENERAL ORDER

The General is sorry to be informed that the foolish and wicked practice of profane cursing and swearing, a vice heretofore little known in an American army, is growing into fashion. He hopes the officers will, by example as well as influence, endeavor to check it, and that both they and the men will reflect, that we can have little hope of the blessing of Heaven on our arms, if we insult it by our impiety and folly. Added to this, it is a vice so mean and low, without any temptation, that every man of sense and character detests and despises it.

•

SURRENDER AT APPOMATTOX

Horace Porter

Great leaders display certain virtues when the end comes, no matter what the outcome. Here is grace in victory and grace in defeat. The account comes from an eyewitness at Appomattox Courthouse, Virginia, where on April 9, 1865, General Robert E. Lee surrendered the Confederate Army of Northern Virginia to General Ulysses S. Grant, effectively ending the Civil War.

General Grant began the conversation by saying: "I met you once before, General Lee, while we were serving in Mexico, when you came over from General Scott's headquarters to visit Garland's brigade, to which I then belonged. I have always remembered your appearance, and I think I should have recognized you anywhere." "Yes," replied General Lee, "I know I met you on that occasion, and I have often thought of it and tried to recollect how you looked, but I have never been able to recall a single feature." After some further mention of Mexico, General Lee said: "I suppose, General Grant, that the object of our present meeting is fully understood. I asked to see you to ascertain upon what terms you would receive the surrender of my army." General Grant replied: "The terms I propose are those stated substantially in my letter of yesterday—that is, the officers and men surrendered to be paroled and disqualified from taking up arms again until properly exchanged, and all arms, ammunition, and supplies to be delivered up as captured property." Lee nodded an assent, and said: "Those are about the conditions which I expected would be proposed." General Grant then continued: "Yes, I think our correspondence indicated pretty clearly the action that would be taken at our meeting; and I hope it may lead to a general suspension of hostilities and be the means of preventing any further loss of life."

Lee inclined his head as indicating his accord with this wish, and General Grant then went on to talk at some length in a very pleasant vein about the prospects of peace. Lee was evidently anxious to proceed to the formal work of the surrender, and he brought the subject up again by saying: "I presume, General Grant, we have both carefully considered the proper steps to be taken, and I would suggest that you commit to writing the terms you have proposed, so that they may be formally acted upon."

"Very well," replied General Grant, "I will write them out." And calling for his manifold order book, he opened it on the table before him and proceeded to write the terms. The leaves had been so prepared that three impressions of the writing were made. He wrote very rapidly, and did not pause until he had finished the sentence ending with "officers appointed by me to receive them." Then he looked toward Lee, and his eyes seemed to be resting on the handsome sword that hung at that officer's side. He said afterward that this set him to thinking that it would be an unnecessary humiliation to require the officers to surrender their swords, and a great hardship to deprive them of their personal baggage and horses, and after a short pause he wrote the sentence: "This will not embrace the side-arms of the officers, nor their private horses or baggage." When he had finished the letter he called Colonel (afterward General) Ely S. Parker, one of the military secretaries on the staff, to his side and looked it over with him and directed him as they went along to interline six or seven words and to strike out the word "their," which had been repeated. When this had been done, he handed the book to General Lee and asked him to read over the letter. . . .

Lee took it and laid it on the table beside him, while he drew from his pocket a pair of steel-rimmed spectacles and wiped the glasses carefully with his handkerchief. Then he crossed his legs, adjusted the spectacles very slowly and deliberately, took up the draft of the letter, and proceeded to read it attentively. . . .

When Lee came to the sentence about the officers' side-arms, private horses, and baggage, he showed for the first time during the reading of the letter a slight change of countenance, and was evidently touched by this act of generosity. It was doubtless the condition mentioned to which he particularly alluded when he looked toward General Grant as he finished reading and said with some degree of warmth in his manner: "This will have a very happy effect upon my army."

General Grant then said: "Unless you have some suggestions

to make in regard to the form in which I have stated the terms, I will have a copy of the letter made in ink and sign it."

"There is one thing I would like to mention," Lee replied after a short pause. "The cavalrymen and artillerists own their own horses in our army. Its organization in this respect differs from that of the United States." This expression attracted the notice of our officers present, as showing how firmly the conviction was grounded in his mind that we were two distinct countries. He continued: "I would like to understand whether these men will be permitted to retain their horses."

"You will find that the terms as written do not allow this," General Grant replied; "only the officers are permitted to take their private property."

Lee read over the second page of the letter again, and then said: "No, I see the terms do not allow it; that is clear." His face showed plainly that he was quite anxious to have this concession made, and Grant said very promptly and without giving Lee time to make a direct request: "Well, the subject is quite new to me. Of course I did not know that any private soldiers owned their animals, but I think this will be the last battle of the war—I sincerely hope so—and that the surrender of this army will be followed soon by that of all the others, and I take it that most of the men in the ranks are small farmers, and as the country has been so raided by the two armies, it is doubtful whether they will be able to put in a crop to carry themselves and their families through the next winter without the aid of the horses they are now riding, and I will arrange it in this way: I will not change the terms as now written, but I will instruct the officers I shall appoint to receive the paroles to let all the men who claim to own a horse or mule take the animals home with them to work their little farms." (This expression has been quoted in various forms and has been the subject of some dispute. I give the exact words used.)

Lee now looked greatly relieved, and though anything but a demonstrative man, he gave every evidence of his appreciation of this concession, and said, "This will have the best possible effect upon the men. It will be very gratifying and will do much toward conciliating our people." He handed the draft of the terms back to General Grant, who called Colonel T. S. Bowers of the staff to him and directed him to make a copy in ink. . . .

General Lee now took the initiative again in leading the conversation back into business channels. He said: "I have a thousand

or more of your men as prisoners, General Grant, a number of
them officers whom we have required to march along with us for
several days. I shall be glad to send them into your lines as soon as
it can be arranged, for I have no provisions for them. I have, indeed,
nothing for my own men. They have been living for the last few
days principally upon parched corn, and we are badly in need of
both rations and forage. I telegraphed to Lynchburg, directing several trainloads of rations to be sent on by rail from there, and when
they arrive I should be glad to have the present wants of my men
supplied from them."

At this remark all eyes turned toward Sheridan, for he had
captured these trains with his cavalry the night before, near Appomattox Station. General Grant replied: "I should like to have our
men sent within our lines as soon as possible. I will take steps at
once to have your army supplied with rations, but I am sorry we
have no forage for the animals. We have had to depend upon the
country for our supply of forage."

At a little before four o'clock General Lee shook hands with
General Grant, bowed to the other officers, and with Colonel Mar-
shall left the room. One after another we followed, and passed out
to the porch. Lee signaled to his orderly to bring up his horse, and
while the animal was being bridled the general stood on the lowest
step and gazed sadly in the direction of the valley beyond where his
army lay—now an army of prisoners. He smote his hands together a
number of times in an absent sort of a way; seemed not to see the
group of Union officers in the yard who rose respectfully at his
approach, and appeared unconscious of everything about him. All
appreciated the sadness that overwhelmed him, and he had the
personal sympathy of everyone who beheld him at this supreme
moment of trial. The approach of his horse seemed to recall him
from his reverie, and he at once mounted. General Grant now
stepped down from the porch, and, moving toward him, saluted
him by raising his hat. He was followed in this act of courtesy by all
our officers present; Lee raised his hat respectfully, and rode off to
break the sad news to the brave fellows whom he had so long
commanded.

•

"You Have Done Your Duty"

When the Civil War erupted in 1861, thousands of black men tried to enlist in the Union army but were turned away by the government. Only after the Emancipation Proclamation in 1863 did the North begin recruiting large numbers of black soldiers. Eventually almost 200,000 blacks served in the Union forces, in segregated units known as the U.S. Colored Troops. No heroism in our nation's history surpasses the selflessness and loyalty of these men, many who had known freedom for so short a time, yet who immediately offered their own lives so others might be free.

This farewell address was issued after the close of the war to the 1st South Carolina Volunteers at Morris Island, South Carolina, scene of the famous bloody assault against Fort Wagner. There the 54th Massachusetts Colored Infantry had suffered a 40 percent casualty rate while spearheading the attack.

HEADQUARTERS 33RD UNITED STATES COLORED
TROOPS, LATE 1ST SOUTH CAROLINA VOLUNTEERS

MORRIS ISLAND, S.C.
February 9, 1866

GENERAL ORDERS, NO. 1

Comrades—The hour is at hand when we must separate forever, and nothing can ever take from us the pride we feel, when we look back upon the history of the 1st South Carolina Volunteers—the first black regiment that ever bore arms in defence of freedom on the continent of America.

On the ninth day of May, 1862, at which time there were nearly four millions of your race in a bondage sanctioned by the laws of the land, and protected by our flag—on that day, in the face of floods of prejudice, that wellnigh deluged every avenue to manhood and true liberty, you came forth to do battle for our country and your kindred. For long and weary months without pay, or even the privilege of being recognized as soldiers, you labored on, only to be disbanded and sent to your homes, without even a hope of reward. And when our country, necessitated by the deadly struggle with armed traitors, finally granted you the opportunity *again* to come forth in defence of the nation's life, the alacrity with which you responded to the call gave abundant evidence of your readiness to strike a manly blow for the liberty of your race. And from that little band of hopeful, trusting, and brave men, who gathered at Camp Saxton, on Port Royal Island, in the fall of 1862, amidst the terrible prejudices that then surrounded us, has grown an army of a hundred and forty thousand black soldiers, whose valor and heroism has won for your race a name which will live as long as the undying pages of history shall endure; and by whose efforts, united with those of the white man, armed rebellion has been conquered, the millions of bondsmen have been emancipated, and the fundamental law of the land has been so altered as to remove forever the possibility of human slavery being reestablished within the borders of redeemed America. The flag of our fathers, restored to its rightful significance, now floats over every foot of our territory, from Maine to California, and beholds only freemen! The prejudices which formerly existed against you are wellnigh rooted out.

Soldiers, you have done your duty, and acquitted yourselves like men, who, actuated by such ennobling motives, could not fail; and as the result of your fidelity and obedience, you have won your freedom. And oh, how great the reward!

It seems fitting to me that the last hours of our existence as a regiment should be passed amidst the unmarked graves of your comrades—at Fort Wagner. Near you rest the bones of Colonel Shaw, buried by an enemy's hand, in the same grave with his black soldiers, who fell at his side; where, in future, your children's children will come on pilgrimages to do homage to the ashes of those that fell in this glorious struggle.

The flag which was presented to us by the Rev. George B. Cheever and his congregation, of New York City, on the first of January, 1863—the day when Lincoln's immortal proclamation of freedom was given to the world—and which you have borne so nobly through the war, is now to be rolled up forever, and deposited in our nation's capital. And while there it shall rest, with the battles in which you have participated inscribed upon its folds, it will be a source of pride to us all to remember that it has never been disgraced by a cowardly faltering in the hour of danger or polluted by a traitor's touch.

Now that you are to lay aside your arms, and return to the peaceful avocations of life, I adjure you, by the associations and history of the past, and the love you bear for your liberties, to harbor no feelings of hatred toward your former masters, but to seek in the paths of honesty, virtue, sobriety, and industry, and by a willing obedience to the laws of the land, to grow up to the full stature of American citizens. The church, the schoolhouse and the right forever to be free are now secured to you, and every prospect before you is full of hope and encouragement. The nation guarantees to you full protection and justice, and will require from you in return the respect for the laws and orderly deportment which will prove to everyone your right to all the privileges of freemen.

To the officers of the regiment I would say, your toils are ended, your mission is fulfilled, and we separate forever. The fidelity, patience, and patriotism with which you have discharged your duties, to your men and to your country, entitle you to a far higher tribute than any words of thankfulness which I can give you from the bottom of my heart. You will find your reward in the proud conviction that the cause for which you have battled so nobly has been crowned with abundant success.

Officers and soldiers of the First South Carolina Volunteers, I bid you all farewell.

By order of Lt.-Col. C. T. Trowbridge, commanding Regiment.

E. W. Hyde,

Lieutenant and Acting Adjutant

•

DUTY, HONOR, COUNTRY

Douglas MacArthur

These words come from a speech General Douglas MacArthur delivered at West Point on May 12, 1962. Every cadet entering the United States Military Academy receives a copy of the address. They are great words not only for every soldier, but for every citizen.

Duty. Honor. Country. Those three hallowed words reverently dictate what you ought to be, what you can be, what you will be. They are your rallying points, to build courage when courage seems to fail, to regain faith when there seems to be little cause for faith, to create hope when hope becomes forlorn. . . .

The unbelievers will say they are but words, but a slogan, but a flamboyant phrase. Every pedant, every demagogue, every cynic, every hypocrite, every troublemaker, and, I am sorry to say, some others of an entirely different character, will try to downgrade them even to the extent of mockery and ridicule, but these are some of the things they do. They build your basic character. They mold you for your future roles as the custodians of the nation's defense. They make you strong enough to know when you are weak, and brave enough to face yourself when you are afraid.

They teach you to be proud and unbending in honest failure, but humble and gentle in success; not to substitute words for actions, not to seek the path of comfort, but to face the stress and spur of difficulty and challenge; to learn to stand up in the storm, but to have compassion on those who fail; to master yourself before you seek to master others; to have a heart that is clean, a goal that is high; to learn to laugh yet never forget how to weep; to reach into the future, yet never neglect the past; to be serious, yet never to take yourself too seriously; to be modest so that you will remember the simplicity of true greatness, the open mind of true wisdom, the meekness of true strength.

They give you a temper of the will, a quality of the imagination, a vigor of the emotions, a freshness of the deep springs of life, a temperamental predominance of courage over timidity, of an appetite for adventure over love of ease.

They create in your heart the sense of wonder, the unfailing hope of what next, and the joy and inspiration of life. They teach you in this way to be an officer and a gentleman.

•

AMERICA IS GREAT
BECAUSE SHE IS GOOD

This brief reflection has been attributed to Alexis de Tocqueville, one of the greatest observers of early American democratic life. In the end, the state of the union comes down to the character of ‚ its citizens.

I sought for the greatness
and genius of America
in her commodious harbors
and her ample rivers,
and it was not there;

in the fertile fields
and boundless prairies,
and it was not there;

in her rich mines
and her vast world commerce,
and it was not there.

Not until I went
into the churches of America
and heard her pulpits,
aflame with righteousness,
did I understand the secret
of her genius and power.

America is great
because she is good,
and if America ever ceases to be good,
America will cease to be great.

•

A GENERAL THANKSGIVING
From *The Book of Common Prayer*

Learning to say thank you is one of the most important lessons of
life. It's not just a matter of manners. Gratitude is a virtue that
helps us remember the obligations and responsibilities we owe
others in return for the gifts we have received. It makes us better
citizens.

Almighty God, Father of all mercies, we, thine unworthy servants, do give thee most humble and hearty thanks for all thy good-

ness and loving-kindness to us, and to all men. We bless thee for our creation, preservation, and all the blessings of this life; but above all, for thine inestimable love in the redemption of the world by our Lord Jesus Christ; for the means of grace, and for the hope of glory. And, we beseech thee, give us that due sense of all thy mercies, that our hearts may be unfeignedly thankful; and that we show forth thy praise, not only with our lips, but in our lives, by giving up our selves to thy service, and by walking before thee in holiness and righteousness all our days; through Jesus Christ our Lord, to whom, with thee and the Holy Ghost, be all honor and glory, world without end. *Amen.*

Seven

·

WHAT WE LIVE BY

W H O am I? Why am I here? What should I do? What is my destiny? What does it all mean?

These are some of the profound questions we ask ourselves as we undertake life's journey. The search for meaning is intrinsic to human nature. As thinking creatures, we want to understand why we find ourselves on this road and where the journey is taking us. Will that place make us truly happy and fulfilled? "If we could first know where we are, and whither we are tending, we could better judge what to do, and how to do it," Abraham Lincoln observed. Without answers to these questions, we feel a bit disoriented. We are wanderers, searching and striving for end and aim, for purpose and connection.

And clearly, if we are to be true to ideas like courage and perseverance and responsibility and loyalty, it helps to know *why* we should go to the trouble. What ultimate good does it do? What do the virtues have to do with our place in the universe, our reason for being here, and our nature as human beings? Why *should* we be moral creatures?

This final chapter does not give all the answers. But it helps us think about the questions. It challenges us to think deeply about our actions, reminding us that in many respects life is an inward journey. The ancient Greek philosophers believed that self-knowledge is the highest end: "The unexamined life is not worth living," they told us. It is easy to assume that you know quite a bit about your own life. But in fact, a feeling of being adrift in the world can be in no small measure the result of failing to live by the ancients' dictum: "Know thyself." Knowing yourself takes effort, and for that reason we prize it highly enough to place it in that category of knowledge we call wisdom.

For many people, however, such wisdom about one's self can never be enough. They seek not only knowledge of the self but also knowledge of God's will. For them, answers to the most important questions come through faith, through revelation, not reason. So in this chapter we also find stories about how faith can guide us on life's journey. Here we see people who draw strength from above, trusting in God for help in the large and small tasks of life. We see them living in readiness to answer God's call, and finding direction by seeking ways to serve Him. And we see them discovering answers to the question "Why am I here?" by serving their fellow man, by helping others along life's way according to the dictates of their faith.

Because this is the final chapter, we also find here two or three selections about approaching the end of life. Wisdom and faith can help us face our mortality. This section does not deal predominately with death, however, because even though death may be the end of life, it is neither its purpose nor its meaning. Life in one sense is indeed a journey from the cradle to the grave, but in a more important respect, it is a journey of understanding one's self, one's fellow creatures, and God's will.

And in this sense, courage and compassion and honesty and loyalty and all the other virtues can make the difference. They can be *the* difference. They can be a destination, because *how* we journey is more important than how far we manage to go. As Samuel Johnson said, "Life, like every other blessing, derives its value from its use alone. Not for itself, but for a nobler end the eternal gave it; and that end is virtue." At the end, we may discover that those things we call virtues are among the very reasons we find ourselves here. They are not just means; very frequently they are the ends themselves. And when they become what we live by, our own actions turn out to be some of the best answers to those great questions of life.

THE SEED

He who sows trusts in God.

One warm autumn day a little girl dropped a seed into a hole in the ground, covered it up, and waited for her flower to grow.

But before long the winter snows arrived, and left a thick white blanket all over the ground. And the poor seed could not grow at all.

After waiting patiently for weeks and months, the little girl peeked outside her door and said, "Now, seed, hurry and grow, grow, grow, until you have a tall stem covered with pretty green leaves and big yellow blossoms."

But the seed answered, "I am still icy and cold. You must ask someone else."

"Who?" asked the little girl.

"The hard ground whose bed I lie in," said the seed.

"I will!" cried the little girl. "Ground, ground, won't you grow soft, so my little seed can be warm, and grow into a flower?"

But the ground answered, "You must ask someone else."

"Who?" asked the little girl.

"The snow who covers me," said the ground.

"I will!" cried the little girl. "Snow, snow, won't you melt away, so the ground can grow soft, and my little seed can be warm, and grow into a flower?"

But the snow answered, "You must ask someone else."

"Who?" asked the little girl.

"The sun that melts me," said the snow.

"I will!" cried the little girl. "Sun, sun, won't you come out, so the snow will melt, and the ground can grow soft, and my little seed can be warm, and grow into a flower?"

But the sun answered, "You must ask someone else."

"Who?" asked the little girl.

"The clouds that cover me," said the sun.

"I will!" cried the little girl. "Clouds, clouds, won't you go away, so the sun can come out, and the snow will melt, and the ground can grow soft, and my little seed can be warm, and grow into a flower?"

But the clouds answered, "You must ask someone else."

"Who?" asked the little girl.

"The wind that blows us," said the clouds.

"I will!" cried the little girl. "Wind, wind, won't you blow, so the clouds will go away, and the sun can come out, and the snow can melt, and the ground can grow soft, and my little seed can be warm, and grow into a flower?"

But the wind whispered in her ear, "You must ask someone else."

"Who?" asked the little girl.

"God, who makes all things grow," said the wind.

"I will!" cried the little girl. "I should have thought of that."

So she got down on her knees, and folded her hands, and prayed.

"God," she prayed, "won't you tell the wind to blow, so the clouds will go away, and the sun can come out, and the snow can melt, and the ground can grow soft, and my little seed can be warm, and grow into a flower?"

And God smiled down on the little girl.

She looked out her door again. A warm breeze played in the air. The clouds were gone, the sun was shining, the snow was melting, and the ground was turning soft and green.

And before long her flower came up.

•

THE LITTLE LOST LAMB

Everyone counts in God's eyes. This story is based on Luke 15:3–7.

The mother sheep loved her little lamb just as your mother loves you.

It was a wee little lamb with a thin coat of wool and slender legs. At night it slept in the sheepfold close to its mother's warm fleece. All day long it nibbled grass, and drank from a running stream, and played in the meadow.

"Take care of my lamb," the mother sheep tried to say to the shepherd of the flock. "It is too little and weak to take care of itself."

The shepherd understood, and he watched over the little lamb although there were a hundred sheep in his flock.

He was a good shepherd or he would not have been able to care for them all. Every morning he opened the gate of the fold and they crowded out. Then he led them up a hill to a green meadow where he watched them all day. There were wolves in the mountains close by, watching for a chance to kill the little lambs. The shepherd kept the wolves away.

When the sun began to drop down behind the hill, the shepherd led his flock home to the fold. And before he closed the gate, he always counted the flock to see if there were a hundred sheep.

A storm in high places is very terrible. There was a storm with wind, and cold rain, and fire in the sky one day. The mother sheep was too frightened to know which way to go. She followed the other sheep, who pushed and almost crushed each other as they ran down the hill. But the shepherd led them all gently, pointing the way with his crook. He called them by the names he had given them. He went first to keep the storm from beating them back until they knew they were safe, for the sheepfold was in sight.

As they went through the gate, one by one, he counted them.

There were only ninety-nine.

Then the shepherd looked down into the pleading eyes of the mother sheep. She was trying to tell him that her little lamb was lost in the storm.

If he had not been a good shepherd, he might have thought

that so little a lamb was no great loss. But he thought only about how cold the lamb must be with its thin fleece, out in the storm. He remembered that, above the storm, he had heard the howling of wolves.

So the good shepherd went out in the wind and rain to find the little lamb.

It had grown so dark that he could hardly see. The wind was cold, the rain soaked his cloak, and the stones cut his feet. Another shepherd would have turned back. But the good shepherd could see, through the storm, the sorrowful eyes of the little lamb's mother. So he went on until he found the little lost lamb, lying so cold and frightened beside the road.

The shepherd took the lamb in his arms. It was too cold to walk home. All the way back he carried it, just as carefully as your mother carried you when you were a baby. He was very happy when he reached the sheepfold and gave it back to its mother. He asked his neighbors to come and be glad with him because not even one lamb was lost from the flock.

They wondered a little that the shepherd was so glad.

"Ninety-nine is almost a hundred," they said. "What difference would one little lamb have made in so large a flock?"

The good shepherd knew. The little lamb who was lost was one of his sheep, and he loved them all.

●

SAMUEL IN THE TEMPLE
Retold from 1 Samuel 3:1–21

Samuel's simple words to God—"Speak, for thy servant heareth" —remind us that if we live to do the Lord's will, then we must live in readiness to answer his call. This beautiful story comes from the first book of Samuel in the Bible.

Once upon a time, a long while ago, when wonderful things used to happen, there was a man named Elkanah and his wife, Hannah, who lived in the hill country of Ephraim.

Hannah loved children very much indeed. But she had no little children of her own, although she wanted one very much.

Those were the days when people were beginning to learn that all good things are given by the Heavenly Father. Hannah knew this, too, and while she worked she prayed that God would give her a little child. After she had made this prayer many times, God answered it. A little boy was born to Elkanah and Hannah. They named him Samuel, which means "name of God," because he had come in answer to his mother's prayer.

As Samuel grew from a baby to a little boy, good and strong and a comfort to his father and mother, Hannah thought a great deal about what he should do and be when he grew up. Every year Elkanah and Hannah made a journey to the temple, where the old priest Eli was, to make an offering to the Lord. When Samuel was grown and it drew near time to go again to the temple, Hannah said to herself: "For this child I prayed, and the Lord hath given me my petition which I asked of him. I will bring him that he may appear before the Lord forever."

So Hannah took Samuel, who was still only a little boy, to the temple, and gave him to the old priest Eli to be his helper in the house of the Lord. Although Hannah loved little Samuel very much, she knew that the best thing he could do would be to serve Eli there in the temple.

It was a very great, still place, this temple. It was different from the white house in the hills with vines and flowering trees around it that had been Samuel's home. His father and mother left him, after they had made their offering of three bullocks and some meal and the juice of the grape. Samuel never saw his mother, Hannah, again, except once a year when she came to bring him a new little robe to wear. The linen of this she had spun and woven with her own hands. And there was no other child there with Samuel.

The priest Eli became very old. His own sons had left him, and Samuel found a great deal to do to help him. At last there came a time when Eli's eyes grew so dim that he was not able to see whether the lamp that was always kept lighted in the temple, night and day, was burning or not. So Samuel kept watch of the lamp, and slept, every night, in the great, dim temple.

It was a very lonely, cold place for a little boy to stay alone at night. The tall stone pillars cast long shadows on the floor, which trembled, and moved, and seemed almost alive. Samuel could be very brave and not miss his mother too much in the daytime, when the sun shone and everything was bright. But at night he was like any other little boy. Samuel was afraid of the dark, and it seemed to him that he could not stay, all by himself, there in the temple.

. . .

One night as Samuel lay in the dark of the temple, but not sleeping, because he was afraid, he was suddenly startled to hear a voice calling to him.

"Samuel, Samuel," called the voice.

"Here am I!" Samuel answered. He jumped up, ran in to Eli, and said, "Here am I, for you called me."

But Eli said, "I did not call you, Samuel. Lie down again."

So Samuel went and lay down, but soon he heard the voice again, calling to him.

"Samuel, Samuel!"

So Samuel ran again to Eli and awoke him, and said, "Here am I. You called me."

But Eli said, "I called you not, my son. Lie down again."

Now Samuel did not yet know the voice of the Lord, or he might not have been so afraid. He went back into the dark temple and lay down, and tried to go to sleep for the third time. But a third time he heard the voice calling to him, "Samuel, Samuel!"

"Eli, Eli, here I am. You did call me!" he cried, as he ran again into the old priest's room. And now Eli understood that it had been the voice of God speaking to Samuel. So he said to the little boy: "Go, lie down, and it shall be, if He call thee, that thou shalt say, 'Speak, Lord, for Thy servant heareth.'" So Samuel went and lay down in his place.

And the Lord came, and stood, and called as at other times, "Samuel, Samuel." Then Samuel answered, bravely, as Eli had told him to, "Speak, for Thy servant heareth." And the Lord talked to Samuel a long time in the temple, telling him true and wonderful things.

Samuel listened, and understood. After the voice had stopped speaking, he felt comforted, and no longer afraid or lonely. He knew then that he was never alone, for his Heavenly Father was with him, even in the dark. So he slept without any fear until it was morning, and time to open the doors of the house of the Lord.

And Samuel grew, and the Lord always spoke with him, and all Israel knew that Samuel was established to be a prophet of their God.

•

BABOUSCKA

Edith M. Thomas

Like the story of Samuel in the temple, this touching old legend from Russia reminds us that with faith, as with other virtues, readiness is all. Faith entails seizing the chance to serve God when an opportunity presents itself.

The tradition of Babouscka leaving presents in the houses of good children on Christmas Eve is an old one in Russia.

> Babouscka sits before the fire,
>   Upon a winter's night,
> The driving winds heap up the snow,
>   Her hut is snug and tight;
> The howling winds, they only make
>   Babouscka's fire more bright!
>
> She hears a knocking at the door,
>   So late—who can it be?
> She hastes to lift the wooden latch
>   (No thought of fear has she):
> The wind-blown candle in her hand
>   Shines out on strangers three.
>
> Their beards are white with age, and snow
>   That in the darkness flies;
> Their floating locks are long and white,
>   But kindly are the eyes
> That sparkle underneath their brows,
>   Like stars in frosty skies.
>
> "Babouscka, we have come from far;
>   We tarry but to say,
> A little Prince is born this night
>   Who all the world shall sway.
> Come join the search; come, go with us
>   Who go these gifts to pay."

Babouscka shivers at the door:
  "I would I might behold
The little Prince who shall be King;
  But ah, the night is cold,
The wind so fierce, the snow so deep,
  And I, good sirs, am old!"

The strangers three, no word they speak,
  But fade in snowy space—
Babouscka sits before the fire,
  And looks with wistful face:
"I wish that I had questioned them,
  So I the way might trace!

"When morning comes, with blessed light,
  I'll early be awake.
My staff in hand, I'll go—perchance,
  Those strangers overtake.
And for the Child, some little toys
  I'll carry for His sake."

The morning came, and, staff in hand,
  She wandered in the snow:
And asked the way of all she met,
  But none the way could show.
"It must be farther yet," she sighed,
  "Then farther will I go."

And still 'tis said, on Christmas Eve,
  When high the drifts are piled,
With staff and basket on her arm,
  Babouscka seeks the Child.
At every door her face is seen—
  Her wistful face and mild!

At every door her gifts she leaves,
  And bends, and murmurs low,
Above each little face half hid
  By pillows white as snow:
"And is *He* here?"—then softly sighs:
  "Nay, farther must I go!"

•

THE SILVER CROWN
Adapted from Laura E. Richards

In this story we find that we make our own crown as we make our way through life.

"And shall I be a king?" asked the child, "and shall I wear a crown?"

"You shall surely wear a crown," said the Angel, "and a kingdom is waiting for you."

"Oh, joy!" said the child. "But tell me, how will it come about? For now I am only a little child, and the crown would hardly stay on my curls."

"That I may not tell," said the Angel. "Only ride and run your best, for the way is long to your kingdom, and the time short."

So the child rode and ran his best, crossing hills and valleys, broad streams and foaming torrents. Here and there he saw people at work or at play, and on these he looked eagerly.

"Perhaps, when they see me," he said, "they will run to meet me, and will crown me with a golden crown, and lead me to their palace and throne me there as king!"

But the folk were all busy with their tasks or their sport, and none heeded him, or left their business for him; and still he must fare forward alone.

Also, he came upon many travelers like himself, some coming toward him, others passing him by. On these, too, he looked earnestly, and would stop now one, now another, and question him.

"Do you know," he asked, "of any kingdom in these parts where the crown is ready and the folk wait for a king?"

Then one would laugh, and another weep, and another jeer, but all alike shook their heads.

"I am seeking crown and kingdom for myself," cried one. "Is it likely that I can be finding one for you, too?"

Another said: "You seek in vain. There are no crowns, only fools' caps with asses' ears and bells that jingle in them."

But others who had been longest on the way only looked on him, some sadly, some kindly, and made no answer. And still he fared onward.

Now and then he stopped to help some poor soul who had fallen into trouble, and when he did that the way lightened before him, and he felt the heart light within him. But at other times the hurry was strong on him, so that he would turn away his face, and shut his ears to the cries that rang in them; and when he did that, the way darkened, and oftentimes he stumbled himself, and fell into pits and quagmires, and must cry for help, sometimes on those to whom he had refused it.

By and by he forgot about the crown and the kingdom; or if he thought of them, it was but as a far-off dream of dim gold, such as one sees at morning when the sun breaks through the mist. But still he knew that the way was long and the time short, and still he rode and ran his best.

At last he was no longer a child, but an old and weary man. Just when his feet could carry him no farther, he looked up and saw that the way came to an end before him, and there was a gate and one in white sitting by it who beckoned to him. Trembling, yet glad, the old man drew near, and knew the Angel who had spoken to him at the beginning.

"Welcome!" said the Angel. "You come in good time."

"I came as fast as I could," said the man, "but many things hindered me, and now I am weary, and can go no farther."

"But what did you find on the way?" asked the Angel.

"Oh! I found joy and sorrow," said the man, "a good measure of both, but never a crown, such as you promised me, and never a kingdom."

"But look," said the Angel. "You are wearing your crown. It is of the purest silver and shines like white frost. And as for your kingdom, the name of it is Heaven and here is the entrance to it."

•

THE LEGEND OF SAINT CHRISTOPHER

*Adapted from retellings by
Eleanor Broadus and Peggy Webling*

Shakespeare wrote: "It is excellent to have a giant's strength, but it is tyrannous to use it like a giant." This old legend about Saint Christopher, the patron saint of travelers, reminds us that we should use our God-given strengths in the service of God and our fellow travelers in life.

Long ago there lived a man who was so tall and strong he seemed like a giant. He could lift almost any weight, and people gave him the name Offero, which meant "the Bearer." Offero was proud of his strength, and it is perhaps not strange that he made up his mind to serve no one but the mightiest ruler in the world.

"I, Offero, do swear to be servant to only the greatest king on earth," he vowed, "and I will serve him all the days of my life."

Then he set out on his quest, passing through kingdom after kingdom in search of the most powerful of all monarchs. He wandered through forests, crushing with his strong arms the wild beasts that attacked him. He uprooted great trees and threw them across deep, swift streams, and over these rude bridges he passed into lands lying farther and farther away. He crossed seas with merchants in their vessels, and passed over deserts with slow caravans, and trudged alone down the highways of the world.

At last he heard of a king whom all believed the richest in the world. He went to him to offer his services.

"Great monarch!" said Offero, towering before the throne, "I have sworn to serve only the most powerful king. Will you accept me?"

The king, admiring the stranger's giant form and fearless gaze, welcomed him and placed him beside the throne. There Offero stood day after day, amidst his sovereign's gold and treasures, rejoicing in a master worthy of his strength.

But one day a stranger from another land came to the court. He stood before the throne and spoke with fiery zeal in words Offero could not understand. As the stranger turned to leave, Offero saw his monarch cowering in his high seat.

"Great king," he cried, "this man has come here with strange words on his lips, and you tremble before him. Why? I could kill him with one blow of my hand."

"I tremble because of the news he brings me," the king cried. "He speaks of another king, an ancient enemy of mine, who even now approaches my land with a vast army."

"If you are afraid of him, he must be more powerful than you," Offero said scornfully. "I must find him, for I have sworn to serve only the greatest of kings."

So Offero set out to find this new master. He traveled many

days until, coming to the top of a bleak mountain, he saw a wide, dark valley opening before him. Through this valley marched a mighty army; rank after rank filed along with glittering weapons and bloodstained banners. In the rear, surrounded by men in fierce armor, rode a warrior in a heavy chariot. On his head was a crown of jewels that gleamed like fire.

Offero walked boldly down the mountainside and presented himself to the commander of the host.

"I have traveled many miles to enter your service," he said, "because you are the strongest of all kings, and I will serve none but the mightiest."

This terrible king gladly accepted Offero's services and put his strength to work at once. The vast army marched forward, destroying whole peoples and leaving lands barren and burned. Always Offero fought in the front ranks. His heart sank to be in the company of such a bloody master, but he had vowed to serve only the greatest monarch. And certainly no people could stand against this cruel king, who subdued all with terror and bloodshed.

Then one day the warrior king was wounded in battle, and as he lay bleeding a shadow of fear passed across his face.

"What is it you fear?" Offero asked.

"The Prince of Evil," answered the pale king. "I fear he will seize my soul. He calls me in whirlwinds, in the thunder and darkness."

Offero watched the king with wonder. "You are a child to fear storms," he said.

"No," whispered the king, "in spite of your great body, it is you who are a child. You do not understand these things. Even you, with your great strength, must fear Satan."

"My heart knows no fear," Offero said. "Farewell, oh fainthearted king. I pass on to seek this one who is mightier than you."

He strode away, seeking the Prince of Evil.

The following day, when the sun was high in the heavens, Offero found himself in the depths of a great forest. It was almost black with the branches of the trees overhead, and the earth was cold underfoot. There, on a great stone, sat a shadow. It was the Evil One.

"I seek the one who rules the world," Offero announced boldly.

"Good!" laughed Satan. "You have found him. Come with me, and I will keep you busy."

It was not pleasant work. It meant that every minute was spent in making trouble for other people. But Offero did as he was told, because everyone they met was afraid of Satan, and he believed he was serving the strongest of kings at last.

But one day, as they traveled along, they came in sight of a small, rough-hewn cross by the side of the road. At once Satan left the path and went a long way around, over rocks and through bushes, and at last came back to the road with the cross well behind him.

"Why did you do that?" asked Offero, for although Satan often took roundabout paths, he had never before made so much trouble for himself.

"I do not like to go near the cross," Satan admitted. "I fear Him whose sign it is."

Offero's heart leapt with joy.

"What is his name?" he demanded.

"I dare not say his name," Satan answered, trembling. "But some call him the Prince of Peace."

"If you fear him, he must be stronger than you," Offero said. "I will leave you and serve him."

Once again he set off in search of this new master. He traveled far, for he did not know the way, but hope and courage never failed him. At last he found a man, an ancient hermit, who looked as if he might know how to find the Prince of Peace. Offero told him his story.

"I will serve him, if I can find him," he told the old man. "Where is he? I will kill all his enemies, if he wishes."

"Be not in haste," the hermit said quietly. "You are through with killing now. This king differs from all others. I will show you how to serve him."

He led Offero to the bank of a swift, wide river.

"Here many travelers have lost their lives, for no boat can live in its waters," he said. "If you will stand here on the bank, and carry people across, you will be serving the Prince of Peace. He will know of your service, and in time you will see him."

So Offero built a hut beside the river, and cut a mighty staff to guide his feet among the sunken rocks, and waited for the coming of travelers. They found him always at the door of his hut, ready to carry them across on his broad shoulders. Many a weary soul would have perished without his aid. Month after month, year after year, in summer heat and winter frost he labored. It seemed strange to him that he should be serving his king this way. Sometimes he would sigh and wonder if the Prince of Peace really knew of his service. But the people he helped became his friends, and he was no longer lonely as he had always been before.

One night, when the cold winds were howling around his little hut, Offero lay down to sleep. No traveler, he knew, would seek his help to ford the stream in such a storm.

He heard the beat of rain and the rising tide.

As he was sinking into sleep there came the sound of a voice outside.

"Offero! Rise and bear me over the river!"

The strong man sprang up. He opened his door, curious to see the traveler who dared to cross on such a night.

He peered into the darkness, but there was no one there.

"I must have fallen into a dream," he thought, and once more shut out the wind and rain before stretching himself on the ground.

"Offero! Rise and bear me over the river!"

The voice was louder this time. The words sprang out, like a deep bell, through the howling blast.

Offero stood at his door wondering. He was all alone. The sky was black with clouds. He heard the rushing river and the dull murmur of thunder in the far distance.

For the second time, amazed by the echo of the ringing voice in his heart, he went into his hut and closed the door. This time he did not lie down but waited.

"Offero! Rise and bear me over the river!"

The giant leapt into the night and saw, standing on the river-bank below him, the figure of a child.

Offero's wonder changed to doubt. He knew well the dangers of the river at flood. But three times the child had called upon him. The child was waiting for him now. So he lifted the boy upon his shoulders, grasped his tall staff in his right hand, and slowly, cautiously, boldly, stepped down into the waters.

The current was swifter, the waves higher than ever before. He felt the stones slipping beneath his feet. The stormclouds burst over his head in torrents of blinding rain.

The weight of the child was much greater than he had expected, and it grew even greater with every step. Offero's broad shoulders ached and drooped, but he pressed forward, every muscle taut.

The waters were swirling as high as his waist, breaking against his chest, splashing his face, rushing through his hair. His back ached beneath the weight on his shoulders. His huge staff bent under his hand like a reed. All around him, giant trees, uprooted from the banks, came whirling and crashing downstream. The skies were emptied of rain, but lightning flashed unceasingly and thunder roared over his head.

Onward and onward he struggled, gasping and shaking the water from his face. At last he staggered up the opposite bank, and gently lifted the child from his shoulders.

"Who are you, my child?" he panted. "It seemed as if I were carrying the weight of the whole world!

"Do you not know me?" the sweet voice answered. "I am He you have promised to serve. Did you not know that in this humble, hard work of aiding so many weary travelers, you were serving Me all along? And from now on you will be called not Offero, the Bearer, but Christopher, the Christ-bearer, for I have accepted you as my faithful servant."

And Christopher fell to his feet and worshipped in silence. When he opened his eyes, he was alone by the river.

He rose, and picked up his staff, and found it had blossomed with leaves and flowers. Then he went back to his holy work of serving men for the rest of his days.

•

THE WIDOW'S MITES

Retold by Frances M. Dadmun

To a large extent, living well entails giving well—a giving of some portion of your time, or talent, or money, or all three. This story from Luke 21:1–4 in the Bible shows us that the value of giving lies not simply in the amount given but in the sacrifice it requires and the love that prompts it.

It was one morning during Passover week, and Jesus and his disciples were sitting in a court of the great temple at Jerusalem. They were watching the people as they passed by. Many of them were rich men. You could tell this from their clothes and from the way they walked with their chins in the air.

Fastened to columns that supported the roof were trumpet-shaped boxes where people put their offerings for the temple. Jesus noticed that the richly dressed people threw in a good deal of money, which rattled noisily as it fell into the boxes. Everyone else noticed it too—they couldn't help it. Probably they thought how generous the givers were and wished they had more money themselves to give away. But Jesus saw something else which other people overlooked—a thin-faced, poorly dressed widow, who stepped shyly up to a box and dropped in two mites, the smallest coin the Jews had. Jesus saw also that she had no more to give— her pocket was empty. She looked hurriedly about her, for fear someone might have seen how little she could give, but she need not have been troubled. Her coins were too small to make a noise, and her dress was so poor that no one cared what she might do. It was the rich people whom the crowd admired.

Jesus looked about for his disciples, but they were watching the rich men, too. It all seemed very wonderful to the disciples after their simple country homes. So Jesus had to call their attention to the poor widow. And he said, "This poor widow gave more than all the rest; for they gave only a part while she gave all she had."

Then the disciples forgot to watch the rich men, who did not seem interesting anymore. But they looked reverently after the poor widow until she slipped through the crowd and was gone.

•

THE BOY AND THE ANGEL

Retold by Joel H. Metcalf

"All service ranks the same with God," the poet Robert Browning wrote. This unusual and touching story is based on a poem by Browning.

Theocrite, though only a little boy, nevertheless had to earn his living. His days were long and his work was hard, but his spirit was dauntless and he was forever singing, "Praise God." Morning, noon, and night he sang at his work, and this brought joy to his own heart and to the hearts of those with whom he lived and worked. And it brought joy to the heart of God, who heard him from on high.

One day, as he was singing at his work, a monk passed by, and, touched by his song's sweetness and charm, came in, and said: "Well done, my son. I do not doubt your praise is heard by God as well as if thou wert Pope of Rome and in St. Peter's Church singing the glad songs of praise at Easter time."

Theocrite was happy in his work, but, at the suggestion of singing in the cathedral of St. Peter's, he said, "Would to God that I might praise him in the great St. Peter's before I die!"

The angel Gabriel heard his pious wish, and the next day Theocrite was gone, for the angel had started him on the way to become nothing less than the Pope of Rome.

But immediately God said, "How is it I do not hear the voice of Theocrite singing at his work?"

Then the angel Gabriel left the heavenly sphere and became a boy like Theocrite, taking his place as well as he could. The boy's work he could easily do, and he tried to sing his song of praise. But he could not.

God said: "I hear a voice of praise, but in it there is no doubt and fear, like that of the song of Theocrite. I miss my little human praise."

Then the angel Gabriel cast off his disguise. No man can fill another's place, and even the angel found that he could not entirely fill the place of a little boy with curls.

And so he went to Rome at the Easter-tide, where the new

Pope, Theocrite, was about to praise God in the great way, and said: "I took thee from thy trade, and made thee pope of Rome, but it was all a mistake. I did not do well. Thou couldst be a great pope, but no one can take thy place in the old home.

"I have tried to take thy place. I left my angel sphere to do thy work.

"Thy voice seemed to me weak, but, alas! when it stopped, I could not take up thy song. God was not satisfied.

"All the songs of praise rise as a wondrous chorus to the ear of God, but without you the great chorus was incomplete, and He missed your little voice of praise.

"Therefore, come back with me to your old cell and your old work—come back to your boyhood and sing again your song, 'Praise God.'"

And so Theocrite grew old at home. He never sang the praises of God "the great way" in St. Peter's at Rome; but when he and the new pope came to die, they went to heaven, side by side.

•

A LATE BLOOMER

For some people, finding a mission in life proves a long struggle.
This tale from Mexico assures us that we will find our work if we
keep looking.

A cactus stood all alone in the desert, wondering why it was stuck in the middle of nowhere.

"I do nothing but stand here all day," it sighed. "What use am I? I'm the ugliest plant in the desert. My spines are thin and prickly, my leaves are rubbery and tough, my skin is thick and bumpy. I can't offer shade or juicy fruit to any passing traveler. I don't see that I'm any use at all."

All it did was stand in the sun day after day, growing taller and fatter. Its spines grew longer and its leaves tougher, and it swelled here and there until it was lumpy and lopsided all over. It truly was strange-looking.

"I wish I could do something useful," it sighed.

By day the hawks circled high overhead.

"What can I do with my life?" the cactus called. Whether they heard or not, the hawks sailed away.

At night the moon floated into the sky and cast its pale glow on the desert floor.

"What good can I do with my life?" the cactus called. The moon only stared coldly as it mounted its course.

A lizard crawled by, leaving a little trail in the sand with its tail.

"What worthy deed can I do?" the cactus called.

"You?" the lizard laughed, pausing a moment. "Worthy deed? Why, you can't do anything! The hawks circle way overhead, tracing delicate patterns for us all to admire. The moon hangs high like a lantern at night, so we can see our ways home to our loved ones. Even I, the lowly lizard, have something to do. I decorate the sands with these beautiful brushstrokes as I pull my tail along. But you? You do nothing but get uglier every day."

And so it went on, year after year. At last the cactus grew old, and it knew its time was short.

"Oh, Lord," it cried out, "I've wondered so long, and I've tried so hard. Forgive me if I've failed to find something worthy to do. I fear that now it's too late."

But just then the cactus felt a strange stirring and unfolding, and it knew a surge of joy that erased all despair. At its very tip, like a sudden crown, a glorious flower suddenly opened in bloom.

Never had the desert known such a blossom. Its fragrance perfumed the air far and wide and brought happiness to all passing by. The butterflies paused to admire its beauty, and that night even the moon smiled when it rose to find such a treasure.

The cactus heard a voice.

"You have waited long," the Lord said. "The heart that seeks to do good reflects my glory, and will always bring something worthwhile to the world, something in which all can rejoice—even if for only a moment."

•

HOW THE WISE MAN FOUND
THE KING

*Retold by Christine Chaundler
and Eric Wood*

In this old legend we see that there are many ways to serve God,
countless opportunities to give him thanks and praise.

When Christ was born in Bethlehem, three kings set out from
their homes to find Him and worship Him. They had seen a wonderful new star in the eastern countries where they lived, and they
knew that it meant that a great King was born—a King whose
kingdom would never come to an end, who was mightier than the
sun and greater than the stars—a King who was the Lord of earth
and sky and sea.

These three kings had studied old books and prophecies, and
they knew that God had promised to send this mighty King into the
world one day, and when they saw the star they rejoiced with
exceeding great joy. And gathering together all the richest treasures
they possessed, gold and frankincense and myrrh, they set out at
once to follow the guiding of the star until it led them at last to the
lowly cattle shed where the Holy Child lay.

But in the country they had left there was another king. He too
had studied the old prophecies with his brother-kings, and he too
was waiting for some sign to tell him that the Saviour of the world
had come. Something had happened to delay him when at last the
star brought the glad tidings of Christ's birth. He was not ready to
start with the other wise men, and so he was left behind. And when
he had gathered together his treasures and was ready to set out
upon his journey, he was too late to follow the star that was guiding
the others, and so he was obliged to find his own way as best he
could across the world.

He had brought with him three jewels to give to the great King
whom he was going to worship. One of them was a ruby, as red as
the last rays of the setting sun. One was a sapphire, holding in its
depths all the blue in sea and sky. And the third was a pearl, as pure
and white as the peak of a snow-clad mountain. No money in the
world was enough to buy these precious gems, so valuable were

they; yet the king was ready to give them all to the God whom he was seeking.

For many long months he travelled, asking wherever he went for tidings of the other three kings. He could not catch them; they were too far ahead for that. But by inquiring diligently of everybody he met the king managed to keep more or less upon their track.

It was a long journey and a very weary one, and the dangers and difficulties through which the other wise men had passed were ten times greater for him, all alone and unattended as he was. But his longing to reach the Christ-Child and to bow himself down in worship before Him spurred the king on. With his three jewels hidden in his bosom he rode bravely through all the dangers and surmounted all the difficulties, until at last he arrived in Judea, and knew that he could not be far from his goal.

As he rode through the country he heard on every side sounds of mourning and distress. Cruel Herod, frightened at what the wise men had said of the King who was born in Bethlehem, had determined to find and kill the Holy Child, lest when He grew older He should try to snatch the throne of Israel from him. So he had told the three wise men to come and tell him when they had found the Messiah, that he also might come and worship Him. But God had warned the wise men in a dream, and they had returned to their country by another way.

When Herod found that the wise men had returned to their own country by another way, and did not mean to come and tell him where Christ was hidden, he sent forth an order that all the children in that part of the country under two years of age were to be killed. And the rough soldiers had gone out and, tearing the children from their mothers' arms, had killed them ruthlessly.

But there was one Child they did not kill—the one of all others that they wanted. Joseph had been warned by God in a dream, and taking the young Child and His mother, had fled with them into Egypt. And there the little family lived for many years, until Herod was dead, and it was safe for them to return to their own land again.

So when the wise man who was too late arrived at last at Bethlehem, he found that the King of the Jews whom he had come so far to worship was there no longer. He had gone, no man knew where.

The wise man was at first in despair. He had come so far and dared so much, and now it seemed that he would never be able to offer his gifts to the King after all. Then he took heart again. Since he had come so far, what did a little farther matter? He had set out to worship the King, and he would travel through the world, if need be, until at last he found Him.

So he rode bravely on again.

He had not gone very far when he heard a woman screaming, crying bitterly for help. The king hurried to the place from where the sound came, and there he saw a poor mother witn a little baby in her arms, whom a cruel soldier was trying to take from her and kill. The mother had hidden the little one safely all through the terrible massacre, and now, when she thought the danger was past, this soldier had found the child and, in spite of her prayers and cries, was about to kill it.

The king spurred forward and sprang to the ground beside the poor woman, begging the soldier to spare the little one's life. But the soldier only laughed roughly, and said that it was his duty, he must do his duty whatever happened. And again he tried to snatch the child from the woman's arms.

Then the king drew from his bosom the ruby which he was carrying to Christ. He uncovered the jewel and flashed it before the man's astonished gaze.

"I will give you this if you will spare the child's life," he said.

The soldier fixed his eyes upon the wonderful jewel, and the temptation was too great for him. He let the child and its mother go unharmed, and he himself went away with the ruby in his possession, rich beyond anything he had ever dreamed or hoped to be.

Then, a little sadly, the king rode on. He had no ruby now to offer to the Christ-Child when he found Him. Still, there were the other two jewels left. He need not be ashamed of his gifts even now, and he went on his way with renewed courage.

After many more weary months of travelling he came to a place where there was a terrible famine. The poor people were dying of sickness and hunger. They had no one to help them, and the king, overcome with pity, parted with his second jewel in order to buy food for the starving, care and comfort for the sick, and clothes and raiment for the naked. He stayed in the famine-stricken place until he had done all that he could for the poor, starving people. Then he rode on again, poorer by the loss of his jewel, but rich with the blessings of those whom he had saved from death and misery.

Now the wise man had only the pearl left of all his costly offerings with which he had started on his journey. He did not regret the loss of the other two gems, for he knew that if he had

had the choice over again he would still have parted with them. Only he wished, so very, very much, that he had more treasures to offer to the King.

But the pearl that was left was of even greater value than the other two jewels, and although he longed for it to be a thousand times rarer and more precious, yet he knew that it was a present fit for a king, even for the King of all the earth. And so he rode on, still seeking the Christ-Child.

Long years passed away, and the king still journeyed on, seeking the Saviour, yet never finding Him. After many years he came to a place where a poor slave girl was to be sold to a brutal master. The king tried to persuade the master to let the girl go free. But the man only laughed at him, and at last the king, finding that words were of no avail, and determined to save the poor, trembling girl from the dreadful life ahead of her, drew forth his last remaining jewel and bought the girl's freedom with the precious pearl, though it went to his heart to give it away.

Then once more he started on his search, grieving that he had now no present at all to bring to the King, yet determined never to give up his quest until he had found the Lord for whom he had looked so long and faithfully.

Thirty-three years he wandered through the world, until at last, old and worn and dying, he reached Jerusalem on the very day of Our Lord's crucifixion. And there, on the Cross of Calvary, he found the King for whom he had searched so long. In spite of the cross and the crown of thorns, in spite of the scornful, mocking words of those who stood around, the wise man recognized his Saviour, and he knew that he had reached the end of his journey at last. This was not the little Baby whom he had set out to seek such a long, long time ago, but still it was the King.

He pushed his way through the crowd and sank down, exhausted, and made the confession that he had come empty-handed. He had found the great King at last, but he had nothing at all to offer Him.

But had he nothing at all? Legend says that as he knelt at the foot of the cross, this man who had searched so faithfully and earnestly heard a heavenly voice come from afar—simple, tender words that filled his longing heart.

"Inasmuch as thou hast done it unto the least of these My brethren, thou hast done it unto Me."

And the wise man knew that his long, weary journey had not been in vain.

•

GOD WILL SEE

Flannery O'Connor wrote: "A work of art is good in itself. What is
good in itself glorifies God because it reflects God." This story
reminds us of who the really important audience is as we go about
our daily work.

Long ago in ancient Greece an aged sculptor was laboring over
a block of stone. He carved with utmost care, probing the rock with
his chisel, chipping away a fragment at a time, gauging the marks
with sinewy hands before making the next cut. When it was finished, the piece would be hoisted high into the air and set on top
of a towering shaft, and so would become the capital, or uppermost
part, of a column. And the column would help support the roof of
a lofty temple.

"Why spend so much time and effort on that section?" asked a
government official who passed by. "It will sit fifty feet high. No
human eye will be able to see those details."

The old artist put down his hammer and chisel, gazed steadily
at his questioner, and replied: "But God will see it!"

•

ROBERT OF SICILY

Retold by Sara Cone Bryant

Hopefully, as we get further along in life, we win some of the rewards of long, hard work—better jobs, higher offices, larger reputations, fatter paychecks. As we accumulate the trappings of success, this old tale may help us remember the lesson of Proverbs 16:18—"Pride goeth before destruction, and a haughty spirit before a fall." The story comes from the *Gesta Romanorum,* a collection of ancient tales compiled most probably in England in the early fourteenth century. It was a source mined for inspiration by many great writers, including Shakespeare and Chaucer.

An old legend says that there was once a king named Robert of Sicily, who was brother to the great Pope of Rome and to the Emperor of Allemaine. He was a very selfish king and very proud. He cared more for his pleasures than for the needs of his people, and his heart was so filled with his own greatness that he had no thought for God.

One day, this proud king was sitting in his place at church, at vesper service. His courtiers were about him, in their bright garments, and he himself was dressed in his royal robes. The choir was chanting the Latin service, and as the beautiful voices swelled louder, the king noticed one particular verse which seemed to be repeated again and again. He turned to a learned clerk at his side and asked what those words meant, for he knew no Latin.

"They mean, 'He hath put down the mighty from their seats, and hath exalted them of low degree,'" answered the clerk.

"It is well the words are in Latin, then," said the king angrily, "for they are a lie. There is no power on earth or in heaven that can put me down from my seat!" And he sneered at the beautiful singing, as he leaned back in his place.

Presently the king fell asleep, while the service went on. He slept deeply and long. When he awoke the church was dark and still, and he was all alone. He, the king, had been left alone in the church, to awake in the dark! He was furious with rage and surprise, and, stumbling through the dim aisles, he reached the great doors and beat at them, madly, shouting for his servants.

The old sexton heard someone shouting and pounding in the church, and thought it was some drunken vagabond who had stolen in during the service. He came to the door with his keys and called out, "Who is there?"

"Open! Open! It is I, the king!" came a hoarse, angry voice from within.

"It is a crazy man," thought the sexton, and he was frightened. He opened the doors carefully and stood back, peering into the darkness. Out past him rushed the figure of a man in scanty, tattered clothes, with unkempt hair and wild white face. The sexton did not know that he had ever seen him before, but he looked long after him, wondering at his wildness and his haste.

In his fluttering rags, without hat or cloak, not knowing what strange thing had happened to him, King Robert rushed to his palace gates, pushed aside the startled servants, and hurried, blind with rage, up the wide stair and through the great corridors, toward the room where he could hear the sound of his courtiers' voices. Men and women servants tried to stop the ragged man who had somehow gotten into the palace, but Robert did not even see them as he fled along. Straight to the open doors of the big banquet hall he made his way and into the midst of the grand feast there.

The great hall was filled with lights and flowers. The tables were set with everything that is delicate and rich to eat. The courtiers, in their gay clothes, were laughing and talking. And at the head of the feast, on the king's own throne, sat a king. His face, his figure, his voice were exactly like Robert of Sicily. No human being could have told the difference; no one dreamed that he was not the king. He was dressed in the king's royal robes, he wore the royal crown, and on his hand was the king's own ring. Robert of Sicily, half naked, ragged, without a sign of his kingship on him, stood before the throne and stared with fury at this figure of himself.

The king on the throne looked at him. "Who art thou, and what dost thou here?" he asked. And though his voice was just like Robert's own, it had something in it sweet and deep, like the sound of bells.

"I am the king!" cried Robert of Sicily. "I am the king, and you are an impostor!"

The courtiers started from their seats, and drew their swords. They would have killed the crazy man who insulted their king. But he raised his hand and stopped them, and with his eyes looking into Robert's eyes he said, "Not the king; you shall be the king's jester! You shall wear the cap and bells, and make laughter for my court. You shall be the servant of the servants, and your companion shall be the jester's ape."

With shouts of laughter, the courtiers drove Robert of Sicily from the banquet hall. The waiting-men, with laughter, too, pushed him into the soldiers' hall; and there the pages brought the jester's wretched ape, and put a fool's cap and bells on Robert's head. It was like a terrible dream. He could not believe it true. He could not understand what had happened to him. And when he woke next morning, he believed it was a dream, and that he was king again. But as he turned his head, he felt the coarse straw under his cheek instead of the soft pillow, and he saw that he was in the stable, with the shivering ape by his side. Robert of Sicily was a jester, and no one knew him for the king.

Three long years passed. Sicily was happy and all things went well under the king, who was not Robert. Robert was still the jester, and his heart became harder and more bitter with every year. Many times during the three years, the king who had his face and voice had called him to himself, when none else could hear, and had asked him the one question, "Who art thou?" And each time that he asked it his eyes looked into Robert's eyes, to find his heart. But each time Robert threw back his head and answered proudly, "I am the king!" And the king's eyes grew sad and stern.

At the end of three years, the Pope bade the Emperor of Allemaine and the King of Sicily, his brothers, to a great meeting in his city of Rome. The King of Sicily went, with all his soldiers and courtiers and servants—a great procession of horsemen and footmen. Never had there been a gayer sight than the grand train: men in bright armor, riders in wonderful cloaks of velvet and silk, servants carrying marvelous presents to the Pope. And at the very end rode Robert the jester. His horse was a poor old thing, many-colored, and the ape rode with him. Everyone in the villages through which they passed ran after the jester and pointed and laughed.

The Pope received his brothers and their trains in the square before Saint Peter's. With music and flags and flowers he made the King of Sicily welcome and greeted him as his brother. In the midst of it, the jester broke through the crowd and threw himself before the Pope. "Look at me!" he cried, "I am your brother, Robert of Sicily! This man is an impostor who has stolen my throne. I am Robert, the king!"

The Pope looked at the poor jester with pity, but the Emperor of Allemaine turned to the King of Sicily, and said, "Is it not rather dangerous, brother, to keep a madman as jester?" And again Robert was pushed back among the serving-men.

It was Holy Week, and the king and the emperor, with all their trains, went every day to the great services in the cathedral. Something wonderful and holy seemed to make all these services more beautiful than ever before. All the people of Rome felt it: it was as if the presence of an angel were there. Men thought of God and felt his blessing on them. But no one knew who it was that brought the beautiful feeling. And when Easter Day came, never had there been so lovely, so holy a day. In the great churches, filled with flowers, and sweet with incense, the kneeling people listened to the choirs singing, and it was like the voices of angels. Their prayers were more earnest than ever before, their praise more glad; there was something heavenly in Rome.

Robert of Sicily went to the services with the rest and sat in the humblest place with the servants. Over and over again he heard the sweet voices of the choirs chant the Latin words he had heard long ago: "He hath put down the mighty from their seat, and hath exalted them of low degree." And at last, as he listened, his heart was softened. He, too, felt the strange blessed presence of a heavenly power. He thought of God, and of his own wickedness; he remembered how happy he had been, and how little good he had done; he realized that his power had not been from himself at all. On Easter night, as he crept to his bed of straw, he wept, not because he was so wretched, but because he had not been a better king when power was his.

At last all the festivities were over, and the King of Sicily went home to his own land again with his people. Robert the jester came home too.

On the day of their homecoming, there was a special service in the royal church, and even after the service was over for the people, the monks held prayers of thanksgiving and praise. The sound of their singing came softly in at the palace windows. In the great banquet room, the king sat, wearing his royal robes and his crown, while many subjects came to greet him. At last, he sent them all away, saying he wanted to be alone; but he commanded the jester to stay. And when they were alone together the king looked into Robert's eyes, as he had done before, and said, softly, "Who art thou?"

Robert of Sicily bowed his head. "Thou knowest best," he said, "I only know that I have sinned."

As he spoke, he heard the voices of the monks singing, "He

hath put down the mighty from their seats"—and his head sank lower. But suddenly the music seemed to change. A wonderful light shone all about. As Robert raised his eyes, he saw the face of the king smiling at him with a radiance like nothing on earth, and as he sank to his knees before the glory of that smile, a voice sounded with the music, like a melody throbbing on a single string: "I am an angel, and thou art the king!"

Then Robert of Sicily was alone. His royal robes were upon him once more. He wore his crown and his royal ring. He was king. And when the courtiers came back they found their king kneeling by his throne, absorbed in silent prayer.

•

THE GOLDEN TRIPOD

Retold by James Baldwin

This story is about the Seven Sages of ancient Greece, seven famous rulers, legislators, and philosophers who lived between 620 and 550 B.C. It reminds us that the wiser we get, the more we recognize our own limitations.

Tripods were kettles standing on three legs. They were ordinary domestic utensils in ancient Greece, but they were also sometimes elaborately decorated as works of art. Homer mentions tripods as prizes awarded to victors in various contests.

One morning, long ago, a merchant of Miletus was walking along the seashore. Some fisherman were pulling in a large net, and he stopped to watch them.

"My good men," he said, "how many fish do you expect to draw in this time?"

"We cannot tell," they answered. "We never count our fish before they are caught."

The net seemed heavy. There was certainly something in it. The merchant felt sure that the fishermen were having a good haul.

"How much will you take for the fish that you are drawing in?" he asked.

"How much will you give?" said the fisherman.

"Well, I will give three pieces of silver for all that are in the net," answered the merchant.

The fishermen talked in low tones with one another for a little while, and then one said, "It's a bargain. Be they many or few, you may have all for three pieces of silver."

In a few minutes the big net was pulled up out of the water. There was not a fish in it. But it held a beautiful golden tripod that was worth more than a thousand fishes.

The merchant was delighted. "Here is your money," he said. "Give me the tripod."

"No, indeed," said the fishermen. "You were to have all the fish that happened to be in the net and nothing else. We didn't sell you the tripod."

They began to quarrel. They talked and wrangled a long time and could not agree. Then one of the fishermen said, "Let us ask the governor about it and do as he shall bid us."

"Yes, let us ask the governor," said the merchant. "Let him decide the matter for us."

So they carried the tripod to the governor, and each told his story.

The governor listened but could not make up his mind as to who was right.

"This is a very important question," he said. "We must send to Delphi and ask the oracle whether the tripod shall be given to the fishermen or to the merchant. Leave the tripod in my care until we get an answer."

Now the oracle at Delphi was supposed to be very wise. People from all parts of the world sent to it, to tell it their troubles and get its advice.

So the governor sent a messenger to Delphi to ask the oracle what should be done with the tripod. The merchant and the fishermen waited impatiently till the answer came. And this is what the oracle said:

> "Give not the merchant nor the fishermen the prize,
> But give it to that one who is wisest of the wise."

The governor was much pleased with this answer.

"The prize shall go to the man who deserves it most," he said. "There is our neighbor, Thales, whom everybody knows and loves. He is famous all over the world. Men come from every country to see him and learn from him. We will give the prize to him."

So with his own hands he carried the golden tripod to the little house where Thales lived. He knocked at the door and the wise man himself opened it.

Then the governor told him how the tripod had been found, and how the oracle had said that it must be given to the wisest of the wise.

"And so I have brought the prize to you, friend Thales."

"To me!" said the astonished Thales. "Why, there are many men who are wiser than I. There is my friend Bias of Priene. He excels all other men. Send the beautiful gift to him."

So the governor called two of his trusted officers and told them to carry the tripod to Priene and offer it to Bias.

"Tell the wise man why you bring it, and repeat to him the words of the oracle."

Now, all the world had heard of the wisdom of Bias. He taught that men ought to be kind even to their enemies. He taught, also, that a friend is the greatest blessing that anyone can have.

He was a poor man and had no wish to be rich. "It is better to be wise than wealthy," he said.

When the governor's messengers came to Priene with the tripod, they found Bias at work in his garden. They told him their errand and showed him the beautiful prize.

He would not take it.

"The oracle did not intend that I should have it," he said. "I am not the wisest of the wise."

"But what shall we do with it?" said the messengers. "Where shall we find the wisest man?"

"In Mitylene," answered Bias, "there is a very great man named Pittacus. He might now be the king of his country, but he prefers to give all of his time to the study of wisdom. He is the man whom the oracle meant."

The name of Pittacus was known all over the world. He was a brave soldier and a wise teacher. The people of his country had made him their king, but as soon as he had made good laws for them he gave up his crown.

One of his mottoes was this: "Whatever you do, do it well."

The messengers found him in his house talking to his friends and teaching them wisdom.

He looked at the tripod. "How beautiful it is!" he said.

Then the messengers told him how it had been taken from the sea, and they repeated the words of the oracle:

"Give not the merchant nor the fishermen the prize,
  But give it to that one who is wisest of the wise."

"We present the prize to you" said the messengers, "because you are the wisest of the wise."

"You are mistaken," answered Pittacus. "I should be delighted to own so beautiful a piece of workmanship, but I know I am not worthy."

"Then to whom shall we take it?" asked the messengers.

"Take it to Cleobulus, King of Rhodes," answered the wise man. "He is the handsomest and strongest of men, and I believe he is the wisest also."

The messengers went on until they came at last to the island of Rhodes. There everybody was talking about King Cleobulus and his wonderful wisdom. He had studied in all the great schools of the world, and there was nothing that he did not know.

"Educate the children," he said, and for that reason his name is remembered to this day.

When the messengers showed him the tripod, he said, "That is indeed a beautiful piece of work. Will you sell it? What is the price?"

They told him that it was not for sale, but that it was to be given to the wisest of the wise.

"Well, you will not find that man in Rhodes," said he. "He lives in Corinth, and his name is Periander. Carry the precious gift to him."

Everybody had heard of Periander, King of Corinth. Some had heard of his great learning, and others had heard of his selfishness and cruelty.

Strangers admired him for his wisdom. His own people despised him for his wickedness.

When he heard that some men had come to Corinth with a very costly golden tripod, he had them brought before him.

"I have heard all about that tripod," he said, "and I know why you are carrying it from one place to another. Do you expect to find any man in Corinth who deserves so rich a gift?"

"We hope that you are the man," said the messengers.

"Ha! ha!" laughed Periander. "Do I look like the wisest of the wise? No, indeed. But in Lacedæmon there is a good and noble man named Chilon. He loves his country, he loves his fellow men, he loves learning. To my mind he deserves the golden prize. I bid you carry it to him."

The messengers were surprised. They had never heard of Chilon, for his name was hardly known outside of his own country. But when they came into Lacedæmon, they heard his praises on every side.

They learned that Chilon was a very quiet man, that he never spoke about himself, and that he spent all his time trying to make his country great and strong and happy.

Chilon was so busy that the messengers had to wait several days before they could see him. At last they were allowed to go before him and state their business.

"We have here a very beautiful tripod," they said. "The oracle at Delphi has ordered that it shall be given to the wisest of wise men, and for that reason we have brought it to you."

"You have made a mistake," said Chilon. "Over in Athens there is a very wise man whose name is Solon. He is a poet, a soldier, and a lawmaker. He is my worst enemy, and yet I admire him as the wisest man in the world. It is to him that you should have taken the tripod."

The messengers made due haste to carry the golden prize to Athens. They had no trouble finding Solon. He was the chief ruler of that great city.

All the people whom they saw spoke in praise of his wisdom.

When they told him their errand he was silent for a little while; then he said: "I have never thought of myself as a wise man, and therefore the prize is not for me. But I know of at least six men who are famous for their wisdom, and one of them must be the wisest of the wise."

"Who are they?" asked the messengers.

"Their names are Thales, Bias, Pittacus, Cleobulus, Periander, and Chilon," answered Solon.

"We have offered the prize to each one of them," said the messengers, "and each one has refused it."

"Then there is only one other thing to be done," said Solon. "Carry it to Delphi and leave it there in the Temple of Apollo; for Apollo is the fountain of wisdom, the wisest of the wise."

And this the messengers did.

• • •

The famous men whom I have told you about in this story are commonly called the Seven Wise Men of Greece. They lived more than two thousand years ago. Each one helped to make his country famous, and each one remembered that no matter how much he knew, there was much more he did not know.

•

A LITTLE LEARNING

Alexander Pope

As we journey further into the world, we discover this important piece of wisdom: The more we learn, the more we know there is much left to learn. These verses come from *An Essay on Criticism* by Alexander Pope (1688–1744). The second line refers to springs in Pieria at the foot of Mount Olympus. According to Greek mythology, these fountains were the haunts of the Muses, the inspiring nymphs of the arts and sciences.

A little learning is a dangerous thing;
Drink deep, or taste not the Pierian spring:
There shallow draughts intoxicate the brain,
And drinking largely sobers us again.
Fired at first sight with what the Muse imparts,
In fearless youth we tempt the heights of Arts,
While from the bounded level of our mind
Short views we take, nor see the lengths behind;
But more advanced, behold with strange surprise
New distant scenes of endless science rise!
So pleased at first the towering Alps we try,
Mount o'er the vales, and seem to tread the sky,
The eternal snows appear already past,
And the first clouds and mountains seem the last;
But, those attained, we tremble to survey
The growing labors of the lengthened way,
The increasing prospects tire our wandering eyes,
Hills peep o'er hills, and Alps on Alps arise!

•

THE LEGEND BEAUTIFUL

The next three stories deal explicitly with the question: How can
I live most perfectly? None of the tales imply that anyone can
actually live perfectly, but they do hold forth a vision toward
which we can strive. This first story, an old legend from Germany,
says, "Do thy duty, and leave the rest to God," and helps us understand the nature of some of those obligations. The retelling is
based in part on a rhymed version of the story from Henry Wadsworth Longfellow's *Tales of a Wayside Inn.*

A monk was kneeling alone in his cold, bare cell, praying most
fervently. He was a gentle, devout man who had gone into a secluded monastery, hoping to live an existence acceptable to God.
Several times a day he prayed, thanking the Lord for all the blessings of life, seeking forgiveness for his sins, and asking for the
strength to deny temptation.

As the noon hour approached, the narrow stone cell suddenly
filled with a bright glow. And at once, lifting his eyes, the holy man
had a vision. It seemed to him that he saw Christ, dressed in a
simple garment, walking through village streets and harvest fields,
just as he must have done so long ago when he taught in Galilee.
As the good monk watched, he saw Jesus healing the lame and the
blind, blessing the little children, and preaching the word of God
to the crowds who pressed close around him.

The monk gazed at the vision in awe and exaltation. He felt
himself blessed beyond all deserts, and his heart filled with love
and thanks that the Lord should show himself to his humble servant
this way.

"How wonderful it is," he thought, "that a poor monk should
be granted this divine vision, and that Jesus of Nazareth should visit
my lonely cell!"

He remained kneeling on the hard, cold stones, rejoicing that
he should be a witness to such glory, and scarcely daring even to
breathe for fear that the heavenly vision would depart.

But suddenly his joy was interrupted by a familiar sound. The
chapel bell began to clang loudly and persistently, calling for him
to leave his cell and do his daily work. For now it was the appointed

hour when, rain or shine, in winter cold or summer heat, the sick and poor and lame and blind gathered outside the monastery gates. There they received a daily portion of bread, which the good brothers baked especially for the needy. And it was this monk's duty to go each afternoon and distribute the charity.

The holy man was filled with sorrow and doubt. What should he do? How could he turn his back upon this magnificent sight? Had not Jesus himself come to grace his cold, narrow cell? Surely he should not insult this divine vision by getting up and deserting the room for a crowd of ragged beggars outside the gate. They could wait a little while, after all. There would be no harm in that. Surely it was better to stay kneeling in prayer before this glorious sight, as long as it remained before him.

But the thought of the poor people waiting at the gates would not leave the monk's mind. He remembered the anxious, careworn looks on their faces, the sadness in their eyes, the feebleness with which they stretched forth their arms. Many of them had no other food than the bread they received once a day from the good brother's hands. Certainly they could wait, but was it right to leave them waiting in hunger and doubt even for a few minutes when their lives were already full of so much sad waiting?

It seemed to the monk that two sensations now warred within his soul—ecstasy over the radiant vision before him, and deep distress for the people who waited outside. Should he go, or should he stay? If he turned his back, would the radiant vision remain, or would it flee? If it disappeared, would it ever come again? He searched his heart for an answer, and he tried to think of what Jesus himself would have done in his place. Would the Master, whose work on this earth was healing the sick and comforting the afflicted, who showed men how to love their neighbors, who spoke of charity and mercy and brotherhood—would he leave his brothers and sisters waiting cold and hungry outside the gates, even for an instant?

And as the monk put all these questions to himself, he seemed to hear a voice whisper within his breast: "Do thy duty, and leave the rest to God."

At once he knew what he must do. Rising from his knees and taking one last, longing look at the blessed vision, he departed his cell, and hurried out to feed the poor.

There were so many in need that day! The monk worked as quickly as he could, passing among the huddled figures, placing the precious loaves in their trembling hands. Yet every time he emptied his basket, more pleading faces appeared. It seemed he would never finish his task! He longed to be back in his secluded cell, where he could reflect undisturbed on the wonderful vision that had been sent to him. He worried that he had slighted the radiant visitor by turning his back. Should he have stayed? The question burned in his conscience. If only this duty would end quickly, so he could return to the solitude of his chamber and examine his decision, to know that he had made the right choice.

At last, after a long hour, the day's work was over, and he was free to return to his cell. As he turned his face toward the cloister, it seemed as though its high walls glowed with a gentle light. He caught his breath as a sudden hope swelled in his breast. Hurrying down the long, narrow hallway toward his room, he threw open the door and stopped on the threshold with an awestruck gasp.

There, in his chamber, the radiant vision still stood, just as before. Throughout the long hour of absence, Jesus had waited for the good monk to return.

The holy man felt a surge of joy in his heart, and he sank to his knees before the heavenly image.

As he bowed his head, the vision spoke: "Hadst thou stayed, I must have fled."

And at last the monk knew he had made the right decision when he turned to help his brothers and sisters.

•

TRUE SAINTLINESS

Adapted from a retelling by Joel H. Metcalf

Justice Oliver Wendell Holmes said: "It is one thing to utter a happy phrase from a protected cloister, another to think under fire—to think for action upon which great interests depend. The great problems are questions of here and now." For most of us, the "great interests" and "great problems" of here and now are the well-being of our family, friends, and community. True saintliness lies in our attention to these places.

There was once a hermit, living in a cave of the desert, whose only food consisted of roots and acorns and a little bread the peasants gave him. He spent all his days praying and reading the holy Scriptures, and every hour of the night he would get up and offer a short prayer.

He did this because he wanted to live a life acceptable to God and to be a true saint—one of the greatest and best the world had ever known.

Finally, when he grew to be an old man, and had been faithful in his prayers, fastings, and vigils for many years, he asked the Lord to show him what progress he had made in the spiritual life.

"Oh God," he prayed, "show me one who has attained more sanctity than I, that I may see how I can improve my life." And immediately his prayer was answered.

A white-robed angel came to him, and said: "Tomorrow go to the nearest town, and in the marketplace you will find a clown performing tricks and making the people laugh. He is the man you seek."

The hermit was astonished and humbled, for he had a suspicion that there were none better than he. But he did as he was bidden, and in the public square he found a man who would first play a tune, then sing a song, then perform a few tricks of magic, after which he would pass his fool's cap around for pennies.

The hermit watched him in disgust, but, after the performance was over, he drew him aside, and asked him if he had always been a clown, what good deeds he had done, and what prayers and penances he had performed which made him beloved of God.

The grin on the clown's face vanished, and he said: "Do not mock me, holy father. I am ashamed to confess I have forgotten how to pray. I don't remember ever having done any good works. All I do is to play my flute and laugh and sing, for the few pennies I can earn, even when my heart is sad."

But the hermit would not take this answer, for the angel had told him the clown was a greater saint than he. So he insisted. "Remember! Sometime you must have performed some great act of goodness."

But the minstrel said: "No, I cannot remember doing any good act. I never deserved any praise from God or man."

"But," persisted the hermit, "have you always been a vagabond? Have you always been a beggar, as you are now?"

"Oh, no," said the clown. "I will tell you how I became poor.

Years ago, when I was a young man, and had just received my share of my father's estate, in the far-off city where I lived, I saw a woman by the roadside, tired out and weeping, as though pursued by enemies. I asked her what was the matter, and she said her husband and children had been sold into slavery for debt. Not only was she homeless and poor but evil men were after her to carry her away into slavery also. Of course there was nothing else to do but to buy her freedom and that of her family, which took all the money I had. This explains my poverty. There was no special merit in it. Anybody would have done the same, and I had almost forgotten about it."

The hermit, however, understood why the Lord thought the clown a greater saint than he.

"All my life I have been striving to save myself, and men call me a saint. But this poor piper, by one good deed, has far outstripped me in the heavenly race. He may forget what he has done, but God does not."

Then the hermit went back to his cave, a sadder but a wiser man, for he knew now that true saintliness could not be selfish. He added to his prayers and fastings a desire to help others all he could, but still he lived alone in his cave.

Ten years after, he prayed again for God to show him a greater saint than he, that he might imitate him in righteousness.

Then the angel came, as before, and told him that on a small farm nearby, two women lived, and in them he would find two souls who could show him the higher call of duty and saintliness.

So he made a second pilgrimage. When he reached the little farm, the two women received him gladly. They were greatly honored to receive a visit from so perfect a saint. His fame had gone before him. They brought him food and drink, and entertained him as lavishly as their small stores would permit.

The hermit, however, could hardly wait to find out from them the secret of their acceptableness to God, so he asked them about their lives. "We have no history," they said. "We have always worked hard in the house and the fields, with our husbands. We have many beloved children, for whom we have cared. We have seen poverty and sickness and death, but so have all the families about us, so we are no different from the rest."

"Yes," said the hermit, "but what about your good deeds? What have you done for God?"

"Why, nothing," they said. "We had no money to give away. We were too poor. We had no time to do much of anything for other people, for our families kept us busy from morning until night, but we are very happy and contented."

With all his questioning the monk could not get any other answer, so he gave up and was going away disappointed, when he thought to call at a neighbor's house and ask there about the two women.

"Why," they said, "they are the best people you ever saw. They have lived here for twenty-five years, and no one ever heard angry words from them, and they have had many crosses to bear, I can tell you. They mind their own affairs, and they have a kind word and a pleasant smile for all."

Then a great light seemed to break upon the mind of the hermit.

He saw how many ways there are of serving God. Some serve Him in churches and hermits' cells by praise and prayer. Some serve Him on the highway, helping strangers in desperate need. Some live faithfully and gently in humble homes, working, bringing up children, remaining kind and cheerful. Some bear pain patiently, for His sake. Endless, endless ways there are, that only the Heavenly Father sees.

And the hermit thought: "I have lived all alone these many years, and kept my temper, and been patient and uncomplaining. But could I have done the same with the worries of family life? I can get along with very little, but how would I be in poverty when others suffer besides myself? The strain and stress of bread-winning for others might have been too much for me. I know now what God meant to tell me. It is harder to be a saint in the home than in the desert, and to those who faithfully follow the harder way the greater credit belongs. Perhaps it was wrong and selfish of me to go into the desert when the common life would have furnished me all I ought to ask—room to deny myself and a road to lead me daily nearer to God."

•

THREE QUESTIONS

Leo Tolstoy

Complicated questions sometimes have simple answers, as this old folktale retold by Tolstoy reminds us. Here is a king who wishes to rule perfectly. The hermit in this story teaches him the same lesson learned by the hermit in the last tale: "If we love one another, God dwelleth in us, and His love is perfected in us" (1 John 4:12).

It once occurred to a certain king that if he always knew the right time to begin everything, if he knew who were the right people to listen to and whom to avoid, and, above all, if he always knew what was the most important thing to do, he would never fail in anything he might undertake.

And this thought having occurred to him, he had it proclaimed throughout his kingdom that he would give a great reward to anyone who could teach him what was the right time for every action, and who were the most necessary people, and how he might know what was the most important thing to do.

And learned men came to the king, but they all answered his questions differently.

All the answers being different, the king agreed with none of them and gave the reward to none. But still wishing to find the right answers to his questions, he decided to consult a hermit, widely renowned for his wisdom.

The hermit lived in a wood which he never quitted, and he received none but common folk. So the king put on simple clothes, and before reaching the hermit's cell, he dismounted from his horse and, leaving his bodyguard behind, went on alone.

When the king approached, the hermit was digging the ground in front of his hut. Seeing the king, he greeted him, and went on digging. The hermit was frail and weak, and each time he stuck his spade into the ground and turned a little earth, he breathed heavily.

The king went up to him and said, "I have come to you, wise hermit, to ask you to answer three questions: How can I learn to do the right thing at the right time? Who are the people I most need, and to whom I should, therefore, pay more attention than to the rest? And what affairs are the most important and need my first attention?"

The hermit listened to the king but answered nothing. He just spat on his hand and recommenced digging.

"You are tired," said the king; "let me take the spade and work awhile for you."

"Thanks!" said the hermit, and, giving the spade to the king, he sat down on the ground.

When he had dug two beds, the king stopped and repeated his questions. The hermit again gave no answer but rose, stretched out his hand for the spade, and said: "Now rest awhile—and let me work a bit."

But the king did not give him the spade and continued to dig. One hour passed and another. The sun began to sink behind the trees, and the king at last stuck the spade into the ground and said: "I came to you, wise man, for an answer to my questions. If you can give me none, tell me so, and I will return home."

"Here comes someone running," said the hermit; "let us see who it is."

The king turned round and saw a bearded man come running out of the wood. The man held his hands pressed against his side, and blood was flowing from under them. When he reached the king, he fell fainting on the ground, moaning feebly. The king and the hermit unfastened the man's clothing. There was a large wound in his side. The king washed it as best he could, and bandaged it with his handkerchief and with a towel the hermit had. But the blood would not stop flowing, and the king again and again washed and rebandaged the wound. When at last the blood ceased flowing, the man revived and asked for something to drink. The king brought fresh water and gave it to him. Meanwhile the sun had set, and it had become cool. So the king, with the hermit's help, carried the wounded man into the hut and laid him on the bed. Lying on the bed the man closed his eyes and was quiet, but the king was so tired with his walk and with the work he had done that he crouched down on the threshold and also fell asleep—so soundly that he slept all through the short summer night. When he awoke in the morning, it was long before he could remember where he was, or who was the strange bearded man lying on the bed and gazing intently at him with shining eyes.

"Forgive me!" said the bearded man in a weak voice, when he saw that the king was awake and was looking at him.

"I do not know you and have nothing to forgive you for," said the king.

"You do not know me, but I know you. I am that enemy of yours who swore to revenge himself on you, because you executed his brother and seized his property. I knew you had gone alone to see the hermit, and I resolved to kill you on your way back. But the day passed and you did not return. So I came out from my ambush to find you, and I came upon your bodyguards, and they recognized me, and wounded me. I escaped from them but would have bled to death had you not dressed my wound. I wished to kill you, and you saved my life. Now, if I live and if you wish it, I will serve you as your most faithful servant and will bid my sons do the same. Forgive me!"

The king was very glad to have made peace with his enemy so easily and to have gained him for a friend, so he not only forgave him but said he would send his servants and his own physician to attend him, and promised to restore his property.

Having taken leave of the wounded man, the king went out onto the porch and looked around for the hermit. Before going away he wished once more to beg an answer to the questions he had put. The hermit was outside, on his knees, sowing seeds in the beds that had been dug the day before.

The king approached him and said: "For the last time, I pray you to answer my questions, wise man."

"You have already been answered!" said the hermit, still crouching on his thin legs and looking up at the king, who stood before him.

"How answered? What do you mean?" asked the king.

"Do you not see?" replied the hermit. "If you had not pitied my weakness yesterday, and had not dug these beds for me, but had gone your way, that man would have attacked you, and you would have repented of not having stayed with me. So the most important time was when you were digging the beds; and I was the most important man; and to do me good was your most important business. Afterward, when that man ran to us, the most important time was when you were attending to him, for if you had not bound up his wounds he would have died without having made peace with you. So he was the most important man, and what you did for him was your most important business. Remember then: there is only one time that is important—now! It is the most important time because it is the only time when we have any power. The most necessary man is he with whom you are, for no man knows whether he will ever have dealings with anyone else; and the most important affair is to do him good, because for that purpose alone was man sent into this life!"

•

I SOUGHT MY SOUL

> I sought my soul,
>   But my soul I could not see.
> I sought my God,
>   But my God eluded me.
> I sought my brother,
>   And I found all three.

•

SAINT AUGUSTINE BY THE SEASHORE
Adapted from a retelling by Peggy Webling

The next three stories remind us that the wisdom of man has limits, and the fullest understanding of our world and our existence comes in humility before God's creation. This first legend is about Saint Augustine of Hippo (354–430).

It chanced on a fair summer's day that Saint Augustine was walking alone on the seashore.

The sun sparkled on the ocean and white sands. Now and then a seagull flew across the sky or swept downward to the waves. Soft, fleecy little clouds were floating beneath the blue of heaven, and the whisper of the water was the only sound.

The lonely man was thinking deeply on a subject that even he could not understand, although he was one of the most wise and learned of men. He was pondering the acts of God, and trying to look into their hidden meaning. He struggled to comprehend the

Divine Plan behind events, and his heart filled with frustration and anguish when he failed to find unclouded explanations.

Suddenly he came across a little child who had dug a hole in the sand. He filled a little bucket at the edge of the water, ran and emptied it into the hole, then returned to the sea for more water. Bucket after bucket he poured into the hole.

"What are you doing, my boy?" asked the wise man.

The child did not show any surprise at the question, or even raise his head.

"I am going to empty the waters of the sea into this hole, my Father," he replied.

"That is impossible, little one!" exclaimed the wise man, with a smile.

The boy looked up into his face.

"No more impossible than for you to fathom the mysteries of God," he answered quietly.

The holy man was struck by the truth of the simple words. His heart was humbled. At once the frustrations lifted from his mind. He covered his eyes with his hands, and he gave thanks that faith could fill voids where understanding fell short.

When he raised his head, after a moment, he found himself alone with the sea and sky.

•

THE MELON AND THE PROFESSOR

*Retold by Mary Hayes Davis
and Cheow-Leung*

This tale is from China, but different variations are told all over the world. It reminds us that there is an order in creation which we do not fully see.

Wu-Kiao was a professor in a large Chinese university, and a very proud and learned man. Hundreds of students were under his teaching, and many thousands honored him. When he went out of his house, five people followed, singing and playing the drum all the way down the street, and eight men carried his chair. At home he had six servants about him. During each meal, thirty dishes were served at his table.

The professor was a great man. Through his wisdom and out of his deep knowledge, he explained all questions to the people.

One day Wu-Kiao sat in the shade of a tree in his garden. He turned his head and saw a watermelon lying on the ground, nearly covered by its green leaves. Then, seeing the fig tree with many figs on it, he said, "I think the Creator should have made the melon grow on this tree."

He touched the tree and said, "How strong you are; you could bear larger fruit like the watermelon." And he said to the vine, "You, so thin and small, should bear small fruit like the fig. Things are not well ordered. Mistakes are made in creation."

Just then a fig dropped from the tree on his nose, and he was a little bruised.

Then he said: "I was wrong. If the fig tree bore fruit as large as the watermelon and dropped it on my nose, I think I would be killed. It would be a dangerous tree to all people. I must study more carefully. I know many things and many people; and if I study and think more deeply, it may be I shall come to know that the Creator's works are perfect."

•

THE WONDER TREE

Adapted from
Friedrich A. Krummacher

This legend about the prophet Nathan and the young Solomon reminds us that miracles surround us every day, whether we choose to see them or not.

One day in the springtime, Prince Solomon was sitting under the palm trees in the royal gardens when he saw the Prophet Nathan walking near.

"Nathan," said the Prince, "I would see a wonder."

The Prophet smiled. "I had the same desire in the days of my youth," he replied.

"And was it fulfilled?" asked Solomon.

"A Man of God came to me," said Nathan, "having a pomegranate seed in his hand. 'Behold,' he said, 'what will become of this.' Then he made a hole in the ground, and planted the seed, and covered it over. When he withdrew his hand the clods of earth opened, and I saw two small leaves coming forth. But scarcely had I beheld them, when they joined together and became a small stem wrapped in bark; and the stem grew before my eyes—and it grew thicker and higher and became covered with branches.

"I marveled, but the Man of God motioned me to be silent. 'Behold,' said he, 'new creations begin.'

"Then he took water in the palm of his hand, and sprinkled the branches three times, and lo! the branches were covered with green leaves, so that a cool shade spread above us, and the air was filled with perfume.

" 'From whence come this perfume and this shade?' cried I.

" 'Dost thou not see,' he answered, 'these crimson flowers bursting from among the leaves, and hanging in clusters?'

"I was about to speak, but a gentle breeze moved the leaves, scattering the petals of the flowers around us. Scarcely had the falling flowers reached the ground when I saw ruddy pomegranates hanging beneath the leaves of the tree, like almonds on Aaron's rod. Then the Man of God left me, and I was lost in amazement."

"Where is he, this Man of God?" asked Prince Solomon eagerly. "What is his name? Is he still alive?"

"Son of David," answered Nathan, "I have spoken to thee of a dream."

When the Prince heard this he was grieved to the heart. "How couldst thou deceive me thus?" he asked.

But the Prophet replied: "Behold in thy father's gardens thou mayest daily see the unfolding of wonder trees. Doth not this same miracle happen to the fig, the date, and the pomegranate? They spring from the earth, they put out branches and leaves, they flower, they fruit—not in a moment, perhaps, but in months and years. But canst thou tell the difference betwixt a minute, a month, or a year in the eyes of Him with whom one day is as a thousand years, and a thousand years as one day?"

•

THE THREE HEAVY STONES

This story comes from a school reader of the mid-nineteenth
century. It warns against living to serve certain preoccupations—
preoccupations still very much alive in a modern world full of
such slogans as "If it feels good, do it" and "Image is everything."

It was in the confines of the desert, amid barren and almost
inaccessible rocks, that Ben Achmet, the Dervish, led a life of auster-
ity and devotion. A cave in the rock was his dwelling. Roots and
fruits, the scanty products of the sterile region he inhabited, satisfied his hunger, and the fountain that bubbled up from the lower
part of a neighboring cliff slaked his thirst.

He had once been a priest in a magnificent mosque, and had
scrupulously conducted the ceremonies of the Mohammedan faith.
But seeking a life of total devotion, he abandoned the mosque and
his authority as priest, betaking himself to the desert to spend his
days as a hermit.

Years rolled over the head of Ben Achmet, and the fame of his
sanctity spread abroad. He often supplied the traveler of the desert
with water from his little well. In times of pestilence, he left his
solitary abode to attend to the sick and comfort the dying in the
villages that were scattered around. Often did he stanch the blood
of the wounded Arab and heal him of his wounds. His fame was
spread abroad; his name inspired veneration, and even the plunder-
ing nomad gave up his booty at the command of Ben Achmet, the
Dervish.

Akaba was an Arabian robber. He had a band of lawless men
under his command, ready to do his bidding. He had a treasure
house stored with ill-gotten wealth, and a large number of prisoners. The sanctity of Ben Achmet arrested his attention; his conscience smote him on account of his guilt, and he longed to be as
famed for his devotion as he had been for his crimes.

He sought the abode of the Dervish, and told him his desires.

"Ben Achmet," said he, "I have five hundred thieves ready to
obey me. I have any number of slaves at my command. And I have
a goodly treasure house filled with riches. Tell me how to add to
these the hope of a happy immortality."

Ben Achmet led him to the base of a neighboring cliff that was steep, rugged, and high. Pointing to three large stones that lay near together, he told him to lift them from the ground, and to follow him up the cliff.

Akaba, laden with the stones, could scarcely move. To ascend the cliff was impossible.

"I cannot follow thee with these burdens, Ben Achmet," said he.

"Then cast down one of the stones," replied the Dervish, "and hasten after me."

Akaba dropped one of the stones but still found himself too heavily encumbered to proceed.

"I tell thee it is impossible," cried the robber chieftain. "Thou thyself could not proceed a step with such a load."

"Let go another stone, then," said Ben Achmet.

Akaba readily dropped another stone and, with great difficulty, clambered up the cliff for a while. But soon, exhausted from the effort, he again cried out that he could come no further.

Ben Achmet directed him to drop the last stone, and no sooner had he done this than he mounted with ease and soon stood with his conductor on the summit of the cliff.

"Son," said Ben Achmet, "thou hast three burdens that hinder thee in thy way to a better world. Disband thy troops of lawless plunderers. Set thy prisoners at liberty. Restore thy ill-gotten wealth to its owners. It is easier for Akaba to ascend this cliff with the stones that lie at its foot than for him to journey onward to a better world with lust for power, pleasure, and riches in his possession."

●

THE BUNDLE

He carried a bundle of false beliefs,
Musty and heavy as a lawyer's briefs;
Prejudice, jealousy, bitterness, strife—
These were the wares of his troubled life.

He carried the bundle wherever he went—
Anger, suspicion, and selfish intent;
He saw what he sought, injustice and sin.
Life was a tempest without and within.

He mumbled and stumbled; the world was all wrong.
His bundle grew heavy as he shuffled along.
Worry, impatience, discord, and doubt—
These were the things that he dragged all about.

Tired of his bundle, he set the load down,
He prayed long to God; his face lost its frown.
In his eyes dawned a light by which he could see.
He forsook his old bundle and walked away free.

•

THE PHARISEE AND THE
TAX COLLECTOR

Adapted from a retelling by
Eva March Tappan

Jesus told this parable to help us understand correct and incorrect
ways to show our faith. The Pharisee in this story was a member
of a religious group noted for strict observance of rites and ceremonies of the law. Someone once noted that he came to the
Temple not to pray but to bray. His self-righteousness seems to
revolve around one word: "I." The parable comes from Luke
18:9–14.

Jesus told a parable to some people who thought they were
more righteous than anyone else and regarded others with scorn.
He said: "There were once two men who went up to the Temple to pray. One was a Pharisee and the other a tax collector."
Here the people began to listen closely, for many of them felt
that a tax collector was so wicked that he hardly had a right to go
into the Temple. The Pharisees, on the other hand, were known for
their strict observance of holy ceremonies.
"This is the way they prayed," Jesus continued. "The Pharisee
stood by himself and said loudly, so that all might hear: 'God, I
thank you that I am not like other men. I am glad I am not greedy
for money and not unjust, like that tax collector. I fast twice a week,
and I give to the Temple one-tenth of all my money.'

"The tax collector did not venture to come far into the Temple but stood at the edge of the court. He dared not lift his eyes toward heaven, but as he said his prayer, he beat upon his breast in sorrow and thought, 'I am a sinner, but may God have mercy on me.'

"Then," said Jesus, "this tax collector went home accepted by God, but the Pharisee was not accepted, for he had not truly repented. For everyone who exalts himself will be humbled, but he who humbles himself will be exalted."

•

THE PRAYER

This dervish tale cautions us against another wrong way to pray. Honesty is no small part of faith—honesty with self, honesty with God. We should not negotiate with God through legalisms or sophistry.

A perfectly healthy man suddenly grew very ill and lay at death's door. The doctors stood around his bed, poked and prodded, shook their heads, and told him there was nothing they could do.

"If only I can keep my life," the man prayed, "I promise I'll sell my house and give all the money to the poor."

Soon he grew better, and his health was restored. He knew he should keep his promise, but he couldn't stand the thought of losing so much money. So he came up with a plan.

He advertised his house for sale for one silver coin. Whoever bought the house, however, also had to buy his cat. The price of the cat he set at one hundred gold coins.

Before long he found a buyer. He said goodbye to his cat, shut the door behind him, and set off down the street with one hundred gold coins in his purse. He rounded a corner, dropped the silver coin into a beggar's cup, and felt quite relieved that everything had turned out so well.

•

ABRAHAM AND THE OLD MAN

Retold by Horace E. Scudder

This little parable was in circulation during colonial times, and
many people mistakenly thought it was part of the Bible. It has
been attributed to the English scholar and churchman Jeremy
Taylor (1613–1667). It reminds us that faith gives us a means to
act virtuously toward all we meet on life's journey, not just those
who share our faith.

The patriarch Abraham sat at the door of his tent. It was evening, when he was wont to watch for any strangers who might pass
by, for all such he bade enter his tent. He espied an old man coming
toward him, leaning on his staff, weary with travel and bent with
age, for he was a hundred years old.

Abraham rose and asked the old man to come into the tent. He
washed the old man's feet, gave him the best seat, and set meat
before him. The old man ate his supper in silence, but he offered
no prayer before he ate.

"Why dost thou not first worship the God of heaven?" asked
Abraham.

"I worship fire only; I know no other God," said the old man.

At that Abraham was very angry and drove his guest out into
the dark night. Then God called Abraham and said to him: "Where
is that stranger who was in thy tent?"

"I thrust him out," said the patriarch, "because he did not
worship Thee."

Then God answered Abraham out of heaven: "I have suffered
him these hundred years, although he did not honor me, and
couldst thou not endure him one night when he gave thee no
trouble?"

Then was Abraham very sorry, and went and brought the old
man back, and gave him rest, and sent him on his way in the
morning.

•

SELF-DEPENDENCE

Matthew Arnold

Self-knowledge and self-reliance are sources of strength.

Weary of myself, and sick of asking
   What I am, and what I ought to be,
At this vessel's prow I stand, which bears me
   Forwards, forwards, o'er the starlit sea.

And a look of passionate desire
   O'er the sea and to the stars I send:
"Ye who from my childhood up have calm'd me,
   Calm me, ah, compose me to the end!

"Ah, once more," I cried, "ye stars, ye waters,
   On my heart your mighty charm renew;
Still, still let me, as I gaze upon you,
   Feel my soul becoming vast like you!"

From the intense, clear, star-sown vault of heaven,
   Over the lit sea's unquiet way,
In the rustling night air came the answer:
   "Wouldst thou *be* as these are? *Live* as they.

"Unaffrighted by the silence round them,
   Undistracted by the sights they see,
These demand not that the things without them
   Yield them love, amusement, sympathy.

"And with joy the stars perform their shining,
   And the sea its long moon-silver'd roll;
For self-poised they live, nor pine with noting
   All the fever of some differing soul.

"Bounded by themselves, and unregardful
   In what state God's other works may be,
In their own tasks all their powers pouring,
   These attain the mighty life you see."

O airborne voice! long since, severely clear,
A cry like thine in mine own heart I hear:
"Resolve to be thyself; and know that he,
Who finds himself, loses his misery!"

•

PRAYER FOR TRUE KNOWLEDGE

Thomas à Kempis

Seeking God's will brings strength too.

Grant me, O Lord, to know what I ought to know,
To love what I ought to love,
To praise what delights Thee most,
To value what is precious in Thy sight,
To hate what is offensive to Thee.

Do not suffer me to judge according to the sight of my eyes,
Nor to pass sentence according to the hearing of the ears of ignorant men;
But to discern with a true judgment between things visible and spiritual,
And above all, always to inquire what is the good pleasure of Thy will. Amen.

•

THREE WORDS OF STRENGTH

Friedrich von Schiller

And virtue brings strength.

There are three lessons I would write,
Three words, as with a burning pen,
In tracings of eternal light,
Upon the hearts of men.

Have Hope. Though clouds environ round,
   And gladness hides her face in scorn,
Put off the shadow from thy brow:
   No night but hath its morn.

Have Faith. Where'er thy bark is driven,
   The calm's disport, the tempest's mirth,
Know this: God rules the hosts of heaven,
   The inhabitants of earth.

Have Love. Not love alone for one,
   But man, as man, thy brother call;
And scatter, like a circling sun,
   Thy charities on all.

●

YOUR SECOND JOB

As told to Fulton Oursler
by Albert Schweitzer

One of the truly remarkable figures of the twentieth century,
Albert Schweitzer (1875–1965) had by age thirty already become
Europe's premier organist, an acclaimed biographer, and a first-
rate theologian when he decided to study medicine in order to
devote his life to helping people in Africa. In 1913, Schweitzer
and his wife, Helene, traveled to what was then French Equatorial
Africa to found the Schweitzer Hospital on the Ogooué River,
where thousands of people received treatment during the following decades. In this selection, the man whose work inspired the
world challenges us to seek adventures for the soul.

Often people say: "I would like to do some good in the world.
But with so many responsibilities at home and in business, my nose
is always to the grindstone. I am sunk in my own petty affairs, and
there is no chance for my life to mean anything."

This is a common and dangerous error. In helpfulness to others, every man can find on his own doorstep adventures for the

soul—our surest source of true peace and lifelong satisfaction. To know this happiness, one does not have to neglect duties or do spectacular things.

This career for the spirit I call "your second job." In this there is no pay except the privilege of doing it. In it you will encounter noble chances and find deep strength. Here all your reserve power can be put to work, for what the world lacks most today is men who occupy themselves with the needs of other men. In this unselfish labor a blessing falls on both the helper and the helped.

Without such spiritual adventures the man or woman of today walks in darkness. In the pressures of modern society we tend to lose our individuality. Our craving for creation and self-expression is stifled; true civilization is to that extent retarded.

What is the remedy? No matter how busy one is, any human being can assert his personality by seizing every opportunity for spiritual activity. How? By his second job: by means of personal action, on however small a scale, for the good of his fellow men. He will not have to look far for opportunities.

Our greatest mistake, as individuals, is that we walk through our life with closed eyes and do not notice our chances. As soon as we open our eyes and deliberately search we see many who need help, not in big things but in the littlest things. Wherever a man turns he can find someone who needs him.

One day I was traveling through Germany in a third-class railway carriage beside an eager youth who sat as if looking for something unseen. Facing him was a fretful and plainly worried old man. Presently the lad remarked that it would be dark before we reached the nearest large city.

"I don't know what I shall do when we get there," said the old man anxiously. "My only son is in the hospital, very ill. I had a telegram to come at once. I must see him before he dies. But I am from the country and I'm afraid I shall get lost in the city."

To which the young man replied "I know the city well. I will get off with you and take you to your son. Then I will catch a later train."

As they left the compartment they walked together like brothers.

Who can assay the effect of that small kind deed? You, too, can watch for the little things that need to be done.

During the First World War a cockney cab driver was declared too old for military service. From one bureau to another he went, offering to make himself useful in spare time and always being turned away. Finally he gave himself his own commission. Soldiers from out-of-town camps were being allowed leave in the city before going to the front. So at eight o'clock the old cabby appeared at a railroad station and looked for puzzled troopers. Four or five times every night, right up to demobilization, he served as a volunteer guide through the maze of London streets.

From a feeling of embarrassment, we hesitate to approach a stranger. The fear of being repulsed is the cause of a great deal of coldness in the world; when we seem indifferent we are often merely timid. The adventurous soul must break that barrier, resolving in advance not to mind a rebuff. If we dare with wisdom, always maintaining a certain reserve in our approach, we find that when we open ourselves we open doors in others.

Organized welfare work is, of course, necessary; but the gaps in it must be filled by personal service, performed with loving kindness. A charitable organization is a complex affair; like an automobile, it needs a broad highway to run on. It cannot penetrate the little bypaths; those are for men and women to walk through, with open eyes and hearts full of comprehension.

We cannot abdicate our conscience to an organization, nor to a government. "Am I my brother's keeper?" Most certainly I am! I cannot escape my responsibility by saying the State will do all that is necessary. It is a tragedy that nowadays so many think and feel otherwise.

Even in family life children are coming to believe they do not have to take care of the old folks. But old-age pensions do not relieve children of their duties. To dehumanize such care is wrong because it abolishes the principle of love, which is the foundation in upbuilding human beings and civilization itself.

You may think it is a wonderful life my wife and I have in the equatorial jungle. That is merely where we happen to be. But you can have a still more wonderful life by staying where you happen to be and putting your soul to the test in a thousand little trials, and winning triumphs of love. Such a career of the spirit demands patience, devotion, daring. It calls for strength of will and the determination to love: the greatest test of a man. But in this hard "second job" is to be found the only true happiness.

•

WHAT IS SUCCESS?

Ralph Waldo Emerson

To laugh often and much;

To win the respect of intelligent people
    and the affection of children;

To earn the appreciation of honest critics
    and endure the betrayal of false friends;

To appreciate beauty;

To find the best in others;

To leave the world a bit better,
    whether by a healthy child, a garden
    patch or a redeemed social condition;

To know even one life has breathed easier
    because you have lived;

This is to have succeeded.

•

GIVE UNTIL IT HURTS

Mother Teresa

Here is a modern-day heroine for the whole world. In 1948,
Mother Teresa of Calcutta founded the Order of the Missionaries
of Charity, a Roman Catholic congregation of women dedicated
to helping the needy, especially the destitute of India. She is sometimes called "the saint of the gutters" because of her work rescu-
ing people from the streets. Here is someone whose words and
deeds can inspire us all to strive for lives of spiritual fullness.

It is not enough for me to say: "I love God." I also have to love my neighbor. St. John says that you are a liar if you say you love God and you don't love your neighbor. How can you love God, whom you do not see, if you do not love your neighbor, whom you see, whom you touch, with whom you live? And so it is very important for us to realize that love, to be true, has to hurt. I must be willing to give whatever it takes not to harm other people and, in fact, to do good to them. This requires that I be willing to give until it hurts. Otherwise, there is no true love in me and I bring injustice, not peace, to those around me.

It hurt Jesus to love us. We have been created in His image for greater things, to love and to be loved. We must "put on Christ," as Scripture tells us. And so, we have been created to love as He loves us. Jesus makes Himself the hungry one, the naked one, the homeless one, the unwanted one, and He says, "You did it to Me." On the last day He will say to those on His right, "Whatever you did to the least of these, you did to Me," and He will also say to those on His left, "Whatever you neglected to do for the least of these, you neglected to do it for Me."

When He was dying on the Cross, Jesus said, "I thirst." Jesus is thirsting for our love, and this is the thirst of everyone, poor and rich alike. We all thirst for the love of others, that they go out of their way to avoid harming us and to do good to us. This is the meaning of true love, to give until it hurts.

I can never forget the experience I had in visiting a home where they kept all these old parents of sons and daughters who had just put them into an institution and forgotten them—maybe. I saw that in that home these old people had everything—good food, a comfortable place, television, everything, but everyone was looking toward the door. And I did not see a single one with a smile on the face. I turned to Sister and I asked: "Why do these people who have every comfort here, why are they all looking toward the door? Why are they not smiling?"

I am so used to seeing the smiles on our people—even the dying ones smile. And Sister said: "This is the way it is nearly every day. They are expecting, they are hoping that a son or daughter will come to visit them. They are hurt because they are forgotten." And see, this neglect to love brings spiritual poverty. Maybe in our own family we have somebody who is feeling lonely, who is feeling sick, who is feeling worried. Are we there? Are we willing to give until it hurts in order to be with our families, or do we put our own interests first? These are the questions we must ask ourselves, especially as we begin this year of the family. We must remember that love begins at home and we must also remember that "the future of humanity passes through the family."

I was surprised in the West to see so many young boys and girls given to drugs. And I tried to find out why. Why is it like that, when those in the West have so many more things than those in the East? And the answer was: "Because there is no one in the family to receive them." Our children depend on us for everything—their health, their nutrition, their security, their coming to know and love God. For all of this, they look to us with trust, hope, and expectation. But often father and mother are so busy they have no time for their children, or perhaps they are not even married or have given up on their marriage. So the children go to the streets and get involved in drugs or other things. We are talking of love of the child, which is where love and peace must begin. These are the things that break peace. . . .

Those who are materially poor can be very wonderful people. One evening we went out and we picked up four people from the street [in India]. And one of them was in a most terrible condition. I told the Sisters: "You take care of the other three; I will take care of the one who looks worst." So I did for her all that my love can do. I put her in bed, and there was such a beautiful smile on her face. She took hold of my hand as she said one word only: "Thank you"—and she died.

I could not help but examine my conscience before her. And I asked: "What would I say if I were in her place?" And my answer was very simple. I would have tried to draw a little attention to myself. I would have said: "I am hungry, I am dying, I am cold, I am in pain," or something. But she gave me much more—she gave me her grateful love. And she died with a smile on her face.

Then there was the man we picked up from the drain, half eaten by worms, and, after we had brought him to the home, he only said, "I have lived like an animal in the street, but I am going to die as an angel, loved and cared for." Then, after we had removed all the worms from his body, all he said, with a big smile, was: "Sister, I am going home to God"—and he died. It was so wonderful to see the greatness of that man who could speak like that without blaming anybody, without comparing anything. Like an angel—this is the greatness of people who are spiritually rich even when they are materially poor.

We are not social workers. We may be doing social work in the eyes of some people, but we must be contemplatives in the heart of the world. For we must bring that presence of God into your family, for the family that prays together stays together. There is so much hatred, so much misery, and we with our prayer, with our sacrifice, are beginning at home. Love begins at home, and it is not how much we do but how much love we put into what we do.

And so here I am talking to you. I want you to find the poor here, right in your own home first. And begin love here. Bring that good news to your own people first. And find out about your next-door neighbors. Do you know who they are?

I had the most extraordinary experience of love of neighbor with a Hindu family. A gentleman came to our house and said: "Mother Teresa, there is a family who have not eaten for so long. Do something." So I took some rice and went there immediately. And I saw the children—their eyes shining with hunger, I don't know if you have ever seen hunger. But I have seen it very often. And the mother of the family took the rice I gave her and went out. When she came back, I asked her: "Where did you go? What did you do?" And she gave me a very simple answer: "They are hungry also." What struck me was that she knew—and who are they? A Muslim family—and she knew. I didn't bring any more rice that evening because I wanted them, Hindus and Muslims, to enjoy the joy of sharing.

But there were those children, radiating joy, sharing the joy and peace with their mother because she had the love to give until it hurts. And you see this is where love begins—at home in the family.

•

THE MAGIC MILL

The next few selections touch on the subject of old age. One of the great benefits of growing older is the opportunity to learn from the mistakes of our youth. If we take those opportunities, age brings wisdom.

At Apolda, I have been told, there is a magic mill. In appearance it is very much like a huge coffee mill, but it is turned from beneath instead of from above. Two large beams form the handles, by which two stout serving men keep the mill in motion.

And what kind of grain is ground in the mill? I will tell you the story as it was told to me, but I will not vouch for its truth. Old women are thrown in at the top, wrinkled and bent, without hair and without teeth, and when they come out below they are quite young and pretty, with cheeks as rosy as an apple.

One turn of the great mill does it all. Crick crack, it goes, and the whole magical change is made. And when those who have become young again are asked if it is not a painful process, they answer: "Painful? Oh, no! On the contrary, it is quite delightful! It is just like waking in the morning after a good night's rest, to see the sun shining in your room, and to hear the trees rustling and the birds twittering in the branches."

A long way from Apolda, as the story runs, there once lived an old woman who had often heard of the magic mill. She had been very happy in her youth, and she wished above all things to be young again. So, at length, she made up her mind to try what the mill would do for her. The journey to Apolda was a long and hard one, for the road led up and down many steep hills and through boggy meadows and over a stony desert where there was no cooling shade.

But by and by the woman stood before the mill.

"I want to become young again," she said to one of the serving men, who was quietly sitting on a bench puffing rings of smoke into the still blue air.

"And, pray, what is your name?" asked the man.

"The children call me Mother Redcap," was the answer.

"Sit down, then, on this bench, Mother Redcap," and the man went into the mill and, opening a thick book, returned with a long strip of paper.

"Is that the bill?" asked the old woman.

"Oh, no!" answered the other. "We charge nothing here; only you must sign your name to this paper."

"And why should I do that?" asked the woman.

The man smiled, and answered: "This paper is only a list of all the follies you have ever committed. It is complete, even to the present hour. Before you can become young again you must pledge yourself to commit them all over again in the very same order as before. To be sure, there is a long list. From the time you were sixteen until you were thirty, there was at least one folly every day, and on Sunday there were two; then you improved a little until you were forty; but after that the follies have been plentiful enough, I assure you."

The old woman sighed and said: "I know that what you say is all true. And I hardly think it will repay one to become young again at such a price."

"Neither do I think so," answered the man. "Very few indeed could it ever repay. And so we have an easy time of it—seven days of rest every week! The mill is always still, at least of late years."

"Now, couldn't we strike out just a few things?" pleaded the old woman, with a tap on the man's shoulder. "Suppose we leave off about a dozen things that I remember with sorrow. I wouldn't mind doing all the rest."

"No, no!" answered the man. "We are not allowed to leave off anything. The rule is, all or none!"

"Very well, then, I shall have nothing to do with your old mill," said she, turning away.

When she reached her home again, the good folk who came to look at her exclaimed: "Why, Mother Redcap, you come back older than you went! We never thought there was any truth in the story about that mill!"

She coughed a little dry cough, and answered: "What does it matter about being young again? If one will only try to make it so, old age may be as beautiful as youth!"

•

Father William

Robert Southey

Youth can learn from age about the right way to be young and grow old.

"You are old, Father William," the young man cried,
"The few locks that are left you are gray.
You are hale, Father William, a hearty old man;
Now tell me the reason, I pray."

"In the days of my youth," Father William replied,
"I remembered that youth would fly fast;
And abused not my health and my vigour at first,
That I never might need them at last."

"You are old, Father William," the young man cried,
"And pleasures with youth pass away,
And yet you lament not the days that are gone,
Now tell me the reason, I pray."

"In the days of my youth," Father William replied,
"I remembered that youth could not last;
I thought of the future, whatever I did,
That I never might grieve for the past."

"You are old, Father William," the young man cried,
"And life must be hastening away;
You are cheerful, and love to converse upon death,
Now tell me the reason, I pray."

"I am cheerful, young man," Father William replied,
"Let the cause thy attention engage;
In the days of my youth I remembered my God,
And He hath not forgotten my age!"

•

FRIENDSHIP SWEETENING TO THE
EVENING OF LIFE

Thomas Jefferson

Friendship is one virtue that may grow more dear to us in the
twilight of life. This letter from Thomas Jefferson to John Adams
gives us a glimpse into one of the most remarkable friendships in
our nation's political history. These men were long-time political
adversaries, but they were also wise enough and great-hearted
enough to know that honest philosophical differences do not have

to scar personal friendships. When he learned of schemes to "draw a curtain of separation" between the two of them, Jefferson wrote this eloquent letter to his old comrade.

Less than three years later, lying on his deathbed, John Adams reassured himself with the words, "Thomas Jefferson survives!" He did not know that five hundred miles away at Monticello, Jefferson was dying as well. On July 4, 1826, exactly fifty years after the birth of the nation they had helped create, two great friends and patriots departed this earth together.

To John Adams
Monticello, October 12, 1823

Dear Sir,

I do not write with the ease which your letter of September the 18th supposes. Crippled wrists and fingers make writing slow and laborious. But while writing to you, I lose the sense of these things in the recollection of ancient times, when youth and health made happiness out of everything. I forget for a while the hoary winter of age, when we can think of nothing but how to keep ourselves warm, and how to get rid of our heavy hours until the friendly hand of death shall rid us of all at once. Against this *tedium vitæ,* however, I am fortunately mounted on a hobby, which, indeed, I should have better managed some thirty or forty years ago; but whose easy amble is still sufficient to give exercise and amusement to an octogenary rider. This is the establishment of a University, on a scale more comprehensive and in a country more healthy and central than our old William and Mary, which these obstacles have long kept in a state of languor and inefficiency. But the tardiness with which such works proceed may render it doubtful whether I shall live to see it go into action.

Putting aside these things, however, for the present I write this letter as due to a friendship coeval with our government, and now attempted to be poisoned, when too late in life to be replaced by new affections. I had for some time observed in the public papers dark hints and mysterious innuendoes of a correspondence of yours with a friend, to whom you had opened your bosom without reserve, and which was to be made public by that friend or his representative. And now it is said to be actually published. It has not yet reached us, but extracts have been given, and such as seemed most likely to draw a curtain of separation between you and myself. Were there no other motive than that of indignation against the author of this outrage on private confidence, whose shaft seems to have been aimed at yourself more particularly, this would make it the duty of every honorable mind to disappoint that aim, by opposing to its impression a sevenfold shield of apathy and insensibility. With me, however, no such armor is needed. The circumstances of the times in which we have happened to live, and the partiality of our friends at a particular period, placed us in a state of apparent opposition, which some might suppose to be personal also; and there might not be wanting those who wished to make it so, by filling our ears with malignant falsehoods, by dressing up hideous phantoms of their own creation, presenting them to you under my name, to me under yours, and endeavouring to instill into our minds things concerning each other the most destitute of truth. And if there had been, at any time, a moment when we were off our guard, and in a temper to let the whispers of these people make us forget what we had known of each other for so many years, and years of so much trial, yet all men who have attended to the workings of the human mind, who have seen the false colors under which passion sometimes dresses the actions and motives of others, have seen also those passions subsiding with time and reflection, dissipating like mists before the rising sun, and restoring to us the sight of all things in their true shape and colors. It would be strange indeed if, at our years, we were to go back an age to hunt up imaginary or forgotten facts, to disturb the repose of affections so sweetening to the evening of our lives. Be assured, my dear Sir, that I am incapable of receiving the slightest impression from the effort now made to plant thorns on the pillow of age, worth and wisdom, and to sow tares between friends who have been such for near half a century. Beseeching you then, not to suffer your mind to be disquieted by this wicked attempt to poison its peace, and praying you to throw it by among the things which have never happened, I add sincere assurances of my unabated and constant attachment, friendship and respect.

•

THE MANDARIN AND THE TAILOR

This tale from Vietnam reminds us that clothes don't make the
man. More important, it reminds us that experience should bring
wisdom and humility. Just as life has stages, so does the ego.

One day a man received word he had just been appointed a
mandarin. He was so excited, he could barely contain himself.

"I will be a great man now," he told his friend. "I must have a
new robe made immediately, one that does justice to my new station in life."

"I know the perfect tailor for you," his friend replied. "He is
an old, wise man who knows how to give every customer the perfect fit. Let me give you his address."

So the new mandarin went to the tailor, who carefully took his
measurements. After he had put away his tape measure, the old
man said: "There is one more piece of information I need to know.
Tell me, sir, how long have you been a mandarin?"

"Why? What does that have to do with the fit of my robe?" his
client asked in surprise.

"Ah, I can't make the robe without knowing that, sir. You see,
a newly appointed mandarin is so impressed with his office, he
holds his head high in the air, tilts his nose up, and sticks his chest
out. So I must make the front of his robe longer than the back.

"A few years later, when he is busy with his work, and level-
headed from the stings of experience, and looks straight ahead to
see what is coming and what must be done next, then I cut the robe
so the front and back are the same length.

"And later, after he is stooped by old age and so many years of
weary service, not to mention the humility learned from a lifetime
of endeavor, then I must cut the robe so the back is longer than the
front.

"Therefore, sir, I must know your seniority if I am to fit you
properly."

The new mandarin walked out of the tailor's shop thinking less
of his robe and more of why his friend had sent him to see just this
man.

•

THE BED QUILT

Dorothy Canfield Fisher

This touching story about an elderly woman's triumph helps us
remember that life keeps its richness—whether we're young or
old—so long as we can devote ourselves to some ideal, some
worthy work. Here is the dignity of achievement.

Of all the Elwell family Aunt Mehetabel was certainly the most
unimportant member. It was in the New England days, when an
unmarried woman was an old maid at twenty, at forty was everyone's servant, and at sixty had gone through so much discipline that
she could need no more in the next world. Aunt Mehetabel was
sixty-eight.

She had never for a moment known the pleasure of being
important to anyone. Not that she was useless in her brother's
family; she was expected, as a matter of course, to take upon herself
the most tedious and uninteresting part of the household labors.
On Mondays she accepted as her share the washing of the men's
shirts, heavy with sweat and stiff with dirt from the fields and from
their own hard-working bodies. Tuesdays she never dreamed of
being allowed to iron anything pretty or even interesting, like the
baby's white dresses or the fancy aprons of her young lady nieces.
She stood all day pressing out a tiresome, monotonous succession
of dishcloths and towels and sheets.

In preserving-time she was allowed to have none of the pleasant responsibility of deciding when the fruit had cooked long
enough, nor did she share in the little excitement of pouring the
sweet-smelling stuff into the stone jars. She sat in a corner with the
children and stoned cherries incessantly, or hulled strawberries
until her fingers were dyed red to the bone.

The Elwells were not consciously unkind to their aunt—they
were even in a vague way fond of her—but she was so utterly
insignificant a figure in their lives that they bestowed no thought
whatever on her. Aunt Mehetabel did not resent this treatment; she
took it quite as unconsciously as they gave it. It was to be expected
when one was an old-maid dependent in a busy family. She gathered what crumbs of comfort she could from their occasional care-

less kindnesses and tried to hide the hurt which even yet pierced her at her brother's rough joking. In the winter when they all sat before the big hearth, roasted apples, drank mulled cider, and teased the girls about their beaux and the boys about their sweethearts, she shrank into a dusky corner with her knitting, happy if the evening passed without her brother saying, with a crude sarcasm, "Ask your Aunt Mehetabel about the beaux that used to come a-sparkin' her!" or, "Mehetabel, how was't when you was in love with Abel Cummings?" As a matter of fact, she had been the same at twenty as at sixty, a quiet, mouse-like little creature, too timid and shy for anyone to notice, or to raise her eyes for a moment and wish for a life of her own.

Her sister-in-law, a big hearty housewife who ruled indoors with as autocratic a sway as did her husband on the farm, was rather kind in an absent, offhand way to the shrunken little old woman, and it was through her that Mehetabel was able to enjoy the one pleasure of her life. Even as a girl she had been clever with her needle in the way of patching bed quilts. More than that she could never learn to do. The garments that she made for herself were the most lamentable affairs, and she was humbly grateful for any help in the bewildering business of putting them together. But in patchwork she enjoyed a tepid importance. She could really do that as well as anyone else. During years of devotion to this one art she had accumulated a considerable store of quilting patterns. Sometimes the neighbors would send over and ask "Miss Mehetabel" for such and such a design. It was with an agreeable flutter at being able to help someone that she went to the dresser, in her bare little room under the eaves, and extracted from her crowded portfolio the pattern desired.

She never knew how her great idea came to her. Sometimes she thought she must have dreamed it, sometimes she even wondered reverently, in the phraseology of the weekly prayer-meeting, if it had not been "sent" to her. She never admitted to herself that she could have thought of it without other help; it was too great, too ambitious, too lofty a project for her humble mind to have conceived. Even when she finished drawing the design with her own fingers, she gazed at it incredulously, not daring to believe that it could indeed be her handiwork. At first it seemed to her only like a lovely but quite unreal dream. She did not think of putting it into execution—so elaborate, so complicated, so beautifully difficult a pattern could be only for the angels in heaven to quilt. But so curiously does familiarity accustom us even to very wonderful things that as she lived with this astonishing creation of her mind, the longing grew stronger and stronger to give it material life with her nimble old fingers.

She gasped at her daring when this idea first swept over her and put it away as one does a sinfully selfish notion, but she kept coming back to it again and again. Finally she said compromisingly to herself that she would make one "square," just one part of her design, to see how it would look. Accustomed to the most complete dependence on her brother and his wife, she dared not do even this without asking Sophia's permission. With a heart full of hope and fear thumping furiously against her old ribs, she approached the mistress of the house on churning-day, knowing with the innocent guile of a child that the country woman was apt to be in a good temper while working over the fragrant butter in the cool cellar.

Sophia listened absently to her sister-in-law's halting, hesitating petition. "Why, yes, Mehetabel," she said, leaning far down into the huge churn for the last golden morsels—"why, yes, start another quilt if you want to. I've got a lot of pieces from the spring sewing that will work in real good." Mehetabel tried honestly to make her see that this would be no common quilt, but her limited vocabulary and her emotion stood between her and expression. At last Sophia said, with a kindly impatience: "Oh, there! Don't bother me. I never could keep track of your quiltin' patterns, anyhow. I don't care what pattern you go by."

With this overwhelmingly, although unconsciously, generous permission Mehetabel rushed back up the steep attic stairs to her room, and in a joyful agitation began preparations for the work of her life. It was even better than she hoped. By some heaven-sent inspiration she had invented a pattern beyond which no patchwork quilt could go.

She had but little time from her incessant round of household drudgery for this new and absorbing occupation, and she did not dare sit up late at night lest she burn too much candle. It was weeks before the little square began to take on a finished look, to show the pattern. Then Mehetabel was in a fever of impatience to bring it to completion. She was too conscientious to shirk even the smallest part of her share of the work of the house, but she rushed through it with a speed which left her panting as she climbed to the little room. This seemed like a radiant spot to her as she bent over the innumerable scraps of cloth which already in her imagination ranged themselves in the infinitely diverse pattern of her masterpiece. Finally she could wait no longer, and one evening ventured to bring her work down beside the fire where the family sat, hoping that some good fortune would give her a place near the tallow candles on the mantelpiece. She was on the last corner of the square, and her needle flew in and out with inconceivable rapidity. No one noticed her, a fact which filled her with relief, and by bedtime she had but a few more stitches to add.

As she stood up with the others, the square fluttered out of her trembling old hands and fell on the table. Sophia glanced at it carelessly. "Is that the new quilt you're beginning on?" she asked with a yawn. "It looks like a real pretty pattern. Let's see it." Up to that moment Mehetabel had labored in the purest spirit of disinterested devotion to an ideal, but as Sophia held her work toward the candle to examine it, and exclaimed in amazement and admiration, she felt an astonished joy to know that her creation would stand the test of publicity.

"Land sakes!" ejaculated her sister-in-law, looking at the many-colored square. "Why, Mehetabel Elwell, where'd you git that pattern?"

"I made it up," said Mehetabel quietly, but with unutterable pride.

"Now!" exclaimed Sophia incredulously. *"Did* you! Why, I never see such a pattern in my life. Girls, come here and see what your Aunt Mehetabel is doing."

The three tall daughters turned back reluctantly from the stairs. "I don't seem to take much interest in patchwork," said one listlessly.

"No, nor I neither!" answered Sophia, "but a stone image would take an interest in this pattern. Honest, Mehetabel, did you think of it yourself? And how under the sun and stars did you ever git your courage up to start in a-making it? Land! Look at all those tiny squinchy little seams! Why the wrong side ain't a thing *but* seams!"

The girls echoed their mother's exclamations, and Mr. Elwell himself came over to see what they were discussing. "Well, I declare!" he said, looking at his sister with eyes more approving than she could ever remember. "That beats old Mis' Wightman's quilt that got the blue ribbon so many times at the county fair."

Mehetabel's heart swelled within her, and tears of joy moistened her old eyes as she lay that night in her narrow, hard bed, too

proud and excited to sleep. The next day her sister-in-law amazed her by taking the huge pan of potatoes out of her lap and setting one of the younger children to peeling them. "Don't you want to go on with that quiltin' pattern?" she said. "I'd kind o' like to see how you're goin' to make the grapevine design come out on the corner."

By the end of the summer the family interest had risen so high that Mehetabel was given a little stand in the sitting-room where she could keep her pieces, and work in odd minutes. She almost wept over such kindness, and resolved firmly not to take advantage of it by neglecting her work, which she performed with a fierce thoroughness. But the whole atmosphere of her world was changed. Things had a meaning now. Through the longest task of washing milk-pans there rose the rainbow of promise of her variegated work. She took her place by the little table and put the thimble on her knotted, hard finger with the solemnity of a priestess performing a sacred rite.

She was even able to bear with some degree of dignity the extreme honor of having the minister and the minister's wife comment admiringly on her great project. The family felt quite proud of Aunt Mehetabel as Minister Bowman had said it was work as fine as any he had ever seen, "and he didn't know but finer!" The remark was repeated verbatim to the neighbors in the following weeks when they dropped in and examined in a perverse silence some astonishingly difficult *tour de force* which Mehetabel had just finished.

The family especially plumed themselves on the slow progress of the quilt. "Mehetabel has been to work on that corner for six weeks, come Tuesday, and she ain't half done yet," they explained to visitors. They fell out of the way of always expecting her to be the one to run on errands, even for the children. "Don't bother your Aunt Mehetabel," Sophia would call. "Can't you see she's got to a ticklish place on the quilt?"

The old woman sat up straighter and looked the world in the face. She was part of it at last. She joined in the conversation and her remarks were listened to. The children were even told to mind her when she asked them to do some service for her, although this she did but seldom, the habit of self-effacement being too strong.

One day some strangers from the next town drove up and asked if they could inspect the wonderful quilt which they had heard of, even down in their end of the valley. After that such visitations were not uncommon, making the Elwells' house a notable object. Mehetabel's quilt came to be one of the town sights, and no one was allowed to leave the town without having paid tribute to its worth. The Elwells saw to it that their aunt was better dressed than she had ever been before, and one of the girls made her a pretty little cap to wear on her thin white hair.

A year went by and a quarter of the quilt was finished; a second year passed and half was done. The third year Mehetabel had pneumonia and lay ill for weeks and weeks, overcome with terror lest she die before her work was completed. A fourth year and one could really see the grandeur of the whole design; and in September of the fifth year, the entire family watching her with eager and admiring eyes, Mehetabel quilted the last stitches in her creation. The girls held it up by the four corners, and they all looked at it in a solemn silence. Then Mr. Elwell smote one horny hand within the other and exclaimed: "By ginger! That's goin' to the county fair!" Mehetabel blushed a deep red at this. It was a thought which had occurred to her in a bold moment, but she had not dared to entertain it. The family acclaimed the idea, and one of the boys was forthwith dispatched to the house of the neighbor who was chairman of the committee for their village. He returned with radiant face. "Of course he'll take it. Like's not it may git a prize, so he says; but he's got to have it right off, because all the things are goin' tomorrow morning."

Even in her swelling pride Mehetabel felt a pang of separation as the bulky package was carried out of the house. As the days went on she felt absolutely lost without her work. For years it had been her one preoccupation, and she could not bear even to look at the little stand, now quite bare of the litter of scraps which had lain on it so long. One of the neighbors, who took the long journey to the fair, reported that the quilt was hung in a place of honor in a glass case in "Agricultural Hall." But that meant little to Mehetabel's utter ignorance of all that lay outside of her brother's home. The family noticed the old woman's depression, and one day Sophia said kindly, "You feel sort o' lost without the quilt, don't you, Mehetabel?"

"They took it away so quick!" she said wistfully. "I hadn't hardly had one real good look at it myself."

Mr. Elwell made no comment, but a day or two later he asked his sister how early she could get up in the morning.

"I dunno. Why?" she asked.

"Well, Thomas Ralston has got to drive clear to West Oldton to see a lawyer there, and that is four miles beyond the fair. He says if you can git up so's to leave here at four in the morning he'll drive you over to the fair, leave you there for the day, and bring you back again at night."

Mehetabel looked at him with incredulity. It was as though someone had offered her a ride in a golden chariot up to the gates of heaven. "Why, you can't *mean* it!" she cried, paling with the intensity of her emotion. Her brother laughed a little uneasily. Even to his careless indifference this joy was a revelation of the narrowness of her life in his home. "Oh, 'tain't so much to go to the fair. Yes, I mean it. Go git your things ready, for he wants to start tomorrow morning."

All that night a trembling, excited old woman lay and stared at the rafters. She, who had never been more than six miles from home in her life, was going to drive thirty miles away—it was like going to another world. She who had never seen anything more exciting than a church supper was to see the county fair. To Mehetabel it was like making the tour of the world. She had never dreamed of doing it. She could not at all imagine what it would be like.

Nor did the exhortations of the family, as they bade good-bye to her, throw any light on her confusion. They had all been at least once to the scene of gayety she was to visit, and as she tried to eat her breakfast they called out conflicting advice to her till her head whirled. Sophia told her to be sure and see the display of preserves. Her brother said not to miss inspecting the stock, her nieces said the fancywork was the only thing worth looking at, and her nephews said she must bring them home an account of the races. The buggy drove up to the door, she was helped in, and her wraps tucked about her. They all stood together and waved good-bye to her as she drove out of the yard. She waved back, but she scarcely saw them. On her return home that evening she was very pale, and so tired and stiff that her brother had to lift her out bodily, but her lips were set in a blissful smile. They crowded around her with thronging questions, until Sophia pushed them all aside, telling them Aunt Mehetabel was too tired to speak until she had had her supper. This was eaten in an enforced silence on the part of the children, and then the old woman was helped into an easy-chair before the fire. They gathered about her, eager for news of the great world, and Sophia said, "Now, come, Mehetabel, tell us all about it!"

Mehetabel drew a long breath. "It was just perfect!" she said. "Finer even than I thought. They've got it hanging up in the very middle of a sort o' closet made of glass, and one of the lower corners is ripped and turned back so's to show the seams on the wrong side."

"What?" asked Sophia, a little blankly.

"Why, the quilt!' said Mehetabel in surprise. "There are a whole lot of other ones in that room, but not one that can hold a candle to it, if I do say it who shouldn't. I heard lots of people say the same thing. You ought to have heard what the women said about that corner, Sophia. They said—well, I'd be ashamed to *tell* you what they said. I declare if I wouldn't!"

Mr. Elwell asked, "What did you think of that big ox we've heard so much about?"

"I didn't look at the stock," returned his sister indifferently. "That set of pieces you gave me, Maria, from your red waist, come out just lovely!" she assured one of her nieces. "I heard one woman say you could 'most smell the red silk roses."

"Did any of the horses in our town race?" asked young Thomas.

"I didn't see the races."

"How about the preserves?" asked Sophia.

"I didn't see the preserves," said Mehetabel calmly. "You see, I went right to the room where the quilt was, and then I didn't want to leave it. It had been so long since I'd seen it. I had to look at it first real good myself, and then I looked at the others to see if there was any that could come up to it. And then the people begun comin' in and I got so interested in hearin' what they had to say I couldn't think of goin' anywheres else. I ate my lunch right there too, and I'm as glad as can be I did, too, for what do you think?"—she gazed about her with kindling eyes—"while I stood there with a sandwich in one hand didn't the head of the hull concern come in and open the glass door and pin 'First Prize' right in the middle of the quilt!"

There was a stir of congratulation and proud exclamation. Then Sophia returned again to the attack. "Didn't you go to see anything else?" she queried.

"Why, no," said Mehetable. "Only the quilt. Why should I?"

She fell into a reverie where she saw again the glorious creation of her hand and brain hanging before all the world with the mark of highest approval on it. She longed to make her listeners see the splendid vision with her. She struggled for words; she reached blindly after unknown superlatives. "I tell you it looked like—" she said, and paused, hesitating. Vague recollections of hymn-book phraseology came into her mind, the only form of literary expression she knew; but they were dismissed as being sacrilegious, and also not sufficiently forcible. Finally, "I tell you it looked real *well!*" she assured them, and sat staring into the fire, on her tired old face the supreme content of an artist who has realized his ideal.

●

ULYSSES

Alfred Tennyson

This is a great poem for any time of life, but particularly for old age. Homer's *Odyssey* ends with the great hero Ulysses returning to his island home of Ithaca after long years of adventures; there, presumably, the rest of his days will be quiet and untroubled. But here Tennyson presents a Ulysses full of courage and determination "to strive, to seek, to find, and not to yield." The image is, of course, metaphorical. We can keep learning, growing, working, and exploring wherever we are. The point is to keep striving.

It little profits that an idle king,
By this still hearth, among these barren crags,
Match'd with an aged wife, I mete and dole
Unequal laws unto a savage race,
That hoard, and sleep, and feed, and know not me.

I cannot rest from travel: I will drink
Life to the lees: all times I have enjoy'd
Greatly, have suffer'd greatly, both with those
That loved me, and alone; on shore, and when
Thro' scudding drifts the rainy Hyades
Vext the dim sea: I am become a name;
For always roaming with a hungry heart
Much have I seen and known; cities of men
And manners, climates, councils, governments,
Myself not least, but honor'd of them all;
And drunk delight of battle with my peers,
Far on the ringing plains of windy Troy.

I am a part of all that I have met;
Yet all experience is an arch wherethro'
Gleams that untravel'd world, whose margin fades
Forever and forever when I move.
How dull it is to pause, to make an end,
To rust unburnish'd, not to shine in use!
As tho' to breathe were life. Life piled on life
Were all too little, and of one to me
Little remains: but every hour is saved
From that eternal silence, something more,
A bringer of new things; and vile it were
For some three suns to store and hoard myself
And this gray spirit yearning in desire
To follow knowledge like a sinking star,
Beyond the utmost bound of human thought.

This is my son, mine own Telemachus,
To whom I leave the scepter and the isle—
Well-loved of me, discerning to fulfill
This labor, by slow prudence to make mild
A rugged people, and thro' soft degrees
Subdue them to the useful and the good.
Most blameless is he, centered in the sphere
Of common duties, decent not to fail
In offices of tenderness, and pay
Meet adoration to my household gods,
When I am gone. He works his work, I mine.

There lies the port; the vessel puffs her sail:
There gloom the dark broad seas. My mariners,
Souls that have toil'd, and wrought, and thought with me—
That ever with a frolic welcome took
The thunder and the sunshine, and opposed
Free hearts, free foreheads—you and I are old;
Old age hath yet his honor and his toil;
Death closes all: but something ere the end,
Some work of noble note, may yet be done,
Not unbecoming men that strove with Gods.
The lights begin to twinkle from the rocks:
The long day wanes: the slow moon climbs: the deep
Moans round with many voices. Come, my friends,
'Tis not too late to seek a newer world.
Push off, and sitting well in order smite
The sounding furrows; for my purpose holds
To sail beyond the sunset, and the baths
Of all the western stars, until I die.
It may be that the gulfs will wash us down:
It may be we shall touch the Happy Isles,
And see the great Achilles, whom we knew.
Tho' much is taken, much abides; and tho'
We are not now that strength which in old days
Moved earth and heaven; that which we are, we are;
One equal temper of heroic hearts,
Made weak by time and fate, but strong in will
To strive, to seek, to find, and not to yield.

•

THE ANGEL

Hans Christian Andersen

The next two stories may help us deal with life's closing. Hans
Christian Andersen suggests that the end is a homeward journey,
in the company of angels. He also suggests that the kindnesses
neighbors give to one another become treasures laid up in
heaven.

Whenever a good child dies, an angel from heaven comes down to earth and takes the dead child in his arms, spreads out his great white wings, flies away over all the places the child has loved, and picks quite a handful of flowers, which he carries up to the Almighty that they may bloom in heaven more brightly than on earth. And the Father presses all the flowers to his heart; but He kisses the flower that pleases Him best, and the flower is then endowed with a voice, and can join in the great chorus of praise!

"See"—this is what an angel said, as he carried a dead child up to heaven, and the child heard, as if in a dream; and they went on over the regions of home where the little child had played, and came through gardens with beautiful flowers—"which of these shall we take with us to plant in heaven?" asked the angel.

Now there stood near them a slender, beautiful rosebush. But a wicked hand had broken the stem, so that all the branches, covered with half-opened buds, were hanging around, quite withered.

"The poor rosebush!" said the child. "Take it, that it may bloom up yonder."

And the angel took it, and kissed the child, and the little one half opened his eyes. They plucked some of the rich flowers, but also took with them the wild pansy and the despised buttercup.

"Now we have flowers," said the child.

And the angel nodded, but he did not yet fly upward to heaven. It was night and quite silent. They remained in the great city. They floated about there in a small street, where lay whole heaps of straw, ashes, and sweepings, for it had been garbage-removal day. There lay fragments of plates, bits of plaster, rags, and old hats, and all this did not look well. And the angel pointed amid all this confusion to a few fragments of a flowerpot, and to a lump of earth that had fallen out and was kept together by the roots of a great dried field flower, which was of no use, and had therefore been thrown out into the street.

"We will take that with us," said the angel. "I will tell you why as we fly onward.

"Down yonder in the narrow lane, in the low cellar, lived a poor sick boy. From his childhood he had been bedridden. When he was at his best he could go up and down the room a few times, leaning on crutches. That was the most he could do. For a few days in summer the sunbeams would penetrate for a few hours to the ground of the cellar, and when the poor boy sat there and the sun shone on him, and he looked at the red blood in his three fingers, as he held them up before his face, he would say, 'Yes, today he has been out!' He knew the forest with its beautiful vernal green only from the fact that a neighbor's little son brought him the first green branch of a beech tree, and he held that up over his head, and dreamed he was in the beechwood, where the sun shone and the birds sang.

"On a spring day the neighbor's boy brought him also field flowers, and among them was, by chance, one to which the root was still hanging. And so it was planted in a flowerpot, and placed by the bed, close to the window. The flower had been planted by a fortunate hand; and it grew, threw out new shoots, and bore flowers every year. It became a splendid flower garden to the sickly boy— his little treasure here on earth. He watered it, and tended it, and took care that it had the benefit of every ray of sunlight, down to the latest that struggled in through the narrow window. And the flower itself was woven into his dreams, for it grew for him and gladened his eyes, and spread its fragrance about him. And toward it he turned in death, when the Father called him.

"He has now been with the Almighty for a year. For a year the flower has stood forgotten in the window, and is withered; and thus, at the garbage-removal, it has been thrown out into the dust of the street. And this is the poor flower which we have taken into our bouquet; for this flower has given more joy than the richest in a queen's garden."

"But how do you know all this?" asked the child.

"I know it," said the angel, "for I myself was that boy who walked on crutches. I know my flower well."

And the child opened his eyes and looked into the glorious, happy face of the angel; and at the same moment they entered the regions where there is peace and joy. And the Father pressed the dead child to his bosom, and then it received wings like the angel, and flew hand in hand with him. And the Almighty kissed the dry, withered field flower, and it received a voice and sang with all the angels hovering around—some near, and some in wider circles, and some in infinite distance, but all equally happy. And they all sang—little and great, the good, happy child, and the poor field flower that had lain there withered, thrown among the dust in the rubbish of the garbage-removal day, in the dark, narrow lane.

•

THE INDIAN GIRL AND
HER MESSENGER BIRD

George W. Ranck

Love restores, even at times of death.

Once upon a time, there was an Indian who lived in a big wood on the banks of a beautiful river, and he did nothing all day long but catch fish and hunt wild deer. Well, this Indian had two lovely little daughters, and he named one Sunbeam, because she was so bright and cheerful, and the other he called Starlight, because, he said, her sweet eyes twinkled like the stars.

Sunbeam and Starlight were as busy as bees, from morning till night. They ran races under the shady trees, made bouquets of wild flowers, swung on grapevine swings, turned berries and acorns into beads, and dressed their glossy black hair with bright feathers that beautiful birds had dropped. They loved each other so much, and were so happy together, that they never knew what trouble meant until, one day, Starlight got very sick, and before the big moon came over the treetops the sweet Indian child had closed her starry eyes in death, and rested for the last time upon her soft little deer-skin bed.

And now, for the first time, Sunbeam's heart was full of grief. She could not play, for Starlight was gone, she knew not where. So she took the bright feathers out of her hair, and sat down by the river and cried and cried for Starlight to come back to her. But when her father told her that Starlight was gone to the Spiritland of love and beauty, and would be happy forever and ever, Sunbeam was comforted.

"Now," said she, "I know where darling Starlight is, and I can kiss her and talk to her again."

Sunbeam had heard her people say that the birds were messengers from the Spiritland. So she hunted through the woods until she found a little songbird that was too young to fly, fast asleep in its nest. She carried it gently home, put it into a cage, and watched over it and fed it tenderly day after day until its wings grew strong and it filled the woods with its music. Then she carried it in her soft little hands to Starlight's grave; and after she had loaded it with kisses and messages of love for Starlight, she told it never to cease its sweetest song or fold its shining wings until it had flown to the Spiritland. She let it go, and the glad bird, as it rose above the tall green trees, poured forth a song more joyful than any that Sunbeam had ever heard. Higher and higher it flew, and sweeter and sweeter grew its song, until at last both its form and its music were lost in the floating summer clouds.

Then Sunbeam ran swiftly over the soft grass to her father and told him, with a bright smile and a light heart, that she had talked with dear Starlight, and had kissed her sweet rosy mouth again. And Sunbeam was once more her father's bright and happy little Indian girl.

•

THE DEATH OF THOMAS MORE
James Anthony Froude

A statesman, scholar, and deeply religious Roman Catholic, Thomas More (1478–1535) resigned his office as chancellor of England in 1532 when the clergy of England accepted King Henry VIII as their head. He retired to his home, where he pursued his writing, but in 1534 he was summoned to swear to the Act of Succession, which implied a denial of papal supremacy. More refused to take the oath and was imprisoned in the Tower of London. In 1535 he was tried for treason and sentenced to death. Here is a man who lived by the dictates of his conscience and died by them, too, when the time came.

At daybreak he was awakened by the entrance of Sir Thomas Pope, who had come to confirm his anticipations and to tell him it was the king's pleasure that he should suffer at nine o'clock that morning. He received the news with utter composure.

"I am much bounden to the king," he said, "for the benefits and honors he has bestowed upon me; and, so help me God, most of all am I bounden to him that it pleaseth his majesty to rid me so shortly out of the miseries of this present world."

Pope told him the king desired that he would not "use many words on the scaffold." "Mr. Pope," he answered, "you do well to give me warning, for otherwise I had purposed somewhat to have spoken; but no matter wherewith his grace should have cause to be offended. Howbeit, whatever I intended I shall obey His Highness's command."

Afterwards he discussed the arrangements for his funeral, at which he begged that his family might be present, and, when all was settled, Pope rose to leave him. He was an old friend. He took More's hand and wrung it, and, quite overcome, burst into tears.

"Quiet yourself, Mr. Pope," More said, "and be not discomfited; for I trust we shall soon see each other full merrily, when we shall live and love together in eternal bliss."

As soon as he was alone, he dressed in his most elaborate costume. It was for the benefit, he said, of the executioner, who was to do him so great a service. Sir William Kingston remonstrated, and with some difficulty induced him to put on a plainer suit; but, that his intended liberality should not fail, he sent the man a gold angel in compensation, "as a token that he maliced him nothing, but rather loved him extremely."

So about nine of the clock he was brought by the lieutenant out of the Tower, his beard being long, which fashion he had never before used, his face pale and lean, carrying in his hands a red cross, casting his eyes often towards heaven. He had been unpopular as a judge, and one or two persons in the crowd were insolent to him; but the distance was short and soon over, as all else was nearly over now.

The scaffold had been awkwardly erected and shook as he placed his foot upon the ladder. "See me safe up," he said to Kingston. "For my coming down I can shift for myself." He began to speak to the people, but the sheriff begged him not to proceed, and he contented himself with asking for their prayers, and desiring them to bear witness for him that he died a faithful servant of God and the king. He then repeated the Miserere prayer on his knees; and when he had ended and had risen, the executioner, with an emotion that promised ill for the manner in which his part in the tragedy would be accomplished, begged his forgiveness.

More kissed him. "Thou art to do me the greatest benefit that I can receive," he said. "Pluck up thy spirit, man, and be not afraid to do thine office. My neck is very short. Take heed therefore that thou strike not awry, for saving of thy honesty." The executioner offered to tie his eyes. "I will cover them myself," he said, and binding them in a cloth that he had brought with him, he knelt and laid his head upon the block.

The fatal stroke was about to fall, when he signed for a moment's delay while he laid aside his beard. "Pity that should be cut," he murmured, "that has not committed treason." With such strange words, the strangest perhaps ever uttered at such a time, the lips most famous through Europe for eloquence and wisdom closed forever.

•

THE STUDENT

Anton Chekhov

This is a story that lifts the spirit. It speaks of the deep mystery of compassion ("her whole being was interested in what was passing in Peter's soul"). It speaks of the mystery that is the interconnectedness of all lives and events. And it speaks of the mystery that is the peace that passes all understanding.

At first the weather was fine and still. The thrushes were calling, and in the swamps close by something alive droned pitifully with a sound like blowing into an empty bottle. A snipe flew by, and the shot aimed at it rang out with a gay, resounding note in the spring air. But when it began to get dark in the forest a cold, penetrating wind blew inappropriately from the east, and everything sank into silence. Needles of ice stretched across the pools, and it felt cheerless, remote, and lonely in the forest. There was a whiff of winter.

Ivan Velikopolsky, the son of a sacristan, and a student of the clerical academy, returning home from shooting, walked all the time by the path in the waterside meadow. His fingers were numb and his face was burning with the wind. It seemed to him that the cold that had suddenly come on had destroyed the order and harmony of things, that nature itself felt ill at ease, and that was why the evening darkness was falling more rapidly than usual. All around it was deserted and peculiarly gloomy. The only light was one gleaming in the widows' gardens near the river; the village, over three miles away, and everything in the distance all around was plunged in the cold evening mist. The student remembered that, as he went out from the house, his mother was sitting barefoot on the floor in the entry, cleaning the samovar, while his father lay on the stove coughing. As it was Good Friday nothing had been cooked, and the student was terribly hungry. And now, shrinking from the cold, he thought that just such a wind had blown in the days of Rurik and in the time of Ivan the Terrible and Peter, and in their time there had been just the same desperate poverty and hunger, the same thatched roofs with holes in them, ignorance, misery, the same desolation around, the same darkness, the same feeling of oppression—all these had existed, did exist, and would exist, and the lapse of a thousand years would make life no better. And he did not want to go home.

The gardens were called the widows' because they were kept by two widows, mother and daughter. A campfire was burning brightly with a crackling sound, throwing out light far around on the ploughed earth. The widow Vasilisa, a tall, fat old woman in a man's coat, was standing by and looking thoughtfully into the fire; her daughter, Lukerya, a little pockmarked woman with a stupid-looking face, was sitting on the ground, washing a caldron and spoons. Apparently they had just had supper. There was a sound of men's voices; it was the laborers watering their horses at the river.

"Here you have winter back again," said the student, going up to the campfire. "Good evening."

Vasilisa started, but at once recognized him and smiled cordially.

"I did not know you; God bless you," she said. "You'll be rich."

They talked. Vasilisa, a woman of experience who had been in service with the gentry, first as a wet nurse, afterwards as a children's nurse, expressed herself with refinement, and a soft, sedate smile never left her face. Her daughter, Lukerya, a village peasant woman who had been crushed by her husband, simply screwed up her eyes at the student and said nothing, and she had a strange expression like that of a deaf-mute.

"At just such a fire the Apostle Peter warmed himself," said the student, stretching out his hands to the fire, "so it must have been cold then, too. Ah, what a terrible night it must have been, granny! An utterly dismal long night!"

He looked around at the darkness, shook his head abruptly,

and asked: "No doubt you have been at the reading of the Twelve Gospels?"

"Yes, I have," answered Vasilisa.

"If you remember, at the Last Supper Peter said to Jesus, 'I am ready to go with Thee into darkness and unto death.' And our Lord answered him thus: 'I say unto thee, Peter, before the cock croweth thou wilt have denied Me thrice.' After the supper Jesus went through the agony of death in the garden and prayed, and poor Peter was weary in spirit and faint; his eyelids were heavy and he could not struggle against sleep. He fell asleep. Then you heard how Judas the same night kissed Jesus and betrayed Him to His tormentors. They took Him bound to the high priest and beat Him, while Peter, exhausted, worn out with misery and alarm, hardly awake, you know, feeling that something awful was just going to happen on earth, followed behind.... He loved Jesus passionately, intensely, and now he saw from far off how He was beaten...."

Lukerya left the spoons and fixed an immovable stare upon the student.

"They came to the high priest's," he went on. "They began to question Jesus, and meantime the laborers made a fire in the yard as it was cold, and warmed themselves. Peter, too, stood with them near the fire and warmed himself as I am doing. A woman, seeing him, said: 'He was with Jesus, too'—that is as much as to say that he, too, should be taken to be questioned. And all the laborers who were standing near the fire must have looked sourly and suspiciously at him, because he was confused and said, 'I don't know Him.' A little while after again someone recognized him as one of Jesus' disciples and said, 'Thou, too, art one of them,' but again he denied it. And for the third time someone turned to him, 'Why, did I not see thee with Him in the garden today?' For the third time he denied it. And immediately after that time the cock crowed, and

Peter, looking from far off at Jesus, remembered the words He had said to him in the evening. . . . He remembered, he came to himself, went out of the yard and wept bitterly—bitterly. In the Gospel it is written: 'He went out and wept bitterly.' I imagine it: the still, still, dark, dark garden, and in the stillness, faintly audible, smothered sobbing. . . ."

The student sighed and sank into thought. Still smiling, Vasilisa suddenly gave a gulp, big tears flowed freely down her cheeks, and she screened her face from the fire with her sleeve as though ashamed of her tears, and Lukerya, staring immovably at the student, flushed crimson, and her expression became strained and heavy like that of someone enduring intense pain.

The laborers came back from the river, and one of them riding a horse was quite near, and the light from the fire quivered upon him. The student said goodnight to the widows and went on. And again the darkness was about him and his fingers began to be numb. A cruel wind was blowing; winter really had come back and it did not feel as though Easter would be the day after tomorrow.

Now the student was thinking about Vasilisa: since she had shed tears, all that had happened to Peter the night before the Crucifixion must have some relation to her. . . .

He looked around. The solitary light was still gleaming in the darkness and no figures could be seen near it now. The student thought again that if Vasilisa had shed tears, and her daughter had been troubled, it was evident that what he had just been telling them about, which had happened nineteen centuries ago, had a relation to the present—to both women, to the desolate village, to himself, to all people. The old woman had wept, not because he could tell the story touchingly but because Peter was near to her, because her whole being was interested in what was passing in Peter's soul.

And joy suddenly stirred in his soul, and he even stopped for a minute to take breath. "The past," he thought, "is linked with the present by an unbroken chain of events flowing one out of another." And it seemed to him that he had just seen both ends of that chain, that when he touched one end the other quivered.

When he crossed the river by the ferryboat and afterwards, mounting the hill, looked at his village and towards the west where the cold purple sunset laid a narrow streak of light, he thought that truth and beauty, which had guided human life there in the garden and in the yard of the high priest, had continued without interruption to this day, and had evidently always been the chief thing in human life and in all earthly life, indeed; and the feeling of youth, health, vigor—he was only twenty-two—and the inexpressible sweet expectation of happiness, of unknown mysterious happiness, took possession of him little by little, and life seemed to him enchanting, marvelous, and full of lofty meaning.

•

WHAT MEN LIVE BY

Leo Tolstoy

This beautiful parable is an adaptation of an ancient tale found in different versions in the Koran, the Talmud, the Apocrypha, and *The Arabian Nights*. Tolstoy originally introduced this story with a series of verses from the first letter of John in the Bible, including verse sixteen of chapter four: "God is love; and he who abides in love abides in God, and God abides in him."

I

A shoemaker named Simon, who had neither house nor land of his own, lived with his wife and children in a peasant's hut and earned his living by his work. Work was cheap but bread was dear, and what he earned he spent for food. The man and his wife had but one sheepskin coat between them for winter wear, and even that was worn to tatters, and this was the second year he had been wanting to buy sheepskins for a new coat. Before winter Simon saved up a little money: a three-ruble note lay hidden in his wife's box, and five rubles and twenty kopeks were owed him by customers in the village.

So one morning he prepared to go to the village to buy the sheepskins. He put on over his shirt his wife's wadded nankeen jacket, and over that he put his own cloth coat. He took the three-ruble note in his pocket, cut himself a stick to serve as a staff, and started off after breakfast. "I'll collect the five rubles that are due me," thought he, "and add the three I have got, and that will be enough to buy sheepskins for the winter coat."

He came to the village and called at a peasant's hut, but the

man was not at home. The peasant's wife promised that the money
would be paid next week, but she would not pay it herself. Then
Simon called on another peasant, but this one swore he had no
money, and would pay only twenty kopeks which he owed for a
pair of boots Simon had mended. Simon then tried to buy the
sheepskins on credit, but the dealer would not trust him.

"Bring your money," said he, "then you may have your pick of
the skins. We know what debt-collecting is like."

So all the business the shoemaker did was to get twenty kopeks
for boots he had mended, and to take a pair of felt boots a peasant
gave him to sole with leather.

Simon felt downhearted. He spent the twenty kopeks on vodka,
and started homewards without having bought any skins. In the
morning he had felt the frost, but now, after drinking the vodka, he
felt warm even without a sheepskin coat. He trudged along, striking
his stick on the frozen earth with one hand, swinging the felt boots
with the other, and talking to himself.

"I'm quite warm," said he, "though I have no sheepskin coat.
I've had a drop and it runs through all my veins. I need no sheepskins. I go along and don't worry about anything. That's the sort of
man I am! What do I care? I can live without sheepskins. I don't
need them. My wife will fret, to be sure. And, true enough, it *is* a
shame; one works all day long and then does not get paid. Stop a
bit! If you don't bring that money along, sure enough I'll skin you,
blessed if I don't. How's that? He pays twenty kopeks at a time! What
can I do with twenty kopeks? Drink it—that's all one can do! Hard
up, he says he is! So he may be—but what about me? You have
house, and cattle, and everything, I've only what I stand up in! You
have corn of your own growing, I have to buy every grain. Do what
I will, I must spend three rubles every week for bread alone. I
come home and find the bread all used up and I have to fork out
another ruble and a half. So just you pay up what you owe, and no
nonsense about it!"

By this time he had nearly reached the shrine at the bend of
the road. Looking up, he saw something whitish behind the shrine.
The daylight was fading, and the shoemaker peered at the thing
without being able to make out what it was. "There was no white
stone here before. Can it be an ox? It's not like an ox. It has a head
like a man, but it's too white; and what could a man be doing
there?"

He came closer, so that it was clearly visible. To his surprise it really was a man, alive or dead, sitting naked, leaning motionless against the shrine. Terror seized the shoemaker, and he thought, "Someone has killed him, stripped him, and left him here. If I meddle I shall surely get into trouble."

So the shoemaker went on. He passed in front of the shrine so that he could not see the man. When he had gone some way he looked back, and saw that the man was no longer leaning against the shrine but was moving as if looking towards him. The shoemaker felt more frightened than before, and thought, "Shall I go back to him or shall I go on? If I go near him, something dreadful may happen. Who knows who the fellow is. He has not come here for any good. If I go near him he may jump up and throttle me, and there will be no getting away. Or if not, he'd still be a burden on one's hands. What could I do with a naked man? I couldn't give him my last clothes. Heaven only help me to get away!"

So the shoemaker hurried on, leaving the shrine behind him —when suddenly his conscience smote him and he stopped in the road.

"What are you doing, Simon?" said he to himself. "The man may be dying of want, and you slip past, afraid. Have you grown so rich as to be afraid of robbers? Ah, Simon, shame on you!"

So he turned back and went up to the man.

II

Simon approached the stranger, looked at him, and saw that he was a young man, fit, with no bruises on his body, but evidently freezing and frightened, and he sat there leaning back without looking up at Simon, as if too faint to lift his eyes. Simon went close to him and then the man seemed to wake up. Turning his head, he opened his eyes and looked into Simon's face. That one look was enough to make Simon fond of the man. He threw the felt boots on the ground, undid his sash, laid it on the boots, and took off his cloth coat.

"It's not a time for talking," said he. "Come, put this coat on at once!" And Simon took the man by the elbows and helped him to rise. As he stood there, Simon saw that his body was clean and in good condition, his hands and feet shapely, and his face good and kind. He threw his coat over the man's shoulders, but the latter could not find the sleeves. Simon guided his arms into them, and drawing the coat well on, wrapped it closely about him, tying the sash round the man's waist.

Simon even took off his torn cap to put it on the man's head, but then his own head felt cold and he thought, "I'm quite bald, while he has long curly hair." So he put his cap on his own head again. "It will be better to give him something for his feet," thought he, and he made the man sit down and helped him to put on the felt boots, saying, "There, friend, now move about and warm yourself. Other matters can be settled later on. Can you walk?"

The man stood up and looked kindly at Simon, but could not say a word.

"Why don't you speak?" said Simon. "It's too cold to stay here; we must be getting home. There now, take my stick, and if you're feeling weak, lean on that. Now step out!"

The man started walking and moved easily, not lagging behind.

As they went along, Simon asked him, "And where do you belong to?"

"I'm not from these parts."

"I thought as much. I know the folks hereabouts. But how did you come to be there by the shrine?"

"I cannot tell."

"Has someone been ill-treating you?"

"No one has ill-treated me. God has punished me."

"Of course, God rules all. Still, you'll have to find food and shelter somewhere. Where do you want to go to?"

"It is all the same to me."

Simon was amazed. The man did not look like a rogue, and he spoke gently, but yet he gave no account of himself. Still Simon thought, "Who knows what may have happened?" And he said to the stranger, "Well then, come home with me and at least warm yourself awhile."

So Simon walked towards his home, and the stranger kept up with him, walking at his side. The wind had risen and Simon felt it cold under his shirt. He was getting over his tipsiness by now and began to feel the frost. He went along sniffling and wrapping his wife's coat around him, and he thought to himself: "There now— talk about sheepskins! I went out for sheepskins and come home without even a coat to my back, and what is more, I'm bringing a naked man along with me. Matrena won't be pleased!" And when he thought of his wife he felt sad, but when he looked at the stranger and remembered how he had looked up at him at the shrine, his heart was glad.

III

Simon's wife had everything ready early that day. She had cut wood, brought water, fed the children, eaten her own meal, and now she sat thinking. She wondered when she ought to make bread: now or tomorrow? There was still a large piece left.

"If Simon has had some dinner in town," thought she, "and does not eat much for supper, the bread will last another day."

She weighed the piece of bread in her hand again and again, and thought: "I won't make any more today. We have only enough flour left to bake one batch. We can manage to make this last till Friday."

So Matrena put away the bread, and sat down at the table to patch her husband's shirt. While she worked she thought how her husband was buying skins for a winter coat.

"If only the dealer does not cheat him. My good man is much too simple; he cheats nobody, but any child can take him in. Eight rubles is a lot of money—he should get a good coat at that price. Not tanned skins, but still a proper winter coat. How difficult it was last winter to get on without a warm coat. I could neither get down to the river, nor go out anywhere. When he went out he put on all we had, and there was nothing left for me. He did not start very early today, but still it's time he was back. I only hope he has not gone on a spree!"

Hardly had Matrena thought this than steps were heard on the threshold and someone entered. Matrena stuck her needle into her work and went out into the passage. There she saw two men: Simon, and with him a man without a hat and wearing felt boots.

Matrena noticed at once that her husband smelt of spirits. "There now, he has been drinking," thought she. And when she saw that he was coatless, had only her jacket on, brought no parcel, stood there silent, and seemed ashamed, her heart was ready to break with disappointment. "He has drunk the money," thought she, "and has been on a spree with some good-for-nothing fellow whom he has brought home with him."

Matrena let them pass into the hut, followed them in, and saw that the stranger was a young, slight man, wearing her husband's coat. There was no shirt to be seen under it, and he had no hat. Having entered, he stood neither moving nor raising his eyes, and Matrena thought, "He must be a bad man—he's afraid."

Matrena frowned, and stood beside the stove looking to see what they would do.

Simon took off his cap and sat down on the bench as if things were all right.

"Come, Matrena; if supper is ready, let us have some."

Matrena muttered something to herself and did not move, but stayed where she was, by the stove. She looked first at the one and then at the other of them and only shook her head. Simon saw that his wife was annoyed, but tried to pass it off. Pretending not to notice anything, he took the stranger by the arm.

"Sit down, friend," said he, "and let us have some supper."

The stranger sat down on the bench.

"Haven't you cooked anything for us?" said Simon.

Matrena's anger boiled over. "I've cooked, but not for you. It seems to me you have drunk your wits away. You went to buy a sheepskin coat, but come home without so much as the coat you had on, and bring a naked vagabond home with you. I have no supper for drunkards like you."

"That's enough, Matrena. Don't wag your tongue without reason! You had better ask what sort of man—"

"And you tell me what you've done with the money?"

Simon found the pocket of the jacket, drew out the three-ruble note, and unfolded it.

"Here is the money. Trifonov did not pay, but promises to pay soon."

Matrena got still more angry; he had bought no sheepskins, but had put his only coat on some naked fellow and had even brought him to their house.

She snatched up the note from the table, took it to put away in safety, and said: "I have no supper for you. We can't feed all the naked drunkards in the world."

"There now, Matrena, hold your tongue a bit. First hear what a man has to say—!"

"Much wisdom I shall hear from a drunken fool. I was right in not wanting to marry you—a drunkard. The linen my mother gave me you drank, and now you've been to buy a coat—and have drunk it too!"

Simon tried to explain to his wife that he had spent only twenty kopeks; tried to tell how he had found the man—but Matrena would not let him get a word in. She talked nineteen to the dozen, and dragged in things that had happened ten years before.

Matrena talked and talked, and at last she flew at Simon and seized him by the sleeve.

"Give me my jacket. It is the only one I have, and you must needs take it from me and wear it yourself. Give it here, you mangy dog, and may the devil take you."

Simon began to pull off the jacket, and turned a sleeve of it inside out; Matrena seized the jacket and it burst its seams. She snatched it up, threw it over her head, and went to the door. She meant to go out but stopped undecided—she wanted to work off her anger, but she also wanted to learn what sort of a man the stranger was.

IV

Matrena stopped and said: "If he were a good man he would not be naked. Why, he hasn't even a shirt on him. If he were all right, you would say where you came across the fellow."

"That's just what I am trying to tell you," said Simon. "As I came to the shrine I saw him sitting all naked and frozen. It isn't quite the weather to sit about naked! God sent me to him or he would have perished. What was I to do? How do we know what may have happened to him? So I took him, clothed him, and brought him along. Don't be so angry, Matrena. It is a sin. Remember, we must all die one day."

Angry words rose to Matrena's lips, but she looked at the stranger and was silent. He sat on the edge of the bench, motionless, his hands folded on his knees, his head drooping on his breast, his eyes closed, and his brows knit as if in pain. Matrena was silent, and Simon said, "Matrena, have you no love of God?"

Matrena heard these words, and as she looked at the stranger, suddenly her heart softened towards him. She came back from the door, and going to the stove she got out the supper. Setting a cup on the table, she poured out some *kvas.* Then she brought out the last piece of bread and set out a knife and spoons.

"Eat, if you want to," said she.

Simon drew the stranger to the table.

"Take your place, young man," said he.

Simon cut the bread and crumbled it into the broth, and they began to eat. Matrena sat at the corner of the table, resting her head on her hand and looking at the stranger.

And Matrena was touched with pity for the stranger and began to feel fond of him. And at once the stranger's face lit up; his brows were no longer bent, he raised his eyes and smiled at Matrena.

When they had finished supper, the woman cleared away the

things and began questioning the stranger. "Where are you from?" said she.

"I am not from these parts."

"But how did you come to be on the road?"

"I may not tell."

"Did someone rob you?"

"God punished me."

"And you were lying there naked?"

"Yes, naked and freezing. Simon saw me and had pity on me. He took off his coat, put it on me, and brought me here. And you have fed me, given me drink, and shown pity on me. God will reward you!"

Matrena rose, took from the window Simon's old shirt that she had been patching, and gave it to the stranger. She also brought out a pair of trousers for him.

"There," said she, "I see you have no shirt. Put this on, and lie down where you please, in the loft or on the stove."

The stranger took off the coat, put on the shirt, and lay down in the loft. Matrena put out the candle, took the coat, and climbed to where her husband lay on the stove.

Matrena drew the skirts of the coat over her and lay down but could not sleep; she could not get the stranger out of her mind.

When she remembered that he had eaten their last piece of bread and that there was none for tomorrow, and thought of the shirt and trousers she had given away, she felt grieved; but when she remembered how he had smiled, her heart was glad.

Long did Matrena lie awake, and she noticed that Simon also was awake—he drew the coat towards him.

"Simon!"

"Well?"

"You have had the last of the bread and I have not put any to rise. I don't know what we shall do tomorrow. Perhaps I can borrow some from neighbor Martha."

"If we're alive we shall find something to eat."

The woman lay still awhile, and then said, "He seems a good man, but why does he not tell us who he is?"

"I suppose he has his reasons."

"Simon!"

"Well?"

"We give, but why does nobody give us anything?"

Simon did not know what to say, so he only said, "Let us stop talking," and turned over and went to sleep.

V

In the morning Simon awoke. The children were still asleep; his wife had gone to the neighbor's to borrow some bread. The stranger alone was sitting on the bench, dressed in the old shirt and trousers, and looking upwards. His face was brighter than it had been the day before.

Simon said to him, "Well, friend, the belly wants bread and the naked body clothes. One has to work for a living. What work do you know?"

"I do not know any."

This surprised Simon, but he said, "Men who want to learn can learn anything."

"Men work and I will work also."

"What is your name?"

"Michael."

"Well, Michael, if you don't wish to talk about yourself, that is your own affair, but you'll have to earn a living for yourself. If you will work as I tell you, I will give you food and shelter."

"May God reward you! I will learn. Show me what to do."

Simon took yarn, put it around his thumb, and began to twist it.

"It is easy enough—see!"

Michael watched him, put some yarn around his own thumb in the same way, caught the knack, and twisted the yarn also.

Then Simon showed him how to wax the thread. This Michael also mastered. Next Simon showed him how to twist the bristle in, and how to sew, and this, too, Michael learned at once.

Whatever Simon showed him he understood at once, and after three days he worked as if he had sewn boots all his life. He worked without stopping and ate little. When work was over he sat silently, looking upwards. He hardly went into the street, spoke only when necessary, and neither joked nor laughed. They never saw him smile, except that first evening when Matrena gave them supper.

VI

Day by day and week by week the year went by. Michael lived and worked with Simon. His fame spread till people said that no one sewed boots so neatly and strongly as Simon's workman, Michael. From all the district around, people came to Simon for their boots, and he began to be well off.

One winter's day, as Simon and Michael sat working, a carriage on sledge-runners, with three horses and with bells, drove up to the hut. They looked out of the window. The carriage stopped at their door, a fine servant jumped down from the box and opened the door. A gentleman in a fur coat got out and walked up to Simon's hut. Up jumped Matrena and opened the door wide. The gentleman stooped to enter the hut, and when he drew himself up again, his head nearly reached the ceiling and he seemed quite to fill his end of the room.

Simon rose, bowed, and looked at the gentleman with astonishment. He had never seen anyone like him. Simon himself was lean, Michael was thin, and Matrena was dry as a bone, but this man was like someone from another world: red-faced, burly, with a neck like a bull's, and looking altogether as if he were cast in iron.

The gentleman puffed, threw off his fur coat, sat down on the bench, and said, "Which of you is the master bootmaker?"

"I am, your Excellency," said Simon, coming forward.

Then the gentleman shouted to his lad, "Hey, Fedka, bring the leather!"

The servant ran in, bringing a parcel. The gentleman took the parcel and put it on the table.

"Untie it," said he. The lad untied it.

The gentleman pointed to the leather.

"Look here, shoemaker," said he, "do you see this leather?"

"Yes, your honor."

"But do you know what sort of leather it is?"

Simon felt the leather and said, "It is good leather."

"Good, indeed! Why, you fool, you never saw such leather before in your life. It's German, and it cost twenty rubles."

Simon was frightened, and said, "Where should I ever see leather like that?"

"Just so! Now, can you make it into boots for me?"

"Yes, your Excellency, I can."

Then the gentleman shouted at him: "You *can,* can you? Well, remember for whom you are to make them, and what the leather is. You must make me boots that will wear for a year, neither losing shape nor coming unsewn. If you can do it, take the leather and cut it up, but if you can't, say so. I warn you now, if your boots come unsewn or lose shape within a year I will have you put in prison. If they don't burst or lose shape for a year, I will pay you ten rubles for your work."

Simon was frightened and did not know what to say. He glanced at Michael and nudging him with his elbow, whispered, "Shall I take the work?"

Michael nodded his head as if to say, "Yes, take it."

Simon did as Michael advised and undertook to make boots that would not lose shape or split for a whole year.

Calling his servant, the gentleman told him to pull the boot off his left leg, which he stretched out.

"Take my measure!" said he.

Simon stitched a paper measure seventeen inches long, smoothed it out, knelt down, wiped his hands well on his apron so as not to soil the gentleman's sock, and began to measure. He measured the sole, and around the instep, and began to measure the calf of the leg, but the paper was too short. The calf of the leg was as thick as a beam.

"Mind you don't make it too tight in the leg."

Simon stitched on another strip of paper. The gentleman twitched his toes about in his sock, looking around at those in the hut, and as he did so he noticed Michael.

"Whom have you there?" asked he.

"That is my workman. He will sew the boots."

"Mind," said the gentleman to Michael, "remember to make them so that they will last me a year."

Simon also looked at Michael, and saw that Michael was not looking at the gentleman but was gazing into the corner behind the gentleman, as if he saw someone there. Michael looked and looked, and suddenly he smiled, and his face became brighter.

"What are you grinning at, you fool?" thundered the gentleman. "You had better look to it that the boots are ready in time."

"They shall be ready in good time," said Michael.

"Mind it is so," said the gentleman, and he put on his boots and his fur coat, wrapped the latter around him, and went to the door. But he forgot to stoop and struck his head against the lintel.

He swore and rubbed his head. Then he took his seat in the carriage and drove away.

When he had gone, Simon said: "There's a figure of a man for you! You could not kill him with a mallet. He almost knocked out the lintel, but little harm it did him."

And Matrena said: "Living as he does, how should he not grow strong? Death itself can't touch such a rock as that."

VII

Then Simon said to Michael: "Well, we have taken the work, but we must see we don't get into trouble over it. The leather is dear, and the gentleman hot-tempered. We must make no mistakes. Come, your eye is truer and your hands have become nimbler than mine, so you take this measure and cut out the boots. I will finish off the sewing of the vamps."

Michael did as he was told. He took the leather, spread it out on the table, folded it in two, took a knife, and began to cut it out.

Matrena came and watched him cutting, and was surprised to see how he was doing it. Matrena was accustomed to seeing boots made, and she looked and saw that Michael was not cutting the leather for boots, but was cutting it around.

She wished to say something, but she thought to herself: "Perhaps I do not understand how gentlemen's boots should be made. I suppose Michael knows more about it—and I won't interfere."

When Michael had cut up the leather he took a thread and began to sew not with two ends, as boots are sewn, but with a single end, as for soft slippers.

Again Matrena wondered, but again she did not interfere. Michael sewed on steadily till noon. Then Simon rose for dinner, looked around, and saw that Michael had made slippers out of the gentleman's leather.

"Ah!" groaned Simon, and he thought, "How is it that Michael, who has been with me a whole year and never made a mistake before, should do such a dreadful thing? The gentleman ordered high boots, welted, with whole fronts, and Michael has made soft slippers with single soles, and has wasted the leather. What am I to say to the gentleman? I can never replace leather such as this."

And he said to Michael, "What are you doing, friend? You have ruined me! You know the gentleman ordered high boots, but see what you have made!"

Hardly had he begun to rebuke Michael, when "rat-tat" went the iron ring that hung at the door. Someone was knocking. They looked out of the window; a man had come on horseback and was fastening his horse. They opened the door, and the servant who had been with the gentleman came in.

"Good day," said he.

"Good day," replied Simon. "What can we do for you?"

"My mistress has sent me about the boots."

"What about the boots?"

"Why, my master no longer needs them. He is dead."

"Is it possible?"

"He did not live to get home after leaving you, but died in the carriage. When we reached home and the servants came to help him alight, he rolled over like a sack. He was dead already, and so stiff that he could hardly be got out of the carriage. My mistress sent me here, saying: 'Tell the bootmaker that the gentleman who ordered boots of him and left the leather for them no longer needs the boots, but that he must quickly make soft slippers for the corpse. Wait till they are ready and bring them back with you.' That is why I have come."

Michael gathered up the remnants of the leather, rolled them up, took the soft slippers he had made, slapped them together, wiped them down with his apron, and handed them and the roll of leather to the servant, who took them and said, "Good-bye, masters, and good day to you!"

VIII

Another year passed, and another, and Michael was now living his sixth year with Simon. He lived as before. He went nowhere, spoke only when necessary, and had smiled only twice in all those years—once when Matrena gave him food, and a second time when the gentleman was in their hut. Simon was more than pleased with his workman. He never now asked him where he came from, and only feared lest Michael should go away.

They were all at home one day. Matrena was putting iron pots in the oven; the children were running along the benches and looking out of the window; Simon was sewing at one window and Michael was fastening on a heel at the other.

One of the boys ran along the bench to Michael, leaned on his shoulder, and looked out of the window.

"Look, Uncle Michael! There is a lady with little girls! She seems to be coming here. And one of the girls is lame."

When the boy said that, Michael dropped his work, turned to the window, and looked out into the street.

Simon was surprised. Michael never used to look out into the street, but now he pressed against the window, staring at something. Simon also looked out and saw that a well-dressed woman was really coming to his hut, leading by the hand two little girls in fur coats and woolen shawls. The girls could hardly be told one from the other, except that one of them was crippled in her left leg and walked with a limp.

The woman stepped onto the porch and entered the passage. Feeling about for the entrance she found the latch, which she lifted, and opened the door. She let the two girls go in first, and followed them into the hut.

"Good day, good folk!'

"Pray come in," said Simon. "What can we do for you?"

The woman sat down by the table. The two little girls pressed close to her knees, afraid of the people in the hut.

"I want leather shoes made for these two little girls, for spring."

"We can do that. We have never made such small shoes, but we can make them—either welted or turnover shoes, linen-lined. My man, Michael, is a master at the work."

Simon glanced at Michael and saw that he had left his work and was sitting with his eyes fixed on the little girls. Simon was surprised. It was true the girls were pretty, plump, with black eyes and rosy cheeks, and they wore nice kerchiefs and fur coats, but still Simon could not understand why Michael should look at them like that—just as if he had known them before. Simon was puzzled, but went on talking with the woman and arranging the price. Having fixed it, he prepared the measure. The woman lifted the lame girl onto her lap and said: "Take two measures from this little girl. Make one shoe for the lame foot and three for the sound one. They both have the same-sized feet. They are twins."

Simon took the measure and, speaking of the lame girl, said: "How did it happen to her? She is such a pretty girl. Was she born so?"

"No, her mother crushed her leg."

Then Matrena joined in. She wondered who this woman was and whose the children were, so she said, "Are not you their mother, then?"

"No, my good woman, I am neither their mother nor any relation to them. They were quite strangers to me, but I adopted them."

"They are not your children and yet you are so fond of them?"

"How can I help being fond of them? I fed them both at my

own breast. I had a child of my own, but God took him. I was not so fond of him as I now am of these."

"Then whose children are they?"

IX

The woman, having begun talking, told them the whole story.

"It is about six years since their parents died, both in one week. Their father was buried on the Tuesday, and their mother died on the Friday. These orphans were born three days after their father's death, and their mother did not live another day. My husband and I were then living as peasants in the village. We were neighbors of theirs, our yard being next to theirs. Their father was a lonely man, a woodcutter in the forest. While he was felling trees one day, one fell on him. It fell across his body and crushed his bowels out. They hardly got him home before his soul went to God, and that same week his wife gave birth to twins—these little girls. She was poor and alone; she had no one, young or old, with her. Alone she gave them birth, and alone she met her death.

"The next morning I went to see her, but when I entered the hut, she, poor thing, was already stark and cold. In dying she had rolled onto this child and crushed her leg. The village folk came to the hut, washed the body, laid her out, made a coffin, and buried her. They were good folk. The babies were left alone. What was to be done with them? I was the only woman there who had a baby at the time. I was nursing my firstborn—eight weeks old. So I took them for a time. The peasants came together, and thought and thought what to do with them, and at last they said to me, 'For the present, Mary, you had better keep the girls, and later on we will arrange what to do for them.' So I nursed the sound one at my breast, but at first I did not feed this crippled one. I did not suppose she would live. But then I thought to myself, why should the poor innocent suffer? I pitied her and began to feed her. And so I fed my own boy and these two—the three of them—at my own breast. I was young and strong and had good food, and God gave me so much milk that at times it even overflowed. I used sometimes to feed two at a time, while the third was waiting. When one had had enough I nursed the third. And God so ordered it that these grew up, while my own was buried before he was two years old. And I had no more children, though we prospered. Now my husband is working for the corn merchant at the mill. The pay is good and we are well off. But I have no children of my own, and how lonely I would be without these little girls! How can I help loving them! They are the joy of my life!"

She pressed the lame little girl to her with one hand, while with the other she wiped the tears from her cheeks.

And Matrena sighed, and said, "The proverb is true that says, 'One may live without father or mother, but one cannot live without God.'"

So they talked together, when suddenly the whole hut was lighted up as though by summer lightning from the corner where Michael sat. They all looked towards him and saw him sitting, his hands folded on his knees, gazing upwards and smiling.

X

The woman went away with the girls. Michael rose from the bench, put down his work, and took off his apron. Then, bowing low to Simon and his wife, he said: "Farewell, masters. God has forgiven me. I ask your forgiveness, too, for anything done amiss."

And they saw that a light shone from Michael. And Simon rose, bowed down to Michael, and said: "I see, Michael, that you are no common man, and I can neither keep you nor question you. Only tell me this: how is it that when I found you and brought you home, you were gloomy, and when my wife gave you food you smiled at her and became brighter? Then when the gentleman came to order the boots, you smiled again and became brighter still? And now, when this woman brought the little girls, you smiled a third time and have become as bright as day? Tell me, Michael, why does your face shine so, and why did you smile those three times?"

And Michael answered: "Light shines from me because I have been punished, but now God has pardoned me. And I smiled three times, because God sent me to learn three truths, and I have learned them. One I learned when your wife pitied me, and that is why I smiled the first time. The second I learned when the rich man ordered the boots, and then I smiled again. And now, when I saw those little girls, I learned the third and last truth, and I smiled the third time."

And Simon said, "Tell me, Michael, what did God punish you for? And what were the three truths so that I, too, may know them?"

And Michael answered: "God punished me for disobeying Him. I was an angel in heaven and disobeyed God. God sent me to fetch a woman's soul. I flew to earth, and saw a sick woman lying alone who had just given birth to twin girls. They moved feebly at their mother's side, but she could not lift them to her breast. When she saw me, she understood that God had sent me for her soul, and she wept and said: 'Angel of God! My husband has just been buried, killed by a falling tree. I have neither sister, nor aunt, nor mother, no one to care for my orphans. Do not take my soul! Let me nurse my babes, feed them, and set them on their feet before I die. Children cannot live without father or mother.' And I hearkened to her. I placed one child at her breast and gave the other into her arms, and returned to the Lord in heaven. I flew to the Lord, and said: 'I could not take the soul of the mother. Her husband was crushed by a tree; the woman has twins and prays that her soul may not be taken. She says: "Let me nurse and feed my children, and set them on their feet. Children cannot live without father or mother." I have not taken her soul.' And God said: 'Go—take the mother's soul, and learn three truths: Learn *What dwells in man; What is not given to man;* and *What men live by.* When thou hast learned these things, thou shalt return to heaven.' So I flew again to earth and took the mother's soul. The babes dropped from her breast. Her body rolled over on the bed and crushed one babe, twisting its leg. I rose above the village, wishing to take her soul to God, but a wind seized me and my wings drooped and dropped off. Her soul rose alone to God, while I fell to earth by the roadside."

XI

And Simon and Matrena understood who it was that had lived with them, and whom they had clothed and fed. And they wept with awe and with joy. And the angel said: "I was alone in the field, naked. I had never known human needs, cold, or hunger till I became a man. I was famished, frozen, and did not know what to do. I saw, near the field I was in, a shrine built for God, and I went to it hoping to find shelter. But the shrine was locked and I could not enter. So I sat down behind the shrine to shelter myself at least from the wind. Evening drew on; I was hungry, frozen, and in pain. Suddenly I heard a man coming along the road. He carried a pair of boots and was talking to himself. For the first time since I became a man I saw the mortal face of a man, and his face seemed terrible to me and I turned from it. And I heard the man talking to himself about how to cover his body from the cold in winter, and how to feed wife and children. And I thought: 'I am perishing of cold and hunger and here is a man thinking only of how to clothe himself and his wife, and how to get bread for themselves. He cannot help me.' When the man saw me he frowned and became still more terrible, and passed me by on the other side. I despaired, but suddenly I heard him coming back. I looked up and did not recognize the same man: before, I had seen death in his face, but now he was alive and I recognized in him the presence of God. He came up to me, clothed me, took me with him, and brought me to his home. I entered the house; a woman came to meet us and began to speak. The woman was still more terrible than the man had been. The spirit of death came from her mouth; I could not breathe for the stench of death that spread around her. She wished to drive me out into the cold, and I knew that if she did so she would die. Suddenly her husband spoke to her of God, and the woman changed at once. And when she brought me food and looked at me, I glanced at her and saw that death no longer dwelt in her. She had become alive, and in her too I saw God.

"Then I remembered the first lesson God had set me: *'Learn what dwells in man.'* And I understood that in man dwells Love! I was glad that God had already begun to show me what He had promised, and I smiled for the first time. But I had not yet learned all. I did not yet know *What is not given to man,* and *What men live by.*

"I lived with you and a year passed. A man came to order boots that would wear for a year without losing shape or cracking. I looked at him, and suddenly, behind his shoulder, I saw my comrade—the angel of death. None but me saw that angel, but I knew him, and knew that before the sun set he would take that rich man's soul. And I thought to myself, 'The man is making preparations for a year and does not know that he will die before evening.' And I remembered God's second saying, *'Learn what is not given to man.'*

"What dwells in man I already knew. Now I learned what is not given him. It is not given to man to know his own needs. And I smiled for the second time. I was glad to have seen my comrade angel—glad also that God had revealed to me the second saying.

"But I still did not know all. I did not know *What men live by.* And I lived on, waiting till God would reveal to me the last lesson. In the sixth year came the twin girls with the woman, and I recognized the girls and heard how they had been kept alive. Having heard the story, I thought, 'Their mother besought me for the children's sake, and I believed her when she said that children cannot live without father or mother, but a stranger has nursed them and has brought them up.' And when the woman showed her love for the children that were not her own, and wept over them, I saw in her the living God, and understood *What men live by*. And I knew that God had revealed to me the last lesson, and had forgiven my sin. And then I smiled for the third time."

XII

And the angel's body was bared, and he was clothed in light so that eye could not look on him; and his voice grew louder, as though it came not from him but from heaven above. And the angel said: "I have learned that men live not by care for themselves but by love.

"It was not given to the mother to know what her children needed for their life. Nor was it given to the rich man to know what he himself needed. Nor is it given to any man to know whether, when evening comes, he will need boots for his body or slippers for his corpse.

"I remained alive when I was a man not by care of myself but because love was present in a passerby, and because he and his wife pitied and loved me. The orphans remained alive not because of their mother's care but because there was love in the heart of a woman, a stranger to them, who pitied and loved them. And all men live not by the thought they spend on their own welfare but because love exists in man.

"I knew before that God gave life to men and desires that they should live; now I understood more than that.

"I understood that God does not wish men to live apart, and therefore he does not reveal to them what each one needs for himself. He wishes them to live united, and therefore reveals to each of them what is necessary for all.

"I now understand that though it seems to men that they live by care for themselves, in truth it is love alone by which they live. He who has love is in God, and God is in him, for God is love."

And the angel sang praise to God, so that the hut trembled at his voice. The roof opened, and a column of fire rose from earth to heaven. Simon and his wife and children fell to the ground. Wings appeared upon the angel's shoulders and he rose into the heavens.

And when Simon came to himself, the hut stood as before, and there was no one in it but his own family.

•

THE CHILD'S STORY

Charles Dickens

**What are we here for, if not to walk with each other along life's
journey?**

Once upon a time, a good many years ago, there was a traveler,
and he set out upon a journey. It was a magic journey, and seemed
very long when he began it, and very short when he got halfway
through.

He traveled along a rather dark path for some little time, without meeting anything, until at last he came to a beautiful child. So
he said to the child, "What do you do here?" And the child said, "I
am always at play. Come and play with me!"

So he played with that child, the whole day long, and they
were very merry. The sky was so blue, and the sun was so bright,
the water was so sparkling, the leaves were so green, the flowers
were so lovely, and they heard such singing birds and saw so many
butterflies, that everything was beautiful. This was in fine weather.
When it rained, they loved to watch the falling drops, and to smell
the fresh scents. When it blew, it was delightful to listen to the wind,
and fancy what it said as it came rushing from its home—where
was that, they wondered!—whistling and howling, driving the
clouds before it, bending the trees, rumbling in the chimneys, shaking the house, and making the sea roar in fury. But when it snowed,
that was best of all, for they liked nothing so well as to look up at
the white flakes falling fast and thick, like down from the breasts of
millions of white birds, and to see how smooth and deep the drift
was, and to listen to the hush upon the paths and roads.

They had plenty of the finest toys in the world, and the most
astonishing picture books—all about scimitars and slippers and
turbans, and dwarfs and giants and genii and fairies, and Bluebeards
and beanstalks and riches and caverns and forests and Valentines
and Orsons—and all new and all true.

But one day, of a sudden, the traveler lost the child. He called
to him over and over again, but got no answer. So he went upon
his road, and went on for a little while without meeting anything,
until at last he came to a handsome boy. So he said to the boy,

"What do you do here?" And the boy said, "I am always learning. Come and learn with me."

So he learned with that boy about Jupiter and Juno, and the Greeks and the Romans, and I don't know what, and learned more than I could tell—or he, either, for he soon forgot a great deal of it. But they were not always learning; they had the merriest games that ever were played. They rowed upon the river in summer, and skated on the ice in winter; they were active afoot, and active on horseback, at cricket, and all games at ball; at prisoner's base, hare and hounds, follow my leader, and more sports than I can think of. Nobody could beat them. They had holidays, too, the Twelfth Night cakes, and parties where they danced till midnight, and real theaters where they saw palaces of real gold and silver rise out of the real earth, and saw all the wonders of the world at once. As to friends, they had such dear friends and so many of them that I want time to reckon them up. They were all young, like the handsome boy, and were never to be strange to one another all their lives through.

Still, one day, in the midst of all these pleasures, the traveler lost the boy as he had lost the child, and, after calling to him in vain, went on upon his journey. So he went on for a little while without seeing anything, until at last he came to a young man. So he said to the young man, "What do you do here?" And the young man said, "I am always in love. Come and love with me."

So he went with that young man, and presently they came to one of the prettiest girls that was ever seen—just like Fanny in the corner there—and she had eyes like Fanny, and hair like Fanny, and dimples like Fanny, and she laughed and colored just as Fanny does while I am talking about her. So the young man fell in love directly—just as Somebody I won't mention, the first time he came here, did with Fanny. Well! He was teased sometimes—just as Somebody used to be by Fanny; and they quarreled sometimes— just as Somebody and Fanny used to quarrel; and they made it up, and sat in the dark, and wrote letters every day, and never were happy asunder, and were always looking out for each other and pretending not to, and were engaged at Christmastime, and sat close to each other by the fire, and were going to be married very soon—all exactly like Somebody I won't mention, and Fanny!

But the traveler lost them one day, as he had lost the rest of his friends, and, after calling to them to come back, which they never did, went on upon his journey. So he went on for a little while without seeing anything, until at last he came to a middle-aged gentleman. So he said to the gentleman, "What are you doing here?" And his answer was, "I am always busy. Come and be busy with me!"

So he began to be very busy with that gentleman, and they went on through the wood together. The whole journey was through a wood, only it had been open and green at first, like a wood in spring, and now began to be thick and dark, like a wood in summer. Some of the little trees that had come out earliest were even turning brown. The gentleman was not alone, but had a lady of about the same age with him, who was his wife; and they had children, who were with them, too. So they all went on together through the wood, cutting down the trees, and making a path through the branches and the fallen leaves, and carrying burdens and working hard.

Sometimes they came to a long green avenue that opened into deeper woods. Then they would hear a very little distant voice crying: "Father, father, I am another child! Stop for me!" And presently they would see a very little figure, growing larger as it came along, running to join them. When it came up, they all crowded around it, and kissed and welcomed it; and then they all went on together.

Sometimes they came to several avenues at once, and then they all stood still, and one of the children said, "Father, I am going to sea," and another said, "Father, I am going to India," and another, "Father, I am going to seek my fortune where I can," and another, "Father, I am going to Heaven!" So, with many tears at parting, they went, solitary, down those avenues, each child upon its way; and the child who went to Heaven rose into the golden air and vanished.

Whenever these partings happened, the traveler looked at the gentleman and saw him glance up at the sky above the trees, where the day was beginning to decline, and the sunset to come on. He saw, too, that his hair was turning gray. But they never could rest long, for they had their journey to perform, and it was necessary for them to be always busy.

At last, there had been so many partings that there were no children left, and only the traveler, the gentleman, and the lady went upon their way in company. And now the wood was yellow; and now brown; and the leaves, even of the forest trees, began to fall. They came to an avenue that was darker than the rest, and were pressing forward on their journey without looking down it when the lady stopped.

"My husband," said the lady, "I am called."

They listened, and they heard a voice, a long way down the avenue, say, "Mother, mother!"

It was the voice of the first child who had said, "I am going to Heaven!" and the father said: "I pray not yet. The sunset is very near. I pray not yet!"

But the voice cried, "Mother, mother!" without minding him, though his hair was now quite white, and tears were on his face.

Then the mother, who was already drawn into the shade of the dark avenue and moving away with her arms still around his neck, kissed him, and said, "My dearest, I am summoned, and I go!" And she was gone. And the traveler and he were left alone together.

And they went on and on together, until they came to very near the end of the wood; so near that they could see the sunset shining red before them through the trees.

Yet once more, while he broke his way among the branches, the traveler lost his friend. He called and called, but there was no reply, and when he passed out of the wood, and saw the peaceful sun going down upon a wide purple prospect, he came to an old man sitting on a fallen tree. So he said to the old man, "What do you do here?" And the old man said with a calm smile: "I am always remembering. Come and remember with me!"

So the traveler sat down by the side of that old man, face to face with the serene sunset; and all his friends came softly back and stood around him. The beautiful child, the handsome boy, the young man in love, the father, the mother, and the children: every one of them was there, and he had lost nothing. So he loved them all, and was kind and forbearing with them all, and was always pleased to watch them all, and they all honored and loved him. And I think the traveler must be yourself, dear Grandfather, because this is what you do to us, and what we do to you.

•

THE GREAT COMMANDMENT
Matthew 22:37–40

Thou shalt love the Lord thy God with all thy heart,
   and with all thy soul, and with all thy mind.
This is the first and great commandment.
And the second is like unto it;
Thou shalt love thy neighbor as thyself.
On these two commandments hang all the law and the prophets.

Acknowledgments

For permission to reprint copyrighted material, grateful acknowledgment is made to the following publishers, authors, and agents:

"A Worn Path" from *A Curtain of Green and Other Stories.* Copyright 1941 and renewed 1969 by Eudora Welty. Reprinted by permission of Harcourt Brace & Company.

"The Story of the Two Friends" from *The King of the Snakes and Other Folklore Stories from Uganda* by Rosetta Baskerville, The Sheldon Press, 1922. Used by permission of the publishers.

"The Conquest of Everest" from *The Age of Mountaineering* by James Ramsey Ullman. Copyright © 1941, 1954, 1982 by the Estate of James Ramsey Ullman. Reprinted by permission of Harold Matson Co., Inc.

"The Man Who Broke the Color Barrier" from *Sports Heroes Who Wouldn't Quit* by Hal Butler. Copyright © 1973 by Hal Butler. Reprinted by permission of Julian Messner, a division of Simon & Schuster, Inc.

"Kaddo's Wall" reprinted from *The Cow-Tail Switch and Other West African Stories* by Harold Courlander and George Herzog. Copyright © 1975 by Harold Courlander. Reprinted by permission of Henry Holt and Co., Inc.

"End of the Tiger" from *End of the Tiger and Other Stories* by John D. MacDonald. Reprinted by permission of Maynard MacDonald.

"No Greater Love" by John W. Mansur. Reprinted with permission from the August 1987 *Reader's Digest.*

"An Excellent Wife" taken from the *New American Standard Bible* ®, © Copyright The Lockman Foundation 1960, 1962, 1963, 1968, 1971, 1972, 1973, 1975, 1977. Used by permission.

"The Bravest Man" from *The Quality of Courage* by Mickey Mantle. Copyright © 1964 by Bedford S. Wynne, Trustee of four separate trusts for the benefit of Mickey Elven Mantle, David Harold Mantle, Billy Giles Mantle and Danny Murl

Mantle. Used by permission of Doubleday, a division of Bantam Doubleday Dell Publishing Group, Inc.

"Distance" from *Fires* by Raymond Carver. Copyright © 1983. Reprinted by permission of Capra Press, Santa Barbara.

"My Very Dear Sarah" by Sullivan Ballou. Reprinted by permission of the Chicago Historical Society.

"Your Second Job" as told to Fulton Oursler by Albert Schweitzer from the October 1949 *Reader's Digest.* Reprinted by permission of Fulton Oursler, Jr., and April Armstrong.

"Give Until It Hurts" by Mother Teresa. Reprinted by permission of Missionaries of Charity, Inc.

The author also gratefully acknowledges the endeavors of scholars and collectors who in a past age devoted their energies to preserving the best of our heritage, and whose works have supplied this volume with many truly great stories.

Reasonable care has been taken to trace ownership and, when necessary, to obtain permission for each selection included.

Index

A

"About Angels" (Richards), 73–75
"Abraham and the Old Man" (Scudder), 752
"Achilles Heel, The" (Baldwin), 218–21
Adams, Elmer, 660–64
Adams, John, 764–66
Adams, Laura M., 540–42
Addams, Jane, 554–57
"Admetus and Alcestis" (Baldwin), 565–67
Aesop, 176, 177, 218, 224, 522, 616
Alcott, Amos B. and Abigail May, 538–39
Alden, Raymond M., 255–60, 392–393
Alexander the Great, 601–2, 657–658
"All God's Creatures Have Work to Do" (Southeast Asian folktale), 193–95
"All the World Is Sleeping" (song), 485
"America Is Great Because She Is Good" (Tocqueville, attrib.), 694–95
"American Army of Two, An" (Farmer), 634–36
"American Boy, The" (Roosevelt), 216–17
Andersen, Hans Christian, 118–20, 778–80
"Angel, The" (Andersen), 778–80

B

"Appius" (Twitchell), 75–76
Appomattox, 687–90
"Apron String, The" (Richards), 52–53
"Arachne" (Cooke), 183–85
Armfield, Constance, 666–69
Arnold, Benedict, 644–46
Arnold, Matthew, 753–54

B

"Babouscka" (Thomas), 707–8
Babrius, 86
"Baby, The" (MacDonald), 515–16
"Baby, The" (Richards), 522–23
Balder, 531–35
Baldwin, James, 69–70, 82–85, 152–59, 211–13, 218–22, 227–31, 269–74, 279–84, 405–8, 565–67, 601–2, 677–79, 729–34
Ball, Francis, 651–52
Ballou, Sullivan, 578–79
Baskerville, Rosetta, 196–200
"Bat," 643–44
Bates, Abigail and Rebecca, 634–636
Baumbach, Rudolf, 581–87
"Beautiful Hands" (Evans), 29–30
Becket, Thomas, 357–60
"Bed Quilt, The" (Fisher), 768–76
"Beethoven's Triumph," 336–39
"Before Hull House" (Addams), 554–57
"Believe Me, If All Those Endearing Young Charms" (Moore), 588

"Betsy Ross and the First Flag"
(Humphrey), 630–32
"Birds Who Befriended a King,
The" (Armfield), 666–69
Blaisdell, Albert, 651–52
"Blind Men and the Elephant, The,"
192–93
Boutet de Monvel, Louis Maurice,
620–24
"Boy and the Angel, The" (Metcalf),
717–18
"Boy Who Brought Light into a
World of Darkness, The," 437–41
"Boy Who Kissed His Mother, The"
(Rexford), 72–73
Brahms, Johannes, 21
Braille, Louis, 437–41
"Bravest Man, The" (Mantle), 543–
547
Broadus, Eleanor, 710–15
"Brotherhood of Long Ago, The"
(Coe), 658–59
"Brother to the Lepers" (Stoddard),
442–46
Brown, Henry Box, 309–11
"Brownies, The," 30–36
Bryant, Sara Cone, 150–51, 163–65,
177–78, 435–37, 647–48, 725–
729
Bryce, Catherine T., 254
Buckham, James, 380–83
Buckley, Elsie F., 320–22
"Bundle, The," 749–50
Bunner, Henry Cuyler, 114–15
Burgess, Thornton W., 596–99
"Busy Man, The," 615
Butler, Hal, 348–52

C

Cabot, Ella Lyman, 260–62, 486–87,
657
"Camel's Nose, The," 237–38
Canton, William, 274
Carlyle, Thomas, 339–41
Carpenter, Edmund, 318
Carver, Raymond, 557–65

"Cat and the Parrot, The" (Bryant),
163–65
Cather, Katherine D., 189–91
"Character of Leadership, The"
(Jefferson), 684–86
"Charge of the Night Brigade, The,"
526–27
"Charlemagne and the Robber
Knight" (Frary and Stebbins),
653–55
"Chattering Aspen, The" (Stewart),
496–97
Chaucer, Geoffrey, 233–37
Chaundler, Christine, 720–23
Chekhov, Anton, 457–61, 467–73,
784–88
Cheow-Leung, 174, 215–16, 745–
746
"Chevalier D'Assas, The," 637–38
"Child's Story, The" (Dickens),
807–10
"Christmas at Sea" (Stevenson),
120–21
Christopher, Saint, 710–15
Church, Francis P., 240–42
Claudy, C. H., 312–17
Coe, Fanny E., 408–11, 658–59
Columbus, Christopher, 294–98
"Conquest of Everest, The"
(Ullman), 346–47
Conrad, Joseph, 594
Cooke, Flora, 183–85, 367–68,
408–11, 527–31
Cooper, George, 145
Copernicus, Nicolaus, 329–33
Corbett, Richard, 539–40
"Cornelia's Jewels" (Baldwin and
Sly), 69–70
"Cost of One Seed, The" (African
folktale), 519–20
Courlander, Harold, 427–32
"Courtship and Marriage of Cock
Robin and Jenny Wren, The,"
492–95
Cowdery, M. F., 24
Cowles, Julia Darrow, 498–500

"Crab and His Mother, The" (Aesop), 522
"Cradle Song" (Brahms), 21
"Crisis, The" (Paine), 298–99
Curius, Manius, 648–49

D

Dadmun, Frances, 421–23, 617–20, 624–26, 716
Damien de Veuster, Joseph, 442–46
"Dancing Horses of Sybaris, The," 211–13
Davis, Mary H., 174, 215–16, 745–746
Dayre, Sydney, 166
"Death of Balder, The" (McCaleb), 531–35
"Death of Becket, The" (Stanley), 357–60
"Death of Thomas More, The" (Froude), 782–84
De Morgan, Mary, 603–6
Dickens, Charles, 447–53, 807–10
"Discontented Pig, The" (Cather), 189–91
"Discontented Stonecutter, The" (Japanese folktale), 179–81
"Distance" (Carver), 557–65
Dix, Dorothea, 671–75
"Dog in the Manger, The" (Aesop), 176
"Dog of Montargis, The" (Baldwin), 279–84
"Dr. Johnson and His Father" (Baldwin), 82–85
Donner, Virginia, 77–82
"Drover's Wife, The" (Lawson), 98–105
"Duty, Honor, Country" (MacArthur), 693–94

E

Eells, Elsie, 159–61
Elizabeth, Saint, 502–5
"Emerald Lizard, The," 433–34
Emerson, Ralph Waldo, 758

"End of the Tiger" (MacDonald), 462–65
Essenwein, J. Berg, 63–67
Evans, Lawton B., 29–30
Everest, Mount, 346–47
Ewing, Juliana Horatia, 30–36
"Excellent Wife, An," 508–9

F

Farmer, Florence, 634–36
"Father" (Guest), 97–98
"Father's Return, A" (African folktale), 86–88
"Father William" (Southey), 763–64
Field, Eugene, 57–58, 122–26
"Fire Bearer, The" (Coe and Cooke), 408–11
Fisher, Dorothy Canfield, 768–76
"Fish or Cat?" (Arab folktale), 232
"For Remembrance" (Richards), 512–13
"For the Love of a Man" (London), 286–94
"Fortune, A" (Richards), 524–25
"Fortune and the Beggar" (Krylov), 169–70
Forum, Roman, 636–37
"For You and Me" (Richards), 203–204
Foster, Warren, 660–64
"Four Daughters" (South American tale), 53–55
"Fox and the Cat, The," 148
Frary, Marie, 653–55
"Friend of a Friend of a Friend, The" (Arab folktale), 166–67
"Friendship Sweetening to the Evening of Life" (Jefferson), 764–766
Froude, James Anthony, 782–84

G

"Galileo and the Leaning Tower," 333–35
"Garden of the Frost Flowers, The" (Olcott), 58–62

Gask, Lilian, 424–27, 474–76
Gates, Ellen, 201–3
"General Thanksgiving, A," 695–696
"George Pickett's Friend" (Moores), 656
"Gideon and His Brave Three Hundred" (Dadmun and Hurlbut), 624–26
"Give Until It Hurts" (Mother Teresa), 758–61
"God and the Soldier," 637
"God Will Provide" (Mexican folktale), 265–66
"God Will See," 724
"Going to School" (Martin), 146
"Gold Bread, The" (Wiggin and Smith), 185–89
"Golden Tripod, The" (Baldwin), 729–34
"Golden Windows, The," 41–43
"Good King Wenceslaus," 649–50
"Gordian Knot, The" (Baldwin), 601–2
"Gorgon's Head, The" (Baldwin), 269–74
Gould, F. J., 149–50, 213–15
"Grandfather Stork" (Pyle), 139–141
Grant, Ulysses S., 687–90
"Gratefulness" (Herbert), 616
"Great Commandment, The," 811
"Greatest of These Is Love, The" (Paul), 590
"Greedy" (Dayre), 166
"Grief" (Chekhov), 457–61
Grimm Brothers, 368–70
"Grumble Family, The," 610
"Grumble Town," 608–9
Guest, Edgar, 97–98

H

"Habit" (James), 239–40
"Hampshire Hills, The" (Field), 122–26
"Hans the Shepherd Boy" (Cabot), 260–61

"Happy Prince, The" (Wilde), 413–421
Harrison, Elizabeth, 43–47, 275–79, 373–78, 394–401, 488–90
Harte, Bret, 547–54
Haughery, Margaret, 435–37
Hawthorne, Nathaniel, 115–18
"Heedless Man at the Gates of Paradise, The" (Dervish tale), 267
"He Gave His Life for His Country" (Tyrolian tale), 633–34
"Henry Box Brown's Escape" (Brown), 309–11
Herbert, George, 616
"Hercules Kills the Hydra," 284–85
"Hermit of the Himalayas, The" (Dadmun), 421–23
"Heroes" (Canton), 274
Herzog, George, 427–32
"High-Water Mark" (Harte), 547–54
"Hill, The" (Richards), 26–27
"Hill Mother, The" (Pyle), 247–53
Holbrook, Florence, 70–71, 383–385, 386–87
"Honest Farmer, The" (Cabot), 262
"Honorable Estate, Instituted of God, An," 505–8
"How Five Little Angels Lost Their Wings" (Stewart), 135–39
"How Hippo Was Humbled" (African folktale), 181–83
Howitt, Mary, 222–24
"How the Animals Got Sunlight" (Native American folktale), 389–391
"How the Brazilian Beetles Got Their Coats" (Eells), 159–61
"How the Indians Learned to Heal" (Powers), 411–12
"How the Ostrich Got His Long Neck" (African folktale), 225–26
"How the Robin's Breast Became Red" (Cooke), 367–68
"How the Wise Man Found the King" (Chaundler and Wood), 720–23

"How They Built the Walls" (Tweedy), 627–30
Humphrey, Grace, 405–8, 630–32
Hurlbut, Jesse Lyman, 624–26
"Hush, Little Baby" (song), 21
Hyde, E. W., 691–93
Hydra, 284–85

I

"I Know of a Lovely Garden" (Luther), 535–36
"In *Adam's* Fall . . . ," 146–47
"Indian Girl and Her Messenger Bird, The" (Ranck), 781–82
"Industry and Sloth," 204
"Ingratitude and Injustice of Men Towards Fortune, The" (La Fontaine), 209
"In Regard to Duty" (Lee), 536–37
"In the Uttermost Parts of the Sea" (Andersen), 118–20
Irving, Washington, 204–9
"I Sought My Soul," 744
"Is There a Santa Claus?" (Church), 240–42

J

James, William, 239–40
Jefferson, Thomas, 684–86, 764–66
Jeffreys, Charles, 589
Jerome, Harriet Louise, 388–89
"Jinkyswoitmaya" (Claudy), 312–17
Joan of Arc, 620–24
"John Smith at Jamestown," 401–4
Johnson, Samuel, 82–85, 700
Jonson, Ben, 580, 581
"Joseph and His Brothers" (Essenwein and Stockard), 63–67

K

"Kaddo's Wall" (Courlander and Herzog), 427–32
Kaufman, Rosalie, 657–58
Kempis, Thomas à, 754
Kerr, Hugh T., 22–23
Key, Francis Scott, 304–6

"Keys of Calais, The" (Yonge), 639–642
"King and the Shirt, The," 611
"King John and the Magna Carta" (Baldwin), 677–79
Kingsley, Charles, 115–18
"King Solomon and the Ants" (Whittier), 669–70
"Knights of the Silver Shield, The" (Alden), 255–60
Krummacher, Friedrich, 200–201, 746–47
Krylov, Ivan, 169–70
Kupfer, Grace H., 323–24

L

"Lady with the Lamp, The" (Adams and Foster), 660–64
Lafayette, Marquis de, 658–59
La Fontaine, Jean de, 209–10
Lamartine, Alphonse de, 294–98
"Lame Boy, The" (Lane), 378–79
Lane, Mrs. Charles A., 378–79
Langton, Stephen, 677–79
Lanier, Henry W., 77–82
"Last Fight in the Colosseum, The" (Yonge), 453–56
"Late Bloomer, A" (Mexican folktale), 718–19
Lawson, Henry, 98–105
Lear, Edward, 491
Lee, Robert E., 536–37, 687–90
"Legend Beautiful, The" (German tale), 735–37
"Legend of Saint Christopher, The" (Broadus and Webling), 710–715
"Legend of the Christ Child, The" (Harrison), 43–47
"Legend of the Roman Forum, A," 636–37
"Life Heroic, The," 360
"Lift Up Your Soul" (Alcott), 538–539
Lincoln, Abraham, 264–65, 651–52, 656, 699
"Lincoln Licks the Bullies," 264–65

"Line of Golden Light, The" (Harrison), 373–78

"Lion's Hair, The," (African folktale) 513–15

"Little Eyes upon You," 523–24

"Little Fish That Would Not Do As It Was Bid" (Taylor), 144

"Little Girl Who Dared, The" (Lanier), 77–82

"Little Learning, A" (Pope), 734

"Little Loaf, The," 175

"Little Lost Lamb, The," 703–4

London, Jack, 286–94, 364

Longfellow, Henry Wadsworth, 664–66

Luther, Martin, 535–36

M

MacArthur, Douglas, 693–94

McCaleb, Anna, 531–35

MacDonald, George, 515–16

MacDonald, John D., 462–65

"Magic Cavern, The" (Olcott), 520–521

"Magic Mill, The," 761–63

"Magic Sword, The," 268–69

Magna Carta, 677–79

"Maid of Orléans, The" (Boutet de Monvel), 620–24

Mallory, George, 346–47

"Man, the Boy, and the Donkey, The" (Baldwin), 221–22

"Man and His Piece of Cloth, The" (Raju), 195–96

"Mandarin and the Tailor, The" (Vietnamese tale), 767

"Man Enough for the Job" (Cabot), 657

Mansur, John W., 466–67

Mantle, Mickey, 543–47

"Man Who Broke the Color Barrier, The" (Butler), 348–52

"Man Who Dined on Turnips, The," 648–49

"Man Who Loved Money Better Than Life, The" (Davis and Cheow-Leung), 174

"Man Who Loved War Too Much, The" (Gould), 213–15

"Man Who Moved the Earth, The," 329–33

"Man Who Would Not Drink Alone, The" (Kaufman), 657–58

"Man Without a Country, The," 644–46

Marathon, 307–9

"Margaret of New Orleans" (Bryant), 435–37

"Marines' Hymn, The," 306–7

Marriage Vows, 505–8

Martin, John, 146

"Matsuyama Mirror, The" (Japanese tale), 49–51

Maupassant, Guy de, 89–96

"Melon and the Professor, The" (Davis and Cheow-Leung), 745–746

Metcalf, Joel H., 717–18, 737–40

Michelangelo Buonnaroti, 325–29

Mill, John Stuart, 339–41, 484

Miller, Francis T., 671–75, 679–82

Miller, Mrs. E. R., 150

Milton, John, 336

"Miser, The" (Aesop), 176

"Molly Pitcher," 301–3

"Monica, Mother of Augustine" (Adams), 540–42

Moore, Thomas, 588

Moores, Charles W., 656

More, Saint Thomas, 782–84

"Most Precious Thing, The," 511–512

"Mouse Tower, The" (Southey and Gask), 424–27

"Mouse Who Was Afraid, The" (Bryce), 254

"Mr. Nobody," 36–37

"Mr. Straw" (Japanese folktale), 370–73

Mutiny, The" (Lamartine), 294–98

"My Native Land" (Scott), 646–47

"My Two Homes" (Tweedy), 47–48

"My Very Dear Sarah . . ." (Ballou), 578–79

N

"Nails in the Post" (Cowdery), 24
Narrative of Sojourner Truth, The,
675–77
Nehemiah, 627–30
Neri, Saint Philip, 149–50
New England Primer, The, 146–
147
"New Leaves, The" (Richards), 55–
56
"Night Wind, The" (Field), 57–58
Nightingale, Florence, 660–64,
664–66
"No Greater Love" (Mansur), 466–
467
"Northwest Passage" (Stevenson),
25–26

O

O'Connor, W. P., 171–73
Oedipus, 320–22
Olcott, Frances Jenkins, 58–62,
520–21, 527–31
"Old Man and Death, The" (Aesop),
616
"Old Mother Webtoes" (Pyle), 141–
143
"One, Two, Three!" (Bunner), 114–
115
"One Word Against Another" (Arab
folktale), 231–32
"On His Blindness" (Milton), 336
"On My First Daughter" (Jonson),
580
"On My First Son" (Jonson), 581
"Opportunity" (Sill), 268
"Orpheus and Eurydice"
(Turnbull), 567–70
Oursler, Fulton, 755–57
"Owl and the Pussy Cat, The"
(Lear), 491

P

Paine, Thomas, 298–99
Paul, Saint, 590
"Peddler's Pack, The" (De Morgan),
603–6

Perseus, 269–74
"Pharisee and the Tax Collector,
The" (Tappan), 750–51
Philoxenus, 323–24
Picket, George, 656
"Pig Brother, The" (Richards), 161–
163
"Pioneer Family, The"
(Tocqueville), 352–56
"Pioneer of Compassion, A"
(Miller), 671–75
Pitcher, Molly, 301–3
"Place of Brotherhood, The"
(Jewish tale), 67–68
"Plowman Who Found Content,
The" (Cowles), 498–500
"Pocahontas" (Baldwin and
Humphrey), 405–8
Pope, Alexander, 734
Porter, Horace, 687–90
Powers, Mabel, 411–12
"Prayer, The" (Dervish tale), 751
"Prayer at Valley Forge, A," 299–
301
"Prayer for Home and Family"
(Stevenson), 128–29
"Prayer for True Knowledge"
(Kempis), 754
"Prince Harweda and the Magic
Prison" (Harrison), 394–401
"Prince's Happy Heart, The," 38–
40
"Princess Who Wanted to Be
Beautiful, The," 365–66
"Problem, A" (Chekhov), 467–73
"Procrustes the Pitiless" (Baldwin),
227–31
Prometheus, 408–11
"Proserpina" (Cooke, Olcott, and
others), 527–31
"Proteus" (Harrison), 275–79
Pyle, Katharine, 139–43, 247–53,
501–2
Pyrrhus, 213–15

Q

"Quails, The" (*Jataka* tale), 595–96

R

"Race from Marathon, The," 307–9
Raju, P. V. Ramaswami, 195–96
Ranck, George W., 781–82
Rexford, Eben E., 72–73
Richards, Laura E., 26–27, 41–43, 52–53, 55–56, 73–75, 161–63, 203–4, 512–13, 522–23, 524–25, 709–10
"Rip van Winkle" (Irving), 204–9
"Robert of Sicily" (Bryant), 725–29
"Robin to His Mate, The," 495
Robinson, Jack Roosevelt, 348–52
Roosevelt, Theodore, 216–17
"Roses of Saint Elizabeth, The," 502–5
Ross, Betsy, 630–32
"Rules of Behavior," 159

S

"Sacajawea" (Miller), 679–82
"Saint Augustine by the Seashore" (Webling), 744–45
"Saint Catherine and the Silver Crucifix," 476–78
"Saint Francis and the Wolf" (Dadmun), 617–20
"Saint Martin and the Beggar" (Webling), 478–80
"Samuel in the Temple," 704–6
"Santa Filomena" (Longfellow), 664–66
Schiller, Friedrich von, 754–55
Schweitzer, Albert, 755–57
Scott, Sir Walter, 646–47
Scott, William, 651–52
Scudder, Horace E., 752
"Sculptor and the Sistine Chapel, The," 325–29
"Scylla and Charybdis" (Carpenter), 318–20
"Seed, The," 701–2
"Self-Dependence" (Arnold), 753–754
"Sheltering Wings" (Jerome), 388–389

"Shipwreck, The" (Dickens), 447–453
Sill, Edward Rowland, 268
"Silver Crown, The" (Richards), 709–10
"Simon's Father" (Maupassant), 89–96
Sistine Chapel, 325–29
"Sleep Baby, Sleep" (song), 485
"Sleeping Sentinel, The" (Blaisdell and Ball), 651–52
Sly, William J., 69–70
Smith, John, 401–4, 405–8
Smith, Nora Archibald, 185–89
"Sojourner Truth," 675–77
Solomon, King, 67–68, 666–69, 746–47
"Someone Must Pay" (Arab tale), 606–8
"Sound for a Smell, A," 226–27
Southey, Robert, 424–27, 763–64
Speckbacher, Albert, 633–34
"Sphinx, The" (Buckley), 320–322
"Spider and the Fly, The" (Howitt), 222–24
"Spider's Two Feasts" (African folktale), 167–69
"Squirrel's Devotion, The" (Cabot), 486–87
"Stag at the Pool, The" (Aesop), 218
Stanley, Arthur Penrhyn, 357–60
"Star Jewels, The" (Grimm Brothers), 368–70
"Star-Spangled Banner, The" (Tappan), 304–6
Stebbins, Charles, 653–55
Stevenson, Robert Louis, 25–26, 120–21, 128–29
Stewart, Mary, 135–39, 496–97, 573–78
Stockard, Marietta, 63–67
Stoddard, Charles Warren, 442–446
"Stone in the Road, The," 613–14

"Stone Lion, The" (O'Connor), 171–73

"Story of the First Diamonds, The" (Holbrook), 70–71

"Story of the Small Green Caterpillar, The" (Harrison), 488–90

"Story of Two Friends, The" (Baskerville), 196–200

"Stronger Than Death" (Stewart), 573–78

"Student, The" (Chekhov), 784–88

Sun (New York), 341–45

"Surrender at Appomattox" (Porter), 687–90

"Sweet and Low" (Tennyson), 22

Sybaris, 211–13

T

"Talkative Tortoise, The" (Bryant), 150–51

Tappan, Eva March, 304–6, 750–51

"Tarpeia" (Bryant), 647–48

Taylor, Ann, 144

Tennyson, Alfred, Lord, 22, 486, 776–78

Teresa, Mother, 758–61

Theseus, 115–18, 227–31

"Theseus and the Stone" (Kingsley and Hawthorne), 115–18

Thomas, Edith M., 707–8

"Thomas Carlyle and *The French Revolution,* 339–41

"Three Billy Goats Gruff, The" (Norse tale), 27–28

"Three Heavy Stones, The," 748–49

"Three Questions" (Tolstoy), 741–744

"Three Rioters, The" (Chaucer), 233–37

"Three Things," 68

"Three Wishes, The" (Pyle), 501–2

"Three Words of Strength" (Schiller), 754–55

"Titanic, The" (from *The Sun*), 341–45

Tocqueville, Alexis de, 352–56, 694

"To His Son, Vincent Corbet" (Corbett), 539–40

Tolstoy, Leo, 741–44, 788–806

"Tongue and How to Use It, The" (Gould), 149–50

"Tower to the Moon, The" (Dominican tale), 599–601

"Town Mouse and the Country Mouse, The" (Bryant), 177–78

"Tree That Was Lonesome, The," 37–38

"True Saintliness" (Metcalf), 737–740

Truth, Sojourner, 675–77

"Truth Speaker, A" (Kupfer), 323–324

Turnbull, V. C., 567–70

Tweedy, Henry Hallam, 47–48, 627–30

"Twelve Months, The" (Baldwin), 152–59

"Twenty Froggies" (Cooper), 145

Twitchell, H., 75–76

"Two Gifts, The" (Gask), 474–76

"Two Surprises," 612–13

"Two Travelers and the Oyster, The," 238

U

Ullman, James Ramsey, 346–47

Ulysses, 318–20, 776–78

"Ulysses" (Tennyson), 776–78

"Unfruitful Tree, The" (Krummacher), 200–201

V

Valley Forge, 299–301

"Vice Grown into Fashion, A" (Washington), 686–87

W

Washington, George, 299–301, 303, 631, 657, 683–84, 684–86, 686–687

"Washington's Glasses," 683–84

"Water of Youth, The" (Baumbach), 581–87

"Waukewa's Eagle" (Buckham), 380–83

"We Are Seven" (Wordsworth), 126–28

Webling, Peggy, 478–80, 710–15, 744–45

"We Have Lived and Loved Together" (Jeffreys), 589

Welty, Eudora, 105–13

Wescelas, Saint, 649–50

"We Thank Thee," 40

"What Bradley Owed" (Kerr), 22–23

"What Does Little Birdie Say?" (Tennyson), 486

"What Is Success?" (Emerson), 758

"What Men Live By" (Tolstoy), 788–806

"When Mother Reads Aloud," 525

"When Mr. Bluebird Won His Coat" (Burgess), 596–99

"White Stone Canoe, The" (Chippewa Tale), 570–73

Whittier, John Greenleaf, 669–70

"Why Evergreen Trees Never Lose Their Leaves" (Holbrook), 386–387

"Why the Baby Says 'Goo' " (Wilson), 517–18

"Why the Chimes Rang" (Alden), 392–93

"Why the Thumb Stands Alone" (African folktale), 263–64

"Why the Water in Rivers Is Never Still" (Holbrook), 383–85

"Widow's Mites, The" (Dadmun), 716

Wiggin, Kate Douglas, 185–89

Wilde, Oscar, 413–21

Wilson, Gilbert L., 517–18

"Wise Old Owl, The," 152

"Wives of Weinsberg, The" (Yonge), 510

"Wolf and the Lamb, The" (Aesop), 224

"Wonder Tree, The" (Krummacher), 746–47

Wood, Eric, 720–23

"Woo Sing and the Mirror" (Davis and Cheow-Leung), 215–16

"Words Are Wonderful Things" (Miller), 150

Wordsworth, William, 126–28

"Worn Path, A" (Welty), 105–13

"Wounded Pine Tree, The" (Babrius), 86

Y

Yonge, Charlotte, 453–56, 510, 639–42

"You Have Done Your Duty" (Hyde), 691–93

"Your Mission" (Gates), 201–3

"Your Second Job" (Oursler/ Schweitzer), 755–57

WILLIAM J. BENNETT served as Director of the Office of National Drug Control Policy under President Bush, and as Secretary of Education and Chairman of the National Endowment for the Humanities under President Reagan. He holds a bachelor of arts degree in philosophy from Williams College, a doctorate in political philosophy from the University of Texas, and a law degree from Harvard. Dr. Bennett is currently a co-director of Empower America, and the John M. Olin Distinguished Fellow in Cultural Policy Studies at the Heritage Foundation. He, his wife, Elayne, and their two sons, John and Joseph, live in Chevy Chase, Maryland.